Human conduct

AN INTRODUCTION TO THE PROBLEMS OF ETHICS

For no light matter is at stake; the question concerns the very manner in which human life is to be lived.

Plato, *Republic*, Book I, 352-D.

Human conduct

AN INTRODUCTION TO THE PROBLEMS OF ETHICS

JOHN HOSPERS

Rupert Hart-Davis
London 1970

FOR MARIANNE

British edition 1962
Second impression 1970

Printed in Great Britain by The Anchor Press Ltd, Tiptree, Essex

ISBN 0 246 63875 3

Preface

In what way should a person conduct his life? What things in life count most—pleasure and enjoyment, truth and knowledge, moral courage and conscientiousness? What makes some things good and others bad, some acts right and others wrong? Have we obligations to others? What are they and why should we perform them? In what circumstances can we rightly be praised, blamed, punished, or excused for our actions? Do we possess freedom—of action, of choice, of desire? How do we know any of these things, and how can we prove them?

It is to such questions that this book is addressed. The proponents of each of the major historical views on these subjects are described and assessed, although no attempt is made to treat the views in chronological order. The attempt is rather to present them in a logical order, with no acquaintance with the literature of the subject presupposed. To some extent each chapter assumes an acquaintance with those preceding, so the chapters are best studied in the order given; nevertheless the order can be changed without great damage to comprehension, except in the case of Chapters 3-7, which form a continuous series.

Every topic discussed is illustrated by numerous examples, so that the reader will be assisted in applying the principles involved to the problems of the contemporary world: problems of personal morality, political and economic problems, problems of war and peace. Numerous exercises containing further examples are to be found at the end of the numbered sections, of which there are twenty-eight in all. Where controversial issues arise, dialogues have been constructed which represent each of the main positions on the problem under discussion.

I am enormously indebted to Professors Elizabeth Beardsley of Lincoln University and Paul Taylor of Brooklyn College, who read painstakingly through the entire manuscript and gave me the benefit of many valuable suggestions; and to my colleagues Professors Howard Hintz, Martin Lean, and Julius Portnoy, all of Brooklyn College, who read some of the chapters and gave me advice and encouragement.

John Hospers

Los Angeles, California
January, 1961

$\mathcal{C}$ontents

1. Moral problems

Would you be willing to put your arm into a blazing fire and keep it there for ten minutes if by so doing you could save the life of your next-door neighbor? Would you want him to do so to save your life?

If someone irritates you continually and needles you to the point of madness, and if you could give him a painless but lethal poison without the slightest chance of ever being found out, would you do it?

If someone approached you with a gun and there was a 50 per cent chance that he would shoot, would you shoot him first?

Suppose that you are promised a million dollars in cash for just pressing a button, with the result that a person somewhere in the United States, entirely unknown to you, dies instantly. No one can ever trace the cause back to you. You don't even have to see the man die. Would you press the button?

To relieve all the hunger in India for one day, would you be willing to walk naked down the street in broad daylight for two hours (or until the police caught you) without any explanation to anyone then or at any time in the future?

Would you be just as willing to give to a worthy cause if the gift were strictly anonymous — no one would ever know that you gave it so no one would praise you or think better of you for it? Would you do it even if you knew you would be hated for it?

Would you rather be dishonest and thought honest, or be honest and thought dishonest?

The hero of a movie by herculean efforts extricates the beautiful heroine from an impossible situation, thus saving her life. He later marries her. Now suppose the situation were the same except that the person to be rescued is an ugly old hag. Would you admire the hero the same, less, or more for saving her? If you were the hero, would you still have saved her?

An old person condemns the enjoyments of the young. Would he still condemn them if he himself were young again and able to have another fling?

You are not likely to find yourself in many of these situations. Nevertheless, it is of some interest to ask yourself these questions to find out how far your sense of duty or heroism would extend.

In the next set of problems, ask yourself not what you *would* do but what you honestly think you *should* do.

1. You are a brilliant student with a great talent for medicine, and your aim is to become a physician. But medical school is expensive, and costs are so high that even by working eight hours a day you can earn only a fraction of the amount needed. Your parents can help you just enough to get you through, *if* they do not help your grandmother. But your grandmother has a chronic illness which requires constant care and expensive medication and which may continue for five or ten years. If your parents declared their inability to provide for her, she *might* be able to get into a free hospital, where, however, she would not be nearly so well taken care of. Should you forego medical school for years and perhaps forever so that your parents can provide your grandmother with the kind of care and attention they want her to have?

2. You are sitting alone on a high rock overlooking the ocean, and suddenly you hear, or think you hear, a scream for help uttered by someone drowning in the turbulent waters below. You are a reasonably good swimmer, but you doubt your ability to get far in such choppy water, and there is a good chance that if you tried to rescue the person, both of you would drown. It will take at least two minutes, even at top speed, for you to get down the rocky slope to the water's edge, by which time it may be too late. Besides, you aren't sure you hear someone calling; twice before, you thought you heard the same thing and you turned out to be mistaken. Should you wait for another call to make sure you heard right the first time? But that may mean a fatal delay. If you do go at once and really do see someone crying for help, should you risk your life in a perhaps vain attempt to save his? Would it make any difference if you knew that the person drowning was a confessed murderer who had recently escaped from the penitentiary?

3. You, a physician, are examining a patient suffering from poor blood circulation; you conclude that the patient has advanced arteriosclerosis. There is a partial block in the thigh where the arteries branch out to carry blood to the legs. By means of an arterial graft the condition can be corrected, but it is first necessary to locate the exact position of the block. This can be done by means of a dye injected into the bloodstream, which will make the block visible under X-rays. There are medical risks, but they seem well worth taking.

Nevertheless, you hesitate. Once before, confronted by a similar case, you used the dye, and something went wrong: the patient was paralyzed from the waist down. He sued both you and the hospital for malpractice, and the jury returned an award of a quarter of a million dollars to the patient. It clearly seems foolish to stick your neck out and take such a risk again. The safest thing for you to do is not even to tell the patient that the technique is available. Still, there is a 95 per cent chance of recovery if the technique is used. What should you do?

4. A famous German musician is going to play his first concert in America after World War II. Though he had known that before and during the war the Nazis had tortured and killed millions of Jews and political prisoners in concentration camps, he had not openly opposed them. True, if he had opposed them, he would probably have been killed; and his resistance wouldn't have stopped the Nazis anyway. Besides, he wasn't an active Nazi; he was just a musician who wanted to go ahead with his work unmolested. He could do so by declaring his allegiance and keeping quiet, letting others fight the battles. So that's what he did. Can you blame him? Still, some men did resist, and many of them were artists just as great as he. Should you condemn him now, five years later, or should you let bygones be bygones? After all, the dead won't come back to life if you judge him harshly now. Yet it doesn't seem as if you should welcome him with open arms the way you do more courageous men. Furthermore, he is without doubt a great musician, Nazi sympathizer or not; and isn't music music whoever plays it? Should you join the picket line that is boycotting and protesting the concert (the pickets won't succeed, but concert-goers passing the picket lines will at least know that others are supporting a principle), or should you attend the great musician's performance of the compositions you love and try not to think of his past affiliations?

5. T. E. Lawrence describes his engagements in a military expedition with the Arabs against the Turks during World War I. When the army was encamped for the night at Wadi Kitan, Hamed the Moor, in a rage, murdered Salem, a member of the Ageyl tribe. Although Lawrence was sick and very weak, he had tried to prevent Hamed. Lawrence knew of the Arab custom of seeking justice through the feud. When the relatives of the dead Salem demanded blood for blood, he realized that to prevent endless future violence, Hamed must die. Lawrence therefore killed Hamed.

Did Lawrence do wrong? He had not wished to commit murder, but he felt that it was his first duty to keep unity in the army. His act did succeed in preserving unity. Still, he had doubts. What if the blood cry of the relatives was only a threat? Then Lawrence had destroyed a life needlessly. But in view of the Arab custom, it was very unlikely that their demand was a mere threat. What if Hamed's relatives had then issued a blood cry for Lawrence? Would that not have been worse?

He might, of course, have sent Hamed away and told the relatives that he was dead. This plan might have worked. Hamed would have been getting away with a crime, but isn't one death better than two? Then, however, Hamed might have continued his rages and killings. Or, Lawrence might have tried to explain the Western procedure of trial before punishment.

Although it wouldn't have convinced them, he might have made a bit of progress. But even that bit was not very probable. Or perhaps the situation was none of his business at all?

What would you have done in Lawrence's place?

1. The scope of ethics

The preceding examples are only a few of the countless moral problems which may or do confront people. The study of moral problems is called *ethics*. But before we embark on this study, it will be well to dispel a few confusions at the start.

A. A definition of ethics

1. Some people have said, "Ethics is the study of right and wrong." This definition is too narrow; ethics is concerned with much more than that. Ethics is concerned not only with the question "When is an act right and when is it wrong?" but with much more besides. Specifically, ethics is also concerned with the following questions:

a. One question is, "What things are good?" (Or, in other words, "What things are desirable?" "What things are worthwhile?") For example, if an increase in human knowledge is something desirable or worthwhile, then it would, presumably, be right to aim at such an increase; but if an increase is not desirable, then the rightness of attempts to achieve knowledge would be questioned. What *acts* are right, then, would seem to depend on what *things* (objects, processes, events, states of mind, goals) are good. We cannot decide what is right or wrong without considering what things are worth having or striving for. (This is not the only possible view of the relation between the right and the good, as we shall see in later chapters. But, whatever may be the relation between them, this example will help to show that they are not the same.)

In daily conversation the words "right" and "good" are not always used in this clear-cut manner: they are not used interchangeably (it would sound strange to say "a right thing" rather than "a good thing"), but they are not carefully distinguished either. In ethics, however, we shall try to observe this distinction carefully: we shall use the word "right" to refer only to actions and "good" to refer to whatever is desirable as the aim, end, or goal of actions.

We shall not use the word "good" only for this purpose: we shall also speak, as we do in daily life, of a good person, a good moral character, a good character trait, and also of good motives, good intentions, good desires. What makes a goal or end a good one to aim at will not necessarily be the same as what makes a person or character good, or a motive or desire good.

The difference between the good and the right can perhaps be illustrated best in this way: imagine a race of beings on Mars whose behavior we could examine in detail through powerful telescopes but with whom we had no chance of communicating in any way. We might say that it would be good if they were happier than they are; but since, according to our hypothesis, there is nothing we can possibly do about it anyway, the question of right or wrong action on our part does not arise. We might say that it *would* be right to help them *if* we were able to do so; but since we cannot, there are no actions of ours with regard to them that we can speak of as right or wrong. The situation is even clearer with regard to the past. Suppose that ten million years ago on this very spot, a lion was eating an antelope, causing the still living antelope great pain. We might believe that it would have been better if this incident had not occurred (or at least if the antelope had died suddenly, so that it would not suffer pain); but since there is absolutely nothing we can do to change the past once it has happened, it would be pointless to say that it is wrong of us *now* not to try to snatch the antelope from the lion's clutches. The most we can say is that it would (or might) have been wrong of us not to have done so *if* we had been there at the time.

One other point of terminology is this: there is, in ordinary moral discourse, some difference between saying "This act is right" and "You ought to do this." The second is the stronger of the two. When we say that it is right to do something, we usually mean no more than that it is permissible —in other words, that it is *not wrong* to do it. But when we say that you ought to do it, or have a duty or an obligation to do it, we are saying something more: that it is *wrong not* to do it. Since it is the second of these two concepts that has most concerned ethical thinkers, this part of ethics is called "theory of right" less often than it is called "theory of obligation."

b. Another question we shall ask in our study of ethics is, "When does a person deserve blame, praise, punishment, or reward?" This question introduces a whole new area of considerations — moral responsibility, avoidability, determinism, and freedom of the will. These questions will concern us only after we have discussed the good and the right in some detail.

At first it may seem that this topic falls under the heading of right action or obligation. When we ask whether someone deserves blame for some act he has performed, aren't we simply asking, "Would it be right to blame him?" Sometimes the question is interpreted in this way. But it may mean something else as well: not "Should he be blamed?" but "Does he deserve to be blamed?" This will take us into the difficult problem of deserts.

2. Other people say, "Ethics is not the same as morals but is the *study* of morals." As far as it goes, this distinction is correct. Morals — people's beliefs about right and wrong, good and bad, punishment and desert, and so on, together with their actions in consequence of these beliefs — are human phenomena which are there to be studied and would be there even if nobody were interested in studying them. Ethics uses them as material for study, just as biology uses living organisms as its material for study.

But ethics is not just any study of morals. Anthropology studies morals too — the moral beliefs, customs, and practices of past and present cultures, tribes, and civilizations. Anthropologists describe these morals and sometimes find patterns and regularities amongst them which can be used to state scientific generalizations. But anthropologists, as scientists, pass no judgment upon them; they do not even say, in their professional capacity at any rate, that some morals are better than others. But ethics is not content merely to say, "This is what the ancient Etruscans did, and that is what the Australian bushmen do." Using the data of anthropology, ethics goes on to ask, "When one culture considers a certain practice, such as killing the aged, right and another considers it wrong, are they both right, and if not, which really is right?" "If one person or group considers pleasure the object most worth striving for in life and if another eschews pleasure and values only resignation and retirement from the world, which of these ideals is more worth pursuing?" In other words, ethics is concerned with pronouncing judgments of value upon human behavior, not merely in describing the behavior. Anthropology, psychology, and sociology, whose findings are all of interest to ethics, are *descriptive;* ethics is *prescriptive.* This distinction leads to still another suggestion.

3. The statement "Ethics is not the study of what *is* but of what *ought* to be" is another conception of ethics. In a sense this statement is true, but, like most slogans, it is misleading. First: in a way, the study of what is right and wrong is the study of what is; if it is a fact that murder is wrong, then this is a fact about what *is.* "Is" is such an inclusive word that every study that has some object-of-study (and what study has not?) could be described as a study of some aspect or other of what is. Second: "what ought to be" is not a very clear phrase. As we have just observed, we usually employ "ought" words when we are talking about human actions: you ought to do this but not that. But when we say that this or that ought to *be,* what do we mean? that one or another person ought to *do* it or bring it about? What meaning can "ought" have if it isn't applied to actions that someone ought to perform? But if "X ought to exist" means the same as "Someone ought to do or bring about X," then the definition is much too narrow; for ethics is also concerned with what is good and what is deserved.

In any event, the statement is correct insofar as it points out the difference between judgments of fact and judgments of value. There are many ways of putting this distinction, but this one is perhaps the easiest: "Ethics is concerned not only with what a certain individual or group considers right but with what *is* right. Ethics not merely describes moral ideals held by human beings but asks which ideal is *better* than others, more worth pursuing, and why." Here we see clearly the difference between ethics on the one hand and empirical science on the other. If you say that more promises are broken than kept, this is an empirical statement, that is, one that can be verified (discovered to be true or false) by observing people and compiling statistics concerning the keeping and breaking of promises. But if you say that promises *should,* or ought to, be kept, you cannot test your assertion by observing people's actions or compiling statistics. Even if 99 per cent of all promises made were broken, this fact would not prove that promises *ought* not to be kept; in fact the defender of promises might make his defense more vigorous than before, since he would feel that his defense was more needed. It may be an empirical fact, that is, empirically verifiable, that Smith is incurably ill, and every physician may agree that this is true. But this does not settle the question whether the physician *ought* to keep Smith alive as long as possible no matter how much he suffers, or whether he should be given the slight overdose of morphine that would put him out of his misery, or whether he should merely be kept under heavy sedation which will relieve him of some of his pain but weaken his heart and thus shorten his days. All these are moral questions. Two people might agree on the empirical facts of the case and yet disagree about what course of action to follow in view of these facts. Here lies the great difference between ethics (along with its sister discipline, aesthetics) on the one hand and the empirical sciences — physics, chemistry, biology, psychology, and so on — on the other.

"If statements about good and bad and right and wrong cannot be verified empirically," one may ask, "how *can* they be verified?" This is a large and difficult question, which we must postpone until the last chapter of the book, after we have surveyed all the major theories concerning the problems we have outlined. The question is so complex that adequate treatment of it would require another book. It is complex because to ask, "How do you know that this statement is true?" presupposes another question, "What do you mean by the terms in your statement?" There are many theories about the meanings of "good," "right," and other ethical terms, which have to be fully thrashed out before we are in a position to answer the question "How do you know?" This difficult and highly technical discipline of the meanings of ethical terms is called *metaethics,* or, sometimes, ethical theory, as opposed to the study of *normative ethics,* a critical study of the major theories about what things are good, what acts are right, and what actions deserve blame. Normative ethics will occupy us throughout all but the last chapter of this book.

4. "Ethics is the study of what is moral and what is immoral." As it stands, this statement is most misleading. The term "moral" is ambiguous. It has two opposites, "immoral" and "nonmoral." (1) In one sense, to call a person or an action "moral" is to use a term of praise or commendation, and to use the opposite term, "immoral," is to use a term of condemnation and disapproval. "Immoral," when applied to actions, usually means very much the same as "wrong," and when applied to situations and people, usually means the same as "bad"; but in either case it is a term of condemnation. (2) In another sense, the term "moral" simply puts a question or issue into the category of ethics as opposed to other questions which are not in this domain. Thus, on the one hand, committing murder is said to be immoral;

but the *question* whether it is immoral is a moral question, it is one of the questions in the domain of ethics. On the other hand, whether I put my right foot or my left foot down first when I get out of bed in the morning is a nonmoral matter which is no concern of ethics. We distinguish moral from immoral *behavior* and moral from nonmoral *questions,* issues, controversies, problems. (The word "amoral" has still a different use. People, not issues, are described as amoral. A person is said to be amoral when he has no sense of right and wrong, or acts as if he didn't.)

Where is the line between moral and nonmoral questions to be drawn? This is a difficult question, which we cannot attempt to answer here, for different people have different views on this point. Some say that a question or problem is a moral one if it concerns behavior that affects the happiness or well-being of any other person (or, sometimes, of any other living creature). Others say that it is a moral question only if it concerns behavior that can be universalized, behavior of which one can legitimately ask whether everyone else in the same position ought to do the same. In any event, moral questions are very inclusive, and we shall not be at a loss to discover a vast array of questions which are moral by anyone's criterion.

It would be easy to resolve the problem of how a moral problem differs from a nonmoral one simply by saying that moral issues are those in which such terms as "right," "good," and "ought," are used. But all of these words are used in contexts which everyone would agree are nonmoral. We ask not only, "Is this act right?" but also, "What is the right answer to this algebraic problem?" We say, "You ought to do this," but we also say, "There ought to be a side road just about here" and "This problem in long division ought to have come out without a remainder." As for "good," its nonmoral uses far exceed the moral ones: we speak of a good baseball player, a good day, a good school, a good way to solve a problem, a good way to relax, even a good way to murder someone. In most, if not all, of these examples, we are concerned with an activity that has some aim or function, and we call something or somebody "good" if it regularly or efficiently fulfills that function. The function may have nothing whatever to do with morality. It is, of course, the moral use of these terms that we shall be concerned with in ethics. But it will not do to define moral questions as those employing moral terms, since all these terms are also used in nonmoral contexts. We still haven't answered the question "When is the term being used in a moral way?" It would be circular to define moral questions in terms of their use of moral words and then distinguish the moral sense of these words by referring back to moral questions.

5. "Ethics is concerned with encouraging people to do what is right." This statement is not only misleading but false. We shall try to come to some true and defensible conclusions about what is right and what is good, but finding true principles is not the same thing as acting upon them. People can be made to act in certain ways by moral advice, exhortation, persuasion, sermons, propaganda, hypnosis, or psychiatric therapy. But none of these

means is the concern of ethics; ethics is concerned to find the truth about these moral questions, not to try to make us act upon them. We may, in fact, honor our moral principles more in the breach than in the observance; and nobody, of course, always practices what he preaches. Perhaps *doing* right is more important than *discovering* what is right. But at least the second is a necessary means to the first. Unless you first know what is right, how will you know what to do or what to persuade others to do? You cannot act upon knowledge unless you first have the knowledge. Of course, you may act without knowledge at all; many people act ignorantly, and many do not even care what is right but just do as they please. Nevertheless, acting in moral matters without knowledge is surely just as dangerous as an engineer's trying to build a bridge without knowledge of the principles of engineering. Before you drink what's in the bottle, it is wise to know what the bottle contains.

Ethics, then, is interested in discovering true statements, just as is any other domain of inquiry. But ethics, unlike other disciplines, is interested in finding these truths in the special area of the right and the good. It is concerned not directly with practice but with finding true statements about what our practices ought to be — statements which, it is hoped, will then be acted upon. "Propositions about practice are not themselves practical, any more than propositions about gases are gaseous." [1] Nevertheless, ethical propositions can be said to be practical in an indirect way that the others are not, just *because* they are propositions about practice. It is difficult to think of questions which, in the long run, are more practical than questions about how to live, how to conduct oneself, how best to spend the few short years that are the most that anyone can enjoy in this world.

6. "Ethics should be able to tell you exactly which acts are right and which ones are wrong." But even this statement is a mistake. We shall search for moral *principles,* i.e., rules of behavior, (we shall be more precise about this later on) having to do with matters of right and wrong. But it would be hopeless to attempt to answer every moral question confronting every human being; for in order to do so, we would have to know not only true moral principles but also a vast array of empirical facts about the person and his situation and the circumstances of his action and the probable effects of the action. Suppose that we take as an example of a moral principle, "The infliction of needless suffering is wrong." (There are questions we could raise about when something is needless, but let that pass for the moment.) Let us assume for the moment that the principle is true. The full argument would be as follows:

    1. The infliction of needless suffering is wrong.
    2. This act is a case of the infliction of needless suffering.
Therefore, 3. This act is wrong.

[1] Bertrand Russell, "The Elements of Ethics," in Sellars and Hospers, *Readings in Ethical Theory,* p. 1.

The third statement does give us the desired conclusion, and the first statement is, as we have agreed, a true moral principle. But the second statement is also required in order to arrive at the conclusion; and this second statement, let us note, is not a statement in ethics at all but an empirical statement about a specific act or situation. Every situation is somewhat different from every other, and no ethical philosopher could possibly be acquainted with them all. All the ethical philosopher can tell us, in the above example, is that *if* some proposed act will cause needless suffering, *then* it is wrong. He cannot, of course, tell us whether *this* particular act *is* the infliction of needless suffering. Only a person who is there at the time, such as the agent ("agent" in ethics means the doer of the act) himself, is in a position to know the particular circumstances of the individual case.

B. Moral rules

Most people most of the time assent to a conglomeration of moral rules which they do not bother to question or examine. These rules are usually those they have been taught to believe, such as "Don't tell lies" and "Don't cheat your friends," plus a few which they find convenient or agreeable, such as "Mind your own business" and "Never give a sucker an even break." Usually these rules are not stated explicitly; they come out into the open only when the person is questioned. Very often one of the rules contradicts another, thus enabling the user to resort first to one and then to the other to suit his convenience or to accord with his pre-existing prejudices.

The unspoken moral code of many Americans consists, in part, of such directives as these: It is good to help out your friends and neighbors, but not so much that it causes you any great discomfort or keeps you from buying that second television set. It is not proper to argue with others about morals or religion because argument might cause ill will and hurt people's feelings. (Implication: it is more important for people to feel comfortable all the time than to explore together the truth about life and death, God and immortality, right and wrong.) It's not a good idea to question where a person's money comes from; if he has it, you look up to him, that's all. If a person keeps a low-paying job which he likes and turns down a high-paying job which he likes less, he ought to have his head examined. If he spends his money on books instead of on lavish cocktail parties, he must really be out of his mind. Negroes should never be permitted to go beyond the eighth grade in school or to attend the same schools with whites because Negroes are an inferior race. The United States is the best country in the world, and anybody who criticizes it ought to be deported.

The following is the implicit code of large numbers of television viewers, especially of the younger generation: Giving a rotten character a break, especially if it happens to be a pretty girl, is the right thing to do even if it endangers the lives of others. A simple, direct man is the best for any job, even though he may not be very smart. A man who pretends that some political issue is complicated is only trying to cover up his ignorance with a lot of fáncy double-talk. A hard-riding square-shooting cowboy is a better judge of right and wrong or of national policy and legislation than any lawyer or professor. To think about anything is a sign of weakness; it is better just to act. The best man is the one who is fastest with a gun; that's why the right side always wins out. If you are on the right side, you'll always win out in the end. Our country is always in the right; and since the right must win, we are not in any danger and never can be. To deny this is un-American.

Perhaps the most conspicuous example of how little we think through the rules of conduct by which we profess to live runs as follows: The majority of Americans profess to be Christians and therefore to accept the Christian way of life; yet very few of them practice these rules. Few even reflect on the moral directives of Christianity which they have heard many times. They pay lip service to the moral commands found in the Gospels, but they would not dream of putting these precepts into practice; and if any of their neighbors did so, they would consider the neighbors fools. Officially these professed Christians believe it is their duty to turn the other cheek, but in daily life they retaliate even for small injuries. They consider it unmasculine to discuss anything rationally; the way to settle things is to see who wins in a fair fight. Officially they believe they should forgive, not once but seventy times seven; but in fact they seldom forgive at all, and when they do they usually make a great show of letting people know how forgiving they are. They are told in the Bible to take no thought for the morrow, what they shall eat or wear; but in fact they spend the greater part of their time in this enterprise. Although they are told that it is easier for a camel to pass through the eye of a needle than for a rich man to enter into the kingdom of heaven, their chief goal is to amass as much money and property as possible, not only for their comfort but to satisfy their exhibitionism and to cause envy among their neighbors. They believe that all men are brothers, but they associate only with those who are in an income group as high as their own. They prefer not to associate with people of different racial or religious background and feel uncomfortable in their presence. The Bible tells these so-called Christians that no man can serve both God and Mammon; but during a lifetime spent in trying to outdo their neighbors in serving Mammon, they assume that their Creator will reward them with eternal bliss for their efforts in His behalf. They are told that the meek shall inherit the earth; but if anyone they know is meek, they consider him a sissy or a sucker. They are told that of faith, hope, and charity, the greatest is charity, but they do not particularly mind that, owing to overpopulation and lack of industrialization, the world does not produce enough to feed its people one square meal a day. While millions starve, these Christians spend more money each year on liquor than on all charitable enterprises combined. They are told to beware of false gods, but they believe in "America First" and frown on any attempt to alleviate world tensions because the enemy is wicked, communistic, and atheistic besides. Attempts at conciliation they brand "appeasement," and in some school systems all books referring favorably to the concept of "One World" are banned. These Christians are supposed to believe that it is wrong to kill, yet ". . . from the time of Constantine to the time of global radiation and the interceptible missile, Christians have killed Christians and been blessed for doing so by other Christians."[1]

Many people who conduct their lives *as if* these statements were true would be shocked and sometimes ashamed to see them listed in cold black and white. Nevertheless, it is important to bring out into the open the moral principles which are *presupposed* in our behavior so that we can have them before us and scrutinize them with care.

C. Applying the rules

"But," one may ask, "what need have I of ethics? Don't I already know what's good and bad, right and wrong? If I already know, what need is there to discuss it? Why not just stick to the good old do's and don'ts I have been brought up with — don't tell lies, don't steal, don't kill, be kind to your parents, be honest, keep your promises? What's wrong with this?"

We shall have a good deal to say about moral rules in the coming pages. At the moment we are not saying that there is anything wrong with those just cited. All the same, in ethics we cannot simply accept rules and leave them at that, for people will question them or even state other rules which contradict them. Therefore we must try to justify them — to try to find out why they are satisfactory, if they are, and why they are not, if they are not. Before examining any specific ethical views, there are a number of questions we can ask about the traditional do's and don'ts.

1. Are we to believe that these traditional moral rules have absolutely *no exceptions?* For example, aren't there situations in which it would be right to tell a lie, even positively wrong not to do so? Imagine that a neighborhood gossip asks you, "Are they really going to give a surprise birthday party for your mother?" You know full well that if you confirm it (and it was told you as a secret), the news will be all over the neighborhood in twenty-four hours. Even if you are silent, your silence will be interpreted as assent and the neighbor will still spread the news. It would seem that the only thing for you to do to keep the secret is to lie and say, "No." Imagine another situation. An escapee from a lunatic asylum, vowing vengeance against Mr. Smith for an imaginary grievance, enters your house armed with a knife, and asks you where Smith lives so that he can go there and kill him. Should you tell the lunatic the truth?

What about keeping promises? You have promised to meet somebody at four p.m., and on the way you are witness to an accident in which you can help in saving someone's life. Aren't you justified in breaking your promise to keep the appointment?

[1] From *The Causes of World War Three.* Copyright © 1958 by C. Wright Mills. By permission of Simon and Schuster, Inc., p. 152.

What about killing? If you had a chance to kill a dictator who, if allowed to live, would kill thousands of people, wouldn't it be right to kill him and wrong not to do so? Would you have saved the life of one of the sadistic torturers in Hitler's concentration camps if you had had a chance to put him into the same gas chamber to which he had already condemned thousands? If you believe it is *always* wrong to kill, you must believe that the 1944 plot against Hitler's life was wrong, even though, had it succeeded, it would probably have ended the war many months sooner and thus saved thousands of lives.

It can be disputed, of course, whether these really are exceptions; and we shall be arguing these matters pro and con in the coming chapters. If you don't like these examples, others could be devised to show that the traditional do's and don'ts require some exceptions. At this point we are in no position to state that exceptions should be made but only that there *might* be exceptions or, at the very least, that these traditional rules need some justifying.

If you insist that there are no exceptions to these rules, you will find particularly difficult the kind of situation in which you have to break one of the rules you accept no matter what you do. Suppose that believing you should never break a promise and also that you should save human life if it is in your power to do so, you are confronted with the situation in which to save a life you have to break a promise. In such a situation, something has to give — when two rules come into conflict, one of them (at least for the moment) must go.

2. Exactly what do the traditional do's and don'ts *mean?* Their area of application is not specified, and there is often a large twilight-zone of cases in which it is far from clear whether these cases are covered by the rule or not.

Exactly when is one lying? Someone says, "I ain't done nothin'." A listener unacquainted with the idiom of the English language, concluding that two negatives make an affirmative, infers that the speaker *has* done something. Was the speaker lying just because, when taken literally, his statement was untrue? You say, "This essay has always struck me as very trivial," and your hearer reports you to someone else as saying that you thought it was trivial when you were five years old (long before you had even read the essay). If you deny it, can your hearer rightly accuse you of having lied? Someone says, "They had her for dinner last night" and another replies, "That's a lie, they're not cannibals." Is the second speaker justified in saying that the first speaker lied? You say, "I wouldn't eat spinach for all the tea in China!" but someone offers you a dollar and you eat the spinach. Is he justified in saying, "You lied — you said you wouldn't do it for all the tea in China"? Are you justified in replying, "But I wouldn't — I don't even like tea. I didn't say I wouldn't do it for a dollar"? Saying that you wouldn't do it for all the tea in China *suggests* that you wouldn't do it for an amount of money equivalent to the value of all the tea in China, but of course you didn't *say* it. Can you be said to have lied because you said something idio‑ matically or metaphorically which was taken literally or because your state‑ ment suggested to most or all listeners some false statement that you did not specifically assert? What if your statement not only suggested but *implied* a false statement? You say, "Unless you give me a raise, I'll quit," and you get no raise and still don't quit. Surely you have lied? Someone asks you, "Have you a dime?" You say "No," and it later turns out that you have a dollar. Have you lied? If you say, "But you only asked if I had a dime," does this exonerate you from the charge?

In most of these examples, it would probably be agreed that the statement was not a lie, even though it was false, because there was no *intent* to de‑ ceive. A lie, you might say, is an intentional falsehood; an unintentionally false statement is no lie. Thus, if you say one thing and mean another, this would be no lie even though it misleads everyone. But what if you say noth‑ ing at all? "He's the one who stole the money, isn't he?" someone asks you, and you say nothing; but since you don't deny it, he assumes that you have assented. Perhaps he shouldn't have assumed this; but what if you *deliber‑ ately* chose not to speak so as to create a mistaken impression? Then you have lied, even though you have made no statement at all! What of the deaf person who automatically replies, "Yes" to every question he is asked. He hasn't really heard the question, but he doesn't want to ask the ques‑ tioner to repeat it, so he says, "Yes" to keep the peace. What of the timid person who says, "Yes" just to avoid an argument? What of the person who says, "Yes" to the question "Was it $5,000?" and only later, on reflec‑ tion, realizes that he misheard the question, which really was, "Was it $500?" He doesn't consider it important enough to go back to it after the subject has been changed; and besides, he has no reason to think it important.

You can devise many examples of your own to show how vague is the area of application of the term "lying." Thus, even if you espouse without exceptions the rule "Never tell a lie," it is not clear in many cases what is covered by this rule. And yet it is important to know what it covers if you want the rule applied without exception.

The same vagueness pervades crucial terms in all the traditional moral rules. "Be honest" — but what is honesty? Does honesty compel you to re‑ turn the one penny too much change that the clerk has given you, even if to do so means driving back fifty miles to the town where the purchase was made? Is a transaction honest as long as you paid the agreed price and got the correct change even if the clerk grossly overcharged you for the merchan‑ dise, or misread the price tag, or if the merchant was swindling you? Some people would go so far as to say that the whole capitalistic system in which merchants charge the highest price they can get away with is one huge system of dishonesty, and that anything we can do to attack it — such as not giving change back which is due the storekeeper — is justified insofar as it, and actions like it, tend to undermine the whole system.

"Do not steal." Are you stealing if you take something that you think belongs to you but, as it later turns out, really does not? Are you stealing if you enter the apartment of someone who has stolen from you and take from him an object of equal value? Are you stealing if someone hands you a five dollar bill, thinking it to be one dollar, and you say nothing about it? Are you stealing land from tenants if you foreclose mortgages which they cannot pay because of your own business practices? Are you stealing from competitors if you engage in monopolistic practices, underselling them at a loss until the competitors go broke, and then jacking up prices? "Business is business," some would say with a shrug; but others would answer that many of the acts performed under the banner of this sacred maxim are such gross examples of stealing and cheating that beside them the daily garden variety examples pale into insignificance. Where *is* one to draw the line between what is stealing and what is not?

"Do not kill." Undoubtedly you kill somebody when he dies as the result of your shooting him at close range. But suppose you only scare him, and as a result he dies of a heart attack. Or suppose that, as in ancient times, you leave a child to die of exposure or, by refusing to feed him, let him starve? There is nothing you have actively *done; death results from what you did *not* do. But if failure to do something can be called killing, what of the man who, knowing that many people will starve, if he does not sign a bill granting more food to starving workers, fails or refuses to sign? Many would say, "He's killing them just as surely as if he shot them himself." In that sense, aren't we guilty of killing whenever we deny help to starving people overseas?

The automobile driver steps on the brakes to avoid hitting a pedestrian and finds that the brakes do not work. Has he killed the pedestrian through negligence in having his brakes taken care of? Suppose he says, "I knew the brakes weren't too good, but I didn't know they were *that* bad." Is he guilty of murder or only of negligence? "Negligence," we may say, but a person died as a result of his negligence. Suppose the garageman didn't repair the brakes well enough the last time or was called to the telephone before the job was completed and forgot to return to it. What is he guilty of? What if a man doesn't shoot his wife but through months of mental torture finally drives her to suicide? What if she is highly suggestible, and he gradually plants the idea of suicide in her mind by a hypnotic reiteration of the suggestion? "Doing it mentally is no different from doing it physically," one may say. Then what about the boss who, through a technicality, takes away all retirement benefits from an employee of long standing who is just retiring, with the result that the employee, now old and with no way of earning money, shoots himself? "The boss killed him just as surely as if he had knifed him" because the man's death occurred as a consequence of the boss's action. But if any person whose act results in another's death is to be called a murderer, then has anybody who tells a person some bitter truth about himself which results in his suicide, killed him? If so, what about his mother, who gave him birth? His death would not have occurred but for his birth — if he hadn't been given life, he couldn't have died. But it would be strange to say that she killed him. Or what of the testing of thermonuclear bombs? Every time one of them is exploded, scientists tell us, hundreds of our descendants will die from the effects of strontium-90 and other side-effects of the explosions. We don't know who they are and they don't know us — most of them haven't been born yet — but they will die just the same, as the result of our actions.

All these concepts then — lying, stealing, killing, and others that we have not mentioned — are fuzzy ones, and their application to specific examples is far from clear. But even if the application were crystal clear, it would not put an end to the questions that could be asked about the traditional do's and don'ts.

3. What about the situations which the rules don't seem to cover at all? What are we to do in entirely new situations which could not have been foreseen at the time the rules were set forth? For example: (1) Large numbers of people are killed every year on our highways because of speeding cars that cannot stop in time. If the speed limits were higher, even more people would be killed. If they were much lower, say, thirty miles per hour everywhere, there would be fewer casualties; but motorists would suffer enormous inconvenience. If cars were prohibited entirely, there would be no fatalities resulting from automobiles. What should be done? How much inconvenience balances against the loss of one life? Should the speed of all cars be reduced to a crawl in order to lower accidents by 75 per cent? (2) The surgeon says that if he operates, there is a 50 per cent chance that your child will live and that if he does not operate, there is an 80 per cent chance for your child's life but the child will be hopelessly crippled. It is up to you to make the decision. What should you do? (3) In 1945 the President of the United States had to decide whether to drop the first atomic bomb on Japan. Thousands would be killed. On the one hand, dropping the bomb would undoubtedly remove the necessity for an invasion of Japan, which, Army authorities estimated, might cost a million American casualties. On the other hand, dropping the bomb would set a ghastly precedent, and it would always be remembered that we were the first nation in history to drop such a bomb; yet might it not also render war obsolete? How was one to know in 1945? A demonstration bomb might have been dropped with the same deterring effect; but at the time there were no more bombs available. Aside from minimizing loss of life — and there was no way of telling which of the alternatives would succeed in doing this — what principles could be used to guide one's decision, in these new and unprecedented circumstances?

Unprecedented situations provide the most dramatic examples, but we need not go far to find others. Suppose that you are receiving large dividends from stock in a certain company but you have reason to question the business practices of that company. Much of its income is derived from cutthroat business methods, from shady deals with underworld characters in violation of the law, from illegally divulging military secrets to potential enemy nations, or from robbing widows and orphans by insisting on a literal reading of certain ambiguous words in the fine print of time-payment contracts. Should you just close your eyes to these practices and keep on receiving the income you desire and need to support your family, or should you stand on principle and sell your lucrative stock in that company, even though your act would not change the company's business practices in the slightest or help in any way the victims of these practices? Which of the traditional do's and don'ts will help you solve this and a thousand other problems that occur in our complex business society? Most people conveniently ignore such situations and do whatever lines their pocketbooks the most because such situations do not fall, at least in any obvious or noncontroversial way, under any of the traditional rules of moral behavior. But are these people justified?

4. Probing more deeply, one may ask, "Why these do's and don'ts rather than others?" Suppose one rule instilled in you from childhood is "Always avenge an injury done you." But now it occurs to you that this may not be a good rule. An act of vengeance on your part will probably lead to someone else's trying to avenge your act with one of his own, and so on indefinitely. Or suppose one person says that no one should ever take another human life even in self-defense, while another person's set of moral rules allows killing in these circumstances. Inevitably these situations raise the question "When one person holds one set of moral rules and another person holds a different, or only partially overlapping, set, what is to decide between them?" Surely they can't both be right? That the first person has been brought up to believe in his set of rules does not make them right because the second person, whose rules contradict the first set, has been brought up to believe in his own set of rules. If being brought up to believe in one's set of inherited rules is a sufficient reason to make them right in the first instance, why not also in the second?

Even if there were no disagreement, if every human being lived by exactly the same set of rules, one might still ask the question "How are these rules to be justified?" If someone asked you to defend them, what would you say?

We shall be discussing this question at length in the coming chapters. Meanwhile, here are a few precautions.

D. Confusions and pitfalls

If we are to traverse intelligently and fruitfully such a complex field as ethics, we shall have to be on guard against certain mistakes to which we may easily fall victim if they are not pointed out in advance. They are stumbling blocks because they prevent us from honestly searching for the truth, especially when the truth is unpleasant. Most people do not want to get at the truth as much as they want to find reasons to support their pet prejudices. Once the reasons are found, they dismiss the philosopher as they would a taxi after they have arrived at their destination. This tendency is so widespread and so deep-seated that no single book on ethics, or even a collection of them, can possibly uproot it. The best we can do is to be constantly on our guard against it, to recognize when we are its victims, and not to deceive ourselves into believing that we are impartial seekers after truth when we are not. It is difficult enough to learn the facts of physics and chemistry, for these subjects are complicated and often abstruse; but at least our emotions are not usually involved and we do not have years of prejudice to fight. We do not so badly want carbon monoxide to be harmless that we come to believe that it is. When, however, the subject is the conduct of our own lives, it is almost inevitable that we shall come to believe what we want to believe, whether or not these beliefs are justified.

1. Since earlier remarks have already suggested it, we may first mention the unduly *narrow concept of morality* held by many people. People tend to identify morality with whatever commands they learned in childhood, the traditional do's and don'ts about such matters as lying, cheating, and stealing. These rules cover, though vaguely, as we have seen, certain classes of actions but only a small fraction of the total. A crooked business deal, a political appointment of a nonentity when a worthy candidate was available, a bill signed into law which will increase our troubles overseas, any one of these can have far more harmful effects than a thousand lies or a million broken promises to Sally or Peter. Yet actions in business and politics are often not associated with morality at all: "That's just politics," people say. If a girl in one's home town engages in premarital intercourse and the fact becomes known, every respectable citizen (including many who have done the same thing) is full of moral condemnation of her action; but if the citizens of the town do not take the trouble to investigate the records of their candidates for public office, as is usually the case, nobody condemns these citizens. No one feels that "politics" — even the exercise of one's duty to vote intelligently, which is the lifeblood of democracy — has anything to do with moral action. No one thinks that a person who does not vote intelligently or who votes at the dictation of his own personal interest or of pressure groups is doing anything wrong.

Why this curious incongruity? It stems partly from the fact that we were not taught as children to desist from unfair business practices or to sign bills into law only after due consideration of all the consequences. Children are in no position to do these things, and many adults never get into that position; so, of course, there are no parental commands against these things. At the time of life when feelings of guilt were first instilled, there were, therefore, no feelings of guilt applied to these adult activities. Moreover, most moral rules are passed on from generation to generation with very little change. When our grandmothers were young, there were very few problems of a complex industrial society on which to offer moral rules.

In many people the concept of morality never develops beyond the childhood stage. Consequently they feel no guilt about committing acts in public life, where the victims of their greed or negligence are often unseen, which they would never commit in private life. They can swindle the stockholders of a large corporation with never a tremor of guilt, but their consciences would so strongly object to stealing money from a personal friend that they would not dream of doing it. A man may be an exemplary father and at the same time a vicious and underhanded business competitor who treats a public trust as a sport.

We have not yet examined any ethical theories, but perhaps it would not be going out on a limb to say that this childhood concept of morality, which strains at the gnat and swallows the camel, is a grossly insufficient one, and the sooner we get rid of it, the sooner we shall be in a position to evaluate impartially where our duties lie.

2. A device involved in moral decisions to which everyone falls victim, not once or twice but constantly, is *rationalization*. We usually profess to make our choice of action depend on prior *reasons,* but in practice we are likely *first* to decide what we want to do and *then* think up reasons for doing it. We find reasons for doing what we would have done anyway without reasons.

When we want to arrive at work late, we say that people should be given a break once in a while; when someone else is late, we say people ought to have the decency to be punctual. When someone picks a fight with us, we say he had no right to do it, and we display considerable moral indignation; but when we want to pick a fight with someone else, we say it is our duty to teach him a lesson. When we want badly to go to a party instead of waiting on Grandfather, who is ill, we say that we need a bit of relaxation, or that Grandfather isn't that sick anyway, or that others can do it better; but if others used the same excuses, we would accuse them of shirking their duty.

Rationalization is especially insidious when it masquerades under the banner of Duty. "It's my duty to punish you," says the father who wants to take out his aggression on somebody that morning. Perhaps he really does feel that it is his duty, but it is also what he *wants* to do. When what you say you ought to do happens to coincide with what you want to do, it is always wise to ask yourself, "Am I really doing it because I ought to or only because I want to? Are the reasons I give for saying I ought to actually rationalizations of my desire to do it?" Most people will not embark on a course of action, no matter how obvious it is to others that it is what they want to do, without indulging themselves in some rationalization or other in an attempt to justify their action, though the reasons by themselves would seldom be enough to initiate the action without a desire in that direction antecedent to the reasons.

In this area it is so tempting and so easy to delude ourselves, to think that our official motives are our real motives, that even if we are as impartial and as honest with ourselves as we can be, we are still in danger of rationalizing our behavior. Consider the district judge who has just been elected governor of the state. His first official act as governor is to deny a commutation of the death sentence to a condemned prisoner, though the prisoner was his boyhood friend. "It is my sworn duty to be impartial," he says. "Since no new evidence in the case has come up, I must stand by the sentence of the judge who gave the verdict. Under these circumstances I would not commute the sentence of a total stranger; therefore, neither should I commute the sentence of my boyhood friend just because I happen to know him personally." Perhaps he *is* being impartial; perhaps his decision *is* the result of honest moral reflection rather than a rationalization of his desire. But perhaps not. His wife wonders. Surely, she thinks, he cannot forget that he and the prisoner were rivals and that she and the prisoner were once lovers. Could it not be that now, years later, the governor still harbors, even if unconsciously, some resentment over these facts and that they, not his noble reasoning, are really the motive power behind his refusal to commute the sentence? How can one be sure? It is so fatally easy to believe what we want to believe in order to do what we want to do.

> No one who has examined the repertory of arguments of the average man can fail to notice how persistently some are applied in one context and some in another. It is a good thing that he, himself, should have a large income because (a) the amount he saves increases the capital of the country, (b) the part he spends, even on luxuries, is good for trade and increases employment. It is good because (c) the country cannot afford the burden of high wages, (d) poverty and hardship produce sturdy, manly characters, and (e) if the gardener were paid more, he would only spend it on useless luxuries like going to the pictures. This is only a small sample of what one can draw from him in a few minutes' conversation, but it is enough to show the prevalence of special pleading. (b) and (e) are inconsistent with one another; the view that luxury expenditure is socially valuable being applied to himself, while the view that it is a social evil is applied to his gardener. (a) is not applied to his gardener, while (c) and (d) are not applied to himself. We may further ask whether he really believes (a) and (e), which imply that the thing of greatest social value to do with money is to save it, or (b) which implies that the right thing is to spend it on no matter what. It is useless to ask which he believes. He believes both propositions and will employ either in different contexts. Men have a much larger power of believing inconsistent propositions than is commonly supposed.[1]

3. Moral judgments are often based on nothing more than *emotional appeals*. It often happens that a child will not do what he is commanded unless all the engines of persuasion available to the parents, and sometimes force as

---

[1] From *Straight and Crooked Thinking,* by Robert Thouless. Copyright 1939, Simon and Schuster, Inc., pp. 227-28.

well, are employed to make him do so. Reason makes very little appeal to
the small child, and yet he must be made from his earliest years to do certain things and refrain from doing others. Thus one can hardly object on
occasion to persuasion, emotional appeal, and even outright coercion. Nevertheless, when we are trying to find acceptable moral principles rather than
to get people to practice them, the appeal to emotion is not desirable; indeed,
it is usually employed when the person can think of no good reason for saying what he does. The trouble with emotional appeal is that it is double-
edged: it can be used on both sides of the fence — and the same is true also,
of course, of the use of force. If a person can be persuaded by emotional
appeals to do right, he can also be persuaded by the same means to do
wrong. Emotional appeal can instill propaganda for race-hatred as easily as
it can instill pleas for racial equality and tolerance. Thus, the use of emotional
appeal to recommend a proposition shows nothing one way or the other
about the truth or acceptability of the proposition. To distinguish right from
wrong, then, we need other means.

4. Moral rules are often *diluted into tautologies* through successive interpretations to make them coincide with what one already approves. Consider
the rule "Do not kill." (Presumably this rule refers to human beings; but
many would extend it to animals, at least the animals they like, such as
dogs and horses; and others, such as the Hindus, extend it to all forms of
life.) The extreme pacifist takes the rule literally: he will not take life, at
least human life, for any reason whatever. He may or may not be right
in acting thus, but at least he is consistent. Most people, possibly for excellent reasons, do not want the rule to apply in all the situations that the pacifist does. For example, they wish to permit killing in self-defense and killing in war or in certain types of war. The rule becomes, in effect, "Do not
kill, except in war (those on the other side, not your own side) and in self-
defense." What constitutes self-defense is a thorny problem. Is it self-defense
to kill somebody to keep him from robbing your house? But then you may
wish to make another kind of exception. For example, someone asks you
whether the man who presses the button in the death house, thus electro-
cuting the prisoner, ought to be considered guilty of murder, or, perhaps,
the governor who refuses to commute his sentence, or the legislators who
refused to abandon the death penalty for condemned prisoners, or the judge
who sentenced him. But the moment you have included this new class of
exceptions into the rule, revising it to read ". . . and in cases of capital
punishment . . . ," other possible exceptions occur to you. You remember
your friend in the Korean war who was pinned hopelessly under the wreck-
age of his burning plane, crying, "Shoot me, somebody, shoot me!" knowing that in a minute or less the gasoline tanks would explode and he would
be burned to death. One of his friends shot him and was therefore court-martialed. Should he have been? Was this killing really wrong? But it doesn't
fall under any of the already mentioned classes of exceptions.

Not being able to think of any new class of exceptions under which this instance belongs, and fearful lest still other classes of possible exceptions may present themselves, you cut the Gordian knot by saying, "It's not killing per se but *murder,* that's always wrong." But murder is — what? the deliberate taking of a human life other than in self-defense? By this criterion your friend is guilty of murder, which you just said is always wrong. You will have to revise your definition of murder if you want it to cover a situation such as this. So you seize upon an easy way out: you say that murder is always wrong because murder is *unjustified killing* and what your friend did was justified, so it wasn't really murder. But this explanation, of course, only pushes the question one step further back: for when is killing justified, and when, on the other hand, is it murder?

At any rate, your new-found rule, "Murder is always wrong," has become an empty tautology. Since "Killing is wrong" seems to demand exceptions and the rule "Murder is wrong" does not, you favor the latter. But what does this rule now say? Murder is unjustified killing, and murder is always wrong, so it follows logically that unjustified killing is always wrong. But what does the term "unjustified" mean in this context? When is an act unjustified? Presumably when it's wrong. So all that the fine new exceptionless rule tells you is that unjustified killing is wrong — in other words, killing that's wrong is wrong. And this is no more informative than Calvin Coolidge's famous statement, "When large numbers of people are out of work, unemployment results."

If you want moral rules to be guides to action, they must be rules that say something, rules with teeth in them, rules that permit some actions and prohibit others, not empty tautologies masquerading as moral rules, to which everyone can agree simply because the rules *are* empty and vacuous. "You should always do what is your duty" may be a fine and noble sentiment; but unfortunately, being a tautology, it tells you absolutely nothing about what specific actions or kinds of actions you should perform.

EXERCISES

1. Which of the following would you look upon as a matter of *moral* concern? Why? (See J. Hartland-Swann, *An Analysis of Morals,* Chapter 3.)

a. cheating at cards

b. cheating on examinations

c. jaywalking

d. keeping your car washed

e. keeping your car in good running condition

f. stopping your car in a traffic jam simply for the fun of it and letting the cars behind you try to get past

g. eating healthful foods

h. doing two hours' work for eight hours' pay

i. getting drunk every couple of days

2. What are the presuppositions of the following statements? What do you think of them? Why?

a. But he can't have taken the money; he was an Eagle Scout.

b. Of course I won't help her — she's only a servant.

c. He can't be doing the right thing because it means criticizing his own father.

d. Get everything you can from others but never give anything in return.

3. In daily life we often hear the slogan, "It's none of your (or my) business." In which of the following situations would you say that the matter in question is none of the person's business? Why?

a. It's none of your business, Mother, whom I date or marry.

b. Fellow Congressmen, it's strictly my own business how I got my money.

c. It's none of my business if the neighbor's children are in rags.

d. If I choose to eat squirrel meat for breakfast, that's nobody's business but my own.

e. If I choose not to mow my front lawn, that's strictly my own business.

f. If I refuse to see a doctor when I'm sick, that's nobody else's business.

4. Which side of the following dispute are you inclined to agree with? Why?

A: People are always violating in practice what they preach. They believe something is wrong, and yet they do it.

B: I doubt this. People usually do what they *think* is right — at least at the time they do it they have convinced themselves that it is right. No, the trouble is not so much that they act contrary to their beliefs as that they aren't careful enough in arriving at their moral beliefs in the first place.

5. Which of the following moral rules are, in your opinion, tautologies? Explain.

a. You should always do what's best.

b. Follow reason.

c. Let your conscience be your guide.

d. It is wrong to inflict needless pain.

e. Women must be chaste, because virtue demands it.

f. Always do what you ought to do.

g. Justice demands that criminals should not go unpunished.

6. Which of the following actions do you consider the worst? Why?

a. Because of graft and corruption among high officials in the city government, city taxes have to be raised 35 per cent.

b. The ambulance brings to the hospital a man bleeding to death. The hospital, being a free city hospital, does not admit him. "We don't have room," the man at the receiving desk says, falsely; "take him to the other city hospital." At the other city hospital he is also refused, on exactly the same grounds. So he is returned to the first hospital, but by that time he is dead.

c. A group of Negro soldiers in the South going home on leave, is riding in a bus. An intoxicated white soldier on the bus becomes sick and vomits. The bus driver accuses one of the Negroes of doing it and has the bus evacuated while the Negro soldiers clean it up. While they are working the driver calls the local sheriff and has the Negro soldiers locked up for disorderly conduct. The judge sentences them to thirty days on the chain gang. They are not permitted to get in contact with Army headquarters or with their families, who are expecting them home for Christmas the next day. (This actual incident is described in *New Republic*, Vol. III, No. 1569 [December 25, 1944], pp. 871-72.)

d. "Preachers, rabbis, priests . . . use religion to cloak and to support impersonal, wholesale murder — and the preparation for it. They condone the intent to murder millions of people by clean-cut young men flying and aiming intricate machineries toward Euro-Asia, zeroing in on cities full of human beings — young men who, two years before, were begging their fathers for the use of the family car for a Saturday-night date." (From C. W. Mills's *The Causes of World War Three.* Copyright © 1958 by C. Wright Mills. By permission of Simon and Schuster, Inc., p. 126.)

e. The communist youth turns in his parents to the Secret Police for suspected activity hostile to the aims of the Party.

7. In which of the following sentences do you think the word "ought" is being used in a specifically moral (as opposed to non-moral) way? Where the use is non-moral, indicate as well as you can what "ought" means in the sentence; try to translate the sentence without using the "ought."

a. There ought to be another closet somewhere on this floor.

b. You ought to chew your food properly for the sake of your health.

c. You oughtn't to leave the house without first eating a hearty breakfast.

d. You ought to save a portion of your salary each week.

e. When you make a promise you ought to keep it.

f. You ought to be more cooperative.

8. Assess the role of rationalization in the following excerpt from Henry Fielding's novel *Tom Jones* (New York: Modern Library), pages 4-5.

Miss Bridget Allworthy . . . very rightly conceived the charms of a person in a woman to be no better than snares for her as well as for others; and yet so discreet was she in her conduct, that her prudence was as much on the guard as if she had all the snares to apprehend which were ever laid for her whole sex. Indeed, I have observed, though it may seem unaccountable to the reader, that this guard of prudence, like the Trained Bands, is always readiest to go on duty where there is the least danger. It often basely and cowardly deserts those paragons for whom the men are all wishing, sighing, dying, and spreading every net in their power; and constantly attends at the heels of that higher order of women for whom the other sex have a more distant and awful respect, and whom (from despair, I suppose, of success) they never venture to attack.

9. What would you say of someone who said, with regard to the example of the escapee from the asylum (p. 12), "It is my duty to tell him the truth. That way, at least I am absolved. If he then goes on, as a result of the information I gave him, to Smith's house and kills Smith, that's his own responsibility."

10. Evaluate the following:

A: You believe stealing is wrong, don't you?

B: Of course.

A: Well, we white men stole this continent from the Indians. Don't you think it's our moral duty to give it back to them?

11. Do you consider the following individuals guilty of killing? If so, why?

a. A multimillionaire sells some of his surplus ships to the government. The ships are no longer safe; even when new they were capable only of limited use on inland waterways. The man has secret information from an unimpeachable source to the effect that the ships will be used for ocean travel by American troops. He knows, therefore, that in all probability some of the ships (and human lives) will be lost because of his sale. But he sells the rotten ships anyway, not mentioning that they are unfit for ocean travel. (This and many similar incidents are related in Gustavus Myers, *The History of the Great American Fortunes* [New York: Modern Library].

b. Some automobile manufacturers, in order to cut corners and reap added profits, fail to put certain safety devices in their new cars. For every device they fail to put in, they can accurately predict that hundreds or thousands of motorists will be killed in otherwise avoidable automobile accidents, but of course the manufacturers don't know which ones will be killed. (The same applies to the inclusion of defective parts.)

12. Try to arrive at a satisfactory definition of the following:

a. lying	*c*. promise-keeping
b. killing	*d*. stealing

(Try to separate in your mind the questions "Is this an instance of X" and "Is X always wrong?")

(*The reading list is at the end of the chapter.*)

2. *Moral standards and ethical relativism*

We have already made some remarks about moral rules and moral actions and have ventured to criticize certain instances of human conduct. One might well ask, "From what point of view, or by what moral standard, have these criticisms and evaluations been made?" We shall be pursuing this theme at length in the coming chapters, but let us first break the ground by considering a few of the more obvious candidates.

A. Moral standards

1. *Parental authority*. This argument can hardly be a sufficient reason for adopting a moral rule. There are many different parents imposing many different moral rules on their children, and some of these rules often contradict others. When we want to know which of two conflicting rules is to be preferred, we cannot answer in terms of parental authority because both the rules have that as their source. Besides, even if all parental commands agreed with one another, we would still have to face the question "What is there about parental commands that makes them always right?" In fact, doesn't it seem clear that some parental commands are wrong and mistaken? At the very least, aren't some of them better than others? But if some are better, they are not better by virtue of their being parental commands, for they are all equally parental commands.

2. *Custom and public opinion.* The same objections could be given here. Custom approves now one thing and now another, varying enormously from time to time and place to place. What indication is there that the customs that happen to be prevalent at one's own particular time and place are always and invariably right? Custom has approved torture, intolerance, persecution, hatred; does custom make them right? Public opinion can tear innocent men to pieces. It can destroy a man's reputation and his very life. If you hold that custom is always right, you must hold that all these practices are right. But if so, would it be wrong to try to change the custom? Doesn't it make sense to speak of *improving* existing customs or the existing climate of public opinion? Indeed, one might say that the moral leaders of mankind have been those who, on occasion, flouted public opinion, rose above it, tried to change and mold the customs of their community or nation. Public opinion is the opinion of the majority; why should the majority always be right? There are more of them, but does their number make their word more reliable? In scientific matters no one would dream of saying that public opinion determines what is true and what is false. Everyone today agrees that in the Middle Ages, the majority, who believed the earth was flat, was wrong. Why should it be any more likely that the majority is always right in moral matters? On the contrary, in moral matters the majority tends to be unreflective, given to rationalizing, and easily swayed by passion and prejudice. The majority may be stupid, intolerant, and bound by fear, habit, or moral inertia. We recognize these weaknesses when we do not always accept the majority's opinions. For example, we no longer believe, as the majority of certain societies once did, in witch-burning. It would seem that what is right and what is wrong will have to be decided, if at all, by some criterion other than custom or public opinion.

3. *The law of the land.* One might suggest that legality is the test of the rightness or wrongness of an act: what is right is what the law permits, what is wrong is what the law prohibits, and what the law doesn't mention is neither right nor wrong. What the law says is written in the law books, so the problem is simple: just look it up. But this solution won't do either, for several reasons:

a. Law and morality are not coextensive. Laws are often concerned with things which have nothing to do with morality (or at least seem not to), such as sitting on the grass or parking overnight in a residential area. Conversely, morality covers many things that the law does not. Most of the activities of domestic life, such as how to bring up one's children, are not covered — at least not yet! — by laws. If you have promised to do something for your neighbor which would mean a great deal to him, and you break your promise, the law says nothing about this one way or the other. You can't be haled into court for the breaking of a promise unless there was a written contract; but it doesn't follow from this provision that it is not wrong of you to break your promise. A thousand details of personal life are not matters of law, but they are in the realm of right and wrong.

b. Laws differ from nation to nation, state to state, city to city. In the state of New York it is unlawful to drive over fifty miles per hour, but when you cross the border into Connecticut it is unlawful to drive over forty-five miles per hour. Are you willing to say that it is not just illegal but morally wrong to travel fifty miles per hour in Connecticut but not in New York? Most states differ in their divorce laws. Some permit divorce only on grounds of adultery; others allow divorce for almost any reason including a sixty-day absence from one's spouse. Are we really prepared to say that divorce for mental cruelty is wrong in New York but not in Nevada? Morality would be a strange thing indeed if what is right on one side of a river is wrong on the other side just because a state boundary had been crossed.

c. Laws are repealed. When that happens, do we want to say that what was wrong yesterday is right today? If human slavery is prohibited by law today but was not yesterday, does this change mean that slavery is morally wrong today but was not yesterday? Wasn't slavery just as wrong yesterday as today, but today there are laws prohibiting it whereas yesterday there were not? In other words, the law yesterday permitted something that was morally wrong. But if that is so, morality and the law cannot be identical. The law usually moves so slowly that many years may elapse before something we believe to be wrong becomes prohibited by law.

d. We speak of bad laws and good laws, better laws and worse laws. This kind of talk wouldn't make sense if being right and being lawful were identical. Would we consider it morally right to sell heroin if the law prohibiting it were repealed? Indeed, what point would there be in trying to get a law enacted or repealed if the existing law is always by definition good? Can't something that is not yet a law be better than something that now is a law?

e. The law is often far from clear. Its meaning is very much a matter of interpretation, as every judge knows; and interpretations change from year to year and court to court. To what extent is Congress empowered by the Constitution to regulate interstate commerce? The Constitution gives the federal government the power to enact whatever legislation is necessary to regulate relations between the states. Does this power include, for example, empowering the FBI to investigate the private life of any human being it chooses on the chance that he may cross state boundaries, an action that would bring him under the interstate commerce proviso, and be a menace in another state? According to the Constitution, to take another example, everyone is entitled to "due process of law," but no one has ever given a precise answer to the question "When is a legal process *due* process?"

4. *Reason.* This sounds like a more promising candidate. But "reason" is disconcertingly vague. If someone said to you, "I'll give you some good moral advice: Follow reason," how would your future behavior be different because of the advice? What, in fact, would the advice mean? What exactly *is* reason, anyway, which you are supposed to follow?

a. Perhaps "reason" means "Follow reason*ing*." In deductive reasoning, we proceed from certain statements which we call the premises of the argument to another statement which we call the conclusion. Reasoning can be valid or invalid — valid when the conclusion follows logically from the premises, invalid when it does not. (In inductive reasoning, it is enough if the conclusion acquires a certain degree of probability on the basis of the premises.) But everything depends on what the premises are. You can logically arrive at any conclusion you want, no matter how absurd it is, provided you choose premises suitable to your purpose. Thus:

> All acts committed in the light of the full moon are right.
> This act was committed in the light of the full moon.
Therefore, This act is right.

This reasoning is perfectly valid, for the premises do yield the conclusion; yet there is not the slightest reason to suppose that the premises (especially the first one) are true. How then are we to guarantee that we have true premises? This cannot be established on the basis of reasoning alone, for that would only mean using that premise as the conclusion of an earlier deduction based on other premises — and then we would have to ask the same question about *these* premises. Reasoning is very important in ethics, as we shall see, but reasoning *alone* cannot establish the truth of premises — ethical or any other. The premises are the meat, whether healthful or poisonous, that has gone into the meat grinder. Reason simply grinds out the meat, of whatever kind it may be.

b. But perhaps "reason" is taken in a sense allied to "reasonable," and the command to "follow reason" simply comes to this: "Do that act which, in these circumstances, is the most reasonable." This advice may sound laudable, but unfortunately it is not very helpful. If your army unit takes a great many prisoners and there is already a serious food shortage, one person will say that the most reasonable thing to do is kill the prisoners. Another, shocked at this suggestion, will contend that the most reasonable thing to do is share the food with the prisoners even though the weakest among both soldiers and prisoners will probably die. Someone asks for your opinion, and you say, "Do the reasonable thing." People are forever forcing their moral dicta upon others by saying "This is the reasonable thing to do," but how will their advice enable us to settle controversies about which particular act *is* the most reasonable one?

c. Perhaps, then, the command means the same as "Follow that course of action which can be defended with the best *reasons* in its *favor.*" This interpretation sounds still better, and probably no one has any wish to deny that the act most in accordance with reason in this sense is the one we should perform. But again the troublesome question arises, "How are we to determine which one that is?" People can produce arguments on both sides of a question, and each person will say that his reasons are the best reasons. Then what are we to do?

In a way the entire remainder of this book can be considered an attempt to answer this question. We shall be constantly considering not only alternatives among actions but *reasons* for and against doing them. Different theories, as we shall see, give different accounts of what the best reasons are. We shall simply have to wait, then, to see what these theories have to say. Until we have filled in the general principle "Do the act for which the best reasons can be given" with some specific content, the principle will be too vague to be of much use to us.

5. *Conscience.* "Do whatever your conscience tells you," one often hears, "and whatever it tells you will be right."

But the matter is not quite that easy. Different people's consciences give notoriously differing verdicts, depending on their training and temperament. What if my conscience tells me that it is wrong for anyone to take human life, even that of an enemy in wartime, and your conscience tells you that under certain circumstances the taking of life is permissible? Superficial students of *Hamlet* sometimes think that Hamlet's conscience bothered him at the thought of murdering his uncle and was the reason that he failed to do so; but the fact is that Hamlet's conscience bothered him *because* he failed to commit the murder, to discharge what he considered to be the sacred duty of vengeance. Not everyone's conscience, however, approves such acts of vengeance — the verdict of many consciences is that vengeance is always wrong.

In general, what a person's conscience approves depends on how he has been brought up. As children we have received certain commands from our parents, and feelings of guilt are aroused in us if we do not do the things we are commanded to do. Since parental commands vary considerably from family to family and from culture to culture, what the conscience of the offspring approves and disapproves varies accordingly. True, people often outgrow their early consciences. Children who have been taught to feel guilt at the thought of stealing sometimes lose this guilt feeling in later years when they earn their living by this means. Your conscience may bother you when you do certain things, like eating pork, which you may have been brought up not to do but no longer consider wrong. But there seems to be just about as much variation among adults in what their consciences "tell them" as there is among children.

There is probably no kind of crime in history that has not been condoned by the consciences of a great many people. People have burned others at the stake, frozen them to death, baked them in ovens, and thrown them to the lions, all with the full sanction of conscience and with the firm conviction that if they failed to do these things, they would be shirking their sacred duty. It is sometimes argued that these people knew all the time that they were doing wrong; they were indulging their sadistic and murderous impulses and camouflaging them with appeals to duty and conscience. Doubtless this is sometimes true. But there is no evidence whatever that it is *always* true, and much evidence that it is not. Many of those who burned others at the stake for heretical beliefs sincerely thought that it was their sacred duty to do so, even against their humanitarian instincts; doubtless they thought that burning for a few minutes now would be a small thing compared with burning in hell-fire forever after. Furthermore, there was a chance that at the point of death the victims would repent, and others viewing the event might take warning from this spectacle and refrain from sin. It is possible, of course, that some of the authorities were sadists who reveled in the sight of other human beings being burned alive, and that their talk of duty was only a rationalization. But we can hardly accuse all of them of this. We may think they were wrong in what they did, but we can hardly doubt their sincerity, or the fact that these actions were fully approved by their consciences; in fact they were convinced that this was a sacred duty, even though an unpleasant one, which God required of them.

It may be said that this argument is inconclusive because we have not yet shown that burning people at the stake or throwing them to the lions is wrong. True: all we have done so far is to try to show that *if* you believe that doing these things is wrong, and *if* these acts were approved by conscience (as they were), then it follows that conscience cannot always be right.

Many people would argue as follows: "But *their* consciences told them that it was right for *them* to do these things. And *our* consciences tell us that it is wrong for *us* to do these things. So where's the contradiction? Both *may* be correct: maybe it was right for them and wrong for us." We shall discuss this point of view under the heading of Relativism, below. At the moment it need only be remarked that people's consciences often tell them much more than this. The conscience of many a pacifist, for example, tells him not only that it is wrong *for him* to take human life but that it is wrong *for anyone* to do so. And if one person's conscience is opposed to taking human life under all circumstances and another's approves it in some circumstances, there is still conflict between the verdicts of the two consciences.

There is, however, another possible maneuver: "I mean, of course, an *enlightened* conscience, not just any conscience. Conscience can easily be misled, to be sure, but when the conscience has emerged from a state of ignorance to one of enlightenment, then it is an infallible guide to right and wrong. It is only the enlightened conscience whose dictates we should follow."

The trouble with this argument is that it begs the question. How are we to tell whose conscience is enlightened? Everyone tends to think that his own conscience is enlightened and that the consciences of those who disagree with him are not. In practice "an enlightened conscience" becomes equivalent to "a conscience that agrees with mine." How are we going to settle disputes between various claimants to the title of "enlightened conscience"? Is there some superconscience that arbitrates, like a Supreme Court, the conflicting claims of competing individual consciences? If so, what is to be done if two people each claim to have such a superconscience? Shall there be a super superconscience to arbitrate these claims? And by what criterion are they to be so arbitrated? Such questions could go on endlessly, in an infinite regress.

The mention of a superconscience may give rise to another idea, "Your conscience is the voice of God in you." It is often alleged that conscience draws its authority from the fact that it is of divine origin; the voice of conscience is to be followed, not because it is conscience, but because it is the voice of God.

This claim moves the argument from the heading of Conscience to that of Revelation. For the claim here is that the command of God is the criterion of moral authority and that conscience is to be followed only insofar as it is indeed the voice of God; a conscience which is not truly the voice of God is not to be obeyed. Thus we turn from Conscience to Revelation.

6. *Revelation.* The most widespread view of all regarding the criterion of right and wrong is that God has issued certain commands which we should obey. Conscience comes in only secondarily, in that, according to some, at least, it is God's way of speaking to us. Many people, however, who believe that God speaks infallibly would admit that conscience does *not* speak infallibly — that conscience is to be relied on only when its dictates are in accord with those of Revelation, but that when they are not, it is revelation and not conscience that should be our guide. The conscience of one man may disagree with that of another, but Revelation speaks with a single voice. Consciences may contradict one another, but it is hardly likely that God would contradict Himself.

This claim, simple though it seems, contains several related points which must be discussed separately, and we cannot complete a discussion of them all in this brief chapter. The question "Why should we obey it?" will be discussed in Chapter 4. But a few remarks can be made here about the claim that Revelation is the criterion for judging matters of right and wrong.

a. There is a difficulty about the alleged revelation itself. Presumably it is the *true* revelation that is to be regarded as infallible, not the many alleged revelations which also exist. A believer in one true revelation must condemn all the others as frauds. The majority of believers in revelation, for example, do not believe that Joseph Smith received the revealed will of God on golden plates from heaven, yet devout Mormons believe that he did. How is one to establish the claim that one and only one of these revelations is genuine? Everything depends upon this choice, but how is it to be made? This is a ticklish problem, and in a book on ethics we can hardly take time out to consider the epistemological problems involved. Yet if the moral criterion is to be found in revelation, *the* one and only true revelation (and each one contradicts the others at some points), then we must have a way of finding which one that true one is. Christianity, Judaism, Mohammedanism, and many other religions each claim to possess the one and only true revelation.

The competing claims would have to be somehow ironed out before we could proceed.

b. Even if we have agreed which alleged revelation is genuine, our problems are not over. There is also the problem of interpreting the frequently vague and cryptic pronouncements made in each allegedly revealed book. Does the commandment against killing impose pacifism upon us? Most Christians have not thought so, but some have; and those who have not thought so have disagreed as to the circumstances under which killing was permitted. If one's eternal salvation is to depend on following the commandments, it is more important than ever that we know exactly to what classes of acts they are designed to apply. Yet on this point there is no end of controversy.

c. The claim of revelation, then, cannot be settled in any simple manner. We have already considered two difficulties: which revelation? and which interpretation? But there is another problem which at first may seem so trivial and academic as to be not worth discussion. When we appeal to revelation as the basis of moral authority, do we mean that an act is right because God, as revealed in a sacred book, commands it or that God commands it because it is right? A great deal turns on which of these alternatives we adopt.

Let us consider the first alternative: if an act is right simply because God commands it and for no other reason, then no matter what God commands, it is *ipso facto* right. If God commands the slaughter of ten thousand Canaanites who, it would seem, have committed no crime other than that of living in the land the Israelites desire to occupy, then killing these Canaanites was right, and that is the end of the matter. True, one may believe that God does not command such things, though at least one alleged revelation says that He did; but the point is not whether God commanded this or not but that *if* He did, then (on this interpretation) it *would* be right. Any command, no matter what its contents might be, even if it required the infliction of torture on thousands of other human beings, would be right provided that, according to the true revelation, God commanded it.

One may, of course, say, "I wouldn't accept a revelation as true which said that God commanded such things. I would look around among the alleged revelations and find that one which contained the moral commands I found to be the most humane, merciful, edifying, and noble. And whatever 'sacred book' contained these to the highest degree, I would accept as containing the true revelation." This line of argument, however, would be a most curious procedure. Such a person would be accepting a certain revelation as genuine because it happened to agree with *his* moral views. But this is not at all what our first alternative specifies. It specifies, rather, that we should examine whatever revelation is true — this would, presumably, have to be discovered on *other* grounds, such as "For which is there the most evidence?" — and then we should take the moral commands contained therein as true, *no matter what their content is.* What God commands according to that revelation may or may not agree with what you previously thought; if it doesn't, that's just too bad, for you have to accept it *just because* it was God who commanded it. If you *first* look for a moral code that agrees with your own and *then* select the "true" revelation on the basis of that, you are accepting that revelation, not because it is revelation, but because it agrees with what you already believe, which is quite a different reason. Is it not going round in a circle to say, first, that you should accept a set of moral rules because God commands them and for no other reason, and then that this "sacred book" must contain God's commands because it contains moral views that coincide with yours? If you already had the views before you searched for the true revelation, did you believe them to be God's commands then? You could hardly have believed this, for by your own admission you had not yet discovered what God's commands were; yet you must have believed it, for according to your other statement something cannot be right or wrong unless it is God's command, this being what *makes* it right or wrong. You cannot make God's command the criterion of right and then turn around and make a certain standard of right the criterion for discovering what God's command is.

One other thing should be noted about this first interpretation. It says that what makes an act right or wrong is the fact that God commands it. But what of the atheist or agnostic, or, for that matter, a believer in a religion other than your own, who tells you that he believes killing is wrong but does *not* believe that it goes contrary to God's command? Can you honestly say to him, "Revelation is the one and only criterion of right and wrong; and since you don't accept revelation, you can have no criterion of right and wrong?" You are, after all, committed to saying that there is no right or wrong whatever apart from God's commands; thus a person who did not believe in God could not, according to your theory, have any views about right and wrong. "But," the person insists, "I do have views about right and wrong, although they are not views about God's will or command." What will you say to him now? You can say, "Since all views of right and wrong are views about what God commands and you don't believe in God (or at least that God commands anything), you don't *really* have moral views about right and wrong at all." If the person is sincere, he will find your statement very difficult to accept. Or, more plausibly, you may say, "You really do have views about right and wrong, you just *don't know* what I know, namely that these are views about what God commands."

Let us turn to the second interpretation, which says, "God commands it because it's right" (rather than the other way round). God, then, has a *reason* for commanding something, namely that it is right. But if that is so, the rightness of an act no longer depends on God's commanding it; it would be right even if God did *not* command it, or even if there were no God at all. The fact of God's commanding it is not what *makes* it right; it is right for some *other* reason. If this is so, then we could do the act directly for that reason and not because God commands it. God, being good, commands us to do what is right, but His commanding the act is not what makes it right. God commands us to do certain things, but they would be right even if He didn't command them. (Presumably a God who was not good might command us to do things that were wrong.) If the will of God does not determine what is right but only commands us to do what would be right regardless of God's action, then what does determine right? This second interpretation may well be the preferable one of the two, but it leads us beyond revelation to discover a criterion of rightness.

B. Relativism

We have just examined various moral norms, or standards, which have been suggested by various people; and during the course of this book we shall examine many more. But first we should examine a view, called "relativism," which is popularly believed to deny the existence or possibility of any moral standard whatever. Relativism, when analyzed, breaks down into several different views.

1. *Sociological relativism* is simply the view that different groups of people — different tribes, different cultures, different civilizations — have different moral standards for evaluating acts as right or wrong. For example, in our society we believe that it is better to be caught for stealing than to escape capture; but the Spartan youth who allowed the fox to gnaw at his vital organs rather than be caught for stealing it reflected a popular belief that being caught was bad but stealing was not. The Dobu tribesmen of New Guinea believe that growing your own vegetables is honorable but stealing your neighbor's vegetables is still more honorable. The ancient Romans, unlike the Christians, had more respect for honor than for pity. They could be forgiving if they could gain some advantage from being so; otherwise they had virtually no feeling for victims, such as prisoners of war. Courage was prized; mercy and humility were not. Some desert tribes, such as those discussed in our previous example of T. E. Lawrence, think it a sacred obligation, when one of their number has been killed or captured by an opposing tribe, to capture and kill (by slow torture) a member of that tribe, even if he is not the same man who committed the offense — a perfectly innocent man will do just as well. The Eskimos think it right to kill their parents after the parents have reached a certain age — indeed, the parents expect this — rather than take them along on their hazardous journeys.

Here is one more example of sociological relativism:

> The Peruvian calls the brave Indian treacherous, a subhuman object fit only
> for destruction. It should be understood that the Indian is not treacherous, in

the sense implied, but is only carrying out his conviction that he is doing right. "Doing right" seems to be a universal instinct; but what constitutes right, and what constitutes wrong, differs with society and what it considers best for the majority. The [Indians], feeling no obligation to the tribe, kill each other whenever an individual's interests seem threatened, and this is called "good." [1]

Thus, they kill members of their own tribe by slow torture if the priest has pronounced a curse on him. Children thus cursed die a slow death by whipping and branding with hot irons to exorcise the demons gradually so that the soul, when it leaves the body, will be pure. [2]

Even within one society, of course, there are many differences. In parts of the American South it is considered not only undesirable but wrong for Negro children to sit in the same classrooms with white children. And in one city, even in one block, there are individual differences: some think there is nothing wrong with presenting a false claim for damages to an insurance company (including the paying of physicians and witnesses to swear to false statements about the extent of someone's injuries), as long as it is only the company and not an individual that is being sued; whereas the members of the family next door are horrified at such practices and see no moral difference between false claims against individuals and false claims against companies or cities.

No one is likely to deny relativism in this sense. It would ill become the moral philosopher to say, "You sociologists and anthropologists are all wrong in the alleged facts which you report. It is all a tissue of lies!" Those who are best qualified to know what the Dobu tribesmen believe are those who have lived among the Dobu and seen for themselves.

Even so, the term "sociological relativism" is ambiguous. If the term merely means that there are moral beliefs held by one group which are not held by another, this is obviously true — an empirical fact. But if the term means that different groups have different *basic* moral principles, the statement is not so obviously true and may even be false. Different groups *may* be using the same basic moral principles but applying them in different ways to different situations. Imagine two tribes, each believing that they should do what is most conducive to the survival of as many people as possible within the tribe. One of the tribes lives in the desert, and the other where there is plenty of water. In the first tribe wasting even a small amount of water is considered a grave moral offense, perhaps even a capital offense; in the second tribe there are no rules at all about wasting water. This is an example of sociological relativism in the first sense; the one believes that wasting water is wrong and the other does not. But it is not an example of sociological relativism in the second sense, for both moral rules equally illustrate one basic moral principle, that what is right is what promotes sur-

[1] From *The Rivers Ran East* by Leonard Clark. New York: Funk & Wagnalls, 1954, p. 164. Reprinted by permission of the publisher.
[2] *Ibid.*, pp. 56-57.

vival. On this assumption they do not differ at all; what differs is the application of this one principle to different circumstances.

We tend to believe that what happened to Oedipus was wrong, since he acted in ignorance of the facts and he could not possibly have known these facts. Here, we think, is another example of relativism. But is it? The Thebans believed that if Oedipus were not punished, the gods would take vengeance upon their entire city; punishing him, even for something he couldn't have foreseen, was a way to stave off the vengeance of the gods — one man would be lost but an entire city might be saved. If we shared this belief (a religious, not a moral belief), would we too have considered it right to punish Oedipus? They had different beliefs from ours about the gods and the world; but did they have different *moral* beliefs? It is not easy to say; whether or not sociological relativism in the second sense applies here is far from obvious, even though many people tend to assume that it does because they do not distinguish the two senses in the first place.

We shall have more to say about this point in later chapters. Meanwhile, there are other things that have been meant by the term "relativism."

2. Sociological relativism is not an ethical doctrine at all; it tries to describe what people's moral beliefs *are;* it says nothing about whether any of them are preferable to others. *Ethical relativism,* however, goes further; it has a definite view about right and wrong, and thus it enters the domain of ethics. According to ethical relativism, if there are two tribes or societies, and in one of them it is believed that acts of a certain kind are wrong while in the other it is believed that acts of that same kind are right, *both beliefs* are true: in the first society acts of that kind *are* wrong and in the other society they *are* right. Polygamy is right in polygamous societies but not in monogamous societies. Thus there is no overall standard of right and wrong — what is right and what is wrong depends on the society of which you are a member.

Here at once we have an ambiguity. Let us suppose, for the moment, that slavery is right in one society and wrong in another — not just that it is thought to be so, which would be sociological relativism, but that it really is so, as ethical relativism says. But a person who holds this belief need not be a relativist at all. He may believe in some one over-all standard of right, such as the maximum happiness of the people concerned (a view we shall examine in Chapter 5). And if so, since he has one standard of rightness, he is no relativist. A certain practice might make for the happiness of one society but not of another, and in that event it would be right in the one society but not in the other; only the application of the moral principle differs from one society to another, not the principle itself. Probably most people who call themselves ethical relativists are not so at all, for they believe in one moral standard which applies in different ways to different societies because of the various conditions in which they live. One might as well talk about gravitational relativism because a stone falls and a balloon rises; yet both events are equally instances of one law of universal gravitation.

But suppose that the person believes that there *is* no one over-all standard and that what is right and what is wrong varies from one society to another without reference to any one overall moral principle. A person might believe that what is right for one group may be wrong for another and what is right for one individual may be wrong for another, though *not* because there is one over-all moral principle of which these are different applications. The relativist will be hard put to it to give any reason *why* he believes this to be so, but he may state the position without any attempt to give reasons. In that event he can truly be called a relativist. But now he must face certain problems:

a. If we ask him *why* a practice that is right in one society is wrong in another, he will have no reason to present. There seems to be no general principle from which his position follows. This weakness, to put it mildly, will leave many people dissatisfied.

b. "What is right in one group is wrong in another," he says. But what exactly is a group? and which group is one to select? Every person is a member of many different groups — his nation, his state, his city, his club, his school, church, fraternity, or athletic association. Suppose that most of the people in his club think that a certain kind of act is wrong and that most of the people in his nation think it is right; what then?

c. How many of the group — whatever group it turns out to be — must think it is wrong before it really is wrong? The usual answer is, "The majority." Presumably this means anything over 50 per cent. If 51 per cent of his countrymen think adultery is wrong, then it is wrong for the people in that country; but if only 49 per cent of them think it wrong, then it isn't. This conclusion is strange, to say the least. Can't a majority be mistaken? A minority view may sometimes spread and become a majority view later; in that event, was the act wrong before and right now? It is very easy to say, "Head hunting is right in a headhunting society, and if most of the people in the United States became headhunters, then headhunting would be right for us," and the same with such practices as polygamy, witch-burning, conviction without a trial, cannibalism. But is there any reason why what most people believe should be true?

d. If what the majority of a society or group approves is *ipso facto* right in that society, how can there be any such thing as moral improvement? If someone in a headhunting society were convinced that headhunting was cruel, barbarous, and wrong and proceeded to share these sentiments with his chieftain, the relativistic chieftain would reply, "But the majority in our tribe considers it right, so it *is* right." In a society in which most people cheated the government on their income tax, it would be right to do so, though it would no longer be right once the percentage of cheaters dropped below 50. If ethical relativism is correct, it is clearly impossible for the moral beliefs of a society to be mistaken because the certainty of the majority that its beliefs were right would prove that those beliefs *were* right for that society at that time. The minority view would therefore be mistaken, no matter what it was. Needless to say, most people who state that "in morals everything is relative" and who proceed to call themselves ethical relativists are unaware of these implications of their theory.

3. There are, however, other possible views to take. One possibility is that there is no such thing as right and wrong at all, that the words "right" and "wrong" have no meaning. This view should hardly be called "ethical relativism"; for according to relativism, right and wrong are relative to societies, and this view says that right and wrong do not even exist. It is better called *ethical nihilism,* a denial of ethics, "reducing it to nothing," rubbing out all moral categories entirely. But this particular view is plainly mistaken. There is a great deal of controversy about the meaning of ethical terms, and we shall pursue this controversy in Chapter 11; but we *do* use them to say *something.* When we say, "Murder is wrong," it is not as if we were uttering nonsense syllables, saying, "Murder is glubglub" or something of the sort. Even a small child attaches *some* meaning to the word and would never interchange the words "right" and "wrong" in a sentence. For that matter, neither would he use "wrong" synonymously with other words such as "book" and "red." Something is meant by moral words; so whatever this may be, the words are not meaningless.

"But that isn't what I mean either," someone may say. "What I mean is that words like 'right' and 'wrong' don't refer to *qualities* of actions. There is no quality of rightness the way there is a quality of redness." This indeed may be the case, not all adjectives are the names of qualities. (It is even a controversial question what qualities are.) We shall examine this possibility in Chapter 11. Meanwhile, even if these words are not the names of qualities, they are far from meaningless. Is "nice" the name of a quality? or "boring"? Yet these words are not meaningless.

4. Still another view is *ethical skepticism.* Ethical skeptics do not hold that ethical terms are meaningless; rather, they hold that there is no way anybody can ever discover what things they apply to—that is, nobody can ever say, with any justification, what things are good or bad, right or wrong. People have different theories, but nobody is ever justified in holding any of them. This is, indeed, a possible position, and we shall do well to keep ethical skepticism in mind throughout our study. But there is nothing decisive we can say about it at this point. Our main concern will be to advance various ethical views and see which ones can be justified and in what respects; and it will take quite some time to consider what can be said for or against each of these views. One cannot simply condemn them all at the outset and say that we are never justified in believing any of them. That is the sort of thing one might be able to say at the *end* of an investigation but not a priori at the beginning.

We turn, then, to the task of considering various ethical theories—first, to present them, and second, to make critical evaluations of them. We shall begin, in Chapter 2, with the least systematic views, those which do not attempt to give a *complete* ethical theory. (A theory about right and wrong is said to be complete when it provides a principle or criterion for classifying *all* acts as either right or wrong.) They present, instead, a general "view of life," or *Weltanschauung,* but do not attempt to cover all the details of action. Then, in Chapter 3, we shall begin a systematic account of ethical theories which make a claim to completeness.

EXERCISES

1. The following practices are usually considered wrong in our society. Do you think you would still consider them wrong if you were living in the social or physical conditions in which they are not considered wrong? Can you think of any general moral principle of which the two rules (in one society, "It's wrong to do this"; in another society "It's right to do this") can be considered applications?

a. The Eskimo's killing his aged parents because they would endanger the entire tribe if they were permitted to go along on the long journey from winter to summer quarters. (Travel would be slowed down by caring for the sick and infirm, and the trip is dangerous enough even for the strong.)

b. Mass executions without a trial or with only the pretense of one in a country undergoing a revolution.

c. Tormenting trapped or captured birds and animals for sport.

d. Eating human flesh, assuming that it will give one strength and virility on the next hunting expedition.

e. Polyandry, in a country in which (owing to casualties in war) the women outnumber the men by five to one.

f. The poor man's thinking it worse to spend his hard-earned savings on medical care than to go to a doctor to see what's the matter with him.

g. Using torture to extract military secrets from prisoners of war.

h. Refusing to eat the flesh of cattle from religious conviction, even when refusal means starvation.

i. Killing those who do not belong to the master race.

j. The moral code of some indigent students, especially with regard to affluent roommates: When I have money, I should share what I have with my rommate; and when he has money, he should share what he has with me.

k. Stealing, provided that those stolen from are personal enemies, have done me an ill turn, or belong to a class hostile to the people (e.g. the bourgeoisie), but of course not from relatives or friends.

2. Take a poll of people who call themselves relativists (possibly some class members) and, by questioning them, try to discover to what group and sub-group of relativists they belong, or whether, on analysis, their position is no longer classifiable as relativism.

3. Try to discover, among those of your friends who hold a religiously based ethic, whether they believe that God commands it because it's right or whether it's right because God commands it. Then read Plato's dialogue *Euthyphro* for further clarification on this question.

4. Give a critical analysis of the view set forth in E. A. Westermarck's book *Ethical Relativity*.

5. "The moral rules of a society should be relative to the needs of that particular society." Do you consider such a position relativistic? Why?

6. Consider the people you know who always agree with the majority. Do you think that they (1) use public opinion as a criterion of rightness, (2) prefer to keep their views to themselves out of timidity or desire for peace, or (3) just don't think at all?

7. Here are some verbatim examples of moral situations from L. Hatch's *Dilemmas* (copyright 1931 by Leonard Hatch. Reprinted by permission of Simon and Schuster, Inc.). In each example, ask yourself (1) what you would do in this situation and (2) why — that is, justify your answer with reasons.

a. You are a physician, a specialist on cancer. One of your patients, who is also a close friend of yours, is irretrievably doomed. He is certain to die within a short time, after appalling suffering.

You are on your way abroad. After your boat has sailed, you find a letter from this patient telling you that because he knows there is no hope for him he is going to kill himself on a certain date. You know he is telling the truth, and that an early death will spare him inevitable suffering.

Should you send a wireless back to his family informing them of his intention to commit suicide on such a date? Or should you do nothing?

b. You are a druggist's clerk, supporting your wife and two small children by that job, which consists chiefly in putting up prescriptions. One day, in going over some old files of prescription copies, you realize to your horror that the mysterious death of a man in your town six months previous must have been due to a mistake of yours in compounding a prescription for him.

You had never been suspected and the case has been closed, except that the widow of the dead man has been left under a cloud of suspicion. Should you come forward now and reveal that you were to blame? Or should you let the passage of time gradually keep on effacing the whole matter?

c. You have become a murderer in spirit and intent. Or, to be more exact, you have been so unjustly and repeatedly humiliated and cruelly injured by a certain contemptible specimen of humanity that you are convinced that he should be done away with.

Just at the time when you have worked yourself into a state where you could kill him without a qualm, he *is* murdered. Murdered on that very night upon which you had gone to his home for that purpose, only to be anticipated by somebody else.

And you know who that somebody else is. And the prosecuting attorney knows that you know. Have you the moral right to testify against this person whose crime has merely forestalled the same crime by yourself?

d. You are an editor confronted with the following situation: A widow has an only daughter who imagines that her health will not permit her to work. Her only interest is in writing poetry, in which field she imagines she has a great future. The mother indulges her in this selfish point of view, and drudges to support this daughter as well as herself.

The years pass. None of the girl's verse is ever accepted, and in time she becomes consumptive — a hopeless case. Her one thought is to have some poem of hers accepted and printed by a certain magazine (yours) before she dies. It is also her mother's wish for her.

One of her poems — a hopelessly mediocre one — is now in your hands as editor of the magazine. The mother comes to you, tells you the whole story, and begs you to print the poem.

The poem is unquestionably below the magazine's standard, but printing it will in no way imperil that paper's reputation.

Should you follow your impulse to print it? Or should you steel yourself against that impulse, on the ground that you have no right to offer your subscribers something you know to be utterly worthless merely for the sake of giving yourself a personal gratification?

READING LIST, SECTIONS 1 AND 2

Anthologies of readings in ethics
Johnson, Oliver A., ed. *Ethics: A Source Book*. Rev. ed. New York: Holt, Rinehart, Winston, 1961.
Melden, Abraham I., ed. *Ethical Theories*. Englewood Cliffs, N. J.: Prentice-Hall, 1955.
Munitz, Milton K., ed. *A Modern Introduction to Ethics*. Chicago: Free Press, 1958.
Selby-Bigge, Sir Lewis A., ed. *British Moralists*. New York: Oxford Univ. Press, 1897.
Sellars, Wilfrid, and John Hospers, eds. *Readings in Ethical Theory*. New York: Appleton-Century-Crofts, 1952.

Other general references in ethics
Brandt, Richard. *Ethical Theory*. Englewood Cliffs, N. J.: Prentice-Hall, 1959.
Broad, C. D. *Five Types of Ethical Theory* (1935).* New York: Humanities Press, 1960. (Littlefield, Adams.)
Carritt, Edgar F. *Ethical and Political Thinking*. New York: Oxford Univ. Press, 1947.
Dewey, John. *Human Nature and Conduct*. New York: Modern Library, 1930.
————, and James Tufts. *Ethics*. Rev. ed. New York: Holt, 1932.
Edel, Abraham. *Ethical Judgment*. Chicago: Free Press, 1955.
Everett, Millard S. *Ideals of Life*. New York: Wiley, 1954.
Ewing, Alfred C. *Ethics*. New York: Macmillan, 1953.
Field, Guy C. *Moral Theory*. 2nd ed. rev. London: Methuen, 1932.
Garvin, Lucius. *A Modern Introduction to Ethics*. Boston: Houghton Mifflin, 1953.
Ginsberg, Morris. *On the Diversity of Morals*. New York: Macmillan, 1956.
Hartland-Swann, John. *An Analysis of Morals*. London: Allen & Unwin, 1960.
Joseph, Horace W. B. *Some Problems in Ethics*. New York: Oxford Univ. Press, 1931.

* Dates in parentheses are dates of first publication.

Ladd, John. *The Structure of a Moral Code*. Cambridge: Harvard Univ. Press, 1957.

Lecky, W. E. H. *A History of European Morals from Augustus to Charlemagne* (1866). New York: Braziller, 1955.

Leys, W. A. R. *Ethics for Policy Decisions*. Englewood Cliffs, N. J.: Prentice-Hall, 1952.

Mackinnon, D. M. *A Study in Ethical Theory*. London: Black, 1957.

Mandelbaum, Maurice. *The Phenomenology of Moral Experience*. Chicago: Free Press, 1958.

Mayo, Bernard. *Ethics and Moral Life*. New York: St. Martin's, 1958.

Montefiore, Alan. *Introduction to Moral Philosophy*. New York: Praeger, 1956.

Nelson, Leonard. *A System of Ethics*. New Haven: Yale Univ. Press, 1956.

Nowell-Smith, Patrick. *Ethics*. Baltimore: Pelican Books, 1954.

Pratt, James B. *Reason in the Art of Living: A Textbook of Ethics*. New York: Macmillan, 1949.

Rashdall, Hastings. *Theory of Good and Evil*. 2nd ed. New York: Oxford Univ. Press, 1924. 2 vols.

Schlick, Moritz. *Problems of Ethics*. Englewood Cliffs, N. J.: Prentice-Hall, 1939.

Sidgwick, Henry. *The Methods of Ethics*. 7th ed. New York: Macmillan, 1874.

———. *An Outline of the History of Ethics*. 6th ed. London: Macmillan, 1931.

Stace, Walter T. *The Concept of Morals*. New York: Macmillan, 1937.

Urban, Wilbur Marshall. *Fundamentals of Ethics*. New York: Holt, 1930.

Warnock, Mary. *Ethics Since 1900*. London: Oxford Univ. Press, 1960.

Westermarck, Edvard A. *Ethical Relativity*. New York: Harcourt, Brace, 1932.

2. *Ideals of life*

3. *The Epicurean way of life*

How should one conduct his life? What is the most desirable way for an individual to live? Perhaps the simplest answer to this question, though it may not be the most satisfactory, as we shall see, is that each person should consider only himself; such a view is called *egoism*. But in his own life what should each person seek? Most of us would probably say, "Many things." But the simplest view says, "One thing and one thing only — pleasure, and as much of it as possible." The view that pleasure is the only thing worth seeking is called *hedonism* (taken from the Greek word *hedone,* meaning pleasure). The first theory we shall examine, then, is egoistic hedonism.

A. Egoistic hedonism

Let us assume, for the time being, that one should always seek pleasure and that he should seek no one's pleasure but his own. (If it gives him pleasure to provide pleasure for others, then of course that is consistent with the view — not because others receive pleasure, but because the person himself gets pleasure from giving it.) But when is this pleasure to be enjoyed? In general, two views on this point should be distinguished:

1. *Egoistic hedonism of the present moment.* According to the first view, I should always do, at any moment, what will give me the most pleasure at that moment. If doing A will give me the most pleasure now, I should do A; but if doing B will, then I should do B. Notice that the view does not say that I should do what *I think* will give me the most pleasure now but what *will* actually give me the most pleasure now. I may be misinformed about how to gain the maximum amount of immediate pleasure for myself. If I am misinformed, it is up to me to correct that misinformation as soon as possible, since, obviously, doing what I think will give me the most pleasure now will not, if I am misinformed, actually give me the most pleasure now. If for some reason I think that I shall get pleasure from placing my hand on a hot stove, it would be wise for me to correct this misinformation before trying the experiment; for I shall most assuredly not get pleasure if I do.

Nor does the view say that I should do what I *want* most at the moment to do. I might want to do something which yet will give me no pleasure; if so, I should refrain from doing it for that reason, even though I want to do it. The achievement of maximum pleasure for oneself in the immediate present should be one's aim; if what one happens to want does not coincide with this aim, one should bring his desires into line, as far as he can, with what *will* produce the most immediate pleasure.

The pleasure to be achieved should be *now,* in the immediate present. I should behave at each moment as if there were not going to be a next moment. Most adults willingly postpone pleasures they might have had today in order to insure greater or continued pleasures later; but small children find it very difficult to do this — they are interested only in the *now.*

Adults sometimes act according to this principle of immediate pleasure, as is reflected in sayings such as "Today is all that matters — let tomorrow take care of itself" and "Eat, drink, and be merry, for tomorrow we die." Yet these same people continue to pay installments on their life insurance policies and give up many of their nights out in order to buy a new car next year. Indeed, no adult acts upon the immediate pleasure principle consistently. A baby can do so because his parents feed and support him; but I as a provider who did so would not remain alive for long, since I would not even work during the day in order to get money for food in the evening. Even if I consider no one but myself, if I do only what gives me pleasure at this moment, I shall do things that will give me much displeasure — pain, distress, misery — later on. Eating exotic food may give me great pleasure now, but in an hour or two I shall suffer the pangs of indigestion. Spending my money on riotous living now may give me pleasure this evening, but tomorrow I shall be penniless and unable to support myself. Getting drunk may be a pleasant experience, but there is always "the morning after the night before." I may not *like* to take into consideration all the moments that will follow the present moment, but for my own comfort tomorrow I must.

In fact I have to consider many tomorrows. Unless I study hard and long for a good many years, I shall not be able to find an enjoyable job and earn the amount of money I want. If I don't protect my health now while I am young, I shall later have no health to protect. No matter how egoistic I am, I soon discover that egoistic hedonism of the present moment simply does not pay off. In countless situations throughout life, doing what gives me pleasure at the moment will lead to such future misery that I have to give up the present pleasure in order to avoid the future displeasure. If I think only about the present, the future will see to it that I shall have no pleasure then. That's the way the world is, and there is nothing I can do about it but accept it and conform to it, for my own sake.

This harsh fact, that present pleasure often leads to future displeasure, spells the doom of egoistic hedonism of the present moment. Even the most shortsighted of selfish individuals soon learn to be concerned to some extent with their future selves. When a person has suffered the pangs of indigestion several times, he learns to forego the rich and spicy delicacy in favor of one less tasty that won't have the unpleasant aftereffects. After he has illegally double-parked a few times and had to appear in court as a result, he learns to hunt for a legal parking place, even though it gives him no pleasure at all to search. He may not feel like driving carefully — it is so much more pleasant to pay no attention — but if he does not, he may crash into an on-coming car and be maimed or killed. In such ways every egoistic hedonist learns not to pay exclusive attention to the present moment. Many notorious egoists of history, such as those who hatch intricate Machiavellian plots, have been steadfast, almost heroic, in giving up momentary pleasures in order to achieve greater ones in the future.

Egoistic hedonism of the present moment can pay off only under one set of conditions: when life is so insecure that there is no likelihood that there will be a future, not even a tomorrow. That is why "Eat, drink, and be merry, for tomorrow you die" is not unreasonable advice, egoistically speak-ing, if tomorrow you *are* going to die. There is no use saving money for yourself in the future if you will have no future. But most of the time we are not in such a situation: even if, perchance, you or I will not have a tomorrow, we don't *know* that we won't have one, and the odds are that we will. It is quite understandable, however, that egoistic hedonism of the present moment should become widespread when times are so uncertain and life so insecure that it seems at least as likely as not that there will be no tomorrow to enjoy. In such circumstances large numbers of people will live only for today.

2. *Egoistic hedonism of the long run.* Everyone who acts on the advice "Don't scratch it now, even though it itches, or it will feel worse tomorrow" is going beyond egoism of the present moment and is considering his long-run pleasure or satisfaction rather than the immediate present. But people vary a great deal in their views about how long the run is that they ought to consider. How far into the future should they calculate their hedonistic satisfactions? If tomorrow, why not the day after tomorrow, next week, next year? People who invest in insurance policies are considering a much longer run than just next year. If a man is to consider his future, why not his *whole* future — that is, his lifetime? If you knew that you would live fifty years more, would you be willing to enjoy all the pleasures you wanted for the first twenty-five years on the condition that you would be in pain and dis-tress for the other twenty-five? Very few would. They would want to con-sider their entire life span in deciding what to do and what not to do. (One might say, "I'll enjoy the first twenty-five years to the hilt and then commit suicide," but this plan would be to defeat the condition of the example, namely, that you have fifty years more to live.)

It is a fact of human nature, however, that we visualize the present and the immediate future more intensely than we do the more distant future. What is far away in time tends to fade into insignificance. You would do more to get a hundred dollars tomorrow than you would to get a hundred dollars a year from now, even though you were just as sure to get it a year from now. Most people would do more to get a hundred dollars tomorrow than they would to get two hundred dollars a year from now, even if they were equally sure to get it in both cases. Most people are not egoistic hedonists of the present moment, but many are not egoistic hedonists of the really long-run variety either. Their long-run considerations usually, though not with regard to such things as life insurance policies, encompass less than their probable life span. The further a reward is placed in the future, the less it tends to affect their calculations. Though very few would ignore the immediate future in favor of the present moment — as in the indigestion example — there are many who would ignore the remote future in favor of the near future. The same psychological principle applies, of course, to future punishments. Many thousands of people believe quite literally in hell-fire; but they are not much influenced by this belief now because the danger is so far in the future, not because they feel uncertain about their belief. Then too, they have never seen others suffer this torment, so it is not present with great vividness before their minds.

There is, however, another reason, which is not a psychological weakness but is realistically based on the fact that the further away something is in time, the less likely it is to happen. This is not always true, of course. You would probably be just as willing to accept a wager that an eclipse of the sun which astronomers had predicted for ten years hence would really occur as a wager on an eclipse predicted for next week. You know that astronomers' calculations are very precise and they have not been known to make mistakes about these things. But the vast majority of events predicted for the future are far less certain to occur than eclipses. When there is a considerable time lapse between the present and the predicted event, many things occurring between now and then may prevent its happening. That is why a friend's visit promised for tomorrow is better than the same thing promised for next year. The risk that a time lapse involves is also a good reason for accepting a smaller benefit now in preference to a much greater benefit promised for the distant future. By that time the promiser may have changed his mind or be dead; the one promised may no longer need the promised benefit, or even want it, or be there to receive it. At least the smaller benefit is more certain. "A bird in the hand is worth two in the bush."

Does this caution make it unreasonable to plan for *any* long-term rewards for yourself? Surely not. It would be unwise to stop putting a part of your monthly paycheck into retirement benefits, at least if the interest rates are good and the economy is stable; for in that way you will be comparatively certain to have money in hand when you retire. Of course it isn't certain; before you reach that age, you may be dead (though at least your family will be protected), or the company issuing the benefits may be nonexistent or insolvent, or the entire city may have been wiped out by a nuclear missile. But, as long as these dire events do not seem overwhelmingly probable, you are (egoistically speaking) wise in giving up a certain small percentage of your income now to make sure, or relatively sure, that you will not be caught short later. At any rate, to most people it seems worth the gamble. If they stay alive, they will have enough to live on when they are old; and if everything is destroyed, it won't make any difference anyway for they won't be here to miss it. People would be considered imprudent if they refused to put something aside for a rainy day just because a rainy day *might* never come.

How is one to calculate an immediate reward against a much greater reward promised for the future? If $100 were promised you for tomorrow or $1,000 were promised you for a year hence, which should you take? To reap the maximum possible benefit, you would multiply the *amount* of the offer by the *probability* of its occurring. Thus, the $100 promised for right now is, let us say, a sure thing, with a probability of 100 per cent; but there is only a 50 per cent chance of the $1,000 a year hence. Since the product in the first alternative is 100 and in the second alternative, 500, it would, according to this calculation, be prudent for you to forego the present $100 in favor of the less certain but far greater amount in the future. This calculation, of course, considers only the material reward, which is merely one aspect of the benefit. If you badly need the money now and have reason to believe that you will not need it as much a year from now, if you are likely to spend the year worrying whether the $1,000 will really come through, or if you can invest the $100 now so shrewdly that it will produce much more than $1,000 in a year's time, or even if you just enjoy the manipulation of money, any or all of these things may weight your decision in favor of taking the $100 now. It is the pleasure, not the money per se, which the hedonist values.

The trouble is, of course, that probabilities are notoriously difficult to estimate. In most cases we just don't know how probable or improbable a future event is, nor do we find it easy to weigh the pleasure of possession against the pleasure of manipulation, and so on. Seldom indeed can we assign any mathematical value to the weights or probabilities. We can often say that this event is more probable or likely to occur than that is, but we cannot say how much more. We shall bump into this difficulty again and again, but it is not the fault of ethics: it is the fault of (1) the empirical world for being so complex that the consequences of actions are difficult and often impossible to discover and of (2) the state of our *knowledge,* which is incomplete chiefly because the empirical world *is* so complex, though of course as knowledge increases, we are increasingly able to predict what will probably happen. Meanwhile, since we are not omniscient, we have to do the best we can with the knowledge we have.

Estimates of probability are sufficiently uncertain that there will never, in all likelihood, be general agreement on them. One person will be so impressed with the certainty of the present, as opposed to the uncertainty of the future, that he will usually take what he wants at that moment, even though he may be depriving himself of many things in the future which he might otherwise have had. He will "take the cash and let the credit go." At the other end of the spectrum, some people are so impressed with the necessity of long-range planning that it becomes an unbreakable habit with them to sacrifice and keep sacrificing what they want in the here and now so that they can enjoy peace, comfort, and security much later in their lives. Each of these extremes can be self-defeating.

Here is an example of the first extreme: An immigrant laborer has to change his habits if he is to work in industry. He must learn to be more efficient, less disposed to spend half his time chatting on the job, and able to obey commands instantly and precisely. Yet he doesn't change his ways and, as a result, is fired. His life in the past has been so insecure that promises of greater financial rewards in the future just don't touch him. He accepts the loss of a job and consequent poverty with resignation and adjusts easily to a condition he has experienced often in the past. True, he *need* not adjust to it in this case, for he could avoid it by putting forth some effort now. But doing so would make the present uncomfortable for him, and he is unable to project his mind very far into the future. So, by not putting forth a relatively small effort now, he makes large future benefits impossible.

Here is an example of the second extreme: A business executive has spent half his life planning and scheming and outwitting his competitors so that he can enjoy peace and luxury in his later years. Now he has achieved his goal, he has all the money he can ever use, and he has a bad case of ulcers to reward him for his efforts. It would seem wise for him now to take things easier and enjoy some of the pleasures he has worked so hard for. But instead he keeps on scheming and planning and worsening his ulcers, just as if he were still poor and had to engage in a life-and-death battle against poverty to insure that he would have enough to live on. Planning has become such a habit with him that he has apparently forgotten what all the planning was for.

Let us now cast these remarks into a different terminology, that of *means* and *ends*. As we shall see, these terms will be constantly used in our study of ethics. As long as we stick to egoism of the present moment, we do not have to make the distinction between means and ends. But only then. In life, people are always taking *means* to attain *ends* they wish to secure: you study today (means) so that you will pass the course later (end); you undergo medical treatment now (means) so that your ailment can be cured (end). The vast majority of the acts we perform every day are merely means toward the attainment of other things which we desire. The world being what it is, this must be so, since almost everything we want in life requires us to take some steps (means) in order to attain it.

The pure egoist of the present moment would have no need of ends, toward which he would have to adopt means, since he tries to attain nothing in the future. But, as we have seen, virtually all human beings do try to attain things in the future which are not yet present. Even a person who swats the fly so that the fly won't bother him any more is adopting a present means toward a future end.

Some people have only a very limited capacity for adopting means toward future ends. A student may want to become a physician and earn a physician's income, but he cannot bring himself to go through the years of hard study and financial deprivation which are the necessary means to that end. Others find it very easy to visualize long-term ends, such as founding a vast business enterprise, but they are relatively incapable of enjoying the present — to them everything in the present is only a means. To plan to attain long-term ends when the path toward these ends is lengthy and laborious and involves much sacrifice, and at the same time to enjoy the here and now without "putting all your eggs in one basket" and sacrificing all pleasure now for the sake of something that may after all never come to pass — this is a most difficult achievement. Probably the best solution (when this is possible) is to select ends which you desire very much but toward which you *also* enjoy the means; that way the effort expended will not be a complete waste if the end is never attained. For instance, if you want to become a distinguished scholar but also enjoy the long process of study required to attain this end, then even if you never quite attain your goal, you will at any rate have had years of enjoyable study.

The egoistic hedonist, then, wants to maximize his total pleasure, or enjoyment. But because to obtain pleasure later he must often sacrifice it now, the art of maximizing his own pleasure throughout his entire life span is a most difficult one.

B. Epicureanism

Historically, the most famous version of egoistic hedonism is *Epicureanism,* which derives its name from its founder, the Greek philosopher Epicurus (342-270 B.C.). The Epicureans were rational egoistic hedonists who believed that there is only one thing worth aiming at, namely the maximum pleasure for oneself. But by pleasure they meant long-run pleasure, as estimated over an entire life span. The Epicureans condemned most pleasure-seekers because they sought the immediate pleasures, such as food and drink and sex, instead of the long-term pleasures, such as aesthetic satisfaction and knowledge. The rational egoistic hedonist considers not only today's pleasures but tomorrow's and next year's. Most pleasure seekers, the Epicureans thought, make two great mistakes: (1) they seek those sources of pleasure which give immediate pleasure, such as alcohol, but bring in their train a vast surplus of displeasure in the long run, like stocks that bring in large dividends for a year or so and then become valueless; and (2) they seek pleasures where, in the long run, they are not to be found at all — for instance, they wait in line to get into a crowded, smoky night club where the food is bad and they can't see the floor show; where people *think* they can find the most pleasure is often very far from where it can *actually* be found. The Epicureans objected not to the pursuit of pleasure or even its pursuit for oneself alone but to the blind and short-sighted way in which people go about seeking their pleasure. Either they do not sacrifice short-term pleasures for greater long-term ones, thus cheating themselves in the long run; or they do not properly examine where the true sources of pleasure are to be found, so that even if they do try to get long-term pleasures, they seek them in the wrong places and pay the price of misery for their mistakes.

The *general* thesis of Epicureanism is the principle of egoistic but long-range pleasure-seeking. We must separate the general thesis clearly from the *specific* thesis, which is the Epicureans' account of exactly *how* this long-term pleasure for oneself is to be attained. One might agree with the general thesis of Epicureanism about what one should try to attain in life without agreeing with the specific thesis about how it is to be attained. Let us turn now to the specific thesis.

With regard to the specific thesis, history has done the Epicureans a grave injustice. The very mention of the terms "epicure" and "epicurean" today brings to most people's minds images of a gourmand, one who fills himself to overflowing with food and drink, or of a rank indulger of his sensual appetites, or of a decadent wastrel suffering from overrefinement of taste. This was the sort of thing Chaucer meant when he characterized the Franklin (in *The Canterbury Tales*) as "Epicurus' owne sonne," and it is what the contemporary restaurateur has in mind when he names his establishment "The Epicurean Restaurant." The Epicureans, however, believed just the opposite. They condemned a life of sensual indulgence and believed that long-term pleasure could best be achieved by developing calmness, freedom from worry or distress, virtual absence of the physical appetites, and a cultivated mind. They were convinced that the pleasures most easily attained and most intense at the moment are the very ones that produce the most misery in the end — they are snares and delusions, hedonistic booby traps. So studious were the Epicureans in avoiding momentary pleasures that might have unpleasant aftereffects that they ended up well on the way to a complete asceticism.

On the matter of food, for example, the historical Epicurean was at the opposite extreme from the Epicurean of the popular mind who wants more and more exotic delicacies to titillate his taste buds. Epicurus argued that if you cultivate a taste for delicacies, you will be embarking on a road on which there is no returning and no long-run satisfaction but a dead end of unfulfilled and unfulfillable desire. The more new taste combinations you try, the more you will want; your jaded palate will become so accustomed to dishes that were recently exciting that you will crave ever more bizarre and impossible taste combinations. Eventually nature will no longer be able to satisfy you. Besides, the habit becomes expensive. If you cultivate a taste for peacock's tongues, you may find that other foods will taste so bland by comparison that you will be driven to seek more peacock's tongues and delicacies even rarer. In so doing, you will soon bankrupt yourself or at least suffer from constant anxiety lest there should be insufficient money or insufficient supply to provide you with these delicacies. Furthermore, most of these dishes, when indulged in frequently, lead to indigestion and ill health. They are simply not worth the trouble. It is wisest never to start indulging in them. Fortunately, thought Epicurus, the foods that are most healthful for us are also the least expensive. He claimed that he lived in perfect contentment on cheese and water. Nothing more, he contended, was needed for the healthful continuance of life, and he disciplined himself at an early age to the point where he desired nothing more.

On physical passion, Epicurus had similar advice. People very easily and naturally come to *want* sexual satisfaction, but it is an irony of nature that what people want most intensely and derive greatest pleasure from at the moment is seldom what will give them the most long-term pleasure. Nature traps us: she implants in us this desire, together with a high degree of momentary pleasure, and we anticipate the immediate pleasure so strongly that either we don't think of any long-term consequences or we rationalize ourselves into saying (against our better judgment) that these things *will* bring long-term satisfaction. But in giving in to these desires, we are mistaken; we cheat only ourselves. If we indulge in a life of sexual abandon, we soon become miserable. We always want more such satisfaction than we can have, we come to desire many sources of this pleasure which are not attainable to us, and we suffer the pangs of frustrated desire as a result. Our tastes finally become so overrefined that nothing really satisfies us, and we wind up in a frantic search for the unattainable. We would do well never to embark upon this fatal road. Nature lures us on to greater self-indulgence only to frustrate and defeat us in the end.

Even if one is married to one person, Epicurus thought, the chances are that he still won't enjoy long-run satisfaction. Two people are bound to become tired of each other and seek other company, in secret if not openly. Then jealousies arise, and the corrosive force of one single attack of jealousy costs us more grief and misery than a thousand pleasant encounters cause us satisfaction. The miseries, both physical and mental, that accompany constant sexual exploits are incalculably greater than the fleeting and evanescent pleasure which those exploits give us. The solution is simply to pare down our desires at the outset and never to start out on the fateful road that can lead to no happy destination. Once one is on this road, more and more impossible or nearly impossible conditions have to be fulfilled in order to produce even a minimum of pleasure, until finally even that minimum is no longer possible to us. Yet once we have started on that road, it beckons us on so powerfully with promises and allurements that it is almost impossible to turn back. The wisest course is the one that is most difficult at the outset, namely, to exert a considerable effort of will and not start indulging in the desires that can lead us only to disaster.

What pleasures, then, does Epicurus recommend? In general, the intellectual and the aesthetic. The self-defeating character of most pleasures does not apply to these. Knowledge requires careful cultivation and the initial expenditure of effort; but once this hurdle has been overcome, there is virtually all gain and no loss. Once we have knowledge, we have an enduring source of satisfaction which nothing, not bankruptcy or bereavement or even disease, but only death, can take away. Once one has trained himself to enjoy these pleasures, the pleasures last; and they are not followed, as the others are, by pain and misery. Reading Homer in the original requires mastery of a difficult foreign language, and you will not enjoy it in the beginning — many times you will throw the book aside and wonder whether it is worth the effort. But once acquired, the mastery is there to stay, and it will not desert you as long as you exercise it. The first time you hear a great symphony you may be bewildered and even repelled, but if you stick with it you will derive from it an aesthetic experience which is pleasurable to a degree that few things in life can ever be, and you will continue to be able to do so. These sources of pleasure are like gold coins which do not shine until you rub them thoroughly, but the more you rub them the brighter they will shine. Nor do they have the ball-and-chain of accompanying pain and distress: since these pleasures are relatively impersonal, they are not subject to the fluctuations of an unstable market or to the whims of an individual who knows that she is wanted and will use every resource in her power to make you jealous and frustrated until you give her exactly what she wants and who, having gained her ends, will throw you overboard. The "higher" pleasures are, unlike these "lower" ones, relatively pure and unmixed. They carry no agony and anguish with them — they are pure wheat and no chaff. Accordingly, these "higher" pleasures are far more worthy of cultivation than the "lower" ones, even though the "lower" ones are more intense, more alluring, and more easily enjoyed at the beginning.

C. Comments on Epicureanism

Let us leave unquestioned, for the moment, the claim of hedonism, which will be examined in Chapter 3, and of egoism, which will be examined in Chapter 4. Assuming, then, the general thesis of Epicureanism (which is simply egoistic hedonism), let us examine its specific thesis. Does the Epicurean path to long-term pleasure actually and always lead to it? This of course is an empirical claim, and, like all empirical claims of a general nature, it could be disputed endlessly. Nevertheless, a few remarks may be in order to indicate the direction which a critic of the specific thesis of Epicureanism might take.

1. To the Epicurean claim that the "lower" pleasures are self-defeating one might make the empirical counterclaim that the "lower" pleasures are not such hedonistic booby traps as the Epicureans thought. The pleasures of married life, for example, are fraught with dangers: danger of loss of the beloved, danger of disaffection with all its accompanying bitterness and sorrow, danger that love will diminish and that the relationship will develop into a tragicomedy of mutual recriminations. Still, it seems to most people that in spite of all these dangers the enterprise is worth the risk. Married life at its best can be the happiest of which people are capable, and even when it does not work out well, it can still bring more pleasure — or at the very least, less misery — than a life of loneliness and noninvolvement. The majority of married couples will probably testify that even when conditions are considerably less than ideal, they are still better than if husband and wife were living apart. He may be unhappy with her but he is even more unhappy without her.

The same may be said for the other sources of pleasure. Indulgence in food and drink does have the dangers against which Epicurus warned. But he was so anxious to avoid all unpleasant consequences of food and drink that he went too far in the other direction and recommended a diet of such utter simplicity as to be absurd and unnecessary, particularly today when countless foods can be produced quite cheaply. Moderation, one might suggest, would be a wiser thing to recommend than the abstemiousness preached by the Epicureans.

In general, then, a critic of Epicureanism might well say, "Even if the 'lower' pleasures have anything like as small a chance of paying off in the long run as you say, I still prefer to cultivate them. I know that there is a considerable risk involved in their pursuit, but I am willing to take that risk, even to live dangerously at times. I would rather gratify my natural wants, though in moderation, than to deny them entirely and have the peace of abstinence — even if it *is* peace and not utter frustration. If, to win a victory, I must walk through a mine field (exercising due care), I prefer to walk through the mine field rather than win no victories." Epicureans are confident that once we know the risks involved in the pursuit of these things, we shall no longer wish to indulge in them; but may it not be better to take the gamble and proceed, knowing the risks full well? Isn't it better to have some hits, together, of course, with some errors, than to live a life of no hits, no runs, no errors?

2. In reply to the Epicurean statement that the lower pleasures are more transitory, another critic might ask, "Are they? The pleasure of eating a juicy steak is more transitory than that of hearing Beethoven in that you can't eat *this* steak again tomorrow whereas you can listen to the same composition by Beethoven tomorrow. But then, if tomorrow you have a

steak just like the one you had today, what's the difference?" "You tire of the 'lower' pleasure more easily," say the Epicureans. But doesn't this depend on the person? Some people tire of art very quickly (even if indeed they enjoy it at all), but they never seem to tire of food and drink and sexual satisfaction, quite apart from the fact that they need *some* food and drink just to survive. If you were to eat a steak for dinner every evening or listen to the same Beethoven composition every evening, which would you more quickly tire of? Probably, one might suggest, the Beethoven. Most people, perhaps even most aesthetes, might not enjoy having their favorite musical composition repeated as many times a month as their favorite dish.

3. "Moreover," the critic may continue, "the 'higher' pleasures depend on the previous satisfaction of the 'lower' ones, not the other way round. If you have to do without a few meals, the most intense source of aesthetic or intellectual satisfaction brings no pleasure at all. Nor can you enjoy aesthetic or intellectual pleasures when you are in a state of fear, terror, jealousy, or other emotional convulsion." (This observation is true only to a degree, however. When we are in a state of extreme emotion, enjoyment may actually be intensified — consider the ability of music "to soothe the savage breast." And as for hunger, it would indeed be difficult to enjoy music or study while starving; yet some of the greatest works of art have been appreciated — and, for that matter, composed — on something less than a full stomach.)

4. A critic might also object that the "higher" pleasures take a great deal of time to cultivate. Often they require years of preparation, involving much labor and energy, initial confusion of mind, and heavy expenditure of money. And the payoff is uncertain. One may not enjoy these things even after all this preparation — witness the student who is sent to college by his parents but doesn't enjoy it at all. Furthermore, when years of one's life have gone into the preparation, one expects greater rewards at the end: "This had better be good!" says the student trying to enjoy a Béla Bartók string quartet after listening to it several times in bewilderment and frustration. Epicurus thought that the "lower" pleasures were the risky ones, but one might make an argument for saying that the "higher ones" are really riskier because of the long time that the capacity to enjoy them is in preparation. The further away from the present, the less certain a thing is; and doesn't this condition apply to the "higher" pleasures also? (Again, this is only part of the story. One may enjoy having complete mastery of a field of knowledge, but one may also have considerable enjoyment along the way, while one is still in the process of acquiring that mastery.)

5. The Epicurean view that *constant* indulgence in the "lower" pleasures usually brings misery (there seem to be exceptions even to this statement) is true; continuous overindulgence is a condition that calls for a psychoanalyst. A critic could say, however, that to many people, limited indulgence in

the "lower" pleasures tends to bring a great deal of satisfaction, sometimes more even in the long run than indulgence in the "higher" pleasures does. Individuals vary so much from one to another that it is difficult to generalize; but couldn't one argue quite plausibly that the "lower" pleasures do more to make life enjoyable than all the "higher" ones put together? The historian W. E. H. Lecky, in his *History of European Morals,* published in 1869, had some interesting comments on this question. He may have exaggerated and he may have been mistaken on some points, but his comments are an undeniable challenge to the champion of exclusively "higher" pleasures:

> No painter or novelist, who wished to depict an ideal of perfect happiness, would seek it in a profound student. . . . Bodily conditions have in general more influence upon our enjoyment than mental ones. The happiness of the great majority of men is far more affected by health and temperament, resulting from physical conditions, which again physical enjoyments are often calculated to produce, than by any mental or moral causes, and acute physical sufferings paralyze all the energies of our nature to a greater extent than any mental distress. It is probable that the American inventor of the first anaesthetic has done more for the real happiness of mankind than all the moral philosophers from Socrates to Mill.[1]

6. Finally, a critic might note that on the whole, Epicureans seem to have been more anxious to avoid experiences which would cause them pain and distress than to seek experiences which would cause them pleasure. They seem to have identified pleasure with a kind of vanilla-flavored state of quiescence and tranquillity — the absence of disturbances, not a positive enjoyment of anything. At least, they talked of avoiding more than they talked of seeking, of refraining more than of doing. But pleasure is much more than this. Pleasure is usually understood by most people to be a positive state, not merely the absence of something. It is a plus, not a zero. (The concept of pleasure will be analyzed further in Chapter 3.)

There is, however, a useful caution constantly expressed by Epicureans: the warning that what you want and what gives you pleasure (at least in the long run) are often not the same. You may want something so badly that you would do anything to get it, yet that very thing may bring you no end of misery later on. People are often not competent judges of their own sources of pleasure. When left to themselves they will usually do what they want at the time; but nature cheats them, for what they want turns out to be very different from what would give them pleasure, at least continued pleasure. People who follow the whims of their moment-to-moment cravings for pleasure are their own slaves, for they do not attain the things which they themselves want in the long run.

[1] W. E. H. Lecky, *A History of European Morals* (New York: Braziller, 1955), p. 88.

D. *The calculation of pleasures*

An exact device for calculating quantities of pleasures was attempted by the English philosopher Jeremy Bentham (1748-1833) many hundreds of years after Epicurus. Bentham devised what is called the *hedonistic calculus* for calculating the amount of pleasure or pain that would occur as a result of one's actions. (Bentham used the word "pain" as the opposite of pleasure. As we shall see in Chapter 3, this was a mistake.) Bentham was no egoist, for his ethical theory, which we shall discuss in Chapter 5, requires that we consider the pleasurable and painful effects of our actions on everyone, not just on ourselves. But that point is incidental here. What matters at the moment is that he undertook to provide a method of estimating pleasures and pains which can be used by the hedonist, whether he is egoistic or not.

a. Bentham's first criterion is the *intensity* of a pleasure. Between two pleasures — all other things being equal — the more intense one is to be preferred; and between two pains, if one must choose between them, the less intense one is to be preferred.

b. His second criterion is *duration*. Other things being equal, the preferable pleasure is the one that lasts the longest. Unfortunately, the most intense pleasures are usually those of the shortest duration, and we often have to choose between a short intense pleasure and a longer but milder one. (Epicurus thought that we are almost always justified in sacrificing the short intense pleasure for the long milder one, but as we have just seen, this position can be questioned.)

c. In addition there is the criterion of *certainty*. Between a pleasure certain to occur and one less certain, we should of course prefer the certain one. The more probable is to be preferred to the less probable. But we often have to choose between a longer or more intense pleasure that is less certain to occur and a shorter or milder one that is more nearly certain to occur. Thus the first two factors have to be weighed against the third.

d. The fourth criterion is *propinquity*. Other things being equal, the nearby pleasure is to be preferred to the one far off in the future. But this raises a question: are the far-off pleasures to be preferred less *because* they are far off or because, being far off, they are usually less certain to occur? If they were just as certain to occur, should we still prefer the nearby one? Is propinquity to be taken as a separate criterion or only as a corollary of certainty and uncertainty? If the latter, the criterion of propinquity is not a separate one at all.

e. Next is *fecundity* of pleasures, their tendency to promote or lead to more pleasures. Some pleasures, such as sexual pleasures not accompanied by mutual affection and trust, are less fecund than sexual pleasures that do have these accompaniments. That is why the latter are to be preferred. Pleasures that lead to more pleasures are to be preferred to those which lead to fewer or none.

f. Last is the *purity* of pleasures, the degree to which they occur *unmixed* with pain. Clearly, of two pleasures, the unmixed one is to be preferred to the mixed one. (Bentham listed one more criterion, *extent,* or the number of persons who can enjoy the pleasures. But since we are operating just now in the domain of egoism, without considering other people, we shall not consider this last factor here.)

To keep all these six criteria in mind in deciding each action of our lives seems like such a complicated business as to be utterly unrealistic. But Bentham says,

> It is not to be expected that this process should be strictly pursued previously to every moral judgment, or to every legislative or judicial operation. It may, however, be always kept in view; and as near as the process actually pursued on these occasions approaches to it, so near will such process approach the character of an exact one.[1]

Does Bentham's hedonistic calculus really enable us to give an exact mathematical calculation of pleasures and pains? Here the answer is surely "No." Of all the criteria, duration is the only one that can be calculated precisely, for example, by looking at one's watch. Intensity of pleasure or pain cannot be measured in the same way — one can say this one was more intense, or much more intense, than that one, but that's about all. We cannot say that this pleasure was twenty-three times as intense as that one, the way we can say it lasted twenty-three times as long. Propinquity can be calculated, for again it involves time, which is mathematically divisible with great precision. Degrees of probability (certainty or uncertainty) are very difficult to calculate: we can say it is 50 per cent probable that the next throw of the coin will come up heads, but there are very few situations in which we can be that precise. In short, the hedonistic calculus is an ideal that is very far from being realized and bids fair never to be realized.

Does this improbability of realization imply that Bentham's calculus is useless or that his six criteria have no value? Far from it. It is useful to have pointed out the separate criteria that can be taken into consideration before we act. If more people took Bentham's list seriously, fewer people would act rashly and reap the bitter reward of pain and misery. In daily life there are very few things that can be estimated in advance with great precision, but we do not consider the estimation useless on that account. You may know that you want a new piano more than you do a stereo hi-fi set, but if you told somebody you wanted the piano just 53 per cent more, he would probably raise an eyebrow or two.

There are two views one may hold about the impossibility of quantification of pleasures and pains. (1) The impossibility is only a technical one which may in time be remedied. Just as, once upon a time, we could say

[1] Jeremy Bentham, *Introduction to the Principles of Morals and Legislation* (Many editions), Ch. 1.

with regard to temperature only, "It's hot" or "It's cold" or "This is cooler than that," but now, by means of thermometers, we can say exactly how hot or how cold it is — "It's 86° F."; so we may one day be in a similar position with regard to the measurement of pleasures and pains. (2) The impossibility is inherent and not technically remediable. Even if we were able to measure precisely the intensity of certain chemical-electrical currents passing through the cerebral cortex (those which appear to be connected with the experience of pleasure), we would have measured not the pleasure itself but only the strength of these currents. Pleasure, according to this view, is intrinsically unquantifiable, unlike electrical currents.

To consider this interesting question in detail would take us into epistemology and metaphysics. For ethics, however, it doesn't much matter which alternative we accept, for the net effect is the same: a hedonistic calculus is a present impossibility. But — so what?

> I am quite prepared to admit that the notion of a *calculus* of satisfactions and dissatisfactions is impossible. But I cannot conceive why any philosopher should want to have one. . . . It is said that if you cannot make a calculation of the relative amounts of pleasure and pain which your actions will produce in the world, you cannot know which actions are good, which bad. This, however, is a very shallow argument. In the first place, even if you cannot measure pleasures and pains, this does not prevent you from knowing that some pleasures or pains are greater than others. A man does not need a thermometer to know that he is being frozen to death or boiled alive. And without any such instrument he can detect the difference between a hot day and a cold one. So too a man knows that some pains are terrible, some slight; that some pleasures are great, some small; although he cannot measure either the pleasures or the pains.[1]

Bentham did not draw any Epicurean conclusions from his calculus. His aim was simply to render more precise the ideal of careful, long-term pleasure-calculation. He was, however, convinced that when judged by *all* the criteria he listed, the pleasures of friendship and affection and good books paid off more than those of high drinking and fast living. "Is pushpin [bowling] as good as poetry, provided that it causes equal pleasure?" Bentham was asked. Bentham's answer was, "Yes, *if* it causes equal pleasure [in the long run, etc.]"; but he was convinced that poetry, in its total effects, direct and indirect, does cause more pleasure than pushpin. This empirical conclusion could, however, be disputed.

Bentham's follower John Stuart Mill (1806-73), was so concerned that certain kinds of pleasure should come out as *better* than others that he supplemented Bentham's list of criteria with another one, that of *quality*. Mill held that the "higher" pleasures, in addition to being greater in dura-

---

[1] From Walter T. Stace, *The Concept of Morals.* New York: Macmillan, 1937, pp. 131-32. Reprinted by permission of the author.

tion, fecundity, and richness, were also of a better quality than the others. But this characteristic of being "better" or "higher" is not easy to explain on Mill's officially hedonistic account.

If I am asked what I mean by difference of quality in pleasures, or what makes one pleasure more valuable than another merely as a pleasure, except its being greater in amount, there is but one possible answer. Of two pleasures, if there be one to which all or almost all *who have experience of both* give a decided preference, irrespective of any feeling of moral obligation to prefer it, that is the more desirable pleasure. If one of the two is, by those who are competently acquainted with both, placed so far above the other that they prefer it, even though knowing it to be attended with a greater amount of discontent, and would not resign it for any quantity of the other pleasure which their nature is capable of, we are justified in ascribing to the preferred enjoyment a superiority in quality, so far outweighing quantity as to render it, in comparison, of small account.[1]

Of course, Mill was quite certain that the "higher" pleasures would be preferred by those who were "competently acquainted with both."

According to some critics, however, this "qualitative" principle of Mill's is a blunder: partly because if something is (in the long run) *less* pleasurable and yet *better,* then one has already deserted pleasure as the sole criterion of desirability and whatever we have left is no longer hedonism; and partly because, in these critics' opinion, the qualitative principle is unnecessary anyway. Bentham was sure that certain pleasures would emerge as more worthwhile than others as a result of his list of factors, without any need of assistance from a separate principle of quality. To say that the "higher" pleasures, in addition to being more long-lived, more certain, more pure, were also "higher" by a qualitative principle seemed to Benthamites like so much excess baggage — a way of unnecessarily complicating and obscuring the original hedonistic position. For if the first barrel of criteria (Bentham's) already hit the mark by showing certain sources of pleasure to be preferable to others, why the need to employ the second barrel, Mill's qualitative principle?

EXERCISES

1. Try to clarify the concept of "higher" vs. "lower" pleasures. In which class do you think the following would be included: playing baseball? plowing a straight furrow in rich black soil? taking a walk in the country? sailing? giving love and affection? Do you think the distinction is a good one nonetheless?

2. Write a few paragraphs defending the "higher" pleasures against the "lower," or vice versa.

3. A moral theory is *egoistic* when it is concerned with the agent and no one else. A person is said to be *egotistic* (or egotistical) when he is consciously self-

[1] J. S. Mill, *Utilitarianism* (Many editions), Ch. 2.

centered and conceited, usually offensively so. Can a person be an egoist and yet not egotistical? Explain or illustrate.

4. Which of the following points of view would the Epicurean agree with? Explain.

a. We should never pay attention to the pleasures of other people.

b. Sardanapalus, the Assyrian king: "Eat, drink, and play; for nothing else would I give a snap of the fingers. The dinners I have eaten, the wanton acts I have exulted in, the delights of love I have enjoyed — all these things still belong to me, although my blessings have now disappeared."

c. Edward Fitzgerald, *The Rubaiyat of Omar Khayyam:*

> Ah, my Beloved, fill the cup that clears
> Today of past regret and future fears.
>   Tomorrow! — why, tomorrow I may be
> Myself with yesterday's sev'n thousand years.

d. Old man: Have your fling while you're young, my boy; I can't any more and am glad I did when I was young. The other pleasures you can always have later.

5. Evaluate Bentham's criteria for the calculation of pleasures.

6. Do you think that Mill's "qualitative principle" with respect to the calculation of pleasures is a necessary supplement to Bentham's account or not? Give reasons for your answer.

7. Do you think that the quantification of pleasures is only technically impossible (impossible now, with our present methods of measurement) or is logically impossible ("impossible in principle")? Give reasons for your answer.

8. Read Walter Pater's novel, *Marius the Epicurean,* noting especially how the hero, Marius, is led from his tribal religion into Epicureanism, and from Epicureanism into Stoicism.

9. The Epicureans believed that religious belief is evil, not because it is false (though they believed this too), but because such belief disturbs man's tranquility and peace by forcing him to give up the pleasures of this life in favor of those of another life (which they believed did not exist), and because fear of punishment in an after-life is extremely disturbing to one's happiness in this life. The best expression of this view is to be found in Lucretius' great poem, *On the Nature of Things.* Evaluate this view. Does it follow from the premises of the Epicurean ethics?

(The reading list on Epicureanism is combined with the one on Stoicism at the end of the next section.)

4. *The Stoic way of life*

Officially, Stoicism is not egoistic. Nevertheless, its first concern is not with other people or with the world but with the individual — with how the individual is to find peace in a troubled world.

A. The ethics of Stoicism

The Stoic school was founded by the Greek philosopher Zeno (336?-264? B.C.) and was carried from Greece to Rome, where it flourished for several centuries into the Christian era alongside Christianity. Its influence is marked in many Christian writers such as St. Paul, and it has put an indelible stamp on Western thought. "Bear your troubles stoically" has become a cliché. The Stoics had an elaborate metaphysical doctrine; we shall have space here only to consider their ethics, although a full appreciation of Stoic ethics is impeded somewhat by abstracting it from its underpinning in Stoic metaphysics.

Happiness, not pleasure, is of importance in the Stoic view of life. (Most people do not carefully distinguish between the terms "happiness" and "pleasure." We shall make the distinction as sharp as we can in Chapter 3.) But the chief characteristic of Stoic ethics is the Stoics' view of how happiness is to be attained. Happiness is not to be found in anything that the outside world can give — mingling with the world and becoming involved in its activities leads only to disillusionment and despair. Society is so set up that no one can find happiness by staking his hopes upon the world. Any personal involvement in its affairs brings one to grief in the end. Fame, fortune, even the respect of one's fellow men, are here one day only to vanish the next; and he who is dependent on these things is the most miserable of men. One falls in love, and the loved one finds another or else is struck down by death or disease. One becomes involved in public life, and one's noblest efforts are frustrated by little men who dash one's highest aims and aspirations to the ground. The hopes and ideals of bright burning youth are one by one made to bite the dust. Whatever sources of pleasure we have, like meteors, burn brightly for an instant and then are reduced to ashes and forgotten forever, ending in bitterness and disillusionment for those who cherished them. "Vanity of vanities, all is vanity." (The author of Ecclesiastes was nine-tenths a Stoic.)

In this dark world there is no satisfaction to be found of our deepest desires; the satisfactions we may find one day are brought crumbling into ruin the next. Since our desires cannot find lasting satisfaction in this world, and since, the Stoics believed, there is no other, our only recourse is not to have desires — to suppress them until they no longer exist. If we expect nothing of this world, we shall not be disappointed; if we expect a great deal we shall face only bitterness and defeat. Our degree of happiness is sometimes said to be what we have, divided by what we want. Most people want far more than they have, and the more they have the more they want. The solution is not to *want* anything, then we shall never be distressed at not having it.

Nature has instilled in us a large number of powerful and insistent desires: for food and drink, for sexual conquest, for fame, for power, for possession of the world's goods. All these desires will bring us to ruin if we let nature take its course and pursue them. Salvation is to be found only in systematically, rigorously, and uncompromisingly rooting them out. To do so requires a herculean effort of will, but it must be done; for only when it is done can we find peace. Once we have achieved peace, nothing can touch us any more: our crops and lands may be destroyed in fire or plague, our family killed by disease, our security and livelihood taken away from us by economic chaos or the collapse of our civilization; none of these calamities will faze us, for the loss of something that doesn't matter to us anyway can cause us no pain. We should develop toward the outside world a calm and steadfast attitude of what the Stoics called *apatheia* (literally, lack of feeling or emotional involvement). Once we have developed *apatheia* toward everything in the outside world, nothing that happens in that world can possibly hurt us: come what may, we shall have an inner reserve of Stoic fortitude which will not desert us. "World, do your worst," we may say, and it will not perturb us.

The English word "apathy" is derived from the Greek *apatheia,* but it is a poor translation. We think of people as apathetic when they are listless, bored, uncaring. A state of apathy reminds us of the ennui people may feel at dull cocktail parties. But this is not at all the kind of thing the Stoics meant. They did not recommend the cultivation of boredom. They recommended, rather, a heroic act of will by which we cast out all our desires, so that, once these were eradicated from our natures, nothing that happened to us could affect us inwardly. Apathy is associated in our minds with laziness; but the state of Stoic *apatheia* could never be achieved by being lazy. Indeed, it required the very opposite.

The Stoics believed that nothing that occurs in the outside world, no matter what it may do to us, is in itself good or evil. Famine, disease, plague, war, torture, the fall of civilization itself — none of these are evils. The only good or evil things are *in us* — in our attitude of mind, not in what happens to us but in how we take what happens to us. Even if, like Job, we are deprived of all our possessions and our dear ones, even if we are tortured on the rack, there is no evil in these mishaps. The only evil is in our personal involvement in these things so that we depend upon them, care about them, and miss them when we no longer have them. This personal involvement in the things of the world is the greatest possible evil, for it is incompatible with *apatheia.* But if we face the world with true *apatheia,* refusing to bend our will to it even for a moment, retaining a deep and imperturbable inner calm in the face of everything, then we have achieved the highest good possible in life. Our bodies may be rotting with disease and pain, but this state is not evil so long as we preserve inviolate the *sanctum sanctorum* of our minds and our spirit remains unmoved, heroic, and unquenchable.

This outlook, one may say, is a philosophy for heroes and martyrs. It is, however, an outlook that springs eternal within us whenever the outside world has little to offer and the inner world of one's own spirit is all that is left. Over the years, people come to depend on countless things outside their own control: money, property, conveniences, other people. But when time after time one or another of these things fails us, Stoicism, as a kind of secondary line of defense, tells us not to desire these things in the first place. Our only recourse is to rely on that which *is* within our control — our own will. Once our fingers have been burned by contact with the things in the world outside, and especially if they have been burned many times, we do not reach out to touch the world again. We try hard not to desire it, or anything that belongs to it, lest we be burned once more.

Such a view of life, to be sure, goes contrary to the basic drives of human nature and can hardly be practiced by many thousands of people in its pure, original, undiluted form. Early Stoicism, which has just been described, was so rigorous and demanding in the total suppression of human desires that few people, even those repeatedly struck down by adversity, could put it into practice: "hope springs eternal. . . ." So the early, extreme Stoicism gave way to a more moderate Stoicism. Extreme Stoicism tells us to renounce the world and all desires for things of the world, to uproot such desires completely from our natures. The more moderate Stoicism that gradually came to supplant it softened this demand. Moderate Stoicism requires that our primary allegiance be given to that aspect of our nature which is under our control, so that we in no way come to depend on the outside world; moderate Stoicism recommends the cultivation of *apatheia,* the exhibition of heroic fortitude in the face of adversity and ruin, the determination never to be humbled by external circumstances and to preserve one's equanimity and inner calm regardless of what happens. But in moderate Stoicism a secondary allegiance can be given to some things of the world, such as good food, good company, and good reading, provided always that we never become dependent on these things, that we never become so accustomed to them that we are unhappy when they are denied us, that when we have to do without them, we can live as before, unperturbed by the loss. If we can maintain our independence of the things of the world, then, according to moderate Stoicism, we may be permitted a temporary indulgence in them. The danger is, of course, that once we become accustomed to these things, it becomes increasingly difficult to do without them, and when we are forced to do so, we have to go through the same herculean ordeal of developing *apatheia* all over again. It would almost seem preferable to purge our souls of desire once and for all rather than to go through the painful process every time the world frowns upon us.

Not all the Stoics, however, acted in accordance even with moderate Stoicism. The most famous of all the Stoics was the Roman emperor Marcus Aurelius (121-180 A.D.), whose famous book, *Meditations,* has been a handbook of the Stoic way of life for many centuries. He tried to practice Stoicism in his personal life but also to remember that he was governing an empire composed chiefly of non-Stoics. In trying to reduce the amount of political corruption, in instigating humanitarian measures and in fighting poverty and disease in his empire, he was, strictly speaking, not being consistently Stoic. For if nothing in the outside world is either good or bad, then neither is poverty or disease bad — so why fight them? Indeed, their occurrence might well be encouraged, for does not adversity provide the best possible soil for the cultivation for *apatheia*? Why neglect such a delicious opportunity for developing Stoic fortitude and calm in the face of misfortune?

There was one side effect of Stoicism which deserves mention. Since all men are born with the same desires and instincts against which they must do constant battle if they are to develop *apatheia,* all men are in this very important respect alike. All men are brothers, fellow sufferers from desire, fellow soldiers in the same battle against desire, a battle on which their only hope of happiness depends. All distinctions of social class and rank are therefore of no consequence: the slave can be as free as the king if they are both swept clean of the desires which have heretofore made their lives equally miserable. (The two most famous Stoics were Epictetus, a slave, and Marcus Aurelius.) The external trappings of wealth, position, fame, and fortune make no difference whatever. Stoicism was the first doctrine in the history of the world to preach the brotherhood of all mankind, and in this respect it had a considerable influence upon Christianity. This doctrine had an interesting effect upon the institution of slavery. On the one hand, the slave was equal to the king, for external things like social position were not of the slightest consequence. The king without *apatheia* was more miserable than the slave with it. On the other hand, since one's social position was not of any consequence, there was no incentive to change it. Why agitate for the removal of an institution that didn't matter anyway?

B. Interpretations of Stoicism

Superficially, Stoicism and Epicureanism are quite different. Epicureanism is selfishly pleasure-seeking, and Stoicism requires complete renunciation. Yet they are not as unlike as these descriptions would make it appear. The Epicurean, as we have already observed, had to discipline himself; for most of the immediately pressing desires had to be given up in favor of long-term ones which at the moment seemed less promising. To forego immediate desires in favor of long-term ones might require almost as much self-discipline as to stamp out all desires. At any rate, both took as their ideal a state of being in which the avoidance of pain and distress was more important than the positive cultivation and acquisition of satisfactions. Both recommended ways of life which required one to abandon those sources of gratification which led one to depend on the outside world and to cultivate only those things which were within the control of one's will. "Learn to do without those things that the world may take away from you" is a motto that suited them both. Both were so afraid of getting hurt by the "slings and arrows of outrageous fortune" that they preferred not to be involved in matters of fortune at all. If one had to infer what a person's moral code was from observing his behavior from day to day, it would have been difficult in practice to distinguish a Stoic from an Epicurean.

There is, however, more than one way of interpreting the Stoic teaching, and even if this difference of interpretation may make no difference in Stoic practice, it makes a great deal of difference to the kind of comment and criticism one may make of the Stoic ethics. It is this: what did the Stoics really consider worth while, worth having for its own sake, the end toward which their other activities were means? One might interpret Stoicism as holding any one of the following three views on this point:

1. Only *apatheia* is worth cultivating. Happiness is not something worthy of being sought, even if it were attainable in this world.

2. Happiness is what is desirable, but since the world is so organized that happiness is impossible in it, one had better renounce the search for it and cultivate *apatheia* (thus settling for second best) rather than struggle endlessly in a morass of happiness-seeking that can end only in bitterness and ruin.

3. Happiness is what is desirable, and it *can* be achieved, but only through the renunciation of desire, not by its gratification, in other words, only by the cultivation of *apatheia*.

In the third interpretation, happiness can be sought and gained, but only through *apatheia*. In the first two interpretations, happiness should not even be sought, but the reasons are different. For the first interpretation the reason would be as follows: don't seek happiness because it is not worthy of being sought. For the second interpretation: don't seek happiness because you won't find it anyway.

1. If the first interpretation is accepted, it is difficult to reply to the Stoic claim other than to ask why *apatheia* should be considered such a good thing to have. The critic may argue as follows: "Would *apatheia* be worth cultivating if the world were organized in such a way as to fulfill our desires rather than to frustrate them?" The Stoic who supported this first interpretation, would have to say, "Yes. Even if there were a world full of potential for happiness, one should develop *apatheia,* not happiness." "But then," the critic and most of us would say, "the Stoic would develop his *apatheia* quite uselessly; his efforts and his heroism would be pointless, tragically comic to behold. Why develop *apatheia* against the slings and arrows of outrageous fortune if fortune is not outrageous? Why should *apatheia* be cultivated for its own sake? The best one can say for it is that, in a hostile world and in the face of desires that are bound to be frustrated anyway, one can make the best of a bad situation by developing *apatheia* to keep from courting disaster. But good for its own sake? Between two worlds, the first filled with happy people and a certain amount of *apatheia* and the second filled with unhappy people and the same amount of *apatheia,* there

would be nothing to choose according to the Stoic, since both worlds contain the same amount of *apatheia,* which alone is worth having. The greater happiness of the first world would make no difference to the evaluation. But isn't this position rather absurd? Stranger still, between one world containing much happiness but little *apatheia* and a second world containing very little happiness and a great deal of *apatheia,* the Stoic would be committed to preferring the second world. But in a world in which a great deal of happiness was possible without *apatheia,* what would all the *apatheia* be *for?*"

2. Let us turn, then, to the second interpretation of Stoicism — that happiness is what is really desirable but that the world is such as to make it impossible of attainment. This view can be more easily attacked than the first view, since the second involves an empirical claim — the claim that the world is of such a nature as to render happiness impossible. This empirical claim very few people would agree with. They might reply to the Stoic somewhat as follows: "Even under adverse external conditions, such as the dying Roman Empire under which Stoicism flourished, happiness drawn from external things is possible to some degree. Love is a good thing and is worth trying to attain, even though the object of one's love may later prove unfaithful or fall sick of an incurable disease and die. Love is a calculated risk, but the experience is worth the risk. True, if one values a possession or a relationship, it is much harder for him to do without it later on. But even if he has to adjust to doing without it, it is still better to have had it and at least have the memory of some happiness than not to have had it at all. Those mothers who have lost sons in war almost always say that if they had it to do over again they would rather have the son and lose him than not to have had him at all. And the same with engagements and marriages which end in one's being jilted or divorced: ''tis better to have loved and lost than never to have loved at all.' Is it better not to develop a passion for good reading for fear that one may become blind and unable to read any more, or is it better to develop the love of reading even though there is always some danger of blindness or other disability that would prevent its continuance? Who would hesitate to prefer the latter?"

"The Stoic, however," our critic continues, "would in consistency have to prefer the former. Would he be justified in doing so? 'Nothing ventured, nothing gained,' says a favorite aphorism; but the Stoic is so afraid that venturing would mean losing that he is compulsively afraid to venture. Far more even than with the Epicurean, who avoids only *some* this-worldly satisfactions, we may describe the Stoic as holding a view of 'no hits, no runs, no errors.' But to live this way is to deprive oneself of even the limited happiness that life has to offer. True, when you stick your neck out there is always some danger that it will be chopped off; and when that danger is considerable, only a fool would stick his neck out. But the Stoic won't stick his neck out even when the danger is small, or even when it seems quite certainly worth the risk. If you *never* stick your neck out, what can you get out of life? You are reduced to sitting apart in splendid isolation, watching the other people in the world playing the game of life while you can have no part in it because you are so afraid of getting hurt in the game. Now what is better — participating in the game even if there is dan-.ger or sitting apart in sneering contempt for the game and the players? We have only one life to live (to this the Stoic himself agrees), and we should incorporate into that life a wide variety of experiences. This will mean that sometimes we shall be disappointed, hurt, frustrated, even bitter; but at least we shall have played the game and known what the experience of living is like, taking both its joys and its sorrows in our stride, instead of sitting in a glass house apart from it all. The Stoic is such a compulsive safety seeker that he deprives himself of what life has to offer, and thereby he cheats himself. He takes a rule of life that is applicable only under the most adverse and unusual circumstances — say when one is being tortured or one's entire family has been slaughtered — and converts it into a universal maxim to be employed in all situations. He is like the agoraphobe who is so afraid of the street, because some people are killed by cars, that he will never venture on the street at all. Surely he is just as much of a fool as his opposite number, the man who unthinkingly and blindly dashes into every situation that offers excitement regardless of whether it will kill him or maim him or send him to jail for twenty years."

The argument above is the kind of criticism that is most likely to be brought to bear against the Stoic who supports the second interpretation: that he is guilty of a factual error about the world in saying that it offers no chance for happiness; he is in error because the world does offer some chance. This factual error leads him to make a strategical error as well, for he retreats from every possible situation of involvement in the world even when the danger to his happiness is small. He takes a piece of advice that is useful in a few situations a part of the time and tries to apply it to all situations all of the time.

The Stoic is not without a reply. Just as his critic accuses him of making a factual mistake about the world, so the Stoic will accuse his critic of making a factual mistake about the world. "You say that the world is such that happiness, more than an occasional smattering of it, is possible in it; but I, who have experienced the world in all its aspects, deny this. I agree with you that happiness is desirable, but I disagree with your optimism about the possibility of having it in a world such as ours. Let me cite the theory of the German philosopher Arthur Schopenhauer (1788-1860), who, though he wrote in the nineteenth century, shares the Stoic evaluation of the world and human nature and their effect on man's happiness. Man, says Schopenhauer, is a creature cursed with endless desires, in a world which inevitably frustrates them. Desires

. . . are limitless, [their] claims inexhaustible, and every satisfied desire gives rise to a new one. No possible satisfaction in the world could suffice to still its longings, set a goal to its infinite cravings, and fill the bottomless abyss of its heart. Then let one consider what as a rule are the satisfactions of any kind that a man obtains. For the most part nothing more than the bare maintenance of this existence itself, extorted day by day with unceasing trouble and constant care in the conflict with want, and with death in prospect. Everything in life shows that earthly happiness is destined to be frustrated or recognized as an illusion. . . . The life of most men is troubled and short. Those who are comparatively happy are so, for the most part, only apparently, or else, like men of long life, they are the rare exceptions, a possibility of which there had to be — as decoy-birds. Life presents itself as a continual deception in small things as in great. If it has promised, it does not keep its word, unless to show how little worth desiring were the things desired; thus we are deluded now by hope, now by what was hoped for. If it has given, it has done so in order to take. The enchantment of distance shows us paradises which vanish like optical illusions when we have allowed ourselves to be mocked by them. Happiness accordingly always lies in the future, or else in the past, and the present day may be compared to a small dark cloud which the wind drives over the sunny plain: before and behind it all is bright, only it itself always casts a shadow. The present is therefore always insufficient; but the future is uncertain, and the past irrevocable. Life with its hourly, daily, weekly, yearly, little, greater, and great misfortunes, with its deluded hopes and its accidents destroying all our calculations, bears so distinctly the impression of something with which we must become disgusted, that it is hard to conceive how one has been able to mistake this and allow oneself to be persuaded that life is there in order to be thankfully enjoyed, and that man exists in order to be happy. Rather that continual illusion and disillusion, and also the nature of life throughout, presents itself to us as intended and calculated to awaken the conviction that nothing at all is worth our striving, our efforts and struggles, that all good things are vanity, the world in all its ends bankrupt, and life a business which does not cover its expenses. . . .

Human existence, far from bearing the character of a *gift,* has entirely the character of a *debt* that has been contracted. The calling in of this debt appears in the form of the pressing wants, tormenting desires, and endless misery established through this existence. As a rule, the whole lifetime is devoted to the paying off of this debt; but this only meets the interest. The payment of the capital takes place through death. And when was this debt contracted? At the begetting.[1]

"Examples of the kind of thing Schopenhauer has in mind," continues the Stoic, "are not far to seek. We are hungry, and we desire food; but as soon as we have eaten what we want, we are tired of the food and its very odor is repellent, until hunger comes again and we desire it once more. We fall in love and are torn by longing; but we can never have the beloved object

[1] A. Schopenhauer, *The World as Will and Idea* (London: Routledge & Kegan Paul, 1883), Vol. 3, pp. 390-93.

and must grind out our years in frustration and bitterness or do with a second-best while thinking of the one we really want. Or, if we do attain the object of our longing, the satisfaction is short-lived: we soon tire of her and become bored; we may desire instead someone else whom we cannot have. We are chained to a treadmill of desires — desires that exist only to be frustrated or if satisfied then replaced by still other desires which are frustrated in turn. We want what we do not have, and once we have it we do not want it any more. Yet the desires, each more burning than the last, keep coming one by one; only death puts an end to them all. The fruit of the forbidden tree lures us onward with desire, only to turn to dust and ashes in our mouths. The state of desire is painful, for it is a state of want; the state of repletion and satiety is also painful, for what we have we no longer desire; where in all this is happiness? The only release from nature's treadmill is the total escape from all desire, which, for most of us, is possible only in death."

Such is Schopenhauer's picture of human life. But the critic will question it at many points. He will say, for example, "(1) The state of desire is not necessarily painful or even unpleasant. Acute hunger is painful, but a mild hunger, carrying with it anticipations of satisfaction may be quite pleasant. It is not true that every satisfaction of desire presupposes a previous state of dissatisfaction. Delight in study *may* have been preceded by a painful desire for it, but it may not.

"Moreover, (2) the process of satisfying the desire may itself be pleasant. A student of medicine may aim at becoming a good physician, and the attainment of the goal may bring him happiness; but (as we have indicated before) this is not to say that he has no happiness along the way — the process of working toward his goal may bring him as much happiness as the fulfillment will. A philosopher once said, 'If you offered me the choice between the Truth and the Search for Truth, I would choose the Search!'

"Still further, (3) people often *do* achieve their goals and experience great happiness in so doing. Nor need the happiness be evanescent; it may be enduring, lasting as long as life. Aren't there many people who have attained at least some of their life's goals and who would not wish their lives to be different if they could live them again? True, everyone has some frustration and unhappiness, and nobody can have everything he wants; but sometimes the unhappiness only accentuates the happiness and makes the experience more poignant — instead of the bits of happiness (very small ones, Schopenhauer says) acting as a decoy for the vast quantity of unhappiness. It is true that sometimes a man desires a woman and tires of her as soon as he weds her; but this change itself, psychologists tell us, may be a neurotic symptom — at any rate, it is far from universal. There are thousands of happily married couples who remain so year after year and who from their personal experience can give the lie to Schopenhauer's universal pessimism about human relations. To someone who told them that human happiness is impossible of attainment, they would reply, 'Speak for yourself!' "

3. But the preceding line of argument is not conclusive for the third interpretation of Stoicism — that we can indeed be happy in this world but that this happiness can be achieved only through a complete renunciation of desire. (Even Schopenhauer left this escape valve, happiness — or at least peace — through complete renunciation of desire.) The critic would say, "The third interpretation too makes an empirical claim, and if it is to be refuted, it must be refuted by adducing empirical facts. The facts to adduce are not far to seek. A human being has certain basic needs which cannot be denied or squelched without severe detriment to his happiness. People can be happy without going to the movies, they can be happy without having much material wealth (if they can't at the time, they can gradually become adjusted to it — 'remember how happy we were when we were poor?'), they can even be happy without sexual satisfaction.

"But one should not infer that people can be happy while renouncing *all* desires, that there is *nothing* of which they can be deprived without loss of happiness. There is a limit to what people can adjust themselves to. A person can train himself to be indifferent to small degrees of pain, but he cannot train himself to be indifferent to torture; the Stoic who says that a man can be happy while being tortured on the rack, as long as he has *apatheia,* is simply fooling himself. He can train himself to subsist on bread and water, but not on sticks and stones. There are some things which he cannot do without, no matter how much he disciplines himself, and still be happy. Clearly a person cannot live entirely without food and drink. But can a person be happy without any satisfaction of the desire for recognition — the desire to be somebody, to be looked up to even by only one other person in the whole world? A person is able, if necessary, to do without sexual gratification. Can he do equally well without any affection or respect or esteem of any kind — without being cared for by any living creature, even a dog or a horse? Can one do entirely without new experience of any kind — without some excitement, some novelty, or something interesting to occupy his time — and still be happy? Opinions may differ on *which* desires cannot remain unsatisfied without loss of happiness, and they may differ also as to the *degree* to which happiness is impaired by the frustration of these desires. But happiness *is* impaired to some extent by the denial of these desires and will be impaired no matter how much self-discipline one exerts." This last statement is all that the critic of the third interpretation of Stoicism needs to show. If that claim is true, then the supporter of the third interpretation is mistaken when he says that man can discipline himself to expunge all of his desires and attain happiness through this complete renunciation.

The Stoic may, of course, question these "findings" by psychologists. On the other hand, he may "give" a bit at one point: he may admit, without surrendering his basic Stoic position, "A certain degree of happiness is possible in this world even apart from complete renunciation of desire, but it is far outweighed by the unhappiness. Petrarch said, 'A thousand pleasures are not worth one torment.'" Consider all the things that are required in order to make a person happy, even briefly: a certain degree of physical health, friends, affection, the wherewithal to live without worry about the morrow; and even with all this good fortune a person may yet be unhappy. But let just one thing go wrong, and one is miserable. Suppose one is wealthy and has no fear of want, has family and friends and success, but has a violent toothache. That one discomfort is enough to spoil the happiness derived from all the rest. Or if a person has wealth and health and vitality and friends, and everyone envies him his lot; yet he may be miserable because of just one thing — his son has turned out to be a wastrel. Happiness, on those rare occasions when it does occur, requires such a precarious balance of conditions that it does not long endure.

> All the goods of life united would not make a very happy man; but all the ills united would make a wretch indeed; and any one of them almost (and who can be free from every one), nay often the absence of one good (and who can possess all), is sufficient to render life ineligible.[1]

"Life for most people," our Stoic will continue, "is a desperate struggle for existence; even today two-thirds of the human race is undernourished and in perpetual fear of starvation. For the remaining third, happiness hinges on the slenderest of threads which may snap at any moment. Even while the brief enjoyment lasts, one cannot but think of the time when it will have vanished. Year after year a man struggles to attain a financial goal; perhaps he dies without reaching it, or perhaps he attains it and the next year he dies and his ungrateful children squander in a few months what he has built up through the years. Or war comes, and all those precious to him are killed; nothing is left but bereavement and poverty. The world is cruel and often seems to punish most those who have tried hardest to improve it. Thousands of men, with the potential to increase by even a little the small degree of happiness to which man can attain, die before their time from some stupid accident or painful disease. A widowed mother of five small children contracts polio and there is no money to take care of the children. A physician, after a life of service to the poor in his community, contracts a painful and incurable disease; and in spite of every sedative that can be administered, he screams in pain for many months until death releases him. Who of us knows that this will not be our own lot? Remember Tolstoy's remarkable story, "The Death of Ivan Ilyitch." Millions of incidents like this occur in every country in every generation of human history. Let me quote the Scottish philosopher David Hume (1711-76):

---

[1] David Hume, *Dialogues concerning Natural Religion*, ed. by Norman Kemp Smith, 2nd ed. (New York: Social Sciences, 1948), Pt. 10, p. 196.

The whole earth, believe me . . . is cursed and polluted. A perpetual war is kindled amongst all living creatures. Necessity, hunger, want, stimulate the strong and courageous: fear, anxiety, terror agitate the weak and infirm. The first entrance into life gives anguish to the newborn infant and to its wretched parent; weakness, impotence, distress, attend each stage of that life; and 'tis at last finished in agony and horror.

Observe too, said Philo, the curious artifices of nature, in order to embitter the life of every living being. The stronger prey upon the weaker, and keep them in perpetual terror and anxiety. The weaker too, in their turn, often prey upon the stronger, and vex and molest them without relaxation. Consider that innumerable race of insects, which either are bred on the body of each animal, or flying about infix their stings in him. These insects have others still less than themselves, which torment them. And thus on each hand, before and behind, above and below, every animal is surrounded with enemies, which incessantly seek his misery and his destruction.

Man alone, said Demea, seems to be, in part, an exception to this rule. For by combination in society, he can easily master lions, tigers, and bears, whose greater strength and agility naturally enable them to prey upon him.

On the contrary, it is here chiefly, replied Philo, that the uniform and equal maxims of nature are most apparent. Man, it is true, can, by combination, surmount all his *real* enemies, and become master of the whole animal creation: but does he not immediately raise up to himself *imaginary* enemies, the demons of his fancy, who haunt him with superstitious terrors, and blast every enjoyment of life? His pleasure, as he imagines, becomes, in their eyes, a crime; his food and repose give them umbrage and offense; his very sleep and dreams furnish new materials to anxious fear; and even death, his refuge from every other ill, presents only the dread of endless and innumerable woes. Nor does the wolf molest more the timid flock, than superstition does the anxious breast of wretched mortals.

Besides, consider, Demea; this very society, by which we surmount those wild beasts, our natural enemies; what new enemies does it not raise to us? What woe and misery does it not occasion? Man is the greatest enemy of man. Oppression, injustice, contempt, contumely, violence, sedition, war, calumny, treachery, fraud: by these they mutually torment each other; and they would soon dissolve that society which they had formed, were it not for the dread of still greater ills, which must attend their separation.

But though these external insults, said Demea, from animals, from men, from all the elements, which assault us, form a frightful catalogue of woes, they are nothing in comparison of those, which arise within ourselves, from the distempered condition of our mind and body. How many lie under the lingering torment of diseases? . . . The disorders of the mind . . . though more secret, are not perhaps less dismal and vexatious. Remorse, shame, anguish, rage, disappointment, anxiety, fear, dejection, despair; who has ever passed through life without cruel inroads from these tormentors? How many have scarcely ever felt any better sensations? Labor and poverty, so abhorred by everyone, are the certain lot of the far greater number; and those few privileged persons, who enjoy ease and opulence, never reach contentment or true felicity . . .

Were a stranger to drop, on a sudden, into this world, I would show him as a specimen of its ills, a hospital full of diseases, a prison crowded with malefactors and debtors, a field of battle strewed with carcasses, a fleet floundering in the ocean, a nation languishing under tyranny, famine, or pestilence. To turn the gay side of life to him, and give him a notion of its pleasures; whither should I conduct him? to a ball, to an opera, to court? He might justly think, that I was only showing him a diversity of distress and sorrow.[1]

"Imagine," our Stoic will continue, "a drama in which the first act, though sometimes happy, is not appreciated even for that happiness; imagine too that from then on the play runs down and finally fizzles out. The early years are healthful and (sometimes) relatively happy, but the youth is in no position to appreciate them. (Remember G. B. Shaw's remark 'Youth is such a wonderful thing it's a pity to waste it on young people.') By the time a bit of wisdom comes into life to temper the passions, the organism has already begun to slow down and develop the maladies of middle age. And by the time the person has grown old enough to know a bit about the art of living (if indeed he ever does), his best years are past and his body is already preparing for the grave, and there is nothing to look forward to but pain, suffering, and death. Is this dismal drama the best that life has to offer?

"One can finally come to say, as we Stoics do, 'I don't care any more. No matter what happens to me, I am resigned.' And in this thought there is perhaps some peace. But think what a quantity of misery, frustration, loneliness, and disillusionment must have taken place before the bright burning flame of desire has at last been quenched to make such an attitude possible! For we all did care once, we hoped for much from the world and were filled with love and ambition and yearning. Gradually, one by one, with great pain and bitterness, our hopes and expectations were crushed, spat upon, tramped into the ground.

"Have you ever had thoughts like these?" our Stoic goes on. "A hundred years from now I won't be here any more, no matter what I do during my lifetime, no matter what I may achieve. My happiness and unhappiness, my hopes and fears — they will all be gone forever. If I make great plans, and even if I succeed in carrying them out, still the end of them all is death, and it will all be as if it had never been. So what's the use of anything? Is life, with all its vicissitudes and suffering, worth the struggle? Whether or not one takes the Stoic way out by renouncing all desire, is the whole play worth the price of admission — particularly when we didn't ask to see the play in the first place? Wasn't Ivan (in Dostoevski's *The Brothers Karamazov*) justified in simply 'returning the ticket'? Are the few frantic bits and scraps of happiness that the lucky ones among us can pick up along the way enough to make up for the suffering and the dying, the disease and

[1] *Ibid.*, pp. 195-96.

pain and bereavement, the frustration and the gradual but inexorable extinction of expectation and hope which life forces upon us?"

All these remarks made by the supporter of the third interpretation of Stoicism present a searing indictment of the conditions under which happiness is possible on earth. But, as with the second-interpretation Stoic, a critic may grant all or most or the points in this empirical description of life and yet not share the same attitude toward it. "In the first place," he may say, "human happiness, which you now grant does exist, is not as fleeting and evanescent as you think. At least, for many people it isn't. But even if there is more misery than happiness in most lives, and even if there isn't a life after this one, things are not as bad as you think. Perhaps I haven't had a predominantly happy life; yet I am glad I am alive, and I welcome the thought of living a good many years more even if my fondest hopes are never fulfilled and I die a painful death. Do I have this cheerful outlook because I am still immature and have unrealistically optimistic expectations of life? Perhaps, but I don't think so. I don't know what may happen tomorrow, and I count on nothing. But even though all my hopes may be dashed to earth, still I do not renounce all desire. I want to be a part of it all and share life's burdens and struggles. And I take satisfaction in trying in my small way to improve the lot of mankind on the earth even if I do not live to see the fruits of my labors.

"In the second place," the critic goes on, "I take a different attitude toward death. It would be easy to beat a fatalistic drum and, no matter what activity was suggested to me, to repeat the dreary refrain, 'I'm going to die anyway, so what difference does it make?' Even if I were going to live for five hundred years I could still repeat that same refrain. 'You want me to work for man's improvement? But I'm going to die anyway, so what difference does it make?' Such a gloomy outlook would be foolish. By holding it I would be destroying whatever happiness I might otherwise enjoy during my few years here. 'But you're going to die, so it isn't worth it.' True, it isn't worth painting my house if I'm going to move out of it tomorrow, or next week, or next month, perhaps even next year. But if I'm not going to move out of it for many years or several years, is it still not worth it? During those years we will enjoy living in a painted house rather than an unpainted one, and that does make a difference, during those years. You Stoics want to extend a principle — 'it isn't worth it' — that is sometimes true to *all* occasions, and that extension is surely unjustified.

"It's not that I don't dislike having to die. I regret that I must leave this life and can't see what happens to the world after I am gone. Since I know it is inevitable, I do not grieve over it but put it out of my mind and devote myself to things which I *can* do something about. Nor do I take the attitude that death is only a release from suffering and pain — for if so I would count it a blessing rather than a misfortune and would look forward to it with anticipation. What would you have? Should people just sit around waiting to die? The choice before us is not whether to die or not to die but whether to use these few fleeting years uselessly or in constructive activity. If I try to leave the world, even in some small way, better for my descendants than I found it, I shall take some comfort in that thought. Indeed, it is probably in working for the well-being of others as well as myself that I shall find the greater part of whatever happiness I shall ever enjoy in this life, until death puts an end to happiness and unhappiness alike."

C. *Psychological criticisms of moral theories*

There is another kind of criticism of Stoicism, psychological criticism. We shall briefly consider it, for it is brought against many other moral theories, and its validity is not easy to assess.

The Stoic, though he seems strong and brave and imperturbable, is really an emotional weakling who cannot stand to get hurt and so takes out insurance against failure in advance by toning down his desires and hopes to the point where he knows they can be fulfilled. He is afraid to gamble lustily and play for great stakes . . . In his fear of suffering the death of great disappointment, he chooses to live half-dead rather than taste the full joy of living, with all its possibilities of tragic ending. . . .

From a diagnostic and therapeutic standpoint, any philosophy like Stoicism, which is able to transmute evil into good and call submission to defeat "happiness," plays into the hands of an unconscious will-to-failure. This prevents shy and retiring persons especially from coming to grips with the real problems of their unhappiness. . . . It is more wholesome . . . to admit to themselves that they are unhappy so that they will be stimulated to find the source of their frustration and correct it, instead of running away from it into the easy pseudo-happiness of resignation, humility, and inner peace.[1]

We could spend considerable time disputing whether this charge is a justified attack against Stoicism. But let us ask a more general question: Is it a valid criticism of a moral theory that its proponents are neurotic and maladjusted? Are these terms any more than bits of name-calling, sneering at others because they are not like oneself or the majority? And even if one is not simply name-calling but pointing out genuine facts about people or their views, how is this ethical criticism? Suppose a person is described as neurotic — is this somehow bad? Can terms like "neurotic" and "abnormal" be used as a club for hitting over the head other people who do not follow a certain way or pattern of life?

When someone calls another "neurotic," "mentally disturbed," "maladjusted," whether or not these terms are more than emotive epithets depends on the speaker and the occasion. If one person is simply castigating someone else, he may use these terms with little if any empirical meaning. But when

[1] Millard S. Everett, *Ideals of Life* (New York: Wiley, 1954), pp. 107-08. Reprinted by permission of the publisher.

a professional psychologist uses these terms, he uses them to describe a quite definite condition of mind or body whose existence over a period of time can be empirically verified.

The term "normal" has two main senses. In one sense, it refers only to statistical frequency; what is normal is what is most usual. Thus it is normal for a human being to have two eyes, two ears, two arms, two legs. But in the other sense, "normal" means living up to or fulfilling a *norm,* or standard; in this sense it doesn't matter whether the majority of people fulfill it or not. Although 20-20 vision is considered normal eyesight, the majority of people do not have it. In the statistical sense 20-20 vision is not normal, but in the second sense it is considered so. It is this second sense that psychologists have in mind when they call people normal or abnormal. It is quite possible for the majority of individuals in a given society to be abnormal in many respects. (Not only possible, but actually true!) Unfortunately the nature of this norm can be described accurately only in complex psychological-psychiatric terms. In Western society, at least, a normal person is moderately self-confident, thinks himself to be good but not terribly good, reacts with aggression when he is crossed but not overdimensionally (he doesn't reply to a minor insult with murder), is considerate of other people but not exactly a saint (he helps people in trouble up to a point but doesn't lend money to an acquaintance who has already swindled him ten times), and is relatively happy except in unusual circumstances when something beyond his control gives him cause for unhappiness (if his fortune is wiped out, if a loved one dies — and even then he adjusts to it in time). This is the norm; and it is, of course, an empirical question how many people live up to this norm, and to what extent.

So far, no question of good or bad in any moral sense has arisen. But when a person criticizes another person, or his moral views, for being neurotic, abnormal, escapist, and the like, he usually does intend such an inference: "It is abnormal, *therefore* it is bad." But this conclusion does not follow. Why might not certain forms of abnormality, at least, be good? Or why may not other norms be set up which are in some ways preferable to the one described in the previous paragraph? A society composed entirely of "normal" people would not, to say the least, be very interesting; the vast majority of "normal, well-adjusted" people tend to be dullards. Moreover, if one examines the biographies of great men, very many admittedly great painters and poets and composers and even scientists and mathematicians are quite abnormal, neurotic, and maladjusted by any psychiatric standard. Yet is their abnormality a condemnation? One might suggest that if Beethoven, Van Gogh, and Dostoevski were neurotic, and neuroticism is what it takes to produce such great works, then long live abnormality, and let us have more of it! Genius is always abnormal: it is certainly abnormal in the statistical sense, for there are not many geniuses; and it is abnormal in the other sense as well, for virtually no geniuses (when one examines their life histories) turn out to live up to the psychiatric standard or norm for the human personality.

Why, then, present such a combination of characteristics as we described above as the norm, and why recommend such a norm to others as something desirable? This norm is recommended because (and for this psychiatrists have ample evidence), as a rule, a person who fulfills it is *happier* — freer from conflicts, depressions, and tensions — than other people are: *Why* he is happier is a long story which can be told in detail only in terms of the language of the unconscious (id, superego, ego; unconscious desire, guilt, cathexis, transference, and so on). But the conclusion itself (which, of course, is the special task of psychological science) is that a person possessing the characteristics described, owing to an equilibrium of forces within his unconscious, is a *happier* person, and is consequently in a position to use his energy and vitality and whatever ability he has in a constructive way. He is free from the energy-sapping inner conflicts that impair, to varying degrees, the lives of neurotic and psychotic individuals.

What, then, of the creative artists, at least those to whom some of the vocabulary of neuroticism are applicable? Beethoven, Van Gogh, and Dostoevski added immeasurably to the happiness of millions of people who appreciate their works; but it would be difficult to believe, after reading their biographies, that they were, on the whole, happy human beings. They were sacrificial lambs on the altar of human happiness — the happiness of others, not of themselves. Should there be more of such persons in the world? For their own sake, perhaps no; but for the sake of others, definitely yes. Even for those who were unhappy in their personal lives, many people consider that their misery is compensated many thousandfold by the increased delight of the human race.

However this may be, the creative geniuses among the psychiatric class of neurotics are the rare exception: the vast majority of neurotics are quite uncreative. Their condition impedes their own happiness, and they add little happiness to the lives of others: indeed, being on the whole unpredictable and demanding people with countless irritating idiosyncrasies, they tend to make life unhappy for their friends, families, and neighbors. They contribute neither to the world's happiness nor to their own.

Now back to Stoicism. Since such terms as "neurotic," "defeatist," and "abnormal" can be understood in different lights, the critic will not, if he is wise, simply apply these terms to Stoicism and certain other "life-denying" ideals of life or to the people who hold them. Instead, he will restrict himself to empirical descriptions that can be tested: he will allege that such people, by detaching themselves from the world and its problems, are not only being parasitic by leaving those problems to others but they are also cheating themselves by needlessly denying themselves whatever happiness life does have to offer; that if they cultivated a more positive attitude toward the world than merely *apatheia,* the world *could* give them a measure of happiness, although of course not everything they want. *Assuming* that happiness is worth having and that the attitude of such people unnecessarily deprives them (as well as those around them) of it, the critic points out that these people actually diminish the amount of happiness that could exist in a world that already contains far more unhappiness than it needs to contain.

EXERCISES

1. Do you think that the following excerpt from Alexander Pope's *Essay on Man* contains a just evaluation of Stoicism? Explain your answer.

> In lazy apathy let Stoics boast
> Their virtue fix'd; 'tis fix'd as in a frost;
> Contracted all, retiring to the breast;
> But strength of mind is Exercise, not Rest;
> The rising tempest puts in act the soul;
> Parts it may ravage, but preserves the whole.

2. To what extent, and in what respects, do you think that the following readings reflect the basic attitude of Stoicism? Justify your answer.

a. The Book of Job.

b. The Book of Ecclesiastes.

c. B. de Spinoza. *Ethics,* Books 4 and 5.

d. B. Russell. *Mysticism and Logic.*

e. William James, "The Sick Soul," in *The Varieties of Religious Experience* (Gifford lectures, 1901-02 [London: Longmans, Green, 1952], pp. 127-65).

f. Marcel Proust's theory of love, as contained in his *Remembrance of Things Past* (Many editions).

g. A. E. Housman. "When I Was One and Twenty." (From *Complete Poems of A. E. Housman,* published by Holt, Rinehart and Winston, Inc. Copyright 1959 by Holt, Rinehart and Winston, Inc. Also reprinted by permission of The Society of Authors as the Literary Representative of the estate of the late A. E. Housman, and Messrs. Jonathan Cape, Ltd., publishers of A. E. Housman's *Collected Poems.*)

> When I was one-and-twenty
>   I heard a wise man say,
> 'Give crowns and pounds and guineas
>   But not your heart away;
> Give pearls away and rubies
>   But keep your fancy free.'
> But I was one-and-twenty,
>   No use to talk to me.
>
> When I was one-and-twenty
>   I heard him say again,
> 'The heart out of the bosom
>   Was never given in vain;
> 'Tis paid with sighs aplenty
>   And sold for endless rue.'
> And I am two-and-twenty,
>   And oh, 'tis true, 'tis true.

h. K. Baier, *The Meaning of Life,* Section 3.

3. Read one of the following books and try to separate the descriptions of case histories from the value judgments pronounced upon them. What seem to be the criteria for arriving at these judgments? What relevance do you think they have to the study of ethics?

a. Karl Augustus Menninger, *Man against Himself* (New York: Harcourt, Brace [Harvest Books], 1956).

b. Edmund Bergler, *Principles of Self-damage* (New York: Philosophical Library, 1959).

c. E. Fromm, *Man for Himself.*

d. Albert Ellis, *How To Live with a Neurotic at Work or at Home* (New York: Crown, 1957).

4. Compare the list of "basic human needs" in M. S. Everett, *Ideals of Life,* Chapter 2 with that of Anatol Rapoport in *Operational Philosophy; Integrating Knowledge and Action* (New York: Harper, 1953).

5. Discuss the thesis that individual human lives can have meaning even if life as a whole has no meaning. (See K. Baier, *The Meaning of Life,* Section 3.)

READING LIST, SECTIONS 3 AND 4

Baier, Kurt. *The Meaning of Life.* Canberra, Australia: Commonwealth Government Printer, 1957.

The Book of Ecclesiastes. Introductory essay by Irwin Edman. New York: Odyssey Press, 1946.

Epictetus. *Discourses.* Many editions.

Epicurus. *Writings.* In Oates, Whitney J., ed. *The Stoic and Epicurean Philosophers.* New York: Random House, 1940. This is a valuable book to own because it contains the complete extant writings of the Epicureans and Stoics.

Lucretius. *On the Nature of Things.* Many editions.

Marcus Aurelius. *Meditations.* Many editions.

Pater, Walter. *Marius the Epicurean.* Many editions.

Russell, Bertrand. *Mysticism and Logic* (1911). In Russell, B., *Selected Papers.* New York: Modern Library, pp. 16-55.

Schopenhauer, Arthur. "On the Sufferings of the World" and "On the Vanity of Existence." In Schopenhauer, A., *Studies in Pessimism.* New York: Modern Library, pp. 1-49.

Spinoza, Benedict de. *Ethics.* Many editions, especially Bks. 4 and 5.

5. Self-realization

Let us now turn from these rather one-sided views and consider an ideal of life which includes all aspects of human nature — an ideal that does not try to stunt the personality or force it into one single track and ignore all the rest but permits it a well-rounded development in accordance with the basic needs and desires of human nature.

Representatives of such a view are to be found, once again, in classical civilization. We shall examine first the view of Aristotle. (Plato's view, which in some ways belongs in this category and in some ways not, will be examined in a somewhat different connection in Chapter 4.)

A. Aristotle

According to Aristotle (384-322 B.C.), the highest good (*summum bonum,* it is usually called in the literature of ethics) which man can seek or attain is happiness (*eudaimonia,* "well-being"). All men aim at happiness, but they vary considerably in their methods of pursuing it. Aristotle's choice of ideal is not particularly newsworthy, but he has some interesting suggestions as to how the ideal is to be attained. It is his view of the *means* toward happiness that distinguishes Aristotle's view from others. And if even his view of the means is not especially startling, it may be because Aristotle's view is so much an embodiment of Greek "common-sense ethics" and Greek civilization has come to have such an enormous influence upon our own that we have absorbed this kind of view through our pores, as it were, for many years before we knew that it was stated by Aristotle. (Aristotle was far from indifferent to public welfare — "the general good" — but since his *Nicomachean Ethics* is devoted almost entirely to the question of how an individual should conduct his life, we shall consider his view under the heading of "ideals of life.")

According to Aristotle, the best way of finding out how man can gain happiness is to discover wherein his peculiar virtue (*arete,* better translated as "excellence") really lies. The peculiar excellence of a knife is that it cuts; the peculiar excellence of a clock is that it tells the time. Each kind of thing has a peculiar excellence (*arete*) that distinguishes it from other things. If we follow this line of reasoning, what is the peculiar excellence of man? Not the fact that he is alive, for life is something he shares with all animals and plants; besides, it is *how* he lives that matters, not just *that* he lives. Not in the fact that he is sentient (can perceive the outside world by means of his sense organs), for the animals, though not the plants, have this power also. Man's excellence lies in something that he alone possesses: his *rational faculty,* or power of reason. Man is the rational animal. His happiness is to be sought, then, in his exercise of reason. A man who does not exercise this peculiarly human capacity is not exercising his capacity as a man and is not realizing within himself the kind of happiness of which only human beings are capable.

Man exercises his rational powers in many ways. It would seem that building bridges, plowing fields, and shoveling coal would be examples of rational activity, since man would never undertake them if he did not figure out what means to take toward certain ends. But these are not the activities that Aristotle had in mind in speaking of rational activities. He was referring to abstract reasoning such as studying philosophy, working with his head

with no practical implications for working with his hands. The Greeks aristo-
cratic ideal held it to be beneath one's dignity as a citizen to work with
one's hands (such work was for servants and slaves). Thus even if the
manual arts are guided and made possible by reason, they are not the kind
of pursuits Aristotle is recommending to us as the exercise of reason.

Even if we ignore this theoretical-intellectual bias, however, it is difficult
to find Aristotle's argument thus far conclusive. The fact that some property is peculiar to man is no proof that it is (1) better than any other or
(2) more conducive to man's happiness. Let us admit that the rational
faculty is peculiar to the human species, though some of the "lower" animals
appear to possess it to some degree. There are other qualities which are also
peculiarly human, perhaps more so than reason: for example, the moral
sense. Man is the only creature we know of that has a sense of right and
wrong. The dog puts his tail between his legs when he is scolded for taking
meat off the table, but whether he acts from the conviction that he has done
wrong, rather than from the dread of punishment, could easily be disputed.
The American theologian Paul Tillich (1886-) has defined man as the
only creature with a moral sense and as the only creature with a sense of anguish. The French philosopher Henri Bergson (1859-1941) has defined him
as the laughing animal, and the American theologian Reinhold Niebuhr
(1892-) has defined him as the only animal that is always in heat. Man is
also the only creature that performs axe-murders, that puts empty milk bot-
tles on the back porch in the evening, and that saves up his hatred for years
while he plots and plans to avenge himself against an enemy. There are
many characteristics peculiar to man, some good and some bad; and the
fact that some property or faculty is peculiar to man is therefore no evidence that it is good or desirable.

That reason is peculiar to man does not show in any way that man's
happiness is to be found in the exercise of his rational faculty. There is no
doubt that without a rational faculty man would have far fewer avenues
of happiness open to him than he has now; but he would also have far
fewer avenues of *un*happiness. In artistic creation, in scientific and other
types of discovery, in the mastering of ideas and concepts, there is a happiness that is perhaps as great as anything the material world can give. Yet
for many more people, the pursuit of intellectual matters causes far more
unhappiness than happiness. Sometimes the person is unhappy because he
has some intellectual ability but not enough: he cannot grasp ideas easily,
and the feeling of just being on the verge or just barely understanding concepts that come easily to others can be an important source of distress and
discomfiture, even of despair. The possession of a rational faculty can lead
to either happiness or unhappiness, depending on the person and the conditions.

But this emphasis on reason, though it sets the tone for Aristotle's ethics,
is only a small part of his theory. Aristotle continues that although man's

exercise of his powers of reason are his peculiar source of happiness, there are many other things required to make this happiness possible. To be happy, a man must have a certain amount of financial security, material possessions, a congenial home life, good looks (at least he must not be repulsive in appearance), friends on whom he can rely, a certain amount of personal freedom. A slave cannot possibly be happy, thought Aristotle, and neither can a woman (at least not in the Greek society of which Aristotle spoke). Clearly the conditions for enjoying happiness are considerable, and only a minority of the human race are so situated that they can be truly happy. The Stoics could speak of happiness as a matter of will only, of a man being happy while he is being tortured, but Aristotle considered this view to be rank nonsense. According to Aristotle, a man cannot be happy if he is in pain, or diseased, or blind, or unfree. To be happy, a man must be in full possession of his powers of reason. Moreover, he must exercise them (and thus, of course, he must have the leisure to do so) and all the other conditions must be fulfilled besides. It would appear that the majority of people cannot be happy.

Among the conditions for a man's happiness is the exercise of the moral qualities, or *virtues*. In these matters Aristotle's view is that a man will be happiest if he observes the rule of "moderation in all things" — Aristotle's famous "doctrine of the mean." Virtue is a Golden Mean — a *mean between extremes*. For example, courage is a virtue, but this virtue is a mean between the extremes of cowardice on the one hand and rashness on the other. The man who is too afraid to engage in the battle is not courageous, nor is the man who dashes into the fray without even considering whether there are impossible odds against him. Generosity is a virtue, but it too is a mean between extremes. One can be so ungenerous that he never gives at all (niggardliness) or so overgenerous that he gives to one and all, whether the person or the cause is worth anything or not, and has nothing left to give when a worthwhile cause comes along (prodigality). Neither of these extremes is virtuous; virtue in the matter of giving lies in the area between the two extremes. A man who indulges in pleasures all the time — always "out on the town" — is not leading a virtuous life; but neither is the man who never allows himself any relaxation, any pleasurable outlets. The virtuous state is again a mean between extremes. The virtue of temperance is neither that of total abstinence on the one hand nor of constant self-indulgence on the other. And so on through many other qualities. One is being virtuous if he pursues a path between two opposite extremes of behavior.

(We see how different the sense given to terms such as "temperance" and "virtue" is today. We tend to associate temperance with total abstinence and the W.C.T.U., but to Aristotle total abstinence would have seemed almost as bad as a life of frenzied indulgence. We also tend to associate virtue with abstinence from certain pleasures, the virtuous life being (to our minds) rather drab and dull because of its abstemiousness; whereas Aristotle would not have called such total abstinence a virtue at all but simply pointless self-denial.)

According to Aristotle, virtue is not always to be found half way between the extremes. Courage is closer to rashness than it is to cowardice, and generosity is closer to prodigality than it is to niggardliness. Moreover, the mean is not to be located at the same point for every individual. A person tending toward timidity will do well to aim at self-assertion and go further in this direction than the man who is self-assertive by nature. There is no formula that can be given for discovering the mean in each individual case. Each person through trial and error must discover it for himself. Aristotle is giving us very general advice, but this, he says, is all that can be done in the nature of the subject: a treatise on ethics can not possibly tell us where the mean is to be located with respect to each virtue and each individual. "Be generous" is easy advice to give. But to be generous to the right person, at the right time, in the right amount — that is the difficult part, and no exact specifications can be given. Such things must simply be learned anew by each individual, gradually and often painfully, in the hard school of experience, which seems to mean careful observation of the consequences of one's past actions. Swimming can be learned only to a small extent by reading manuals on swimming; the rest must be learned by doing, by getting in the water and practicing. So it is with the virtuous life; men can attain to virtue (the Golden Mean) by practicing virtuous actions constantly until they are skilled in their performance. When skill has been achieved, a man will be happy, at least insofar as happiness depends on virtue. With respect to virtue, then, happiness is found by following the doctrine of the mean.

Aristotle hastens to tell us, however, that there are some virtues which are not means between extremes. One cannot plausibly argue, "I shall be moderate in the number of murders I shall commit. Not too many, but not too few either. Say three per month." Some actions such as murder, betrayal, and adultery, are not subject to the mean at all; these are wrong whenever and wherever they occur. Such acts are the acts of an unvirtuous man always.

His account, however, raises some questions:

a. Are the virtues that Aristotle mentions really means between extremes? Cowardice is doubtless lack of courage, but is rashness too much courage? It would appear that it is not courage at all, and therefore should not be placed on the same continuum. One might prefer to say, "Lack of bravery is cowardice. Bravery with knowledge is courage. And bravery without knowledge is rashness." The same objections could be made with the other virtues. Is being stupidly or uncritically generous the same as being *too* generous?

b. If virtue is a mean between extremes, how is one to know when he has found the satisfactory mean in his own case? Does he just introspect and see? and if so *what* does he see? What is the criterion for the achievement of the mean? If the mean belongs at a different point for some people than for others, how are we to know where it belongs for us?

c. And if virtue is *not* always a mean between extremes, as Aristotle says — if it is in the case of generosity but not in the case of adultery — how is one to tell in which category a particular action belongs? what criterion is there for determining when a virtue is a mean between extremes and when it is not? Lastly,

d. The whole doctrine is presented without proof or evidence. It is an explicit statement of Greek "common-sense" ethics, but it answers no questions about whether and why this view is to be preferred to any other view.

Aristotle's view does, however, present an interesting contrast to the ethics of self-denial. Aristotle does not deny any of man's basic needs or desires; he tries to give adequate, though not unlimited, expression to them all. He does not picture man as an inhabitant of a world in which his every desire is doomed to defeat and frustration. Happiness, he assumes, is possible to man (though not to all men, as we have seen), and by a life of moderation and the development of all the aspects of his nature, with emphasis on reason because it must control all the rest, man can achieve this happiness. Life must include material things, security, health, and the cultivation of our natural faculties — not just any one of these but all. To many persons today these recommendations of Aristotle seem so obvious as not to be worth stating. Indeed, Aristotle's ethics has been called the biggest collection of clichés, truisms, and tautologies in the history of ethics. This, of course, does not impugn their truth (what could be more indubitably true than a tautology?) but only its novelty. And if something has become a truism there must have been a great many people who have come to consider it true.

If many of Aristotle's remarks seem to be either obvious or vacuous, the comments that can be made about them are almost equally so. Yet it may be of some importance to point out a few of them.

a. All the things that Aristotle mentions are matters of *degree*: it is not that we can't be happy entirely without money, it is that we can't be *as* happy if we don't know where the next meal is coming from as we can be if we do know. A person is surely happier if he has friends on whom he can rely than if he has none; but this is not to say that without friends he can't be happy *at all* — it is only far more difficult. Some degree of happiness is doubtless possible to some men even in this unfavorable circumstance.

b. Besides, for Aristotle, happiness depends upon the individual involved. It is useless to say *in general* that people can't be happy without this or that or another thing, even to a certain degree. It all depends on who is being referred to. Some people would be extremely and irreparably unhappy without being able to read books; others would never miss them. One person can be amazingly happy even in the face of loss of money, loss of friends, loss of family, loss of eyesight, loss of health; whereas another person, of a different temperament, may be utterly and permanently shattered by the loss of even one of these things. Maybe some people *can* be (relatively) happy even in penury and want; can we say definitely that they can't? If so, what evidence can we give? How do we really know? On the one hand, it is not only futile but false to state categorically that a person who loses his money or friends or family and is unhappy as a result *could* adjust to these adversities and still be happy in the face of them if only he tried as hard as other people; it is equally false, on the other hand, to state that he couldn't. Happiness seems to be at least as much a matter of one's "natural temper" as of the situations one must confront during his life. Some people have it in them to remain happy in spite of mountains of adversity, whereas other people are, as it were, knocked out by things that would scarcely affect others. Most of the general talk about what is needed to make people happy and what they can and cannot do without is rendered useless from the start by the simple fact that people *differ*. What, indeed, *is* one to say in general about how to be happy? People make the mistake of assuming that everyone else is like themselves. Armed with this assumption, they give forth endless moral advice, pronouncements, and generalizations about the way to be happy — all with a considerable sense of righteousness and duty. They speak, if they but knew it, with almost complete futility; for each man's personality is, to a far greater extent than most people realize, a law unto itself. As a result, true generalizations about these matters are well-nigh impossible.

B. "Realizing yourself"

A generalized form of Aristotle's view, without his special emphasis upon man's peculiar nature or the doctrine of the mean, has been advanced as the doctrine of self-realization. "To realize" usually means the same as "to make real," and since each of us is already real — in the sense that we exist — what does it mean for us to realize ourselves? If someone were to give you two words of advice, "Realize yourself," what specifically would he be suggesting?

The view of ethics as self-realization is concerned with realizing our *capacities,* or *potentialities.* A person has an aptitude for medicine, and he is told to realize this capacity, to actualize this potentiality which he has and which many others have not. By realizing (making real or actual) his potentiality, he may perhaps, in a metaphorical sense, realize "himself."

Yet if we do not qualify it in some way, the advice "Realize your potentialities" does not come to much. Are we to try to actualize *all* our potentialities? But of these we have an infinite number. There are many things we *could* do, and many traits we *could* develop, it we had the time and wanted to take the trouble. We probably have within ourselves the potentiality for painting over windows, eating snake-meat, preparing sandwiches containing sawdust, counting all the dandelions within a mile's radius of our residence, and barking like a dog for fifteen minutes each morning. But what point would there be in actualizing such potentialities? Even if there were, we could not in a thousand lifetimes actualize every potentiality we possess. If we actualize some of them, it must always be at the expense of most of the others. Besides, is it being suggested that we actualize our potentialities toward cruelty, sadism, deceitfulness, hypocrisy, pig-headedness, and asininity? These potentials are usually far easier to develop than their opposites, yet it would be usual to maintain that we should try to discourage the development of these qualities. Clearly, then, some selectivity will have to be exercised in the matter of which potentialities to work on.

One suggestion would be: "Try to actualize those potentialities within you which, if actualized, will make you the happiest." Of course, you can't know in advance just which ones these will turn out to be. Sometimes you may think you will be happiest developing one capacity and then it turns out after you have spent years developing it that you are tired or bored with it and would now be happier developing a different one. Still, the suggestion seems fruitful: through trial and error if necessary, actualize those potentialities which will give you the maximum of happiness.

To this end, two different patterns of development have been suggested:

a. "Develop a wide *range* of your potentialities; realize yourself in as large a number of different ways as you can. Don't stick to just one thing; be a well rounded personality; go in for some sports (don't try all of them, of course, it would take several lifetimes), go in for some intellectual activity but not too much, cultivate some social interests, divide your studies between practical and theoretical interests. Don't try to develop all your capacities, but do try to develop some from each of the main branches or departments of human interest and endeavor. Try a little of everything, and then pursue those things in each line of endeavor which seem most likely to bring you happiness."

This advice would result in what has been called a "smorgasbord" pattern of life: a little of this, a little of that, some here and some there. Some people like to live life in that way. Many of us cannot, for our work may be demanding and may require us to spend a disproportionate amount of time at one thing — for example, studying philosophy or digging ditches. But even if the necessities of work did not require some specialization, it is not likely that everyone would *want* to live a smorgasbord type of life or even think it desirable to do so. They would say that to live in this way would be like designing a dress in such a way as to include a little bit of every color in the spectrum or designing a cathedral so as to include all the different architectural styles. They suggest a more *organized* pattern.

b. "Concentrate on one thing, the thing of greatest interest to you, and then build everything else around that — and often the 'everything else' will not include very much. The mathematician may be so absorbed in mathematics that he will care for very little else, in extreme cases, perhaps for nothing else. And what is wrong with that, as long as he is happiest that way? At any rate, there should be some dominant center to your life. Your life should revolve around the satisfaction of your major interest; everything else should be incidental to that."

Doubtless the first pattern would be preferred by some people and the second by others. Both, however, have been suggested as patterns of self-realization.

Thus far, only a part of the story has been told. Let us look more carefully at the relations among the capacities themselves. There are some capacities which, if developed, will hinder the development of others. By their very existence these *hindering* capacities will render impossible the development of other ones. If you become a perennial drunkard, you have developed one kind of capacity, but by doing so you have closed off the opportunity for developing, at least beyond a rudimentary stage, your capacity for concentrated study of any subject-matter whatever. Some capacities, once developed, are so all-devouring that they leave no room for anything else; drug addiction is an example. Such developments of capacities are called *obstructive*. On the other hand, some capacities when developed are mutually *cooperative* — they not only do not interfere with the development of other capacities but positively enhance them. Alcoholism interferes with study, but eating healthful foods does not. Habits of self-discipline developed in concentrating on one subject are cooperative in that they help in enabling one to concentrate on other subjects later; a capacity developed in one area also may be helpful in another. In the art of a novelist the development of a fine style of writing cooperates in a high degree with the development of the ability to observe human nature; the two together are far more than twice as valuable as either of them is taken alone.

This distinction between hindering, or obstructive, and cooperative capacities is useful in evaluating one's various potentialities. You may, for example, desire the actualization of two potentialities about equally; but if one of them is on the whole cooperative with the development of your other capacities and the second one is on the whole obstructive of them, you will do well to develop the first capacity rather than the second; for by so doing you will not be hindering a realization of other potentialities which you may also wish sometime to actualize. If you want to spend five hours a week in some sport or exercise but also desire to spend about the same amount of time painting the town red, it is somewhat more likely that the achievement of the first aim will cooperate better with the fulfillment of your other capacities than will the achievement of the second — unless, of course, you are a gossip columnist who gets material while eavesdropping in bars or unless you need relaxation and find that exercise does not relax you. Your desire for a serious affair with Miss X may be no greater or less than your desire for an affair with Miss Y; but if Miss X will give you affection and emotional equilibrium at the same time, so that you can pursue your other activities just as well or even better, you are well advised to cultivate her in preference to Miss Y, who will take more and more of your leisure, begrudge you the time spent on your work, and embroil you in a passionate and jealousy-ridden *affaire de coeur* into the bargain. A girl may not find it difficult to develop her potentiality for becoming a prostitute; but if she continues this course for long, she may seal off any possibility of feeling genuine love in a legal marriage. If you develop your capacity for enjoying heroin, you may wreck the realization of all the rest of your potentialities. When you contemplate developing some aspect of your nature, the question to ask yourself is, "Would the actualization of this particular potentiality be cooperative with, or obstructive of, the actualization of other potentialities which I also value?"

It is not enough, of course, to know what one potentiality, A, will, if actualized, cooperate with the others, B, C, and D. If the development of B, C, and D will not increase your happiness anyway, then their incompatibility with A need not worry you. But suppose that B is, on the whole, cooperative with A. You will still want to know whether the achievement of A and B will lead to a relatively permanent or enduring happiness or satisfaction; if the satisfaction is very evanescent, you will do well to develop some other capacities instead which *will* be more satisfying in the long run. The ideal would be a *harmonious system* of developed capacities whose mutual fulfillment will bring the maximum possible amount of *enduring* happiness or satisfaction. Some people's lives exhibit very well this harmonious development of a large number of capacities, each reinforcing the other; whereas many other people, though they develop certain valuable capacities, also develop others which are obstructive of these, so that their lives are, as it were, split asunder by the simultaneous development of two or more groups of relatively incompatible capacities.

Is the description of a human being fulfilling to a maximum degree the ideal of self-realization enough? Perhaps it is, if you are concerned only with your own self-realization. But if you want to consider other people as well, more will have to be added. Thus far our description has had a rather egoistic sound: you should actualize those potentialities which will act cooperatively so as to bring *you* the maximum fulfillment; you are considering yourself only. For example, let us suppose that the activity for which you are best suited is robbing banks; your potentiality for this rather intricate art is more easily developed to a high degree than any other of your potentialities (your abilities are indifferent in everything else). Let us also suppose that robbing banks brings you great satisfaction — both the result (the money gained) and the process that leads to this result (you enjoy the risk, you have a strong gambler's instinct, and you set about opening safes with all the fascination that some people have for crossword puzzles). Moreover, if you concentrate on this pursuit for only a few hours a day and suffer no qualms of conscience, your work may not interfere with the development of other aspects of your personality; indeed, the money received from your professional activity enables you to buy many books and paintings, give lavish parties, belong to an exclusive tennis club, and travel abroad each summer. So your profession is far less obstructive of these other things than if you worked ten hours a day hauling rubbish for a living and came home every evening too tired to do anything but sleep. To be sure, your chosen profession is obstructive of the realization of *some* other wishes (as what profession is not?), for if you rob banks in the evening (you would hardly do it during banking hours) you cannot at the same time go to night clubs or watch the late movie on television. But you don't care much about these activities anyway and prefer the challenge of safe-cracking even when there is no financial reward. Thus the system of your interests forms a harmonious whole, with safe-cracking as the center and all the others harmoniously grouped around it. What more could one ask for? If you have achieved this way of life, have you not achieved far more than most people by way of self-realization? Isn't your degree of self-realization well-nigh perfect?

As long as we are talking about self-realization on an *individual* level, it is very difficult to attack such a way of life on the ground that it lacks self-realization. But some theorists have gone on to talk not about individual but about *social* self-realization. Full self-realization, they say, is possible only in the context of one's society; self-realization is not complete unless it is not merely *your* fulfillments which constitute a harmonious whole but those of your society. According to this view, it may be possible for you personally to achieve a high degree of self-realization, as in the example above; but unless your own personal fulfillments are an ingredient in a harmonious system of fulfillments incorporating all of your society (some would say, the entire human race), your own self-realization has been at the expense of others, and your personal self-realization should be forfeited in the interest of the broader whole; true self-realization is possible only in the context of society, and our bank robber has therefore not achieved self-realization at all. Just as each of your own activities should fit into a harmonious pattern of such fulfillments which are not obstructive of each other (individual self-realization), so the totality of your fulfillments is only an ingredient in the entire pattern of social fulfillments encompassing all the members of society (social self-realization).

Social self-realization works in much the same way as individual self-realization. The fulfillments of some individuals, which would be quite complete and satisfactory if one considered their personal lives only, are obstructive when one considers the entire range of fulfillments of society as a whole. However harmonious the bank robber's personal life may be, his activities obstruct, stand in the way of, the equally legitimate fulfillments of a large number of other people, since he cannot actualize his potentialities without interfering with their attempts to actualize theirs. True, he doesn't obstruct all of them; his activity actually facilitates the development of their capacities at sleuthing; but his activity does interfere with their attainment of financial security and peace.

Doubtless this scheme of harmonious self-realization could be worked out in greater detail for society just as for the individual. But a question arises concerning the whole attempt. Extending the scheme to society is very neat, but what right has it to be called *self*-realization? Suppose you give up your activity as a bank robber and spend the rest of your life doing something you have less aptitude for and enjoy much less and which, like hard physical labor, tends to be obstructive of many other fulfillments which you desire. Your activity is now not obstructive of society, but in what way are you realizing yourself more than you did before? Doesn't it seem false, or at the very least over-optimistic, to call this change an improvement in *self*-realization? Let us take an even more obvious instance: suppose you give up your life, say in wartime, so that certain social goals such as freedom may continue to be realized. This is certainly the ultimate in self-sacrifice, but is it self-realization? Can you be said to have realized yourself when you are not even alive any more to do any realizing? To use the phrase in such a situation sounds like a bad joke.

There are those who say that even though you don't know it at the time, when you do something that promotes social realization, you are in reality realizing yourself. This contention, however, would have to be proven. (We shall discuss the alleged harmony of personal interest with public interest in Chapter 4.) It is a convenient assumption, but is there a shred of evidence to justify it? If you give up your life in order to make certain social or societal fulfillments possible, we may say that your action is self-sacrificing, noble, worthy, and all the rest; but how is it a realization of one's *self* when it certainly looks like the extinction of the self? Should we say to someone about to go on a suicide mission, "Remember, you are only realizing yourself"? Would it not be more honest to say, "You will probably be killed, but in so doing you will be helping to make possible a continued realization of the interests of a free society"? At least the last statement, though perhaps not very consoling to the individual concerned, would not be confusing the realization of society with the realization of the self. To telescope the two into one by talking about "social *self*-realization" sounds like double talk.

Once the concept of self-realization has been extended to include social realization, it is a very different kind of concept from what it was when it began. In the social form, it is virtually indistinguishable from the utilitarian ethics which we shall be discussing in Chapter 5.

EXERCISES

1. Try to formulate Epicurus' theory of pleasures in the language of individual self-realization.

2. Consider the following four propositions describing Aristotle's ethics. Does any of them follow logically from any of the others? Do they stand or fall together? Are they related at all? Evaluate each one in turn.

a. Happiness is the supreme good of man.

b. Happiness is brought about by pursuing that which is peculiar to man, his rational faculty.

c. Happiness requires many conditions — money, looks, friends, and so on.

d. Virtue is a mean between extremes.

3. Does the thought of the following poem, "They Do Not Live," by Irwin Edman, conflict with the ethics of Aristotle? of self-realization? Explain your answer. (From *Poems* by Irwin Edman. Copyright 1925-1958 by Irwin Edman. By permission of Simon and Schuster, Inc.)

> They do not live who choose the middle way,
> Whom ecstasy and anguish have not known,
> Who scale no trembling heights nor plumb the lone
> Depths of an aching darkness in bright day.
> They miss the passion with the pain, the
> High tides that lift the spirit to its own,
> The lifting surge of music, the dear tone
> Of a loved voice in pleading or in play.
> They miss the hurts and stumblings; surely fear
> Is never theirs, nor groping in the night;
> In their serene cool weather come no dread
> Torrents or tempests to corrupt their sight,
> Nor any rainbow; neither do they fear
> The sea, nor does the thunder wake these dead.

4. Give a description of the kind of the life which, in your opinion, contains the realization of the maximum number of cooperative capacities and the minimum of destructive ones. (To what extent does your account coincide with Aristotle's doctrine of the mean?)

READING LIST, SECTION 5

Aristotle. *Nichomachean Ethics.* Many editions, especially Bks. 1, 2, and 10.

Bradley, Francis Herbert. *Ethical Studies* (1876). New York: Oxford Univ. Press, 1927.

Campbell, Charles A. "Moral and Non-Moral Values" (1935). In Sellars, Wilfrid, and John Hospers, eds. *Readings in Ethical Theory.* New York: Appleton-Century-Crofts, 1952, pp. 340-62.

———. "Moral Intuition and the Principle of Self-realization." (Henrietta Herz lecture, 1948) *Proceedings of the British Academy,* Vol. 34 (1948), pp. 23-56.

Einstein, Albert, and others. *Living Philosophies.* New York: Simon and Schuster, 1937.

Fromm, Erich. *The Art of Loving.* New York: Harper, 1956.

———. *Man For Himself: An Inquiry into the Psychology of Ethics.* New York: Rinehart, 1947.

Green, Thomas Hill. *Prolegomena to Ethics.* New York: Oxford Univ. Press, 1890.

MacIver, Robert Morrison, ed. *The Pursuit of Happiness.* New York: Simon and Schuster, 1955.

Randall, John H. Jr. *Aristotle.* New York: Columbia Univ. Press, 1960.

Ross, Sir William David. *Aristotle* (1923). 5th rev. ed. New York: Barnes & Noble, 1953.

Russell, Bertrand. *The Conquest of Happiness* (1930). New York: New American Library.

Sidgwick, Henry. *Lectures on the Ethics of T. H. Green, Herbert Spencer, and J. Martineau.* London: Macmillan, 1902, especially Lecture 5 in the section on Green, pp. 60-79.

6. Following nature

In the Stoic ideal of life, man's victory is to be found in adjusting his will to the bitter facts of external nature. In one way, then, Stoicism might be said to be recommending "following nature." Yet this is far indeed from the meaning that has come to be attached to this phrase in the literature of the last two centuries. "Be natural," "Get close to nature," "Do what comes naturally," "Let nature be your guide," are all watchwords of a nature-based ideal of life. Since we are a part of nature and a product of nature's processes, the thought that somehow the processes of nature constitute a good guide for human action has been an alluring one. But this talk about nature is too vague to be manageable unless we pin it down to specific assertions. Here are the principal ones:

1. First of all, "Follow nature" could mean the same as "Obey the laws of nature." If this statement means what it seems to mean, it is hardly advice at all, much less moral advice. For it is pointless to advise people to do what they cannot help doing anyway. How can we help "obeying" the Law of Gravitation? If you fall out of a window, you cannot help going downward; to advise a person to go downward would be considered a distasteful joke. Besides, strictly speaking, we do not obey laws of nature, for laws of nature are simply generalized descriptions of the processes of nature themselves. They are not prescriptions as to how nature ought to behave as laws of Congress prescribe how we are to behave. It would be more accurate to say that everything we do is an instance of some law (or laws) of nature. If we eat, the subsequent processes are instances of biochemical laws of digestion; if we step off a roof, our fall is an instance of laws of physics;

if we free-associate, our action is an instance of certain laws of psychology. Follow nature" in this sense, then, is misleading and superfluous advice.

But most people who talk about "obeying nature's laws" do not mean it in quite this sense. They mean that the laws of nature are such that if we do certain things we shall enjoy or suffer certain consequences. If we do not observe certain elementary rules of health, we shall suffer from malnutrition and disease. The laws of nature do not say that we must or ought to follow certain rules of health but only that *if* we don't, then certain other things will happen to us in consequence. In this sense, it is unlikely that anyone (except those who do not care whether they live or die) would recommend that we ignore the facts about the natural world on which these "rules of health" are based.

2. "Do what's natural" may mean roughly the same as "Go primitive." Romanticism expressed a yearning to return to the primitive, the "natural" (Wordsworth's "vernal wood"); and Rousseau considered the state of "the noble savage" to be the ideal state of man. (He had never lived among savages.) In a life dominated by the constant irritations of busses and subways, strikes and shortages, smoke and hideous factory buildings mushrooming all about us, it is "natural" to rebel against all this and cry out for a return to nature. City dwellers feel this urge more strongly than country dwellers, who for their part often crave more nearness to people, more culture, more big stores and night clubs and the other things that cities afford. But should the whole of our lives be dominated either by city life or by nature? To enjoy the city while living in the country seems to most people to be more desirable than either extreme taken alone, and many of those who cry the most vociferously for a return to "life in the raw" would not wish to do without electric lighting, plumbing, automobiles, and television sets.

How far should this goal of being primitive be carried? Is it enough to picnic in the woods on alternate Sunday afternoons?

> . . . But where shall such Sabbath forays into nature's jungle end? How aboriginal should one get? Shall one play Indian and creep through the woods in a loincloth? Or should one identify oneself with more primitive natural species and go about barking, growling, or chirping? But why stop here? Why not go the limit in the direction of biological simplicity and, like Diogenes, bask in the sun, quietly thermotropic? Or if this is still too complicated, give oneself up like a stone to the eternal forces of gravitation? [1]

3. "Follow nature" may be identified with "Do what's natural" and "Avoid the artificial." This interpretation, like the second, is closely connected with the primitive, though perhaps avoiding some of its extremes. The queston here, of course, is, "What is meant by 'artificial'?" Andre Gide said, "The only unnatural thing in the world is a work of art." But he used

---

[1] L. Garvin, *A Modern Introduction to Ethics*, p. 374.

the phrase "work of art" as the Greeks did, for any work of *techne,* any work resulting from human activity. Thus paintings are artificial, cities are artificial, sewage systems and electric power plants are artificial, cosmetics and hearing aids and manufactured drugs (as opposed to natural herbs) are artificial. Should we then refrain from making things, from devising new inventions and cures, from using our intelligence in employing the materials present in nature to make new things to satisfy our needs and desires? The result of such procedure would be much the same as "going primitive."

It is true that all (or almost all) the chemical elements are to be found in nature; but is there any good reason why they should be used by us only in the form in which they are found in nature? Why should we limit ourselves in this way? Why are herbs to be used in cures but not the results of man's medical research? (Indeed, finding the right herbs for the right disorders is itself a product of medical research.) One may say, perhaps, that herbs are better for us in their natural form. Possibly this view may be true; but what about penicillin, anesthetics, surgery, and countless other medical advances which have saved thousands of lives? Our non-artificialist must condemn these artificial cures because, since they are the result of man's inventive ingenuity, they are not "natural." Should the "natural" products be used even in those cases when they are *not* medically better but simply because they are "natural"? This view seems quite irrational — surely the best products should be used, whether they happen to be "natural" or not. Indeed, medical research is required partly because nature itself is insufficient. If all men naturally had good eyesight, they would not need eyeglasses; but because some men do not have good eyesight, other men devise a clearly artificial product, eyeglasses, to remedy this deficiency of nature.

4. "Follow nature" may be taken to be synonymous with "Follow *your* nature," that is, presumably, "Do those things toward which you have a natural bent or propensity." When people talk about "your nature" as opposed to just "nature," the meaning has shifted once again. "Follow your nature," in the sense of do what you are best equipped to do — or, in other words, fulfill the potentialities you have or that nature gave you — will lead you to do many things that are quite "artificial." If you have a natural ability at engineering, you will design or construct buildings and tunnels; thus you will be doing what is "natural" in this fourth sense, though it is most unnatural in the third sense, which we have just finished discussing, for bridges and tunnels are, if anything is, "artificial." In fact, if "following nature" means doing those things for which you have the greatest potentiality, we have already discussed that view in the preceding section on self-realization.

5. "Follow nature" may also mean, "Take nature and nature's processes as *models for imitation* by man." According to this view, we are to scru-

tinize the processes of nature — the wind and the waves, or the birds and the bees — as they occur without man's interference and then follow suit. Take your cue from nature — do as nature does and you'll be all right.

When stated in general terms, this advice may sound alluring. But what are its specific implications? What sort of things does nature do? Or, if we do not wish to personify nature, what sort of events and processes occur in the world apart from man? Is nature a worthy model for imitation by man? Nature provides moisture, warmth, and nutrients for the crops to grow; but nature also provides droughts, floods, famines, plagues, earthquakes, and volcanic eruptions. Nature permits life to occur, though under very re- stricted conditions — a sudden change in climate, an increase of predatory organisms, and a whole species may be obliterated. With individual lives nature is even more careless: for every hundred creatures born or hatched, only a small percentage, in a state of nature, live to maturity; most of them starve or are eaten by other animals or drown in floods or in other ways fall victim to the catastrophes of nature; very few of them die a "natural" death.

> These endowments (of animals) are bestowed with so scrupulous an economy that any considerable diminution must entirely destroy the creature. Whenever one power is increased, there is a proportional abatement in the others. Ani- mals, which excel in swiftness, are commonly defective in force. Those, which possess both, are either imperfect in some of their senses, or are oppressed with the most craving wants. The human species, whose chief excellency is reason and sagacity, is of all others the most necessitous, and the most deficient in bodily advantages; without clothes, without arms, without food, without lodg- ing, without any convenience of life, except what they owe to their own skill and industry. In short, nature seems to have formed an exact calculation of the necessities of her creatures; and like a rigid master, has afforded them little more powers or endowments, than what are strictly sufficient to supply those necessities. An indulgent parent would have bestowed a large stock, in order to guard against accidents, and secure the happiness and welfare of the creature, in the most unfortunate concurrence of circumstances. Every course of life would not have been so surrounded with precipices, that the least de- parture from the true path, by mistake or necessity, must involve us in misery and ruin. Some reserve, some fund would have been provided to ensure happi- ness; nor would the powers and the necessities have been adjusted with so rigid an economy. . . . A builder is never esteemed prudent, who undertakes a plan, beyond what his stock will enable him to finish.[1]

Are the processes of nature, then, to be taken as rules for imitation by man? In nature, life lives on other life; as Tennyson put it, "Nature, red in tooth and claw with ravine shriek'd against [man's] creed." Do the propo- nents of nature really suggest that we should return to the "code of the jungle" — that is to say, no code at all — and kill as nature kills, maim and torture as nature maims and tortures?

[1] David Hume, *Dialogues concerning Natural Religion*, Pt. 11, pp. 207-08.

In sober truth, nearly all the things which men are hanged or imprisoned for doing to one another, are Nature's every day performances. Killing, the most criminal act recognized by human nature, Nature does once to every being that lives; and in a large proportion of cases, after protracted tortures such as only the greatest monsters whom we read of ever purposely inflicted on their living fellow-creatures . . . Nature impales men, breaks them as if on the wheel, casts them to be devoured by wild beasts, burns them to death, crushes them with stones like the first Christian martyr, starves them with hunger, freezes them with cold, poisons them by the quick or slow venom of her exhalations, and has hundreds of other hideous deaths in reserve, such as the ingenious cruelty of a Nabis or a Domitian never surpassed. All this, Nature does with the most supercilious disregard both of mercy and of justice, emptying her shafts upon the best and noblest indifferently with the meanest and worst; upon those who are engaged in the highest and worthiest enterprises, and often as the direct consequence of the noblest acts; and it might almost be imagined as a punishment for them. She mows down those on whose existence hangs the well-being of a whole people, perhaps the prospects of the human race for generations to come, with as little compunction as those whose death is a relief to themselves, or a blessing to those under their noxious influence.

Such are Nature's dealings with life. Even when she does not intend to kill, she inflicts the same tortures in apparent wantonness. In the clumsy provision which she has made for that perpetual renewal of animal life, rendered necessary by the prompt termination she puts to it in every individual instance, no human being ever comes into the world but another human being is literally stretched on the rack for hours or days, not unfrequently issuing in death. Next to taking life (equal to it according to a high authority) is taking the means by which we live; and Nature does this too on the largest scale and with the most callous indifference. A single hurricane destroys the hopes of a season; a flight of locusts, or an inundation, desolates a district; a trifling chemical change in an edible root, starves a million of people. The waves of the sea, like banditti seize and appropriate the wealth of the rich and the little all of the poor with the same accompaniments of stripping, wounding, and killing as their human antitypes. Everything, in short, which the worst men commit either against life or property is perpetrated on a larger scale by natural agents. Nature has Noyades more fatal than those of Carrier; her explosions of fire damp are as destructive as human artillery; her plague and cholera far surpass the poison cups of the Borgias. Even the love of "order" which is thought to be a following of the ways of Nature, is in fact a contradiction of them. All which people are accustomed to deprecate as "disorder" and its consequences, is precisely a counterpart of Nature's ways. Anarchy and the Reign of Terror are overmatched in injustice, ruin, and death, by a hurricane and a pestilence.[1]

If we do not really mean to say that man should do all these things just because nature does them, then we should not suggest "following nature" as a guide to conduct.

[1] From Mill, John Stuart: *Nature and the Utility of Religion,* edited by George Nakhnikian. New York, 1958. Reprinted by permission of the publisher, The Liberal Arts Press, Inc., pp. 20-22.

Though his criticism is made from the point of view of another moral theory which we have not yet examined, Mill continues to argue that almost everything we consider worthwhile in human life consists not in following nature but in improving upon and transcending nature. If we used nature as a model for our own behavior, we would kill, maim, and torture indiscriminately; but instead of following nature in this respect, we should seek to improve upon it, to lengthen life and decrease suffering. If there is any characteristic of human beings which is "natural," which is part of our inherited make-up and which we do not have to learn to cultivate, it is complete selfishness. But should we cultivate selfishness just because nature implants this tendency so strongly in us? We may grant that we should try to survive, but we should help others to survive too. Human well-being, indeed, to a large extent, human society, is possible only if we try to help our fellow men, consider the welfare of others, fulfill certain tasks as part of the social structure. It is "natural" for ants and bees to work for the good of the antheap or the beehive; but predatory animals are usually "rugged individualists" which work for their own survival even at the expense of others of their species. Which kind of behavior should we imitate, since nature presents us with both? Neither bees nor lions exhibit any compassion to those who do not belong to their species; should we therefore follow their example?

On the one hand, to take, to grab, to receive without giving is, in Mill's eyes, the most "natural" behavior in the world; consider small children. The virtue of gratitude, on the other hand, is cultivated with extreme difficulty and requires years of parental precept and example to make an impression; even then the attempt is not always successful. Always we must learn to check and inhibit our natural impulses to selfishness and savagery. Almost all the traits we consider to be virtues in any society above the headhunter level (and even headhunters must inhibit their natural tendencies somewhat, as in refraining from killing members of their own tribe) are traits which are not "natural" to us — they must be inculcated in us with endless patience, diligence, and effort.

Thus, either we admire nature and should therefore do as nature does — kill as nature kills, be ruthless as nature is ruthless, be wasteful of life and achievement as nature is wasteful; *or* we realize that nature is not a fit model for human imitation and we should therefore stop talking about "following nature." According to Mill, once we clearly see how nature behaves, there is no warrant left for believing that we should follow nature. Mill is not denying that *sometimes* we should do things that are also done by nature — for example, we may have to kill in defending our country against an invader, and we regularly kill animals in order to eat them, just as animals kill one another for the same purpose. Still, even when we are justified in doing these things, it is not *because* nature does them. So even then nature is not a fit model for human imitation. That nature does something is, by itself, no reason for believing that we should or should not do it. Nature simply has nothing to do with the matter one way or the other.

6. There is, however, a related interpretation of "Follow nature" which may survive Mill's criticism. Perhaps "Follow nature" does not mean simply that we should do as nature does but that we should look to the *evolutionary process* manifest in nature, observe in which direction this process is tending, and seek to follow in the same direction.

Unfortunately, however, the direction in which nature is tending is far from clear. To derive any specific conclusions from observing the evolutionary process we have to "read into the script." The evolutionary process has many aspects, and everything depends on which aspects we select. Organisms grow, and in this growth and vitality we may find much to emulate. But organisms also deteriorate and die; should we do our best to emulate in our own lives this model of deterioration as well as that of growth? Many organisms evolve, and in the course of millions of years they achieve a far greater organic complexity than they began with; but other organisms stay the same for countless centuries — many insects have not changed in evolution for millions of years. The "static" and the "dynamic" are thus both illustrated in nature, so which should we imitate? There is no one direction of evolution; nature's processes tend in many directions, and everything depends on which direction we seize upon as models for our own behavior. Yet what is to determine our selection? We cannot say, "The direction of evolution is what determines our selection," because, as we have just seen, there are many directions. We may say, "The *best* direction," but now we have given the show away. The best by what criterion? Not the criterion of nature, which is quite impartial among the various directions and contains them all. Nature never says that a dynamic form of life that changes through the generations is any better than the well-adjusted ant that never changes throughout millions of years of evolution.

The English philosopher Herbert Spencer (1820-1903), following in the footsteps of Charles Darwin, tried to attach moral strings to Darwin's doctrine of evolution. Spencer seized upon two aspects of the evolutionary process, (1) increasing complexity of structure and (2) increasing integration of function. Since evolution tends in both these directions, we human beings, who are products of nature, should assist nature and reinforce this tendency. We should not go back to "the law of the jungle" because, in evolving organisms as complex as human beings, nature has produced something that has gone beyond this "law," and to return to it now would therefore be a retrogression. However things may stand with tigers and boa constrictors, in human beings nature has evolved something better. Human beings are social animals, and they can achieve certain peculiarly human values by ignoring the jungle and forging ahead to attain a degree of cooperation, harmony, peace, and welfare which are unknown at the earlier stages of evolution. In fact, the direction of evolution seems to be toward mutual cooperation and a harmonious fulfillment of our diverse tendencies and potentialities.

But at once problems arise in Spencer's position:

a. Is it an empirical fact that integration and complexity *are* the directions of evolution? There is some reason for doubting it. For example, suppose that next year the human race destroys itself in a thermonuclear war. Is destruction then the direction of evolution? Empirically the answer would seem to be, "Yes," because that was in fact the direction which evolution finally took. Or suppose, without war, that the human race gets fat and comfortable, neglects the use of the intellect, and enjoys nothing more than watching television six nights a week. Then apparently watching television is the direction of evolution. Yet is watching television therefore better than destroying mankind? The conclusive proof of the direction in which something is tending, it would seem, is the course that it actually takes.

b. But if Spencer means not the direction that evolution *does* take but the direction which it *should* take, or would *ideally* take, then other problems confront us. How do we know what direction it should take? All we can infer from watching nature is the direction (or directions) which it actually *does* take. Indeed, when we cease to use the *actual* direction(s) of evolution as a criterion and use the *ideal* direction instead, we are no longer using nature as a "touchstone for ethics." For according to what criterion is a certain direction desirable or ideal? The actual direction of evolution, as we have just seen, is no guide. We must then be appealing to some *other* standard, not that of nature (direction of evolution) at all.

Spencer thought that the democratic values of harmony, individual survival and longevity, and mutual cooperation among mankind were the direction of evolution. A German philosopher of the same era, Friedrich Nietzsche (1844-1900), had almost diametrically opposed views.[1] He said that in nature there are individuals who are "naturally superior": through strength or craft they dominate the other members of the species and have no interest in their inferiors except to use them for their own purposes. Working on this assumption, Nietzsche held that the natural state of war and cutthroat competition among organisms is the desirable state and that the character traits to which this state of affairs gives rise — strength, craft, resourcefulness, ruthlessness — should be encouraged in human behavior. These traits should be manifested in the life of the mind and not merely in the struggle to survive as living organisms; life is best when they are exhibited at a maximum in both mind and body. Daring, courage, and imagination in intellectual matters should be prized as highly as strength and resourcefulness in the physical domain. True, only a minority of people

[1] We shall consider only the traditional (and usual) interpretation of Nietzsche's ethical views. For a newer and quite different interpretation of Nietzsche, see Walter Kaufmann, *Nietzsche*. Whether or not the traditional interpretation of Nietzsche's view is the correct one, it is well to consider it just the same as a *type* of ethical view falling under the heading "Following nature."

can achieve success in the attempt to "ride high" over the wishes of the majority; but the very fact that they succeed in "riding high" is evidence of their capacity to do so. The ideal state of affairs is for an able minority to dominate a weak and passive majority. The mass of human beings should be led by a relatively small number of supermen who exhibit intellectual and physical achievement to the maximum degree and who have shown their ability to outmaneuver and dominate the passive and incompetent majority who lack the will, the imagination, and the intelligence to achieve a position of dominance. (Many have thought that Nietzsche's ideal leader would have been Adolf Hitler, but this is most improbable. Hitler was used by others who put him at the top to satisfy their own ends, until at last he achieved the power on his own. Nietzsche would probably have called Hitler a contemptible little rabble-rouser. A man of more heroic stature like Napoleon would have fulfilled his ideal much better.)

The unnatural character traits such as sympathy, humility, love, cooperation are those valued by the majority; Nietzsche had only contempt for these qualities. It is easy to see, he thought, why the majority cherish such ideals, which are roughly those of Christianity. Lacking the wit and the imagination to do what the strong, ruthless superman does, they band together against him. Individually they could never survive against him, but by sheer force of numbers the worthless may often (as in democratic countries) become victorious over the superior few, in an attempt to make their passive and "nay-saying" traits dominant over the active and "yea-saying" traits of the "natural aristocracy." The result, thought Nietzsche, is mediocrity multiplied a million times. Nature discloses no such pattern as the weak triumphing over the strong, shopkeepers over supermen. This victory is strictly a perversion of nature's ideal. Man should return to the primitive competitive virtues, to a life of daring and danger and ruthlessness in mental and physical struggle — like the lion, trampling down his enemies, always watchful, always ready, always victorious by strength and cunning. Only then are men really alive, not puny, shivering sheep banding together against the mighty lions of the world to protect their own miserable and futile lives. Better for the natural slaves to be really slaves and the natural leaders to be the actual leaders. Such is the pattern of nature.

Much more could be said about Nietzsche's views; but since most of his works consist largely of passionate appeals rather than reasoned conclusions and since in ethics we are chiefly interested in the reasons which people adduce in defense of their views, we need not pursue his views much further at this point. Nevertheless, perhaps a few brief remarks are in order.

If Nietzsche's ideal is recommended in the name of "nature," it no more follows from the facts of evolution than Spencer's milder view does. The same criticisms made there are applicable here.

Moreover, one may well ask *why* Nietzsche wants the few to have what they want while the majority cannot have what they want. Does he believe that in the long run the majority will be better off if the few dominate over them? That is a possibility; some men have held this, and their views will be discussed in Chapter 8. But in that case he is espousing universal welfare (which we shall discuss in Chapter 5) as an ideal, the domination of the many by the few being only a means to this end. But it is inconceivable, in the light of Nietzsche's writings, that he held such a thing; he had nothing but contempt for the wishes of the majority, and if the majority were to be permanently miserable, poverty-stricken, unhappy slaves, he would not have had the slightest compunction about it.

Why, then, should the desires of a few be fulfilled and those of the many trampled upon? Because, according to Nietzsche, the few are more able, and their ability to rule is demonstrated by the fact that through violence, craft, and ruthless competitiveness they *have* achieved the summit of power. But how is this achievement any guarantee? If someone is crafty or lucky enough to arrive at a position where he can rule a nation, does his achievement of the position show that he is better *able* than another to carry out its functions? Surely ruling requires the exercise of other capacities than those which enabled him to get to a position of power in the first place. (This is the "tragedy of power," which we shall discuss in Chapter 8.) Why is it then that the wishes of only a comparative few should be granted? Why are not all people entitled to something in this world? Through many pages of ravings, condemnations, and entreaties, Nietzsche never gives a clear answer to this question. About all we can conclude is that ability (specifically, ability to get to the top, by whatever means) should be promoted just because its exercise is good and that power and ruthlessness should be encouraged just because it is a good thing to manifest these traits. But this answer is no answer at all; or if it *is* considered an answer, why can it not be used to say the opposite: that humility and cooperation should be encouraged because it is a good thing to manifest these traits? (Perhaps ruthlessness builds character; but don't other qualities do so as well or better? and why only the characters of some preferred individuals?) Perhaps then the qualities that Nietzsche prizes as desirable can be recommended, at least sometimes, for the sake of achieving *something else;* but what is their value simply *for their own sakes?* The concept of "X for X's sake" takes us directly into the subject of Chapter 3, in which we shall try to clarify the distinction between what is desirable for its own sake and what is desirable only for the sake of something else.

EXERCISES

1. Try to clarify the distinction between what is natural and what is artificial. Is the attempt to shorten life when the person is in great pain and dying slowly from an incurable disease bad because it is "unnatural"? Is the attempt on the part of physicians to lengthen human life by means of surgery and medication also to be condemned as "unnatural"? Can you defend some methods of birth control as "natural" as opposed to others that are "artificial"?

2. "Man is the animal for whom it is natural to be artificial" (L. Garvin, *A Modern Introduction to Ethics,* p. 378). How is the word "natural" being used in this sentence? (It must be a different sense from "nonartificial," or the sentence would be self-contradictory.)

3. Can either one of the choices in the following pairs be said to be (1) more natural, and (2) therefore better, than any other choice? Organically grown vegetables, vitamin pills; crude oil, gasoline; horses, automobiles.

4. Read Mill's essay "Nature," concentrating especially on the last half, in which he criticizes the view that a benevolent Deity is the author of nature.

5. Evaluate the following sonnet by Matthew Arnold, "To an Independent Preacher Who Preached That We Should Be in Harmony with Nature" (1888):

> "In harmony with nature?" Restless fool,
> Who with such heat dost preach what were to thee,
> When true, the last impossibility—
> To be like Nature strong, like Nature cool!
> Know, man hath all which Nature hath, but more,
> And in that *more* lies all his hopes of good.
> Nature is cruel, man is sick of blood;
> Nature is stubborn, man would fain adore;
> Nature is fickle, man hath need of rest;
> Nature forgives no debt, and fears no grave;
> Man would be mild, and with safe conscience blest.
> Man must begin, know this, where Nature ends;
> Nature and man can never be fast friends.
> Fool, if thou canst not pass her, rest her slave!

6. Evaluate the following passage from G. L. Dickinson, *The Meaning of Good,* p. 46:

I'm not much impressed by the argument you attribute to Nature, that if we don't agree with her we shall be knocked on the head. I, for instance, happen to object strongly to her whole procedure: I don't believe much in the harmony of the final consummation . . . and I am sensibly aware of the horrible discomfort of the intermediate stages, the pushing, kicking, trampling of the host, and the wounded and dead left behind on the march. Of all this I venture to disapprove; then comes Nature and says, "but you ought to approve!" I ask why, and she says, "Because the procedure is mine." I still demur, and she comes down on me with a threat—"Very good, approve or not, as you like; but if you don't approve you will be eliminated!" "By all means," I say, and cling to my old opinion with the more affection that I feel myself invested with something of the glory of a martyr. . . . In my humble opinion it's Nature, not I, that cuts a poor figure!

7. Read Walter Kaufmann's *Nietzsche* and indicate in what ways his interpretation of Nietzsche's views differs from the traditional one which we have presented in this chapter.

READING LIST, SECTION 6

Carritt, Edgar F. *The Theory of Morals: An Introduction to Ethical Philosophy.* New York: Oxford Univ. Press, 1928.

Dickinson, Goldsworthy Lowes. *The Meaning of Good* (1906). New York: Dutton. 1921.

Garvin, Lucius. *A Modern Introduction to Ethics.* Boston: Houghton Mifflin, 1953, Ch. 14.

Huxley, Thomas Henry. *Evolution and Ethics* (1894). In Huxley, T. H. *Selections from the Essays of T. H. Huxley.* Ed. by Albury Castell. New York: Appleton-Century-Crofts, 1948.

————, and Julian Huxley. *Touchstone for Ethics.* New York: Harper, 1947.

Kaufman, Walter Arnold. *Nietzsche.* Princeton: Princeton Univ. Press, 1950. (Meridian Books.)

Mill, John Stuart. "Nature" (1874). In Mill, J. S. *Nature and the Utility of Religion.* New York: Liberal Arts Press, 1958, pp. 3-44.

Nietzsche, Friedrich. *Beyond Good and Evil.* Other writings of his are also relevant. See Nietzsche, F. *The Philosophy of Nietzsche.* New York: Modern Library.

Sidgwick, Henry. *Lectures on the Ethics of T. H. Green, Herbert Spencer, and J. Martineau.* London: Macmillan, 1902, especially the section dealing with Spencer's ethics, pp. 138-312.

Spencer, Herbert. *The Data of Ethics* (1888). New York: McKay, n. d.

3. *Intrinsic good*

We have now examined several "ideals of life" and ventured a few preliminary comments about them. But the result so far has been indecisive. Not only have we found no way of establishing one of them at the expense of another (a topic we shall examine much later in our discussion); but we have not even (thus far) examined any ethical theory that attempts to be complete. A complete ethical theory is one that, in principle at least, is able to tell us what to do under any circumstances. The Stoic tells us what attitude to take in times of adversity; but what, specifically, can he tell us to do if we have made a promise which would cost us a very great sacrifice to keep? or if we have to compromise a principle in order to gain a desirable end? In these situations he has nothing to say to us; indeed, he recommends very few specific kinds of action, he rather tells us what kind of attitude to adopt to the world in general. We must now try to go beyond the Stoic view and consider some ethical theories which attempt to be complete. We have not even introduced, thus far, most of the central terms which occur in systematic discussions of ethics and which will enable us to cast our thoughts into a clear conceptual framework. These terms we shall start to present at once by discussing the all-important concept of intrinsic good. If we want to know what acts should be performed, we should first find out what ends we should try to achieve by doing these actions — in other words, what goals are worth pursuing — before we can determine what acts to perform in the pursuit of these goals.

If you were asked to make a list of things you considered good, desirable, or worthwhile, you might include such things as financial security, recognition by others, material comfort, kindness to others, affection, knowledge, the appreciation of art. But at the outset, in compiling such a list, we come across a distinction which will turn out to be of the greatest importance. Our question, "What things are good?" is ambiguous. There are some things which we consider good (or desirable) only for their results — for what they lead to. There are other things which we consider good not because of what they lead to but because of what they are in themselves: we consider them worth having or pursuing not merely as ways of getting other things but because of their own intrinsic nature. The first kind of good is called *instrumental* good because the goodness or worthwhileness of these things lies in their being instruments toward the attainment of the other things which are considered good not merely as instruments. The second kind of good is called *intrinsic* good because we value these things (whatever they may turn out to be) not for what they lead to but for what they are.

When speaking of instrumental good, it is important to distinguish between what is instrumentally good and what is a good instrument. If something, call it B, is intrinsically good, then something else, A, is instrumentally good if it leads to the attainment of B. But suppose that B is intrinsically bad, or evil. Then A is an instrumental evil because it leads to what is intrinsically bad. This A is, nevertheless, a *good instrument* toward the achievement of B. Something may be a good instrument toward the achievement of an end, even if that end is far from good: the use of a gun is a better instrument for killing somebody than is a handful of pins. When we say a gun is a good instrument, we mean that it is an efficient means of achieving a given end (and when we say it is the *best* means we mean that it is the *most* efficient instrument), but we are making no judgment about whether the end is good. When, however, we say that A is instrumentally good, we are saying that (1) it leads (the more efficiently the better) to the achievement of B and that (2) B either is itself intrinsically good or leads in turn to something that is.

If you ask yourself which of the things on your list of good or desirable things are intrinsically good and which are instrumentally good, you will probably find that you consider most of them to be instrumentally good. Money is an obvious example. Almost everyone desires money. This of course isn't the same as saying that we think that money is always *desirable* — whether it is desirable depends on what it leads to, for example, whether it leads to peace and comfort or to dissension and discontent. Money, then, is not under all circumstances instrumentally good; but when it *is* good, it is good instrumentally, not intrinsically. When it is desirable, it is desirable for the other things which it can bring. When it cannot bring other things — as on Robinson Crusoe's island — it is of no value whatever.

Doesn't the miser consider money to be intrinsically good? No, even he values it for what he can get out of it. The difference between him and the rest of us is that we value it because of the things we can purchase with it — a house, new clothes, a life insurance policy — whereas he values it because he enjoys looking at it or just thinking about it. For him, the money is directly instrumental to this enjoyment; for us, the money is indirectly instrumental to enjoyment but directly instrumental to the things we can purchase with it which will help give us the enjoyment.

Are the things we can buy with money intrinsically good? Are new cars and houses, clothes, and life insurance policies intrinsically good? There seems to be no doubt that the answer again is, "No"; for in each case we can ask what these things are good *for;* and when we say they are good *for* something, we are saying that they are instruments toward something. Houses and lands are often good instruments for the attainment of other things such as (possibly) joy or pleasure. But of course houses and lands are instrumentally good only if what they lead to is intrinsically good. Money is a good instrument toward the purchase of houses and lands, and houses and lands are good instruments for the achievement of financial security, and financial security is a good instrument (though not always) toward enjoyment or pleasure. And *if* enjoyment or pleasure is intrinsically good, then these other things are instrumentally good — directly or indirectly — in that they lead, the one through the other, toward this enjoyment. But, it would seem, none of these other things is *intrinsically good.* If you had a beautiful house and yacht and limitless financial security, but all these things brought you only worry, unpleasant responsibility, and suspicion of everyone because of the fear that every so-called friend was really out to get your money; would you still consider a house and yacht worth having? Perhaps you would if you thought that the situation might change and that you might still get some pleasure out of your money. But suppose you knew that your money never had given you and never would (in the future) give you one spark of enjoyment, would you still consider it desirable or worth having in itself? The answer would seem to be clearly in the negative — unless you cherished the vain hope that your money would still be good *for* something — that is, a good instrument.

What, then, about the enjoyment itself? Is *it* intrinsically good? Many people, including many moral philosophers, have thought that it is. Whether enjoyment is the *only* thing that is, is a subject we shall discuss in detail later in this chapter; but that it *is* intrinsically desirable would be agreed to by most people. We seem to value enjoyment and desire it for itself alone; we do not desire it for what it will bring — rather, we desire other things because they will help to bring *it*. The question "What do you want money for?" can be easily answered; so can the question "What do you want property for?" or "What do you want new clothes for?" But if someone asked us, "What do you want enjoyment for?" the question would sound very strange. We might ask, "What do you mean, what do I want it for? I don't want it *for* anything at all. I just like to have it, that's all."

Might we say the same thing about health? If we are asked why we want to go ahead with the surgery, we can hardly say that surgery is desirable in itself; we shall say that only by having it can we achieve what we want, namely the restoration of health. But suppose someone asked us, "Well, what's so good about health? What do you want health for?" This question too might sound a bit strange, for we ordinarily take health as something desirable without question. But if pressed we might reply, "Because I can't enjoy life, at least not as much, if I'm not at least reasonably healthy;

certainly I can't enjoy it if I'm in constant pain or dread of pain." So we come back to enjoyment once more as an intrinsic good.

Before proceeding further, it is important to forestall an almost inevitable confusion by asking one question: "Is the distinction between intrinsic and instrumental good the same as the distinction between means and ends which we considered in Chapter 2? The distinctions seem to be the same: enjoyment is an end toward which financial security is a means; enjoyment is intrinsically good, whereas these other things, when good at all, are instrumentally good. Don't the two distinctions reduce to one?"

The answer is, "No," and the reasons are not far to seek. People adopt all sorts of means — A, B, C — to achieve all sorts of ends — X, Y, Z. What means people take to achieve what ends is a question for empirical observation. What means people adopt to get-rich-quick, or how they proceed to insure their financial security, or what system of government will be most likely to achieve certain ends — these are matters for economists and sociologists and political scientists to investigate. But the question of what is intrinsically good cannot be empirically settled in this way. What means people adopt is a question of fact; what ends are good is a question of value. What means are used to pursue what ends is a question of only incidental interest to ethics; what things are instrumentally good is a question of the very greatest importance to ethics. When you ask questions about what ends people pursue, you are asking what things they *desire;* and these things may be bad as well as good. When you ask questions about intrinsic good, you are asking what things are *desirable,* whether or not they happen to be desired.

Let us return, then, to our discussion of intrinsic good. We shall consider first whether pleasure, or enjoyment (or some of its synonyms), are always intrinsically good; and second, whether other things besides pleasure are also intrinsically good. We shall postpone until the next chapter the question "Who should have these goods?" for there a number of separate arguments will arise. We shall, at times, tend to assume, in this chapter, that whatever is intrinsically good should be available equally to all.

7. Hedonism

The business man works hard every day and comes home tired every evening. What for? To improve the business and keep it going, he says. And what does he want to do that for? To keep himself and his family financially secure. And why does he want financial security? So that his family will never be in want, so that they need have no fear of poverty, so that they can buy the things they need. And why does he want to achieve these ends? So that he and his family can enjoy life more—in the belief that having some of the good things of life will provide them at least with a greater chance of enjoying it.

This kind of reasoning—we could multiply examples indefinitely— seems to lead us to the conclusion that pleasure, or enjoyment, is desirable for its own sake, whereas the other things mentioned are not. This conclusion is precisely the contention of the ethical *hedonist*. We have already encountered one form of hedonism—Epicureanism; now we can recast the hedonist's main contention in a clearer form by saying that according to the hedonist, first, *all* pleasure or enjoyment is intrinsically good and, second, *only* pleasure or enjoyment is intrinsically good—that is, nothing else but pleasure is intrinsically good. We shall examine these two contentions in order.

A. Pleasure as an intrinsic good

HEDONIST: I claim, first of all, that all pleasure is intrinsically good.

OPPONENT: I should think that whether pleasure is good or not depends on what the pleasure is. The pleasure you get from helping someone or from contemplating a beautiful work of art is, I would say, good; but the pleasure a person gets from committing the perfect crime or from wreaking vengeance on his enemy is not good at all. Are you denying this?

H: I don't deny this. But when you say "good" or "bad" you must specify whether you mean intrinsically or instrumentally. I am not saying that all pleasure is good; I am saying that all pleasure is *intrinsically* good. The pleasure a criminal gets from committing his crime is bad *instrumentally*. If he enjoys killing one person and the law does not catch up with him to bring him some displeasure, he is more likely to kill others in order to get more pleasure. And of course acts of murder cause no end of pain, sadness, and grief to both actual and potential victims, misery which far outweighs the temporary pleasure of the murderer. But I hold that the pleasure *taken by itself* is not bad; it is bad only because of what it leads to, that is, it is only bad instrumentally. The act of murder is instrumentally bad, but the accompanying pleasure is still intrinsically good. Considered *by itself* without reference to its consequences (and this is what we are doing when we consider it not instrumentally but intrinsically), pleasure is good.

O: I see your point, but I still can't escape the conviction that the pleasure accompanying an act of murder is not only instrumentally but intrinsically bad.

H: But why intrinsically? I hold that such a pleasure is bad because of what it leads to—because of its consequences. And I can't think of a better reason. Surely that is sufficient reason for condemning murder!

O: Perhaps so, and of course I don't deny that pleasure in committing murder is instrumentally bad. I am only contending that it is intrinsically bad as well. My basic position is that it's immoral to hold that pleasure is the only thing in the world that is intrinsically good; later I shall want to say that other things ought to be desired too, such as moral behavior.

H: But I don't hold that pleasure is the only thing that ought to be desired! Many things ought to be desired — kindness as opposed to cruelty, eating foods conducive to health rather than those conducive to sickness, and so on. All these things ought to be desired, but that doesn't mean that they are intrinsically good. You confuse what is intrinsically good with what ought to be desired. What is intrinsically good is what ought to be desired *for its own sake* rather than for the sake of something else that can be achieved by means of it. I say we ought to desire many things (such as peace and goodwill) because, in general, an increase in them leads to an increase in the intrinsic good (pleasure or enjoyment) in the world. More people will experience pleasurable states of consciousness if these kinds of action are encouraged and the opposite ones condemned.

O: When we decide to do what we are convinced is right, do you really believe that we should do it because it will give us pleasure?

H: Of course not. I am not an ethical egoist like the Epicureans. Doing the good deed may give *me* no pleasure at all, but if it will give pleasure to many others or avoid displeasure, I should do it regardless. I do it so as to increase, in the long run, the total amount of pleasure in the world, including the decrease of displeasurable states like pain, distress, misery, suffering, although it may not be *my* pleasure that I am increasing.

O: I understand what you mean. But there are many objections to ethical hedonism which I find convincing. Writers have not been slow in pointing them out. For example, A. E. Taylor writes:

> A man is not morally good because his career has been marked by extraordinary cases of unexpected good luck, nor is the life of the lower animals to be reckoned morally good because it may contain a vast number of pleasant moments.[1]

H: Here again there is a complete misunderstanding. You are confusing *intrinsic* goodness with *moral* goodness. We hedonists all hold that moral goodness is instrumental — something is morally good when it leads to more intrinsic good. Hedonists do not say that moral goodness consists in enjoyment of pleasure.

O: But even though you don't believe that moral goodness consists in the enjoyment of pleasure, aren't you committed to believing that what is good about right actions is the pleasure accompanying their performance?

H: If right acts are accompanied by pleasure, then that pleasure, like all pleasure, is intrinsically good. But the performance need not be accompanied by your pleasure to be right. If an act will cause great pleasure to others, although none to the agent, there will be more total intrinsic good

[1] Alfred E. Taylor, *The Problem of Conduct* (New York: Macmillan, 1901), p. 327.

(pleasure) in the consequence of that act than in the consequence of an act that is pleasurable to the agent but causes no pleasure to others.

o: I still can't stomach you hedonists' saying that *all* pleasure without exception is good. Oh, I know you mean intrinsically good, and I know that lots of the pleasures we call bad (or so you will say) are bad not in themselves but because they, or the acts which they accompany, lead to displeasure which more than counterbalances the pleasure enjoyed. But I doubt whether something is even *intrinsically* good in proportion to the amount of pleasure it brings. Let's try G. E. Moore's famous experiment: "Let us imagine one world exceedingly beautiful. Imagine it as beautiful as you can . . . and then imagine the ugliest world you can possibly conceive. Imagine it simply as one heap of filth." [1] And now suppose that nobody receives any pleasure from either world, because there are no conscious beings in either world. Still, if we had the choice, shouldn't we do what we can to produce the first world rather than the second one?

h: Of course not. If neither world contains one iota of pleasure, what is there to choose between them? You are tempted to say that the first world contains more intrinsic good than the second only because beautiful objects and scenes usually *cause* people to experience pleasure more than "heaps of filth" do. But by your hypothesis neither of these worlds is experienced by anyone, and as long as that is the case I can only say "It couldn't matter less which one you create." The beautiful world would have only a *potential* for enjoyment; but if part of your hypothesis is that it is not and never will be enjoyed by anyone, then what possible good is it?

There is another point too which is easily lost sight of: according to the conditions of the example, no pleasure is experienced. But *you yourself,* in contemplating these two imaginary worlds, can hardly help experiencing pleasure in imagining the first world rather than the second. Besides, the expression "heap of filth" which is used to describe the second world, is not so much a description of the world itself as of people's reactions to it; and the same with the term "beautiful." So you see, it is almost impossibly difficult to keep out a reference to our *experience* of such a world, even in the act of describing it as existing unexperienced. But if you rigidly exclude from your consciousness the pleasure in contemplating the one world and the displeasure in the other and if you keep securely in mind the fact that neither world is experienced now or in the future (according to the conditions of the example), then I think you will find that there is nothing — as far as intrinsic goodness is concerned — to choose between them.

o: According to you, then, an ideal state of affairs would be the maximum enjoyment of the intensest possible pleasure continuing without interruption for the longest possible time. But

Let us imagine a moment of the most intense pleasure we have ever known. . . . Now imagine that moment of experience continued without change and

[1] G. E. Moore, *Principia Ethica* (1903), p. 8.

without further activity for the whole span of a normal lifetime. If it is pleasure and pleasure alone that gives to experience its character of intrinsic goodness, then such a life span should, as a whole, have the greatest intrinsic good imaginable in any life span. But, I think, few of us will agree that it has. We would gladly exchange some of the pleasure content for a little variety, for an opportunity for genuine activity.[1]

H: But that's ridiculous! In the first place, the whole example contradicts itself: first it speaks of intense pleasure, and then it says that a continued intense pleasure would no longer be pleasurable! Very well, then it *wouldn't* be pleasure any more, would it? Pleasure has to be pleasurable! What the person giving the example ought to say, and perhaps means to say, is that when something is the *source* of pleasure, it doesn't remain a source of pleasure forever because we grow tired or bored with it and want some other source of pleasure. This statement is probably true enough. But to say that pleasure itself finally is no longer pleasurable — this is self-contradictory. At the moment that the experience is no longer pleasurable, then it is not pleasure but displeasure, and the objection no longer applies.

I agree that we would gladly exchange one continuous unchanging source of pleasure for a variety of sources, precisely because the most pleasure in the long run is obtainable that way. But this is a far cry from saying that pleasure itself becomes displeasurable. I think the confusion is, once again, between the pleasure itself and the source of the pleasure.

O: Another point has been bothering me. You speak only of pleasure as intrinsically good; you have never yet mentioned the word "happiness." Why not? Don't you believe that happiness is intrinsically good?

H: I don't deny it; but this introduces a long story. Everything depends now on how you conceive the relation of pleasure to happiness.

B. Pleasure and happiness

Leaving our two disputants for a short time, we must try to clear up a few problems concerning pleasure, pain, and happiness. Two senses of "pleasure" must first be distinguished:

We may speak of pleasure — let us call it pleasure$_1$ — in the sense of a pleasurable state of consciousness, one with "positive hedonic tone." It seems to be impossible to define it further, for the term refers to an experience which, like so many experiences, no words are adequate to describe. We can only cite typical circumstances under which this experience occurs: we may derive this kind of pleasure from such sources as a refreshing swim, from reading a good book, from grappling with a philosophical problem, from creating a work of art, or from talking with congenial persons. Pleasure in this sense is, as Aristotle said, an accompaniment of an activity; of course different people experience pleasure and experience it to widely different degrees and from widely varying activities: some people experience pleasure

---

[1] A. C. Garnett, "Intrinsic Good: Its Definition and Referent," in Ray Lepley, ed., *Value: a Cooperative Inquiry* (New York: Columbia Univ. Press, 1949), p. 85.

from mathematical pursuits, for example, and others do not. From whatever sources it may be derived, pleasure is an accompaniment of an activity, like a frosting on a cake — the frosting tops the cake but is not found by itself apart from the cake. (Whether we eat this cake only in order to get the frosting is a question which we shall pursue in Chapter 4.)

Opposed to pleasure₁ is, let us say unpoetically, "displeasure," since there is no convenient term other than the negative one in our language. Displeasure would include all unpleasant states of consciousness, such as we experience from bodily pain, from hearing bad news, from situations involving distress, anger, terror, and jealousy. In general, the pleasant states are those which we like to have continued, and the unpleasant ones are those we would prefer to terminate as soon as possible.

Pleasure₁ may also come from another kind of source, the pleasure derived from bodily *sensations*. Let us call pleasure in this sense pleasure₂. There are pleasurable sensations, such as those of being tickled, stroked, and rubbed; since these pleasures have a definite bodily location, here it makes sense to ask, *"Where* do you feel the pleasure?" — whereas it does not make sense to ask, "Where do you feel the pleasure you get from reading a good book?"

The opposite of pleasure₂ is pain. Pain is a sensation, experienced at a definite place; a pain in my tooth, an ache in my side, a stabbing sensation in my big toe. You can always sensibly ask, "Where (in what part of your body) do you feel the pain?" Sometimes, misleadingly, people use the term "pain" as the opposite of pleasure₁, as if pain were the same as displeasure instead of a usual *source* of displeasure. In this sense, the "pain" is not a sensation and thus not locatable, and it makes no sense to ask, "Where did you feel the pain you experienced at hearing the bad news?"

One great confusion of the traditional hedonists, such as Bentham and Mill, was to talk of pleasure and pain as if they were opposites. They failed to recognize the double sense of the word "pleasure" and thus tended to assume that the opposite of pleasure₁ (hearing a concert) is the sensation pain. The truth is rather that pain is a *cause* of pleasant or unpleasant states of consciousness (displeasure). For instance, pain-sensations ordinarily cause in people an unpleasant state of consciousness so that they do not wish its continuance — but not always, as with the masochist, who enjoys (derives pleasure₁ from) the infliction of pain. Pleasure-sensations ordinarily cause in people a pleasurable state of consciousness so that they wish its continuance — but not always, as when the prolonged continuance of pleasure-sensations causes us to desire their cessation or when someone we dread or dislike produces these sensations in us. It is probably because pleasure-sensations *usually* cause pleasurable states of consciousness that the two have been confused with one another. Some sensations, such as that of scratching an itch and tickling, can be both pleasurable and painful at the same time.

If pain were the opposite of pleasure₁, the masochist's situation would be, to say the least, puzzling: how could he take pleasure in the opposite of pleasure, pain? But in fact there is no puzzle at all; the infliction of pain on his body *causes* him (for reasons familiar to psychoanalysts) to experience pleasure₁, whereas such pain causes most persons displeasure. True, he does not want the pain for the pain's sake; he wants it for the sake of the pleasure₁ he derives from it. But the infliction of the pain is precisely what gives him the pleasure. To say that pain is pleasant sounds paradoxical; but the paradox disappears when we distinguish the double sense of "pleasure." Once we say that pain (painful sensations) sometimes causes pleasure (pleasant states of consciousness), there is no puzzle at all. Clearly, it is pleasure₁ that is of relevance to ethics, and it is pleasure₁ which people have (however dimly) in mind when they say that pleasure is intrinsically good.

What of the relation of pleasure to happiness? The word "pleasure" is associated in our culture with attitudes of disapproval, chiefly because of our Puritan background. Many people, when they hear the word "pleasure," think of something evil and sinful, especially in such phrases as "a life of pleasure"; but they do not react so when they think of a life of happiness. Heaven offers eternal happiness, but the devout would be shocked to think that happiness meant eternal pleasure. They disapprove of pleasure because "pleasure" has become identified with *sources* of pleasure₁, and only with some of these sources at that: not with such sources as good books, symphony concerts, and doing one's duty (all of which are undeniably sources of pleasure₁), but with such pleasant sensations as debauchery and drunken revelry (both of which also undeniably can be sources of pleasure₁). It does not seem strange in our society to speak of the pleasures of food and drink, but it seems stretching the word to speak of the pleasures of worshiping God; yet there seems to be no reason why the activity of worship should not cause just as much pleasure₁ as gluttony would. It is no wonder, then, that many people, confusing pleasure with sources of pleasure, and only with some of the sources at that, hold that pleasure is "sinful" and come to condemn hedonism as a "pig-philosophy."

It should be plain by this time that no such thing is intended by hedonists. Solving a mathematical problem, acquiring scientific knowledge, and helping one's fellow men, can be just as much sources of pleasure as the things that pigs do. But because of the traditional, unfavorable associations attaching to the word "pleasure," it has been suggested that a more neutral word, such as "satisfaction," should be used in preference to the loaded word "pleasure."

Even this substitution will not solve our present problem; for after we have presented "satisfaction" as a neutral synonym for "pleasure," we still want to know what is the relation of this state — by either name — to happiness.

What is happiness? It is popular to say, "Nobody knows. Your happiness

may lie in building bridges, mine in studying philosophy." But this statement contains a double confusion.

(1) In the first place, the second sentence is concerned not with what
happiness is but with how it can be acquired. Perhaps one person can acquire it in one way and another in another way, but knowing the method
of acquisition does not yet tell us what happiness is.

(2) In the second place, even if no one can give a definition of "happiness" (any more than of "pleasure"), it by no means follows that nobody
knows what it is. There are several senses of the word "definition." In the
broadest sense, to define a word is to indicate what we mean by the word;
we must be able to give the meaning of any word whatever, else it could
never be learned and thus could never become a part of a public language.
In a narrower sense of "definition" some words cannot be defined: they
cannot be defined in the sense of giving a set of words which, taken together, are synonymous with the original word so that every time the original
word appears in a sentence it could be replaced with the defining phrase
without any change of meaning. Probably no group of words can be
used in place of the word "happiness" (or the word "pleasure") in every
context of its occurrence in the way that the word for the unit of measure
"yard" can always be replaced by the phrase "three feet." To many people
this lack seems fatal: "Then how can you ever know what the word
means?" they ask. But these people identify one type of definition (which
semanticists call "definition by designation") with definition in general. It
may be that no combination of words we can devise will do just the job
that the word "happiness" does in our language — indeed, why should there
be for every word such a combination of other words? But this lack in no
way shows that we cannot know what people mean by the word "happiness"
—indeed, we obviously *have* learned to use the word and to attach some
meaning to it. We have learned, not by being given a bunch of words which
are together synonymous with "happiness" (parents do not teach children
the meaning of most words in this way), but by observing the situations and
contexts in which the word was used. When the child smiles and claps his
hands in anticipation of the candy, the parent says, "Now you're happy"
and so repeats the statement in countless other instances. Thus the child
recognizes a kind of state or experience to which the word can be applied
in common, and he comes to use the word himself, in spite of the fact that
he cannot describe the state of happiness in words (only, perhaps, the situations in life which produce it). Probably, he will never be able to do so.
He has learned the meaning of the term by "ostensive definition," not by
any kind of *verbal* definition.

If someone says, then, "Nobody knows what happiness is," one might
reply

. . . everyone knows what happiness is. For everyone knows in his own experience the difference between being happy and being unhappy. He knows

whether he is happy or not at this moment. He knows whether he is happy ór unhappy in his relations with his wife. He knows that in some periods of his life he was happier than in other periods. He knows that he is happy to-day, and was unhappy yesterday. And how can he have all this knowledge if he does not know what happiness is? [1]

Still, even though we are acquainted with countless instances of the word's application, we may want to know more precisely how it is distinguished from other words which are also used for labeling mental states. Though we cannot produce a set of substitute words, perhaps we can indicate with greater precision the area in which the term operates in our language. Let us try.

On one point almost everyone would be agreed: happiness is more of a long-term affair than is pleasure. You can feel pleasure one moment and not the next. This is true not only of pleasure$_2$ (you can have a pleasurable sensation one moment and not have it the next) but also, to almost the same degree, of pleasure$_1$ (you can feel pleasure when you hear the first item in the reading of the will but extreme displeasure when you hear the second item). Pleasant and unpleasant states of consciousness are extremely evanescent; one can pass from the one to the other (with varying degrees of both) hundreds of times a day. Still, it would seem strange to say that one alternated between happiness and unhappiness hundreds of times a day. One can judge that a person is experiencing pleasure$_1$ at a certain moment without yet being able to judge that he is happy; to determine a man's state of happiness one needs much more observation over a longer span of time. Some have thought that this span should cover a lifetime: Darius of Persia said, according to Herodotus, "Call no man happy until he is dead," for one can never be sure that some reversal of fortune will not change his state so abruptly that a man who was thought to be happy would have to be judged unhappy after all. But after he is dead is a poor time to call him happy; surely one can say, at least sometimes, that he was happy prior to his reversal of fortune and unhappy afterwards. One can say that he is happier this year than last year or that he is happier when at school than at work. What then, specifically, is the relation between happiness and pleasant states of consciousness?

a. According to one view, pleasures$_1$ may *lead* to happiness but do not, even when taken together, *constitute* happiness. A person may experience many pleasures and yet be unhappy, may experience few pleasures and yet be quite happy; pleasurable states, when they occur, may or may not bring happiness. Some sources of pleasure — perhaps the traditional, "lower" sources such as food and drink, and sex when divorced from affection and mutual esteem — produce pleasures which are intense but seldom lead to happiness; whereas other sources such as intellectual and aesthetic activity more often do produce pleasures that lead to happiness. Some pleasures are like copper coins — they are heavy but they add very little to one's

---

[1] From Walter T. Stace, *The Concept of Morals.* New York: Macmillan, 1937, p. 128. Reprinted by permission of the author.

wealth; whereas other pleasures are like gold coins — they are light and small and have great value.[1]

b. According to the other view, pleasures are not merely possible means to happiness; they are the *ingredients* of happiness. The more pleasurable states of consciousness a person experiences, the happier he is. The relation of pleasant states to happiness is that of parts to a whole. The whole is composed of the parts, and happiness consists of the aggregation of pleasant states. These pleasant states may, as we have already seen, be *caused* by many different things, depending on the type of person in question: by friendship, affection, sensual love, learning, problem-solving, creative activity. But whatever be their cause, the more pleasant states you have during the course of a year or a lifetime, the happier you are during that period. This, of course, is not the same thing as saying that the more pleasurable *sensations* you have during a year the happier you are. Pleasures$_1$ ordinarily result from pleasures$_2$, pleasurable sensations (though in the masochist, from painful sensations); but, as we have already seen, many pleasures$_1$ come from sources that are not sensations at all, like books and symphony concerts and telegrams containing good news. It is pleasures$_1$, not pleasures$_2$, that are the ingredients of happiness, though of course pleasures$_2$, by causing pleasures$_1$, may thereby sometimes contribute to happiness.

Of course, as Aristotle said, one swallow does not make a summer, and neither does one pleasure$_1$ constitute happiness. A person may enjoy books and not be happy, and he may have a pleasant sex life and not be happy; it is the conjunction of a large number of these pleasures$_1$ that constitutes happiness.

The second view of happiness seems to be definitely preferable to the first one, for the first one appears to be confusing (1) pleasure with pleasurable sensations and (2) pleasure with the "lower" sources of pleasure. It is true that pleasurable sensations are not ingredients of happiness; but if happiness is not composed of pleasures$_1$, of what *is* it composed? Once we bear in mind that art, knowledge, worship, and human affection may produce pleasures$_1$ just as much as (and in the long run, probably more than) food and drink and fame and fortune may, there seems to be no objection left to saying that happiness is composed of pleasures$_1$ and that the more such pleasures$_1$ a man experiences the happier he is. A person may have some pleasures$_1$ and yet be unhappy because happiness requires a combination of *many* pleasures$_1$ as its ingredients; but a person cannot have a few or no pleasures$_1$ and still be happy — though of course he may lack pleasures of a certain *kind* (such as sex) and still be happy.

C. Happiness as an intrinsic good

Assuming, now, that this analysis of happiness is acceptable, what of the contention that happiness is intrinsically good? Since happiness is composed

[1] *Ibid.*, pp. 155-59.

of pleasures₁, which the hedonist says are intrinsically good, there would seem to be no reason why the whole of these pleasures₁ should not be intrinsically good. If each part of the pie is delicious, presumably the whole pie will be delicious. Indeed, reasoning thus, many persons who are inclined to object to the view that pleasure is intrinsically good — perhaps through a confusion between intrinsic and instrumental good, perhaps through confusing pleasure₁ with pleasure₂, perhaps through confusing pleasure with certain sources of pleasure — would look more favorably upon the view that the whole pattern of pleasures which constitutes happiness is intrinsically good: they might say, for example, that a happy life is intrinsically good even though they might not agree that a certain pleasure₁ in it is intrinsically good.

But let us return to the controversy between the objector and the hedonist — the hedonist now understood in an extended sense which includes the whole pattern of pleasures, or happiness, as intrinsically good.

OBJECTOR: In general, I would agree that happiness is intrinsically good, but not always. Happiness is good when it is *deserved;* but what about undeserved happiness? Suppose that someone has committed a robbery or a murder, is never caught, has no qualms of conscience, and spends the money enjoyably during the ensuing years. Isn't this situation to be looked upon with extreme disfavor?

HEDONIST: Of course it is; the question is, whether the disfavor is on account of the intrinsic badness of the situation or its instrumental badness. I would say that the evil in that situation is instrumental. When people get away with robbery and murder, there are usually serious consequences for the happiness of the people involved (and usually for the agent himself). Moreover, people who have got away with one crime are likely to commit another, thus adding more unhappiness than happiness to the world's balance.

O: I agree that a criminal's escaping punishment is instrumentally bad; but I insist that in addition to this, such things are bad or evil in themselves — not because the situation of a man committing a crime and enjoying the spectacle of policemen vainly seeking the guilty party contains no happiness, for it does (the criminal's), but because the situation contains happiness *conjoined with evil,* and the conjunction of evil with happiness, or for that matter of good with unhappiness, is, I think, always intrinsically bad and morally repugnant to contemplate.

H: Bertrand Russell was once asked whether criminals should be sent to South Sea islands instead of suffering incarceration in prison, since they would just as effectively be sealed off from society in that way. He replied that this retribution would be quite all right, provided that they did not endanger the security of others (the South Sea islanders) and provided that the news of their going there never leaked out. If it did, there might well be a rash of crimes by people tired of civilized life and desirous of a free ticket to Tahiti. In other words, Russell's view was that there should be as much happiness as possible in the world and that *if* criminals could be happy in Tahiti without interfering with the Tahitians and without encouraging crime by their transmigration, this happiness would be all to the good — there would be just so much more happiness in the world without any compensating unhappiness. As an empirical fact, however, the news probably *would* leak out, thus triggering off a crime wave, and for this reason the scheme would not be feasible.

o: But Russell does not, I fear, recognize anything *intrinsically* evil about crime; he believes that the evil is only instrumental.

h: It is bad enough instrumentally without trying to make it intrinsic as well.

o: Here we go again. Let me try to make my point in a different way while we are arguing about whether happiness is *always* intrinsic good. I have cited an instance of undeserved happiness; let me now cite a somewhat different kind of situation — one in which the happy state itself is of an unusual kind, which we would not ordinarily consider good. In Mark Twain's *The Mysterious Stranger* an angel promises perfect and unalloyed happiness to an old man. He then fulfills his promise by making the old man insane. The old man, in an asylum, sees his friends and relatives who visit him, and he gives away (imaginary) dominions and principalities in sheer delight at doing what circumstances had always prevented him from doing before. He is completely happy doing just what he wants to do, with no worries in the world, no problems to face and solve. Yet wouldn't we view such a situation with horror? In fact we would probably say that the old man was better off sane and unhappy than now being insane and happy. Surely the happiness of insanity is not intrinsically good?

h: A very interesting example. Let me propose this first: let me say, for the moment, that the happiness of the insane old man *is* intrinsically better. Maybe for most people the world is so full of tensions, frustrations, and insoluble problems that only those who can escape from it into a dream world of fantasy (and only the insane man can make this escape) can be really happy. I mean this seriously; isn't it possible? I could go into quite a disquisition at this point on the state of modern man in a complex industrial society, surrounded by personal and international tensions which are bound to make him unhappy a considerable part of his life and even to drive him insane if he is a sensitive person who cannot help feeling that the real world is too much for him.

Considered *by itself,* then, apart from its consequences (which is what we do when we ask whether something is intrinsically good), perhaps the state of the insane man *is* better. But now consider the effects of his state on other people: the distress of the family and friends, the wrench it makes in the lives and happiness of those around him who can't communicate with him in the ways they have for years past. Isn't their unhappiness greater than his happiness? Then too, being insane, he can contribute nothing to the world's work, and he must still be given a share in the world's goods: he must be fed and clothed and waited on, and someone must do these things, someone whose energies might better have gone into more socially fruitful activities. Moreover, his happiness is parasitic: not everyone can enjoy it and have society still survive. If everyone were as deranged as he is, who would provide for him and wait on him and grow the crops that feed him? The happiness of the insane man rests, like the slave-dependent economy of ancient empires, upon the work and sweat of other people whose happiness (or a part thereof) must be sacrificed in order to make his possible.

o: But do you really think that apart from the effects on other people the insane man's happiness is intrinsically just as good as, or better than, the happiness of "normal" human beings?

h: Never having been insane, I cannot speak from personal experience about the state of consciousness of insane people. Perhaps in seeing the behavior of the insane, we are projecting — attributing to them states of happiness which we think we would feel if we were rid of the worries that he is rid of. Who knows? Anyway, as I have tried to show, however intrinsically good his state of consciousness is and however desirable it is considered by itself, there is reason to deplore it when we consider all the accompanying circumstances. Of two worlds, one containing only the happiness of an insane man and the other the happiness of a normal man, I would not know which to choose, being unable to compare the two. But of two worlds, one containing the happiness of the insane man and the *un*happiness of those around him and the other containing the possibly smaller degree of happiness of the normal man but *not* accompanied by the unhappiness of the others, there is no doubt that I would choose the latter. Even if the state of happiness-in-insanity is better than some unhappiness-in-normality, the state of happiness-in-insanity-of-one-plus-unhappiness-of-everyone-else is certainly worse.

o: I wonder how you would get around this one: let us suppose that I were offered as alternatives (1) thirty more years of life as happy as the happiest week I have ever experienced, on condition that I could enjoy only the unruffled and unconcerned happiness of an insane man or a pig or (lest you say that a pig isn't capable of happiness) of a human being on the lowest level, say a cave man, or (2) twenty-nine years of the happiness of a good and reasonably cultivated human being. Wouldn't it be better to choose the second alternative even though the total amount of happiness was *ex hypothesi* less and even if my choice neither increased nor decreased the happiness of others? (The fact that I might soon get bored by the life of a pig or a cave man and cease to enjoy it is irrelevant; I could be subjected to psychological treatment that would change my nature and make me totally content with it.) [1]

---

[1] From Alfred Ewing, *Ethics*. New York: Macmillan, 1953. Reprinted by permission of the publisher.

H: First, let me question whether the conditions of your hypothesis could be fulfilled. I doubt whether a person with the mentality of a pig or even a cave man could be as happy as we can be, for we have many avenues to happiness available to us which cave men do not have. The happiness that comes from knowledge, from mastery over nature and unlocking nature's secrets, from contemplating the ocean and the stars, from friendship and the devotion of other human beings, all or most of this happiness is unknown to the cave man. You can't play a beautiful composition on one octave of the scale. No doubt the cave man can be *contented,* more so than we, because most of the sources of *un*happiness we have are unknown to him: he has no neuroses, his problems are simple, his universe is painted in hues of black and white, he has no overwhelming anxieties, and he does not need to fear any political revolutions or thermonuclear bombs. But happy? "If you try to make yourself content with the happiness of a pig, your suppressed potentialities will make you miserable." [1]

O: But may not the absence of these unhappiness-making factors far outweigh the presence of the positive factors that make for happiness?

H: Possibly; well, then he *is* happier. But even so his life cannot be of much instrumental good. Creative people, happy or not, usually do more to improve the world than dolts and dullards, who simply live on the improvements that others have made. Even if the creators aren't happier themselves, they increase the happiness of others — and thus the total quantity of happiness in the world. But that statement conflicts with another condition in your hypothesis — that the happiness of the cultivated man in this case won't affect anyone else at all. I find this condition hard to conceive of and contrary to empirical fact. But *if* the happiness of the cave man were as complete as ours, *if* he could get as much happiness from his few sources of it as we from those same sources plus a hundred times as many more (and can you imagine that?), then the happiness of the cave man would be intrinsically just as good, month for month and year for year, as ours is. And *if* the happiness of the cultivated man didn't tend to increase the world's happiness, then the cave man's happiness would be instrumentally just as good. In these circumstances what reason would there be left to prefer the happiness of the cultivated man? Usually we value it more highly because we believe that it is (1) greater — richer and deeper — and also (2) better instrumentally for the well-being of others. But if these two conditions are removed, as they are in the extremely hypothetical case which you describe, then I see nothing left to prefer in the cultivated man's happiness; I would say that the thirty years of happiness of the one is better, by one year's experience of happiness, than the twenty-nine years of happiness of the other.

[1] From *Human Society in Ethics and Politics* by Bertrand Russell. Copyright © 1955 by Bertrand Russell. Reprinted by permission of Simon and Schuster, Inc. and Allen & Unwin, Ltd., p. 238.

o: There I disagree. The happiness of the cultivated man is intrinsically better than that of the cave man even though the happiness of the cave man is purer because he is not disturbed by the cultivated man's worries and anxieties.

h: But why? When you say that an unfruitful happiness is not as good intrinsically as a fruitful happiness, your assertion carries a *seeming* plausibility only because you still, in the back of your mind, haven't got rid of the *usual* condition, namely that the cultivated man's happiness is more fruitful; and it is *because* it is more fruitful that you consider it better, forgetting that by your own hypothesis in *this* instance it is *not* more fruitful. Once you are quite clear about this hypothesis, I can see no reason remaining why you should prefer the twenty-nine years of the one to the thirty years of the other.

(*The exercises and the reading list are at the end of the chapter.*)

8. Other possible intrinsic goods

o: Thus far I have contended that happiness (pleasure) is not always, or under all conditions, intrinsically good. But that is not my main objection to hedonism. My main point is one that I have not yet brought up: namely, that even if happiness *is* always intrinsically good, it is not the *only* thing that is. I would insist on a plurality of intrinsic goods. Can it really be true that nothing but pleasure (or happiness, if happiness is a sum of pleasures) is intrinsically good? If hedonism is true, it

> . . . involves our saying . . . that a world in which absolutely nothing but pleasure existed — no knowledge, no love, no enjoyment of beauty, no moral qualities — must yet be intrinsically better — better worth creating — provided only the total quantity of pleasure in it were the least bit greater, than one in which all these things existed *as well as* pleasure.[1]

You see, I can't escape the conviction that it's a mistake to say that nothing but pleasure or happiness is intrinsically good. There are so many things of great value in the world that it seems inconceivable to me to say that only one of them should be classified as worth having for its own sake.

h: Of course there are many good things in the world besides happiness. For example, freedom is good. But I deny that it is intrinsically good. A certain amount of political, economic, and religious freedom is necessary, I suppose, for any considerable amount of happiness to be possible. The happiness that comes from being able to travel where you please, think what you please, and exchange opinions with others without fear would not be possible in a police state. So I value freedom very highly — it is worth fighting

[1] G. E. Moore, *Ethics* (New York: Oxford Univ. Press, 1911), pp. 237-38.

for, even dying for. Nevertheless, its worth is not intrinsic. Its absence guarantees the impossibility of certain deep and lasting sources of human happiness, but its presence does not guarantee that anything worth having on its own (intrinsically good) will result.

It is the same with, say, the institution of marriage. Marriage is not intrinsically good, but it can sometimes bring about a great deal of happiness; if it does, it is an instrumental good. An unhappy marriage I do not consider good at all; the unhappiness it brings is in fact intrinsically bad. I can't think of a single exception to the principle that happiness and happiness alone has intrinsic worth.

A. Beauty

o: What about works of art and other objects of beauty? Don't they possess intrinsic worth?

h: No, only the appreciation of them does. If mountains and lakes and sunsets continued but with nobody around to enjoy them, what good would they be? It's true, of course, that the appreciation of art often involves displeasure, especially in the early stages — bewilderment, shock, and so on; but the displeasure may be instrumental to more enduring and positive appreciation later on.

o: Suppose that one person experiences satisfaction in the presence of an admittedly great work of art; and suppose that another person experiences an equal amount of satisfaction in the presence of a work that is a fraud, or a cheap imitation, or has no aesthetic value at all, say a calendar picture. Isn't the first appreciation intrinsically better than the second, even though there is an equal amount of satisfaction in the two situations?

h: The satisfaction in the cheap imitation probably will not last. One outstanding characteristic of great works of art — and one reason why they are called great — is that, however difficult they may be to appreciate at first, they provide more constant and enduring satisfaction over many years than do the cheap or trivial works.

o: But for some people, the cheap imitation may provide more complete and lasting satisfaction than a masterpiece can. Many people go through their lives enjoying the homely sentiments of Edgar Guest, whereas they get not one whit of satisfaction from Shakespeare.

h: Possibly; but this question is more tangled than one might think. It may be that the greatest art isn't the art that produces the most complete pleasure or satisfaction, even aesthetic satisfaction, or the most lasting satisfaction. Perhaps there are other criteria for great art than its pleasure-potential. Doubtless art has other functions as well, such as giving a vivid picture of life or developing psychological insight or social consciousness, and the fulfilling of these functions would make art instrumentally good in many other ways. At least not everyone would agree that the sole function of art is the production of pleasure, even aesthetic pleasure. Until that question is decided — and it is a question for aestheticians, not for us here — your reference to great art is rather confusing.

Whether or not art has other functions besides giving pleasure, those who champion the cause of art will quite certainly hold that great art gives more aesthetic satisfaction in the long run than calendar pictures or doggerel like Edgar Guest's. People may get pleasure from the fakes for a while, even for a long while, but when they do develop the taste for great art (Shakespeare, for example) — and of course many people never even try — they find in it so much that they consider worthwhile (not only pleasure but other things which are instrumentally good) that they would never go back to the trash that they enjoyed before.

o: That's possible. Maybe great art does produce more enjoyment in the long run. But this doesn't end our difficulties. Consider one and the same work of art, say Bach's *B Minor Mass*. Suppose one person hearing it is just "emoting" — he is using the tones he hears simply as a backdrop for his private reveries, as a springboard for an emotional debauch of his own; he is one of those people whose appreciation of music Santayana described as "a drowsy reverie interrupted by nervous thrills." Now consider a second person hearing the same work and gaining an equal pleasure from it; he is listening carefully to the music, admiring every new complication in the melody and its development, the harmonic structure, the counterpoint, and he follows with rapt attention the tonal intervals, the modulations, the interweaving of melodic elements. Surely the second person's appreciation is much more to be valued, even though the amount of pleasure in the two cases is *ex hypothesi* the same.

h: I think you have rather stacked the cards. The way you describe it, it seems pretty certain that the second person is enjoying it far more than the first. But even if he isn't — even if the first person is just getting as much satisfaction from his emotional debauch as the second is getting from his careful listening — there are, again, consequences in the two cases. The appreciation of the second will grow and grow, while the first person is not paving the way for any increased satisfactions. He is cheating himself by not getting the satisfaction that is to be had from *the music*. He is enjoying something *other* than the music, something which has very little to do with the music at all. Perhaps that is just as satisfying as the music, you say? Perhaps. But you see the second person is enjoying the music and presumably can *also* enjoy private reveries on occasion, whereas the first person can enjoy only his reveries and not the music. Besides, the first person probably *could* enjoy the music much more (again, in the long run) than he now enjoys the private reverie, if he but let himself develop the *listening* habit (as opposed to the hearing habit). He is cheating himself just like the person who eats bacon and eggs all his life when he could enjoy a great variety of foods if he only opened himself up to these further avenues of enjoyment.

o: I wouldn't put as much stock as you do in the enjoyment. Not that enjoyment is not good — but so, I contend, are other things as well. Let's try some.

B. Knowledge

. . . How about truth? Isn't that an intrinsic value?

H: Do you mean truth just by itself? Suppose it is true that there is a sunken treasure at the bottom of the sea, but nobody knows about it; what value is this true proposition as long as it is not known by anyone? Consider: how can anything be intrinsically good (or bad) which is not some state of consciousness or other? We just saw that beauty itself is not intrinsically good, but our appreciative enjoyment of it is; a world full of objects, however beautiful, which no one is there to enjoy would have no value whatever. So here: suppose there were all sorts of facts about the world which would offer enjoyment or happiness to sentient beings *if* they knew about them, but no one knew about them; their mere presence (without anyone to know them) would be of no value whatever. Surely it must be the *consciousness* of truth, in other words, *knowledge* rather than truth itself, which is intrinsically good. Knowledge of truth is a state of consciousness. It's what philosophers call a *dispositional* state; — for you can be said to know that two and two make four even when you're not thinking about it or in any way having it before your mind, but the proper stimulus can always bring it back again; it is there, ready to be recognized again (literally, re-cognized). I think, therefore, that you should say that it is knowledge of truth, and not truth per se, that is intrinsically worthwhile.

o: Very well, I accept your amendment. Let's say that it is knowledge that is intrinsically good. And I think it is. I don't value knowledge only for what it brings; I value it for itself. Scientific knowledge, for example, is valuable not only when it leads to more practical inventions conducive to our convenience and comfort (and ultimately, I hope, our happiness); it is valuable also just because it represents an addition to what we know about the universe we live in. We don't always acquire knowledge merely as an instrument; we acquire it also for the sheer joy of *having* it, whether we ever use it or not.

H: Aha — for the *joy* of having it. But then the knowledge *is*, after all, instrumental to happiness. Let us distinguish two things: first, there is knowledge that is *directly* instrumental to happiness, like going through a geometrical exercise just for the pleasure of doing it, not for any use to which we will put it — such knowledge is directly instrumental to the happiness of him who has it; second, there is knowledge that is *indirectly* instrumental to happiness, like acquiring the knowledge to build a bridge to facilitate transportation across a lake or river and thus indirectly contribute to happiness. Both kinds of knowledge are instrumental, but the one is so directly and the other indirectly.

o: I admit that when I acquire knowledge "for the sheer joy of having it" it is still instrumental to that joy. But suppose I say that knowledge is intrinsically valuable or desirable even when it doesn't lead to happiness at all. For example, knowledge of astronomy is of no practical use to me — I shall never use it professionally. It happens that I do enjoy having such knowledge — I feel that I have unlocked some more of nature's doors; I know more about the universe I live in, and I am happier for that knowledge. But suppose that astronomical knowledge didn't make me happier. Wouldn't it still be worth having? Even if knowledge of astronomy made me feel so insignificant, tiny, and dwarfed in comparison with the vast universe that it depressed me and rendered my already tottering ego even more insecure, wouldn't such knowledge still be worth having for its own sake — not for any practical utility, not even because it made me or others happier, but just because it *was* knowledge, the recognition of truth?

h: I must say I don't see how. It seems to me that knowledge is good (instrumentally) when it adds to the sum of human happiness and bad (instrumentally) when it tends to decrease that sum. It seems to me that the enormous advances in medical knowledge are good because they have lengthened life and enabled many people to enjoy happiness into an old age which otherwise they could never have had. It seems to me that the knowledge which led to the discovery of the hydrogen bomb was a bad thing (right now at least), because it is all too likely sooner or later to lead to the extermination of the human race or at least a considerable part of it (Of course I don't deny that if aggressor nations had the knowledge and we didn't, that knowledge would be, instrumentally, even worse.) The value of knowledge, then, I would say, is entirely instrumental. If I am asked whether a certain piece of knowledge is good or worthwhile, I must first discover whether on the whole it led to an increase of happiness. I cannot tell you whether it is good until I know for what it was an instrument.

o: I can't agree. There are instances in which I would value knowledge even if it did not lead to more happiness. If I have invested in the stock market and the stocks have fallen, I would be happier continuing to think that the stocks have gone up, but I still would rather know the bitter truth. Wouldn't you?

h: Of course, because I would find out later anyway. I would rather know the truth sooner than later in order that I might take action and sell before the stocks dropped still further.

o: Or if you were ill with an incurable disease, wouldn't you rather be told the complete truth quite openly than be lied to by the physicians and told that everything was all right? Yet the knowledge of this truth would surely not be the sort of thing that would increase your happiness.

h: I think too that I would rather be told; still I don't believe that this knowledge is of intrinsic worth. I would rather be told in order that I could make certain preparations for death in my own way. I would rather be told because I don't enjoy being deceived. I would rather be told because sooner or later, when I didn't improve, I would begin to suspect anyway that the physicians were lying to me, and this suspicion would cause me more anguish, discomfort, and suspense than if I had been told the truth in the first place. It's not that knowing this truth would be pleasant, but at least knowing would be less unpleasant in the long run than being lied to.

o: But if you didn't know that you were being lied to and didn't even suspect it, then you couldn't be unhappy from this suspicion. After all, you wouldn't want to know the truth under *all* circumstances, would you? When it's something you can change or do something about, that's different; but suppose it's something you can do nothing about. Would you like to know, right now, the date of your death, supposing that I could tell you with absolute certainty?

h: I think that I wouldn't because of a peculiar psychological fact: even if I knew, from your infallible prediction about the date, that my time would not be up for another seventy-five years — and this knowledge might be a relief if I had suspected that I wouldn't live long — I would still probably start counting the days. As the time drew closer, I would feel far more anxiety and dread than I would if I didn't know the exact date; I would react this way in spite of the fact that I *do* know, in general, that I shall die before another seventy-five years have passed. No, the exact date of one's own death is one of the comparatively few things that I think we are better off not knowing. But please note that this doesn't disprove my view; on the contrary, it provides another illustration of it. For I have contended all along that knowledge is good only when it tends to increase happiness or diminish unhappiness; I would not recommend knowledge of the exact date of my death because I wouldn't be able to do anything about it anyway, and by increasing dread and anxiety such knowledge would only mar the enjoyment of much of my life.

o: Surely you agree with Moore that a world in which people had both happiness *and* knowledge would be better than one in which they had happiness only, without knowledge.

h: Yes, but not intrinsically better. It is precisely because knowledge does usually lead to greater happiness in the long run that I think it is usually worth having. The example, you see, is misleading: we are asked to choose between happiness alone on the one hand and happiness plus knowledge on the other, and we are counted on, naturally, to prefer the second alternative. But please remember that knowledge itself does usually lead to more happiness, so the second world that Moore envisages *would* contain more happiness after all — the happiness that comes from knowledge.

o: It seems to me that knowledge doesn't lead to as much happiness as you think, and still, I would say, it is good and worth having. The Romantics often decried the value of knowledge: they thought that it only made us unhappy and depressed to be such minute atoms in an impersonal and indifferent universe. "The tree of knowledge is not that of life," said Byron, and maybe he was right. Consider, for example, what an exasperatingly difficult thing the study of philosophy is. For every student who gains a real comprehension of it, enough to give him a sense of mastery and the happiness that comes from having conquered a domain of knowledge, there are probably a score of students who try, who grapple with it, frustrated and bewildered and envious, but who cannot comprehend it. All told, I would venture that more unhappiness than happiness has been brought about by the study of philosophy. And yet, I would contend, it is a good thing that the students have what little knowledge of philosophy they do have. Knowledge, then, is good independent of how much happiness it brings in its train.

H: Well, I think you are a bit mistaken in your facts. First, even those who don't in any sense master the field often gain from it a feeling of awe and a thrill of "threading their nimble way along the edge of the incomprehensible" (Maugham); this feeling is a kind of happiness. Second, the study of philosophy may give such people a certain humility and may temper their natural arrogance and conceit; and these results are surely virtues — instrumental goods, to be sure, but goods all the same. But I would admit that *if* the study of philosophy did not produce these or other instrumental goods, then it would not be worthwhile. Just as the Sabbath was made for man and not man for the Sabbath, so philosophy is there for study by man and not man for the study of philosophy. There are plenty of people to whom I would not recommend the study of philosophy — those who would never enjoy it anyway (intrinsic good) and those who would never develop certain desirable habits of mind and traits of character from that study (instrumental good).

O: Well, let's not get bogged down in disagreement over empirical facts. You would hold, at any rate, and I would not, that *if* the study of philosophy did not in the final analysis increase man's happiness, then it should not be studied. But what about those people who don't understand philosophy at all yet think they do and in that false belief are happy? This point bothers me. What if a delusion (false belief) brings happiness? Should it then be encouraged? I would say that it shouldn't, no matter how much happiness it may bring; a false belief is bad even when it makes people happy. But you, as a hedonist, are committed to saying that false beliefs should be encouraged when they are conducive to happiness.

H: True — *if* they lead to happiness; but in the long run they usually don't. Take your example of the stock market. If you tell me the bad news at once, I am unhappy; but if you wait and I find out later, it's even worse. When we know the truth, at least we may be in a position to act accordingly; even when we cannot act, there is a certain satisfaction just in knowing how things really are — at least, more satisfaction, usually, than in not knowing. Usually, when we act on the basis of falsehoods — not knowing that they are falsehoods — these falsehoods will trip us up and cause us more unhappiness in the long run than we would have had if they had been exposed in the first place. There are exceptional situations, of course, in which it *would be better not to have the knowledge.* Let me give you a few examples.

(1) Let us suppose that a child is exceptionally intelligent but that if he is told so, he will become arrogant and conceited. Surely it is better not to tell him or at least wait until later years after he has developed self-discipline and a certain humility and the knowledge will not spoil him. (Of course, the other side of this coin is that if he isn't given any encouragement as a child and is made to think he is mediocre, he may become discouraged and not even develop the capacities that he has.)

(2) A person may say, with justification, "I worked and worked on this research project, never knowing that somebody else was working on the very same problem and would publish his results before I could publish mine. But I'm glad I didn't know, and I'm glad that those who did know didn't tell me; for if I had known, I wouldn't have had the stamina to complete the project myself, and I'm still glad I did finish because I developed a mastery of the technique through that work and am now ready for other projects in a way I wasn't before." (Of course, if the person had been told in time, he might have switched to another project and been the first to complete that one. In that case it would have been better had he been told. It is so hard to tell in advance.)

(3) An insecure and mediocre person comes to live on the basis of certain rationalizations and unconscious defenses which give him a tolerable degree of happiness. If these defenses were exposed, he would be utterly miserable. (Of course, if someone by exposing them could cause him to reject them in favor of something better, as a trained psychiatrist might, then it would be better if they were exposed, even if this exposure made him temporarily miserable. But if he is an aged person who is not able to change his personality structure anyway, it is better to leave him with his inner defenses and not tell him what everyone else already knows.)

o: Those are all interesting examples, but I wonder what you would do about others. Imagine a man who is very happy in the belief that his wife loves him but whose belief is, in fact, false. Isn't it better that he be left with his false belief, which gives him comfort?

h: Perhaps, but not probably. If she doesn't love him, she may one day run off with another man and his life will be wrecked; whereas if he had known in time, he would have been spared that agony — he might even have been able to correct some of his own personality traits so as to make himself more lovable.

o: But my point is this: Imagine one man who is happy in the true belief that his wife loves him; then imagine a second man who is equally happy in the false belief that his wife loves him. (He doesn't know that the belief is false, of course, or presumably he wouldn't believe it.) Surely the first situation is intrinsically better, contains more intrinsic good, than the second *in spite of* the fact that the first does *not* contain more happiness. So there must be something intrinsically good besides happiness to account for this difference. In this situation the difference is, I think, that the first man's belief is true and the second man's is false. The second man can't be said to have knowledge, for knowledge implies, as one of its defining characteristics, that the statement known must be true, and *ex hypothesi* the statement the second man believes isn't true. The belief of the second man is *misdirected,* whereas that of the first man is not. Therefore the first situation contains more intrinsic good than the second.

H: Your example is clever. But again I must say I think you are confusing intrinsic with instrumental good. As far as the satisfactions themselves are concerned, if both are equal, then I would say that both *are* equally intrinsically good. But of course the false belief contains, as false beliefs usually do, a vast potential for unhappiness — the chagrin of having been duped, the mutual recriminations when the truth is discovered, the distrust and suspicion and cynicism about human nature from then on. The two experiences of happiness per se have an equal intrinsic good, but the one (believing the truth) is conducive to more intrinsic good later whereas the other (believing a falsehood) is conducive to much that is intrinsically bad.

o: But don't you agree that a *smaller* happiness derived from a true belief is preferable to a *greater* satisfaction derived from a false belief?

H: By itself, no; but if the total consequences are considered, yes, for the consequences of true belief will contain far more happiness than those of false belief. The consequences of false belief are, as a rule, extremely unpleasant to everyone concerned, even though at the time the false belief may be consoling. Believing a falsehood is almost always short-sighted as far as its potential for happiness is concerned.

o: What of false beliefs whose falsity is never discovered? Of course, you will say, one never knows that the falsity *won't* be discovered. But what if the belief is the kind whose falsity could never be discovered? Consider, for example, a man who is resting secure and happy in the belief that Allah is in His heaven and all's right with the world and that after a disappointing life in this vale of tears, he will have Allah's heavenly rewards when he dies. Now suppose for a moment (let's not argue it here) that this belief about Allah is false. If it is, our man will never know the difference; when he dies thinking of the glory beyond, he will never wake up again to find out that he has been duped. Isn't this satisfaction *worse* than the satisfaction he might get from a belief which is true, even though the satisfaction from the true belief is less, or even nonexistent?

H: You are ingenious. You have taken a really unique case — perhaps the only clear case of a belief which, if it is false, will never be discovered to be so. Perhaps, if you consider the man only, what you say may be true: he has more happiness going on believing what isn't so than he would have disbelieving or questioning lifelong assumptions. (Even here, he *may* not be so: there are plenty of people who are strong enough to derive the most happiness in the long run out of knowing the truth, however unpleasant the truth may be to face at first; and the experience of facing one bitter truth will equip them to face others.) So, to take the circumstances most favorable to you, suppose our man is old and set in his ways and can't be expected to question or probe or look for evidence for his beliefs. I don't think I'd try to change them, not, that is, if I consider him and his happiness alone.

But consider the effect on other people of seeing one man living on the basis of what they know or believe to be comforting delusions. His false belief will tend to make *them* suspicious of whatever sources of happiness they themselves have; they will tend to feel that happiness comes too often from "being had," and they will suspect beliefs of their own even if they have no reason to. Or the effect may be just the opposite; if a person finds happiness in a false belief which will never be discovered to be false, his example may reinforce the tendency of others to find happiness in beliefs which *will* be discovered to be false. The moment this habit is developed — the habit of believing things because they are consoling, not because there is any evidence that they are true — the consequences will be most unfortunate for the person himself and for all those affected by his behavior. I maintain, therefore, that the satisfaction gained from a false belief is intrinsically as good as the satisfaction gained from a true one, but instrumentally, the false belief is only a booby trap.

o: I am quite willing to grant that the satisfaction obtained from a false belief is instrumentally bad. But I am sure that that isn't the end of the story: the pleasure of believing something false is, in addition to its being harmful (instrumentally bad), *intrinsically* bad. Consider our two worlds again: in World A there is nothing but one person getting satisfaction from a true belief, and in World B there is nothing but one person getting satisfaction from a false belief. I think that World A is better, more worth creating, than World B.

h: No, there is nothing to choose between the two worlds, if you include in them *only* what you have specified. If you include the usual harmful *results* of false beliefs, then I agree with you — but then we are including more in the content of the two worlds than you just did in framing your hypothesis. You are still, in the back of your mind, thinking of the usual harmful *potential* that false beliefs possess.

o: We are at loggerheads again. Holding, as I do, that happiness and knowledge are both intrinsic values, I maintain that the ideal situation would be for a proposition *both* to be known to be true *and* to produce happiness. My evaluation is based on two criteria, yours on only one. You are committed to saying that if a piece of knowledge does not produce happiness, it is not intrinsically good; I am not. Of course, if the knowledge produces *great* unhappiness, then this intrinsic evil measured by the criterion of happiness more than counterbalances its intrinsic good measured by the criterion of knowledge. But if the knowledge causes no happiness at all or even a *small* surplus of unhappiness over happiness, it may still be intrinsically worth having, not because it produces happiness (for it doesn't) but because it is knowledge.

h: I can't see an iota of reason for saying such a thing. If I can account for the facts by one criterion (happiness), it is simply superfluous to bring in a second criterion as well, which is what you are doing.

o: I don't think my second criterion is superfluous because I believe that knowledge, in addition to contributing to happiness, also has value simply as knowledge. Its value as knowledge is not to be gauged entirely by its capacity to produce happiness. A world that contains much knowledge is intrinsically better than one that contains little, even if the happiness in the two worlds is the same.

C. Moral qualities

h: I hold that knowledge is entirely instrumental. Aristotle was right: happiness alone is the aim of human endeavor — or, in the language of this discussion, intrinsically good. Moral virtue is also, I think, entirely instrumental. Kindness, honesty, benevolence, fairness, loyalty, courage, generosity, fidelity, conscientiousness — these are qualities we tend to admire; but their goodness is entirely instrumental. If people are kind, they usually bring more happiness into the world than if they are cruel; therefore, kindness is usually instrumentally better than cruelty, but only because of what kindness brings about, not because of what it is in itself. If the world were different, these virtues would not be needed. This is the point of Aristotle's remark that the gods have no need of virtues. Are the gods honest in their dealings with one another? They have no financial or business dealings with one another, so what need is there of honesty? Are they beneficent? There are no poor in paradise to be recipients of their beneficence. Are they courageous? What use is courage to them, seeing that there are no evils to fight, no causes in which they are required to do battle and exercise courage? Virtue presupposes an evil world in which the virtues are exercised; in paradise these virtues would be useless. Can there be any better proof that the virtues are, one and all, instrumental rather than intrinsic goods?

o: I agree that they are instrumentally good, but that doesn't prove that they aren't *also* intrinsically good. For example, consider loyalty. There is, I think, something intrinsically good about it, something worth having for its own sake. The spectacle of someone who is loyal, even against great temptations and at great sacrifice to himself, is somehow admirable — admirable in itself, not for its effects.

h: You think that the loyalty of fanatical Nazis to Hitler was a good thing? Remember that if it hadn't been for them, millions of people would not have died in battle and others by slow torture in concentration camps.

o: No, I agree that it would have been better if fewer people had been loyal to Hitler, instrumentally better, that is. In this example, loyalty is intrinsically good, but the enormous instrumental evil resulting from the loyalty far outweighs the intrinsic good it possesses. But if loyalty produced nothing — no good and no evil — it would still be intrinsically good, the exercise of a valuable moral quality.

h: What's so good about loyalty? It is the first thing that dictators and tyrants set out to create in their subjects. They distort the facts, suppress free opinion, and try to make everyone passionately loyal to them. I must say I fail to see anything particularly good about loyalty in such circumstances. Loyalty to a good cause is good, instrumentally; and loyalty to a bad cause is bad, instrumentally. It's as simple as that. I suggest that if you are tempted to think of loyalty, even to a bad cause, as intrinsically good, you should consider that you may be valuing this loyalty not intrinsically but as a capacity to produce more intrinsic good: to have the ability to be loyal, even to a bad cause, may be better than to be completely wishy-washy and have no such ability at all because loyalty already exercised in a bad or indifferent cause *may* subsequently be used in a good cause, whereas if there is no loyalty at all, it cannot be used for good. This argument, as well as my earlier ones, makes loyalty an instrumental good.

o: Once again, instrumental to happiness. Everything is instrumental to happiness with you. You are the product of a bourgeois society which has lost the pioneer virtues. Everything for happiness — and the moral qualities on which our society has been built, qualities such as industry, iron self-discipline, and other pioneer virtues, are, in your view, only instruments. Let me quote from Thomas Carlyle (1795-1881):

All work, even cotton-spinning, is noble; work alone is noble; be that here said and asserted once more. . . .

"Happy," my brother? First of all, what difference is it whether thou art happy or not? Today becomes Yesterday so fast, all Tomorrows become Yesterdays; and then there is no question whatever of the "happiness," but quite another question. Nay, thou hast such a sacred pity left at least for thyself, thy very pains, once gone over into Yesterday, become joys to thee. Besides thou knowest not what heavenly blessedness and indispensable sanitive virtue was in them; thou shalt only know it after many days, when thou art wiser! . . .

Truly, I think the man who goes about pothering and uproaring for his "happiness," — pothering, and were it ballot-boxing, poem-making, or in what way so ever fussing and exerting himself, — he is not the man that will help us to "get our knaves and dastards arrested"! No; he rather is only the way to increase the number, — by at least one unit and his tail! Observe, too, that this is all a modern affair; belongs not to the old heroic times, but to these dastard new times. "Happiness our being's end and aim," all that very paltry speculation is at bottom, if we will count well, not yet two centuries old in the world.

The only happiness a brave man ever troubled himself with asking much about was happiness enough to get his work done. Not "I can't eat!" but "I can't work!" that was the burden of all wise complaining among men. It is, after all, the one unhappiness of a man. That he cannot work; that he cannot get his destiny as a man fulfilled. Behold, the day is passing swiftly over, our life is passing swiftly over; and the night cometh, wherein no man can work. The night once come, our happiness, our unhappiness, — it is all abolished; vanished, clean gone; a thing that has been: "not of the slightest consequence" whether we were happy as eupeptic Curtis, as the fattest pig of Epicurus, or unhappy as Job with potsherds, as musical Byron with Giaours and sensibilities of the heart; as the unmusical Meat jack with hard labour and rust! But our work, — behold that it is not abolished, that has not vanished; our work, behold, it remains, or the want of it remains; — for endless Times and Eternities, remains; and that is now the sole question with us for evermore! . . . What has thou done, and how? Happiness, unhappiness: all that was but the *wages* thou hadst; thou hast spent all that, in sustaining thyself hitherward; not a coin of it remains with thee, it is all spent, eaten: and now thy work, where is thy work? Swift, out with it; let us see thy work! [1]

You see, Carlyle believes that work is intrinsically good, and whether or not the doing of it produces happiness is of no consequence — people who aren't already morally soft don't think of happiness, only of getting their work done.

H: Work is very necessary, and the products of one's labor may outlast one's life — true; and an idle hand is the devil's workshop — also true. But isn't the point obvious? Surely the work must be *for* something. Even digging ditches in order to fill them up again may have some value in disciplining the soul and hardening the muscles — but its worth is still instrumental. Sometimes work may be instrumentally bad: an old man, tired and diseased, who still has to work fifteen hours a day to avoid starvation, has already had more work in his lifetime than he should have; he should be entitled to spend the rest of his days in relaxation and peace. Even when work is good, it is so only instrumentally: for receiving an income, for disciplining the character, for preventing the idleness that may cause mischief. Why make a fetish out of work and say that it is intrinsically good?

o: I rather thought you'd say that. I suspect that Carlyle's position can be better conveyed by saying that not work but a certain *nobility* of character that arises only from work well done, is intrinsically good. His argument, I think, is that once people start thinking only of their happiness and not of the things that require doing in the world, they are already a civilization gone soft, like the late Roman civilization and our present one. We are a generation of happiness-seekers, and when we seek only our happiness we are in great danger: we have lost the heroic virtues of the pioneer, who always prepared to fight against danger and extinction. Carlyle feared (and

[1] Thomas Carlyle, *Past and Present* (New York: Oxford Univ. Press, 1909), Bk. 3, Ch. 4, pp. 160-62.

his fears are more justified today than they were when he wrote a hundred years ago) that when people who think only of happiness and not of what must be done to preserve society and continue progress are challenged by another nation or coalition of nations that is not happiness-seeking but rigidly self-disciplined and imbued with these pioneer virtues, the happiness-seekers will be defeated.

H: Most of what you say is probably quite true. I don't think I would disagree with Carlyle on this point, though Carlyle thought he disagreed with my view because he was guilty of several confusions:

First, you speak of people seeking their happiness and you call them egoistic. Hedonism need not be egoistic. Seeking happiness needn't mean seeking just your *own* happiness; it may mean seeking the *general* happiness. There is nothing either selfish or defeatist or soft in people seeking the happiness *of other people*. Nations survive, rather than face extinction, by doing that.

Second, no hedonist says that he should seek only happiness. We should seek many things — knowledge, virtue, anything which will in the long run lead to an increase of happiness.

Third, the hedonist does not recommend that people should go about consciously *seeking* happiness. It is one thing to say that happiness is intrinsically good; it is another to say that we should go about looking for it all the time. Looking for happiness is, as it happens, not the best way to find it. This is the so-called hedonistic paradox — happiness to be got must be forgot — only the paradox isn't really a paradox. There are some things that are best got by forgetting about them; remember Maeterlinck's bluebird of happiness that turns black when it is touched. *How* happiness can best be achieved is an empirical matter, and apparently it is not achieved by being pursued. If you go about your daily work, if you don't think about yourself or your happiness but lose yourself in some object or interest outside of yourself, one day you will wake up and realize that you are quite happy — far happier than the frantic happiness-seekers who have to be out on the town every night.

But fourth and most important: I agree in many ways that Carlyle is right about the heroic virtues and that something invaluable is lost when these are gone, especially when our way of life is challenged. But here is the usual confusion between intrinsic and instrumental. After all, *why* do certain things, such as work, have to be done in the world? Certainly there is some purpose in doing them, and I think that this purpose is the increase (either immediate or eventual, depending on the case) of happiness. We are sometimes called upon to be self-sacrificing, to experience pain and misery, even to face death — as in fighting the Nazis in World War II — not because these acts are intrinsically good but because, in these circumstances, *only by performing them can we survive to have any happiness in the future.* Self-sacrifice is not intrinsically good but only a necessary means (sometimes) to good. Self-sacrifice involves much that is intrinsically bad — unhappiness, that is — but it is necessary in order that future happiness will be possible. There are times in the world's history when civilization hangs in the balance; if people are not supremely self-sacrificing, which requires being spiritually prepared for such an ordeal, there won't be any civilization left to enjoy. They must submit to a Spartan regimen to insure their survival. But their self-sacrifice doesn't mean that living like Spartans is good in itself; self-sacrifice and courage are never intrinsically good but are sometimes required as instruments. If they led to no intrinsic good, they would be pointless.

o: Still, I can imagine a happy (or relatively happy) state of society in which I, nevertheless, wouldn't want to live. Imagine the world united into one huge nation in which there are no differences of opinion and hence no conflict — everyone is living in a state from which all political opposition has been extinguished. Because the purges and brainwashings are not widely known about, they cause little public discomfort; only a handful of intellectuals oppose the new regime, and they are quietly and painlessly put to death. Brainwashing tactics, also painless, are used to push the remaining dubious citizens into line so that they no longer oppose the ruling government. Some intellectual pursuits can still be cultivated, principally mathematics and physical science, for the regime needs these. But politically and economically all have been conditioned to think the same way. In this conviction they live in relative peace and quiescence — in fact the younger generation has never known anything else. As far as they are concerned, in matters intellectual, ignorance is bliss. Nobody thinks of revolting against the government because nobody is left who disagrees with the government on any important matter. After a while torture and brainwashing and executions are no longer required because there is no longer any opposition to liquidate. Even science hasn't a destructive aspect any more, for there is no longer any other power strong enough to make war against the state, and nuclear weapons have long since been dispensed with. Since this situation contains a considerable surplus of happiness over unhappiness, you, as a hedonist, ought to think it quite desirable. Do you? For my part, I consider such a world too ghastly to contemplate.

H: So do I — in most ways. The loss of freedom, even in one sector, I consider as horrible as you do. The lack of variety of interests and of the freedom to pursue them — this is horrible also. Freedom is needed to make the world interesting and to bring about the fullest possible happiness of the mind, even if the younger generation do not recognize this truth because they have never tasted the heady wine of freedom. Again, they are like people who think that all musical compositions must be confined to one octave in the scale and who therefore cannot conceive of what musical compositions transcending these limits are like.

I could say many other unpleasant things about the hypothetical state which you describe. But the point here is this: your example doesn't convince me that other things besides happiness are intrinsically good. Your description of a relatively happy world is, in some respects, convincing, even though I claim that it is worse than our present, partially happy one. But is your world really happy, as happy as it could be under other conditions? In the world as we know it, a small infringement upon man's freedom results in an enormous diminution of happiness. The freedom of the speculative mind, ranging over whatever it chooses without fear and without stint, is one of the greatest sources of happiness possible to man; to squelch that freedom is to squelch one of the most abiding sources of intrinsic good. So I suspect that in describing your world as happy and yet lacking in freedom, you are going contrary to the empirical facts of human nature. I agree that *if* more happiness were possible in such a world, it *would* be better; but what follows your "if" is what I doubt.

o: I, for my part, can well conceive that such a world might be a happier one than ours, and yet far worse — which shows me clearly that the intrinsic goodness in such a world is not merely a function of its degree of happiness.

But let us take leave of hypothetical worlds — at least, thank God, they are hypothetical at the present moment — and return to the present. I want to call your attention to one particular virtue, namely that of *conscientiousness,* of acting strictly from motives of duty. A man behaves conscientiously when he does something because he is convinced that it is his duty to act thus. I, along with many others, find conscientiousness to be an intrinsic good. There is something worthy or admirable — intrinsically, not just for its results — in the spectacle of a man behaving strictly from a sense of duty, especially at great personal sacrifice: "Here I stand, I can do no other"; even if we may happen to disapprove of what he does, we still, I think, must admire him for so steadfastly and uncompromisingly doing his duty as he sees it.

h: Suppose your man is a conscientious Nazi or a conscientious killer of everyone who disagrees with him. The participants in religious wars were probably very conscientious, and so are many of the participants in political wars. Would that they were less so!

o: I agree of course that conscientiousness, like loyalty, can be employed in a bad cause and thus can be instrumentally bad. But still, it is also, I contend, intrinsically good. Let me take a kind of example hardest to reconcile with my view: consider a member of a religious sect who refuses to permit his child to have blood transfusions which are needed to save his life. We may believe that the man is quite wrong in refusing to permit the transfusions; but still, surely, we must admire him for doing his duty as he sincerely sees it, without flinching or swerving, when it is agonizing to see his own beloved child die as a result.

h: Poppycock. I wouldn't admire such a man at all. He is probably just being pig-headed and prefers to sacrifice his own child's life rather than to reconsider his moral principles. I would not place such a premium on stubbornness.

o: If he is merely being stubborn and pig-headed, I agree with you. But this may not be true at all. He has searched his conscience, and he is fully aware of the consequences — that the child will die and that he will be unhappy for the rest of his life; but yet, he is convinced, it is his sacred duty not to violate God's will, and God (he is convinced) requires this sacrifice of him.

H: If he feels that way, again I doubt whether his act is intrinsically admirable. He does it to achieve salvation, for he is convinced that he will not achieve it if he disobeys God's will by permitting the transfusion. Thus, to attain his own personal salvation, he is willing to sacrifice his child's life. Nice bargain! And this, you are saying, is admirable?

o: His motive may be selfish as you describe, but it may not be. Remember that he would just as unhesitatingly die himself, if he were the one who needed the transfusions to save his own life. And let's suppose that if he could save his child's life by sacrificing his own, he would gladly do it; indeed, he would much rather that that sacrifice were required of him. But it is his child who is ill, and so it is his child concerning whom he must make the decision.

H: That may be true, but it still looks suspiciously as if he is allowing the child to die in order to achieve salvation for himself, or perhaps for his child as well as for himself. Acting from this motive is acting to win a reward, not acting out of pure conscientiousness.

o: Maybe, but you can't be sure. If the man acts to receive a reward, he certainly isn't acting out of conscientiousness. But perhaps he acts to be obedient to the will of his Creator and would so act even if he were getting no reward at all but only lifelong sorrow.

H: Who knows what his motives really are? He himself probably does not know. But my point is this: even if his act *is* thoroughly conscientious, that doesn't make conscientiousness intrinsically good. Conscientiousness, I hold, is good only instrumentally; when it does not serve an end that brings about intrinsic good (as in this example), then it is not good at all but something to be condemned and regretted, something for which one should weep in shame instead of something which one should praise as intrinsically good.

We must leave the controversy at this point for the present. The problem about conscientiousness will arise again in Chapter 6, and other candidates for the position of intrinsic good will be introduced in Chapters 8 and 9.

Having surveyed various arguments on the issue of intrinsic good, we are finally in a position to consider some views on *human conduct*. We shall now go on to consider the concept of moral obligation (duty, right action). Assuming that X or Y is intrinsically good, what should we do about it?

What should be the influence of this fact upon our actions? In Chapter 4 we shall examine the view known as ethical egoism on this question — roughly, the view that in pursuing intrinsic good we should consider only ourselves; and in Chapters 5, 6, and 7 we shall consider nonegoistic views.

EXERCISES

1. How would you interpret Nietzsche's ethical views, which were considered in the previous chapter, in terms of the distinction between intrinsic and instrumental good? What do you think he considered desirable for its own sake, and what did he consider desirable only instrumentally?

2. How would you attempt to weigh one pleasure against another? (See R. Brandt, *Ethical Theory*, pp. 318-29.)

3. In case of a plurality of intrinsic goods, how would you weigh one of them (such as pleasure) against another (such as knowledge)? (*Ibid.*, pp. 346-52.)

4. Comment on each of the following positions. Do they incline you to be a hedonist or a pluralist with respect to intrinsic good? Why?

a. "Even if it were possible to make all men happy by an operation or a drug that would stultify their development, this would somehow be an impious crime." (Walter Kaufmann, "The Faith of a Heretic," *Harper's Magazine*, Vol. 218, No. 1305 [February, 1959], p. 39.)

b. "Is it at all necessary that a person should be of any value to the world? The justification for living is that you are alive and do not want to die. If one cannot justify life in that way, then it cannot be justified. It would be very dangerous to be able to declare that a man could be executed because he was of no value to the world. If a trial of this sort should be fairly decided, most of the class who advocate such ideas would be found wanting, and therefore guilty." (Clarence Darrow, *The Story of My Life* [New York: Grosset & Dunlap (Universal Library), 1957], p. 240.)

c. Read the chapter "The Grand Inquisitor" (if you have not already read it) in Dostoevski's *The Brothers Karamazov* (many editions). Then consider the following: "Maybe the Inquisitor is right in saying that people are happier just being told what to do rather than exercising their freedom of decision, which is painful and often dangerous. Perhaps more good *is* achieved in the world — human nature being what it is — by the scheme which the Inquisitor favors. Are you quite sure that the happiness resulting from this scheme isn't greater than that resulting from freedom as Christ suggests? Are you sure, in fact, that the happiness doesn't outweigh the good of the free use of the intellect?" "No, such happiness is greater unless the free use of the intellect is considered *intrinsically* good. Therefore, since I favor Christ's plan in preference to the Inquisitor's, I must say that the free play of the intelligence is an intrinsic good."

d. "It's too bad — he knows every ancient language there is to know, he is a trained Egyptologist, and he spends all day every day in the library to increase his knowledge. Yet he is psychologically unable to assume any responsibility, and his personality is such that he cannot impart any of his tremendous knowledge to others. So it's quite useless. He might as well not have it at all." "I don't agree.

Surely it's a good thing just that he *has* the knowledge, even though he can't transmit it to others. If knowledge weren't intrinsically valuable, why have it in the first place? If it's not worthwhile for him to have the knowledge (and I hold that it is), why should it be worthwhile for him to transmit it to others?"

e. "If you save someone's life, you do it because you assume that a life lost means the loss of that much happiness to the world." "Not so. You mean I shouldn't save a life if I had good reason to believe that the person would not be happy in the coming years? No, I should save it if I can, regardless of my expectations about his happiness." "You mean that if you had excellent reasons for believing that by saving him you would cause more unhappiness than happiness, you should still save him?" "Of course. I consider not whether he will probably be happy but whether I can save his *life*. I believe that life itself, and not just happiness, is intrinsically good."

f. Bereaved parent: "Yes, he took all those trips abroad, and he had such a good time. Now, less than a year later, he's dead, and it's all over — what was the good of it?" "Well, at least he enjoyed himself. What if he had worked hard for years in order to prepare himself for his profession and then had died? If that had happened you would have a right to say, 'What was the good of it?' "

g. Philosophers perform their chosen work not to bring themselves happiness, not even to bring others happiness, but to clarify each matter they discuss in their own minds and in the minds of those whom they teach and to arrive at the truth as far as in them lies, be that truth pleasant or unpleasant to those who learn. If philosophers thought that people, including themselves, would be less happy for having achieved truth or clarity, this consideration would probably not deter them.

5. What possible implications for your view of intrinsic good have the following situations, in which (it would usually be thought) knowledge is not desirable. Is the knowledge intrinsically or instrumentally undesirable?

a. The natives are dubious about being vaccinated. If they are told that the vaccine contains blood of the gods, they will consent. If they are told that the vaccine is taken from the blood of horses and cattle, they will not consent, and they will die.

b. "I'm glad I didn't know that Aunt Sarah was so ill; for had I known, I wouldn't have enjoyed my vacation, and there was not a thing I could have done about it anyway — I would only have worried. And I'm glad Mother didn't tell me that Father was as ill as he was while I was taking final exams, for I wouldn't have done as well on my exams had I known."

6. The Puritan is famous for his condemnation of pleasure. Do you think he holds that pleasure is intrinsically bad, or only instrumentally bad? Explain.

7. It is sometimes said that knowledge is intrinsically good. Do you think any of the following formulations would be preferable? Why?

a. The *possession* of knowledge is intrinsically good.

b. The *exercise* of knowledge is intrinsically good.

c. The possession or exercise of knowledge by me is intrinsically good but not the possession or exercise of it by others.

d. Not even the exercise of knowledge is intrinsically good, but the *enjoyment* of acquiring it and possessing it is.

8. Comment on the following suggestions. What bearing have they on the question of what is intrinsically good?

a. "If something is true, it should be told to people regardless of whether it's going to increase their happiness, even in the long run."

b. "People usually want to know the truth, even if it hurts, because they don't like to be duped or even to be left in the dark. Of course if they don't know they're being duped, then it's all right."

c. A few astronomers discover that an opaque star is hurtling toward the solar system and will strike the earth in four days' time, shattering it to bits. There is nothing that anyone can do about it. Should they broadcast the information or not? Why? If you assume that the people have been told of the impending disaster, which laws should they still be required to observe and which not? Why?

READING LIST, SECTIONS 7 AND 8

Aristotle. *Nichomachean Ethics*. Many editions, Bk. 10.

Baylis, Charles A. *Ethics; the Principles of Wise Choice*. New York: Holt, 1958, Ch. 8.

Blake, Ralph M. "Why Not Hedonism?" *Ethics*, Vol. 37 (1926), pp. 1-18.

Brandt, Richard. *Ethical Theory*. Englewood Cliffs, N. J.: Prentice Hall, 1959, Chs. 12 and 13.

Carritt, Edgar F. *Ethical and Political Thinking*. New York: Oxford Univ. Press, 1947, especially Ch. 8.

Dewey, John. *Theory of Valuation. International Encyclopedia of Unified Science*. Chicago: Univ. of Chicago Press, 1939, Vol. 2, No. 4.

Duncker, K. "Pleasure, Emotion, and Striving." *Philosophy and Phenomenological Research*, Vol. 1 (1940), pp. 391-430.

Moore, George Edward, *Principia Ethica* (1903). New York: Cambridge Univ. Press, 1959 (also paperbound), Ch. 6.

Nowell-Smith, Patrick. *Ethics*. Baltimore: Pelican Books, 1954, especially Ch. 17.

Penelhum, Terence. "The Logic of Pleasure." *Philosophy and Phenomenological Research*, Vol. 17 (1957), pp. 488-503.

Rashdall, Hastings. *Theory of Good and Evil*. 2nd ed. New York: Oxford Univ. Press, 1924. 2 vols., Vol. 1, Bk. 1, Ch. 7.

Rice, Philip B. *On the Knowledge of Good and Evil*. New York: Random House, 1955, Ch. 11.

Ross, Sir William David. *Foundations of Ethics*. (Gifford lectures, 1935-36) New York: Oxford Univ. Press, 1939.

————. *The Right and the Good*. New York: Oxford Univ. Press, 1930, Ch. 5.

Ryle, Gilbert, *Dilemmas*. London: Cambridge Univ. Press, 1956, Ch. 4.

————, and W. B. Gallie. "Pleasure." *Aristotlian Society Proceedings*, Supplementary Vol. 28 (1954), pp. 135-64.

Sidgwick, Henry. *The Methods of Ethics*. 7th ed. New York: Macmillan, 1874, especially Bk. 3, Ch. 14.

4. *Egoism*

9. *Psychological egoism*

The previous chapter was devoted to a survey of various theories concerning intrinsic good. Now we must inquire to what use our conclusions are to be put. What are the implications of these views for *conduct?* What consequences have they for our behavior? Assuming that we have made up our minds what is intrinsically good, how are we to apply our knowledge — by trying to achieve as much intrinsic good as possible for all mankind, or for our nation or club or society, or for ourselves individually? This last view — that we should try to maximize our own intrinsic good and ignore everyone else's — is called *ethical egoism,* and we shall examine it later in this chapter.

Before we do so, however, there is a related view to be considered, which is called *psychological egoism.* Psychological egoism is not an ethical doctrine at all but a theory concerning human motivation. The theory says nothing about what is good or bad or right or wrong. There are many versions of it, but the following statements are typical:

> Everyone is fundamentally selfish.
> People always look out for Number One first.
> Everybody always does what pleases him.
> People always do what they want to do.
> The only thing people ever want is their own satisfaction.
> Everyone always does what is to his own interest.

In fact, psychological egoists often go further than this: they say not merely that people always do what pleases them, what they want, etc., but that it is psychologically impossible for them to do anything else — that people invariably do what pleases them by a law of their own nature.

Thus far one might well remark, "So what? Whether true or false, what has such a view to do with ethics? Such views are descriptive (of human behavior), whereas ethics is prescriptive." There is a connection, however, which is to be found in the oft-quoted dictum, "Ought implies can." How can you say that a person *ought* to do something that he cannot possibly do? If it is true that people are so constituted as always to act in their own interest, then it would be absurd to ask them ever to act *contrary* to their own interest. Yet most ethical views — those to be considered in the following chapters — do prescribe just such conduct. If psychological egoism is true, or so it would appear, no such actions are possible; one might as well ask people to jump over the moon. Psychological egoism, then, presents a challenge that must first be met. Indeed, it must be met even before we consider ethical egoism — not because psychological egoism is incompatible with ethical egoism, for of course it isn't, but for an opposite reason: if people are so constituted that they *can* act only in their own interest, it would be pointless and redundant to recommend what ethical egoism recommends, that they *should* always act in their own interest. One might as well urge people who jump out of windows to go downward rather than upward. What is the point of urging people to do what they can't help doing anyway? In order for ethical theories — either egoistic or nonegoistic — to have any point, there must be the possibility of choosing either egoistic or non-egoistic courses of action.

"But surely," it will be objected at once, "it is absurd to say that everyone behaves selfishly — that is, exclusively for himself. Some persons, like the saints, devote their whole lives to behaving unselfishly and serving their fellow men. Most people are inclined to help themselves most of the time, but they do sometimes help others. Even in a crisis, when their own lives are involved, they will often lay down their lives for others or to further a cause in which they strongly believe. Surely you cannot say that such behavior is selfish. Or, if you do, you have extended the use of the word 'selfish' so that it no longer distinguishes anything from anything else. In ordinary life we distinguish selfish behavior from unselfish behavior and predominantly selfish people from predominantly unselfish ones. Since you cannot deny the empirical fact that people sometimes do give up their own interest, what can you mean by 'selfish' if you call even such behavior selfish?"

It is true that there is a distinction between selfish action and unselfish action; the psychological egoist does not deny this distinction. He does not contend that people always *behave* selfishly; rather, he contends that no matter how self-sacrificing their behavior may be, the *desire* behind the action is always selfish. They may behave as unselfishly as you please, but in doing so they always want something out of it for themselves.

There are, however, various versions of psychological egoism.

1. Let us call the first version *cynicism*. The cynic says, "Everybody acts as he does because he wants to get something out of it for himself." Here "something" usually means a reward that is either quite public or tangible or both, such as fame, fortune, power, glamour. "Behind every seemingly unselfish action," the cynic goes on, "there will be found the desire for these

rewards, which explains the action: a person takes insults from his boss and yet does favors for him in order to gain more money and a promotion; a politician pretends to love the people in order to get their votes so that once elected, he can exert his power over them; a man helps his neighbor so that the neighbor in turn will help him. No matter how unselfish the act is when considered by itself, the desire behind it is always selfish — the agent wants something for himself."

The cynic does not say that all people are motivated exclusively by any *one* of these desires, for then he could easily be refuted. If he said that everyone is out to get as much money as he can, his contention could easily be disproved by pointing to thousands of examples in which people are indifferent to money and give it up in order to do things which pay them less. If he said that everyone is animated solely by desire for power, his argument would be stymied by those examples in which people have given up power which they might have had (or continued to have) in order to live a life of leisurely retirement or even of self-sacrifice. Therefore, the cynic wisely leaves the list of actual desires somewhat indeterminate.

Even so, however, the cynic's view is easily attacked. What of those who eschew fame *and* fortune *and* glamour *and* power (and whatever other things the cynic mentions)? What of those who spend their lives ministering to the needy, those who are willing to lose their jobs and their reputations in order to work for a cause they believe in which appears hopeless or which will probably have no visible effects during their lifetime, or those who spend their lives in a leper colony tending the sick and knowing that in all probability they will die a slow death from the very disease of the people they are helping? The cynic may call such people fools, but in so doing he admits that they exist. Or perhaps he will say that they behave as they do in order to enhance their reputations. But what if they are unknown and forgotten and show no particular desire to be known? The cynic would say that perhaps then they do good in order to reap heavenly rewards later on. But what of the people who do good even though they do not believe in heavenly rewards? The cynic might reply that the money impulse or power impulse is still lurking within them waiting for a chance to come out. But what if there are many such chances and they are never taken, and the person spends his entire life in these activities without showing any disposition to acquire wealth or power or any of the other things the cynic mentions as universal human goals?

1-a. Before we turn to more plausible views, let us take note of the cynic's first cousin, the man who says that everybody has his price — that, since everyone desires money or fame or power, everyone is corruptible or bribable by the promise of these things and will give up whatever ideals he has to obtain them. Some individuals' price may be low and some high, but there is a price for which everyone can be bought.

Many people will feel that this view is true. But let us be careful: "Everyone has his price, if it's high enough"— how high is high enough? Doubtless the price differs from person to person; but what of those who, regardless of the price offered or the allurements of power or temptations of fame, have never capitulated and have even shown contempt or indifference toward these rewards? Surely they refute the theory? Not at all, according to our theorist. Their refusal to be bought only shows that the price offered was not high enough, not that there is no such price. But if the person refuses *all* inducements, doesn't his refusal show that no inducement was great enough? It would surely seem so: some people capitulate, showing that they can be bought; others do not, showing that they can't be. But our theorist does not accept this conclusion: it only shows him that the price was not yet high enough. But what, now, does he mean by "high enough"? It seems that "high enough" means "till he accepts." But then his daring claim turns out to be a flat tautology. "If you offer him enough, he will give in" becomes merely "If you offer him enough so that he gives in, he will give in." His claim, when pressed, becomes tautological.

In any event, our theorist is not yet a full-fledged cynic. For he is saying that everyone *can* be corrupted if the asking price is high enough, which is different from saying that he always *is* corrupted. Many of a man's actions, prior to the capitulation point, may be as unselfishly motivated as one wishes; it's just that under pressure they don't remain so. The true cynic, on the other hand, claims that *all* people *all* the time are animated by selfish impulses.

2. Let us now turn to more plausible versions of psychological egoism, such as *psychological hedonism*. "Not everyone," the psychological hedonist admits, "is animated exclusively by the desire for fame, fortune, power, prestige; there are exceptions. But everyone *does* act in order to gain for himself the greatest possible personal *satisfaction* (or pleasure, or happiness). He may not gain money or power from devoting his life to an unpopular cause, but he does derive personal satisfaction from doing something he believes in, and that is why he does it. The man who spends his life in a leper colony enjoys a glow of good feeling in the thought that he is helping others; he enjoys the satisfaction of an arduous and trying job well done, the satisfaction that comes from having done what he feels is his duty. The man who scrimps and saves so that his family will have enough to live on after he is dead is not, obviously, out for his *own* personal gain, for *he* does not benefit from the insurance payable to his family after his death; he saves because it gives him a pleasant feeling to think of his family being provided for. The man who gives up fame in order to engage in artistic endeavor which may not be appreciated until a century or more after his death does so in order to gain the kind of satisfaction to be found in pursuing the work one loves; it is greater satisfaction than he could gain from just making money. The man who gives money to a beggar may not gain anything from his generosity (not even reputation, if no one sees him give it) except the per-

sonal satisfaction of helping out another human being or having done his duty."

This second version of psychological egoism is far more difficult to attack. No matter how much a person may forsake wealthy circumstances for poverty, no matter how much he may ignore his own welfare in preference to that of his fellow men, the psychological hedonist may say that he did it to reap the personal satisfaction following upon these activities. How are we to refute him?

Indeed, the view may not seem worth refuting; why should one refute a view which is so unobjectionable? If a person derives satisfaction from helping others, is that bad? Isn't it better to gain satisfaction out of helping others than *not* to gain it? Furthermore, if he finds satisfaction in helping his neighbor, he will be that much more likely to help him again the next time. Besides, in what way could such a desire be called selfish? If one man gives another money in order to swindle him later, this act is selfish in the good old garden-variety sense (the act itself is altruistic, but it is "interested altruism"); but if he gives the other person money because the deed itself gives him satisfaction or because it distresses him to see others in want, quite apart from their ability to help him in turn, surely his deed is not selfish at all (it is "disinterested altruism"). If the deed is selfish, it is not so in the usual sense. Pointing to a person who derived great personal satisfaction from helping others, would you say, "There goes a selfish man," or even, "There goes a man with selfish desires"?

Thus, if we include among egoistic desires those aimed at personal satisfaction, we may well ask if it *is* really inconsistent with a nonegoistic ethics to believe in psychological egoism? Why shouldn't a nonegoistic ethics recommend unselfish *acts* performed from the *desire* for personal satisfaction?

Bentham held such a view. He was a firm supporter of psychological egoism (of which psychological hedonism is a version), believing that everyone is so constituted that he will act to gain the maximum satisfaction for himself. "It is pointless," Bentham would argue, "to expect people to behave in any other way; to get them to do something, you first have to make them sure that they will gain something out of it — money, position, prestige, or just personal satisfaction or a warm glow inside — for themselves." At the same time, Bentham was a firm champion of a nonegoistic ethics, as we shall see in the next chapter. He believed that people have a duty to promote the happiness of others and not merely their own. How did he reconcile psychological egoism with a nonegoistic ethics? "People," he would say, "can be trained and educated in such a way that they will derive their maximum personal satisfaction out of doing things for others. If you train children properly, their consciences will bother them at the very thought of murder and theft, and they will find satisfaction in being kind and thoughtful to others. Conscience is an *internal sanction* which, when properly developed, will cause people to behave unselfishly, albeit with motives of personal satisfaction. If conscience cannot always be counted on, there is always the *external sanction* of public opinion and the law. Even if the criminal's conscience does not bother him, the laws of the land, when wisely administered and efficiently enforced, will make him conform to certain desirable patterns of social behavior. He will then refrain from committing crimes because of the perfectly egoistic motive of providing more comfort for himself by living outside prison walls. Our techniques of training, our laws, and public opinion, must be so arranged that he will derive the most satisfaction from doing acts that benefit others and refraining from acts that do not."

Will this solution suffice? Many intelligent and high-minded men have thought so. But there is a catch in it. It would work out all right in practice *only* if conscience, law, and public opinion were as Bentham recommends. But what if they are not? If psychological egoism is correct, you will help your neighbor as long as you derive satisfaction (or some egoistic reward) from doing so. But what if you *don't* derive satisfaction from helping your neighbor? You will refrain from crime as long as the law and the police make criminal activity so uncomfortable for you that it is not to your interest to commit crimes. But what if the law becomes lax or full of loopholes, or the enforcement of it inefficient or corrupt? Then you will commit crimes because you can derive your greatest satisfaction, or so you believe, from doing so. Yet — and here is the crucial point — *shouldn't* you do the unselfish act anyway, even though you don't feel like it and even though you don't gain the slightest satisfaction from doing it? and *shouldn't* you refrain from criminal activity, even though the laws are lax and you won't be caught? Surely no nonegoistic ethics is ever going to say that you should help others only *if* you derive personal satisfaction from doing so or that you should refrain from crime only *if* you would otherwise be caught. On the contrary, a nonegoistic ethics will say that you should help others whether you feel like it or not and whether you get satisfaction out of it or not, and that you should refrain from murder even though you knew you could get away with it and would get great satisfaction out of wreaking revenge on your enemies. There's the rub. Psychological hedonism says that we always do what we do in order to derive the maximum personal satisfaction; so how could we help our neighbor when helping does *not* give us personal satisfaction? Our original difficulty of reconciling this version of psychological egoism with nonegoistic ethical theories, then, is still with us. The problem has not been mitigated at all.

If we cannot reconcile this version of psychological egoism with ethical nonegoism and if we want behavior in accordance with a nonegoistic ethics to be at least possible, we shall simply have to look more closely at psychological egoism to see whether it can be attacked. Fortunately, this is not difficult to do. In fact, the arguments against psychological egoism appear to most philosophers to be so decisive that very few of them today would assent to the doctrine. Let us see why.

Notice that those who champion this version of psychological egoism, psychological hedonism, are not always arguing for the same thing. We must distinguish two varieties of psychological hedonism: the variety which says all that people ever desire is pleasure or satisfaction, or, in other words, that pleasure is the sole object of desire and the variety which says that people desire many things but these things are all desired solely *for the sake of* the pleasure or satisfaction which they will bring to the agent.

a. The variety of psychological hedonism which says that the only thing people ever desire is pleasure or satisfaction is easily attacked.

(1) It is an empirical fact that I do not desire only pleasure. When I am thirsty I desire drink; when I am hungry I desire food. I may not even think of the pleasure I can enjoy from these things. In fact, the only food available may taste unpleasant, and I will still eat it because it fills my belly. When I lend you money to tide you over until your check comes, I do not desire simply my own pleasure. What I desire is to help you out so that you will not be caught short for lack of funds. I desire to spare you financial embarrassment, not to give myself pleasure. True, I *may* get pleasure from the loan, but then I may not; perhaps I shall feel only irritation or self-pity. But even if I do get pleasure from helping you, the pleasure is not *what* I desire at the time I lend you the money. In fact I may not be thinking of the pleasure at all. I may desire anything, X, without any thought of whether X will bring me pleasure, so it is not true that I desire only pleasure.

(2) Sometimes I do desire pleasure, but even then it is not pleasure *only* that I desire. When I am starving I desire food, not pleasure. But when I don't much care whether I eat now or later, I may desire food *as well as* the pleasure I hope to get in eating it. Even when I desire the pleasure I hope to get from the food, it is ridiculous to say that I did not desire the food itself! If I did not desire the food I could hardly desire the pleasure that would accompany eating it.

> Granted that, when I desire my glass of port wine, I have also an idea of the pleasure I expect from it, plainly that pleasure cannot be the only object of my desire; the port wine must be included in my object, else I might be led by my desire to take wormwood instead of wine. If the desire were directed *solely* toward the pleasure, it could not lead me to take the wine; if it is to take a definite direction, it is absolutely necessary that the idea of the object, from which the pleasure is expected, should also be present and should control my activity. The theory that what is desired is always and only pleasure must break down.[1]

b. These objections do not touch the other variety of psychological hedonism, which says that we desire things for the sake of the pleasure or satisfaction which they bring, or which we hope they will bring. This interpretation still seems plausible enough: even if money and fame and *external*

---

[1] G. E. Moore, *Principia Ethica*, pp. 447-48.

rewards may not result from our acts, may even be deliberately sacrificed, who can deny that we gain *inner* rewards in the form of personal satisfaction, pleasure, or happiness, from our altruistic deeds? Some remarks must be made, however, about the theory even in this form.

(1) When is the satisfaction, for the sake of which one desires certain things, supposed to be experienced? Does one desire alcohol because it will bring satisfaction immediately (though not later), or does one desire to put a large percentage of his wages into a pension plan because the plan will bring satisfaction much later in life (though not now)? Clearly one cannot cling to the one or the other of these explanations exclusively; some things are done to gain immediate satisfaction and some are done to gain long-run satisfaction. To be at all plausible, then, the theory must be phrased so as to include the possibility of both: "We desire all the things we do desire, for the sake *either* of immediate *or* of long-term satisfaction."

(2) We must beware of confusing the statement that a person received satisfaction from doing something with the statement that he did it *in order to* receive this satisfaction. It may well be true that a person who helps another gains a certain satisfaction from doing so — the peculiar satisfaction of having done one's duty — but this circumstance, even if true, is no proof of psychological hedonism. The psychological hedonist must show that the act was done solely *in order to receive* the satisfaction. Does the person who spends his life in a leper colony ministering to the sick do it in order to receive the satisfaction of having done it, or does he do it for the sake of helping the lepers (with the satisfaction as an incidental accompaniment to his main purpose)? Often it is very difficult to decide this question, for people are prone to hide their selfish acts under the cloak of altruism. But one test, surely, would be this: if continuing to help the lepers no longer gave the person any satisfaction, would he give up doing so? The psychological hedonist must be prepared to say that in every case he would.

(3) Sometimes the future satisfaction for the sake of which the person is supposed to be doing the act could not occur unless the person already desired something *other* than the satisfaction. For example: a person does something which is unpleasant and irksome when he could be doing something more pleasant, but he does it anyway because people will respect him for it after he is dead. "But," says our psychological hedonist, "he has satisfaction while he is alive in the thought that people *will* respect him after he is dead, and *that* is why he does it." But now comes the observation: If he didn't *already* desire to be thought of favorably after his death, the prospect of being respected posthumously would bring no satisfaction to him while he was alive. The psychological hedonist is putting the cart before the horse: he asserts that the desire to be respected posthumously is the result of the satisfaction he thinks it will bring him, whereas the truth is that the desire for posthumous respect is the *cause* of that satisfaction. Without

first desiring posthumous respect, he could feel no satisfaction in the thought that this desire would be fulfilled.

(4) How does the psychological hedonist know that the person acted in order to gain pleasure or satisfaction for himself? In some cases the psychological hedonist can find a plausible reason for the motive of self-satisfaction, and in others he cannot, even if only on grounds of ignorance of the person involved; how then can he be sure about this second group of cases? When I take tea in preference to coffee, the psychological hedonist can obviously claim that I do so because I expect more satisfaction from the tea than from the coffee. But when I lose my reputation and my position in order to stand up for a principle that I believe to be right, how does he know that I do so in order to gain satisfaction for myself — even the satisfaction of having done what I believe is my duty? It does not seem to me that I derive much satisfaction from this course of action; I could have had much more satisfaction in adopting the easier course and forgetting all about the principle. In fact, I may have little or no satisfaction at all from what I did — I may not be one who feels a warm glow inside at having done my duty; perhaps I thought of it as just a nasty job that had to be done. How does the psychological hedonist *know* that I am mistaken in thinking this? Has he any better evidence about my situation than I have? And not only about my example but about all the other examples — past, present, and future — in the entire history of mankind? Has he such intimate knowledge of the desires of every person who has lived, now lives, or ever will live on this planet that he can say with complete confidence that all these countless acts were (and are, and will be) performed for the sake of personal satisfaction?

The psychological hedonist has fallen, perhaps without knowing it, into a convenient logical trap. He has used the fact that a person does A rather than B as the sole and decisive evidence that A gave him more satisfaction than B. How does he know that doing A gave the agent more satisfaction than doing B? He says so just because the person did A.

This conclusion may have escaped us because *at first,* in the obvious examples, the psychological hedonist did not use this question-begging argument. At first he relied on empirical evidence about the person's motivation, and he relied on it as long as he could. When the empirical evidence deserted him, his empirical thesis became an a priori assumption, but the language of his argument still sounded empirical, so we didn't notice. "The worker among the lepers *must* receive satisfaction from his work or he wouldn't be doing it," runs the psychological hedonist's argument; but how does the psychological hedonist know that this is true? Does he know the man so well that he can say with the confidence of a psychoanalyst that the man did it in order to gain personal satisfaction? On the contrary, he does not know the man at all, and he is in no position to say what the man's motives are. In the absence of such knowledge, the psychological hedonist argues that if the man went out among the lepers he *must* have done it to gain personal satisfaction from it; and this, far from proving his argument, begs the whole question.

Even if cynicism and psychological hedonism are false, other versions of psychological egoism may yet be true. The psychological egoist can offer a third version, which will not have much success, as we shall see, but which at least allows him to cover more instances than the cynic or the psychological hedonist can cover.

3. The egoist who proposes the third version of psychological egoism says, "Every act is done not only in order to gain satisfaction from it, but to *avoid* dissatisfaction (pain, feelings of guilt, pangs of conscience, etc.) that would occur if he did *not* do it."

This version is more inclusive. Perhaps the worker in the leper colony does not receive much satisfaction from his work, at least after the first few months; but perhaps he keeps on with it, even so, in order to *avoid* the pangs of guilt which he would have if he did not do this work. Maybe the husband doesn't stay with his wife in order to get happiness out of their life together, for he knows well enough that he will get none; but he stays with her because (at least so he thinks) he will thus avoid even greater displeasures — of being alone, of having no one to sweep and cook for him.

In spite of the improvement offered by this third version, psychological egoism is not saved. Just as in the second version, there are instances in which, judging by the best evidence we have, the theory is empirically false; and the only way to try to maintain it is, once again, to use the very fact of a person's doing something as evidence that he had an egoistic motive in doing it. With this maneuver the psychological egoist once again begs the whole question.

Consider the following case:

A: When the soldier dived his plane into the enemy ship — thus destroying the ship, his plane, and himself — he probably thought that he would be rewarded in heaven for his deed.

B: He didn't think so. I knew him well, and he didn't believe in a life hereafter.

A: Then he acted because he wanted his family to honor his memory, and this thought gave him satisfaction.

B: No; he had no family at all, and anyway he never did go in for this honor-and-glory, pomp-and-circumstance stuff. He never thought much of such heroics.

A: Well, perhaps he had nothing to live for, life didn't offer much to him, and he would just as soon have been dead.

B: On the contrary, life offered him a great deal; and he wasn't psychologically disturbed either — he had no wish to die and he never had suicidal fantasies. He wasn't even given to moods or depressions. He had been promised a very handsome scholarship on his return to civilian life, which would have taken care of all his expenses for four years. And he was looking forward to the university very much. His dream was to be a great surgeon, and he would have become one too.

A: Then the thought of *not* sacrificing his life must have filled him with such guilt feelings that he couldn't have lived with himself afterward if he hadn't done it. Sacrificing his life was the only way he could avoid having pangs of conscience forever after.

B: But that just isn't so. No one would have dishonored him for not doing the heroic deed; it was strictly "beyond the call of duty" and no one would have expected it of him; nor did anyone dishonor the rest of the company because *they* didn't do that or another similar self-sacrificing deed. Besides, he never was one to be troubled much about guilt feelings. He never indulged in guilt feelings about past actions because he didn't think they did any good; instead, when he thought he had made a mistake, he would act differently on the next occasion but not waste his time in fruitless guilt feelings and regrets about the past. Anyway, the displeasure of those guilt feelings would be small indeed compared with the happiness he could have had if he had continued to live. Can you really say that the guilt feelings would have been so prolonged and so intense as to outweigh all the satisfactions life might have offered him forever after that? Anyway, there wasn't much time, in the split second in which he had to make his decision, to have guilt feelings, or to anticipate them for the future, or to contemplate how he would feel if he didn't make the sacrifice.

A: Well, look: he sacrificed himself, didn't he? And the very fact that he did it *proves* that somehow and in some way he *must have* done it to avoid some dissatisfaction. Otherwise he wouldn't have done it.

Here the psychological egoist's technique is exposed: having no further evidence that the person made the supreme sacrifice in order to derive satisfaction or avoid distress, and confronted with the apparently contrary evidence that he did something that put an end to all his satisfactions forever, the egoist converts his empirical contention into an a priori assumption.

The same considerations apply to countless other cases. A woman went to tend the children of a distant cousin, who, with her husband, had previously died of a communicable disease. As a result of her kindness, the woman herself died of the disease. Did she go to the children for financial gain? No; the family was poor and besides she had more than enough money. Did she go because she enjoyed helping others? No; or even if she did normally enjoy helping others, she did not enjoy *this* venture, for she knew the risk full well, and the task was most unpleasant. She went simply because she felt that it was her duty to go. Ah — but didn't she go in order to obtain the satisfaction she would feel at having done her duty? No, that satisfaction (if any) was small compared with what she went through with the children even before she was taken sick and died herself. Anyway, the fact that she may have gained a smattering of moral satisfaction from her deed is a far cry from saying that she did it *in order to gain* that moral satisfaction — which is most implausible. Perhaps she had an unhappy home life and wanted to escape from it? No indeed; she was a devoted wife and mother and was happily married. Then perhaps she went to avoid the pangs of conscience she would suffer if she didn't go. But there is doubt whether she would have felt these pangs — there was no special reason why *she* of all people had to do this job, and in any case the pangs of conscience, if any, would hardly have outweighed the years of happiness she might have had by staying home with her family. Why then did she do it? As a matter of principle: not to get enjoyment, not even to get the moral satisfaction of having done her duty or to avoid the dissatisfaction of not having done it, but simply *to do her duty*. If one had asked her why she did it, that is what she probably would have said; and who is in a position to say that she was mistaken?

Not all cases that contradict the psychological egoist's claims are cases of doing one's duty or acting on principle. Some are cases in which the person acts contrary to his own satisfaction (immediate or long-run), fully realizing what he is doing, without any thought of duty whatever. Many people who behave so are in need of psychiatric help, but they exist nonetheless. A man steals or gambles or kills; and in spite of not gaining anything but disturbance, unhappiness, and inner conflict from such an action, he continues to do it anyway. The thrice-divorced woman marries again, knowing full well that she will find no satisfaction in the marriage. Such cases may be hard for us to conceive of if we are not acquainted with these people personally, but any psychiatrist has dozens of them in his practice. We may think it strange that people should behave thus, because *we* would not do so; but nevertheless *they* do.

4. Our egoist gives us yet a fourth version of psychological egoism: "The person who acts may not act in order to receive *conscious* satisfaction from his deed but in order to derive *unconscious* satisfaction for himself. Let us revise our view, then, to say that a person always does what he does because he expects to derive a conscious *or unconscious* satisfaction from his act." Thus, for example, the thrice-divorced woman experiences no conscious satisfaction from her misalliances, but she continues to wed in order to reap the reward of *unconscious* masochistic pleasure.

This fourth version of psychological egoism must be submitted to the psychiatrists for their verdict. Before doing so, we may make a preliminary remark. When psychological egoists say that people always act in order to gain satisfaction for themselves, the egoists usually do not mean *un*conscious satisfaction, which the people do not consciously experience; the egoists mean ordinary, conscious satisfaction, which, if the people didn't consciously experience it, they wouldn't call satisfaction at all. Once the doctrine that "everyone acts to produce his own maximum satisfaction" has been extended to include *un*conscious satisfaction, the original doctrine has been distorted almost out of recognition and the sting is taken out of it. Even if the woman who helped out her deceased cousin's sick children derive unconscious satisfaction of some kind from doing so, she was no better off for her deed because she did not consciously experience the satisfaction.

Even in this amended (or distorted) fourth version, the doctrine of psychological egoism does not seem to be true. If one says that an act from which we expect no conscious satisfaction always gives *un*conscious satisfaction, he runs headlong into no less an authority than Freud. Freud attacks this assertion in his doctrine that there are some actions, such as those dictated by unconscious repetition-compulsion, which are not even done for the sake of *un*conscious satisfaction. Such actions, according to Freud, are "beyond the pleasure principle." [1] (The non-Freudians are not likely to accept the unconscious pleasure principle at all.)

With these comments, it would seem that the back of the psychological egoist's doctrine has been broken. To clinch the argument, let us attack still another version of the doctrine:

5. In the fifth version of psychological egoism the egoist maintains, "Everyone always does what he really *wants* to do." (Here there is no special reference to pleasure or satisfaction as being what one wants.) For examples: If the pilot hadn't wanted to destroy the enemy ship (page 150), he wouldn't have sacrificed his life in order to dive on the ship. If the woman hadn't really wanted to take care of her deceased cousin's children (page 151), she wouldn't have bothered to do so. Even in cases of extreme self-sacrifice, people always do what they really want to do. (What we want to do may not be selfish — it may be a very altruistic act; but still, we do it because we *want* to.)

But there is an ambiguity in the phrase "doing what we want." In the most usual sense of the term, the sense we all use every day, the egoistic doctrine is empirically false, for we often do what we do *not* want to do. The pilot didn't want to go on the suicide mission, but he did. The woman who took care of her cousin's sick children, contracting the disease herself, certainly didn't want to go in any usual sense of that phrase. If the psychological egoist denies these circumstances, he is flying into the face of a patent empirical fact. "Maybe *you* don't ever do what you don't want to do," we may say to him; "if you've inherited a million and the world is your oyster, you may not ever have to; but thousands of people who have to do unpleasant work for a living are constantly doing what they don't want to do." The person who does only what he wants is usually a ruthlessly selfish person who does not consider other people's wishes but invariably follows his own. A young child is the best example of this attitude: he does what

[1] See Sigmund Freud, *Beyond the Pleasure Principle* (New York: Boni & Liveright, 1924).

he wants to do, and if he is frustrated, he kicks and screams or cries and pouts. But when a child continues to behave thus as an adult, we consider him psychologically abnormal. The training of children consists to a very large extent of getting them to consider other people's wants and to do things other than what they happen to want themselves. To say, then, that in this usual sense everyone always does what he wants to do is patently absurd.

The psychological egoist, usually without knowing it himself, is trading on the ambiguity of a term to make his doctrine plausible. "Well, he did the deed, didn't he?" he will say. "This shows that he must have wanted it. Yes, it meant giving up a scholarship and a medical future and life itself, but he must have wanted to sacrifice himself or he wouldn't have done it. Yes, the woman was sacrificing everything by going to tend the sick children, but if she hadn't wanted to do it she wouldn't have done it." How does the egoist know? Does he adduce any evidence? Not at all; he simply says that the fact that the person performed an act proves that he wanted to perform it. When the egoist plays the game with this kind of loaded dice, it's no wonder we can't win against him. But his victory is an empty, verbal one, not an empirical one, although he claimed it would be empirical when the game started. No matter how many unselfish desires we turn up for him, he says, "Look harder, you'll find a selfish desire lurking behind it." We look and still find none, and then he says, "If you look hard enough, you'll find it" (which means, as we have already observed, "if you look till you find it, you'll find it"), or "The person did this, didn't he? and that shows that he must have wanted it more than anything else."

If the psychological egoist is permitted to argue in this way, an opponent could argue as follows: "All desires are really *un*selfish. Sometimes it doesn't look that way, and sometimes people do seem to desire selfish ends, but look a little deeper and you'll find lurking behind every selfish desire an unselfish one. True, you may not actually find it, but that only shows that you haven't looked hard enough." Probably no one would accept such an argument; yet logically it is exactly parallel to the argument of the psychological egoist.

The psychological egoist's neat technique is once again exposed: Suppose that Smith has to choose between two acts, A and B. A is a selfish act in which he does what he wants to and ignores those around him who need his help; and B is an unselfish act in which he sacrifices something he badly wants in order to help the others. Suppose that Smith chooses A. The egoist then exclaims triumphantly, "You see? another example of egoism. The other people needed his help, but he helped himself anyway! Didn't I tell you that people are always selfish?" Now suppose that Smith does not A but B. The egoist can't use the same argument he did before, so he must rely on his second line of defense: "Well, he did B, so he *must* have done it because he really wanted to, else he wouldn't have done it." Here the egoist has given us no evidence whatever for his claim; he simply relies on the a priori assumption that his claim must be true. This is a favorite technique of the psychological egoist; once it has been pointed out, there is no longer any excuse for being taken in by it. Once we understand it, we shall probably have no more inclination to believe in psychological egoism.

We could discuss still other versions of psychological egoism — for example, "Everyone always acts so as to promote his own interest (advantage), either immediate or long-run, to the exclusion of everyone else's" — but exactly the same considerations would apply to these. The nerve of psychological egoism has been exposed, and it would be idle to pursue the argument any further.

In conclusion, we should mention two other theories which are easily confused with psychological egoism. Psychological egoism as we have thus far discussed it (which could be called "psychological egoism of the future") says that people always act in order to gain pleasure, satisfaction, happiness, fulfillment of desire, and to avoid the opposite of these things. Another theory is concerned not with what the person is trying to obtain in the future but with what he is experiencing in the present. Still another theory is concerned with what he has experienced in the past.

The theory concerning the present ("psychological egoism of the present moment") is that people will attempt to produce certain effects in the future only if the thought of producing them is a pleasant thought in the present. Such a view is probably as untrue as the ones we have discussed and can be defended to the last ditch only by making it a priori like the others; but it is unnecessary to enter upon it here, since it provides no threat to ethics in the way that psychological egoism does. It does not try to show that people always act as they do in order to produce some advantage to themselves, and hence it is no threat to ethical theories which say that people *should* act so as to produce advantage to others. And there is, it would seem, no reason why the thought of doing an unselfish deed, even an unselfish deed from which one expects to gain no pleasure, may not at the same time give pleasure — though, of course, neither is there any reason why it should always do so.

The theory concerning the past ("psychological egoism of the past") is that one's present interest in doing A rather than B is determined by past experiences of A giving him more satisfaction than B. This theory, too, seems to be false, and it is not supported by most psychologists — at least in the form which says that it is *only* past satisfactions that determine present desires. But whether true or false, again it is no threat to ethics, for there is no reason why past enjoyments — such as being praised by one's parents for doing unpleasant tasks — may not cause one in the present to perform actions which are far from pleasant, and from which no future pleasure is expected.

EXERCISES

1. A person suggests that the formula "A person always does what he really wants to do" cannot possibly be false because the specified condition — his doing a certain thing — is really a *definition* of the phrase "what he really wants to do." Do you consider this position satisfactory? Does it solve the psychological egoist's problems?

2. Do you consider the following examples to be favorable to psychological egoism (in any of its forms), unfavorable to psychological egoism, or neither? Why?

a. A man picks up a nail from the highway and says, "Maybe someone will do the same for me some day, before my car comes along."

b. A man picks up a nail from the highway to prevent other cars from getting flat tires. He is not driving that day, and has no plans to return to the vicinity in the future. He has no hopes or thoughts about someone doing the same for him. He does it simply out of habit.

c. The same as *b,* except that he does it not out of habit but because he believes it to be his duty.

d. The driver asks the hitchhiker riding with him, "Which is the way to town A?" The hitchhiker gives him a truthful answer, although he himself is going to town B, and if he had given the driver the directions to town B instead (saying it was the way to town A) the driver would have gone toward town B, where the hitchhiker wanted to go. The driver would, of course, have discovered the lie, but not until the hitchhiker had been taken to where he wanted to go.

e. The driver at night stops his car to replace a sawhorse marked "Open Trench" which has toppled over in the wind. Asked why he did it, he replies, "It's a kind of unwritten rule of the road."

f. The driver stops to pick up an injured dog on the road, saying, "It hurts me to see an animal just lie there and suffer."

3. Read C. D. Broad's essay "Egoism as a Theory of Human Motives" and give a detailed analysis of it, bringing in the various distinctions which he introduces in his exploration of the problem.

4. Try to resolve the following controversy. Can you detect any ambiguity in the way in which the term "selfish" is being used?

A: Cats are selfish. They want you only for the meal-ticket which you supply. But dogs will really sacrifice for you — they will starve at your feet rather than leave you, and they will travel a thousand miles, undergoing great hardship, just to be with you again.

B: I disagree with you. Even dogs are selfish. They won't do anything for you unless there's something in it for *them.* They want your love and affection more than they want food, and they fear insecurity more than hunger.

A: In the Arctic some time ago an explorer was found who had been dead for three weeks. His dog lay starving at his feet, while his cat was eating his eyes out. Don't you consider that evidence for my position?

B: No. Both the dog and the cat were selfish, but in different ways. And the same for human beings. They are always selfish too, but their selfishness more often includes a concern (selfish concern, of course) for the welfare of others.

A: I disagree once again. Dogs are less selfish than cats, and human beings *can* be more unselfish than either. Neither dogs nor cats act contrary to their own interests from principles of duty, but people do. Perhaps the dog finds it easier or less unpleasant to be with his master even if he himself is starving, but people often do the more difficult thing and the thing that they *don't* want. You have commanded the dog not to go outside; although he wants to go out, perhaps he stays indoors because he fears punishment or loss of affection. But people sometimes do things for others without expecting anything in return — not even the satisfaction or security which the dog expects.

B: I think all three species are equally selfish, always. I grant that a person may act from a sense of duty, unlike the dog, but I don't believe he would do so if he didn't think he would derive more satisfaction (or avoid dissatisfaction) by so doing.

READING LIST, SECTION 9

Brandt, Richard. *Ethical Theory.* Englewood Cliffs, N. J.: Prentice-Hall, 1959, pp. 307-14.
Broad, C. D. "Bishop Butler's Conception of Human Nature" (1930). In Sellars, Wilfrid, and John Hospers, eds. *Readings in Ethical Theory.* New York: Appleton-Century-Crofts, 1952, pp. 451-63.
———. "Egoism as a Theory of Human Motives." In Broad, C. D. *Ethics and the History of Philosophy.* New York: Humanities Press, 1952, pp. 218-31.
———. "Remarks on Psychological Hedonism" (1930). In Sellars and Hospers. *Readings in Ethical Theory,* pp. 464-68.
Moore, George Edward. *Principia Ethica* (1903). New York: Cambridge Univ. Press, 1959 (also paperbound), pp. 67-74.
Pratt, James B. *Reason in the Art of Living.* New York: Macmillan, 1949, Ch. 11.
Rashdall, Hastings. *Theory of Good and Evil.* 2nd ed. New York: Oxford Univ. Press, 1924. 2 vols., Vol. 1, Bk. 1, Ch. 2.
Schlick, Moritz. *The Problems of Ethics.* Englewood Cliffs, N. J.: Prentice-Hall, 1939, Ch. 2.

10. Ethical egoism

We have given some reasons for believing that psychological egoism is a false doctrine. But to say that psychological egoism is false in its description of what motives men *have* is not to say that ethical egoism (page 141) is false in its statement of what motives men *should* have. One theory describes matters of fact, the other, matters of value. Could it not be that, contrary to psychological egoism, we sometimes *do* act from unselfish desires yet, according to ethical egoism, we always *ought* to act selfishly? Or could it not be that though empirically we *can* act against our interests, ethically we *should* act strictly in our own interest and ignore the interests of others?

Many people, whether or not they are psychological egoists, are ethical egoists. They act on such maxims as, "I'm out strictly for myself," or, "I'd be a fool to help out the other fellow, especially when my help will enable him to get ahead of me," or, "Don't be a sentimental fool — look out for yourself and you'll get along all right."

Most ethical egoists, however, do not classify themselves as such or publicly profess their principles. Indeed their principles are quite opposed to those publicly professed by Western society. Ethical egoism has aroused the public indignation of countless parents, teachers, preachers, moralists, and statesmen, even though in private life they may act on the basis of this doctrine. Let us, then, ask ourselves, "Can this much criticized doctrine be rationally attacked, or are we condemned to indulging in emotional outbursts against it, or might it even possibly be true?"

A. Arguments for ethical egoism

One word of caution at the outset. Do not confuse "actions conducive to your interest" with "actions which help you but not others" — roughly, selfish actions. There are many *un*selfish actions which surely *are* to your interest to perform. If you do something for someone, he may do something for you some day when you need it badly. If you control your impulses, obey the law, and treat your colleagues nicely even when you don't feel like it, you will earn the respect and esteem of your community, possessions which may stand you in good stead. In short, it is often to your own interest — long-term if not short — to behave in an unselfish manner. Ethical egoism does not deny that you should help others when doing so helps *you*. Perhaps this overlapping of interests occurs most of the time. Ethical egoism only denies that you should help others when *you* will get nothing out of it — neither fame, fortune, nor even personal satisfaction or happiness. Since you should always do what promotes your own interests, and since the unselfish act in these cases does not promote your own interest, there is no reason why you should do it, according to ethical egoism.

Let us first see whether any arguments can be used to *defend* ethical egoism. Most ethical egoists, to be sure, behave egoistically without trying to state any propositions in favor of their doctrine — they do not care about defenses or refutations. If they did want to defend their view, however, what might they say?

We must first distinguish the *personal* ethical egoist from the *impersonal* ethical egoist. The personal ethical egoist is someone who says that *he* should follow his own interests exclusively; he does not say what other people should do. The impersonal ethical egoist, on the other hand, says that *all* men should pursue their own interests exclusively.

1. Let us consider the *personal ethical egoist* first. If he says, "I *shall* fol-

low my own interests," he is only stating what he is going to do and is not giving voice to an ethical theory at all; hence there is as yet no ethical theory to be defended. He is merely making a prediction about how he is going to behave, and a prediction is best defended by its coming true.

But if he says, "I *ought* to pursue my own interests," what reason can he give for making this statement? Suppose that to the question "Why is this wrong?" he answers, "Because it involves the infliction of unnecessary suffering." The reason he gives is a general answer; it covers not only *this* particular act but all other acts which are like it in the specified respect. If this act is wrong, then all acts like it in the specified respect are wrong, regardless of whether they are yours or mine or someone else's. But to give a general reason already goes contrary to the personal ethical egoist's contention. He cannot make any statement about all acts of a certain kind, for he is concerned only with *his own* acts; he says nothing about anyone else's acts. Because he is a personal ethical egoist, he is cut off from being able to state any general reasons or to voice any general ethical principles to uphold his position. Even if he says, "Because *all* persons should pursue their own interest," he is no longer a personal but an impersonal ethical egoist.

He may, however, try to derive his statement "I should pursue only my own interest" from some other statement about what is intrinsically worthwhile or desirable. He may say, *"My* happiness (or whatever else you want to call intrinsically good) is the only intrinsic good there is, and since I should promote the good, I should promote my own happiness." We might then point out to him that if he considers happiness (or anything else) intrinsically good or worth attaining, why is it not worth attaining for everyone else as well as for himself? Why is *he* an exception? The personal ethical egoist is declaring that only *his* happiness, out of that of all the people in the world, is worth striving for; but he gives no reason why he should be thus privileged. In fact, if what he says is true, then not only he but Smith and Jones and you and I and everyone else in the world should do all we can to promote this egoist's happiness; we should promote what is intrinsically good, and his happiness is the only intrinsic good in the world, so we should all neglect our own interests and promote his.

What reasons could he possibly give to back up such a bizarre claim?

a. He may say, "I alone count because there is some characteristic or property which I alone of all men possess and which gives me exclusive title to happiness." Perhaps he is the most talented or brilliant person in the world, or the most powerful, or the most dedicated. But, in the first place, one could question why the possession of these characteristics should entitle him to exclusive attention. And, in the second place, one could point out that even if he possesses the characteristic now, someone else may possess it later (someone else might arise who is more talented than he) and then by his criterion *that* person would be entitled to exclusive attention. (In other words, he would be assenting to the general principle *"Anyone* possessing more of property A than anyone else does should receive exclusive attention.") His view would thus boomerang against him.

b. "But," the personal ethical egoist may say, "there is a way out of this dilemma. I can make sure that it is only to the promotion of my interests to which exclusive attention should be paid. I shall not claim some special property, for someone else might come to possess that property also; I shall say only that I deserve exclusive attention because *I am I.*" But this reasoning, of course, will not do either. It is true that being John Jones is something that is true only of John Jones. Even if John Jones is no longer the most talented person in the world, he is still John Jones. But exactly the same thing could be said for everyone else. Being Sam Smith is something that holds true only of Sam Smith. The plea "I deserve X because I am I" is something that everyone could present; if it is a valid plea for Jones it is equally so for Smith.

If something is intrinsically good, then, it is not intrinsically good only when Jones has it. Why, indeed, should it not be intrinsically good wherever it occurs? Hence Jones cannot use his premise about intrinsic good to support the conclusion that he should consider his own interests exclusively.

The personal ethical egoist, however, may say, "I didn't mean that only my own happiness, of all the happiness actual and possible in the world, is intrinsically good. I meant that only my happiness is intrinsically good *for me,* yours is *for you,* and so on for everyone else." Once he has said this, of course, he is no longer a personal but an impersonal ethical egoist, since he has generalized his view to cover other people as well as himself. Let us see, then, what the *impersonal* ethical egoist might say in defense of this view.

2. Certainly the *impersonal ethical egoist* sounds more plausible than the personal ethical egoist. But let us examine exactly what the impersonal ethical egoist could mean by what he says. If he believes that happiness (or anything else) is intrinsically good, then what is being added by the phrases "for you" and "for me"? If happiness is good, isn't it good no matter who has it? The phrases "for you" and "for me" *are* meaningfully used in the context of *instrumental* values: for example, "Insulin is good for you, since you are a diabetic, but not for me since I am not." This statement merely means that the use of insulin is a means toward a certain end in your case but not in mine. "Good for" ordinarily means "good as a means toward." But what is the phrase to mean when what is discussed is not a means toward anything? It would appear that either happiness is intrinsically desirable or it is not; what sense would it make to say that it is good for one person and not for another, or that one happiness is good for one person and not for another, unless we are talking about it as a means toward something beyond itself — and, consequently, *not* talking about it as an intrinsic good?

"But," the impersonal ethical egoist may object, "this is still not what I mean. What I mean is that the *statement* 'My happiness is good' is true for me but false for you."

What does the impersonal ethical egoist mean this time? How can one and the same statement be both true and false? If it is true that there is a table in this room, then it cannot (at the same time) be false that there is a table in this room; it is nonsense to say that the statement is true for me but false for you. (Something quite different may be meant by it, namely that I see a table in the room and you don't. This statement may be true, of course; but then if it is *true* that I see it and you don't, then it is not also *false* that I see it and you don't.) The same applies to statements about you and me: If it is true that milk is good for you (that is, conducive to your health), then it is not also false that milk is good for you. The statement that milk is good for you is either true or false, but it is not true for you and false for me. Or to put it in still another way, we have two statements:

> Milk is conducive to your health.
> Milk is not conducive to my health.

If both statements are true (as they might be, for example, if I am allergic to milk), then they are true, not *for* you or me or anyone else but simply true, period. And the same holds if one or both of them is false. When you feel inclined to say that a statement is true for you but false for me, what you have on your hands is *two* statements which you have not distinguished from each other. Thus, you may be inclined to say that the statement "Oysters taste good" is a true statement for you (since you like oysters) and false for me (since I don't like oysters). The truth is that there are *two* statements, one that you like oysters (which is true) and the other that I like oysters (which is false). But the true one is not true just for you, or the false one false for me; the first statement is simply true, and the second one simply false. One is true and the other false even when (as in this example) the statements are *about* you or me. Statements *about* you are not true just *for* you (indeed, what would it mean to say this?). If a statement about you is true (such as that you like oysters), then it is not true for you or for me or for anyone else, but true, period.[1]

Nevertheless, our impersonal ethical egoist may once again absolve himself from our charges against him. He may say, "I didn't really mean to talk about 'good for you' and 'good for me' as if I were talking about intrinsic goods, where that language has no place. Nor did I mean that one and the same statement can be both true and false at the same time, true for one person but false for another. What I really meant was something different. What I should have said is that I should pursue *my* happiness exclusively, and that you should pursue *your* happiness exclusively, and so on for every-

[1] For further discussion of this point, see John Hospers, *Introduction to Philosophical Analysis* (Englewood Cliffs, N. J.: Prentice-Hall, 1953), pp. 125-26.

one else in the world. Putting it that way, I do not have to say anything like 'to you' or 'to me.' "

Very well; at last we have the impersonal ethical egoist's claim without the confusing language. What can we say about this claim? How could the impersonal ethical egoist defend it? He can give the obvious defense at once: "For each person to pursue his own interest exclusively is the best policy because everyone will be happier that way. The world would be a better place to live in if people interfered less with one another. True, to follow this principle would mean sacrificing some desired things which we get through cooperation, but the sacrifice would be more than made up for by the fact that our lives would not be interfered with by others except when we wanted them to be. Because you would not help me when I was in trouble, I might be inconvenienced, but then neither would I have to help you when you were in a jam. In short, considering it from all angles, the world would be a happier place if each person were left free to pursue his own interest and ignored those of everyone else. Accordingly, that state of affairs is what I am recommending in my egoistic theory."

Here at last we have a possible, and a seemingly quite plausible, position. It does, however, present us with an *empirical claim* — the claim that there would be more happiness in the world if people all pursued their own interests and ignored those of others; and this claim would have to be defended. It is a claim in favor of a completely laissez-faire policy, a universal "rugged individualism." But is it true that if each of us pursued a policy of "splendid isolation" with regard to the interests of other people, we would all be happier? We would gain certain advantages (freedom from interference), but would these advantages be worth the cost? In the hunting-and-fishing stage of man's development, such a view might have been plausible enough; when the land was sparsely settled and I had my hunting domain and you had yours and there was plenty of room and plenty of game for both of us, a policy of mutual noninterference may have been the most conducive to happiness — at least it would have avoided friction, though it would certainly have caused loneliness. But even if we ignore the need for human companionship and family life, such a policy could produce the maximum happiness only in circumstances where each person could afford to be relatively *independent* of all the others. Such a policy would be disastrous in a complex society such as ours in which each unit is *interdependent* with all the rest. Today people's fates are so tied up with one another — because we are crowded together, because we want things achievable only by cooperation such as industry, medicine, quick transportation, food supply, — that a policy of complete independence (each person making and supplying the foods and clothes he needs for himself) would result in total anarchy. The number of people that exists on this planet today could not possibly continue to exist if everyone were completely independent. John Donne's statement "no man is an island" is far more true today than when he wrote it. More idiomatically, we might say of today's world, "if we don't hang together, we'll all hang separately." (We shall expand on this problem in Chapter 8.)

Whatever might be said about the intrinsic value of complete independence, the important fact here is that the person who argues the position just outlined is no egoist at all. Consider: what reason does the impersonal ethical egoist give for his position? Is it an egoistic reason? Not at all: "The world would contain more happiness if people did so and so," he says. But then he is saying that happiness is a good thing, not just his own but the world's. His reasoning is not egoistic but (as we shall see in the next chapter) utilitarian; he is, however, a utilitarian with a peculiar twist, for though he shares the utilitarian view that universal happiness is good, he holds (unlike most utilitarians) that the *means* toward universal happiness is the pursuit of one's own interests exclusively. He is egoistic only about the means; about the end toward which exclusive self-interest is a means he is not egoistic but universalistic. Our impersonal ethical egoist, in trying to defend his position plausibly, has deserted his egoism in the process.

B. Criticism of ethical egoism

Let us turn, then, to the remaining portion of our discussion of ethical egoism. If we cannot provide any good defense of ethical egoism, can we provide a good attack upon it — possibly a conclusive attack, a disproof of the whole doctrine?

1. The first attack takes the following form: "According to the egoist, I should (that is, it is my duty to) promote only my own interest. But to make this statement is to ignore entirely the difference between *duties* and *interests*. To pursue my own selfish welfare may be to my own interest, but it is not the same as my duty. It might be to my interest to save my own life even if a hundred others thereby perish, but it does not follow that it is my duty to do so. The egoist's mistake is to confuse duty with interest. To be sure, he says that it is my duty to promote my own interest; but what he is really saying is merely the tautology that it is to my interest to do so."

It is true that where most people talk about duties to others, the egoist does not do so — he only talks about interests and conflicts of interest. In the one instance where he does talk about duty — namely, his own duty of pursuing exclusively his own interest — he is, of course, only talking about interest, namely his own interest. It would be much less misleading if the ethical egoist did not talk about duties at all but only about interests and conflicts of interest. In fact, many ethical egoists never *do* speak of duty — they merely talk about interests (what works to my advantage). It hardly even sounds natural for them to speak of duty. Since the only time they do speak of it is in connection with pursuing their own interest, use the term "interest," which we already have, for "duty" in this sense and do not need the additional term "duty" at all.

The ethical egoist may smilingly grant this whole argument. "It is true," he may say, "that I don't talk about duty but only about interests; What difference does it make? I get along very well that way. Why *should* I talk about duty? Why should I play *your* language-game by distinguishing two things, duties and interests? I maintain that there are only interests and conflicts of interest."

This charge by the ethical egoist is not, to say the least, easy to refute. If he persists in talking only about interests and rejects all talk about duty, we may never be able to change his opinion. We may say that he is only talking egoistically in order to rationalize and justify his egoistic way of living, but he will say, "How can it be a rationalization when I have nothing to be ashamed of? You assume that somehow the egoistic way is bad, but you haven't proved your assumption; so you cannot use it as a premise in your argument." Or, we may tell him that he is morally blind, that he cannot see the difference between interest and duty which the rest of us plainly see; and we can ask him to look again within his own conscience for something he has missed. But if, in spite of this appeal to introspection, he still fails to see something that we claim to see, we cannot of course convince him that he has missed anything; he will simply dismiss our claim to see something more than he sees as fraudulent. We shall discuss this matter further in Chapter 11; meanwhile it is enough to say that there is no way we can force the egoist to talk about duties as something over and above interests if he consistently refuses to do so and claims to see no such distinction. The believer in duties cannot force the egoist to play his language-game.

2. One might make a second attack on ethical egoism by attempting to refute it in a different sort of way:

Let B and K be candidates for the presidency of a certain country and let it be granted that it is in the interest of either to be elected, but that only one can succeed. It would then be in the interest of B but against the interest of K if B were elected, and vice versa, and therefore in the interest of B but against the interest of K if K were liquidated, and vice versa. But from this it would follow that B ought to liquidate K, that it is wrong for B not to do so, that B has not "done his duty" until he has liquidated K; and vice versa. Similarly K, knowing that his own liquidation is in the interest of B and therefore anticipating B's attempts to secure it, ought to take steps to foil B's endeavors. It would be wrong for him not to do so. He would "not have done his duty" until he had made sure of stopping B. It follows that if K prevents B from liquidating him, his act must be said to be both wrong and not wrong — wrong because it is the prevention of what B ought to do, his duty, and wrong for B not to do it; not wrong because it is what K ought to do, his duty, and wrong for K not to do it. But one and the same act (logically) cannot be both morally wrong and not morally wrong. . . .

This is obviously absurd. For morality is designed to apply in just such cases, namely, those where interests conflict. But if the point of view of morality were that of self-interest, then there could *never* be moral solutions of conflicts of interest.[1]

The main lines of Baier's attempted refutation are clear enough: One is that since every adequate ethical view must provide for solutions in situations of conflicts of interest, and since ethical egoism does not provide a solution for conflicts of interest, therefore ethical egoism is an inadequate ethical theory. So much for the inadequacy. But the criticism goes even further. The second line of refutation is that any view which is guilty of an inner contradiction is thereby refuted. Ethical egoism is guilty of an inner contradiction. Therefore ethical egoism is refuted.

a. It is true that there is no surer way of refuting a view than by showing that it is guilty of an inner contradiction. When we reflect about it, however, the present example will no longer seem to be an instance of such contradiction. To say that one and the same act is both right and wrong is to say that it is both right and not right, which is a contradiction in terms; for example, to say that Brutus killing Caesar was both right and wrong would involve a contradiction. But the example presented here is not that of one and the same act being both right and wrong. There are *two* acts, one by B and one by K. They are two acts of the same kind, namely attempted murder — or, if we prefer, one act of attempted murder and another of attempting to prevent it — but in either case there is no contradiction involved in two such acts being attempted. It doesn't even matter whether both acts are right; what matters is that there are *two* acts here, and therefore we do not have a case of *one and the same act* being both right and wrong.

b. Let us examine Baier's other objection, that ethical egoism cannot settle conflicts of interest. It is true that often, if not usually, we expect an ethical theory to settle conflicts of interest; for example, if Mr. A and Mr. B both want the same thing, we expect the ethical theory to tell us (in conjunction, of course, with empirical premises) which one should have it — just as we should expect such a decision from any judge. A judge could not possibly use ethical egoism as a way of settling such a case, for if A and B both want the same thing and they can't both have it, he will *have* to decide against the interest of *one* of them; and egoism, which tells each person to follow his own interest, can provide no basis for settling the dispute. Baier's second objection does seem to be a serious criticism.

How will the ethical egoist react to this objection? Need he be moved by them to renounce his theory?

a. The *personal ethical egoist* would not be at all disturbed by the objection. His one duty (as he conceives it) is to pursue exclusively his own interest. If he happens to be B, he will try to kill K; and if he is K, he will

[1] From Kurt Baier, *The Moral Point of View.* Ithaca, N. Y.: Cornell Univ. Press, 1958, pp. 189-90. Reprinted by permission of the publisher.

try to kill B (and foil B's attempts to kill him); and if he is neither B nor K, he will not concern himself with the dispute one way or the other. Of course if there is something in it for him, he will: if he stands to gain a fortune if B wins, then he will do what he can to assist B's victory, in order to obtain the fortune. Otherwise he will simply ignore the conflict of interests. You may ask, "Doesn't an ethical theory have to have a means of deciding what to do in a case of conflict of interests? If the personal ethical egoist had to advise B or K, what would he say?" But the answer is that if there is nothing in it for him, our personal ethical egoist will not bother to advise either party or try to aid either cause. If asked for advice on the matter, he would probably say, "Go away, you bother me."

So far, then, ethical egoism has not been refuted. It has been shown to be inadequate *only if* you expect an ethics to arbitrate conflicts of interest. Thus, the doctrine *would* be insufficient for the judge in a divorce court who had to decide whether to award custody of the children to the wife or to the husband. The judge has nothing to gain either way, but he has to decide on a matter of conflict of interest between the wife and the husband. If the judge were a personal ethical egoist, his principle would be simply to follow *his own* interest. But this principle wouldn't help him at all in dealing with the case at hand. Here he needs instructions, not for promoting his own interest, but for settling cases of *conflict* of interest between *other* people.

This instruction, of course, ethical egoism cannot provide. But the personal ethical egoist wouldn't mind at all. He has no interest in arbitrating other people's conflicts of interest. He will gladly leave such activities to the "fools."

b. How will the *impersonal ethical egoist* deal with the objection? His view, you will remember, is that he should pursue his own interest exclusively, that A should pursue A's, B should pursue B's, and so on for everyone. What will he do with the example of B and K? He will advise K to try to win over B by whatever means he can, and simultaneously advise B to try to win over K by whatever means he can. In other words, he will advise them to settle the matter by force or craft, and may the strongest or cleverest man win. Does his advice to B contradict his advice to K? Not at all; he is urging each one to try to gain victory over the other; his advice is not much different from telling each of two competing teams to try to win the game. He does not presume to settle a case of conflict of interest but simply tells each contestant to *try* to emerge victorious, though of course only one *can* be victorious.

So far, there seems to be no difficulty for the impersonal ethical egoist. But, as an impersonal ethical egoist, he does have a stake in the general acceptance of his doctrine; for he does say of other people, not just himself, that they should each follow their own interest exclusively. If he sees B, he will urge B to try to win over K; and if he sees K, he will urge

K to try to win over B — as we have already seen. But there is, while no outright contradiction, a curious *tactical incongruity* in his view. If the impersonal ethical egoist advises others to pursue their own interest, might not his advice interfere with the promotion of *his own* interest; and yet is he not committed by his own doctrine to pursuing his own interest exclusively? If he advises B and K, but neither B nor K is a threat to him, there is no problem. But if I advise my business competitor to pursue his own interest with a vengeance, may he not follow my advice and pursue his interest so wholeheartedly that he forces me out of business? For the sake of *my own* interest, then, I may be well advised to keep my egoistic doctrine to myself, lest others use it against me.

An impersonal ethical egoist, therefore, may simply prefer to keep his own counsel and not advise others at all. In this event, he escapes the difficulty just as the personal ethical egoist did. He will pursue his own interest regardless of who else opposes it; while he, as an impersonal ethical egoist, advises others to pursue *their* own interests, he will advise them only when doing so does not imperil *his* interest.

Thus, *if* you are an impersonal ethical egoist and *if* as an impersonal ethical egoist you have a stake in advising others, then — and only then — you will feel a conflict between the promotion of your egoistic doctrine and the promotion of your own interests, which will be damaged if others pursue their interests at the expense of yours. But this dilemma hardly refutes the egoist's doctrine; it concerns only a tactical matter of when to publicize it.

3. Ethical egoism is, however, subject to still a third attack. Suppose you are an impersonal ethical egoist and are suggesting courses of action to your acquaintances. Acquaintance A asks you what to do, and you say to him, "Promote your own interest exclusively; if B tries to get the better of you, cut him down. Even if you could save B's life by lifting a finger, there is no reason for you to do so as long as it doesn't promote your interest." Later on, B asks you what you think *he* should do. So you say to him, "Promote your own interest exclusively; if A tries to get the better of you, cut him down. Even if you could save A's life by lifting a finger, there is no reason for you to do so as long as it doesn't promote your interest." You give similar advice to your other acquaintances.

Suppose, now, that an onlooker heard you say all these things. He might wonder (with good reason) exactly what you were advising. Because you tell A to do what he wants and ignore B, our onlooker thinks you are a friend of A and an enemy of B. But then you go on and tell B to do what he wants and ignore A, so the onlooker now concludes that you are a friend of B and an enemy of A. What are you anyway? It sounds to the onlooker as if you are pathologically addicted to changing your mind. Perhaps, like some people, you are so impressed by whomever you are with at the moment that you forget all about the interests of those who aren't right there in front of you. That might explain your sudden shift in attitude.

The really curious thing about your shift is that according to impersonal ethical egoism it is no shift in attitude at all. It is a consistent expression of *one* attitude, namely impersonal ethical egoism. But that is just the point of the objection. *Is* it a single consistent attitude? When you are in the presence of A, it is only A's interests that count; but a moment later when you are in the presence of B, it is only B's interests that count. Isn't this a very strange situation? Can the question of whose interests ought to count really depend on whom you happen to be addressing or confronting at the moment?

x: Do you mean that the impersonal ethical egoist is giving A and B inconsistent directives?

y: No, he is telling A to try and conquer B, and B to try and conquer A. As we saw earlier, that advice is not inconsistent; both can try.

x: What then is the point of your objection?

y: That we have here a case of *inconsistent attitudes.* The impersonal ethical egoist has one attitude toward A when he is in A's presence but not in B's and another attitude toward A when he is no longer in A's presence but in B's. The first attitude is pro-A, the second one is anti-A. I call that inconsistent.

x: I don't see that it's inconsistent at all. Look, suppose he gathered together A and B and C and D etc. all at the same time. Then our egoist simply advises them *all* to pursue their own interest. He is not concealing from the one what he advises the other or changing his attitude to favor the individual he happens to be with. He is telling each one to promote his own interest against all the others.

y: But your explanation doesn't change the situation. If the impersonal ethical egoist sees each one separately, he tells A that A alone counts, tells B that B alone counts, and so on. This advice is inconsistent. If he sees them all together, what he tells them is that *each* of them is the *only* one that counts. Here the inconsistency is even more blatant. You can no more have four people, each of whom is the only one that counts, than you can have four chairs, each of which is the only chair in the room.

x: It's true that you can't have four people, each of whom is the only one that counts. But what does that mean, "count"? If it means that each one has exclusive importance, your objection is valid; not every interest can have exclusive importance, for then none would be exclusive. But perhaps "count" just means that each person is of exclusive importance to himself; or, if you object to that terminology, that each person should act *as if* he were of sole importance. In this interpretation, you will admit, there is no contradiction.

y: But surely that's not what the impersonal ethical egoist is saying. To A he is saying, in effect, "I hope that you, A, win out" and to B he is saying, in effect, "I hope that you, B, win out." Unless he constantly keeps changing his mind in order to favor whichever man he is with — and this possibility you yourself have excluded in saying the egoist is *not* pathologically addicted to changing his mind — you *will* have to say, I fear, that he is making inconsistent remarks. For unless he *is* changing his mind all the time, how can he hope that A wins over B and *also* hope that B wins over A?

x: If our egoist said that, he *would* be inconsistent. But perhaps he's not saying any such thing at all. He is not saying that he *hopes* A wins over B and a moment later that he hopes B wins over A. There is a difference between saying, "I hope you win" and saying, "Try to win!" He can't simultaneously hope that both teams will win, but he can certainly urge both teams to try. Besides, what's wrong with hoping both that A will not raise a finger to save B's life and also that B will not raise a finger to save A's life? Maybe that's the kind of world our egoist wants. His desire may not be a very pleasing one, but at least it is not involved in inconsistency.

y: Well, whether or not an inconsistency is involved, I think we can agree, depends on *exactly* what we take our egoist to be asserting. I think his stronger claim — that he hopes both will win or that each one is the only one that counts — *has* been refuted as inconsistent. But the weaker and less interesting view — that both should try — is still a possible one; at least it has not been shown to be inconsistent.

C. The moral point of view

If ethical egoism has not received a knockout blow by these criticisms (and whether it has or not depends on the exact form which the doctrine takes), at any rate it has received some damaging blows, of which ethical egoists are not usually aware when they glibly and naively propose the doctrine.

Whatever else may have emerged from this discussion, it is quite clear that ethical egoism is not compatible with the moral point of view. The moral point of view is of some importance and must now be explained.

The moral point of view is the *disinterested* point of view — not the same as *uninterested,* for that just means not caring one way or the other, but disinterested, meaning impartial. It is an Olympian point of view which sees the issue from all sides and is not committed to the interest of any special person (including the viewer) of any group. Every judge is supposed to be able to judge the case before him disinterestedly — that is, he is not an interested party to the dispute — and if he is not disinterested (impartial), he is not fit to act as judge. Consider our example of the divorce court: The husband, looking at the matter from one point of view, wants custody of the children; the wife, looking at the matter from another point of view, also wants custody of the children; friends of the husband will be inclined to side with him, friends of the wife to side with her. The judge, however, is supposed to look at the case impartially, in a way that transcends the point of view of either of the disputants.

It may be a fact of human nature that no one can be *entirely* impartial:

the judge may, in spite of himself, favor the wife because she is attractive or the husband because the story of the husband's boyhood is similar in some ways to his own. No one is immune to these influences, but at least he can be aware of them and try to correct his bias. Indeed, he may lean over backwards so far in trying to be impartial that he *over*-corrects for these influences: the judge may make it worse for the wife because he believes he is inclined to favor her on account of her attractiveness. But although it may be no more possible to be perfectly impartial than it is to draw a perfect circle, he approaches this ideal as closely as he possibly can. Nor does impartiality mean that when the judge tries to arbitrate the case he must always find both of the claimants partly right and partly wrong or that he must compromise: the right decision is not always arrived at by deciding on some half-way house between the two competing views. (If one person says that two plus two make four and another that two plus two make five, the correct solution would not be to compromise on four and one-half.) It may be that one party or the other is entirely in the right. But at any rate, the judge will try to adjudicate the claims not from the point of view of one or another of the interested parties but from that of an intelligent and conscientious *impartial* observer. This, of course, is far from easy to do, especially without considerable moral training and long experience.

Take another example: Different residents of New York City had different attitudes toward whether to build a bridge connecting Brooklyn with Staten Island. The homeowners who would have had to find new places to live were vehemently against building the bridge. The people who lived on Staten Island, as well as those who wanted to live there but could not because ferry service was too slow, were strongly in favor of the bridge. Motorists in general were in favor of it, as were those who commuted back and forth. Taxpayers who were not likely to want to go to Staten Island but who would have had to pay increased taxes for the bridge were against it. If egoism were the only ethical philosophy, there would have been no way of settling this dispute other than by force. We could have said to the motorist, "Push for it as hard as you can," and to the disfranchised homeowners, "Oppose it as strongly as you can." But there would have been no over-all policy, only a number of conflicting local or personal policies. Clearly, public officials and those entrusted with the decision had to decide the matter from a point of view transcending that of the various pressure groups. (Decisions are often made from the point of view of some lobby or pressure group, if the group controls the majority of votes on the committee; but then, of course, it's just a matter of one pressure group against another and no one is adopting the moral point of view.)

Most people do not find it particularly difficult to achieve some degree of impartiality when their own interests are not involved. True, they may be ignorant of the facts: they may advise a course of action that leads to disaster because they do not know that such a course of action will have this result. Or, they may identify so much with one person or be so unable (through lack of common experience) to identify with other persons, that they see everything from the first person's point of view and cannot even begin to comprehend the second. For example, the husband may sympathize with a husband he reads about in a newspaper and not with the wife because he knows how the husband feels but not how the wife feels. For the most part, people fail in impartiality when their own interests are involved. After giving all the relevant facts a rather impartial examination, a man may strongly advise his friend to take his mother-in-law into the household; and yet when it comes to taking his own mother-in-law into his household, he will invent all sorts of reasons for not doing so. Of course, there may be good reasons for not doing it in his own situation that do not apply to his friend's situation; but it is more likely that the very same reasons he uses to discourage himself from making the move he used previously to encourage his friend to do so. On countless occasions, people will be fairly impartial until the moment that *they* have to make a sacrifice or do something irksome: then they become bitter champions of a partisan cause — egoists in their own lives even when the advice they give others is far from egoistic. It is most difficult to retain the moral point of view when doing so goes contrary to our own personal interests. A good test of impartiality is this one: would you still urge the same course of action if the roles were reversed? You are irritated by a stutterer who cannot talk with you at the speed you would like; would you consider this irritation justified if you yourself were the stutterer, trying your best to speak as clearly and rapidly as possible? Suppose you were asked to arbitrate a dispute between A and B *before* you knew whether your own position would be that of A or that of B. *After* you were in the position of A or B, would you still offer the same arguments as you did *before* you knew?

The ethical egoist cannot take the moral point of view; for, as an egoist, he can only take *his own* point of view. He does what is to his own interest exclusively. When his interest happens to coincide with that of others, there is no problem — this coincidence usually happens in regard to the welfare of his own family; for if his wife and children are in distress, he too is in distress. But when his interest conflicts with that of others, he considers his own exclusively. For him there is no rational solution of conflicts of interest.

Not everyone who fails to take the moral point of view is an egoist. Some people sympathize and identify with special points of view which are not their own. There are laborers who unconsciously desire to dominate and thus identify with domineering persons; as a result these laborers are strongly procapital and antilabor, even though they belong in the ranks of labor themselves. Sometimes drivers of automobiles (probably because they are occasionally pedestrians themselves) identify sufficiently with the problems of pedestrians at crossings to favor the pedestrians' point of view as against that of the drivers. Sometimes a person may be so meek and humble — not in pose, but in fact — that he may consider the miseries and inconveniences of others without ever thinking of the greater misery and inconvenience brought upon himself.

So much for the moral point of view. However, a person may say, "So what? I know what the moral point of view is, but I see no reason why I should adopt it. Show me why I ought to adopt 'morality' rather than egoism. Especially when a course of action recommended to me calls for personal sacrifice on my part, why should I do it? Why should I consider others and not merely myself? Why should I ever put myself out for other people?" Since "morality" usually involves doing the right thing even when it conflicts with one's own interest, the question becomes, "Why should I behave morally? Why should I be moral when there is no advantage to me, even a long-term advantage, in being so? Granted that many acts which are described as right or as duties are *not* in accordance with my interests, why therefore should I perform them? I agree, at least for the moment, that behaving egoistically is not always right; but I ask you, why should I do what's right?" We shall turn to this topic next.

EXERCISES

1. Distinguish the following positions carefully from one another and comment on each of them.

a. Only my happiness is intrinsically good.

b. My happiness is intrinsically good for me, and yours for you.

c. The statement that my happiness is intrinsically good is true for me but not true for you.

d. My happiness is the only happiness that ought to concern me.

2. Try to think of some formulations of impersonal ethical egoism other than those presented in the text. Are they guilty of inconsistency or not?

3. "Well, it's a nice apartment, but it's not worth $140 a month." "But it is. It has the space I need." "Well, you need the space and I don't. You need the space, so it's worth $140 a month to you, but not to me." Does the use of the phrases "to you" and "to me" in this imaginary conversation violate any of the criticisms of those phrases set forth on pages 160-61?

4. Consider the following quotation in the light of the moral point of view (From *Common Sense and Nuclear Warfare* by Bertrand Russell. Copyright © 1959 by Bertrand Russell. Reprinted by permission of Simon and Schuster, Inc. and Allen & Unwin, Ltd., p. 30): "The Governments of East and West have adopted the policy which Mr. Dulles calls 'brinkmanship.' This is a policy adapted from a sport which, I am told, is practised by some youthful degenerates. This sport is called 'Chicken!' It is played by choosing a long straight road with a white line down the middle and starting two very fast cars towards each other from opposite ends. Each car is expected to keep the wheels of one side on the white line. As they approach each other, mutual destruction becomes more and

more imminent. If one of them swerves from the white line before the other, the other, as he passes, shouts 'Chicken!' and the one who has swerved becomes an object of contempt. As played by irresponsible boys, this game is considered decadent and immoral, though only the lives of the players are risked. But when the game is played by eminent statesmen, who risk not only their own lives but those of many hundreds of millions of human beings, it is thought on both sides that the statesmen on one side are displaying a high degree of wisdom and courage, and only the statesmen on the other side are reprehensible."

5. Do you think that the following example (taken from a student paper) constitutes a refutation of ethical egoism? "Two egoists do piece-work in a factory, and the boss makes them keep the factory floor clean to avoid fire department violations. If the floor is not cleaned, it is a fire hazard, and the building will close down and the workers lose their jobs. The egoists use most of the floor, but they don't want to clean it because they don't want to lose money while they could be turning out pieces of work for money. According to egoism, it is each one's duty to act so as to maximize his own interest. The egoist's doctrine, however, directs each worker to clean the floor and also *not* to clean the floor: for if he does, the other worker will make money while he cleans; and if he doesn't, he'll lose his job. It is each one's duty to clean the floor to keep his job, but yet he should not clean the floor because it is not to his advantage to do so."

6. Do you think that the following example constitutes a refutation of egoism? (From Richard Brandt, *Ethical Theory*. Englewood Cliffs, N. J.: Prentice-Hall, Copyright 1959, p. 373. Reprinted by permission of the publisher.) "Suppose two knights are competing for the hand of a beautiful maiden, who likes both equally. Then does not egoism direct the one, implicitly: 'Kill your rival and have the maiden for yourself'? And does it not direct the other, implicitly: 'Kill your rival and have the maiden for yourself'? But both directives cannot be followed." (Brandt does not consider the example to be damaging to egoism.)

7. In which of the following circumstances would *you* behave egoistically?

a. You know that you will sell your car in a year or two anyway and that by "breaking it in hard" you will probably not be hurting the car during the time that *you* own it but that the person who buys it from you will have many extra repairs because of your early treatment of the car. (Assume also that the results of your mistreatment will not be obvious after a year to the buyer, to prevent him from buying it.)

b. Would you, if you were a car manufacturer, put together a car cheaply and without necessary safety devices, if you had considerable statistical evidence to prove that many more people would be attracted to your product because of its lower price than would refrain from buying it because of its shoddy construction?

c. Would you, a motorist, stop to pick up a piece of jagged metal from the highway, to keep other motorists from getting a flat tire? (Assume that you have already passed the spot and will not pass that way again, so there is no danger to your car.)

d. If you manufactured cancer-producing cigarettes (whose carcinogenic effect you could avoid by an expensive process), would you pay the newspapers to withhold information about the ill-effects of your product from the public (threatening them with loss of your very considerable advertising if they didn't), provided, of course, that the cost of your bribing the newspapers was less than the cost of manufacturing the cigarettes safely?

e. If you had a ring (like the Ring of Gyges in Plato's *Republic*) which would make you invisible, would you steal articles from stores rather than buy them outright, knowing that you could never be detected?

READING LIST, SECTION 10

Baier, Kurt. *The Moral Point of View*. Ithaca, N. Y.: Cornell Univ. Press, 1958, Ch. 8.

Brandt, Richard. *Ethical Theory*. Englewood Cliffs, N. J.: Prentice-Hall, 1959, Ch. 14.

Carritt, Edgar F. *Ethical and Political Thinking*. New York: Oxford Univ. Press, 1947, Ch. 4.

———. *The Theory of Morals: An Introduction to Ethical Philosophy*. New York: Oxford Univ. Press, 1928, Ch. 2.

Medlin, Brian. "Ultimate Principles and Ethical Egoism." *Australasian Journal of Philosophy*, Vol. 35 (1957), pp. 111-18.

Pratt, James B. *Reason in the Art of Living*. New York: Macmillan, 1949, Ch. 10.

Rashdall, Hastings. *Theory of Good and Evil*. 2nd ed. New York: Oxford Univ. Press, 1924. 2 vols., Vol. 1, Bk. 1, Ch. 3.

Schlick, Moritz. *The Problems of Ethics*. Englewood Cliffs, N. J.: Prentice-Hall, 1939, Ch. 3.

Sidgwick, Henry. *The Methods of Ethics*. 7th ed. New York: Macmillan, 1874, Bk. 2.

11. Why be moral?

In the coming chapters we shall examine and evaluate some views about what acts are right. But before doing so, let us first consider the question "Why should we do right acts?" The questioner in our present context is not denying that certain acts, which are not to his own interest, are right; but he is asking what connection there is between their rightness and his obligation to perform them. Suppose someone whom you have known for years and who has done many things for you asks a favor of you which will take considerable time and trouble when you had planned on doing something else. You have no doubt that helping out the person is what you ought to do, but you ask yourself all the same *why* you ought to do it. Or suppose you tell a blind news vendor that it's a five-dollar bill you are handing him, and he gives you four dollars and some coins in change, whereas actually you handed him only a one-dollar bill. Almost everyone would agree that such an act is wrong. But some people who agree may still ask, "Tell me why I shouldn't do it just the same."

A. Self-interest

The most usual answer, and the most popular answer, to the question "Why should we do right acts?" is "Because it *pays* to do so — because it will, later if not immediately, turn out to be *to our interest* to do so." This motive is appealed to so constantly that we are hardly aware of it. We are told to be honest, but not because honesty is a good thing: we are told that "Honesty pays" and "Honesty is the best *policy*"— the best policy, of course, being the one that most benefits us in the long run. "Be helpful to people when they need help, for then they'll help you when you need it." "Drive safely — the life you save may be your own"— the implication being that if the life you save were *not* your own you need not be so anxious to drive safely. Even Biblical commands often include such an appeal: "Cast thy bread upon the waters and it shall return to thee after many days." But suppose it didn't return to you, should you still cast it upon the waters? The president of a large American corporation, who gives two hundred fifty thousand dollars every year to cancer research, was asked why he did so, and he replied, "It costs more than a yacht, but I have more fun out of it." [1] Here at any rate is an unabashedly egoistic motive. Not every such appeal to morality is as crudely egoistic. "Be helpful to others, for if you do they'll help you in turn" is egoistic in a perfectly straightforward way. "Be helpful to others, for it will give you peace of mind" is perhaps less crudely egoistic, but it is egoistic none the less. If you are to be helpful because it will give you peace of mind, the implication still is that if being helpful did *not* give you peace of mind, there would be no obligation to be so. If those who utter these precepts do not mean them egoistically, they are misleading their listeners, for the general impression that is often left upon children and others who hear them is that one should do good deeds simply in order to get something out of it for himself, whether crude rewards like money and services, or intangible rewards like peace of mind. Morality, in short, is presented as an instrument of "enlightened self-interest."

Of course it is possible that justice *does* pay; it may be that when you do acts that are right, you yourself will always be the gainer thereby, even though at the time the act is one of heroic self-sacrifice. At least this possibility is worth examining. When you do something good, are you always rewarded for it sooner or later? Is right action always to the advantage of the doer?

Offhand, it would certainly seem obvious that the answer is "No." We hear that the good die young and that the big-time crooks are the ones who get away with it. Yet a great many people, moral philosophers and others, have answered our question with a "Yes." They have held that in the long run, when all the factors are considered, virtue *does* pay, crime never pays, and right action always brings benefit back to the door of the doer. Plato

[1] *Life*, Vol. 43, No. 8 (August 19, 1957), p. 108.

was the first to have held this view, and he devoted his longest dialogue, the *Republic,* primarily to an attempt to prove it. Let us see briefly how he defended his position.

First of all, according to Plato, it pays to live a just life because only in that way can you have the respect of your neighbors and friends — in fact, only in that way can you *have* any friends. If you are not a trustworthy sort of person who pays his debts and keeps his promises, other people will not trust you and will cease to have dealings with you. If you are trustworthy, you will earn the respect and esteem of those around you. Therefore, if you expect others to do decently by you, you would be wise to behave decently toward them. Only if you give will you also receive. Here, surely, is a perfectly sensible reason for being moral, a reason that will appeal strongly to most people. In fact, it is probably the main reason in practice why people *are* moral.

Nevertheless, Plato does not set much store by this argument for morality. After all, public opinion and public esteem are unreliable and quixotic. Your neighbors may respect you for things they shouldn't respect you for, such as raking in a million dollars in an illegal gambling operation; or they may feel contemptuous of you for *not* making lots of money, by whatever means. Or they may love you for virtues that they *mistakenly* think you possess; or they may hate you for misdeeds which you have never done. Anyway, if you are popular with them today, you may be unpopular tomorrow, though you yourself have not changed. Plato would say that it is on your own true merits that your happiness should be based, not on the ever-shifting and often mistaken attributions of merit given you by other people.[1]

Plato believes that a man is happy when he is moral ("just" is the word usually given in translations), regardless of whether or not his friends and countrymen hold him in high esteem; a truly good man will not be less happy if he is reviled for injustices he did not commit. Plato indeed makes his task extremely difficult by refusing to admit the slightest reward in the outside world as grounds for the happiness of the just man. He asks us to imagine, on the one hand, a just man, who is universally thought to be unjust and who is hated and ostracized by all his former friends for these imagined injustices, and to imagine, on the other hand, a supremely unjust man, a paragon of evil, who is so clever in his injustice that he is universally thought to be the most just of men and is praised, fawned upon, and followed with adulation wherever he goes for his imagined goodness. If the rewards of justice were to be found in the esteem of one's fellow men, then the just man who is wrongly thought to be unjust would be extremely unhappy, and the unjust man who is wrongly thought to be just would be the happiest of men. No, Plato concludes that the happiness enjoyed by the just man is not the result of something as unreliable and subject to error as the

---

[1] Plato, *Republic,* Bk. 1.

opinions of his fellow men. The happiness that the just man possesses is the result of something inside him, not something as external to him as fame, reputation, even respect. His happiness does not depend on whether men like him or dislike him, revere him or persecute him; it does not depend on whether he is rich or poor, king or slave, even on whether he is healthy or ill. It depends only on his inner state, on the state of his own soul.[1]

What is this inner state? Plato divided the human psyche (or soul) into three parts: the *rational* element was the highest, for reason was to be in control of the other parts or elements; second was the *spirited* element, which has been variously interpreted but is probably best conceived as a kind of drive, or will power, an executive branch which puts into action the decisions arrived at by reason; and third, the appetitive element (the bodily appetites), which has to be held in check, though not suppressed entirely, by reason. There is far more to be said about the division of the psyche than this brief description, but the division is a familiar one and it is not necessary to fill in the details here.

A human being such as Plato describes — one with a healthy psyche, that is, one in which each of the three elements plays its proper role in the total personality — is, says Plato, a happy man. Plato has established the· conditions of psychological health just as a physician might set up conditions for physical health. The man who does not possess within himself the conditions of psychic happiness is an unhappy human being no matter how much society may revere him; and a man who does possess within himself the psychical state which Plato describes is happy no matter what society may think of him or do to him.

It is obviously true that Plato's psychology is somewhat out of date. The psyche is not divided into three parts. Furthermore, countless questions could be raised about the application of Plato's psychology to particular situations. But let us ignore these objections and comment briefly on Plato's position thus far.

a. There is a certain undeniable truth in the general position. Some people have what may be called a "happy temperament"; they are relatively happy no matter what happens to them, and they can overcome even the worst of the trials and tribulations that life serves them and come out comparatively unscathed; whereas other people, not blessed with such a temperament, are laid low by even the tiniest vicissitudes of life — they are "knocked out," as far as happiness is concerned, by things which would not bother a person of happy temperament in the slightest.

b. But to say that everyone's happiness is quite independent of external factors is a gross overstatement, at least as far as most people are concerned most of the time. A person may be happy when family and friends are present, unhappy when they are dead or absent. A person may be happy when

[1] *Ibid.*, Bk. 2.

he has no financial worries and is in good health, and he can certainly be unhappy when he doesn't know where his next meal is coming from or when he is in constant pain and discomfort. Can a person be really happy while he is being tortured on the rack, no matter how well-adjusted his disposition may be and no matter how happy he may be by temperamental endowment?

c. In any event, our main question so far has not been answered. Even if we grant for the moment that happiness depends on the state of one's soul and not at all upon the outside world, we must still ask, "What has all this to do with morality?" What we have to prove is that the moral man is also the happy man. Even if Plato's psychology is correct, and even if his claim about happiness being entirely a matter of the inner man is true, he still has to show us that the moral man is the one who is happy and the immoral man unhappy.

To this task, then, Plato proceeds. He does not consider the common garden variety of unjust men — the petty thieves, the men who are cruel to their wives, the cheap swindlers, or the holy hypocrites. He discusses rather, in detail, what he takes to be the epitome of the unjust man: the cruel dictator, the tyrant. The man who is seized with the desire for immense power thinks that once he has attained power over the lives and destinies of other human beings he will be the happiest of men. Actually, as it turns out, Plato says that he is the most miserable of men. In the first place, his desires are such that they can never be satisfied. When he gets power, he wants more; and when he has more, he wants still more; lust for power is an appetite that feeds and grows upon itself and can never be entirely satisfied short of omnipotence. The same applies to lust for sensual gratification, greed for gold, and desire for fame, once these desires are no longer held in check by reason. To try to gratify these desires, once a man has given in to them, is, according to Plato, like trying to pour water into a leaky vessel: the more you pour into it, the larger the leak becomes because of the weight of the water; and the larger the leak becomes, the more water you have to pour in to try to compensate for the leak, and so on indefinitely. Obviously, a man whose life is devoted to the satisfaction of desires which are by their very nature impossible to satisfy completely cannot be a happy man. Indeed, Plato says that he is of all men the most miserable. He thinks that power will satisfy his desires, whereas it only increases his appetite for more of the same.

"Besides," Plato would continue, "who is fit to judge which way of life is the happiest? Only the person who has experienced all the sources of happiness is fit to judge; the tyrant, slave as he is to the basest desires of his nature, is in no position to judge what the best sources of happiness are. The tyrant knows nothing of the sources of happiness open to the man of ideas or to the man who lives a moral life without encroaching upon the rights of his fellows. What appears to the tyrant at the time to offer him the zenith of happiness — the immoral life — is actually what brings him to the nadir of misery. It is the road that does not appear to promise much to begin with that in fact brings most fulfillment, but the immoral man will never know the joys of that journey because he has never even caught a glimpse of the road."

What shall we say of this argument? Though we might cavil at a few points in Plato's description of the life of the tyrant (not all tyrants are alike), let us, for brevity's sake, grant everything that Plato says about the life of the tyrant and the state of his happiness. But what does the argument show? Only that *one* type of immoral man usually winds up miserable instead of happy as he planned. It does not show that all immoral men do so. Even less does it show that all moral men are happy.

Let us notice carefully that there are two separate propositions here: all moral men are happy, a statement which seems to be plainly false; and immoral men are unhappy, a statement which has a certain degree of plausibility.

a. It would be easy to refute Plato's first proposition. We could give many examples showing that moral men — that is, men who generally perform right acts, not necessarily those rare souls who adopt the moral point of view — are not always happy. Of course we might argue about which acts are the right ones, those in accord with the conventional mores of society or perhaps those contributing the most to the happiness of humanity. But in which ever of these senses we take "right," we reach one conclusion which we can best put in this way: "It may be that morality is a *necessary* condition for happiness — that is, happiness is not possible without it — (this we have yet to see) but at any rate, morality cannot possibly be a *sufficient* condition for happiness — that is, morality alone is not enough to ensure happiness. Once we have made the distinction, the point seems fairly obvious. No matter how moral the man may be, he is not happy when he is being tortured on the rack, or when he is suffering from cancer of the bone, or when his family is being fed to the lions, or, at the very least, he is not *as* happy while these things are going on as he would be if he were *not* undergoing these agonies. Our happiness *is* to some extent at the mercy of forces outside us and for most of us, to a very large extent. This observation alone is sufficient to show that, no matter how moral we are, morality *alone* does not guarantee happiness. The most moral people are not necessarily the happiest people. At best, there are certain stumbling-blocks to happiness which are not present in their nature; but the removal of an unfavorable condition does not guarantee the presence of a positively favorable condition, any more than the removal of rocks from a field guarantees that the soil will be fertile once it is opened to the plow. Plato does not even begin to show us that the moral man is always happy — that is, that morality is sufficient for happiness.

b. Plato's second proposition is more plausible, or at any rate more arguable. Is morality a *necessary* condition for happiness? Even if morality alone is not enough to guarantee happiness, perhaps it is a negative condition — that is, perhaps happiness is never attainable without it.

As far as Plato's example of the power-hungry tyrant is concerned, modern psychiatry would bear out a great deal of Plato's contention. The criminal, the murderer, the professional thief, the tyrannical dictator without ideals who merely satisfies his lust for power — all these, psychiatrists will concur, are profoundly unhappy men following in their unconscious minds intricate networks of inner conflicts, chiefly pseudo-aggressive defenses against masochistically tinged impulses of rebellion in early childhood. If one wanted to find happy people, he would not be likely to find them among members of the Mafia. Such men can never know real peace of mind; they can only struggle, plot, scheme, dare, kill, run constant risks; they are never secure of life and limb, never sure that someone won't do them in as they have done in others, always strangers to the relaxation that most people know, always harboring within themselves large reserves of aggressions, undigested conflicts, fear, and guilt. One has only to read case histories of these men in psychiatry books to be convinced anew of Plato's point, with far more evidence than Plato had at his disposal. Perhaps, we will be inclined to think, their chickens always *do* come home to roost sooner or later. Even if the moral man is not always happy, perhaps the immoral man is always unhappy.

Of course these psychiatric findings do not build as strong an argument as the one might desire for the dependence of happiness on morality. The ax falls upon the innocent as much as upon the guilty. Countless moral people have their lives made miserable by unconscious fears, fantasies, or guilt feelings pertaining to wholly imaginary acts performed by them years ago or in early childhood, acts for which they are punishing themselves day after day and year after year throughout their adult lives. Often the highly moral but extremely neurotic person has a far worse time of it, as far as happiness goes, than the far less moral person who is thick-skinned and has more successful inner defenses.

This observation only shows that psychiatry is indifferent to moral categories; it does not show that the immoral person is ever happy. Rather, it only shows us once again what we have already observed, that the moral person is not always happy. Once again, morality may be a necessary condition for happiness, but it is no sufficient condition.

However, even this second proposition — that morality is necessary for happiness — is, taken as a universal generalization, quite surely false. Let us take a few examples to illustrate the point.

(1) Popular novels often tell of people who do good deeds for which, at the moment, they do not seem to be rewarded. A man helps many down-and-outers with money, advice, and valuable time. The recipients seem to be unappreciative. Then, years later when the giver least expects it and most

needs it, one of the many persons he has helped turns up suddenly and helps him. (Remember, for example, Dickens' *Great Expectations*.) Such stories are very warm and very consoling. But what about those thousands of cases in which the giver does *not* run into one of the recipients of his beneficence, either at a critical juncture or at any other time? Perhaps the recipient dies too soon, or never hears of his benefactor's trouble, or his train is delayed until it is too late. These situations go largely unrecorded, for they do not appeal to our sense of the romantic and our deep-seated wish that things turn out in accordance with our desires.

(2) There are two brothers, one hard-working and the other indolent. The older brother cannot have an education because he earns money for his younger brother to use to go to school. The younger brother, however, never makes use of his education; he is always getting into scrapes, and the older brother is always getting him out of jail and paying his bills. The younger brother counts on the older one's helping him out and so gets into trouble without worry: "George always helps me in a pinch." A large portion of the older brother's income goes to the support of the younger brother, whom the state will not support as long as there is a member of his family capable of doing so. The older brother's generosity means a lifelong sacrifice from which he gains nothing, not even personal satisfaction. He could have used the money himself to much better advantage, yet he feels that while he is able to he should take care of his own flesh and blood, even if his benevolence means that he himself will have no savings to draw on in his old age. The older brother has been unlucky in love and lives a comparatively unhappy life in spite of his benevolence, while the younger, much more attractive to the opposite sex, has a much better time out of life in spite of his laziness, shiftlessness, and constant dependence on the good will of his older brother. It would certainly seem that the one is more moral and the other is happier.

(3) There is a young bank clerk who decides, quite correctly, that he can embezzle $50,000 without his identity ever being known. He fears that he will be underpaid all his life if he doesn't embezzle, that life is slipping by without his ever enjoying the good things of this world; his fiancée will not marry him unless he can support her in the style to which she is accustomed; he wants to settle down with her in a suburban house, surround himself with books, stereo hi-fi set, and various *objets d'art,* and spend a pleasant life, combining culture with sociability; he never wants to commit a similar act again. He does just what he wanted to do: he buys a house, invests the remainder of the money wisely so as to enjoy a continued income from it, marries the girl, and lives happily ever after; he doesn't worry about detection because he has arranged things so that no blame could fall on him; anyway he doesn't have a worrisome disposition and is not one to dwell on past misdeeds; he is blessed with a happy temperament, once his daily comforts are taken care of. The degree of happiness he now pos-

sesses would not have been possible had he not committed the immoral act. Apparently, crime sometimes does pay; in fact, sometimes it pays very handsomely indeed; the cinema to the contrary notwithstanding, only a small portion of the crimes committed are ever detected. Nor do those who commit crimes always suffer pangs of conscience or fears of detection; they often suffer far less than neurotics and psychotics who fill our mental hospitals and who have never committed any crimes at all but are innocent victims of situations thrust upon them in the far distant past.

(4) There is a person of great sensitivity and strong humanitarian feelings who is extremely conscientious in fulfilling what he believes to be his duties to his fellow men. Realizing poignantly the state of mankind and the hopelessness of one person's trying to change it, his life is not nearly as happy as that of the comparatively thick-skinned man who is less intelligent and less sensitive to the sufferings of other human beings. The latter person may stumble through life seeing only a small part of it, but he obviously cannot worry about evils that he cannot see or understand, and his level of happiness is considerably above that of the first man.

(5) In a courtroom there is a constitutional psychopath who is extremely clever at inventing stories about his imaginary troubles. He can weep and lie brazenly but with such emotion that the jury is moved to tears and exonerates him from the perfectly true charges against him. There is also a falsely charged man who is genuinely innocent but is not so clever at putting on an act. His story, every word of it true, fails to impress the jury, and he is convicted, even though he is innocent. That justice always triumphs is an aphorism as absurd as it is often quoted. But it is a law of human nature that for every aphorism there is an equal and opposite aphorism — we simply use whichever one suits the occasion. The opposite one in this case is "There ain't no justice" — which, unfortunately, the world being what it is, seems to be true as often as the first one.

(6) Perhaps the most dramatic illustration of all is war. Millions of people are killed in wars, and most of those killed certainly do not deserve to be killed. They are innocent victims of the rapacity of individuals highly placed in the political system of the nation or victims of the disease of nationalism itself, which makes it fatally easy for two nations, neither of which wants war, to blunder into it. Sometimes the guilty parties get their just deserts and sometimes they don't; but nothing seems to be more certain than that the *victims* of war are, for the most part, innocent victims and that they pay with their lives for misdeeds which are not their own.

There is hardly need of further examples. Nothing seems plainer to one who reflects upon the state of the world and the people in it than that there is no due proportion between human merit and human happiness. The main thing that keeps us, Americans especially, from acknowledging this injustice is a sentimental Pollyannaism which makes us believe that "in the long run everything always comes out all right," although experience daily contradicts this smug assumption. We have been exposed to so many movies and television stories that we have turned things upside down: we judge life by whether it is like the fiction instead of judging the fiction by whether it is like life.

It is difficult, in the light of all these examples, to avoid agreeing with Henry Fielding's remark:

> There are a set of religious, or rather moral writers, who teach that virtue is the certain road to happiness, and vice to misery, in this world. A very wholesome and comfortable doctrine, and to which we have but one objection, namely, that it is not true.[1]

One more consideration, however, should be advanced before we leave self-interest as a reason for moral behavior. We have seen that there are good self-interested reasons for moral *action* — one pays one's debts and keeps one's promises in order to gain the respect of others or a reputation in one's community, although these reasons do not operate without exception. But we might make an argument also for adopting an *attitude* other than that of exclusive concern with oneself. There are reasons of self-interest for developing, if one can, attitudes which will lead one to care about the welfare of other human beings and not merely oneself.

Suppose that the range of your interests includes only yourself. You don't care whether anyone else succeeds or fails, lives or dies. You gain happiness from your own triumphs, unhappiness from your own failures, but you regard everyone else with complete indifference except insofar as other people can be used to promote your own selfish ends. The range of your sources of happiness will, then, be very small. But if you can become the kind of person who is happy when others (at least *some* others) are happy, you will have widened greatly your own possibilities of happiness. It is true that you will also have widened your possibilities of sorrow by being hurt when hurts come to others. If, however, you are not so sensitive as to be paralyzed into inaction by these hurts but do your part to remedy them, you will be decreasing the possibility of a repetition of their occurrence. Moreover, you will be increasing the possibility that others will be of help to you when misfortunes come to you. If you genuinely care about other people, they in turn will be more likely to care genuinely about you. Your concern creates mutual good feeling which is far more of a contribution to happiness than one might think until he has personally experienced such feeling.

The ability to share the joys of other human beings will be likely, then, to heighten the level of happiness possible in one's own life. If only one person can win the European trip and one cares only about himself, then all the other competitors for this prize will be disappointed and frustrated. But if the losers are able sincerely to congratulate the winner and even to share in their imagination the enjoyment of the holiday, their own satis-

[1] Henry Fielding, *Tom Jones* (New York: Modern Library), p. 672.

factions will be greatly increased — perhaps not as much as if they had gone themselves but yet far more than if they had been able to experience only envy and resentment. If you lose the trip, you will at any rate have some satisfaction in the knowledge that someone will enjoy it; and if you win it, you will be able to enjoy it more in the knowledge that others are not hating you for having the opportunity that is denied to them. It is, then, to *your own interest* to develop within yourself attitudes that make it possible for you to share the joys of others. Your life will be richer, less mean and grasping, and no longer characterized by the corrosive feelings of hatred and envy. The success of one person will no longer be built upon the resentment and hostility of others. We have, then, another self-interested reason for "being moral": one which asks of us that we not merely *behave* morally with regard to other human beings but that we develop *attitudes* toward them from which the actions will flow without effort and as a matter of course.[1]

B. Divine command

Let us turn, then, to a second answer to the question, "Why should we be moral?"— namely, "Because God will reward me if I am and punish me if I'm not."

1. "Let's grant," one may say, "that in *this* world the just are often unhappy and that the unjust are happy. But this truth doesn't apply to the next world, where all these scores will be set straight. Indeed, the very fact that there are such gross inequities in this world is one of the reasons why many people have argued that there must be a next world in which the inequities are overcome."

Of course, the fact that this world is unjust doesn't prove that there is another world that is just, any more than the fact that people are hungry proves that there will always be food. As an argument for an afterlife, this one is as much of a *non sequitur* as any argument could be. But it would take us too far afield here to consider the various arguments for immortality. However we may have arrived at the conclusion that there is another life in which all the discrepancies between virtue and happiness will be set right, doesn't our conclusion solve our problem? If our conclusion is true, we need only smile at Plato's hopeless attempt to prove the impossible thesis about justice in this world; and when we hear more and more examples of men being good but unhappy or bad but happy we need only say, "But you see, it *doesn't* always pay to be moral, when you consider only *this* life; but when you consider the life to come, you will realize that it *does* pay to be moral. It is only in the life to come that the prophecies will come true, that the bread that you cast on the waters will come back to you, and with compound interest."

---

[1] This view, for which I am indebted to Michael Scriven, will be developed further in Chapter 7. Here we are concerned, not with expounding ethical theories, but with providing "reasons for being moral."

The first thing to observe about this second answer is that it will appeal only to those who already accept the doctrine of an afterlife in which a just God distributes rewards and punishments according to merit. Those who deny the doctrine or aren't sure will not be moved by it as a reason for morality. Since the argument depends on the truth of this doctrine, one had best be quite sure that it is true and that all competing claimants to the true doctrine are false. If one staked his entire moral life upon the truth of a doctrine announcing eternal rewards, and this doctrine turned out to be false (or some competing doctrine true instead), this result would surely seem to be something of a dirty trick.

Moreover, if the only reason you have for being moral is that God will punish you if you aren't or reward you if you are, then the moment you doubt or no longer believe there is a God who will do these things, your only reason for being moral will vanish. Many people, it seems, are in precisely this situation.

Even for those who are already convinced of the afterlife promised by their religion, there is another point they must squarely face: When a man says, "I should be moral because if I'm not, I'll be punished," he is appealing as much to selfish motives, to self-interest, as our first answer did. It is just self-interest pushed into the next world instead of being confined to this one. The person who acts from this motive is just playing the game for higher stakes. He is declaring his willingness to postpone his reward a bit longer in order to collect at a higher rate of interest in the next world — which is as selfish as it could be. It is like working longer hours in order to collect time and a half at the end of the day. Nor is the moral life conceived as something desirable in itself; it's not that the man enjoys or takes pride in the work, it's only that he wants the money. Indeed, his motive for being moral is not much different from his motive in following the commands of a dictator before whom he cringes and trembles. One may or may not approve or like what the dictator commands, but one follows the commands because if one doesn't, he will be beaten or tortured. Once remove the threatened punishments and the promised rewards, and the person will no longer do as he was commanded.

There are many sincere and conscientious people who have believed that there was no good reason for being moral apart from divine punishments and rewards and that once these were removed, the moral fabric of humanity would crumble into dust. Of course, whether the moral fabric of humanity *would* crumble into dust if these threats and promises were removed, is an empirical question, which could be argued pro and con indefinitely. It is possible that most people do have to be prodded constantly with spears to make them go forward. There are, however, reasons for believing (as we shall see in the next chapter) that in general people's morality would not crumble if religious sanctions were removed, so long as the people had not become so accustomed to these religious sanctions that they could no longer operate without them; people who have not been brought up to depend upon religious sanctions seem to be none the less moral. Whatever the answer to the empirical question may be, hope of reward or dread of punishment may offer an *incentive* to those who are too weak or selfish to behave morally without them, but it cannot offer a good *reason* (justification) for being moral. If this statement begs the question of what we mean by a good reason, we can say that it offers a good reason only if completely selfish reasons are good reasons; it is simply an appeal to self-interest. "Be good or I'll punish you"— nothing could be a clearer appeal to naked and unbridled power than this. In fact the moral goodness of anyone who said it might be questioned simply because of the appeal to power unbacked by reasons.

The moral irrelevance of the appeal to power can be brought out best, perhaps, in this way. If there is a God who is the source of moral commands, then *either* God had a reason for commanding what He did *or* He did not.

a. One alternative is to believe that God had *no* reason for commanding what He did but the commands are simply the result of an arbitrary whim or fiat. If so, then what possible evidence do we have for believing that they are good or that we should obey them? We are told to obey them because we'll be punished if we don't. But that is exactly the same kind of reason — a prudential reason — for obeying the commands of a cruel dictator. We obey him in fear and trembling because we fear the consequences of not doing so, not because we revere him or his commandments. We may obey him and yet privately loathe both the dictator and his commands. Surely religious believers do not want their Deity to be obeyed only because He is more powerful than they are. They want to obey Him, not just because He commanded this or that, but because those commands are good. If the only defense that can be given for a command is simply "Do this because I say so," this is not much of a defense — in fact it is the kind of thing that is usually said when no defense can be given; unable to give any good reasons for his commands, the tyrant appeals to naked power.

Thus, if God has no reason for giving the commands He does, there does not seem to be any good reason why we should obey them other than our fear of His power. John Stuart Mill made this point dramatically: he said, in effect, "Why should I obey the commands of a being, however powerful, who gives no reasons for his commands other than the fact that he utters them? Might it not be better and more courageous of me to choose to ignore the commands and be willing to risk the punishment? After all, I should obey only those commands which are good, and what evidence have I that a being who would issue commands, without giving reasons but threatening punishment all the same for not obeying them, *is* good?"

When I am told that I must believe this, and at the same time call this being by the names which express and affirm the highest human morality, I say in plain terms that I will not. Whatever power such a being may have over me, there is one thing which he shall not do: he shall not compel me to worship him. I will call no being good, who is not what I mean when I apply that epithet to my fellow creatures; and if such a being can sentence me to hell for not so calling him, to hell I will go.[1]

b. The other alternative is to believe that God has a *reason* for commanding what He does. This belief will certainly strike us as the more palatable alternative. But if God has a reason for commanding A rather than B, then why could we not do A rather than B directly on account of that reason rather than because God has commanded it? At any rate, if God has commanded A for a reason, then it is for that reason, surely, that we too should do A; God's commanding it only provides an additional incentive, *if* we believe God to be good. (Of course, we *might* not have thought of A if God hadn't commanded it; if so, our lack of thought would be a good reason for God's issuing the command. But our question would still remain: "Was there or was there not a reason for his commanding A rather than B in the first place?") If we don't believe that A is good because God commands it (this belief was our first alternative), then our second alternative is to believe that God commands A because it is good. If that belief is true, as every student of Plato's *Euthyphro* well remembers, A's goodness is logically independent of God's commanding it, and it would have been good even if there had been no God at all to command it. God's commanding A is a result of A's being good, not the cause of its being good. In that event, religion is not *necessarily* tied to ethics, for there is some *criterion* for a thing's being good, a criterion not consisting simply in the fact that God commands it but a criterion which God Himself could use (and presumably so could we) in judging whether or not something is good. (See pages 31-34.)

2. So much, then, for the appeal to divine punishments and rewards. "But," one may say, "self-interest is not the only reason why people follow a religious ethic, though it may be the reason most frequently encountered. One may do good deeds, not because he fears divine punishments or anticipates rewards in a future life, but simply because he loves and adores the God whom he worships. One may act from love and devotion, not merely from fear of punishment or hope of reward."

Of course this observation is true. It is difficult to discover in individual examples how much subconscious fear there may be behind the consciously experienced love — this mixture of emotion also occurs in one's relation to his parents — but let us grant, indeed insist, that very often deeds are done from motives of love, affection, esteem, and adoration. Nevertheless, let us observe here one thing that is often forgotten: those who behave morally out of love for the God they believe in ought surely to do so *only*

[1] John Stuart Mill, *An Examination of Sir William Hamilton's Philosophy* (Boston: Spencer, 1865), p. 131.

if the God they believe in is morally *worthy* of their love and worship. Ought one to obey the commands of the ancient god Moloch, who demanded that children be thrown into the fire as a sacrifice to appease his wrath? One could question too whether one should obey the commands of the ancient Hebrew god Yahweh, who apparently condoned a great deal of plunder and slaughter against other tribes that were only trying to stay alive and can hardly be said to deserve their fate; yet Yahweh even chided the Israelites from time to time for being too merciful and not getting on with the job fast enough. After all, one shouldn't love just anybody, and one shouldn't obey just anybody's commands. A woman may love her husband, but that doesn't mean she should obey him when he tells her to sell her body on the streets to augment the family income. Love can be misplaced, and so can esteem and devotion. It is not good to be devoted to just anything; we must first make sure that what we love is worth loving, else endless harm can come of the love.

If, on the one hand, we love God, or whomever we believe to be God, blindly and without reason, then we have no guarantee that the object of our adoration deserves to be adored. But if, on the other hand, we love God because we believe that God has certain highly desirable and profoundly good moral qualities, then it is not just because we love Him that we do good things but because He has the qualities which entitle Him to our love. Already the answer to the question "Why should we be moral?" has changed. The answer is no longer, "Because I love and adore God," but, "Because God is good, and being Himself good, he desires to promote good in the world, and therefore commands us to do those things which He sees to be good." This answer points to a good that is independent even of God, in the sense that it would exist even if there were no God or if there were no *good* God (if God were evil, then it would be good to *dis*obey His commands, even if punishment were threatened for disobeying).

Even this answer will work only for those who already believe (1) there is a God and (2) He is good. If these two premises are granted, it will be natural to believe that God will try to maximize the good in the world by commanding us to perform it; but if it is good, shouldn't we perform it anyway, God or no God?

3. Still another version of the religious answer has been advanced: "We should be moral," some people say, "not because we expect rewards for being so nor because we love God and do it out of love, but simply because He is the Author of our being — He created us, and this entitles Him to our unquestioning obedience."

> God made us and all the world. Because of that He has an absolute claim on our obedience. We do not exist in our own right, but only as His creatures, who ought therefore to do and be what He desires.[1]

[1] R. C. Mortimer, *Christian Ethics*, p. 7.

Are we entitled to draw this conclusion? Let us assume that there is someone (not merely natural agents) who brought us into being, that this being is God, and that this same being laid down certain moral commands for us to follow — unless one already believed all these things, he would not use this argument. One can still ask *why* we ought to obey these commands. "God created us, therefore we should do as He commands" is an incomplete argument: it requires the additional premise that creatures ought to obey their creator. Suppose that creatures were created by a malevolent creator who brought them into being only to make them suffer (a view that has sometimes been held), would the upholder of this argument still say that he should obey the commands of such a creator? It would seem to depend on what kind of creator it was. The simple fact of the power to create, plus the use of that power, would hardly entitle any being to our unquestioning assent to his commands. Only if the creator were *good* as well as powerful would we be likely to say that we should do as he commands; we should obey him, not simply because of the bare fact that he created us, but because his commands are good ones. If we make this statement, our argument reduces to the one which we have just previously considered.

C. The common interest

Let us turn to another answer to the question "Why should we be moral?" The answer is, "We should be moral, not because there's something in it for us, or because God will reward us for it, or even because we believe God to be good and therefore want to obey the good directives He has set down for our guidance, but because obeying certain moral rules will help to achieve a better society — a society which we would prefer to one in which such rules were not observed."

Suppose that you are playing a game and that when you play it you agree upon certain rules. You cannot change the rules in a pinch just because the game is going against you. You play the game to win, but to win you must abide by the rules. To the extent that you cheat, you are not playing the game at all. If you are interested enough to play, you probably have an interest in continuing the game. Yet the game can be continued only if you play by the rules.

None of us is forced to play baseball or billiards, but the game of life is one which we all have to play in one way or another. Nor can we play it alone, for we are surrounded by other people who also must play the game. What then is the best means of playing it — best for all of us? As long as we are all together on this planet, isn't it better for all of us to find some arrangement whereby we can live together in such a way that we can each pursue as many of our own interests as possible yet not prevent others from pursuing theirs? To live in such a way we all have to stick to certain rules. Certain kinds of rules — those requiring us to consider the safety and welfare of others and those prohibiting us from aggressions against them — will operate to our *mutual* advantage; that is why we should obey them.

Consider two groups of people, of any size you please. In the first group the people live by certain rules — they refrain from killing, stealing, and committing other acts of aggression against one another. In the second group the people do not wish to be tied down by any rules — they commit acts of aggression against one another with no punishment other than retaliations from the injured party or his friends if they happen to catch the aggressor. In the first group, then, certain limitations are placed upon the behavior of each member; in the second group there are no such limitations. But the result of this lack of limitation is that people in the second group are much worse off than they would otherwise have been: their livelihoods and their very lives are in constant danger; at any moment they may be victimized by other people without recourse to law. It is usually agreed that the members of the first group are much better off than the members of the second. (The members of the second are in fact in the "state of nature" described by Hobbes, which we shall discuss in another connection in Chapter 8.) To live in the first group and behave according to its rules, then, will be to the interest of every member of the group.

At least, to behave according to the rules will be to the interest of every member of the group on *most* occasions: for example, it is to my interest to be honest; for by being honest I gain the respect of others and they will trust me in personal relations and in business enterprises. It is to my interest to refrain from aggression against others; for if I damage others, I shall probably be caught and imprisoned, and besides I shall have few, if any, real friends. Nevertheless, it may not be to my personal interest to live by the rules on *all* occasions: suppose, for example, that law-enforcement is lax or that I can bribe the appropriate officials and I can thus get by with taking from you what doesn't belong to me and be quite sure of not being prosecuted for my actions. Then why shouldn't I bribe and steal? I shouldn't commit these crimes, not because they don't work toward my individual advantage (for, according to our hypothesis, in this case they would), but because they work against the interests of the group as a whole — or, in other words, "the general interest." Once I realize that a group in which members obey certain rules is better than one in which they do not, I have a reason for behaving in accordance with these rules even in situations where doing so does not work toward my personal or individual interest.

Moralities are systems of principles whose acceptance by everyone as overruling the dictates of self-interest is in the interest of everyone alike, though following the rules of a morality is not of course identical with following self-interest. If it were, there could be no conflict between a morality and self-interest and no point in having rules overriding self-interest. . . . The answer to the question "Why be moral?" is therefore as follows. We should be moral because being moral is following rules designed to overrule self-interest whenever it is in the interest of everyone alike that everyone should set aside his interest.[1]

To many people this answer to the question "Why be moral?" will seem quite sufficient, but not to everyone; some will still demand a reason why they should behave morally (or according to rules which promote the interests of the group) in those situations, or on those occasions, when their own private interest conflicts with the interests of the group.

x: Why should I help someone else when it's not to my own interest to do so?

y: Because it is to our mutual interest for each person to help others.

x: I know that, but what do *I* care about that, as long as it's not to *my* interest to help?

y: But don't you want to live according to the rules which society has devised for the mutual interests of its members?

x: Not when they go against my own interest.

y: Other people have lived by the rules and sacrificed for you, even when it wasn't to their interest to do so.

x: I know that.

y: If they hadn't done so, you probably wouldn't be here to tell the tale.

x: I know that too.

y: Then isn't it reasonable that since they went against their own interest to serve yours, that you this time should go against your own interest to serve theirs?

x: Maybe it's reasonable, but I don't see why I should do it. So I'm not reasonable. Now what happens?

y: But if they sacrificed for you when you needed help, and now you turn around and desert them when *they* need it, what you are doing is parasitic. Your badness to them is made possible only by their prior goodness toward you.

x: O.K., so I'm a parasite. Now damn me. I'm still not going to do what's against my interest.

y: I'm not saying you will. I'm saying you should.

x: But you still haven't given me an acceptable reason *why* I should.

D. *"Because it's right"*

Is there any further answer that we can give in this maddening situation? At this point some will say, "Look, there's no further reason we can give this individual why he or anyone else *should* behave morally. All we can do is try to enlighten him on the *psychological* question of why people *do* act morally. After we have shown him some psychological facts, perhaps they will help him to act morally. That's all we can do."

[1] From Kurt Baier, *The Moral Point of View*. Ithaca, N. Y.: Cornell Univ. Press, 1958, p. 314. Reprinted by permission of the publisher.

1. Let us try this approach first. Let us ask, "What actually moves people to perform moral actions?" The answer is fairly simple. People do right acts from a vast variety of motives — sometimes from self-interest, such as hope of reward or having someone return the favor or of being socially accepted by doing the deed, but sometimes from the genuine, unselfish desire to help someone without expecting to be helped or rewarded in return, from the desire to do a good deed just because it will increase the good in the world and for no other reason. Human motives are extremely various, and there is probably no point in trying to pin them all down or classify them. If they are all put under one general heading, as the psychological egoists do (pages 141-55), and all of them are labeled "selfish," the word "selfish" would have to be stretched so as to be beyond all recognition; it would lose all its distinctive meaning and would no longer suffice to distinguish any one motive from any other, which was the whole purpose of having such a word in the first place. Therefore, it would be useless to try to limit the variety of motives at work in the human psyche by saying, for example, that people never act from sense of duty. It seems to be perfectly clear, once we are no longer deluded by words that have been distorted from their original meaning, that people often *do* act from sense of duty, even against their own private interests. Not all people act so all of the time, nor do most of the people most of the time, but some people do some of the time. People sometimes perform an act because they are fully and honestly convinced that it is the right thing to do, though they may not at all be convinced that the act will bring the most enjoyment or happiness or even peace to them personally. This observation is all we need to say on the psychological question. People do sometimes act from motives of duty; and if it is asked, "Why do people do right acts?" the answer is "Sometimes at any rate, they do them because they are convinced that what they are doing is the right thing to do, and for no other reason."

"But," our skeptic will continue, "the fact that something is right can never be a *motive* for action. Even the *knowledge* that something is right cannot, in and of itself, *cause* people to behave in a certain manner. There must also be a *desire* to act in the way required. Only desire can *move* people to action, even though the intellect can convince us that a given action is right. The intellect by itself cannot move us in one way or another. As Spinoza said, pure knowledge alone cannot make us act; the only thing that can keep us from acting on one desire is another desire stronger than the first."

We might say many things about this oversimplified picture of human nature according to which people act only from desire. But criticism is not necessary here, for one can accept the picture and still show the irrelevance of its conclusion. "Let's grant, then," we may say, "that the only force that can topple over a desire is another desire stronger than the first — in fact this is definitional, for if the second topples over the first, that is tantamount to saying that the second is stronger. But what does that matter? *One* of the desires we have—at least some of us—is the desire to do the right thing no matter what the cost to ourselves; and this desire is often very strong, particularly in times of crisis when our fellow men are in need of us." This conclusion is all we need. Human beings always act from their strongest desires—very well; but not all their desires are self-centered desires, and one desire that sometimes is dominant is the desire to do the right thing regardless of what it may cost us.

2. So much, then, for the psychological question, "Why, that is from what motives, do people do right acts?" But we are still left with the ethical question, not "Why, that is, from what motives, *are* people moral?" but "Why, that is, for what good reasons, *should* they be moral? Can any good reasons be given why they should be moral? If anyone has not been convinced by the reasons already given, what more can we say?"

The following answer may seem so simple and obvious as not to be worth giving: "We should be moral, simply because it's right." We are not, at the moment, inquiring whether a given act *is* right but rather, *assuming* that it is right, inquiring why we should *do* it. Assume that it is wrong to short-change the blind news vendor, why shouldn't we do it just the same? Our answer now is, "Simply because it's wrong, that's all. Isn't its wrongness itself a good enough reason for not doing it?" Certainly many eminent people have thought so. "Virtue is its own reward," said Spinoza; and indeed, why should one demand rewards for virtue, like a man who does unpleasant work only in order to receive higher pay at the end of the day? Isn't it enough simply that the act is the right one to perform? Perhaps the rightness of the act isn't enough to *cause* us to perform the act (for some the rightness will be enough, for others it won't, depending on our strength of will and moral purpose), but doesn't the rightness provide a sufficient *reason* for performing the act?

Plato's fallacy, it would seem, is that of taking for granted that the only reason why a person should behave morally is that by doing so he will be the gainer. The implication is that if it should turn out that it is not, after all, to his interest to behave morally, then no reason remains why he should do so. Isn't this line of argument a mistake? Plato was trying to reply to his opponents, the Sophists. The Sophists said that one need not behave morally because doing so often does not promote one's own interests and not doing so often *is* to one's interest. Plato, in replying to them, tried his best to show that the Sophists were wrong and that right action *does* promote one's interests, contrary to what they said. It now appears that what Plato *should* have done is something different: instead of trying to show that right action promotes one's interest, he should have questioned the chief presupposition of the Sophists' argument, namely that *if* right action ("justice") doesn't promote one's interest, then one has no reason for doing what is right. Plato, however, never questioned this presupposition; he and the Sophists both shared it. Instead, he set out to challenge their empirical claim that right action does not in fact always promote one's own interest. Had he challenged the presupposition of their argument instead of the argument itself, he would not have been led into such desperate maneuvers in trying to show that "the just man is the happy man." He would have said, "Whether right action is always to one's interest is irrelevant to whether one should perform it"; he would have said, "Granted that, the world being what it is, right action doesn't always lead to happiness; what does it matter? What makes you think that attaining happiness is the only good reason, or even a good reason at all, for doing what is right?"

Let us observe that we are not merely asking, "Why should we perform right actions?" and giving the tautological reply, "Because they're right." We are asking, "Why should we do this act rather than other acts we might have done instead?" and we are answering, "Because it's the right act." Isn't this the best answer and ultimately the only answer? If someone admits that a certain act is right and yet continues to ask why he should perform it, could it be that he is using this question as an excuse for failing to do what he already admits is right? If someone already accepts a certain act as right, doesn't its very rightness *already supply the reason* why he ought to do it?

If it is to a man's interest to perform the act, of course, he probably won't ask the question. (Even here we could ask, "Is the fact that it's to his interest the real reason why he ought to do it? Should he do it *because* it promotes his interest rather than because it is right?") He will ask the question only when the performance of the act is *not* to his own interest. No matter what answer we give him — that the act is conducive to society's interest or simply that it is right — he refuses to accept it as a reason for performing the act in question. He admits that he is a member of a group and has benefited heavily from the sacrifices of others; when his turn comes to perform a sacrifice for them (conducive to their interests, not to his own), he says, "Tell me *why* I should do it. I'm in the game only as long as I win; when I start to lose I quit. At this point the game doesn't pay off for me, so why should I keep on playing?" But what is this questioner demanding? What he wants, and he will accept no other answer, is a *self-interested* reason why he should keep on playing. But the situation is *ex hypothesi* one in which the act required of him is contrary to his interest. Of course it is impossible to give him a reason *in accordance with his interest* for acting *contrary to his interest*. That would be a contradiction in terms. It is a self-contradictory request, and yet people sometimes make it and are disappointed when it can't be fulfilled. The skeptic shows us an example in which he would be behaving contrary to his interest and asks us to give him a reason *why* he should behave thus, and *yet* the only reasons he will accept are reasons of self-interest. It is no wonder that such a questioner must be disappointed. So must the seeker after square circles.

If the skeptic cannot, without self-contradiction, accept a reason of self-interest for doing what is contrary to his interest and yet he will accept no reason *except* one of self-interest, what more can be done? What meaning does his question now have? (Isn't his question an expression of inner weakness, of conflict as to whether he is going to stick by moral principles to which he has originally committed himself or whether he is going to desert them, not because he has found anything intrinsically wrong with the principles, but because in this situation they conflict with his self-interest.) He wants to eat his cake and have it too: he wants a reason of self-interest to justify an act that would be contrary to his interest, or he wants a moral, (nonself-interested) reason to justify an act of pure self-interest. Once we have explained this situation to him, if he still keeps on asking the question, it would seem that either he still does not understand the nature of his question or he is still trying to have it both ways — and this, it must be admitted, is all too frequently a motive for engaging in philosophical reasoning.[1]

One last point: "But what are you going to do if people *aren't* moral?" some people will ask. Perhaps the philosopher cannot do anything about it at all. It has been our task to consider what the philosopher can validly say about the question of why we should act upon moral principles we already believe to be right; but to show why we should act upon them, of course, does not guarantee that we *shall* act upon them. None of us acts upon his moral convictions 100 per cent of the time; and some of us honor our morality more in the breach than in the observance. Some people, owing perhaps to an unfortunate childhood, are in their adult life so unbendingly and calculatingly selfish that nothing can make them behave unselfishly, whether they profess any moral principles or not. It is not the philosopher's task to make them so. The philosopher cannot, to any great extent, turn selfish people into unselfish ones, immoral people into moral ones; he can move people only if they are willing to hear rational arguments and to act on the basis of them. Philosophy works only when people can be appealed to by rational considerations. Many people, perhaps most people when their selfish interests are involved, cannot be appealed to by these rational considerations; on such people, philosophy is powerless. Some people are in fact singularly immune to reason, and have to be threatened, persuaded, or browbeaten into behaving morally. Some people are immune even to those methods. Such people can never be aided by the philosopher; what they need is a very different kind of therapy which they can receive while reclining on the psychoanalyst's couch.

[1] A further point will be made on this issue in Chapter 11 when we discuss various ways of life.

EXERCISES

1. Do you think that Plato was right in his belief (in the *Republic*) that "the just man is always the happy man"? Examine his various arguments, which come to a climax at the end of Book IX. Does the meaning of the term "justice" shift during the argument between its first introduction in Book I and the culminating arguments in Book IX? If so, how? (Be careful, also, to distinguish in Plato between just *acts* and justice as a "state of the soul.")

2. Read Chapters 11 and 12 of W. T. Stace's *The Concept of Morals*. Do you agree or disagree with Stace's account of why we should be moral? Why?

3. Read Chapter 12 of K. Baier's *The Moral Point of View*. Do you agree with Baier's account of why we should be moral? Why?

4. Would you say that the following facts (if they are facts) (1) society needs moral behavior from us and (2) God commands us to behave morally, are *reasons* for, or *incentives* toward, moral behavior? If incentives, what kind? If reasons, good reasons?

5. If there were a God who issued moral commands but who had no power to enforce them, would his lack of power make any difference to your view of divine commands as a reason or incentive for being moral? Explain. Suppose, instead, that there were a God who was omnipotent but either evil or morally indifferent. Would that make a difference? Why?

6. "The moral life is a conflict between reason and desire." Find as many respects as you can in which this statement is incorrect.

7. Try to think of five situations in which, in an unexpected way, the consequences of a person's good deeds or his bad deeds return to visit him — "his chickens come home to roost." Then try to think of five situations in which there were no such consequences — a person made a sacrifice without a return or did something bad without being punished. Which of the two kinds of situation do you consider occurs most frequently? How would you comment on the situations below?

a. During World War II an American flyer in Germany had a weekend pass to London. While in London he met a friend in the Air Transport Command, who said to him, "Why not go home to Baltimore this weekend? I know it sounds crazy, but you are an officer and nobody will question you — you're top security. Get aboard an ATC plane to New York, take another plane to Baltimore, and return to London the same way. If the planes are all on time, you will have exactly eight hours at home with your wife in Baltimore and can still be back in Paris by Monday morning."

The flyer did as directed, and everything worked perfectly. He spent the eight hours at home with his wife, he was back in Paris just in time the following Monday, and no one questioned him along the way. There was only one complication: during those eight hours his wife became pregnant. In a matter of months her pregnancy was obvious to her friends, who also knew that it had been two years since her husband left the United States. She had either to reveal the truth or be considered unfaithful. She chose to be considered unfaithful. But to one of her friends she felt she had to break down and tell the truth. This friend, who happened to be an acquaintance of her husband's commanding officer's wife, proceeded to tell the commanding officer's wife what had happened. In the course of time she informed her husband, with the result that the flyer was court-martialed.

b. "During a recent New York power failure, there was a sudden demand for flashlight batteries. Supplies were running low, so many merchants, knowing that they could sell their product for any price, sold countless ten-cent batteries for five dollars each. They made a killing."

"I know. But do you know, it would have been much more to their own long-run interest if they had given the batteries away free. Think of the good will they could thereby have cultivated among prospective customers. They would have made these people friends for life and made far more money from them in the long run. You see, the egoistic policy didn't pay after all."

c. "During the New York subway strike, there was a terrible drain on taxis. Thousands of people couldn't cross from Manhattan to Brooklyn, since busses don't run across the bridge. So taxis drove people the half mile from the Manhattan end of the bridge to the Brooklyn end, each taxi full of passengers and charging them each five dollars. This was just as much of a holdup as charging five dollars for a flashlight battery. Suppose that the taxi drivers had made the trips for nothing. They might have received thanks and good will, but other than that *they* wouldn't have received anything for their work. For when you hail a taxi in New York, there isn't one chance in ten thousand that you will have the same taxi driver whom you have had before. If *everyone* in the taxi company had given free rides, if it had been company policy, then the company would have cultivated good will and won many customers. But that would not have been the result if only certain individual taxi drivers had been beneficent. So you see, an unselfish policy would not have paid off for the taxi drivers."

d. "Consider the case of a garageman. Perhaps he doesn't particularly want to make thorough repairs on the cars he handles, for many of the customers won't know the difference anyway for a while; but in the long run if he wants to keep his business, he had better be honest and thorough; otherwise he won't keep his business for long. Honesty *is* the best policy."

"Again, not necessarily. In a small town where the garageman is known to everyone, if he makes bad repairs, the word will soon be around and he will indeed be without any business. But in a large metropolitan city there are many dishonest repairmen who do very well fleecing their customers. By the time the customer knows he has been rooked, he may be a thousand miles away and can no longer retaliate. The local people won't come back, of course, after once being cheated, but for every such person that stays away, there may be two new ones coming in (to be cheated in turn). Since the people in a large city very seldom know one another, they can't tell each other to stay away. Many such dishonest garagemen in large cities seem to do a more lucrative business than the honest ones do."

e. "Consider now the farmer who raises chickens for market. If he underfeeds them, he will have no market for them. The customers won't buy from him any more. So it is to his interest to raise good healthy chickens."

"Formerly, perhaps; not any more. There are ways of disguising the truth, through recent scientific advances, which did not use to be possible. Formerly the chicken received its essential vitamins and minerals from scratching in the soil — and thus so did the consumer, by eating the chicken and the eggs; but now the chickens never see the soil — they walk on wire netting inside constantly illuminated chicken houses. They are fed chemicals which will make them prematurely fat and which will also make their skin smooth so that the housewife will admire the dressed product in the supermarket — not knowing, of course, that she is getting more fat and less protein in her healthy-looking chicken. Worst of all, some of these same chemicals which are fed the chicken are carcinogenic (cancer-producing) agents. But what does the farmer care about this? As long as the public does not know and is more inclined to buy his good-looking chickens, which have been raised to maturity at less than half the cost that would be required for making them truly healthy, it is to his interest to adopt the modern methods. Even if certain individual farmers have moral scruples about using such methods, they will be forced out of the market by unscrupulous competitors who can sell their products more cheaply by using these methods. You see, honesty is best, but it is *not* always the best *policy*. Dishonesty just pays off too handsomely."

READING LIST, SECTION 11

Blake, Ralph M. "The Ground of Moral Obligation." *Ethics,* Vol. 38 (1927-28), pp. 129-40.

Brandt, Richard. *Ethical Theory.* Englewood Cliffs, N. J.: Prentice-Hall, 1959, pp. 375-78.

Brunner, Emil. *The Divine Imperative.* Philadelphia: Westminster Press, 1947.

Falk, W. D. " 'Ought' and Motivation" (1948). In Sellars and Hospers. *Readings in Ethical Theory,* pp. 492-510.

Field, Guy C. "A Criticism of Kant" (1920). In Sellars and Hospers. *Readings in Ethical Theory,* pp. 487-91.

Frankena, William K. "Obligation and Motivation." In Melden, Abraham I., ed. *Essays in Moral Philosophy.* Seattle: Univ. of Washington Press, 1958, pp. 40-81.

Mortimer, Robert Cecil. *Christian Ethics.* New York: Rinehart, 1950.

O'Connor, Daniel J. "Some Questions of Morals and Ethics" (1957). In Munitz, Milton, ed. *A Modern Introduction to Ethics.* Chicago: Free Press, 1958, pp. 39-52.

Plato. *Republic.* Trans. by Francis Macdonald Cornford. New York: Oxford Univ. Press, 1945. Many other editions.

Prichard, H. A. "Duty and Interest." In Sellars and Hospers. *Readings in Ethical Theory,* pp. 469-86.

Ramsey, Paul. *Basic Christian Ethics.* New York: Scribner, 1952.

Rashdall, Hastings. *Conscience and Christ.* New York: Scribner, 1916.

Rees, D. A. "The Ethics of Divine Commands." *Aristotelian Society Proceedings,* Vol. 57 (1955-56), pp. 83-106.

Sellars, Wilfrid. "Obligation and Motivation." In Sellars and Hospers. *Readings in Ethical Theory,* pp. 511-17.

Stace, Walter Terrence. *The Concept of Morals.* New York: Macmillan, 1937, Chs. 11 and 12.

5. $\mathcal{T}$he general good

If it is not the agent's own good that is to be considered, then whose good is? The most natural reply would seem to be, "Everyone's." If not one person rather than another, then why one group rather than another? If not one group rather than another, then why not that whole group which constitutes the human race? Once one admits that one's own personal good is not the only consideration, how can one stop short of the good of everyone — "the general good"? This conclusion, at any rate, is the thesis of the ethical theory known as *utilitarianism*. The thesis is simply stated, though its application to actual situations is often extremely complex: whatever is intrinsically good should be promoted, and, accordingly, our obligation (or duty) is always to act so as to promote the greatest possible intrinsic good. It is never our duty to promote a lesser good when we could, by our action, promote a greater one; and the act which we should perform in any given situation is, therefore, the one which produces more intrinsic good than any other act we could have performed in its stead. In brief, the main tenet of utilitarianism is the maximization of intrinsic good.

A utilitarian's view of obligation will naturally depend on his view of what is intrinsically good. There are two main varieties of utilitarianism corresponding to the two main views of intrinsic good which we examined in Chapter 3: *hedonistic* utilitarianism and *ideal,* or *pluralistic,* utilitarianism.

1. *Hedonistic utilitarianism* says that we should pursue the course of action which will bring about the maximum possible happiness (or long-run pleasure) for everyone concerned. This view is often presented by means of Jeremy Bentham's famous phrase, "The greatest happiness of the greatest number." But Bentham's formula is extremely misleading as it stands; for it sounds as if a majority would be justified in inflicting its opinions on a minority (the Nazis exterminating the Jews, for example), whereas, as we shall see, this application was at the farthest possible remove from Bentham's intention. He meant simply that the more good there is in the world the better, and since every human being counts as one, the more widely good is distributed the better.

199

2. If, however, one believes that other things than happiness possess intrinsic worth — knowledge, beauty, moral qualities — one will not restrict his formulation to happiness only. He will say that what ought to be produced is the maximum possible intrinsic good, leaving it an open question what intrinsic good may be. This version has been called *ideal utilitarianism* (by G. E. Moore) or, more accurately, *pluralistic utilitarianism*. (The difference between the two is less than one might think and in most practical contexts is negligible, since the very things pluralistic utilitarianism calls intrinsic goods will be considered instrumental goods by hedonistic utilitarianism and thus in both views will count as a plus value in the estimation of consequences.) In the coming pages we shall be especially concerned with utilitarianism as historically developed by John Stuart Mill, and accordingly we shall sometimes speak of happiness as the sole intrinsic good (as Mill did); but everything we say about Mill's position can be made to cover pluralistic utilitarianism as well by simply substituting the term "intrinsic good" for "happiness."

12. The utilitarian theory

The description just given is so brief that it will almost inevitably be misleading when one attempts to apply it in actual situations unless it is spelled out in greater detail. Let us proceed at once, then, to the necessary explanations and qualifications.

1. When utilitarians talk about right or wrong acts, they mean — and this point is shared by the proponents of all ethical theories — *voluntary* acts. Involuntary acts like the knee jerk are not included since we have no control over them: once the stimulus has occurred the act results quite irrespective of our own will. The most usual way in which the term "voluntary act" is defined is as follows:[1] an act is voluntary if the person *could* have acted differently *if* he had so chosen. For example, I went shopping yesterday, but if I had chosen (for one reason or another) to remain at home, I would have done so. My choosing made the difference. Making this condition is not the same as saying that an act, to be voluntary, must be *premeditated* or that it must be the outcome of *deliberation,* though voluntary acts often are planned. If you see a victim of a car accident lying in the street, you may rush to help him at once, without going through a process of deliberation; nevertheless your act is voluntary in that if you had chosen to ignore him you would have acted differently. Though not premeditated, the action *was* within your control. "Ought implies can," and there is no ought when there is no can. To be right or wrong, an act must

---

[1] This term is most precisely defined by G. E. Moore in Chapter 1, "Utilitarianism," of his book *Ethics.* For the clearest and most rigorous statement of utilitarianism in its hedonistic form, see Chapters 1 and 2 of this book.

be within your power to perform: it must be performable as the result of your choice, and a different choice must have led to a different act or to no act at all. (The extent to which choices are within our control, and the desires which lead to the choices, will be examined at length in Chapter 10.)

2. There is no preference for immediate, as opposed to remote, happiness. If Act A will produce a certain amount of happiness today and Act B will produce twice as much one year hence, I should do B, even though its effects are more remote. Remoteness does not affect the principle at all: happiness is as intrinsically good tomorrow or next year as it is today, and one should forgo a smaller total intrinsic good now in favor of a larger one in the future. (Of course, a remote happiness is often less certain to occur. But in that case we should choose A not because it is more immediate but because it is more nearly certain to occur. We have already touched on this point in examining Bentham's calculus, pages 56-57.)

3. Unhappiness must be considered as well as happiness. Suppose that Act A will produce five units of happiness and none of unhappiness and Act B will produce ten units of happiness and ten of unhappiness. Then A is to be preferred because the *net* happiness — the resulting total after the unhappiness has been subtracted from it — is greater in A than in B: it is five in A and zero in B. Thus the formula "You should do what will produce the greatest total happiness" is not quite accurate; you should do what will produce the most *net* happiness. This modification is what we shall henceforth mean in talking about "producing the greatest happiness" — we shall assume that the unhappiness has already been figured into the total.

4. It is not even accurate to say that you should always do what leads to the greatest *balance* of happiness over unhappiness, for there may be no such balance in any alternative open to the agent: he may have to choose between "the lesser of two evils." If Act A leads to five units of happiness and ten of unhappiness and Act B leads to five units of happiness and fifteen of unhappiness, you should choose A, not because it produces the most happiness (they both produce an equal amount) and not because there is a greater balance of happiness over unhappiness in A (there is a balance of unhappiness over happiness in both), but because, although both A and B produce a balance of unhappiness over happiness, A leads to a *smaller* balance of unhappiness over happiness than B does. Thus we should say, "Do that act which produces the greatest balance of happiness over unhappiness, or, if no act possible under the circumstances does this, do the one which produces the smallest balance of unhappiness over happiness." This qualification also we shall assume to be included in the utilitarian formula from now on in speaking of "producing the greatest happiness" or "maximizing happiness."

5. One should not assume that an act is right according to utilitarianism simply because it produces more happiness than unhappiness in its total consequences. If one did make this assumption, it would be right for ten

men collectively to torture a victim, provided that the total pleasure en-joyed by the sadists exceeded the pain endured by the victim (assuming that pain is here equated with unhappiness and that all the persons died im-mediately thereafter and there were no further consequences). The require-ment is not that the happiness exceed the unhappiness but that it do so *more* than any other act that could have been performed instead. This require-ment is hardly fulfilled here: it is very probable indeed that the torturers could think of something better to do with their time.

6. When there is a choice between a greater happiness for yourself at the expense of others, and a greater happiness for others at the expense of your own, which should you choose? You choose, according to the utilitarian formula, whatever alternative results in the greater total amount of *net* happiness, precisely as we have described. If the net happiness is greater in the alternative favorable to yourself, you adopt this alternative; otherwise not. Mill says, "The happiness which forms the utilitarian standard of what is right in conduct, is not the agent's own happiness, but that of all concerned. As between his own happiness and that of others, utilitarianism requires him to be as strictly impartial as a disinterested and benevolent spectator." [1] To state this in different language, you are not to ignore your own happi-ness in your calculations, but neither are you to consider it more important than anyone else's; you count as one, and only as one, along with everyone else. Thus if Act A produces a total net happiness of one hundred, and Act B produces seventy-five, A is the right act even if you personally would be happier in consequence of B. Your choice should not be an "interested" one; you are not to be prejudiced in favor of your own happiness nor, for that matter, against it; your choice should be strictly *dis*interested as in the case of an impartial judge. Your choice should be dictated by the greatest-total-happiness principle, not by a *your*-greatest-happiness principle. If you imagine yourself as a judge having to make a decision designed to produce the most happiness for all concerned *without* knowing which of the people affected would be *you,* you have the best idea of the impartiality of judg-ment required by the utilitarian morality.

In egoistic ethics, as we have seen, your sole duty is to promote your own interests as much as possible, making quite sure, of course, that what you do will make you really happy (or whatever else you include in "your own interest") and that you do not choose merely what you *think* at the moment will do so; we have called this policy the policy of *"enlightened* self-interest." In an *altruistic* ethics, on the other hand, you sacrifice your own interests com-pletely to those of others: you ignore your own welfare and become a door-mat for the fulfillment of the interests of others. (We shall discuss altruistic ethics later in this chapter.) But the utilitarian ethics is neither egoistic nor altruistic: it is a *universalistic* ethics, since it considers your interests equally with everyone else's. You are not the slave of others, nor are they your

[1] J. S. Mill, *Utilitarianism,* Ch. 2.

slaves. Indeed, there are countless instances in which the act required of you by ethical egoism and the act required by utilitarianism will be the same: for very often indeed the act that makes you happy will also make those around you happy, and by promoting your own welfare you will also be promoting theirs. (As support for this position, consider capitalistic society: the producer of wealth, by being free to amass profits, will have more incentive to produce and, by increasing production, will be able to create more work and more wealth. By increasing production, he will be increasing the welfare of his employees and the wealth of the nation.) Moreover, it is much more likely that you can effectively produce good by concentrating on your immediate environment than by "spreading yourself thin" and trying to help everyone in the world: "do-gooders" often succeed in achieving no good at all. (But, of course, sometimes they do.) You are in a much better position to produce good among those people whose needs and interests you already know than among strangers; and, of course, the person whose needs and interests you probably know best of all (though not always) is yourself. Utilitarianism is very far, then, from recommending that you ignore your own interests.

It is only when your interests cannot be achieved except at the cost of sacrificing the *greater* interests of others that utilitarianism recommends self-sacrifice. When interests conflict, you have to weigh your own interest against the general interest. If, on the one hand, you are spending all your valuable study time (and thus sacrificing your grades and perhaps your college degree) visiting your sick aunt because she wants you to, you would probably produce more good by spending your time studying. But on the other hand, if an undeniably greater good will result from your sacrifice, if, for instance, your mother is seriously ill and no one else is available to care for her, you might have to drop out of school for a semester to care for her. It might even, on occasion, be your utilitarian duty to sacrifice your very life for a cause, when the cause is extremely worthy and requires your sacrifice for its fulfillment. But you must first make quite sure that your sacrifice will indeed produce the great good intended; otherwise you would be throwing your life away uselessly. You must act with your eyes open, not under the spell of a martyr complex.

The utilitarian morality does recognize in human beings the power of sacrificing their own greatest good for the good of others. It only refuses to admit that the sacrifice is itself a good. A sacrifice which does not increase, or tend to increase, the sum total of happiness, it considers as wasted. The only self-renunciation which it applauds, is devotion to the happiness, or to some of the means of happiness, of others; either of mankind collectively, or of individuals within the limits imposed by the collective interests of mankind.

It is noble to be capable of resigning entirely one's own portion of happiness, or chances of it; but, after all, this self-sacrifice must be for some end; it is not its own end; and if we are told that its end is not happiness, but virtue, which is better than happiness, I ask, would the sacrifice be made if the hero or martyr did not believe that it would earn for others immunity from similar sacrifices? Would it be made if he thought that his renunciation of happiness for himself would produce no fruit for any of his fellow creatures, but to make their lot like his, and place them also in the condition of persons who have renounced happiness? All honor to those who can abnegate for themselves the personal enjoyment of life, when by such renunciation they contribute worthily to increase the amount of happiness in the world; but he who does it, or professes to do it, for any other purpose, is no more deserving of admiration than the ascetic mounted on his pillar. He may be an inspiriting proof of what men *can* do, but assuredly not an example of what they *should*.[1]

7. The general temper of the utilitarian ethics can perhaps best be seen in its attitude toward moral rules, the traditional do's and don'ts. What is the utilitarian's attitude toward rules such as "Don't kill," "Don't tell lies," "Don't steal"?

According to utilitarianism, such rules are *on the whole* good, useful, and worthwhile, but they *may* have exceptions. None of them is sacrosanct. If killing is wrong, it is not because there is something intrinsically bad about killing itself, but because killing leads to a diminution of human happiness. This undesirable consequence almost always occurs: when a man takes another human life, he not only extinguishes in his victim all chances of future happiness, but he causes grief, bereavement, and perhaps years of misery for the victim's family and loved ones; moreover, for weeks or months countless people who know of his act may walk the streets in fear, wondering who will be the next victim — the amount of insecurity caused by even one act of murder is almost incalculable; and in addition to all this unhappiness, every violation of a law has a tendency to weaken the whole fabric of the law itself and tends to make other violations easier and more likely to occur. If the guilty man is caught, he himself hardly gains much happiness from lifelong imprisonment, nor are other people usually much happier for long because of his incarceration; and if he is not caught, many people will live in fear and dread, and he himself will probably repeat his act sooner or later, having escaped capture this time. The good consequences, if any, are few and far between and are overwhelmingly outweighed by the bad ones. Because of these prevailingly bad consequences, killing is condemned by the utilitarian, and thus he agrees with the traditional moral rule prohibiting it.

He would nevertheless admit the possibility of exceptions: if you had had the opportunity to assassinate Hitler in 1943 and did not, the utilitarian would probably say that you were doing wrong in *not* killing him. By not killing him, you would be sealing the death of thousands, if not millions, of other people: political prisoners and Jews whom he tortured and killed in concentration camps and thousands of soldiers (both Axis

[1] *Ibid.*

and Allied) whose lives would have been saved by an earlier cessation of the war. If you had refrained from killing him when you had the chance, saying "It is my duty never to take a life, therefore I shall not take his," the man whose life you saved would then turn around and have a thousand others killed, and for his act the victims would have you to thank. Your conscience, guided by the tra-ditional moral rules, would have helped to bring about the torture and death of countless other people.

Does the utilitarian's willingness to adopt violence upon occasion mean that a utilitarian could never be a pacifist? Not necessarily. He *might* say that *all* taking of human life is wrong, but if he took this stand, he would do so because he believed that killing *always* leads to worse consequences (or greater unhappiness) than not killing and *not* because there is anything intrinsically bad about killing. He might even be able to make out a plausible argument for saying that killing Hitler would have been wrong: perhaps even worse men would have taken over and the slaughter wouldn't have been prevented (but then wouldn't it have been right to kill *all* of them if one had the chance?); perhaps Hitler's "intuitions" led to an earlier defeat for Germany than if stabler men had made more rationally self-seeking decisions on behalf of Nazi Germany; perhaps the assassination of a bad leader would help lead to the assassination of a good one later on. With regard to some Latin American nations, at any rate, one might argue that killing one dictator would only lead to a revolution and another dictator just as bad as the first, with the consequent assassination of the second one, thus leading to revolution and social chaos and a third dictator. There are countless empirical facts that must be taken into consideration and carefully weighed before any such decision can safely be made. The utilitarian is not committed to saying that any one policy or line of action is the best in any particular situation, for what is best depends on empirical facts which may be extremely difficult to ascertain. All he is committed to is the statement that when the action is one that does not promote human happiness as much as another action that he could have performed instead, then the action is wrong; and that when it does promote more happiness, it is right. Which particular action will maximize happiness more than any other, in a particular situation, can be determined only by empirical investigation. Thus, it is possible that killing is always wrong — at least the utilitarian could consistently say so and thus be a pacifist; but *if* killing is always wrong, it is wrong not because killing is wrong per se but because it always and without exception leads to worse consequences than any other actions that could have been performed instead. Then the pacifist, if he is a consistent utilitarian, would have to go on to show in each instance that each and every act of killing is worse (leads to worse consequences) than any act of refraining from doing so — even when the man is a trigger-happy gunman who will kill dozens of people in a crowded street if he is not killed first. That killing is worse in every instance would be extremely difficult — most people would say impossible — to prove.

Consider the syllogism:

> The action which promotes the maximum happiness is right.
> This action is the one which promotes the maximum happiness.
> *Therefore,* This action is right.

The utilitarian gives undeviating assent only to the *first* of these three statements (the major premise); this statement is the chief article of his utilitarian creed, and he cannot abandon it without being inconsistent with his own doctrine. But this first premise is not enough to yield the third statement, which is the conclusion of the argument. To know that the conclusion is true, even granting that the major premise is, one must also know whether the second statement (the minor premise) is true; and the second statement is an empirical one, which cannot be verified by the philosopher sitting in his study but only by a thorough investigation of the empirical facts of the situation. Many people would accept the major premise (and thus be utilitarians) and yet disagree among themselves on the conclusion because they would disagree on the minor premise. They would agree that an act is right if it leads to maximum happiness, but they would not agree on whether this action or that one is the one which *will* in fact lead to the most happiness. They disagree about the empirical facts of the case, not in their utilitarian ethics. The disagreement could be resolved if both parties had a complete grasp of all the relevant empirical facts, for then they would know *which* action *would* lead to the most happiness. In many situations, of course, such agreement will never be reached because the consequences of people's actions (especially when they affect thousands of other people over a long period of time, as happens when war is declared) are so numerous and so complex that nobody will ever know them all. Such a disagreement will not be the fault of ethics, or of philosophy in general, but of the empirical world for being so complicated and subtle in its workings that the full consequences of our actions often can not be determined. Frequently it would take an omniscient deity to know which action in a particular situation was right. Finite human beings have to be content with basing their actions on estimates of probability.

According to utilitarianism, then, the traditional moral rules are justified for the most part because following them will lead to the best consequences far more often than violating them will; and that is why they are useful rules of thumb in human action. But, for the utilitarian, this is *all* they are — rules of thumb. They should never be used blindly, as a pat formula or inviolable rule subject to no exceptions, without an eye to the detailed consequences in each particular situation. The judge who condemned a man to death in the electric chair for stealing $1.95 (as in a case in Alabama in 1959) was probably not contributing to human happiness by inflicting this extreme penalty, even though he acted in accordance with the law of that state. The utilitarian would say that if a starving man steals a loaf of bread, as in Victor Hugo's *Les Miserables,* he should not be condemned for violating the rule "Do not steal"; in fact he probably did nothing morally wrong by stealing in this instance because the effects of not stealing would in this instance have meant starvation and preserving a life (the utilitarian would say) is more important to human happiness than refraining from stealing a loaf of bread — especially since the man stole from one who was far from starving himself (the "victim" would never have missed it). He is probably blameless furthermore because the whole episode was made possible in the first place by a system of laws and a social structure which, by any utilitarian standard, were vicious in the extreme. (But see the effects of lawbreaking, below.)

Moral rules are especially useful when we have to act at once without being able adequately to weigh the consequences; for *usually* (as experience shows) better — i.e., more-happiness-producing — consequences are obtained by following moral rules than by not following them. If there is a drowning person whom you could rescue, you should do so without further investigation; for if you stopped to investigate his record, he would already have drowned. True, he might turn out to be a Hitler, but unless we have such evidence, we have to go by the probability that the world is better off for his being alive than for his being dead. Again, there may be situations in which telling a lie will have better effects than telling the truth. But since, on the whole, lying has bad effects, we have to have special evidence that this situation is different before we are justified in violating the rule. If we have no time to gather such evidence, we should act on what is most probable, namely that telling a lie in this situation will produce consequences less good than telling the truth.

The utilitarian attitude toward moral rules is more favorable than might first appear because of the hidden, or subtle, or not frequently thought of, consequences of actions which at first sight would seem to justify a violation of the rules. One must consider *all* the consequences of the action and not just the immediate ones or the ones that happen to be the most conspicuous. For example: The utilitarian would not hold that it is *always* wrong to break a law, unless he had good grounds for saying that breaking the law *always* leads to worse consequences than observing it. But if the law is a bad law to begin with or even if it is a good law on the whole but observing the law in this particular case would be deleterious to human happiness, then the law should be broken in this case. You would be morally justified, for example, in breaking the speed law in order to rush a badly wounded person to a hospital. But in many situations (probably in most) in which the utilitarian criterion at first *seems* to justify the violation of a law, it does not really do so after careful consideration because of the far-flung consequences. For example, in a more typical instance of breaking the speed law, you might argue as follows: "It would make me happier if I were not arrested for the violation, and it wouldn't make the arresting officer any the less happy, in fact it would save him the trouble of writing out the ticket, so — why not? By letting me go, wouldn't the arresting officer be increasing the total happiness of the world by just a little bit, both his and mine, whereas by giving me a ticket he might actually decrease the world's happiness slightly?"

But happiness would be slightly increased only if one considers only the immediate situation. For one thing, by breaking the speed limit you are endangering the lives of others — you are less able to stop or to swerve out of the way in an emergency. Also those who see you speeding and escaping the penalty may decide to do the same thing themselves; even though you don't cause any accidents by your violation, *they* may do so after taking their cue from you. Moreover, law-breaking may reduce respect for law itself; although there may well be unjust laws and many laws could be improved, it is usually better (has better consequences) to work for their repeal than to break them while they are still in effect. Every violation decreases the effectiveness of law, and we are surely better off having law than not having it at all — even the man who violently objects to a law and complains bitterly when he's arrested will invoke the law to protect *himself* against the violations of others. In spite of these cautions, utilitarianism does not say that one should *never* break a law but only that the consequences of doing so are far more often bad than good; a closer look at the consequences will show how true their reasoning is. (Besides, often when we say a violation is justified we are rationalizing. We say a violation of a law is all right not because we really believe violation will have the best consequences for all but because we, for our own selfish interests, *want* to violate the law. So we rationalize our desire by finding reasons for justifying it, even though we would never have favored someone else's, say a total stranger's, violating a law.)

Here is an even better example of the long-range effects of actions: A physician finds that his patient, after surgery, is incurably ill of cancer, but he cannot bring himself to break the bad news to the patient. So he decides to console the patient instead by telling him that he is recovering from the effects of a tumor, which was removed, and that he will be all right in a month or two. A superficial utilitarian might argue that this procedure would make the patient happier and would also prevent some unhappiness on the part of the physician who would not have to break the tragic news. But a utilitarian with an eye on *all* the consequences of his action would offer the following counterconsiderations:

a. Does the physician know that the patient would be happier being deceived? Perhaps the patient would prefer to know the truth, set his affairs in order, and prepare for death in his own way. (Wouldn't you rather know the truth in such a situation? Or would you rather be consoled by a lie?)

b. Should the physician take it upon *himself* to deprive his patient of vital information, no matter of what kind? Isn't doing so tantamount to saying that the physician's authority is more important than the patient's, since the physician is taking vital decisions out of the patient's hands? One could argue that if we lie to people, we are assuming that the people we lie to are weaklings who aren't strong enough to take the information we withhold from them. Are we justified in making this assumption?

c. Lies have a tendency to spread. If one physician tells his patient that he will soon be well, while knowing all the time that the patient is incurably ill, the patient's relatives will know that he is incurable; or at least they will find out when the man dies in spite of the physician's assurances. Now suppose one of these people who are in on the doctor's secret later becomes incurably ill and his physician tells him he will soon be all right; he is aware of the physician's tricks and won't believe him — he will suspect that the physician is lying to him, and the physician's trick will no longer work on him. The process will continue for as many people as hear the physicians tell such lies.

d. Worse still, how many sick people who are *truthfully* told by their physicians that they are not incurably ill will be haunted day and night by the suspicion that the physician is lying? They know that this physician and others have lied to their patients in the past; why not in the present situation? The amount of fear, dread, and insecurity that people can suffer under such circumstances is incalculable.

e. The physician may be conscientious and lie only in extreme circumstances. But does the physician know that he is so much a master of himself that he will not let down the bars and permit himself to tell more lies when it's easier to do so, on future occasions?

In principle, all these moral rules *might* have exceptions because one can never know in advance that there will not be situations in which violating a rule *may* produce better consequences (more total happiness) than abiding by it. So the utilitarian cannot make the exceptionless observance of these rules an article of faith. Note that he is not bound, as a utilitarian, to say that there *are* such exceptions but only that *if* there are situations in which more happiness in the total consequences is brought about by violating the rule, then it is better to violate the rule. The utilitarian can never consistently say that one should tell the truth, be honest, *no matter what the results* because it is the results that provide the criterion for whether the action in question is right, and one can never be sure for all future situations that the results of a certain class of actions, such as lying, will *always* be bad.

Yet there may well be classes of actions which *so regularly* lead to bad results that in practice one should never perform them. The point is that though it is always possible that there will be justified exceptions to these rules, a person who has to decide what to do in a specific situation can never be justified in assuming that the situation before him is one of the exceptions. Examples of such classes of actions might be these: using torture to achieve our ends; railroading an innocent man to the electric chair to win a case or because he is a detriment to society; hanging a man (no matter how much satisfaction it might give those performing the operation) instead of giving him a trial by jury as prescribed by law; taking somebody's property because somebody else needs it more than the owner. If these things were done even in a few instances, the very foundations of society would be in jeopardy. In defense of this position the utilitarian could offer these arguments:

a. In such classes of actions, our knowledge of the total effects or consequences is never great enough to entitle us to say that the situation before us is an exception to the rule.

> Can the individual ever be justified in assuming that his is one of these exceptional cases? And it seems that this question may be definitely answered in the negative. For, if it is certain that in a large majority of cases the observance of a certain rule is useful, it follows that there is a large probability that it would be wrong to break the rule in any particular case; and the uncertainty of our knowledge both of effects and of their value, in particular cases is so great, that it seems doubtful whether the individual's judgment that the effects will probably be good in his case can ever be set against the general probability that that kind of action is wrong.[1]

b. In any event, we are inclined to be biased by the fact that we strongly *desire* one of the results which we hope to obtain by breaking the rules. The fact that we *want* to break the rule will tend to make us calculate the probable consequences in such a way as to justify the action we desire.

> It seems, then, that it ought always to be observed, not on the ground that in every particular case it will be useful, but on the ground that in *any* particular case the probability of its being so is greater than that of our being likely to decide rightly that we have before us an instance of its disutility. In short, though we may be sure that there are cases where the rule should be broken, we can never know which those cases are, and ought, therefore, never to break it.[2]

c. Even if we *can* clearly see (which we usually can't) that the present situation is one in which the violation of the rule is justified and even if we are so studiously impartial as not to be prejudiced in our own favor, the fact still remains that the *example* we set in breaking the rule this time will tend to encourage *other* violations of the rule which are *not* justified. Thus, when our example has any influence, the effect of an exceptional right action will be to encourage wrong ones.

d. The making of this exception will influence not only others but our-

[1] G. E. Moore, *Principia Ethica* (1903), p. 162.
[2] *Ibid.*, pp. 162-63.

selves. If we have violated the rule in a situation in which the violation is justified, the habit of making exceptions will be reinforced, and we will be all the more likely to violate the rule in cases where the violation is *not* justified.

> For it is impossible for any one to keep his intellect and sentiments so clear, but that, if he has once approved of a generally wrong action, he will be more likely to approve of it also under other circumstances than those which justified it in the first instance. This inability to discriminate exceptional cases offers, of course, a still stronger reason for the universal enforcement, by legal or social sanctions, of actions generally useful. It is undoubtedly well to punish a man, who has done an action, right in his case but generally wrong, even if his example would not be likely to have a dangerous effect. For sanctions have, in general, much more influence upon conduct than example; so that the effect of relaxing them in an exceptional case will almost certainly be an encouragement of similar action in cases which are not exceptional.[1]

At this point the utilitarian position may sound as if it is as opposed to exceptions on principle as the most dyed-in-the-wool formalist who, maintaining the rightness of acts regardless of consequences (see Chapter 6), refuses to grant exceptions for any reasons whatsoever. Yet a gulf always separates them, as we can see if we ask these questions: "If we make the stakes high enough, isn't an exception justified? Suppose that by railroading one innocent man to the electric chair, we could thereby make absolutely sure that nobody for the next hundred years would be condemned for a crime that he didn't commit. Suppose that by torturing one human being, or even a hundred, we could put an end to a war which has already snuffed out ten million lives. Or if that isn't enough, suppose that we could prevent the collapse of an entire civilization only by torturing one human being for one week; wouldn't it be worth the price? No matter how much we abhorred torture, could we stand by and see civilization collapse forever if we could prevent it by administering the prolonged torture to one person? In fact, wouldn't the utilitarian have to approve the act of torture even to gain far smaller ends than the rescue of civilization? If it were the only way to prevent a hostile nation from using the hydrogen bomb to wipe out the twenty largest American cities, thus killing forty million civilians, wouldn't we (or would we) be morally justified in throwing a battalion of American soldiers into nests of poisonous snakes?"

8. Since the consequences of our acts are so notoriously difficult to assess, especially when they involve many people and extend far into the future, the practicing utilitarian is often faced with a well-nigh insuperable task of calculation. This difficulty is, of course, no fault of the theory itself. It is, as we have seen, a fault of the empirical world, in that it is so complex and the causal network of events so intricate and extended that the consequences

[1] *Ibid.*, pp. 163-64.

of what we do cannot easily be foreseen by finite human beings, even with the best of intentions and the most knowledge available at the time. The result is that few decisions of great moment will be simple and easy to arrive at. Once again, the utilitarian *principle* is simple enough; what is complicated is the application of this principle to specific situations — finding out which course of action will produce the maximum intrinsic good. The application of the principle is particularly difficult in the following kinds of situations:

a. When the estimation of *probabilities* is difficult or impossible. Examples:

(1) A person is drowned because the only other human being in the vicinity at the time did not know how to swim to rescue him. The failure to know how to swim is hardly considered a crime — unless, of course, one is in a position (like that of a lifeguard) in which one is expected to know; yet it may have catastrophic consequences, more than lying or stealing. Should it be everyone's duty to learn how to swim well enough to take a life-saving test, just on the off chance that he might some time be in a situation to rescue a drowning person? (But if one should be trained for what there is just an off chance of ever doing, it would take several lifetimes of doing nothing else. Should one learn electrical engineering just on the chance that he might someday be in a situation in which power plant machinery required emergency repairs and he was the only person nearby?)

(2) In Nicholas Monsarrat's novel *The Cruel Sea,* the captain of a British vessel in World War II is in a position to rescue many British survivors afloat at sea, but radar indicates that there is an undersea object (presumably a submarine) below the very spot where the men are struggling in the water. The captain is willing to take some chances with the lives of his men to rescue the others, but he is not willing to take such a tremendous chance as is involved in this situation. There is great probability that the submarine would blow up the ship with the entire crew if he dared to stop the ship even momentarily to pick up the men; indeed it looks like a trap devised for that very purpose. Therefore, with great reluctance he leaves the shipwrecked sailors to drown. (Later it turns out that there was no submarine there at all.)

(3) When Scott's famous journey to the Antarctic met with disaster, the only chance for the survivors was to reach the coast at once. But on the way one of them was injured and had to be carried on a stretcher. Though this delay seriously imperiled all their chances of survival, the captain decided that he should not abandon the man to die. The result was that all the men died.

b. When a means, involving considerable intrinsic evil, is the only way to achieve an end containing an even greater intrinsic good. We are all acquainted with the old adage "The end justifies the means," which people repeat parrot-like to rationalize whatever they want to do. What is the utilitarian attitude toward this maxim? If it means what it is often used to mean, that any end you want to achieve is morally justified no matter what means you take to get it — such as a Roman emperor's wanting to enjoy himself (end) by having a hundred people thrown to the lions (means) — the utilitarian would, of course, be utterly opposed to it. And this meaning *is* the one most often attached to this saying, for it is most often quoted in connection with Machiavellian maneuvers for gaining whatever end one wants at no matter what cost to others.

But this meaning is not the only one that can be given to the maxim. It may also be interpreted in a more general manner to mean that some particular end (not necessarily a selfish one) is so valuable (intrinsically good?) that, though the means taken to attain it involves considerable evil, it is worth this cost — the price is worth paying. To this interpretation the utilitarian would say: "It depends on what the end is and on what the means is. Sometimes the end justifies the means and sometimes it doesn't. We have to examine the end and the means that can be taken to achieve it, in each individual situation." To remove the toothache by having the dentist remove the decayed material and put in a filling would be generally agreed to be worth the pain involved; to remove the toothache by killing the patient would not. Even when the means involves agonizing sacrifice, the end may justify it if it can be achieved in no other way and if the end is worth it.

But when is the end worth the means? If the end is removal of war from the face of the earth and the means is the death of a few thousand human beings now, the utilitarian would say that the end is so supremely worthwhile that it justifies the means, *provided* that the means really involves no more evil than the statement indicates (often the evils involved in the means lead to other evils so that in the final analysis the means contains far more evil than the end does good), and *provided* that the end really *will* be achieved once this means is taken (there must be no slip), and *provided* that the end can be achieved by no other means that involves *less* evil than this one. In actual practice, the end doesn't justify the means as often as one might think because these conditions are not met. A revolution breaks out in a poverty-stricken nation governed by a tyrant; its aims are peace, bread for all, work for all at a decent wage, and democratic government. But to achieve this end, several thousand people have to sacrifice their lives in the revolution against the tyrant's armies. Even so, the end is so worthwhile that, the revolutionaries agree, it is certainly worth the means. But it turns out that this means is not enough — thousands more people have to die to make the end possible; the monarch's armies are stronger than was anticipated, and resistance to the revolution occurs in unexpected quarters. But the price still seems worth paying, especially since so many lives have already been lost in the cause. So the price is paid, but things still don't occur as planned: after the mass executions of those who oppose the revolution, there are so many more opponents of the new regime that it can be preserved only by taking the harshest possible measures, and the nation is turned into a police state in which one word breathed against the new regime means the firing squad. This severity was not envisaged at the beginning, but so many lives have already been sacrificed that it seems they would have been sacrificed in vain if the sacrifices do not continue and on an even greater scale. But by this time, quite gradually, something else has happened: the means that the leaders of the revolution have used have themselves made the end impossible to achieve. Those who took it upon themselves to execute thousands of their fellow countrymen have become so used to killing, so drunk with their newly gained power, and so accustomed to demanding any price to keep themselves in power that they are no longer capable of bringing about (or even any longer desiring) the end for which all these lives have been sacrificed; and if they give up their power now or relax the police state, they themselves will be executed by their opponents. The revolutionaries have changed, and the means they have used to bring about the end is the very thing that has changed them. The result is that the lives are lost and the heroic sacrifices made, but the end toward which all these things were means never comes to pass. This useless sacrifice has happened so often in human history that, utilitarians would say, it should give pause to anyone who thinks that the end is so worthwhile that it justifies the means which are taken to fulfill it.

Still, no utilitarian would say that the end *never* justifies the means. In many situations, freedom for a whole nation has been made possible only by revolting against a tyrant and shedding the blood of thousands; but if this blood had not been shed, the nation would still be in the coils of the oppressor. A great deal of human progress is made possible only at a cost of blood, sweat, and tears. The tremendous practical difficulty is, again, that the results of our actions are so complex and far-flung and so difficult to predict with accuracy that we often don't know with even a reasonable degree of probability whether the total results will be worth the cost. In 1945 the American army was prepared to sacrifice the lives of two million American soldiers in an invasion of Japan to end the war; was the end worth that means? (Wise action by the Allied powers after World War I might have prevented war in the first place; but once the war *had* broken out, most of us would say that it had to be won at any price. Or almost any price! Suppose the war could have been won only at the price of turning half the land area of the earth into a desert? Suppose it could have been won only at the price of turning half the women in the world into prostitutes? In any event the Axis powers would not have agreed that we should win at any price; they did not want us to win at all; they would probably have said that *they* should win it, and at *any* price.) In fact the decision to invade Japan did not have to be made, for the atomic bomb was dropped on two Japanese cities, and it did achieve the desired end. But people all over the world are still disputing whether this end was justified by this means — whether it would not have been better to achieve the end in some other way, even with far greater loss of life on the Allied side, and whether, even *if* the end could have been achieved in no other way, the victory was worth this price, in view of the ghastly precedent we set for the world by dropping the bombs and in view of the horrifying "improvements" that have subsequently been made on these first atomic bombs.

Is there any formula that the utilitarian can give for determining when the end justifies the means? It would be tempting to say — and most students on their first acquaintance with utilitarianism *are* tempted to say — that the end justifies the means in those instances where the total intrinsic good in the end (always remembering that the total is what remains after any bad results have been subtracted from it) outweighs the total intrinsic evil in the means, so that when the two (ends and means) are taken together as one whole, this whole contains more intrinsic good than intrinsic evil. But this answer would be saying only that the total plus-and-minus balance must be higher than the result if no act had been performed at all. This answer is not sufficient. What is required is that there must be more of a plus (intrinsic good) balance as a result of this act than as a result of *any other act that could have been performed instead*. But owing to the complexity of the series of causes and effects in the world and to the difficulty of predicting them with accuracy, it is often diabolically difficult to say in advance which acts will live up to this formula. To estimate such probabilities in detail, considering all the psychological, sociological, political, and economic factors, is of course a task for the social sciences. Probably we would say that in the American Revolution of 1775 the end did justify the means but that in the Russian Revolution of 1917 the end did not; even this judgment, however, is difficult to make with safety, partly because of our prejudices in our own favor, partly because we don't know all the facts involved, and partly because the effects of these movements are not yet complete.

c. When you are part of a system in which evils abound, but it is questionable whether your taking a stand alone against the system will accomplish any good. For example:

(1) You are retired and no longer able to work, but you have a modest income from dividends from a certain corporation. You discover that this corporation derives most of its income from bleeding the residents of a slum district of the city, charging them rents that may go as high as 85 per cent of their incomes and giving them no improvements in return. The residents, being Negroes in a city with restrictive housing legislation, have no other place to move without leaving the region entirely; so they have little choice but to pay. You are shocked at this discovery and do not want any part of the organizations that go in for such practices. Yet by protesting, you could accomplish nothing but would only be laughed at; and if you sold your stocks in this well-paying corporation, you would only be cutting off your only source of income. On the one hand, you wonder, since you can do

nothing to change the policies of the corporation, why not just turn a blind eye to these abuses rather than sacrifice yourself uselessly? On the other hand, you reason, if no one had ever put up a fight against seemingly hopeless odds, no form of corruption or malpractice would ever have been remedied.

(2) You are well trained for a high position in your city government, and your firm intention is to do as much good as you can in that position. But the entire system is riddled with bribery and corruption. If you try to buck the system you will be thrown out at once — a heroic action perhaps, but a useless one, since it will not improve the system and a person with fewer scruples than you have will probably take your place. Shall you then go along with the system, doing your job as well as you can within the corrupt framework, confident that you can keep the job and do some good in it as long as you do not try to buck the system at any sensitive point?

(3) A German soldier, in Irwin Shaw's *The Young Lions,* trained to revere Nazi ideals and to fight against Germany's enemies in the war, is horrified when he is commanded to kill all the survivors (the British) in a desert battle instead of taking them prisoner as prescribed by the Geneva conventions. He is even more horrified when he sees the gas chambers and other means of mass extermination and the haggard survivors in the concentration camps. Rather than continue to be a part of this bestiality, he decides to ask for a transfer to another branch of army service. Yet how would a transfer help? It would not change the system; a sadist would probably replace him at his job, and he would only wind up with a court-martial and possible death.

9. So much, then, for the problems encountered in applying the utilitarian principle to the bewilderingly complex empirical detail of actual situations. There are, however, a few distinctions to be drawn before our exposition of utilitarianism is complete. Our obligation, according to utilitarianism, is to perform the act which will produce (in the sense already specified) the maximum intrinsic good. We have already seen how difficult it often is to know which act this is. But now another problem arises: are not many of the consequences of our acts quite outside our control and "in the lap of the gods"? If so, how can we be said to act wrongly when these consequences turn out differently from what we have every reason to expect? I am driving my car and see my great-aunt walking on the sidewalk; I offer to drive her to her destination, since walking is not easy for her. On the way to her destination a drunken driver plows his car into mine, and my great-aunt is maimed as a result. Was it wrong for me to have given her the lift? How could I be accused of acting wrongly when the accident wasn't my fault, when I couldn't possibly have foreseen the accident, or when there wasn't more than a negligible degree of probability that it might occur?

We must now distinguish between *objective duty* and *subjective duty*. Our objective duty is to produce as much good as possible. But often our objective duty requires a detailed knowledge of circumstances and consequences, more than is available at the time of action; so the best we can do is our subjective duty, namely the act which, in those circumstances, was the most *likely* to produce the maximum good. For example, the act of giving my great-aunt a lift was, subjectively, under the circumstances, more likely to produce good consequences than not giving her a lift, and this likelihood remains true, even though, as things turned out, the lift was far from doing her any good at all. The refusal of the captain in Nicholas Monsarrat's *The Cruel Sea* to stop the ship to pick up survivors was probably the subjectively right act in the circumstances, in spite of the fact that, as it later turned out, no enemy submarine was there to blow up the ship if it stopped. In the same way, if I say in mid-June that it will *probably* not snow tomorrow, this judgment is true even if it *does* snow the next day. For, not being omniscient, I can do no more than go by the best evidence available at the time; and the meteorological statistics do not assign much probability to snowfall in this latitude in June. If a surgeon had recommended a heart operation twenty years ago, his recommendation would have been tantamount to killing the patient; but if he recommended a heart operation today, he would be recommending the best possible course of action, assuming that the best evidence available indicated that in similar cases an operation was the best way to cure or alleviate the condition of the patient. His recommendation would be the right one even if it turned out that the patient died, *provided* that the surgeon had not, through carelessness or correctible ignorance, recommended surgery when this particular case was one that would respond better to another type of treatment. He still would have been doing his subjective duty, though if the patient died, he would not have done his objective duty. (In a less usual but somewhat clearer terminology, that of Bertrand Russell, the physician would have performed the *wisest* act, though not the *most fortunate* act.[1])

Before the act takes place, we can only be called on to do our subjective duty — the act which will probably (in the light of the best evidence available at the time) turn out to be our objective duty. Not being omniscient, we cannot always discern our objective duty, since it depends in part on circumstances beyond our knowledge or control. Sometimes, long afterwards, when we know what the consequences of the act actually were, we can say what our objective duty was; but by that time of course the act is long since past, and knowing our duty will not change the act, though it may guide us to perform future acts more wisely. Talk about objective duty usually occurs in post-mortem situations, after the act has been performed and most of its consequences are known; talk about subjective duty usually

[1] B. Russell, "The Elements of Ethics," p. 13.

occurs before the act takes place, in the light of the evidence available at the time.

Do we ever judge an act on the basis of objective duty? Sometimes we do. We may say, for example, after driving a car on an important errand, that it was all right to have passed that car while going up the hill because, as it turned out, there was no car coming anyway and so we got to our destination that much faster. As it happened, the act was objectively right, for it had the best consequences; but still, the act was not subjectively right, for there was no way of knowing whether another car was approaching from the opposite direction, and if there had been one approaching, there might have been a serious accident. Even in post-mortem discussions most observers would probably say that it was *not* right for the driver to have passed on a hill since by doing so, he was inviting possible disaster and endangering the lives of others as well as his own. They would say that the driver, in trying to excuse himself by saying "Well, it turned out for the best, didn't it?" was attempting (without success) to justify his behavior — thus showing that even in this post-mortem situation it is subjective duty, not objective duty, which people are using as a criterion for judging the person's behavior.

We don't always realize that hindsight is easier than foresight. It is a favorite trick of some moralistically minded persons to condemn someone, after he has committed an act, for not having done his objective duty, even though he faithfully performed his subjective duty. "You shouldn't have offered your great-aunt that ride, you see what happened as a result!" But the persons who made this judgment were in no better position before the act was committed to predict its outcome than the driver was. They are condemning as wrong an act which they, at the time the act was performed, had no more reason to believe was wrong (nor would they have condemned it as wrong at the time) than the driver had. The world contains many such "hindsight moralists"—"hindsight moralists" with regard to the actions of others, at any rate, seldom of themselves.

We must be careful, however, not to confuse subjective duty with the act that we *thought* was our objective duty. When a person does what he *thinks* is his objective duty, he may not be performing either his objective or his subjective duty; for his judgment may be based on preventible ignorance or carelessness or prejudice. Suppose that a member of a certain religious cult refused to permit his child to receive blood transfusions, even though the child's life was in danger without the transfusions. The utilitarian would say that the man was not doing his objective duty, for the consequence of this decision was the child's death; but neither was he doing his subjective duty, for he was not even acting in accordance with the knowledge available at the time — every shred of evidence indicates that refusal to allow transfusions will *not* have good results. It is true that the man *thought* it was his duty to prevent his child from receiving transfusions;

but that does not imply that it *was* his duty — in either the objective or the subjective sense. What you *think* is your duty may or may not be the same as what, in the light of the best evidence available, probably *is* your objective duty — just as it is overwhelmingly probable that you cannot run a mile in four minutes, even though in a burst of energy you may think that you can. What a person thinks is his duty has nothing to do with what *is* his duty, for he may not think correctly. Sometimes what the person *thinks* is his duty is considered a "third type of duty" and called *putative* duty. But this category is misleading if it is taken to mean that one's putative duty ever *is* one's duty. Putative duty, by definition, is not what *is* your duty but what you *think* is your duty, and, of course, what you think may be mistaken. There is, therefore, no sense in which it can be said that what you ought to do is your putative duty.

What you should be *blamed* (or praised) for doing is still another question. Should you be blamed for not having done your objective duty? Hardly, if some of the consequences of your act were unforeseeable at the time. Should you be blamed for not having done your subjective duty? Yes — at least this is where blame seems to belong. Should you be blamed for not having done your putative duty? But putative duty is not a duty at all; anyway you can well be blamed for having done *no more than* your putative duty — for example, if you think it your duty to send your child to an orphanage because you don't want to take care of him any more; or if you think you should vote for Candidate X because he assures the voters that all is well, and this is what you like to believe anyway; or if you make any other decision based on avoidable prejudice, ignorance, callousness, and so on. You may think that the act in question is your duty, but you may think so wrongly, and you can rightly be blamed for not bothering to inform yourself in such a way as to think differently. The whole question of what acts should be blamed and praised will be discussed separately in Chapter 10.

Let us apply these distinctions between kinds of duty to a specific case — a case admittedly designed to illustrate it neatly. Mr. A decides to kill Mr. B by shooting him as he passes on the street, but the gun doesn't go off and the attempt on B's life is unsuccessful. At that moment a stranger, Mr. C, is experimenting with his gun nearby, thinking it isn't loaded, and quite unexpectedly the gun goes off and kills Mr. B. A wrong act has been done, but who did it? Mr. C did the objectively wrong act, for his gun killed the passer-by. Though Mr. A pulled the trigger of his gun, his act caused no bad consequences, so it was not objectively wrong. But Mr. A did perform the subjectively wrong act, since it was probable that his firing the gun at Mr. B would cause the latter's death, even though it did not actually turn out that way. How should blame be assigned? We have not yet discussed blame, but we could blame Mr. A for intending as well as attempting to kill Mr. B — it was no thanks to Mr. A that his attempt failed. And though we cannot blame Mr. C for deliberately killing a human being, we can blame him for being careless, for playing around with a gun where other people were present, and for not bothering to investigate whether the gun was loaded.

10. Still another distinction must be mentioned to complete the account of utilitarianism. Thus far we have been talking about acts. Has utilitarianism anything to say about the *motives* that lead to these acts? When is a motive good and when is it bad? The best motives, according to the utilitarian, are those that most regularly lead to right acts, and the worst motives are those that least frequently lead to right acts. If I give financial help to the poor only out of motives of exhibitionism, to show off my beneficence, this motive would be judged a worse one than if I helped the poor out of a genuine concern for their welfare. Why? Because if I help only for the first reason, I shall do so only when others can see me do it, but if I help for the second reason, I shall do the deed of beneficence even when others will not know that I have done it. If I repay a debt only so that I can butter up my creditor for a swindle in the future, I shall be less likely to repay regularly than if I repay because I feel that it is my duty to do so. If I take medicine only when it tastes good, I am less likely to regain health than if I take it because I have it on reliable medical authority that it is likely to cure me. In each instance, acting from the second motive is more likely to lead to future right acts than is acting from the first motive.

The utilitarian judges *traits of character* in much the same way as he judges motives. Which character traits are desirable (virtuous) and which undesirable (vicious) depends on what kind of acts they are most likely to generate. If I am of a benevolent disposition toward my fellow men, I am more likely to perform utilitarian deeds to promote their welfare than if I am hostile, indifferent, or coldly calculating. Therefore benevolence as a trait of character is considered desirable (instrumentally, not intrinsically). If I have human sympathy and feel distress at the suffering of others, I am more likely to help them than if I lack such sympathy; therefore sympathy is considered a desirable trait of character.

Of most character traits, however, the utilitarian would have to say, "It all depends." Is loyalty a desirable character trait? That depends on what one is loyal to. On the one hand, loyalty among gangsters produces worse results for mankind than disloyalty would; on the other hand, loyalty to a good cause, or to people who champion good causes, is desirable. Self-denial is desirable if it serves a good purpose; otherwise it is pointless. Humility is ordinarily a virtue, but if it causes one to deny utterly his own desires and to serve those of people who are foolish or vicious, it may be worse than if humility did not exist. Even benevolence is not always a virtue; it must be accompanied by intelligence, for the uncritical use of benevolence may cause one's good will to be wasted on worthless objects.

EXERCISES

1. To what extent would a utilitarian classify the following as virtues? Explain. (1) self-control; (2) courage; (3) meekness; (4) tendency to self-criticism; (5) pride; (6) gratitude (Is there any utility in gratitude to the dead?); (7) affability; (8) conscientiousness; (9) sense of humor; (10) irritability; (11) optimism.

2. Assume that you are a utilitarian. Go as far as you can toward solving the following problems facing the United States and the world.

a. Since, according to utilitarianism, "everyone counts as one" whether he is a compatriot of yours or a foreigner, would it be your utilitarian duty to favor the revision of our immigration laws so that all foreigners could enter the United States on a permanent basis, without limitation of numbers and without discrimination between one country and another? (Try to keep all the relevant facts of the situation in mind: e.g., that some national groups tend to multiply themselves much faster than others. Would a reduction in our standard of living be beneficial for the world in general?)

b. The United States possesses approximately 47 per cent of the world's wealth and only 6 per cent of the world's population. Is it the duty of citizens of this country to share this wealth with poverty-stricken peoples of the world, for example (1) by outright gifts of food to undernourished peoples, (2) by the export of trained technicians and such materials for increased food-production as fertilizers and farm machinery, thus making their lands more productive, (3) by abolishing protective tariffs, thus permitting the products of cheaper labor overseas to be purchased by us at lower prices, even though the result would in some industries destroy domestic markets and cause both unemployment and lower wages in this country?

c. The rapidly increasing population of the world is fast outrunning the food supply. Even with every acre of arable land used and a 100 per cent efficient use of the land, an increasing percentage of the human race will starve if it continues to multiply at the present rate. By the year 2000 the world will probably contain over three billion people, far more than can be supported by the absolute minimum of two and a half acres of arable land per person. (Read C. L. Walker's "Too Many People," *Harper's Magazine,* Vol. 196, No. 1173 [February, 1948], pp. 97-104.) What steps toward a solution would you suggest?

d. What steps should be taken to remedy the lavish and wasteful expenditure of our natural resources? The United States must import an increasing quantity of vital raw materials each year. Forests are being used faster than they can be grown anew. Oil is being used at such a fantastic rate that we are already becoming an oil-importing country; meanwhile our methods of extracting oil and natural gas are extremely wasteful, and there is no way known of recovering underground the tons of these resources which are annually wasted by our methods of extracting them. (What would a utilitarian say of the adage, "Why should we do anything for posterity? What has posterity ever done for us?")

3. As a utilitarian, what would be your attitude toward the following historical situations?

a. Queen Elizabeth held Mary Queen of Scots prisoner in the Tower of London and finally had her executed on charges of conspiracy against the crown. Elizabeth knew that her specific charges against Mary were groundless, but she also felt that the execution would restore order in the kingdom and set an example to would-be plotters, thus increasing national security at a time when the very existence of the nation was threatened by Spain. Was Elizabeth justified in putting Mary to death?

b. Before the Bolshevik Revolution of 1917 there was a Provisional Government led by Alexander Kerensky. Kerensky was a less fanatical, more lenient, and more democratic man than Lenin or Stalin, and the history of the Soviet Union in the last forty years would almost certainly have been far less bloodthirsty if he had remained in power. But during the brief period that he was head of the government, he decided to show the Russian people that he was earnest and sincere in his claims of tolerance and his opposition to tyranny; so he declared an amnesty for all political prisoners. The result was that his political enemies were released from prison and they took advantage of his leniency to overthrow his government. Would it have been better if Kerensky had not made this generous move but instead had ordered all political prisoners shot?

c. Argue either for or against the justification of the following: (1) the United States developing the first atomic bombs during World War II, (2) United States use of atomic bombs against Japanese cities to end the war.

4. Apply the utilitarian criterion as best you can to the following war situations:

a. In William W. Haines's play *Command Decision* an air force officer can either give his battle-weary men a reprieve or send them into action again. They are exhausted from a grueling quick succession of bombing flights from England deep into German territory, with high casualties. An alarmingly large percentage of the planes have not returned, and those that did have contained many seriously wounded. Some of the men have flown their last required mission and are eligible for leave to go home and see their families in the States, though if they did so at this time, there would be none to replace them. The morale of these men has greatly declined in the face of dangerous flights coming so soon after one another and causing the high percentage of fatalities. Every human inclination drives the officer to call a halt to the withering succession of attacks. At the same time he is in possession of secret information which he cannot pass on to his men: at Schweinfurt the Nazis have almost completed building the factories and equipment for a new type of guided missile which, if used, could kill hundreds of thousands of civilians and troops stationed in England and within half a year would force Britain out of the war — successes which would have serious or disastrous effects on the whole Allied cause. Three weeks from now it will almost surely be too late; the factories must be destroyed before that time. The chances are heavily against clear weather all the way to the target; but just now, on this particular weekend, the weather is perfect and the forecasts unanimously indicate that it will remain so for two more days. Probably there will be no such opportunity again for more than a month, so it is now or never. Is the commander justified in sending these men, weary and exhausted, men whom he knows intimately and greatly admires, into the face of danger (and certain death for many of them) on two all-out attacks deeper into the enemy territory than they have been before, without their knowing *why* there is such an urgent need?

b. You are at war. The enemy systematically resorts to the torture of spies and captured prisoners to gain the information it desires, a practice which gives it a tactical advantage over your side and probably costs your side many lives because of your own unwillingness to use such methods to obtain any information from the enemy. Moreover, some neutrals are likely to be lost to your side as a result of the enemy's practice: if they side with the enemy but fall into your hands, they won't be tortured anyway, but if they side with you and fall into your enemy's hands, they will be tortured mercilessly. Unless you change your tactics, therefore, you may lose the war, or at any rate many thousands of lives. Under these circumstances, are you justified in using torture to expedite victory for your side?

c. During World War II the British allowed a number of women intelligence agents to return to the Continent, although the War Office knew that they would be tortured and killed by the Nazis. When this fact was revealed years after the war, it caused considerable outcry in Britain. But if the women had not been allowed to go as planned, the Nazis would thereby have been able to infer a fact which the British were most anxious to keep secret: the fact that they had cracked the enemy's code. Was their action justified?

d. Should the American soldiers who captured Japanese prisoners in World War II have given them medication and dressed their wounds? Humanitarianism would indicate that the Americans should have done so; even the conventions of war say they should have unless they would thereby be helping the other side to win — and the prisoners were out of the war in any event. But there was a chance that if the Americans had dressed the enemy's wounds, their own very limited supplies would have been used up and later, American casualties might have required them.

e. Should soldiers stop to bury their own dead and save their identity tags, even though some (say 10 per cent) of the bodies have been tampered with by the enemy in such a way as to cause a fatal explosion in the face of the merciful soldier who attempts to do these things? Yet the parents of the dead would want to see their sons given a decent burial and to have the tags as proof of their death.

f. A platoon of soldiers is about to take a bombed house occupied by the enemy, though the house may also contain prisoners belonging to their own side. The soldiers are not sure who is behind a certain closed door. If anyone enters to investigate, he may be shot down. If the attackers fire a machine gun through the door, they will avoid enemy fire because anyone on the other side of that door will be killed; but any prisoners held there by the enemy will also be killed. What should the attacking platoon do?

5. In the above questions, you probably considered only what steps would be most likely to lead to victory for *your* side. Now analyze at least one of the same examples, asking the much more difficult question, What in the circumstances would be best, not for your side only, but for the human race?

6. What would you as a utilitarian do in the following situations and why?

a. You are thrown into jail on a false charge. If you cannot get out at once, you will lose your job, and your family and friends may be suspicious of you (groundlessly) for being in jail. Your family lawyer is scrupulously honest and will not "pull the wires" required to get you out. But a shyster lawyer in the city, who has illegal connections with the gambling ring which involves city officials all the way up to the mayor, can pull the proper wires to get you out within a couple of hours. Are you justified in availing yourself of this lawyer?

b. In Dostoevski's novel *Crime and Punishment,* the main character, Raskolnikov, plots and carries out the murder of an old woman who has a considerable amount of money in her apartment. After killing her, he steals the money. He argues that (*1*) she is a malicious old woman, petty, cantankerous, and scheming, useless to herself and to society (this happens to be true), and her life causes no happiness to herself or to others and (*2*) her money, if found after her death, would only fall into the hands of chiselers anyway, whereas he, Raskolnikov, would use it for his education. Would you, as a utilitarian justify his action?

c. In Sinclair Lewis' novel *Arrowsmith,* Dr. Arrowsmith has perfected a new vaccine which, if used, will end an outbreak of the plague in the West Indies. If he uses the vaccine on everyone, most or all will be cured. But his vaccine will not be accepted in scientific circles (and thus used to prevent later outbreaks) unless he divides the population into two parts, giving vaccine to one half and not to the other half. If he gives vaccine only to some, he will needlessly cause the death of many people; yet must he not to do this to prove to others that it was the vaccine which saved their lives?

d. You are contemplating stealing a large sum of money from a secret hiding place of a friend who is now lying on his deathbed. No one else knows of the hiding place or of the existence of the money. Access to it is easy, and let us assume that there is no chance of being caught. You are not the kind of person whose conscience bothers you. The usual consequences of stealing — effects on society, effects on general respect for law, effects on your conscience — do not exist in this situation. Moreover, you will make excellent use of the money. Would the theft be justified?

e. Would it be justifiable to whip pigs to death if more succulent pork resulted from this process, giving the consumers of the pork more pleasure than the pigs received pain from being flogged?

f. Your neighbor and his family belong to a religious cult which teaches that all nonmembers of the cult will be punished eternally in hell-fire. Your neighbor's children tell this belief to your children, and your children ask you whether it is true. You do not believe it; but if you deny it, your children will tell the neighbor's children, who in turn will tell their parents, creating mistrust and hostility. At the same time, you do not want to tell your children anything that is not only extremely disturbing to them but that is also, you honestly believe, untrue. What should you do?

g. The chairman of the parole board receives a considerable income by releasing men from prison on parole and forcing them to perform criminal acts in his employ. If they obey him, he has them on another charge if he ever wants to get rid of them; if they refuse, he has them put back in prison for violation of parole (on some trumped-up charge). You alone know of the chairman's misdeeds, but you cannot prove them publicly. If you tried, nobody would believe you, and besides you would probably be shot by one of the hired killers whom the chairman employs. You are aghast at this vicious practice, yet for safety's sake you do not want to speak and almost certainly get yourself killed. What should you do?

h. You are a famous night club singer and the members of a white supremacy group offer you $100,000 to sing every night for one week at their club. If you take the job, you will give the proceeds to a needy hospital. "No," someone says to you, "don't take the job — don't corrupt yourself; money from such a source can never really produce good." "But it can," someone else urges; "think of the many lives that may be saved as a result of such a generous gift. If you were one of the persons who would die but for such help, would you still say no?" What would you, as a utilitarian, do?

7. In your opinion, have modern methods of refrigeration rendered out of date the ancient laws forbidding the consumption of pork? Has the invention of modern methods of contraception rendered out of date the commandment forbidding sexual intercourse outside of marriage?

8. Objective vs. subjective duty. Give your considered judgment on the following examples.

a. "Suppose a driver is approaching a crossroad, where trees and buildings block his vision of traffic on the other road. Ought he to stop or may he drive across at sixty miles an hour if he is in a hurry? We think his moral obligation is to stop, irrespective of whether there *is* traffic on the other road, because he does not *know* whether there is or not." (From Richard Brandt, *Ethical Theory.* Englewood Cliffs, N. J.: Prentice-Hall, 1959, p. 361. Reprinted by permission of the publisher.) Would you say that if it happens that there was in fact no traffic on the other road, he did right not to have stopped?

b. An experienced driver may sometimes actually reduce traffic hazards by violating a speed law or some other traffic ordinance. Is doing so justified every time it does reduce the hazard?

c. You see a suspicious-looking person hanging around the gunpowder plant. No one else is in the vicinity, and there is no time to report his presence to anyone. He lights a match; should you wait to see whether he uses it to light the fuse which may set the entire plant on fire? or should you take the law into your own hands and try to stop him forcibly now, on the assumption that his intentions are evil?

d. "A benevolent statesman may settle ten thousand refugees in a rich and promising agricultural region, and the next night an earthquake may destroy them all." (From J. B. Pratt, *Reason in the Art of Living: a Textbook of Ethics.* New York: Macmillan, 1949, p. 205. Reprinted by permission of the publisher.) Evaluate his action.

e. A physician is driving his car on an emergency call. He isn't sure it is a life-and-death case until he arrives at his destination, but the telephone call reported it to be crucial and he dares not assume that it is less serious than it seems to be. On the way he witnesses an automobile accident in which he may be of service to the victims, and indeed a bystander sees the "M.D." sign on his car and waves for him to stop. What should he do? Assume that he is the only physician in the vicinity.

f. "But suppose that if he lives it is *almost* certain that he will kill again." "Then you as a physician are acting wrongly if you don't give him a drug that will painlessly put him out of the way now." Assume that no one would ever find out, or if they did, would not prosecute. What should you do?

g. Officer: "Don't you realize that by taking that boat without permission and rescuing your brother (who had been left behind on the island when the troopship moved out) you were endangering not only your own life but that of all the troops on board, by informing the enemy of our presence?" Enlisted man: "Yes, I know, but I took the chance and nothing happened, and everything turned out all right, didn't it?" Did the enlisted man do wrong?

READING LIST, SECTION 12

Ayer, Alfred J. "The Principle of Utility." In Ayer, A. J., *Philosophical Essays.* New York: St. Martin's, 1955, pp. 250-70.

Bentham, Jeremy. *Introduction to the Principles of Morals and Legislation.* Many editions, especially Chs. 1-4.

Britton, Karl. *John Stuart Mill.* Baltimore: Pelican Books, 1959.

———. "Utilitarianism: the Appeal to a First Principle." *Aristotelian Society Proceedings,* Vol. 60 (1959-60), pp. 141-54.

Carritt, Edgar F. *Ethical and Political Thinking.* New York: Oxford Univ. Press, 1947, Ch. 4.

Ewing, Alfred C. *Ethics.* New York: Macmillan, 1953, Ch. 5.

Mill, John Stuart. *Utilitarianism.* Many editions, especially Chs. 1 and 2.

Moore, George Edward. *Ethics* (1911). Chs. 1 and 2. In Sellars, Wilfrid and John Hospers, eds. *Readings in Ethical Theory.* New York: Appleton-Century-Crofts, 1952, pp. 35-59.

———. *Principia Ethica* (1903). New York: Cambridge Univ. Press, 1959, (also paperbound), pp. 146-71.

Plamenatz, John. *Mill's Utilitarianism; reprinted with a study of the English Utilitarians.* New York: Macmillan, 1949.

Rashdall, Hastings. *Theory of Good and Evil.* 2nd ed. New York: Oxford Univ. Press, 1924. 2 vols., Vol. 1, Bk. 1, Ch. 7.

Russell, Bertrand. "The Elements of Ethics" (1911). In Sellars and Hospers. *Readings in Ethical Theory,* pp. 1-32.

Sidgwick, Henry. *The Methods of Ethics.* 7th ed. New York: Macmillan, 1874, especially Bk. 1, Ch. 9 and Bk. 4, Chs. 1-5.

Stace, Walter Terrence. *The Concept of Morals.* New York: Macmillan, 1937, especially Chs. 7 and 10.

13. Objections and applications

So much for the principal tenets of utilitarian ethics. But the theory has not gone without criticism. We shall now consider some objections to the utilitarian theory to which answers have been given by the utilitarians themselves. Then we shall consider some applications of the utilitarian ethics to practical situations. In the ensuing chapters we shall consider some ethical theories opposed to utilitarianism and the grounds of their opposition.

A. Man's relation to other men

Objection 1. Isn't the utilitarian principle rendered useless by the fact that everyone is going to use it in order to make exceptions in his own favor? Won't everyone, in calculating the probable results of his actions, calculate them so that they will come out in his own favor? Once you leave the area of strict moral rules — never do this, always do that — you have opened to people a freedom which they are not capable of using. Put it in their power to calculate the consequences, make the rightness or wrongness of their actions depend on the consequences, and they will always figure out the consequences so as to make their action right.

Answer. It is true that people often act according to this description (remember Moore's remarks on the subject, pages 210-11). But how is the fact that people will violate a moral theory an objection to the theory? Most people often do act in a way contrary to Christianity every hour of the day, and yet they believe in Christianity all the same. People are likely to honor more in the breach than in the observance *any* moral theory that requires from them any self-sacrifice or any action contrary to their own selfish interests. But surely this weakness doesn't refute the theory! As Browning said, "A man's reach should exceed his grasp, or what's a heaven for?" Utilitarianism presents to people a moral ideal which they should live up to as much as possible or so far as in them lies; more than that we cannot expect. But at least they should know what the ideal is; why should we pare down the ideal to include only what people will always *do*?

One might go even further: it is quite consistent for a utilitarian to encourage others *not* to weigh the probable consequences of each individual action, even to keep others ignorant of the utilitarian principle itself in deciding what to do. Just as in the hedonistic paradox, in which happiness to be got must be forgot (page 134), so here, it *could* be — one cannot say it *is*, for this is an empirical matter and generalizations are dangerous — that people are so hopelessly biased in their own favor all of the time that they are never able to weigh impartially the probable consequences of their actions when their own selfish interests are involved in the decision. It is possible that even if you asked them to weigh the consequences as an impartial judge in a court of law would, they still would be unable to do so. If they are unable, it would be better — i.e., it would have better results — to give them a few moral rules of thumb which would be likely to produce the best consequences in the majority of cases and tell them to go by these rules. In other words, it is conceivable — but not necessarily true — that you would get better utilitarian results — more happiness would be produced in the long run — by having people follow a few simple rules than by expecting them to guide every action by the utilitarian ideal itself. There would be exceptional cases and great injustice would be caused in these — a man who broke the speed limit to save a life would suffer harsh consequences — but on the whole, if people were sufficiently stupid or uninformed or prejudiced, less unhappiness would be caused by having them follow the traditional rules than by having everybody figure out the probable consequences of each action for himself. I hope people are not as I have described them, and I believe they are not, for the utilitarian theory tends to take a more optimistic view of human nature — utilitarianism demands more of people and believes them to be capable of more — than do moral theories which set rules before people and say, "Now obey these, blindly." But a legislator or executive in a backward country could still establish rules and be a utilitarian, for he would want the people to follow these few rules *in order that* most happiness could thereby be achieved. In other words, the moral rules would be only a means to an end, the end being the fulfillment of the utilitarian ideal.

Objection 2. If utilitarianism requires that everyone guide his actions by the utilitarian principle, very few people ever act rightly, for most people have never even heard of utilitarianism. Besides, most people don't perform actions like keeping promises and helping others out of difficulties *in order that* mankind may thereby be benefited; they do it to help a friend or to satisfy themselves that they have done their duty or in order that the friend may return the favor sometime.

Answer. First part of the objection: It is not necessary, of course, that everyone have heard of utilitarianism. What is asked is that their actions conform to the utilitarian principle, and this they may do, even though the people performing the actions have never heard of the principle.

Second part of the objection: We may grant that most people don't do good deeds *in order to* promote the general happiness of mankind. But this motive isn't required either. As long as the action tends to maximize happiness, it doesn't matter (as far as the rightness is concerned) whether it is done in order to promote the greatest happiness of the greatest number or not. Fulfilling the utilitarian criterion need not be our motive in performing the action, and it usually isn't.

Ninety-nine hundredths of all our actions are done from other motives, and rightly so done, if the rule of duty does not condemn them. . . . He who saves a fellow creature from drowning does what is morally right, whether his motive be duty, or the hope of being paid for his trouble; he who betrays the friend that trusts him, is guilty of a crime, even if his object be to serve another friend to whom he is under greater obligations. . . . The great majority of good actions are intended not for the benefit of the world, but for that of individuals, of which the good of the world is made up; and the thoughts of the most virtuous man need not on these occasions travel beyond the particular persons concerned, except so far as is necessary to assure himself that in benefiting them he is not violating the rights, that is, the legitimate and authorized expectations, of anyone else. The multiplication of happiness is, according to the utilitarian ethics, the object of virtue: the occasions on which any person (except one in a thousand) has it in his power to do this on an extended scale, in other words to be a public benefactor, are but exceptional, and on these occasions alone is he called on to consider public utility; in every other case, private utility, the interest or happiness of some few persons, is all he has to attend to.[1]

Objection 3. What with all the calculating of probable effects of actions, it would seem that the consistent utilitarian would have to spend three-quarters of his life just calculating which of the alternatives open to him he should pursue; and if he spent his life in this way, he would be taking valuable time away from the things he ought to be doing.

Answer. It is true that according to utilitarianism you should estimate the probable consequences of your actions a great deal more than most people do: most people just plunge right in and act, blindly and impulsively (shielded by a few rationalizations), without thinking of the consequences, especially the long-term ones. But it does not follow that you should spend most of your life calculating consequences. Suppose you are faced with a choice between two actions, A and B, and you don't know which you should do. If you sit for hours calculating consequences, you are doing *neither* A nor B. In effect you have a three-way choice:

A
B
Calculating the probable consequences of A and B.

Sometimes doing the last-mentioned is worse than doing either A or B. One student asks you to spend the next hour with him helping him on his trigonometry, and another student asks you to spend the same hour helping him with his Greek; you don't know which to do, so you spend the hour biting your nails trying to decide between them. The result is worse than if you had gone ahead with the one or the other. Important actions fraught with huge consequences, of course, deserve and require considerable study prior to a decision. But when the action is too unimportant in its consequences to deserve much study, it is better not to give it much thought but simply to go ahead. Otherwise you will be like the donkey situated at a point equidistant from two piles of hay who starved to death trying to decide which pile to take. Actions should receive only the amount of advance calculation that they deserve; and though this amount is more than is usually given in making decisions, it is less than the above objection would indicate.

Anyway, it is misleading to say or imply that every time we embark on a new action we have to start from scratch in estimating probable consequences, as if we had never observed the effects of people's actions before. People object that

---

[1] J. S. Mill, *Utilitarianism*, Ch. 2.

. . . there is not time, previous to action, for calculating and weighing the effects of any line of conduct on the general happiness. This is exactly as if anyone were to say that it is impossible to guide our conduct by Christianity, because there is not time, on every occasion on which anything has to be done, to read through the Old and New Testaments. The answer to the objection is that there has been ample time, namely the whole past duration of the human species. During all of that time, mankind have been learning by experience the tendencies of actions; on which experience all the prudence, as well as all the morality of life, are dependent. People talk as if the commencement of this course of experience had hitherto been cut off, and as if, at the moment when some man feels tempted to meddle with the property or life of another, he had to begin considering for the first time whether murder and theft are injurious to human happiness. Even then I do not think that he would find the question very puzzling; but, at all events, the matter is now done to his hand. It is truly a whimsical supposition that, if mankind were agreed in considering utility to be the test of morality, they would remain without any agreement as to what is useful, and would take no measures for having their notions on the subject taught to the young, and enforced by law and opinion. There is no difficulty in proving any ethical standard whatever to work ill, if we suppose universal idiocy to be conjoined with it; but on any hypothesis short of that, mankind must by this time have acquired positive beliefs as to the effects of some actions on their happiness.[1]

Objection 4. It would seem that utilitarianism is an immoral doctrine in that, with all its emphasis on calculation of consequences, it encourages one to act from *expediency* rather than from principle.

Answer. Whether utilitarianism is immoral or not depends, of course, on what you mean by "expediency."

Utility is often summarily stigmatized as an immoral doctrine by giving it the name of *expediency,* and taking advantage of the popular use of that term to contrast it with *principle.* But the *expedient,* in the sense in which it is opposed to the *right,* generally means that which is expedient for the particular interest of the agent himself; as when a minister sacrifices the interests of his country to keep himself in place. When it means anything better than this, it means that which is expedient for some immediate object, some temporary purpose, but which violates a rule whose observance is expedient in a much higher degree.[2]

People are often not very precise in the meaning they attach to the word "expedient," but usually the term has a strongly egoistic flavor. What is expedient is (usually) what is to *your own* interest (usually in the long run, not just at the present moment); and in this sense, expediency is sharply opposed to rightness by the utilitarian criterion. It is not *expedient* for you to sacrifice your own work to help your indigent brother out of a jam, nor is it expedient for the woman to tend the sick orphaned children of her recently deceased sister (catching the disease herself) because in neither case

[1] *Ibid.*   [2] *Ibid.*

will such actions be to the person's own advantage; but, if such actions will increase the sum of human happiness, they are nevertheless *right* by the utilitarian criterion. Thus there is a great gulf between what is expedient and what is right. Confusing the two is the last thing the utilitarian can be accused of.

The word "prudence" is most often used in our century in place of "expediency." The prudent action is the one which will contribute to *your own* advantage in the long run; prudence would be the counsel of the rational egoist, which we discussed in Chapter 2. But prudence, being egoistic, is very far from being the same as rightness, which, according to utilitarianism, consists in maximizing intrinsic good, not just your own good.

Objection 5. If everyone practiced utilitarianism, wouldn't we have a society of nothing but do-gooders? What would happen to all those varied activities that make life interesting? If we took utilitarianism seriously, shouldn't we all rush out and do social work, slum clearance, psychiatry, and other such things to help our fellow men?

Answer. No such absurd conclusion follows. The world being what it is, we could stand a lot more physicians and psychiatrists, to be sure. But there would be no point in everyone doing these things: in the first place, if everyone did them, there would be very little need for them (if some people are going to help other people, there have to be other people who need the help); and in the second place, there are plenty of other absolutely essential occupations whose utility is just as great. For instance, we all have to eat, and somebody has to wash the dishes. The hired hand on a farm and the dishwasher in a restaurant may not feel, if they read about utilitarianism, that they are doing their utilitarian duty. Yet they are performing tasks that society cannot do without. Imagine what the world would be like if nobody cut crops or washed dishes! The people who do these jobs, especially if they have no great talent for doing more complicated work which few people are able to do, are probably doing their utilitarian duty by going ahead with their jobs and filling their particular niche in the total social structure.

As to the things that make life interesting, like enjoying the arts and visiting our national parks, as long as they don't hurt other people and thus diminish the total of human happiness, they are all to the good. Imagine the world entirely without literature or music and you see at once how human happiness would be diminished. Since there are not many people in any generation who are really creative geniuses, they should be encouraged in every possible way, even if in other aspects of their lives they are far from exemplary. Wagner may have been a vain, self-seeking individual, and the superficial utilitarian might think it better if he had never lived. But he has left us his music, which many of us at any rate can enjoy and which people will enjoy in generations to come — a reservoir for human happiness far greater than the very local unhappiness he caused to a few people around him during his lifetime. Artists usually create for themselves only — they can create in no other way. If they pandered to the tastes of the public, changing their creations to please the preferences of the majority, their works would bear no creative stamp and would result in dull eclecticism. No great works of art would then be created, and no pioneering works, setting the pattern of public taste for the future, could come into existence. The artist will do well to ignore the taste of the moment and trust to his own artistic judgment. By doing so, he is far more likely to increase the happiness and well-being of the human race in the long run. Some people think that artists should be public servants. But the fact that artists increase human knowledge and enjoyment is an incidental result of their chief aim, which is to produce works of aesthetic value. If they deliberately set out to be public servants, they would produce nothing of long-term value for themselves or anyone else. (Remember the character of Roark, the architect in Ayn Rand's *The Fountainhead*.)

The same considerations apply in the realm of scientific and philosophical ideas. Only *individual* minds can conceive new ideas; and throughout history great ideas have come only from minds who refused to be intimidated by the dead-level mediocrity of majority opinion. Socrates was condemned as a corrupter of youth and morals, and Galileo served mankind by defying it. "The long run" is often very long indeed.

Objection 6. What with all his emphasis on planning, calculating, and estimating probable consequences, the utilitarian seems to be a kind of calculating machine with no other purpose in life but to produce certain desirable effects. Wouldn't one effect of this kind of activity on the person who does these things be to make him an excellent calculator but a rather cold and unsympathizing individual? This effect seems undesirable. Better have him retain his warmth and spontaneity as a human being and make a few more errors in his estimation of effects.

Answer. Mill has already anticipated this kind of objection.

> It is often affirmed that utilitarianism renders men cold and unsympathizing; that it chills their moral feelings towards individuals; that it makes them regard only the dry and hard consideration of the consequences of actions, not taking into their moral estimate the qualities from which those actions emanate. If the assertion means that they do not allow their judgment respecting the rightness or wrongness of an action to be influenced by their opinion of the qualities of the person who does it, this is a complaint not against utilitarianism, but against having any standard of morality at all; for certainly no known ethical standard decides an action to be good or bad because it is done by a good or a bad man, still less because done by an amiable, a brave, or a benevolent man, or the contrary. These considerations are relevant, not to the estimation of actions, but of persons; and there is nothing in the utilitarian theory inconsistent with the fact that there are other things which interest us in persons besides the rightness and wrongness of their actions.[1]

[1] *Ibid.*

For example, as we have just seen, a person's motives may be good and his actions morally good without his actions being *right*. But when it is rightness and not the other things ("the qualities from which those actions emanate") that we are discussing, it is essential to consider the consequences in great detail, since it is these that we should make as intrinsically good as possible.

Anyway, there is no reason why a person cannot be *both* warm and outgoing in his demeanor *and* scrupulously conscientious about trying to make his actions produce the best possible consequences. A person who is pinched and crabbed in disposition is likely to be taking out his personal grievances and frustrations on the outside world, and more often than not he cannot be trusted even in his estimation of consequences: he may be a slave to duty and all that, but (perhaps without being aware of it himself) he will rig the estimate of probable consequences in such a way as to make it seem right to deny to others the joys that he himself has been denied. Not being very permissive, he will act so as to produce something less than the maximum possible happiness for others — however much his decisions may be disguised as "acting for their own good," and the like. It usually takes a happy person really to *want* happiness for others; such a person will not begrudge others their happiness and will not unduly envy them when they achieve more of it or more of the means to it than he has had. Such a person *will* be warm and outgoing, for he will have nothing to hide or repress, nothing to begrudge others; having tasted of life's happiness himself, he will want others to taste it freely also. The person most likely not only to profess but to *practice* the utilitarian ethics will be a strong, vibrant personality, not one who is "cold and unsympathizing."

But there is one assumption to which every utilitarian *will* be opposed, and that is the assumption that benevolent impulses, sparks of human kindness, and having a warm, radiant, kind personality is *enough* — that a person who has such a personality does not have to use it with intelligence and foresight. Utilitarianism will be opposed to the person who is all heat and no light; for such a person, however noble his motives, however pure his intentions, will *act* unintelligently, and his actions will be very unlikely to be the right ones. Consider the young factory worker who is so warm-hearted that he gives away half his hard-earned paycheck every week to every drunken bum who hands him a sob story. The young man thereby not only damages himself but also does not do the recipients of his benevolence any good (they will only use the money to get drunk another time); and, into the bargain, he cheats all possible *worthy* recipients of his benevolence, for by the time they appear on the scene (if they ever do), he has no money left to dole out. The *uncritical* use of his benevolence does more harm than good; he would have done far more good by keeping all the money himself. The possibility that he may be animated by humanitarian ideals — he may be simply running over with the milk of human kindness — does not make his actions right. "If your heart is in the right place, then everything you do will be all right" is a popular American superstition which has been with us from early childhood. In fact it is not enough that your heart is in the right place, it must also aim its shafts in the right direction. But this fact is lost upon those who have a horror of calculation, of detailed knowledge of the effects of one's actions, and of the use of the intellect in general; the typical American anti-intellectualist bias is manifested nowhere more clearly than in this irrational distrust of the calculation of consequences. This failure to estimate carefully the long-term consequences of one's actions, letting one's soft heart alone be sufficient as guide for the moral life, is perhaps as good a definition as can be given of *sentimentalism*.

The utilitarian is opposed to sentimentalism — not sentiment, but sentimentalism. Consider the mother whose daughter of five has a severe leg injury. If the leg is not treated at once, the child will be crippled for life, since the one leg will never grow any longer than it already is. But the treatment will cause severe and prolonged pain; the mother cannot bear to see her child endure such pain, so she refuses treatment for her daughter. For the rest of her life the daughter resents her mother; when she cannot play with the other girls, when later on she is severely handicapped in acquiring the husband and home life which she desperately needs and desires, she thinks of her mother. "But I did it all for you," says the mother tearfully; "I didn't want to cause you pain." However noble her motives may have been, the action was plainly *wrong*. Good will, a benevolent disposition, and kindliness alone are not enough. One must have the strength of will, the intelligence, and the courage to look ahead, completely and impartially, to the consequences of one's actions — not just in the immediate present (the daughter's pain) but in the distant future (the daughter's lifelong unhappiness).

Consider another example. An employer in a factory takes on a worker who turns out to be an escapee from a mental hospital. But the worker pleads, "Don't tell them, please don't tell them. I'm all right, give me a chance, I don't want to go back there." So the employer, moved to compassion, almost in tears himself at the man's story, and feeling a bit intoxicated besides at his own radiant benevolence, says, "O.K., I'll give you a break. You can't always trust those doctors, and you look all right to me." The employer knows nothing about psychiatry and cares less; he has no idea what danger signs to look for in the worker's behavior, so he keeps the worker on. A few weeks later the employee receives a severe tongue-lashing from a fellow worker, and, pathologically unable to endure being crossed, he rushes out, rapes one female employee, and kills another. These disasters occurred because the employer took a hundred-to-one chance and trusted the worker. The employer felt benevolent, he wanted to trust people, his heart was in the right place — but that is not enough. One must temper his sentiments with realism. It seems a noble thing to trust people, but should one trust them even when the probabilities are all against them and when other people will have to pay with their lives for the benevolent man's misjudgment? Trusting the psychotic in this instance meant that his desire to be away from the institution was worth more than the lives of his victims. Was the satisfaction of his wish worth such a price? The man who is a bit more cautious about trusting people may seem like a cold fish by comparison with the benevolently indulgent employer — and the American ideal is to hate cold fish and to love those who are willing to trust others on a sudden generous impulse with the chances a hundred to one against them — but because of his caution he may well save the lives of some and the happiness of others. It is a hard lesson to learn, particularly for those who were brought up on American movies, but sentimentalism is not the way to bring about the greatest good of everyone involved. Benevolence is indispensable, for benevolent actions do not usually spring from a nonbenevolent nature; but if benevolence is not combined with the careful use of one's intelligence in estimating the results of his actions, it can produce far worse results than if it had never existed at all.

Consider one more example. In the same way, the college administrator in charge of grants-in-aid might be so benevolent that he doled them out to the first students who came along and had none left for the really needy students; or he might be taken in by every sob story that came his way and be unsympathetic to the less sentimental but worthier candidate or be unable to recognize merit when he came across it. For such benevolence a high price is always paid; no utilitarian would favor good will unaccompanied by intelligence.

Neither, of course, would he favor intelligence unaccompanied by good will. The results of that particular combination have been too recently manifest in the world. Hitler and many members of the Nazi High Command were intelligent men; but it would certainly have been better (according to the utilitarian) if they had been less intelligent, for then they would have been less able to carry out their purpose of mass destruction. The clever college administrator may be able to hatch the most diabolical schemes and yet succeed in pulling the wool over everyone's eyes about what he is doing. A person may have full knowledge of the facts of a situation and yet act upon them only in order to promote his own interests. It would appear, then, that knowledge and benevolence (good will) are both necessary conditions for moral action.

In this connection, let us briefly examine the famous dictum of Socrates, "Virtue is knowledge." How can this possibly be true in the light of the above considerations? Various interpretations have been put upon this Socratic aphorism, but the most plausible interpretation is this one: If you knew what would make you happy, you would do it; virtue consists of *knowing* what will make you happy — once you know this, the rest can safely be left up to you. People do not knowingly will themselves into unhappiness, they only arrive at that state through miscalculation — they incorrectly *think* that something will make them happy when, in the long run, it won't; they make an error of *knowledge*. To this interpretation we can make two comments:

a. Socrates does not say that if you know what will increase the *general* happiness, you will do it — only *your* happiness. How then can we derive anything remotely utilitarian from such a formula? Only by combining it, as Plato did, with the idea that only by promoting the general happiness will you be able to achieve *your own* happiness. However, we have already had reason (pages 176-83) to suspect this "harmony theory."

b. From a common-sense viewpoint the formula seems to be true enough. Nobody consciously wills his own misery, thought Socrates. If the dictator knew before he achieved supreme power that he would reap only misery therefrom, of course he would not do it; if you knew that you would get indigestion from eating an exotic dish, you would not eat it. The assumption is that everyone is a rational egoist. But unfortunately this assumption too is a false one: (1) Some people can never learn to sacrifice small benefits now to gain greater ones later on; some people are so attracted by a course of action now, even knowing full well its consequences, that they embark upon it anyway. The probable consequences are known by them intellectually but have no impact upon them emotionally. (2) Moreover, there are countless cases known to modern psychiatric science, which were unknown to the extroverted Greeks, in which people behave in an entirely self-damaging manner. They know full well what their action will lead to, but their knowledge does not deter them. Some people behave in such a self-damaging manner that it seems to the careful observer as if they were deliberately willing their own ruination and destruction. Failure in morality does not, then, seem to arise simply from defect of knowledge but also from defect of will. Socrates thought that if you really saw what the good was, you would do it. St. Paul had, perhaps, a greater insight when he wrote, "The good that I would I do not; but the evil which I would not, that I do."

B. Man's relation to the animals

Objection 7. Utilitarianism is dedicated to the maximization of human happiness. But what about nonhuman beings? Specifically, what about the "lower" animals? Surely we are not to ignore their welfare entirely.

Answer. The utilitarian is committed to the maximization of happiness *wherever* it may exist — in animals as well as in men. Human beings, of course, are the only creatures that are *known* to enjoy happiness or to be capable of it; whether, and to what extent, dogs or fish or beetles are capable of happiness is a terribly sticky question, and utilitarians could well disagree about *that* without disagreeing on the principle that happiness is intrinsically good wherever it is found. Since there is no standard utilitarian view on this point, we can best bring out the controversy by means of a dialogue:

A: Maybe dogs and cats aren't capable of happiness in the full sense that human beings are; at least many *sources* of happiness, such as reading and religious experience and *objets d'art,* don't seem to be available to them. But to say that they are incapable of happiness to any degree at all would be going too far. The dog surely *seems* to be happy when his master is with him and unhappy when he is not, happy when he has open fields to play in and unhappy when he is confined.

B: Would you say, then, that people have duties to animals as well as to other human beings?

A: Certainly. If you are driving on the highway and see a dog that will be run over unless you swerve the car, it surely is your duty to avoid hitting the dog, even though no *human* life is at stake. Or if an animal is lying injured on the highway, it would be wrong not to try and help, call a veterinarian, or at worst put it out of its misery. Morality would be very incomplete indeed if it included only the welfare of human beings and not that of the other creatures. To see any creature in pain and be able to help and not do so would be wrong.

B: How far in this direction is morality to go? Is a dog's welfare to be considered equal to that of a human being?

A: No, I would say it isn't, because a dog is not capable of the degree of intrinsic good that a human being is. If you had to choose between running over a human being and running over a dog, you would have to choose the dog, because running over the human being means the destruction of a greater intrinsic good or at least, if it were a small child, the potentiality for intrinsic good. And I don't think I'm saying this just because I am a human being and not a dog: even if the dog in question were my own dog and the human being a total stranger, I would feel duty-bound to avoid hitting the human being because human beings have a potential for happiness much greater than that of dogs.

B: So much for dogs. We like dogs and we have selfish reasons for saving their lives: they amuse us and they are companions to us. In somewhat different ways, so are cats and horses; and cows and pigs are profitable to us as income and as sources of beef and pork, so we are naturally interested in preserving them too. But would you extend this utilitarian benevolence also toward rats? Remember that rats are more intelligent than any of the animals we have mentioned; so they have a greater potential in that direction at least. Monkeys and chimpanzees have even more potential. These animals would provide a far better test case for our utilitarian altruism. Yet very few people would go out of their way to help a rat; they would rather go out of their way to kill one. Is the utilitarian committed to the preservation of life in all its forms, including insect pests and poisonous snakes?

A: It's true that boll weevils and rattlesnakes don't amuse us and keep us company as dogs do, and for this selfish reason we don't feel like preserving them. But if we try to preserve dogs and not boll weevils, we *ought* to do so not because we happen to like dogs but because they are more *worth* preserving. Couldn't we say that even if rats and rattlesnakes *are* capable of happiness to the same degree as dogs, there is a difference, because rats and rattlesnakes are more destructive?

B: So is every form of life. All life lives on other life, including man, who kills the most of all, and not for food as the other animals do but for sport. Have you seen a dog chewing up a rabbit or a cat chewing up a mouse? They are just as destructive as rats and rattlesnakes. It just happens that the rattlesnakes can harm *us* and the insects can destroy our crops, and so, for selfish reasons, we want them exterminated but not the dogs.

A: But the rattlesnake or cobra who kills a man is destroying a greater intrinsic good than the cat who kills a mouse. Therefore I feel justified in saying that we rightly abhor the snake and the insect, not because, selfishly, they constitute more of a threat to us human beings (though they do), but because human beings enshrine more intrinsic good and are on that account more worth preserving.

B: A nice rationalization of our prejudice in our own favor. Offhand I don't see why *all* of God's creatures shouldn't be equally well treated by us human beings. We should try to preserve them *all* to whatever extent we can. Of course nature takes this to a large extent out of our hands; for "Nature, red in tooth and claw," as Tennyson said, is so arranged that living things have to destroy each other in order to stay alive, and there isn't much that we can do about that system. Still, couldn't we take the attitude that Albert Schweitzer and others do, that *all* life ought equally to be preserved and that we should destroy it only when it is absolutely necessary to do so in order to preserve other life? This attitude doesn't mean that we have to *like* all the animals equally but only that we should *treat* them all equally, at least *impartially,* with respect to the amount of happiness possible to them. We should maximize this happiness without regard to our personal sentiments toward the species in question — exactly as we should treat human beings impartially with respect to the maximization of their happiness, even though we can't be expected to like them all equally. To do a duty for those we like is a pleasure; to do it for those we dislike is — just a duty. It is the same, it would seem, with our treatment of animals.

A: I agree that we should be impartial with respect to animals, and I agree that very few of us are: most people who would try to alleviate the pain of an injured dog on the highway would never bother to stop for an injured skunk on the highway. People generally act from selfish motives, helping only those creatures (man or beast) which they enjoy helping rather than those which, impartially considered, it is their duty to help. But this tendency is no news, is it? People don't do what they ought to do most of the time. Right now I am not concerned with what they do; I am concerned with determining what they *ought* to do. Though I can't see any difference between helping the dog and helping the skunk, except insofar as the former may give *us* happiness and the latter wouldn't, I *can* see a difference between the cat eating the mouse and the snake poisoning the man; for the snake who kills the man is destroying a greater intrinsic good than the cat who kills the mouse. I think I make this statement quite objectively, not just because I happen to be a man. (One reason why men are superior to the other animals is that the other animals can't state their superiority, or even think it, at all.) Therefore I think I would be justified in killing the rattlesnake, for it might kill other men if it lived; whereas I would not feel justified in killing a harmless snake; in fact, as every farmer knows, the harmless snakes are quite useful.

B: You mean, they are useful to *us* — they kill off the rats and mice and other vermin that plague the farmer. So we are being selfish again, aren't we? Remember that the harmless snake you let go will seek out the nesting places of mice and moles and swallow them whole. By "harmless" you mean harmless *to us;* but they are extremely harmful to mice, as every mouse would testify. Don't the mice deserve a break in this world?

A: They do, insofar as it's possible to give them one; but I repeat that when it comes to a choice between a mouse and a man, we should save the man because in him lies a greater intrinsic good. When insects destroy the crops on which man's food supply depends, it's too bad for the insects but they have to go — a greater good must take precedence over a lesser good.

B: Again I think you are making a smug rationalization which testifies to our egoism rather than to the facts. You keep saying that a man contains more intrinsic good, or at least the potential for a greater intrinsic good, than other animals do, and you give this opinion as an "objective" reason for saving man in preference to the others. But have you forgotten that, if human beings contain a greater potential for good, they also contain a greater potential for evil? Human beings may be capable of far greater happiness than other creatures, but they are also capable of far greater *un*happiness. No rat in the world can be as unhappy as a psychotic human being. Not only have human beings a greater potential for *being* unhappy, they also have a far greater potential for *producing* unhappiness in other human beings than any of the "lower" animals have. No animal but man is guilty of murdering someone with an ax, or of betraying his friends for money, or of storing up his hatred for years to wreak vengeance on an enemy, or even (as a rule) of killing just for the fun of it. If the animals do not possess moral virtues, neither are they guilty of crimes. I often wonder which aspect of human beings preponderates — their happiness or their unhappiness, their tendency to help others or their tendency to injure others. Many philosophers and theologians have said that man is predominantly and hopelessly evil. If this is so, wouldn't it be our utilitarian duty to run over the man on the highway rather than the dog; for in running over the man, we would be more likely to be destroying (1) a greater unhappiness (a greater intrinsic evil) and (2) a greater potential for inflicting unhappiness on others (a greater instrumental evil)? Assuming that human nature is predominantly (1) unhappy and (2) morally bad, wouldn't you have to recommend such an action, in all consistency?

A: But we don't *know* that the human being we run over is predominantly bad. Maybe he is, maybe he is even an ax-murderer who deserves death far more richly than any dog could, but we don't know this and are not entitled to assume it; we have to assume, rather, that we would be destroying a greater intrinsic good by running over the man.

B: Assume it? What right have we to assume it? If, as you say, we are not entitled to assume that the man is predominantly bad, how can we assume he is predominantly good? We utilitarians are not supposed to make such assumptions — we go by the probabilities. If man is predominantly bad, the probability (in running over a stranger on the highway) would be that we are destroying a greater evil than the dog could possibly be: both an intrinsic evil (since man, in this view, is predominantly unhappy, far more unhappy than dogs) and an instrumental evil (since man, in this view, is more inclined to make other people unhappy than happy).

A: But man can be changed. Even if he is predominantly unhappy and morally evil, he has the potential of change within him as an animal has not; therefore, because of that potential, he is more worth preserving.

B: Many people would say that man is hopelessly evil or hopelessly unhappy (at least for the most part). Even if he is not hopelessly evil or unhappy, remember that as well as having a great potential for happiness and good, man also has a great potential for misery and evil. This second potential should be considered as fully as the first. If you feel he ought to be saved because he has a greater potential for good than he now shows, I can reply that he ought to be destroyed because he has a greater potential for evil than he now shows. Both, I would say, are equally true, and so your argument is double-edged. I often wonder whether it might not be our utilitarian duty to return this planet to the animals whom we disparagingly call "lower." Perhaps they deserve to enjoy it more than we do. At least they will not destroy it with thermonuclear bombs; whereas if we are left to ourselves we may destroy ourselves and the other animals along with us. The animals, at least, do not deserve this fate.

C. Art and morality

Objection 8. Wouldn't the utilitarian have to condemn art, at least fine art, as worthless, since it possesses no utility?

Answer. Of course not. For one thing, the enjoyment of art has an intrinsic value. The work of art itself does not; it has value only insofar as sentient beings can respond to it. Therefore art is worth creating even if it has no instrumental value whatever. Nevertheless, there *are also* instrumental values in art. We shall consider literature first:

a. Literature sometimes teaches moral lessons which are of value to mankind. This value occurs in didactic literature, such as Bunyan's *Pilgrim's Progress,* but not in all literature, and it is easily overemphasized. Shakespeare did not write *Othello* to attack racial prejudice nor *Macbeth* to prove that crime does not pay.

b. Far more often than by explicit statement, literature teaches (in John Dewey's phrase) as friends and life teach — by *being,* not by express intent. The variety of situations presented, the human characterizations, the moral crises through which the characters pass — these alone, when set before us in a work of literature, can produce a moral effect without any explicit moralizing.

How does literature achieve this moral effect? It presents us with characters and situations (usually situations of difficult moral decision) through which we can deepen our own moral perspectives by reflecting on other people's problems and conflicts, which usually have a complexity that our own daily situations do not possess. We can learn from them without ourselves having to undergo in our personal lives the same moral conflicts or to make the same moral decisions. We can view their situations with a detachment that we can seldom achieve in daily life when we are immersed in the stream of action. By viewing these situations "as from afar off" and reflecting on them, we are enabled to make our own moral decisions more wisely when life calls on us in turn to make them. Literature can be a stimulus to moral reflection unequaled perhaps by any other, for it presents the moral choice in its *total* context with nothing of relevance omitted.

c. Perhaps the chief moral potency of literature lies in its unique power to stimulate and develop the faculty of the *imagination*. Shelley said, "The imagination is the great instrument of moral good, and poetry administers to the effect by acting upon the cause." Through literature we are carried beyond the confines of the narrow world which most of us inhabit into a world of thought and feeling more profound and more varied than our own, a world in which we can share the experiences of human beings (real or fictitious) who are far removed from us in space and time and in attitude and way of life. Literature enables us to enter directly into the affective processes of other human beings; and having done this, no perceptive reader can any longer condemn or dismiss *in toto* a large segment of humanity as "'foreigners" or "Russians" or "wastrels" simply as a mass, for they live before us through literature as individuals, animated by the same passions as we are, facing the same conflicts, and tried in the same crucible of bitter experience. Through such an exercise of the sympathetic imagination, literature tends to draw all men together instead of setting them apart from one another in groups or types with convenient labels tagged to each. Far more than preaching or moralizing, more even than descriptive and scientific discourses of psychology or sociology, literature tends to unite mankind and reveal the common human nature which exists in all of us behind the facade of divisive doctrines, political ideologies, and religious beliefs.

This is not to say, of course, that those who read great works of literature are necessarily tolerant or sympathetic human beings. Reading literature alone is not a cure for human ills, and people who are neurotically grasping or selfish in their private lives will hardly cease to be so as a result of reading works of literature. Still, wide and serious reading of literature has an observable effect: people who do this kind of reading, no matter what their other characteristics may be, do tend to be more understanding of other people's conflicts, to have more sympathy with their problems, and to be able to empathize more with them as human beings than do people who have never broadened their horizons by reading literature at all. No one who has read great literature widely and for a considerable period, so as to make it an integral part of his life, can any longer share the same provincialism and be dominated by the same narrow prejudices which seem to characterize most people most of the time. Literature, perhaps more than anything else, exercises a *leavening* influence on the temper of one's moral life. It looses us from the bonds of our own position in space and time; it releases us from exclusive involvement with our own struggles from day to day; it enables us to see our own local problems and trials (in Spinoza's phrase) under the aspect of eternity — we can now view them as if from an enormous height.

To have moral effects, it is not necessary that a work of literature present us with a system of morality. Its moral potency is greatest when it presents us, not with systems, but with human beings in action, so that through the exercise of the imagination we can see our own customs and philosophies as we see theirs, as some among many of the countless proliferations of adjustments and solutions to human problems which varying circumstances and our endlessly varied and resourceful human nature have produced.

Works of literature, then, develop more than anything else the human faculty of the imagination; and Shelley says that the imagination is the greatest single instrument of moral good. Perhaps this sounds like an absurd overstatement, but consider what morality is like *without* the imagination. Consider the average morality of a small community, relatively isolated from centers of culture and unacquainted with any artistic tradition. Their morality is rigid and circumscribed; the details of each member's personal life are hedged about with constant annoyances, and everyone's life is open to the prying eyes of the others who are unfailingly quick to judge, with or without evidence. Outsiders are looked upon askance; people of a different religion, race, or culture, are viewed with suspicion and distrust; and anyone who does not subscribe to whatever moral code is dominant in the community is condemned or ostracized. No doubt these people are sincere—they are dreadfully sincere, deadly sincere. But sincerity without enlightenment can be as harmful to the achievement of good as intelligence without wisdom when that intelligence is possessed by political leaders playing around with hydrogen bombs. The people of a small community have not known the leavening influence of literature. Their morality is rigid, cramped, and arid. If these same people had been exposed from early youth, in the right way, to great masterpieces of literature and had learned through them to appreciate the tremendous diversity of human mores and beliefs which other groups hold with the same degree of sincerity that *they* possess, they would be less likely to be as harsh, intolerant, and rigid as they are.

People are usually inclined to separate art and morality into two hermetically sealed compartments. They talk as if morality were already complete and self-sufficient without art, and that art, if it is to be tolerated at all, can grudgingly be permitted, provided that it conforms to the moral customs of the time and place of those judging it. But this view is surely to conceive the relation between art and morality in far too one-sided a manner. If art must take cognizance of morality, equally morality must take cognizance of art. Almost everything that is alive and imaginative about morality comes from the leavening influence of art.

To consider examples from Greece alone, what would morality be today without the influence of Aeschylus and Sophocles, without Socrates as described in Plato's dialogues, without even the historians Herodotus and Thucydides with their quiet humor and gentle prodding skepticism and tolerance for other customs and views? It is through great works of art that we get our most vivid conception of various ways of life. What is it about other times and places that we most remember? Is it their political squabbles, their wars, their economic upheavals? These events are known in general to intelligent laymen and in detail to historians, but even then such events do not usually make much of a dent in our personal lives in the way that art does. What is alive today about ancient Greece is its sculpture, its poetry, its epic and drama; what is alive today about the Elizabethan period, even more than the defeat of the Spanish Armada and the reign of Queen Elizabeth, is its poetic drama, with its vivid characterizations and boundless energy. Other civilizations and cultures may be sources of facts and theories which enlighten our understanding; but what enables us to share directly their feelings and attitudes toward life is not their politics nor even their religion but their art. Art alone is never out of date: science is cumulative, even the science textbooks of ten years ago are now discarded as obsolete; we study the science of the Greeks and the Elizabethans only as historical curiosities. But great art is never obsolete: it can still present to us its full impact, undiminished by time. Shakespeare will not be out of date as long as human beings continue to feel love, jealousy, and conflict in a troubled world. We might paraphrase a Biblical statement and apply it to past cultures: "By their arts shall ye know them." The artists whose works we now revere may have died unsung; most of them, even those who were appreciated during their lifetimes, were considered far less important than the latest naval victories or the accession of the current king; yet today these things have all passed into history, but art survives with undiminished vigor. The art of the past molds in countless ways the attitudes, responses, dispositions of our daily lives. Most of what is perceptive and imaginative in morality owes its origin to art, and when morality loses contact with the tradition of art it becomes dead and sterile. Yet in spite of this some people tell us that art is the slave of morality.

Already, in the preceding paragraph, we have started to talk about arts other than literature. But how can they have any moral effects on those who view them or listen to them? Yet there are effects of these arts on the observer which, in a broad sense, are moral (as opposed to nonmoral), and which account for the attempts of many people to censor them:

a. Historically the most famous theory about the moral effect of art on its audience is Aristotle's theory of catharsis; Aristotle applied the theory to tragedy only, but many since his day have applied it to art in general. According to this view, art acts as an emotional cathartic and achieves a "purgation of the emotions." Certain emotions which we would be better off without (Aristotle limited them to pity and fear, but they could easily be extended) are generated during the course of daily life. Art is the principal agency that should help us get rid of these emotions. By observing works of art (witnessing a drama, listening to a powerful symphony, looking at certain works of sculpture or painting) we can work off these emotions rather than let them fester inside us or rather than take them out in unpleasant ways on our fellow men. "Music hath charms to soothe the savage breast," especially the breast that is full of pent-up disturbances and needs some channel for their release. Art siphons off these disturbing inner states rather than let them grow rancid within us.

As it stands, this view is undoubtedly somewhat crude, especially in the light of modern psychology; and we could find fault in many respects with the Aristotelian doctrine of catharsis. Yet the experience of reading, viewing, or listening to a work of art does give a peculiar release, a feeling of freedom from inner turbulence. The mere act of plunging ourselves, for a few hours, into an entirely different world when we go to a play or a concert is often enough to transform, however temporarily, the tone of our daily lives. It is not merely that for a few hours we can forget our troubles — any form of entertainment, however worthless, might do this, and alcohol helps many people to do it too. It is not merely that art provides a break or interruption in the course of our lives at the end of which they are exactly what they were before. It is that through the aesthetic process itself, in the very act of concentrating our energies on an art object of great unity and complexity and depth, we achieve a kind of inner *clarification* that was not present before. "Suppose you are in a restless frame of mind, faced by several obligations that all seem to demand attention, but no one of which predominates to give you a singleness of purpose. Sometimes, under these circumstances, you may read a story, or fall into the contemplation of a picture, or hear a piece of music, and after a while, when you go back to your problem, you may find yourself in a very different state of mind, clearer and more decisive. This is the exhilaration, the tonic effect, of art." [1]

Thus, it is not true that reading novels of crime and detection leads people to indulge in a life of crime; on the whole, those who read such novels are law-abiding people, and if anything, the reading of such novels is a *substitute* for aggressive activity (it is aggression vicariously experienced) rather than an incitement to it. Nor do works of art of a licentious nature usually incite people to rape or adultery; far from acting as incitements to action, they are safety-valves against action by providing a kind of substitute-gratification. Thus, it has been said [2] that Shakespeare's *Antony and Cleopatra* is an immoral work because it celebrates the passionate surrender of an illicit love and the victory of this love over practical, political, and moral concerns. But is there any evidence that people who read this play will behave like the lovers in question *because* they read the play? On the contrary: one could argue that reading the play has an *instrumental* value in that it presents us with another example of a complex moral situation, the perusal of which provides many avenues for our own moral reflection, and that the play also possesses the *intrinsic* value of the appreciation of acute characterization, dramatic power, and poetry whose imagery and intensity are among the most splendid in our language. Again, we are told that American youth has been demoralized by such writers as Hemingway and Faulkner in that they set an example of bad behavior. But to say that they are capable of demoralizing an entire generation is certainly to attribute to them too much moral power, especially over people who have never even heard of them; even among those who do read serious literature, the effects are probably more beneficial than harmful: through books the horizons of such readers have been expanded to include other ways of life than they have previously known; books introduce them to characters whom they would do well to emulate and books provide them with reading experiences which are worth having for their own sake. (Those who are incited to lives of sensual abandon by reading the works of such men must have been strongly inclined in this direction to begin with, else the reading of a few novels could hardly have triggered so great a response.) The same objections, of course, could be made to Picasso's "Guernica" and Alban Berg's *Wozzeck*.

b. Indeed, does not the experience itself of giving ourselves to an aesthetic object have a moral effect? If we are really concentrating on the details of

---

[1] M. C. Beardsley, *Aesthetics*, p. 574.
[2] W. K. Wimsatt, Jr., "The Moral Effect of Art," in E. Vivas and M. Krieger, eds., *The Problems of Aesthetics* (New York: Rinehart, 1950), pp. 541-42.

a work of art and not just passively letting it play upon our senses, this effect, the heightening of our sensibilities and the refining of our capacities for perceptual discrimination, will make us more receptive to the world around us; the effect will raise the tone of our daily lives and make our experience of the world richer than it was before. (Would not the whole temper of man's life in a city be transformed if he were able to see beautiful houses, trees, and streets day after day instead of the hodgepodge now forced on his eyes?)

Most of what passes for aesthetic appreciation does not begin to have this effect; but its failure is only because it is not aesthetic appreciation at all—it is a kind of tired reverie rather than an intense absorption in the aesthetic object. Most people, when they hear music, simply allow themselves to be inundated by the sheer flow of sound. Music for them provides only a soothing background—they never listen to it; but by turning on the radio as soon as they enter the house, they ward off the experience of being alone with themselves. Such people do not actively *listen* to the music and are not even aware of the most elementary kind of ebb and flow occurring within it; they only receive it passively, perhaps using it as a springboard for a private reverie or an emotional debauch of their own. Music has for them not an aesthetic effect but an *anesthetic* effect. It is not just *hearing* music that will have the required effect. The aesthetic experience, which involves nothing less than a total concentration on the perceptual details of the aesthetic object, is an experience that heightens our consciousness, exercises our capacity for perceptual awareness and discrimination, and helps us come alive to the sight and texture of the world around us. After you have seen an exhibition of landscapes by Cézanne, the entire world, as it seems to you, has changed its structure and complexion: it almost looks like landscapes by Cézanne. And is not anything that increases our awareness and subtlety of discernment and discrimination a potentially moral effect? Art provides, indeed, the most intense, concentrated, and sharply focused of the experiences available to man in a world which seldom provides such experiences apart from the works of man's own creation.

D. Morality and religion

Objection 9. Utilitarians have a great deal to say about the total consequences of one's actions, but apparently they say nothing about the consequences of one's actions in a life hereafter. Does this lack mean that utilitarianism is an antireligious ethic, denying that there is a life hereafter in which one is punished or rewarded for one's actions in this life?

Answer. As an ethical theory, utilitarianism neither asserts nor denies that there is a life hereafter. One can either assert it or deny it and still be a utilitarian. If the belief in a life hereafter is true, the belief only broadens the scope of the consequences. Utilitarianism says, "Consider *all* the consequences." So if these consequences include a life hereafter, then of course these too have to be taken into consideration. (This view has sometimes been called "theological utilitarianism.") For that matter, utilitarianism is perfectly compatible with belief in successive reincarnations. If one's actions have consequences in a life hereafter or successive hereafters, then of course these consequences have to be figured into the total; that's all.

Objection 10. But since utilitarianism makes no mention of God or of divine rewards or punishments or divine commands, can't we assume that it is an atheistic, or godless, ethic?

Answer. It is true that utilitarianism makes no mention of God or of divine commands, but utilitarianism is quite compatible with such belief. If one believes that God desires the happiness of His creatures, one can surely believe that He wants them to behave in such a way as to maximize their mutual happiness. If a man believes that he should pursue the maximum happiness and if God also believes that man's happiness is the goal to be pursued, why can't one believe that God would instruct His creatures to conduct themselves in such a way as to bring this goal about?

> We not uncommonly hear the doctrine of utility inveighed against as a godless doctrine. If it be necessary to say anything at all against so mere an assumption, we may say that the question depends upon what idea we have formed of the moral character of the Deity. If it be a true belief that God desires, above all things, the happiness of his creatures, and that this was his purpose in their creation, utility is not only not a godless doctrine, but more profoundly religious than any other. . . . In the golden rule of Jesus of Nazareth, we read the complete spirit of the ethics of utility.[1]

This was Mill's reply, but it has been often criticized. For one thing most religions do not lend themselves particularly well to the belief that God desires man's happiness as a supreme end. In many religions, God desires man's obedience to His commands as given in books of revelation, rather than man's happiness. True, happiness is promised as a consequence of this obedience, for it is to be enjoyed forever as a reward. But the commandments themselves are not presented as utilitarian precepts. "Thou shalt not steal," "Thou shalt not kill," "Thou shalt not bear false witness"; and they don't go on to say "because human beings will live together more happily by obeying these commandments." The God of most religions does not seem to be a utilitarian, at least not in His prescriptions for mankind. If there is a utilitarian presupposition in the traditional commandments, it is far from obvious. And the effect of the commandments does not seem to be utilitarian in every case. For example, religious commandments in the Judaeo-Christian tradition condemn without qualification such practices as marriage to certain relatives, fornication and adultery, homosexuality, and suicide. Yet these practices are certainly not contrary to the general happiness in *all* situations. Proceeding on the basis of utilitarianism alone, one

---

[1] J. S. Mill, *Utilitarianism*, Ch. 2.

would certainly not arrive at such moral directives as these, at least not without qualification.

Even the Christianity of the Gospels, which is utilitarian in some respects, seems to be at odds with utilitarianism in others. It is universalistic as utilitarianism is: "Do unto others as you would have them do unto you"; "Love thy neighbor as thyself." (We shall consider this maxim further in the next chapter.) But at the same time it has an altruistic emphasis, recommending self-abnegation and the total abandonment of oneself to the welfare of others: it is the meek (not the industrious or the thrifty) who shall inherit the earth, and "he that vaunteth himself shall be abased, and he that humbleth himself shall be exalted." It has often been alleged that this emphasis in Christian ethics is so extreme as to counteract utility: if you give up your life for someone who is worthless, if you forgive someone not seven times but seventy times seven (even when he counts on your forgiving nature to promote his own evil ends), you are not thereby achieving the most good; you are sacrificing your own worth in order to promote worthlessness. But the Christian may attempt to counter this charge, either by saying that such actions do promote the most good in the final analysis or by denying that the description properly applies to Christianity.

Whatever may be said about the good or bad consequences of living in accordance with the severe and difficult requirements of the Christian ideal, let us see what can be said about its relation to Christian practice. One objection that is often made is that the dedication to others demanded by Christianity is so difficult as to be impossible of attainment. To this objection, however, the Christian will reply that the utilitarian ideal also is difficult, if not impossible, to live up to. But in neither situation, he will add, is this objection leveled at the ideal itself: Isn't it true that an ideal that demands much is more likely to call forth our best efforts than one that demands little? "But," one may object, "doesn't this tension between what a man feels he *should* do and what he *can* do finally result in a schism in the personality? Since he can't live up to it anyway, won't he at last give up the struggle and decide that he won't even try? He will then have a split moral personality — he will have one moral code which he professes and repeats on Sundays and a quite different one, perhaps merely a crude egoism, by which he lives from day to day without even formulating it explicitly, and never the twain shall meet." But the Christian will again reply, "While this schism may unfortunately be true of many people, it is not true of the best: the Christian saint will not be guilty of professing one moral code and living by another."

One of the strongest claims made by Christianity, however (and other religions as well), is that religious belief is indispensable to the moral life — that in the absence of religious belief human beings would have no motivation to do anything for others at all. (It is often not clear whether religious belief means specifically Christian belief or religious belief of any kind.) If this claim is true, then religious belief is justified, if not on grounds of evidence, at least on grounds of utility.

This claim, however, has been questioned by Mill in his essay "The Utility of Religion." Let us examine Mill's main points and then consider the general question of the relation between religion and moral practice. Mill's main points are these:

a. On the one hand the periods of history in which religious belief has been most widespread have not been those which, by virtually any standard, stood highest in moral behavior. For example, in the Middle Ages many people were so concerned with religious worship that they paid little or no attention to their fellow men and allowed others to starve in the streets without having any qualms of conscience about such behavior. On the other hand, powerful moral influences have often been exerted without religion: the Greeks cultivated a high degree of honesty, justice, and temperance ("moderation in all things") without any particular religious motivation at all. Most Greeks had some religious belief, but Greek religion had almost no effect on conduct: there was no sacred book, no moral code handed down to them, no moral commands to be obeyed in the name of religion. Indeed, it is precisely because of this fact that they were free to use their own rational powers to solve moral problems. The Spartans too had a highly effective moral code, instilled not in the name of religion but of the state.

b. Religious education is admittedly an important factor in the moral upbringing of many human beings. But the moral influence of early religious training owes more to its being early than to its being religious. It is true that most early moral training is instilled in the *name* of religion; but the training can be just as effective when it does not have that sanction, provided that it is instilled consistently and repeatedly. When a child is encouraged to put himself in the place of other individuals and develop imaginative sympathy with their problems, he is receiving his first important lesson in morality, regardless of whether he is taught in the name of religion. The specifically religious character of the training ("God commands you to do this") can scarcely have much effect upon the child: only if what God commands is also commanded by the parents and enforced by their authority is it likely to be effective; God becomes, for all practical purposes, the parents.

c. In later life, moral rules tend to be effective when they are backed up by public opinion. Religion alone, without public opinion, has comparatively little effect on most people. Dueling was long practiced without many qualms of conscience, although it was always forbidden by the religious commandment against killing. Illicit sexual intercourse is still more frowned upon in women than in men, although the Biblical injunction against fornication and adultery applies equally to both sexes.

Without the sanctions superadded by public opinion, its [religion's] **own** sanctions have never, save in exceptional characters or in peculiar moods of mind, exercised a very potent influence. . . . If ever any people were taught that they were under a divine government, and that unfaithfulness to their religion and law would be visited from above by temporal chastisements, the Jews were so. Yet their history was a mere succession of lapses into paganism.[1]

d. Those persons for whom religion *is* essential to morality are usually those who have been brought up from early childhood to believe in their inseparability. For such persons, religious belief counts as the only reason why human beings should behave morally toward one another; and if that belief were to be destroyed, they would lapse into a life of immorality. But there is no reason why the two should be instilled as inseparable. Those in whom moral beliefs were instilled *without* religion find it just as easy to behave decently toward their fellow men as those whose morality was instilled in the name of religion. And if someone whose morality depends on religious belief ever comes to doubt or reject this belief, then the morality may (and often does) go down the drain along with the religion — a result which could have been avoided by not tying morality to religion in the first place.

RELIGIONIST: I grant that many people who profess religion do not practice it and are often indistinguishable from unbelievers in their moral lives. Yet religious belief *does* have a great effect on the moral lives of countless people. Its effect is usually to encourage the kind of conduct which the religion prescribes. When religion prescribes sacrificing one's firstborn children to the god Baal or killing members of opposing tribes, then its effects on conduct are, I would agree, unfortunate. But when it asks us to help our fellow men in time of trouble, to have respect for all human life, and to suppress our hatred and aggressiveness and thirst for revenge, then surely you utilitarians would agree that it promotes good.

UTILITARIAN: Of course — only I contend that these same results can be achieved equally without religion, by proper moral training. But I grant you that there are many people who would have no respect for the rights of others, would not treat them as of equal value with themselves, and would not do to others as they would be done by, if they did not believe that God required such behavior of them.

R: But more than this: religious belief, sincerely held, often gives rise to a degree of humility that is unknown without it. I do not mean the false humility that consists of simply pretending to be humble while one's egoism remains as strong as ever underneath the pretense. I do not mean the complete masochistic self-abasement in which one's self-respect is lost, the humility of the please-trample-on-me, why-don't-you-spit-on-me variety, though some of the saints bordered on that also. True religious humility is not an awkward vacillation between utter self-abasement on the one hand and strident egoism with delusions of grandeur on the other. True religious

---

[1] J. S. Mill, "The Utility of Religion," in *Three Essays on Religion* (London: Longmans, Green, 1874), p. 88.

humility means the genuine and deeply felt conviction that others are of equal value with oneself, and it results therefore in a dedication to the interests of others, with oneself as only one among countless others. This state of mind is possible without religious belief, but for many people (I think for most) only religion provides a sufficiently powerful incentive for retaining such an attitude throughout a lifetime, through all the crises and temptations and petty irritations that may beset one.

u: But there is another side to the same coin, spiritual pride, and those who cultivate humility the most assiduously tend most to be guilty of it. People with deep religious convictions who devote their lives to the service of others usually tend sooner or later to develop an attitude of holier-than-thou. They may never make the connection consciously, but I think the unconscious formula goes something like this: "If I am noble enough to help you, I am superior to you; and, being superior, I look down on you as a miserable human being and expect you to accept my advice along with my help. If you aren't grateful to me and if you don't come to me in sackcloth and ashes, you are wicked. And if, in return for my sacrifices in your behalf, you don't believe every word of the doctrine in whose name I give you my help, you are a lost, depraved soul, whom I can condemn and excoriate without guilt." The person who empties himself to give to others sooner or later exacts a very high price for the gift — such is human nature.

r: What you are describing is only a perversion of humility, not its true nature.

u: Whatever you call it, it frequently occurs, and its chief effect on the individual who has it is *intolerance*. Religions are particularly liable to this danger, for each religion professes to have the truth. In past ages, men who thought differently from the reigning orthodoxy were burned at the stake, broken on the rack, or tortured into capitulation. This type of intolerance is no longer as widely practiced as it once was, at least not in the name of religion. But the tyranny of the majority opinion in a society that ostracizes minority opinion — for example, by not giving jobs to "freethinkers" — and even the tyranny of a family group if it is closely knit and isolated from outside ideas, can be almost as bad as physical torture. Consider the effect on alert young minds of their elders' reaction to probing questions about cherished beliefs. "But how do I know that what you tell me is true?" asks the youngster, and his question is squelched by his parents, perhaps with a warning not to ask such questions or even think such thoughts in the future. Usually he will not risk disaffection and disgrace by asking such questions again; he may even succeed in putting them out of his mind entirely and lose his curiosity about the forbidden matters. He then becomes, in later years, an Upright Proper Citizen who stifles in his own children the same intellectual curiosity that once was stifled in him. But sometimes the maneuver boomerangs, and he becomes suspicious of all authority and skeptical even on matters for which skepticism is unwarranted.

r: You are describing only one situation and one reaction to it. Surely you don't wish to impugn a religious belief, or any other, by its most unfortunate manifestations.

u: Of course not — but my point is this: there is a blighting effect upon the mind of being asked to accept something as true in the absence of evidence. Religious beliefs, you see, are not merely held; they are defended. Belief #1 says that it alone is true and all the rest are frauds, and Belief #2 makes the same claim for itself, and so do the others. Members of the first group will point to certain miraculous events as proof of the truth of their belief, but members of the second group will deny these and claim certain miracles of their own. The arguments of each group, if accepted as proof, would also establish the others, and yet they all contradict each other on certain essential points. So what do these various groups do? By trying to defend their own exclusive claim to truth, they tend to encourage habits of intellectual hypocrisy and deception — any argument is justified so long as the belief is accepted. Each accustoms its adherents to the use of sophistical arguments to try to establish its claim in the face of the competition. Each must systematically minimize or distort the claims of the others, presenting them in an unfavorable light to reduce their plausibility, and must find whatever arguments it can, however farfetched, which can possibly be construed as supporting their own. This distortion — what Mill calls the "subornation of the understanding"— is likely to spread to other areas as well and poison one's whole attitude of mind. One's mind becomes used to defend views to which one is already committed rather than to search impartially for the truth wherever that search may lead.

What is the result of this process? Since the evidence for the views of any one group is either nonexistent or inconclusive, the belief must in the final analysis be backed up by the impressiveness of authoritarian figures (parents, priest, pope, state), and if authority is not sufficient, then by force. When a doctrine cannot be held in the final analysis except by an appeal to faith, more than one doctrine is going to make this appeal, and they will be in conflict with each other.

> If you think that your belief is based upon reason, you will support it by argument rather than by persecution and will abandon it if the argument goes against you. But if your belief is based on faith, you will realize that argument is useless, and will therefore resort to force either in the form of persecution or by stunting and distorting the minds of the young in what is called 'education.' [1]

r: But that's absurd. I don't believe in religious persecution any more than you do. Nor is it any longer widespread in the world. Believers in different faiths are no longer as hostile toward one another as they once were: ministers, rabbis, and priests often participate in the same television program and discuss matters of mutual concern.

[1] From *Human Society in Ethics and Politics* by Bertrand Russell. Copyright © 1955 by Bertrand Russell. Reprinted by permission of Simon and Schuster, Inc. and Allen & Unwin, Ltd., p. 220.

u: Of course — but I'm only pointing out what the logic of their position is: if you can bring people to agree with you peaceably, naturally you don't resort to persecution. If you can instill your beliefs in the minds of the young and keep them from asking too many probing questions, you need nothing else. But suppose you can't, or suppose you have the *power* to persecute (as the Church once did — and perhaps it still would if it had the power) and that only by doing so can you prevent people from leaving the fold — what will you do then? Won't you give in to temptation and then call it your sacred duty to use your authority to the uttermost?

r: Of course not. If I cannot persuade them rationally, I must regretfully admit the defeat of my aims.

u: Then you are more heroic than most of the religious leaders of history. But I would still question whether this occasional cooperativeness between conflicting faiths is really consistent with their basic tenets. Remember that each group holds that its own view is true and that all the others are mistaken, tragically mistaken, on a matter of ultimate concern to all believers, the basis of their eternal salvation. If you or others hold this point of view (and if you don't you are not a believer at all), won't you be inclined, the more intense your conviction becomes, to hold that proponents of other beliefs are so wicked or cruelly misguided that any means is justified to convert them to your own faith — particularly if you hold that they will be eternally punished for their error?

r: No — I shall try to reason with them and persuade them, that is all.

u: Very well, but remember that many other believers are not so rational. Let me turn, then, to what I consider another weakness in your position: when you present moral rules as the command of God, it becomes sinful to question them or criticize them or change them; for they represent the will of God, whose commands never change. In this way, commands that have been current and useful at a certain period in the history of a tribe or nation become fossilized by being prescribed in perpetuity, even though the conditions to which the rule was suited have changed in the meantime. As Mill says, "There is a very real evil consequent on ascribing a supernatural origin to the received maxims of morality. That origin consecrates the whole of them, and protects them from being discussed or criticized." [1]

r: But you are assuming in all this discussion that God did *not* give man certain commandments. Do you want to argue this point about revelation instead of a point about morals we were supposed to be discussing?

u: No. At the moment I only want to discuss the *utility* of religious belief. And I am saying that the utility of certain religious commands (like the prohibition against eating pork, a command which had high utility before men had modern methods of refrigeration) is very low in subsequent ages and requires amendment when conditions change.

[1] J. S. Mill, "The Utility of Religion," in *Three Essays on Religion* (London: Longmans, Green, 1874), p. 99.

R: What you are underestimating is the utility of faith itself. To be able to forsake one's own feeble intellect in matters beyond the scope of the finite mind and to accept the revelation of an infinite God — do not underestimate the greatness, the nobility, the exalting effect on the human mind, of such an act of faith. The attitude of faith itself has consequences unknown to those who lack it.

U: As long as we are discussing the utility (not the truth) of religious belief, I shall voice a contrary consideration.

. . . We may define "faith" as a firm belief in something for which there is no evidence. We do not speak of faith that 2 and 2 are 4 or that the earth is round. We only speak of faith when we wish to substitute emotion for evidence. The substitution of emotion for evidence is apt to lead to strife, since different groups substitute different emotions. Christians have faith in the Resurrection, Communists have faith in Marx's Theory of Value. Neither faith can be defended rationally, and each therefore is defended by propaganda and, if necessary, by war. The two are equal in this respect. If you think it immensely important that people should believe something which cannot be rationally defended, it makes no difference what the something is. Where you control the government, you teach the something to the immature minds of children and you burn or prohibit books which teach the contrary. Where you do not control the government, you will, if you are strong enough, build up armed forces with a view to conquest. All this is an inevitable consequence of any strongly held faith unless, like the Quakers, you are content to remain forever a tiny minority. . . .

I do not believe that a decay of dogmatic belief can do anything but good. I admit at once that new systems of dogma, such as those of the Nazis and the Communists, are even worse than the old systems, but they could never have acquired a hold over men's minds if orthodox habits had not been instilled in youth. Stalin's language is full of reminiscences of the theological seminary in which he received his training. What the world needs is not dogma, but an attitude of scientific inquiry, combined with a belief that the torture of millions is not desirable — whether inflicted by Stalin or by a Deity imagined in the likeness of the believer.[1]

R: Needless to say, I disagree utterly with Russell on this point. But even if I agreed with him that faith has a low utility, I would still believe in encouraging it as long as the faith was *true*.

U: If what you mean is that one should not instill a belief as *true* just because you believe that it would, if adopted, have a very high utility, then I agree with you. But this is exactly what many religious leaders have done; they have said that even though we can't prove it to be true, religious belief has a very salutary effect on mankind and should be instilled for that reason. But I question the *ultimate* utility of instilling a doctrine out of a belief in its utility. "Maybe it isn't true, but it's good for people to believe it anyway"

[1] From *Human Society in Ethics and Politics* by Bertrand Russell. Copyright © 1955 by Bertrand Russell. Reprinted by permission of Simon and Schuster, Inc. and Allen & Unwin, Ltd., pp. 215-16, 221.

— to reason thus is to assume (without telling them) that people cannot face the truth, whatever it may be, and therefore must be fed myths or lies — and is this a true assumption? Worse still, it is to run the risk that if the truth ever does come out and the people discover that they have been deceived, they will never again trust those who have deceived them. These disadvantages will surely outweigh any temporary utility there may be in inculcating as true, doctrines which are not known to be true, simply for the sake of their alleged utility.

R: Well, we are agreed, then, that one should not inculcate or instill religious doctrines out of a belief in their utility. We only disagree on whether the doctrines in question are true. And I hold that the doctrines of at least one religion *are* true and should therefore be instilled.

U: Since we have confined our discussion to the utility of religious belief and have not entered upon the far more intricate question of its truth (a question for epistemology rather than for ethics), let me present one final consideration. Surely one effect of religious belief on morality is to instill in human beings a new and different catalogue of virtues which would be unknown without religion — virtues not with regard to one's behavior toward other men but with regard to one's behavior toward God. Doing good to one's fellow men must now divide the field of moral endeavor with doing homage to God. Loving God occupies an even higher place ("thou shalt love the Lord thy God . . .") than loving one's fellow men ("thou shalt love thy neighbor as thyself"); to violate the first of these commands is at least as great a sin as to violate the second. Serving God regularly in places of worship and not taking His name in vain become equal in importance with respecting the rights of one's neighbor and feeding the hungry. Indeed, one of man's duties toward his fellow men, toward which (often, if not always) all the other duties are conceived as means, is that of doing one's conscientious best to convert them all to one's own religious belief. To *doubt,* even for one moment, the exclusive truth of one's own religious belief and the falsity of all the others is often considered the worst sin of all those that can be committed.

Whatever may be said of these virtues as aids to one's spiritual life, from the point of view of morality — which is concerned with man's relation to man — they must be construed as an enormous waste. If time must be divided between duties to God and duties to man, between Sabbath observance and merely human justice, utilitarian ethics, at any rate, would prefer a belief in which one's duties to his fellow men did not receive quite so much competition.

The result of this emphasis on religious virtue is that personal holiness often comes to be regarded as something quite independent of, and often superior to, beneficent action.

> Social virtue came to be excluded from Christian ethics. To this day Christians think an adulterer more wicked than a politician who takes bribes, al-

though the latter probably does a thousand times as much harm. . . . In the Middle Ages the most virtuous man was the man who retired from the world; the only men of action who were regarded as saints were those who wasted the lives and substance of their subjects in fighting the Turks, like St. Louis. The church would never regard a man as a saint because he reformed the finances, or the criminal law, or the judiciary. Such mere contributions to human welfare would be regarded as of no importance. I do not believe there is a single saint in the whole calendar whose saintship is due to a work of public utility.[1]

R: To deny such men as economic and social reformers sainthood is not to deny them virtue. It is only to deny them a specifically *religious* kind of virtue, on which sainthood is based. You assume that all virtue is concerned with man's conduct toward his fellow man, and if you start with that assumption then of course the religious virtues *are* what you call them, "an enormous waste." But if you believe, as I do, that man has duties to God as well as to his fellow men, then they are not a "waste" at all, but the most important virtues there are. You obtain the conclusions that you do only because you assume that no religious doctrine is true; granted that assumption, your conclusions follow. But you have no right to make that assumption until you have established it; and to do so will take you away from a discussion of the utility of religion, and into a discussion of its truth.

EXERCISES

1. Give some utilitarian arguments either for or against the practice of (1) vegetarianism; (2) using dogs and other animals for experimental purposes in medical laboratories.

2. Write a brief essay on the utilitarian attitude toward

a. duties to ourselves

b. duties to posterity

c. duties to animals (continuing the dialogue on that subject where it ends on page 240)

3. Evaluate the following comments on utilitarianism:

a. "It seems to me pretty clear that utilitarian principles, logically carried out, would result in far more cheating, lying, and unfair action than any good man would tolerate." (A. C. Ewing, *Ethics,* p. 40.)

b. "In any actual instance of a kind that could provide a ground for dispute the effects will be very complicated and uncertain, so that it will always leave a loophole for the utilitarian to argue that I am wrong in my view as to their bearing on the general happiness and that the act which seems right to common sense is really after all on a long view that most productive of happiness. And even if there are some instances where this is very unplausible (as indeed I think there are), he may reply by amending common-sense ethics here and saying that the act we ordinarily think right in this case is not really so." (*Ibid.,* p. 41.)

[1] B. Russell, *Why I Am Not a Christian,* p. 33.

c. Utilitarianism cannot be correct, because it "would have the absurd result that we are going wrong whenever we are relaxing, since on those occasions there will always be opportunities to produce greater good than we can by relaxing. For the relief of suffering is always a greater good than mere enjoyment." (Kurt Baier, *The Moral Point of View* [Ithaca, N. Y.: Cornell Univ. Press, 1958], pp. 203-04.)

d. W. E. H. Lecky, *A History of European Morals from Augustus to Charlemagne* [New York: Braziller, 1955], pp. 40-53.

e. "There is a certain degree of correlation between the variations in the moral code from age to age, and the variations in the real or perceived effects on the general happiness of actions prescribed or forbidden by the code. And in proportion as the apprehension of consequences becomes more comprehensive and exact, we may trace not only change in the moral code handed down from age to age, but progress in the direction of a closer approximation to a perfectly enlightened Utilitarianism. Only we must distinctly notice another important factor in the progress . . . the extension, namely, of the capacity for sympathy in an average member of the community. The imperfection of earlier moral codes is at least as much due to defectiveness of sympathy as of intelligence; often, no doubt, the ruder man did not perceive the effects of his conduct on others; but often, again, he perceived them more or less, but felt little or no concern about them. Thus it happens that changes in the conscience of a community often correspond to changes in the extent and degree of the sensitiveness of an average member of it to the feelings of others. Of this the moral development historically worked out under the influence of Christianity affords familiar illustrations." (H. Sidgwick, *The Methods of Ethics,* p. 455.)

4. Keeping in mind the utilitarian attitude toward animals, what would be the utilitarian attitude toward intelligent beings on other planets? (If we had to choose, should we sacrifice our happiness to theirs if it were proved to us that they had a greater potential for happiness than we and were also more likely to actualize this potential?)

5. Evaluate, from the utilitarian point of view, (*1*) the sexual customs described in Richard Lewinsohn's *A History of Sexual Customs* (New York: Harper, 1959); (*2*) the religious practices described in W. E. H. Lecky's *A History of the Rise of Rationalism in Europe* (New York: Braziller, 1955), especially Chs. 1-3.

6. Blessed are the peacemakers; for they shall be called sons of God. (Matthew 5: 9.) But I say unto you, Resist not him that is evil; but whosoever smiteth thee on thy right cheek, turn to him the other also. (Matthew 5: 39.) But I say unto you, Love your enemies, and pray for them that persecute you. (Matthew 5: 44.) Do these passages, in your opinion, commit Christianity to pacifism? Can you quote any passages of an opposite character?

7. What conclusions, if any, do you think the Gospels lead you to adopt on questions of (*1*) obeying the law? (*2*) divorce? (*3*) racial prejudice? (*4*) democracy v. totalitarianism? (*5*) *laissez faire* capitalism v. a planned economy? (*6*) class distinctions on the basis of blood or wealth?

8. Do you think that art has any moral effects on (*1*) the secondary artist — the performer of the work of art? If so, how? The music teacher says to his pupil, "Keep up your violin playing, it is the best influence on your moral character." Is his advice beside the point? (2) the primary artist — the creator of the work of art? (If so, how? What characteristics must he develop within himself in order to create at all? Is the traditional Romantic picture of the artist as an immoral cad an accurate one? Morality in which sense — morality in the sense of the mores of the artist's own time and place?)

9. Evaluate the following quotations on morality and religion:

a. "It is impossible to lead the mass of women and the common people generally to piety, holiness and faith simply by philosophical teaching; the fear of God is also required, not omitting legends and miraculous stories." (Strabo, quoted in Ludwig Friedlander, *Roman Life and Manners under the Early Empire* [New York: Dutton, 1908], Vol. 3, p. 85.)

b. "Total war ought indeed to be difficult for the Christian conscience to confront, but the current Christian way out makes it easy; war is defended morally and Christians easily fall into line — as they are led to justify it — in each nation in terms of Christian faith itself. Men of religious congregations do evil. Ministers of God make them feel good about doing it. Rather than guide them in the moral cultivation of their consciences, ministers, with moral nimbleness, blunt that conscience, covering it up with peace of mind." (From C. W. Mills's *The Causes of World War Three.* Copyright © 1958 by C. Wright Mills. By permission of Simon and Schuster, Inc., p. 149.)

c. "Suppose that we could prove that adherence to a certain religion does tend to encourage good behavior, would it then follow that the religion should be given a privileged position in the social structure, taught to children and maintained as the orthodox creed? Is it not rather the case that religious truths, if such exist, must be maintained and propagated on the ground that they are *true* and not merely that they are *useful?* And their truth can certainly not be proved merely by demonstrating that they are what Lord Chesterfield called 'the collateral security for virtue.' . . . If a religion is true *and can be shown to be so* then it should be taught, whether or not its effects are fortunate. And if it cannot be shown to be true then it ought not to be propagated officially, even though its social consequences are excellent." (Daniel J. O'Connor, *An Introduction to the Philosophy of Education* [London: Routledge & Kegan Paul, 1957], p. 135.)

d. Read the short story by B. Russell, "Zahotopolk," in his *Nightmares of Eminent Persons* (London: Lane, 1954).

e. " 'The good of others' is a magic formula that transforms anything into gold, a formula to be recited as a guarantee of moral glory and as a fumigator for any action, even the slaughter of a continent. . . . Your code hands out, as its version of the absolute, the following rule of moral conduct: If *you* wish it, it's evil; if others wish it, it's good; if the motive of your action is *your* welfare, don't do it; if the motive is the welfare of others, then anything goes. . . . For those of you who might ask questions, your code provides a consolation prize and a booby-trap: it is for your own happiness, it says, that you must serve the happiness of others, the only way to achieve your joy is to give it up to others, the only way to achieve your prosperity is to surrender your wealth to others, the only way to protect your life is to protect all men except yourself — and if you find no joy in this procedure, it is your own fault and the proof of your evil; if you were good, you would find your happiness in providing a banquet for

others, and your dignity in existing on such crumbs as *they* might care to toss
you. . . . A morality that teaches you to scorn a whore who gives her body indiscriminately to all men — this same morality demands that you surrender your
soul to promiscuous love for all comers." (From *Atlas Shrugged* by Ayn Rand.
© Copyright 1957 by Ayn Rand. Reprinted by permission of Random House,
Inc., pp. 1030, 1031, 1033.)

10. The following excerpt contains numerous mistakes in its description of
utilitarianism. Find as many as you can.

. . . Utilitarianism distinguishes between right and wrong solely by reference
to pleasure or expediency. That is right which tends to make me happy. The
rightness of an action is to be judged by whether its consequences will bring
more pleasure than pain, either to me or to society. By that, and that alone. When
a man judges by reference to his own pleasure only, he is called a hedonist. Such
a man is essentially selfish; for even though he may perform actions which give
pleasure to others, his reason for doing so is that he himself derives pleasure
from giving pleasure. That is why he thinks the action right.

Utilitarians, properly so called, are those who think that right conduct consists not in pursuing their own pleasure but in promoting "the greatest happiness
of the greatest number." In either case the decisive objection is that there is no
means of distinguishing between one pleasure and another, except by its intensity.
It is as right, perhaps more right, to indulge a passion for another man's wife
than to listen to a classical concert. Moreover, any action may be justified by its
end: if, on balance, it causes more happiness than pain, it is right. Thus it would
be right to murder an irritating mother-in-law and so restore peace and harmony
to a whole family.

It is a curious irony that in the public mind Christian ethics have become identified with hedonistic utilitarianism. "Christian" conduct has come to mean kindness. And by kindness is meant giving people what they want. Thus it is unkind
and "unchristian" to insist that married people should live together if they do
not want to. It is unkind and "unchristian" to insist that a man should keep his
word, when it has become irksome to do so. He would be so much happier if he
broke his word, and we ought to promote happiness.

The cause of this ironical situation lies in the partial truth contained in Utilitarianism. God does indeed desire men's happiness, and it is a duty to promote
happiness and not to cause pain. But the human happiness which God desires
is the happiness of maturity, of having reached our human goal of perfection.
And for this many lower and transient pleasures have to be sacrificed, the good
giving way to the better. The rightness of conduct has to be judged not in reference to the present only or to the immediate future — though these are relevant —
but in reference also to the total good of the whole man, a good which extends
beyond this life and is only fully realized in the society of heaven. Every man's
true happiness lies in acquiring a full and developed personality, harmonious and
controlled, and in taking his place in a community of such persons. Many of the
things which we call happiness are, when persisted in, fatal obstacles to the
growth of such a personality: many of the things which we call tragedies are its
unavoidable birth-pangs. The distinction between right and wrong is the distinc-

tion between those things which foster and those which fatally hinder man's growth to perfect manhood, his attainment of his eternal destiny to be fully himself. (From R. C. Mortimer, *Christian Ethics,* pp. 8-10.)

11. Which of the following religious manifestations do you consider the best? Why? (Are there some that you would not consider good at all? Explain.)

a. No matter how often he is insulted or assaulted or by whom, he always "turns the other cheek."

b. She eats less than her body requires, giving to the church the money she would have spent on the food.

c. "Greater love hath no man than this, that a man lay down his life for his friend." With this passage in mind, he lays down his life for the sake of someone else, who is more worthy than he is.

d. Same as "c.", only the other person is a drunken vagrant.

e. The father contributes five thousand dollars toward a new church building rather than using it to help put his son through college, reasoning, "The Kingdom of God comes first."

f. During her entire lifetime, because of her strong religious faith, she takes care never to let a single angry word, a single criticism, or a single uncomplimentary remark about anyone, escape her lips.

12. Do you find the following objectionable on utilitarian grounds? on religious grounds? Explain.

a. "The only motive a person ever has for questioning the true religious belief is his desire to take a moral holiday, using religious doubt as an excuse."

b. "Of course I champion religious persecution, whether in Spain or anywhere else. It's all a way of rooting out the unfaithful and making them come to their senses in time."

c. "Anything I care to do against you is justified, for God is on my side."

d. "God is never wrong, you yourself admit. And God told me last night that it was you who double-crossed me."

e. "If you lack faith, all the good works you may perform during your lifetime are of no value in the sight of God."

f. "The Church holds that it were better for sun and moon to drop from heaven, for the earth to fail, and for all the many millions who are upon it to die of starvation in extremest agony, so far as temporal affliction goes, than that one soul, I will not say should be lost, but should commit one single venial sin, should tell one wilful untruth, though it harmed no one, or steal one poor farthing without excuse." (John Henry Cardinal Newman, *Certain Difficulties Felt by Anglicans in Catholic Teaching* [New York: Longmans, Green, 1918], p. 190.)

13. Evaluate the following arguments:

a. Pascal's famous "wager": Religious belief, with its promise of heavenly reward and threat of punishment, may be true or it may not. If it is, you will be made to suffer for not having believed it; whereas if it is false, it won't make any difference anyway after you're dead. Therefore, it is advisable to believe it.

b. It is safer to be a Catholic than a Protestant, for Protestants say that both Catholics and Protestants can inherit salvation, whereas Catholics (at least until recently) said that only Catholics could enter the kingdom of heaven. So if Catholicism turns out to be right you'll be safe either way.

c. Bertrand Russell, commenting on this type of argument, asked, in effect, "How do you know that there isn't a God who respects sincerity and the weighing of evidence so much that he will punish forever anyone who joins a certain party just to be on the winning side?" (Millard Spencer Everett, *Ideals of Life* [New York: Wiley, 1954], p. 30.)

14. Which of the following religious manifestations do you consider the worst? Why?

a. A famous evangelist repeatedly declares that world peace is impossible and that to strive for it is useless until all men accept the Gospel. Advocates of other religions then declare the same thing with regard to the acceptance of their own religious beliefs. Result: no agreement is arrived at, and each group says, "I told you so!"

b. "On the morning of June 1, 1630, Guglielmo Piazza, commissioner of health in Milan, was observed walking down the street writing from an inkhorn at his belt and wiping his ink-stained fingers against walls of houses. Ignorant women of the neighborhood accused him of smearing the houses with the virus of the plague. They took their complaint to the City Council and Piazza was arrested and tortured. This torture was a survival of feudal times and was carried out in a ceremonial procedure prescribed by law. Many of the village officials to whom the legal aspects of torture were intrusted could not read, and to supply them with the necessary information the Constitutio Criminalis of Maria Theresa in 1768 had 17 copper-plate engravings to illustrate the various modes of torture. As a preamble to torture the victim was shaved and purged. If he survived the atrocities inflicted upon his body three times, God was supposed to intervene for him in a miracle showing the victim's innocence. The Commissioner Piazza withstood two applications of the torture, but yielded to the 'third degree.' To save himself from further torture he said that he had spread the plague, and on being threatened with torture unless he divulged the name of his accomplices he accused a barber named Mora. The latter likewise yielded to torture and gave the desired confession of guilt. He incriminated Don Juan de Padilla, son of the commandant of the fortress, whom the barber had treated for syphilis. The victims of this Renaissance justice were then sentenced to death; they were torn with red-hot pincers, had their right hands cut off, their bones broken, were stretched on the wheel, and after six hours of suffering were burned. Their ashes were thrown into the river and their possessions sold; the house which had been touched with ink was razed and on its site was erected a 'column of infamy,' to commemorate the part these men were supposed to have played in the spread of the plague." (Howard W. Haggard, *Devils, Drugs, and Doctors* [1929] [New York: Pocket Books] pp. 208-13.)

c. Though a certain woman has not read the Bible extensively during her early and middle years, when she becomes old, she begins to read with greater regularity and comes to concentrate more and more on the prophecies of doom and destruction. She is convinced that humanity is evil through and through, that there is no hope for its survival, and that the cause of its impending doom is sin. She reads and rereads these passages with relish. She takes increasing satisfaction in the reflection that those who are now young will never live to be old, that divine judgment is about to descend upon the world, that Armageddon will come and the Four Horsemen of the Apocalypse, that the sun will be darkened and the moon turned to blood and mankind will be wiped out in a tremendous holocaust.

Thus, if peace continues for a time, she will say that the great doom is about to descend and that the behavior of wicked men is about to make this occur. But if war comes, she will quote prophecy to prove it, saying that war is only a ful-fillment of God's inexorable command. Nor does she favor the attempts of the world's governments and the United Nations to ameliorate world tensions. These are merely human agencies, she reasons, and cannot prevent the destruction which God's Word says will soon occur. To take steps to avoid such a catastrophe is to use merely human ingenuity in an attempt to circumvent God's decree, thus adding to an already sinful situation the sin of pride and insubordination to di-vine will.

d. "And it is only religious faith," said the orator, "that enables Americans to look forward to the future with certainty and confidence."

The next morning a group of missiles with hydrogen warheads killed half the population of the United States in fifteen minutes.

Among those dead were those who had said, "Yes I know, but we'll have to take them on, and we can lick them; I know we'll have some casualties, but. . . ." "We must not, we cannot, compromise with evil. They are atheists, and they must be wiped from the face of the earth. . . ." "Only when all man-kind falls down on its knees and accepts the one true revelation will the nations of the world find peace."

READING LIST, SECTION 13

Art and Morality

Beardsley, Monroe C. *Aesthetics.* New York: Harcourt, Brace, 1958, Ch. 12.

Dewey, John. *Art as Experience.* New York: Minton, Balch, 1934, especially Ch. 14.

Mill, John Stuart. "Thoughts on Poetry and Its Variations." In Mill, J. S., *Disser-tations and Discussions.* Boston: Spencer, 1865.

Shelley, Percy Bysshe. *A Defense of Poesy.* Many editions.

Stolnitz, Jerome. *Aesthetics and Philosophy of Art Criticism.* Boston: Houghton Mifflin, 1960, Ch. 13.

Zink, Sidney. "The Moral Effect of Art." In Vivas, Eliseo, and Murray Krieger. *The Problems of Aesthetics.* New York: Rinehart, 1953, pp. 545-61.

Morality and Religion

Huxley, Thomas H. "Agnosticism and Christianity" (1889). In Huxley, T. H., *Selections from the Essays of T. H. Huxley.* Ed. by Alburey Castell. New York: Appleton-Century-Crofts, 1948, pp. 91-105.

Lewis, C. S. *The Abolition of Man.* New York: Macmillan, 1947.

Mill, John Stuart. "The Utility of Religion" (1874). In Mill, J. S., *The Nature and Utility of Religion.* New York: Liberal Arts Press, 1958, pp. 45-80.

Mortimer, Robert Cecil. *Christian Ethics*. New York: Rinehart, 1950.
Niebuhr, Reinhold. *An Interpretation of Christian Ethics*. New York: Harper, 1935. (Meridian Books.)
Paine, Thomas. *The Age of Reason*. Many editions.
Rashdall, Hastings. *Theory of Good and Evil*. 2nd ed. New York: Oxford Univ. Press, 1924. 2 vols., Vol. 1, Bk. 3, Ch. 2.
Russell, Bertrand. "Will Religious Faith Solve Our Troubles?" in B. Russell, *Human Society in Ethics and Politics*. New York: Simon and Schuster, 1954.

6. The ethics of duty

The central concept of utilitarianism is that of intrinsic good, and the rightness of an act is determined by whether it maximizes intrinsic good. Therefore, utilitarianism is *teleological,* that is, it maintains that the rightness of an act depends entirely upon its consequences.

In the ethics of Immanuel Kant (1724-1804) the central concept is that of duty, or obligation. The rightness of an act, according to Kant, depends not on the consequences to which it leads but on its own inherent nature. His ethics is therefore *formalistic* — a formalistic ethics being one in which the rightness of an act does not depend (at least not entirely, and in Kant's view, not at all) upon its consequences, actual or probable or intended.

14. Kant's theory of moral goodness

Before considering Kant's theory of obligation, it will be convenient to consider briefly his view on goodness. Kant does not use the terms "intrinsic good" and "instrumental good," but he speaks of what is *good without qualification.* Happiness, according to Kant, is not good without qualification. Happiness, as Aristotle declared and Plato denied, is partly dependent on circumstances which are to a large extent outside one's control: a pleasant disposition, intelligence, favorable early environment, a measure of good luck. A person may be happy but not deserve it, and may deserve happiness but not have it. The only thing Kant says is more repellent to contemplate than someone enjoying happiness which he does not deserve is someone deprived of it who deserves it. Happiness is good only when it is the reward of virtue, and in a perfect world the degree of each person's happiness would be in exact proportion to his virtue. Since happiness which does not accompany virtue is not good, happiness cannot be good without qualification.

What other things are good? Kant mentions "moderation in the affections and passions, self-control, and calm deliberation" as admirable human quali-

264

ties.[1] Yet they too are not good without qualification. They may, on occasion, be thoroughly bad. The coolness of the villain and his complete self-control in planning and perpetrating his crime make him more abominable than he would have been without these qualities. All other traits of character may have a similar effect. Courage is a fine quality, but the world would have been better off with fewer courageous Nazis. Loyalty is admirable, but not loyalty to a bad cause. Charity is admirable, but not in the form of donations to the Ku Klux Klan.

The only thing that is good without qualification is what Kant calls the *good will.*

A good will is good not because of what it performs or effects, not by its aptness for the attainment of some proposed end, but simply by virtue of the volition — that is, it is good in itself, and considered by itself is to be esteemed much higher than all that can be brought about by it.[2]

But if the good will, quite apart from its consequences, is unqualifiedly good, it is very important to know exactly what a good will is. When Kant uses the term, he does not mean by it what we so often mean by it in everyday discourse, namely good *intentions.* "The road to hell is paved with good intentions," and Kant agrees. People who always intend to do their duty and never do so, who are full of kind and benevolent feelings but somehow never put their noble intentions into practice, are far from what Kant has in mind. Nor does the good will consist simply in grim determination or in a moralistic holier-than-thou attitude. A good will, for Kant, is "not a mere wish, but the summoning of all (the) means in our power"[3] to do the deed which is our duty. Nor do the actual consequences of the deed matter, for these are to a large extent outside our control: only the good will (as Kant has defined it) that leads to the doing is of unqualified value.

Even if it should happen that, owing to a special disfavor of fortune, or to the niggardly provision of a step-motherly nature, this will should wholly lack power to accomplish its purpose, if with its greatest efforts it should yet achieve nothing, and there should remain only the good will . . . then, like a jewel, it would still shine by its own light, as a thing which has its whole value in itself. Its usefulness or fruitlessness can neither add to nor take away anything from its value.[4]

We must now be more specific. We shall first discuss the good will in relation to motives of duty, for here lies Kant's doctrine of moral goodness; then we shall consider the good will in relation to the notion of reason, for there lies Kant's doctrine of obligation.

Kant would say that an agent is *morally good* with respect to a certain

---

[1] I. Kant, *Fundamental Principles of the Metaphysics of Morals*, Pt. 1, p. 11.
[2] *Ibid.*, p. 10.
[3] *Ibid.*, p. 11.
[4] *Ibid.*, p. 11.

act if he does the act entirely from motives of duty — "from duty." But here a distinction must be made at once. To do something *from* duty is one thing; to do it merely in *accordance with* duty is another. Suppose that you are playing chess with someone and as you are contemplating your next move, a small child comes along, takes hold of one of the chessmen, and moves it to another position on the board. Suppose too that the move the child makes is in accordance with the rules of the game — it is a permitted move though perhaps not a brilliant one. Yet the move, though in accordance with the rules of chess, is not made from knowledge of the rules of chess. The child has no idea what the permitted moves are, for he has no conception of the rules of the game. Apply this example to the moral realm: Suppose it is your duty to be benevolent toward others, helping them when they are in need. Suppose also that you are by nature a kind and benevolent human being, who is always distressed at seeing those around you unhappy or in want. Therefore, you help them out: you can't be happy unless they are happy; by satisfying them you satisfy yourself also. You don't help others because it is your duty — you don't even think of duty; you just help because you want to, because it makes you feel good. If it didn't make you feel good, you wouldn't help.

Kant would go on to say that such actions may be right (we shall discuss this shortly), but they are not morally good — or more precisely, *you* are not morally good in respect to such an act, and you cannot be accorded any moral merit for doing it. It is no merit of yours that you happen to be benevolently inclined toward your neighbors by temperament. You are just "doing what comes naturally"— and if something entirely different came more naturally to you, you would do that instead. You will help others only as long as it pleases you to do so, and when it doesn't, you won't be moved to help them by considerations of duty. Beneficent behavior may be right, but in the circumstances described, you cannot be credited with moral goodness (virtue) for having it. What you do is *in accordance with* duty, but it is not done *from* duty; that is, it is not performed *because* it is your duty, but for a different reason. Indeed, you are acting not from duty but from inclination.

Sometimes what is our duty coincides with what we are inclined to do anyway. For example, Kant says it is our duty to preserve our own lives, and it would be wrong to commit suicide just in order to avoid pain or because we are tired of living. But most people are inclined to preserve their own lives anyway, so there is no special merit in their acts of self-preservation. In such a situation, duty and inclination propel us in the same direction, and we do not need the sense of duty to make us do the right thing. But there are other — and doubtless more frequent — situations in which duty and inclination conflict. Let's say that it is your duty to keep a certain promise that you have made but that you do not desire to do so; your inclination is to forget about the promise, especially since keeping it would cause you considerable inconvenience. Here is a test of whether you are acting from duty or from inclination: if you keep your promise anyway, in spite of your inclination to the contrary and simply because it is your duty to do so, then you are acting from duty and your action has moral merit; but if you forget about the promise, then of course you are acting from inclination. Most characteristically moral situations are like this: duty pulls you one way and inclination pulls you another, and the test of your moral character is whether you are strong enough to follow duty in spite of your strong inclination not to do so.

The picture presented by Kant seems clear enough when duty and inclination impel us in opposing directions. But when inclination and duty impel us in the *same* direction, must we hold that we always act from inclination and never from duty? There seems to be no need to hold this view. It is possible that we sometimes act from duty even though we are already inclined to perform the act: for example, it is our duty not to steal from our friends, but most of us are not inclined to do so anyway, however we may be inclined toward strangers. We do not usually need a sense of duty to back up our inclinations in such situations. Even so, we *may* be acting from duty just the same — it's just that in such situations it is fearfully difficult to know whether we are or not. The test would be this: *If* your inclination were the other way, would you still do the act because it was your duty? The trouble is, of course, that this test cannot be carried out, for *ex hypothesi* in this situation duty and inclination *do* pull in the same direction. All you could do in such a situation would be to ask yourself, "*If* at this moment my inclinations turned the opposite way, would I still refrain from stealing because it is my duty to refrain?" and then to be as honest with yourself as you possibly could in answering this question. Even so, rationalization would almost inevitably come in, and you could easily convince yourself that you *would* act from duty anyway, whether or not you would do so in fact. Such introspective tests are always dangerous and inconclusive; it is so easy to say that you are doing something because it is your duty, when actually you are inclined toward it anyway and are (consciously or unconsciously) camouflaging your inclinations by talking about duty to make the act seem more respectable. At any rate, there is no contradiction in saying that you are acting from duty even when your natural inclinations propel you in the same direction as duty. But of course many statements which contain no contradiction may be false just the same.

Even after this matter is cleared up, however, many readers of Kant have voiced an objection to Kant's account of moral goodness. "What!" they say, "is there no moral merit attaching to an act if the act is done from inclination? Do you mean that if you are *inclined* to do something, you deserve no moral credit for doing it but that if you are not inclined to do it and have to fight against your inclinations every step of the way, then and then only is your act morally good?" This objection is not exactly accurate as it stands, for as we have just seen, the mere fact that you are inclined to do something is no proof that you are not doing it from duty. "Still," the objectors will persist, "it seems strange that moral merit should attach to those acts which are done from duty and that good inclinations should not count at all. Suppose that at first you don't want to refrain from stealing but that through gradual self-discipline you develop habits of restraint until finally what you originally did from duty becomes 'second nature' to you. You are no longer tempted to steal and have no inclination left to do it. Surely this change in motive can't mean that your action (in refraining) is not morally good! Quite the contrary — isn't it morally *better* not to have to go through a paroxysm of temptation, doubt, and conflict every time before you decide not to steal? Is it really true that refraining from stealing is morally good when you have a strong temptation to steal but is not morally good when you have no such temptation?"

This is, indeed, an objection that moralists from Aristotle to Dewey have felt. They have held that when we are led to do something only out of a sense of duty, we have not yet reached moral maturity; our moral maturity is best shown when we are not even tempted to do the forbidden act, when doing right has become so much a part of our nature that we no longer even have to *think* of duty — doing one's duty has *become* "doing what comes naturally." If we could achieve this state in every aspect of our moral lives, the term "acting from duty" could then drop out of our moral vocabulary.

At this point the utilitarian will add his word. According to him, we remember (page 220), morally good motives are those most likely to lead to right acts. He contends, "If we do right acts from inclination — if doing them is or becomes "doing what comes naturally"— then we shall be far more regularly and steadily likely to do what is right than if we do it from duty.

(1) "In most people at least, the sense of duty operates by fits and starts; most people who act from duty do so only from time to time and are swayed by their inclinations the rest of the time. The sense of duty must be constantly pushed and prodded; compared with influence of duty

> . . . a man's natural inclination works incessantly upon him; it is forever present to the mind, and mingles itself with every view and consideration. . . . It is certain, from experience, that the smallest grain of natural honesty and benevolence has more effect on men's conduct, than the most pompous views suggested by theological theories and systems.[1]

(2) "Moreover, it is so fatally easy to rationalize about matters of duty; 'It's my duty to see to it that you're punished,' 'It's my duty to tell her off, so that she won't be nasty to others.' People who are forever talking about

---

[1] David Hume, *Dialogues concerning Natural Religion,* ed. by Norman Kemp Smith, 2nd ed. (New York: Social Sciences, 1948), Pt. 12, p. 221.

their duty are somewhat suspect: if they were really morally mature individuals, they would simply do what duty required out of an inclination (an inclination molded and developed by habit and self-discipline earlier in life) to do so and would not present every decision to the Bar of Duty every time they had to act. Whom would you be more likely to fear, a neighbor who had no inclination to burn your house down and so never worried about such things or a neighbor who ardently desired to steal from you or to burn your house down while you were away but was only prevented from doing so by an even stronger sense of duty? Clearly the latter, for, you would suspect, sooner or later the second person's inclinations would be likely to get the better of him and he would do what he wanted to do, camouflaging his act perhaps with some elaborate rationalization, whereas the first person had no harmful inclination in the first place. This likelihood would tend to show that, as an empirical fact, inclination is a better spring to action than is a sense of duty; people who are inclined to do right acts anyway are more likely to be depended on in doing them ("a man's natural inclination works incessantly upon him") than are people who are not inclined toward right acts but do them only out of sense of duty. Sense of duty, however, would come in as a valuable accessory in those instances in which a person's inclinations were toward doing the wrong thing: since inclination would not then dissuade him from the wrong, his sense of duty would have to restrain him as best it could."

The Kantian, however, is not without a defense in this matter. (1) "First of all," he would say, "the act done from inclination is not necessarily *wrong;* rightness and wrongness are unaffected by whether or not the act is done from inclination. They depend solely on a quality of the act which we have yet to consider. Moreover, (2) what you're inclined to do is very much a matter of what kind of native temperament you have — whether you are naturally warm and outgoing or naturally cold and unsympathizing. Your temperament, in turn, depends a great deal on what kind of a childhood you've had — what your relation with your parents was, to what kinds of influence you were then subject, and over these circumstances you had virtually no control. Why should you get credit for your temperament? If it's nothing against you that you have a temperament and character that don't lend themselves to doing good deeds easily, so that you have to be constantly conquering temptations in order to do right, then by the same token it is nothing in your favor that you had a sunny childhood and can feel happy and secure in adulthood and consequently can be outgoing and can help people without envying them their happiness."

Opponents of Kantian ethics could reply, "Granted that you can't rightly take credit for what you can't help and granted that there *is* such a thing as native temperament and that it is molded by childhood forces; still, the greater part of our adult character, the part from which our actions spring, is also affected by our *later* development during our "years of discretion." It is influenced by whether we have developed self-discipline, whether we have taken pains to get ourselves into good habit-patterns; and these things *are* to a considerable extent within our control. Wasn't Kant ignoring this development when he said that the nature of our inclinations was very much a matter of what temperament we happened to have and therefore we deserve no credit or discredit for it?"

This matter cannot be finally disposed of until we have explored the concepts of free will, desert, and moral responsibility in Chapter 10. Two final questions, however, can be considered in the specific context of Kant's ethics:

1. "Isn't this whole conception of our moral nature as drawn between duty on the one hand and inclination on the other rather oversimplified, outmoded, and perhaps just plain mistaken?" another opponent might ask. "After all, isn't acting from duty acting from *another* inclination, namely the inclination to do one's duty? Many people have this inclination to duty very strongly — and can't this inclination too be developed? Why picture the situation after the fashion of the old-time penny dreadfuls, as one of Duty on the one hand vs. Inclination on the other? Why not rather picture duty as one inclination among many, one which we may strive to strengthen?"

But this objection, too, will not find the Kantian without a reply. (1) "In the first place," he can say, "what is this interpretation but another way of saying the same thing? The same moral experience is being referred to and the same moral conflict, whether we choose (with Kant) to call it the conflict between duty and desire or (with our opponent) to call it the conflict between the desire to do our duty and other desires. Either way, Kant would say, it is the former member of the pair that, if triumphant, deserves moral credit, not the latter member; so the distinction still stands. (2) In the second place, isn't the Kantian terminology better, in the sense of reporting the fact of moral experience in a more natural way? When we do our duty, especially when doing so is very difficult, isn't our action responding to another 'pull' (a 'higher' one) *against* the main trend of our desires and inclinations? To call the pull of duty just another inclination is to put it in the same class with all the rest of them, whereas it is conspicuously different. (3) In the third place," the Kantian will add, "isn't it true that sometimes the 'pull' of duty does win out, even when the desire to do one's duty is not very strong? Of course, one may reply that if duty does win out, its victory proves automatically that the desire to do one's duty was the strongest desire, otherwise it wouldn't have won out. In a sense this conclusion is true — that is, if you *define* the strongest desire as the one that wins out. [Remember our discussion of psychological egoism, pages 141-55.] But if you so define desire, the whole thing becomes tautological. If you don't settle the matter in advance by definition, you will have to admit that there are instances of moral conflict in which duty wins out, even though your *desire* to do your duty was not particularly strong. It is preferable then to say that duty won out over inclination. Is not this statement more faithful to the facts of moral experience? Isn't there often a war within us between desire, or inclination, and duty, a war in which duty sometimes wins out in spite of our desires? If so, it is 'taking the high priori road' to say that just because duty won out, therefore our desire to do our duty must have been the strongest desire."

2. An act, or an agent who performs the act, is morally good when the act is done *from* duty, according to Kant; the fact that the act happens to be *in accordance with* duty does not make the act morally worthy, it only makes the act right. But now the opponent asks a second question: "In order to be done *from* duty, does an act have to be *in accordance with* duty at all? As long as an act is done from motives of duty (done, that is, because of the conviction that it is one's duty), is it also necessary that the act should actually *be* one's duty?"

This question brings into the open a moral issue on which we are likely to be swayed strongly in both directions. Consider again (page 218) a member of a religious group who refused to allow his child the blood transfusions required to save his life. Or consider parents in ancient times who, with tears and anguish, sacrificed their firstborn son to the god Moloch, whose wrath they hoped thereby to appease. We may feel the utmost horror at what they did. We are quite sure that what they did was not right; but shall we not also be likely to admire them for being so strong of character as to adhere to their conviction of duty even when every human impulse and inclination would lead them to save their child? We are in the position of wishing to condemn their act yet of admiring them for sticking to what they sincerely believe to be their duty no matter how ruinous it may be to their personal well-being.

What would utilitarians say of this situation? Keeping in mind the terminology introduced on pages 217-18, we can say that a utilitarian would speak as follows: "(1) In all probability the act was not *objectively* right, for in all probability it did not have the best consequences — indeed, it had the disastrous consequence of losing the child's life and causing the parents a lifetime of bereavement; moreover, (2) even before the act was performed, one could say that it was not *subjectively* right, for it would *probably* not have the best consequences, and this probability could be ascertained in advance. (Of course, *if* there were any empirical reason to believe, as some religions did, that divine wrath would descend upon the entire community for the failure to do this one deed, then the act was neither objectively nor subjectively wrong, but right — it had the bad consequence of losing the child's life and causing grief to the parents, but this was far outweighed by the disaster averted for the entire community.) (3) As to the motive, assuming that the act was done strictly from duty in Kant's sense, the motive was somewhat less likely to produce right acts regularly than were good inclinations."

What would Kant say about the parents' motive? Kant, as we have seen, says that the only good motive is duty — doing something *because* it is one's duty — in other words, what moralists have called "conscientiousness." The act may have been objectively and subjectively wrong, but still it was morally good or meritorious because it was done from duty. Now we come to the heart of the question: what should we prefer — a right act done from inclination or a wrong act done from duty?

Kant is by no means clear on this point. But perhaps it is sufficient to point out that the question is never one which could be present to the agent at the time of acting. You can never ask yourself, "Should I do my duty or what *I think* is my duty?" You can deliberate carefully as to what your duty is, and you can be charged with acting hastily if you don't deliberate about it; but once you have decided, you can only do what is, to the very best of your knowledge and belief, your duty. You cannot say, "Act A is right because it is my duty, but Act B is morally good because *I think* it is my duty." The moment you say, and mean, that Act A is your duty, you are by that very statement implying that you *believe* that Act A is your duty. If you didn't believe it, you couldn't sincerely say that it was your duty; and if you believe that Act A is your duty, you cannot turn around and say that something different, Act B, is what you *believe* to be your duty. To say sincerely that something is your duty is already to commit yourself to saying that you believe that it is. At the time of your action, therefore, this conflict cannot arise for you. It can arise only in a different context — for someone else who is judging your act or for you yourself judging it at a later time; then and then only can you ask, "I did what I did out of a conviction that it was my duty, but *was* it my duty?" (What would it mean to say, "I *am doing* this act from the conviction that it is my duty, yet I am not convinced that it *is* my duty"?)

According to at least one contemporary writer, this conflict arises from a failure to distinguish different questions from one another. The question "Ought a person to do his duty or what he sincerely believes to be his duty?" is a question which

> . . . can perplex us only because we have no more than a confused understanding of its sense. As soon as we make clear to ourselves the various things it can mean, the problem vanishes. If we mean (1) "Does thinking that something is one's duty make it so?" the answer is obviously "No." If we mean (2) "Does the moral man do what after careful consideration he has worked out to be what he ought to do?" the answer is, of course, "Yes." If it means (3) "Should a person who has worked out what he ought to do as carefully and conscientiously as can be expected be rebuked for acting on his results?" the answer is plainly "No." If it means (4) "Is a man ever to be rebuked for doing what

he thought he ought to do?" the answer is, of course, "Yes, sometimes, for he may culpably have failed in his theoretical task" (of figuring out carefully, impartially, and free from rationalization, where his duty lies).[1]

EXERCISES

1. Do you consider the following criticism justified? Why? "Kant says that only the good will is 'good without qualification,' and he tries to show that nothing else is, because undeserved happiness is bad, the coolness of the villain is bad, the courage of the invading armies is bad. But by this same criterion, a good will can be shown not to be good without qualification either. Consider a person acting in complete ignorance and superstition but with utter devotion to duty: he whips his children every day, not out of inclination but entirely from duty (it hurts me more than it hurts you, but sparing the rod will spoil the child); he persecutes minority groups, because he feels that doing so is a sacred duty; he opposes the concept of a world at peace, for he is convinced that the world is too small to hold both white, Protestant Americans and other people — he would prefer a nuclear war. We try to convince him of the error of these convictions, but he staunchly adheres to what he believes to be his duty and calls us wicked instruments of the devil because we are trying to undermine his moral convictions. However much we try to reason with him, he will not compromise, for he says that compromise is appeasement, and one who appeases is already in league with the devil: duty requires that he stand fast on his principles. He acts soberly, grimly, in deadly earnest, and from duty. Surely such a situation is not 'good without qualification'!"

2. Consider the following examples in the light of the concept of conscientious action (acting from duty):

a. x: When he has made up his mind what's right, he goes ahead and will not swerve or deviate from it; he will not be bribed, he will not compromise, nothing can bend him. Threats and torture would not make him reveal something if he thought it would be wrong to reveal it. That's the kind of man I admire — one who acts on principle and who will not compromise the principles he acts on.

y: And suppose his principles are all wrong?

x: That's unfortunate, but it makes no difference to my admiration.

b. A young man is strongly opposed on moral grounds to the consumption of alcoholic beverages in any form. But he has moved from his home town to the big city, where he aspires to a position on Madison Avenue and hobnobs with many people who drink heavily and constantly offer him drinks. To avoid awkward situations, he tells people that he has ulcers and is therefore prohibited by his physician from drinking alcohol in any form.

c. x: I don't want to deal with a man who acts on his desires or inclinations, I want him to act on principle. Then, if I know what his principles are, I have a more reliable criterion of his behavior.

y: Perhaps. But I find there is nothing more worthy of suspicion than these

[1] From Kurt Baier, *The Moral Point of View.* Ithaca, N. Y.: Cornell Univ. Press, 1958, pp. 146-47. Reprinted by permission of the publisher.

"men of principle." They are righteous people who pride themselves on always doing their duty. They can always do what they want to do and call it duty. They fool themselves, consciously or unconsciously, into thinking that something is their duty, and they make you try to swallow *their* convictions and live up to *their* standards of duty. If you don't, they will excoriate you and take revenge on you without mercy. Having, they think, a moral warrant for their actions and Right behind them, they can now indulge in aggression without guilt. No, I'd rather have a man follow his inclinations every time, especially if they are benevolent inclinations, than have to deal with a "man of principle."

x: Would you rather have your friend, who acts on his inclinations, let you down in a pinch because he "just didn't feel like helping you"? Remember, if he acts on principle, he will help you even if it means self-sacrifice; your man of inclination won't do this. With him it just depends on what his inclinations are.

y: No, the "man of principle" will always trim or interpret his principles so that he can still do what he wants. He will hedge and amend and make exceptions, saying "The present case is unique in that. . . ." or "Under the circumstances, I feel it is my duty to follow my wife's advice and. . . ." They "put on the armor of God" and ram their self-centered convictions down your throat.

d. "Why do you value conscientiousness? Consider the members of the school board — all proper, respectable, God-fearing, conscientious. But they have no idea what qualities are valuable in a teacher of their children and no insight into the judging of candidates. The result is that they turn down many candidates who would be excellent teachers and hire instead people of the 'right' race and religion and social position who are utter drudges and mediocrities and who will kill whatever intellectual interest or curiosity the children have. The loss to the children is incalculable; but the members of the school board are quite unaware of it, and they go to their righteous and proper deaths ignorant of it. Whether a person is conscientious or not tells me very little about his moral character; it is what he is conscientious *about* that matters."

e. "Even if you *did* go around saving guys' lives and all, how would you know if you did it because you really *wanted* to save guys' lives, or whether you did it because what you *really* wanted to do was be a terrific lawyer, with everybody slapping you on the back and congratulating you in a court when the goddam trial was over, the reporters and everybody . . . ? How would you know you weren't being a phony? The trouble is, you *wouldn't.*" (J. D. Salinger, *The Catcher in the Rye* [New York: Signet Books], p. 155.)

f. "If you wish to save the last of your dignity, do not call your best actions a 'sacrifice': that term brands you as immoral. If a mother buys food for her hungry child rather than a hat for herself, it is *not* a sacrifice: she values the child higher than the hat; but it is a sacrifice to the kind of mother whose higher value is the hat, who would prefer her child to starve and feeds him only from a sense of duty." (From *Atlas Shrugged* by Ayn Rand. © Copyright 1957 by Ayn Rand. Reprinted by permission of Random House, Inc., p. 1029.)

3. Regardless of whether you agree with Kant about conscientiousness as the index of moral worth, would you be inclined to say that more *moral credit* belongs to the person for whom (regardless of whether duty was his sole motive) the act was the more *difficult to perform?* Consider two persons, each performing an equally worthwhile task and each achieving equally; but for the second person the achievement was much more difficult than for the first, for whom it was relatively easy. (See E. L. Beardsley, *Philosophical Review,* Vol. 66, No. 3 [July, 1957], pp. 304-28.)

(*The reading list is at the end of the chapter.*)

15. Kant's theory of obligation

The virtuous man, Kant has said, acts from duty. But what actions does duty prescribe? To answer this question is to describe Kant's theory of obligation.

Kant says that a good will is a rational will, one that acts in accordance with reason. Man, unlike the other animals, is a *rational* being; and the moral law — whatever it turns out to be — will be one that is applicable to all rational beings alike. Man's proper end is the development of his rational nature, not the cultivation of his happiness or the titillation of his senses. If our purpose in life were to achieve happiness, says Kant,

> . . . then nature would have hit upon a very bad arrangement in selecting the reason of the creature to carry out this purpose. For all the actions which the creature has to perform with a view to this purpose, and the whole rule of its conduct, would be far more surely prescribed to it by instinct, and that end would have been attained thereby much more certainly than it ever can be by reason.[1]

The achievement of happiness, then, is not the goal of man's life; if it were, it would not have been necessary for man to be endowed with the faculty of reason.

A good man acts in accordance with reason; but now, what is it exactly to act in accordance with reason? The term "reason" is extremely slippery (pages 27-28) and needs to be rendered more precise. Kant, as we shall see, used it in a much narrower sense than did Aristotle, who also, we may remember, had a good deal to say about the development of man's rational faculties.

There are many strands in Kant's concept of reason, but let us begin with this one — one which Kant's view has in common with many eighteenth-century theories: reason, unlike the feelings, must be something *universal.* One person's feelings may incline him in one direction and another's in another, and that is the end of the matter; but the requirements of reason are the same for all rational beings. If we all followed reason correctly, we should all arrive at the same results. There is something about reason which is universal — and universality is what Kant required of a moral theory.

[1] I. Kant, *Fundamental Principles of the Metaphysics of Morals,* p. 12.

A. Universalizability

How does this description of reason apply to moral actions? Every time you act of your own volition, you are operating under what Kant calls a *maxim,* or directive. When, in circumstances C, you do Act A, you are acting on the maxim, "In circumstances C, do A." According to Kant, the Rule of Rules of all morality is this: you should act in such a way that *you could wish the maxim of your action to become a universal law of human conduct.* This rule Kant called the *categorical imperative,* and it is this rule which we shall now discuss.

Let us first observe that the rule is categorical, not hypothetical. A categorical imperative has the form "Do this!" or "Don't do that!" without any qualifications, without any if's, and's, or but's. A hypothetical imperative, by contrast, is always qualified: "If you want to avoid indigestion, don't eat fried foods" or "If you want to be happy, be kind to others." A hypothetical imperative is always contingent upon the fulfillment of some condition — whatever condition is specified in the "if" clause. Sometimes the condition is some external event — for example, "If he comes to the house, don't let him in." But the hypothetical imperatives Kant is interested in always contain "if" clauses having to do with human desires, like "If you want to grow strong, eat raw fruits and vegetables." A person is always free to reject the imperative, even if the facts it states are true: for instance, the person in question might not *want* to grow strong or to avoid indigestion. In ethics, however, Kant says that the situation is otherwise: moral commands are categorical and are not contingent upon one's wanting to achieve the end in question. "If you want to be respected, be honest" is a hypothetical imperative and not a moral rule at all; indeed, its implication seems to be that if you don't care about being respected, you needn't be honest. A moral rule, by contrast, is always categorical: "Be honest!"

The most important aspect of Kant's categorical imperative, however, is its emphasis on the notion of *universalizability.* Before you do something, ask yourself, "Could I wish the maxim of my action to be universalized — could I wish everyone to do as I am doing?" Parents are appealing to universalizability when they say to their children, "Don't be mean to little Johnny, you wouldn't want him to be mean to you, would you?" This early training in universalizability, trying to get the child to put himself in the other child's place and see if he would like done to him what he is doing to others, is an important part (perhaps the most important part) of all moral training. It is also a central rule of Christian ethics as epitomized in the Golden Rule, "Do unto others as you would have them do unto you," as well of Confucianism as stated in the Confucian rule, "Do not do unto others as you would not have them do unto you."

There is a virtually limitless number of situations to which this principle can be applied. Suppose you are about to cheat someone out of a sum of money which you owe him; you ask yourself whether you could honestly wish everyone to act as you are planning to act — for example, whether you could wish others to cheat you as you are about to cheat someone else. If the answer is, "No" (and it probably is), the action you are contemplating is not really universalizable. Or, suppose you are about to break a promise that you have solemnly made; can you truly say that you could wish this action of yours to become a universal practice? Suppose that as a result of your next action you would (perhaps through some sudden hypnotic effect) cause every member of the human race to do likewise — would you not think twice before doing anything to someone else which you would not like to have done to you in turn?

If you break a promise because you find it convenient to do so, you are acting on the maxim "Break a promise when it is convenient." But if this maxim were universalized, others would be just as entitled to break their promises to you as you are to break yours to them. This situation you would probably view with something less than approval. People who don't mind giving an injury usually feel outraged and resentful on receiving one. A person usually wants others to behave morally toward him, even though he doesn't behave morally toward them. Sometimes he may rationalize himself into thinking that his breach of promise is quite all right, even when he would be righteously indignant if others did the same to him. But this rationalization, according to Kant, is precisely what the moral law does not permit: one is not permitted to make himself an exception. If it's all right for you to do it, it's all right for others to do it too; and if it's wrong for them to do it, then it's wrong for you to do it too. The moral law is *universal* in its application: you can't pick and choose, saying, "It's all right for me to do this, but of course it's wrong for everybody else."

Now we must make the rule more specific. "Act so that you *could* wish. . . ." What does this mean? Whatever it is *possible* to wish — psychologically possible or logically possible? What *everyone* might wish or just you? What you wish in any mood or temper or just in your normal moments? One can wish (and some people do) that all humanity, including themselves, would die immediately; is this wish admitted by Kant's criterion? It would appear that what some people could or would or do wish to have universalized, other people do not. George Bernard Shaw objected to the Golden Rule: "Don't do unto others as you would have them do unto you. Their tastes might be different." For example, if I am very fond of pecan nuts, I can argue, "I wish everyone to give me pecan nuts for Christmas. And since I want to give to others what I would want them to give me, I shall give all my friends and relatives pecan nuts for Christmas, even though they hate them."

One might, of course, object to Shaw's criticism that he is not taking the Golden Rule in the spirit in which it was intended. Doing unto others as you would have them do unto you should *include* considering the difference in their tastes. A better application of the rule would be, "I like to receive presents which are pleasant or useful to me. Therefore I shall give others presents which are pleasant or useful to them." Perhaps. Still, one would like to know how Kant conceived his universalizability principle so as to eliminate possible illegitimate interpretations.

Kant had two criteria for judging whether or not an act was right, or, more precisely, for eliminating certain acts as wrong: *consistency* and *reversibility.*

1. The first criterion, *consistency,* brings us back to the concept of reason. Whatever reason may be thought to include — and we could spend much time discussing what it implies — there is no doubt of one thing to which it is unalterably opposed, namely inconsistency. A person has not used reason correctly if he arrives at conclusions which involve him in an inconsistency. Any result involving inconsistency is condemned at once. According to Kant, there are many suggested moral rules which turn out on examination to be guilty of inconsistency.

a. *Maxims inconsistent by themselves.* If you say, "Do this but don't do it" or "Always preserve life but always destroy it," such a maxim cannot possibly be obeyed because it involves a contradiction. Instances like these are so obvious as to be of no serious interest.

b. *Maxims inconsistent when universalized.* Some directives (maxims) of conduct are not inconsistent when applied by one person or some persons but become so when an attempt is made to make them apply to everybody. Consider first a maxim having nothing to do with morality: "Don't buy a newspaper when you go into the subway. Sit beside someone else and read the paper over his shoulder. Everybody else does." It is possible for you to follow this maxim and for many other people to follow it; but it is logically impossible for *everyone* to follow it, for if they tried to, there would be no one who had a newspaper over whose shoulders the others could read.

Similarly the moral maxim "Never help others but always be helped by them" could not possibly be put into practice by everyone. One, a few, or many people could (and do) behave in accordance with this maxim, but everyone could not do so, for if they tried, there would be nobody to do the helping. In other words, certain individuals can operate on this maxim, but the maxim could not be universalized into a *rule* of human conduct. According to Kant, the essence of a moral rule is its universal character, and this particular maxim could never be universalized into a rule.

Many people apparently act on the maxim "I may do anything I want to other people, but they mayn't do anything they want to me." Yet this maxim could never be a universal rule of human conduct for exactly the same reason as in the previous examples. Each person would consider himself, as the recipient of this bit of advice, to be the one who could do what he wanted; but since everyone acted on the same maxim, everyone could do as he wanted, and others could do what they wanted to him just as much as he could do what he wanted to them — thus negating the rule. Such maxims are *parasitic:* some people can act on them only as long as there are others who do not. For everyone to act on them would involve just as much of an impossibility as the ancient myth of the hundred-headed Hydra, each of whose heads was fiercer than any of the other heads. For exactly the same reason, of course, "Be stronger (or more powerful, or more brutal, or more accomplished, more wealthy, etc.) than anyone else" is a logically impossible rule, since only one person can be the most powerful person in the world, though of course it is quite possible for everyone to *try.*

Let us note, however, how many maxims there are which, however *undesirable* it may be for them to be universalized, yet are perfectly *consistent* to universalize. "Always act with exclusive regard for your own interests" and "Always act in utter and ruthless selfishness" are clearly universalizable; there is nothing inconsistent in the universal application of either one — either would make the world a jungle, but no inconsistency is involved. Of course, "Always consider other people's interests" and "Always cooperate with other people" are also universalizable, since it is equally possible for all men to behave in this way. The rule of consistency permits both of these kinds of behavior. The same is true for countless other types.

There are, however, according to Kant, some maxims which at first seem to be consistently universalizable but really are not. Here is one of Kant's own examples: A man signs a contract. In the course of time he finds it inconvenient and unpleasant to live up to its terms, so he breaks the contract. But even though breaking it may be legal, he would still be doing wrong. The maxim of his action is, "Break your contract when you find it inconvenient or disagreeable to keep it." And this maxim, if universalized, would permit everyone to do the same. "But," one may ask, "what is inconsistent about this maxim? Isn't it perfectly possible for everyone to break his contract?" Kant would say, "No," that to do so would be inconsistent with the very concept of what it is to be a contract. A contract is the sort of thing which the parties agree to keep. What would you think of a contract containing, say, four clauses about what the parties agree to do, followed by a fifth one which reads, "Notwithstanding the above stipulations, they shall have no force" or "The above contract can be broken at the pleasure of either party"? Such a so-called contract would be no contract at all but a farce — it wouldn't be worth the paper it was printed on. It would be inconsistent for something to be a contract and yet be subject to being broken in this manner.

The same answer applies to promises. If I can break a promise whenever I feel like doing so or even when I think I can do the most good by breaking it, this qualification would negate the effect of any promise, and people would soon stop making them or trusting them. "I hereby promise to do A" is inconsistent with "I can refuse to do A whenever I feel like it." If the latter were true, there would be no point in having promised at all — indeed, the statement would *be* no promise but empty words.

The same is true of universal lying. It is not just that telling lies is inconsistent with telling the truth or that keeping promises is inconsistent with breaking them. These are inconsistent, of course; but inconsistency alone is not enough to condemn universal lying, for *everything* is inconsistent with something else, namely its own negative. (You could equally argue, "Telling the truth is wrong because truth is inconsistent with falsehood.") But universal lying is inconsistent in a subtler way than that. "Always assert what you believe to be false." In one sense this maxim can be universalized, for everyone *could* follow it, but the moment the practice became universal, everyone would take everyone else as meaning the opposite of what he said. If you said, "It rained here yesterday," others would take you to mean, "It did not rain here yesterday," and they would take this meaning to be the truth. The word "not" would simply reverse its present meaning; when present it would indicate affirmation, and when absent it would indicate negation — taken in *this* sense, the "false" statement *would* be true — so everyone would not be lying after all, and universal lying would be impossible. (In one way this system would be better than the present one, in which people sometimes tell the truth and sometimes lie and we can't tell which; if everyone always lied, we could tell what the truth was by adding or subtracting the word "not.")

2. Kant, however, uses not only the criterion of consistency to judge all acts he wishes to prohibit but also the criterion of reversibility. He regards his categorical imperative as prohibiting not only those maxims which it is impossible to universalize but those which the *agent could not choose* to have universalized — that is, those whose universalization would not be acceptable to the agent after he had thought through what such a universalization would involve. Kant gives us several examples:

> A third [man] finds in himself a talent which could, by means of some cultivation, make him in many respects a useful man. But he finds himself in comfortable circumstances and prefers indulgence in pleasure to troubling himself with broadening and improving his fortunate natural gifts. Now, however, let him ask whether his maxim of neglecting his gifts, besides agreeing with his propensity to idle amusement, agrees also with what is called duty. He sees that a system of nature could indeed exist in accordance with such a law, even though man (like the inhabitants of the South Sea Islands) should let his talents rust and resolve to devote his life merely to idleness, indulgence, and propagation — in a word, to pleasure. But he cannot possibly will that this should become a universal law of nature or that it should be implanted in us by a natural instinct. For, as a rational being, he necessarily wills that all his faculties should be developed, inasmuch as they are given him for all sorts of possible purposes.
>
> A fourth man, for whom things are going well, sees that others (whom he could help) have to struggle with great hardships, and he asks, "What concern

of mine is it? Let each one be as happy as heaven wills, or as he can make himself; I will not take anything from him or even envy him; but to his welfare or to his assistance in time of need I have no desire to contribute." If such a way of thinking were a universal law of nature, certainly the human race could exist, and without doubt even better than in a state where everyone talks of sympathy and good will or even exerts himself occasionally to practice them while, on the other hand, he cheats when he can and betrays or otherwise violates the rights of man. Now although it is possible that a universal law of nature according to that maxim could exist, it is nevertheless impossible to will that such a principle should hold everywhere as a law of nature. For a will which resolved this would conflict with itself, since instances can often arise in which he would need the love and sympathy of others, and in which he would have robbed himself, by such a law of nature springing from his own will, of all hope of the aid he desires.[1]

Many similar examples will doubtless come to mind. At least at first, they sound plausible enough. A rich man may not want to give to the poor; but if he were poor, wouldn't he want others to give to him? The wastrel doesn't mind being idle, but he doesn't want everyone to be idle, for he wants to live off the fruit of their labors. The man on top would like to have rules which keep him in his favored position, but once put him on the bottom and he will sing a different tune. If we invoke the principle of reversibility, we shall see that people on the giving end of aggression don't want to be on the receiving end and therefore will not condone rules which would work against them if the roles were reversed. The employer would not mind the universalization of antilabor practices and legislation, indeed he enthusiastically approves it as long as he is an employer; but it seems doubtful that he would still approve antilabor legislation if he were a laborer. Surely, we feel, people will think twice before giving their assent to the universalization of a maxim which may later be used against them.

Yet on second thought, can we be so sure? Even if the person knows full well what conditions would be like if the roles were reversed, is it certain that he would disapprove a certain maxim? Does the wastrel necessarily want to live off the fruits of other's labor? Usually, but perhaps not always. He may believe that most labor is useless and that the world would be better off if everyone, not just himself, were to sleep and lie in the sun and catch as catch can. Life would not be very productive, but he does not set a high value on productivity. Or again, the rich man might wish the maxim of his action universalized: "Look out for yourself, give no help and expect none." But doesn't he, as Kant says, desire to have help in his own time of trouble? Not necessarily; he might well be content to live by his stern maxim of self-sufficiency. He might not even *want* sympathy or help in time of trouble. He might be perfectly satisfied to stand or fall by the law of the jungle: he would be as willing to apply his maxim of "rugged individualism" when he was victim as when he was victor.

[1] *Ibid.,* pp. 47-49.

A sadist might even want sadism universalized. "Would he really want it if he were the victim and not the aggressor?" one might ask. Probably he would. But if he had a strong masochistic streak as well (most sadists do), he might not mind being on the receiving end. At least he might think it better to have universal sadistic-masochistic practices (with himself being on the receiving end as well as on the giving end) than not to have such practices at all.

Nor would the thief always be deterred if you suggested the following consideration: "You say you wouldn't mind seeing stealing universalized, but you wouldn't want it if you were the victim of the theft; to approve stealing is to approve it both ways, for him who is victim as well as for him who is the thief." We may expect the thief to agree with this statement, but he may not. "No," he may say, "I think it's better to have stealing, and I would approve it even when I'm on the receiving end. Life is much more spicy and interesting that way. I think the best rule is for anyone to be allowed to steal with impunity if he is clever enough to do it without being caught and also for the victim to have no recourse to law but only the privilege of shooting the thief if he catches him. Whether I were stealing or stolen from, I think this arrangement would be much better than that of the bourgeois world we have now with all its emphasis on the sacredness of property values; therefore I would definitely approve theft as a general policy." Kant assumes that all these people would not choose to have the policies he condemns universalized; but in this assumption he may well be mistaken. Considering the vast variety of human motives and temperaments, it would seem that he probably *is* mistaken.

Our thief might, of course, give a reason for his approval of the universalization which would damage his position: "I'm so confident of my cleverness at stealing that I think I would come off better by this arrangement. I'm confident enough of my own abilities to be convinced that for every theft in which I was the victim, there are ten that I could bring off successfully." We could reply, however, "What if you were *not* so clever? What if others were far cleverer thieves than you, so that you would be the victim of theft more often that the agent?" This consideration might indeed cause the thief to change his mind about approving theft as universal policy. Yet it might not. He might, for example, recognize that he would be *financially* worse off if his maxim were universalized; but if (as many thieves do) he got a thrill out of the *attempt* to steal, he would weigh the financial loss against the gain in thrills and would still feel that he would come out the winner by the arrangement. He might, then, still think that the policy of permitting universal stealing would, all things considered, be preferable to its universal prohibition. There does not seem to be any sure way of causing him to change his opinion within the scope of Kant's criterion.

We might, however, try to carry the matter yet one step further (and beyond anything that Kant says or implies). We might say to the thief,

"But suppose that you didn't happen to have an adventurous temperament. Would you then wish stealing to be a universal policy?" Suppose you are in the situation of the souls envisioned by Plato at the end of the *Republic*, drawing lots to see which bodies they will inhabit and consequently which temperaments they will receive. *Before they drew lots,* would they wish to see stealing made a universal policy? They might come off better with such a policy (on both the giving and receiving end) if they turned out to have the temperaments and dispositions of pirates, but not if they drew lots giving them the souls of shopkeepers. Would they then, *before* they knew what their role in society would be or even what temperament they would inherit, approve the rule permitting universal stealing? What is the answer to this question? Shall we still say, "Some would, some wouldn't?" But how can we tell? The trouble here is that before they knew what temperament they would have while in an embodied state, they would have no ground for choosing at all. In order to make *any* choice one way or the other, even as disembodied souls or spirits, they would already have to have *some* temperamental features and predispositions. Can you imagine a being without any temperamental features making a decision? With what kind of emotional and intellectual structure would he make it? It would seem that this last stage of our question about reversibility is not merely open to the charge of having an indecisive answer but to the far more serious charge of being meaningless.

Our initial suspicion, then, remains: Kant's second criterion for condemning certain kinds of acts as wrong because the agent could not choose the maxims of these acts to be universalized, will not yield a set of maxims on whose universalization everyone can agree. Whether everyone agrees or not will depend on his basic temperamental characteristics; and the existence of these characteristics cannot in turn be made (even hypothetically) into an object of choice without rendering meaningless our description of the imagined situation.

B. Criticism of universalizability

Kant's criteria, then, fail to eliminate certain types of actions as always wrong. Kant held, nevertheless, that these types must be wrong: for when we universalize a maxim, we make a rule, and the rule, being universal, applies to all the members of the class without exception. Kant believed that lying could not consistently be universalized and that therefore lying is always wrong. (A person may say nothing, but if he speaks he is duty bound to tell the truth.) Similarly, killing is always wrong, breaking promises is always wrong, theft is always wrong, suicide is always wrong. Rules, being universal, have no exceptions. Most of Kant's critics and commentators have disagreed with his conclusion: they have either agreed with Kant's principle of universalizability but not agreed that such acts as self-seeking, suicide, breaking promises, actually are nonuniversalizable as Kant thought;

or they have disagreed with Kant about the universalizability principle itself.

1. Those who accept universalizability but exempt certain acts. We have already seen how the view that certain types of actions are prohibited by the universalizability rule can be contested. Perhaps the universalizability rule is all right, but it does not imply that lying, killing, and promise-breaking are always wrong. Almost no one believes that *all* instances of these kinds of action are wrong. (1) In the first place, it is not always clear what actions are to be included under the headings of lying and killing (pages 14-17), and so it is not clear what the rule prohibits. (2) Moreover, the well-nigh unanimous consensus of humanity, including reflective and thoughtful humanity, testifies that acts of these kinds are *not* always wrong. This agreement, of course doesn't prove rightness or wrongness, but it is difficult to believe that the "wisdom of the ages" is entirely mistaken on this important point. More serious still, (3) there is a logical difficulty in situations where duties conflict. If it is always wrong to break a promise and always wrong to tell a lie, what happens when I have to tell a lie in order to keep a promise I have made? Or what if I have to break a promise to save a life? In such a situation "something has to give" — I have to violate the one rule or the other. Can we really say that in such situations "you're damned if you do and you're damned if you don't" — that anything we did in such a situation would be wrong? Kant gives us no counsel as to what to do when there is a conflict of duties. As we shall shortly see, other writers have tried to remedy this lacuna in Kant's theory while yet retaining the main outlines of Kant's ethics.

2. Those who reject universalizability. Why should Kant have felt impelled in the first place to hold that the prohibition against lying, killing, and other kinds of action must operate without exception? There is a distinction, which Kant failed to make, between saying that *one should make no exceptions to a rule* and saying that *the rule itself has no exceptions.* Kant held, and most people would agree with him, that when a rule is laid down, a person should not try to make himself (or any other favored individual or individuals) an exception to it: it won't do to say, "Killing is wrong, except when I do it." If it's right for you to do it, your maxim must be universalizable, and then it's right for others to do it, not just you. But, because no one may make an exception for himself, it does not follow that *the rule itself* may not contain *certain classes of exceptions.* For example, "Do not kill" is certainly a universal rule as it stands, without exceptions.

But suppose we decide — on some grounds or other, perhaps the utilitarian grounds that Kant rejected — that killing is *not* always wrong and that there are certain classes of exceptions to the rule: for example, killing is not wrong when done in self-defense. The rule then becomes, "Do not kill except in self-defense." Even this revised rule may not be entirely satisfactory; perhaps it could be improved by including other classes of exceptions as well. But that is not the point just now. The point is that the rule "Do not kill except in self-defense" is *just as much a universal rule,* applying to all the situations falling under it, as is the original rule "Do not kill." The reference to self-defense does not give us exceptions to the rule; it *builds certain qualifications into the rule.* And a qualified rule may be just as good as, or better than, an unqualified rule. A rule is universal as long as it is applied to all the situations to which it is supposed to apply. "All killing other than self-defense is wrong" condemns as wrong *all* the actions the rule covers (namely, acts of killing other than self-defense) just as much as does the original rule "All killing is wrong." If a rule says, "Don't do X other than in circumstances A, B, or C" and you do X in circumstance A, your action is no exception to the rule; in fact it falls under the rule. There seems, then, to be no reason why a maxim prohibiting killing except in self-defense could *not* be universalized into a rule — a "universal rule of human conduct." The qualified rule satisfies the universalizability test as well as the unqualified one. Once this fact is recognized, there no longer appears to be any need to state moral rules in the simple and unqualified manner ("Never break a promise," "Never kill") which Kant did. We shall have much more to say in later sections about rules and their qualifications.

One word of caution, however. A rule is not universal as long as it contains within it any *proper names* — the names of certain individuals. If I say, "Never tell lies unless you are John Jones, in which case lying is all right," the rule contains reference to a specific individual, John Jones, and is not considered universal. Or suppose you tended to favor a rule which read, "All commercial planes may take to the air without a mechanical examination, unless I happen to be one of the passengers." This rule, of course, contains a proper name, a reference to yourself. Both of these rules would fall under Kant's criticism of "making an exception to a rule" and would not be considered acceptable — to accept them would clearly be to "play favorites." Indeed, when a rule contains a pronoun (as the second one does) instead of a noun which is a proper name, the rule is literally impossible to apply: everyone reading or hearing the rule would take the "I" to refer to himself, so everyone would be the exception, and no one would fall under the rule!

However, the prohibition against proper names is not enough to rule out a great many discriminatory rules. It is easy to construct a rule which contains no proper names and yet is tailor-made to suit certain kinds of cases. Consider: "All persons except Negroes may eat in public places." "All planes that do not contain white, male human beings between the ages of twenty and forty may take to the air without a mechanical examination." These are qualified universal rules containing no proper names, just like the rule "It is wrong to kill except in self-defense." The exclusion of proper names, then, in no way guarantees that the rule will be a good one, even when the rule can be applied universally by Kant's criteria. In fact you could make the qualifications and specifications within the rule so precise and demanding that, although the rule contains no proper names, it excepts no one but yourself. "All persons earning over $600 within a given year should pay federal income tax" is a rule accepted by the Internal Revenue Department; it is qualified (it refers not to everyone but to everyone earning $600) but still universal. But the same can be said of this rule: "All persons should pay income tax other than persons who are male, between 5'11" and 5'11½" in height, between 177 and 178 pounds in weight, . . ." and so on, specifying such a long list of conditions that I am the only person fulfilling all these specifications. The maxim "Pay income tax if you don't meet these specifications" can be universalized equally well, whether the specification is earning $600 a year or whether it is living up to the list of requirements. Yet, whatever we may think of the $600-a-year rule, we would take a dim view of the other rule — unless, perchance, we happened to meet all the specifications. The point is that *both* maxims are equally universalizable but when universalized, they do *not* result in equally good or satisfactory rules. By what criterion, then, are we to judge whether a suggested rule is a good one? This criterion, it would appear, is something we have yet to discover. We shall consider one later in this chapter. Kant's criterion of reversability eliminates some suggested rules because their maxims are not universalizable, but it leaves a large residue of other maxims ("Always cooperate with others," "Never cooperate with others") which are perfectly universalizable, yet not all of which can be applied since many of them contradict one another.

Let us approach this same general point by means of a somewhat different line of reasoning. Kant placed every individual act in a *class* (or category) of actions, such as truth-telling, promise-keeping, lying, killing. But every act, like every other thing in the world, can be classified in a variety of ways. This animal can be classified as a mink, as a mammal, as a fur-bearer, as a quadruped, depending on what features of the animal we happen to be interested in. In the same way, a lie told to save a life may be classified as a lie, as a statement, as a speech-utterance by a living organism, as a deliberate deception, as an act of mercy. An escapee from a lunatic asylum comes to my house, knife in hand, and asks where Jones lives so that he can kill Jones; if I give him Jones's correct address, he will almost certainly take Jones unawares and kill him; am I justified therefore in lying to him? Most of us would say, "Yes"; Kant says, "No," that I may tell him nothing but that if I speak, I must tell the truth. Need we accept this conclusion? If I do tell the would-be murderer a lie, my action falls under a variety of classes of actions, including the following:

(1) Lies told to save a life.
(2) Lies (i.e., deliberate falsehoods).
(3) Statements.

In which of these classes of actions should we place this particular act for purposes of universalization? Kant chooses the second: he says in effect,

"This action is a lie, and since lying is not consistently universalizable, all lies are wrong; so this action is wrong." But why could we not just as well choose the first, and say, "This is a lie told to save a life, and lies told to save lives are right, so this act is right"? Or, for that matter, the third: "This lie is a statement, and uttering statements is right, so this act is right"? In fact, nobody classifies the action in the third way, but it is not clear from Kant's doctrine *why* nobody does. We are looking at the same act as a member of three different classes of acts, each more general and inclusive than the one before it — in other words, three different levels of abstractness. It is not clear why we should have to choose the second of these three classes rather than the first or the third.

Many people would say that the first of these three classes, if we must choose one, would be the best one to choose. For example, instead of condemning all lies just because they are lies, let us distinguish between those lies which are told to save lives and those which are not. Or let us make other possible distinctions, such as between lies which will do good and those which will not. Why should *all* lies be wrong because some are, any more than uttering statements should always be right because it sometimes is? Lies do differ from one another in intent, circumstances, and context; and since they differ from one another, may there not be *morally relevant* differences? Must one lump them all together as either all right or all wrong? In fact, don't we distinguish even further: couldn't some lies told to save lives be right and some wrong, depending on still more specific circumstances? Shouldn't we take into consideration *all* the aspects of an act? Shouldn't we refrain from putting the act into a class, thus lumping it together with lots of more or less similar things as Kant does, but rather look at each act in its total specific detail, in all its uniqueness and individuality?

When we label this act a lie told to save lives, we are considering more specific aspects of this act than when we simply call it a lie, but we are not considering all of them; we are still putting it into a class by abstracting one aspect of it — that of being a lie told to save a life — and ignoring all the rest. This procedure is, after all, what abstracting is: seizing upon one aspect and ignoring the others. When we simply call this act a lie, we are putting it into a wider class by abstracting from the individual act a more general aspect than before: we forget everything about this act except that it is an instance of lying (and is the fact that it is an instance of lying enough to base a moral judgment on?).

When we even more simply call this act a statement, we are abstracting from the act an even more general aspect. Abstracting one aspect involves ignoring (for the purpose at hand) all the others; and why, in the moral life, should we do this? Shouldn't we rather consider every possible aspect of an act — not just "Is this a case of divorce?" but "What are the specific conditions in *this* particular divorce?" — in all the act's complexity and individuality before we attempt to judge whether it is right or wrong? There will always be differences between this act and all the other acts of this type or class, and these differences may turn out to be of great importance. If we simply lump the act together with a motley crew of other acts which have just this one aspect in common with it, aren't we ignoring many aspects of the act which may be of vital importance? Doesn't this procedure, in daily life, lead to slovenly "slogan-thinking" — "It's divorce so it must be wrong," "He told the truth so it must be right"? People who think in such careless generalizations do not bother to think in detail about their actions; they simply paste a label on them and automatically classify them as right or wrong. This procedure, of course, makes moral judgments very easy: people do not have to reflect but only to classify.

But isn't a procedure of this sort extremely unfair? If one particular act of divorce is wrong, why then should all acts of divorce in general, performed by very different people in widely differing circumstances, be wrong? What excuse have we, therefore, for pasting the same label on a whole group of acts by calling them lies or divorces and condemning them forthwith without any further attempt at differentiation? Why even classify this particular act together with all lies told to save lives? This narrower classification is better than the broader one, for it does make one added differentiation — the act is recognized as a lie told to save a life, not just as a lie — but still, couldn't one differentiate even further and perhaps arrive at still more relevant differences between this lie-told-to-save-lives and other lies-told-to-save-lives?"

What these people are questioning, then is (1) the value of abstracting one aspect of an action in considering the rightness or wrongness of the action, and (2) even granting the value or necessity of abstracting, why pitch it at just the level of abstractness which Kant chooses?

Someone may suggest a way out of this difficulty: "Don't say that this act is a lie and wrong because all lying is wrong, for to do that is to lump this act together with a lot of other acts and ignore the differences between them. Don't even say that this lie told to save a life is right because all lying told to save a life is right, for even to do that is to lump this act of lying-to-save-a-life with other acts of the same kind, and not all of these might be right. Focus your judgment on the *specific act* as far as you can. Say this: 'If this act done by you is wrong, then an act exactly like it done by me or anyone else would be wrong. And if this act done by me is right, then an identical act done by you or anyone else is also right.' If you say this much and go no further, then you have rescued the main point of Kant's theory of obligation — namely that a person shouldn't make an exception out of himself and that all people who live up to the specifications mentioned fall under the rule — and yet you don't meet the difficulties we have just been considering about levels of abstractness and discriminatory qualifications built into the rule."

What shall we say about this solution? Certainly most people would be inclined to agree that if one act is right, then all other acts just like it are right, no matter who it is that performs them. But even this seemingly innocuous rule must be revised, or at any rate clarified:

(1) Two acts of killing need not be both right or both wrong. For example, one may be the assassination of a Hitler-like dictator and the other, the killing of an innocent person.The two acts differ in *circumstances* — the circumstances just described. We must specify that the total circumstances of the two acts be identical in order that the same moral judgment be passed upon them. Two acts of sticking a knife into the body of another person need not be both right or both wrong either. For instance, one act may be that of a surgeon operating on a patient, and the second may be that of a hoodlum on the city streets. But there again, though the two acts may be similar or even, if you like, identical, the circumstances of their occurrences are vastly different; they wouldn't necessarily be both right or both wrong unless *all* the circumstances were the same. Can we even say that two acts of surgery need both be right? No, for the one operation may be necessary to save the patient's life, and the other one unnecessary and recommended by the surgeon for financial gain, even though cure without surgery would have been possible. There, once again, the circumstances are different. We have to spell out the circumstances in detail; and only if the circumstances are *all* the same can we be assured that if the one act is right, the other is also.

So far, so good. But even this modification must be revised or clarified further: (2) Smith and Jones may each perform an act as nearly identical as you please in circumstances that are as nearly identical as you please; and yet the one may be right and the other wrong, not because of any difference in the act itself or in the circumstances, but because of an internal difference *in the agents*. For example, if Smith is accident-prone and Jones is not, it may be right for the judge to revoke Smith's driving license and allow Jones to retain his, even though the circumstances of their traffic offence are identical. (One might, of course, call this difference too a difference in the circumstances — the *inner* circumstances as opposed to the outer or *external* circumstances.) Understood in this way, then, the principle seems to be acceptable: two acts which are exactly alike and performed by identical agents in identical circumstances must be either both right or both wrong.

But we have paid a high price for our principle; it is now useless. It is impossible to apply, for there never *are* two identical acts performed in identical inner and outer circumstances. Yet if the acts differ from each other in even the slightest detail, there is no guarantee that this difference may not require a difference in moral evaluation: the one right, the other wrong. Someone might object, "But not all differences are *relevant* differences." Perhaps he is right; but the problem is to find a criterion for knowing when a difference *is* a relevant difference. We shall pursue this problem in a later chapter; but it is not answered by Kant.

The only safe way of applying Kant's test of universalizability is to envisage the act in its whole concrete particularity, and then ask "Could I wish that everyone, when in exactly similar circumstances, should tell a lie exactly similar to that which I am thinking of telling?" But then universalizability, as a short cut to knowing what is right, has failed us. For it is just as hard to see whether a similar act by someone else, with all its concrete particularity, would be right, as it is to see whether our own proposed act would be right.[1]

In spite of this failure, the universalizability criterion may have considerable value, although not the value Kant claimed for it.

Logically we gain nothing by posing the question as a question for everyone rather than for oneself; for it is the same question. But *psychologically* we gain much. So long as I consider the act as one which I may or may not do, it is easy to suppose that I see it to be right when I merely see it to be convenient. But let me ask myself whether it would be right for everyone else; their advantage does not appeal to me or cloud my mind as my own does. If the act is wrong, it will be easier to see that it would be wrong for them; and then I cannot reasonably resist the conclusion that it is wrong for me. Other writers before Kant had for this reason advocated the adoption of the attitude of the impartial spectator.[2]

C. A possible revision

A second Kantian rule, about treating people as ends rather than means, will be discussed in the section on Rights. Meanwhile, before we leave the subject of universalizability, let us consider briefly a revised use of Kant's criterion of universalizability suggested by the contemporary writer Kurt Baier.

1. Some acts, according to Baier, are right or wrong when considered by themselves, without appeal to universalizability. To be right, they must fulfill the condition of *reversibility*, that is, they must be acceptable to a person whether he is at the giving or the receiving end of the action. Since the moral point of view is one of strict impartiality, an act's being right can have nothing to do with who happens to be in a favored position with respect to it. According to Baier's argument, "killing, cruelty, inflicting pain, maiming, torturing, deceiving, cheating, rape, adultery are all instances of this sort of behavior"[3] — behavior which is not reversible and is therefore wrong. Whether all these forms of behavior are irreversible could, of course, be disputed. Some of them could be "acceptable to a person whether he is at the giving or the receiving end of it" *if* he is a certain type of person.

---

[1] From Sir William David Ross, *Kant's Ethical Theory*. New York: Oxford Univ. Press, 1954, p. 34. Reprinted by permission of the publisher.
[2] *Ibid.*, p. 34. Italics mine.
[3] From Kurt Baier, *The Moral Point of View*. Ithaca, N. Y.: Cornell Univ. Press, 1958, p. 202. Reprinted by permission of the publisher.

At any rate, his decision about it will depend upon the type of person he is.

2. More interesting, however, is the second point: some acts are wrong, not because of irreversibility, but because they could not be recommended in moral rules applying to everyone. And yet moral rules, by their very nature, are intended for everyone: a cult or secret society might have rules that outsiders were not permitted to know about, but *moral* rules must be publicly stated and inculcated; the whole point of morality is universal adherence to it. " 'Thou shalt not kill, but it is a strict secret' is absurd. 'Esoteric morality' is a contradiction in terms."[1] Moral rules must be universally applicable, and to be universally applicable they must be universally teachable. *Universal teachability* is Baier's criterion for judging moral rules. By this criterion three kinds of rules are invalidated.

a. *Self-frustrating rules.* There are rules whose purpose is frustrated as soon as everyone acts on them. For example, consider the maxim "When you are in need, ask for help, but never help another man when he is in need."

If everybody adopted this principle, then their adoption of the second half would frustrate what obviously is the point of the adoption of the first half, namely, to get help when one is in need. Although such a principle is not self-contradictory — for anybody could consistently adopt it — it is nevertheless objectionable from the moral point of view, for it could not be taught openly to everyone. It would then lose its point. It is a parasitic principle, useful to anyone only if many people act on its opposite.[2]

b. *Self-defeating rules.* A rule is self-defeating if the whole point of having the rule is defeated as soon as a person *lets it be known* that he has adopted it. (Kant failed to distinguish self-defeating rules from self-frustrating rules.) "Give a promise when you know or think that you can never keep it or when you don't intend to keep it" is a maxim on which many people act, at least sometimes; but if a person announced that this was the maxim of his future actions, the whole purpose of making or giving promises would be defeated. Promises are made to furnish a guarantee to the promisee, and a promiser who made such a remark as this would at once be casting doubt on the sincerity of his promise and thus would take away the point of having any promise at all. If such a rule were taught openly — as it must be, to be a moral rule at all — it would be known that everyone would be likely to act on it, and the point of making promises would be lost. Such a rule, therefore, could not belong to the morality of any group.

c. *Morally impossible rules.* There are some rules which it is impossible to teach in the way moral rules must be capable of being taught: for example, self-frustrating and self-defeating rules *could* be taught in this form (though

---

[1] *Ibid.*, p. 196.
[2] *Ibid.*, pp. 196-97.

it would be pointless to do so), but a morally impossible rule such as "Always assert what you think is false" *could* not be so taught. A person might act on this rule *secretly* and do so successfully, since he would always be taken to be saying what he thinks is true whereas he is actually saying the opposite. Such a person would indeed mislead others, but he cannot teach his principle or maxim to others; for if he did, he would be taken as meaning the opposite of what he said. The open teaching of this maxim to everyone, for everyone's acceptance, would be impossible — unless, of course, it is construed simply as a change in the use of the word "not," in which event, as we saw earlier, it would be identical with the maxim "Tell the truth."

We are considering the open teaching of the principle "Always assert what you think is not the case," for open acceptance by everybody, an acceptance which is not to be interpreted as a change in the use of "not." But this is nonsense. We cannot all *openly* tell one another that we are always going to mislead one another in a certain way and insist that we must continue to be misled, though we know how we could avoid being misled. I conclude that this principle could not be embodied in a rule belonging to the morality of any group.[1]

It should be added, however, that occasional or even habitual liars do not act on the maxim "Always lie" or "Always say what you think is false." Those who lie occasionally are acting on maxims like "Lie when you can thereby avoid harming someone" and "Lie when it is helpful to you and harmful to no one else." Habitual liars often act on the maxim "Lie when it's convenient to do so" or "Lie when it's easiest to do so." Pathological liars act on the maxim "Lie whenever you can deceive someone." All of *these* maxims are perfectly capable of being adopted by everybody and taught to everybody. The first two maxims may be useful and acceptable, the others probably are not. But *why* the second two are better than the other ones (if they are) is a question which remains to be investigated. All of them live up to Kant's criteria, consistency and reversibility, and to Baier's criterion, universal teachability, as well. These criteria, then, can be taken, at best, as *excluding* certain types of actions, but they do not tell us which actions can be *included* in an acceptable body of moral rules. (Necessary conditions are not yet sufficient conditions.) In the next chapter we shall consider some changes that have been made in the Kantian ethics with this goal in mind.

EXERCISES

1. Do you think that the following criticisms of Kant are justified? Give reasons for your answer.

a. When Kant talks about happiness not being the end, or purpose, of man, he is using teleological language to which he is not entitled without a specific

[1] *Ibid.,* p. 199.

supernatural theory. For a purpose implies a purposer. If man was designed for some end, someone, presumably God, must have designed him so. But Kant has not begun, or even tried, to show that man *was* designed by a Divine Being to fulfill some end. So all this teleological talk is without foundation.

b. Besides (continuing the above), it isn't true that instinct would be sufficient if our true end were happiness. We would still need reason to tell us which actions are most likely to lead to happiness (either our own or others').

c. In saying that a good will alone is good without qualification — and assuming that "good without qualification" means the same as "intrinsically good" — Kant was confusing instrumental good with intrinsic good. Good will usually leads to intrinsic good, but how can it be intrinsically good itself, in view of such an example as in Exercise 1 on page 273?

d. How can Kant speak of actions as being consistent or inconsistent? It is only propositions which can be consistent or inconsistent with each other.

e. Kant's universalizability rule can't be applied to matters of feeling, like whom one should marry. In the first place, Kant's whole emphasis was on reason, which is at the opposite pole from feelings. In the second place, if I love Miss X and want to marry her, I certainly couldn't wish this universalized, for I certainly don't want *everybody* to marry Miss X! (Expose all the mistakes you find in this criticism. Assuming that the maxim of one's act must be rational in the sense of being universalizable, does it follow that matters of feeling cannot enter in as the subject matter of the maxim?)

f. Kant's distinction between the categorical imperative as a moral imperative and the hypothetical imperative as a nonmoral one is mistaken. Some categorical imperatives have nothing to do with morality: "Shut the door!" "Eat your food!" And some hypothetical imperatives do: "If you're going to do what's right, keep that promise"; "If it is not overwhelmingly probable that he is about to shoot you, don't shoot him first."

2. What do you think of the following as examples of the application of Kant's universalizability rule? Explain your reasons.

a. Since I enjoy playing tennis, I like to be invited by others to play tennis. Since I should do as I would be done by, I should invite others to play tennis with me on all possible occasions, regardless of whether they enjoy the game.

b. For the sake of my health I take liver pills every day. If it is right for me to do this, it is right for everyone to do it; therefore it would be right for everybody to take liver pills every day.

c. I could not wish everyone to become a professional philosopher; the human race would starve if that happened. But no act, according to Kant, is right unless it can be universalized into a general rule. Therefore nobody ought to become a professional philosopher.

d. If I prefer blondes, I should wish everyone else to prefer blondes.

e. Suicide is always wrong, for if universalized, it would be inconsistent with the continuance of life.

f. Lying is always wrong, for if universalized, it would be inconsistent with the function of language, which is to tell the truth. (Do you agree with Kant here?)

g. It cannot be your duty to love your enemies, for if everyone loved his enemies there would be no enemies left to love.

h. It cannot be your duty to give to the poor, since if everyone did so, the recipients would be poor no longer, and there would be no poor left to give to.

i. Kant himself was inconsistent: he was a bachelor and he had no children. If everyone had followed his example, the race would have died out. If suicide is always wrong (as Kant believed it was), why not celibacy, which would have the same result?

j. A teacher says, as he lights a pipe at the opening of a test period, "Since the maxim of my action should be universalizable, you may smoke during this test." A student replies, "I was wondering whether you might not be universalizing a different maxim: 'All teachers may smoke during test periods.'"

3. Are the following maxims universalizable? Would they pass Kant's criteria? Why? (Watch out for proper names.)

a. Everybody except me is bound by moral rules.

b. Don't stand in line; force yourself in at the head of the line so that you won't have to wait for everyone else to be served first.

c. Hurry now, get your tickets today so that you will have them later when everyone else is clamoring to get them.

d. Write the best essay and win First Prize!

e. Be the exception — be there on time.

f. If two trains meet at a crossing, each should wait till the other has passed.

g. Be ruthless to everyone.

h. Be more charitable than anyone else.

i. Whoever disagrees with me should be shot.

j. Whoever disagrees with another person should be shot.

k. Whoever disagrees with Idea X should be shot.

l. Make everyone believe what you believe.

m. Never speak until you are first spoken to.

n. Wait for the hostess to begin eating.

o. Never be the first to start eating — always wait for someone else to start.

4. Think of all the reasons you can why a moral rule should not contain any proper names. Then read pages 19-26 of R. Brandt, *Ethical Theory,* to compare your reasoning on the point with his.

5. Do you agree or disagree with the following assertion? "Kant seems to have held that all particular rules of duty can be deduced from the one fundamental rule 'Act as if the maxim of thy action were to become by thy will a universal law of nature.' But this appears to me an error analogous to that of supposing that formal logic supplies a complete criterion of truth. I should agree that a volition which does not stand this test is to be condemned; but I hold that a volition which does stand it may after all be wrong. For I conceive that all (or almost all) persons who act conscientiously could sincerely will the maxims on which they act to be universally adopted: while at the same time we continually find such persons in thoroughly conscientious disagreement as to what each ought to do in a given set of circumstances." (Henry Sidgwick, *The Methods of Ethics,* 7th ed. [New York: Macmillan, 1874], pp. 209-10.)

6. Is pacifism parasitic? Would you agree or disagree with the following? "Pacifism is very noble and war is very horrible indeed. But in our present state of society, people who announce that they will not bear arms to resist aggression

are only inviting aggression; if everyone acted thus, the good people in the world would be exterminated by the bad ones. Those who are pacifists today have lived to be so and are able to preach their doctrine, because in the period 1939-45 there were enough people who were *not* pacifists: the Allied armies made their pacifism possible by defending them against a tyranny which, had it been victorious, would have taken away most of their liberties, including their right to preach pacifism."

7. In Victor Hugo's *Les Miserables,* the hero, Jean Valjean, is an ex-convict living under an assumed name. He has built up a successful business in which he employs most of his fellow townspeople; he becomes mayor and a public benefactor. Then he learns that another man, a feeble-minded old beggar, has been arrested as Jean Valjean and will be sent to the galleys. The real Jean Valjean then decides that it is his moral duty to reveal who he is, even at the price of being sent back to the galleys.

a. What do you think Kant would say about Jean Valjean's decision? Why?

b. What do you think the utilitarians would say? Why?

c. What would you say? Give your reasons.

8. Evaluate the following examples, using the concept of reversibility.

a. A throws an orange at B's face; B becomes angry; A resents B's anger. B says, "I bet *you'd* be angry if I did it to you." A replies, "Maybe I would, but I'm me, I'm not you."

b. The mother of a juvenile delinquent who has murdered another boy weeps and says her son is not really bad; she asks that he be released in a short time into her care. She is horrified when the judge gives him a thirty-year sentence. How do you think she would feel — or how do you think you would feel — about the situation if you were, not the mother of the aggressor, but the mother of the murdered boy?

c. x says, "How dreadful to arrest that American flyer shot down over Soviet territory!" y replies, "Was it? What would you suggest doing if a Russian plane were shot down over Pittsburgh? Wouldn't the American people be full of righteous indignation about it?" x answers, "Yes, but they are a militaristic dictatorship, and we are a peace-loving democracy."

9. Evaluate the following interchange: "It is wrong to cheat and lie and steal; what if everyone did these things?" "Yes, but what you say is irrelevant, for not everybody *is* going to do these things. Most people will continue to be upright proper citizens, and the universalization you refer to will not take place."

10. Consider the ethics, not of doing one's duty, but of doing *more than* one's duty ("over and above the call of duty"). Read on this point the very interesting essay by J. Urmson, "Saints and Heroes," in A. I. Melden, ed., *Essays in Moral Philosophy* (Seattle: Univ. of Washington Press, 1958), pp. 198-216.

11. Is there any way in which you could defend the view that of two identical acts performed by identical people in identical circumstances, one could not be right and the other wrong? Answer as best you can, then turn to R. Brandt, *Ethical Theory,* pp. 21-24.

READING LIST, SECTIONS 14 AND 15

Baier, Kurt. *The Moral Point of View.* Ithaca, N. Y.: Cornell Univ. Press, 1958, Ch. 8 and pp. 280-89.

Beardsley, Elizabeth L. "Moral Worth and Moral Credit." *Philosophical Review,* Vol. 66, No. 3 (July, 1957), pp. 304-28.

Brandt, Richard. *Ethical Theory.* Englewood Cliffs, N. J.: Prentice-Hall, 1959, Ch. 2.

Broad, C. D. "Conscience and Conscientious Action." In Broad, C. D., *Ethics and the History of Philosophy.* New York: Humanities Press, 1952, pp. 244-62.

———. *Five Types of Ethical Theory* (1935). New York: Humanities Press, 1960 (Littlefield, Adams), Ch. 5.

Carritt, Edgar F. *The Theory of Morals.* London: Oxford Univ. Press, 1928, Ch. 9.

Ewing, Alfred C. *Ethics.* New York: Macmillan, 1953, Ch. 4.

Field, Guy C. *Moral Theory.* London: Methuen, 1921, Pt. 1.

Hare, R. M. "Universalizability." *Aristotelian Society Proceedings,* Vol. 55 (1954-5), pp. 295-312.

Harrison, Jonathan. "Kant's Four Examples of the First Formulation of the Categorical Imperative." *Philosophical Quarterly,* Vol. 7 (1957), pp. 50-62.

———. "When Is a Principle a Moral Principle?" *Aristotelian Society Proceedings,* Supplementary Vol. 28 (1954), pp. 111-34.

Kant, Immanuel. *The Critique of Practical Reason.* Many editions.

———. *Fundamental Principles of the Metaphysics of Morals.* 9th ed. New York: Longmans, Green, 1923. Many other editions.

Körner, Stephen. *Kant.* Baltimore: Pelican Books, 1955, Ch. 6.

Ladd, John. "Must There Be a Desire To Do One's Duty for Its Own Sake?" In Nakhnikian, G., and H. Castaneda. *Morality and the Language of Conduct.* Detroit: Wayne State Univ. Press, 1961.

Mackinnon, D. M. *A Study in Ethical Theory.* London: Black, 1957, pp. 61-120.

Nowell-Smith, Patrick. *Ethics.* Baltimore: Pelican Books, 1954, Ch. 17.

Paton, Herbert James. *The Categorical Imperative.* London: Hutchinson, 1953.

Rashdall, Hastings. *Theory of Good and Evil.* 2nd ed. New York: Oxford Univ. Press, 1924. 2 vols., Vol. 1, Bk. 1, Ch. 5.

Ross, Sir William David. *Kant's Ethical Theory.* New York: Oxford Univ. Press, 1954.

Shwayder, D. S. "The Sense of Duty." *Philosophical Quarterly,* Vol. 7 (1957), pp. 116-25.

Silber, John R. "The Contents of Kant's Ethical Thought." *Philosophical Quarterly,* Vol. 9 (1959), Pts. 1 and 2, pp. 193-207, 309-18.

Singer, Marcus. "Generalization in Ethics." *Mind,* Vol. 64 (1955), pp. 361-75.

7. Rules and consequences

We are now in a position to try to mediate between the ethical views of Kant and those of the utilitarians. Our present situation could be summarized somewhat like this: Kant's criterion of universalizability has some merit — it does seem that if something is right for one person to do, it would be equally right for anyone else in the same position, and that it is wrong for a person in applying a moral rule to make an exception for himself. The concept of universalizable moral rules will be very much with us in the coming pages. At the same time, we cannot find acceptable the entire Kantian system as it stands, with its exceptionless rules and rigorous formalism. But neither can many people rest entirely content with the utilitarian position as developed thus far. This discontent may be less obvious, but it is important to point out that our day-to-day, common-sense ethics, which is admittedly not very thoroughly thought out, markedly disagrees with utilitarianism in some ways. Let us consider some examples.

16. Prima facie duties

When we are asked why we are keeping a certain promise we made, we are inclined to say, "Because I made it." If we said simply, "Because I think that keeping it will produce the most good," our questioner would be a bit surprised and perhaps shocked. He might conclude that on the next occasion we would be likely to break the promise if we thought that doing so would do the most good on that occasion. This is not to say that common-sense ethics insists that we should keep promises on *all* occasions — most people would agree that we should break a promise to save a life, and often for much lesser reasons than that. But at least, most people would hold, we are not justified in breaking it just because, in our considered opinion, doing so will produce the most good in a particular situation.

Again, when we are asked why a certain criminal is being punished, we are likely to say, "Because he committed murder." We are less likely to say, "Because punishing him will do the most good," although we *may* believe this also. Perhaps we believe that both reasons are relevant — but surely not *only* the second. Or consider a man who has been sentenced for a crime which, we happen to know, he did not commit. We may actually believe that keeping him in jail for five years will do the most good — he is a pest, a trouble-maker, a public nuisance, and he would only cause people harm if he were not behind bars. Still, we do not believe it is right to sentence someone for a crime he did not commit, even though the sentence might help him or society or both.

Still further: we believe it is our duty to help our parents and our children (and to a lesser degree other relatives), even though we would do less, or nothing, for those who are not related to us. Most parents consider it their duty to keep their children sound in body and mind insofar as they are able, although they feel no such duty toward the children of others. If parents are required to choose between doing a lesser good for their own children or a greater good for the children of neighbors or strangers, they would without hesitation choose the one for their own children — not as a moral weakness on their part (partiality for their own kin) but as a moral duty. Far from believing that they are violating their duty when they behave thus, they are convinced that they *should* do it.

Blood relationships aside, we generally consider it our duty to help people who are friends of ours more than those who are strangers to us. It is not that we believe we have *no* duties toward strangers: if while driving along the highway we saw a stranger who was the victim of a car accident, we would undoubtedly consider it our duty to stop and be of what help we could. But if a total stranger telephoned us at 3 A.M. and asked us to drive ten miles outside of town where his car had just broken down, most of us would probably feel that we had no obligation whatever to help him; whereas if a personal friend asked, we might feel some obligation. In other words, we do not consider it our duty to confer good impersonally but to confer it only on specific people who are related to us in special ways (blood or friendship). Particularly is this true when the person has done us a good turn: we are more likely to think it our duty to help the person in the broken-down car if that person has done *us* favors in the past. On the face of it at least, this tendency is difficult to square with utilitarianism; for, according to utilitarianism, we should confer our bounties where they will do the most good. If we can do more good for a total stranger by helping him, we should help. But to do so conflicts with our ordinary concept of where our duty lies, for we believe (whether or not we are right in this belief) that we have duties to special persons for special reasons, as distinguished from our one-and-only utilitarian duty to maximize the total good regardless of whether it falls upon friends or strangers.

Suppose that two men, your father and a stranger, are both trapped in a burning building; there is time to rescue (at most) only one of them, and you are the only person nearby. Your father, though he is dear to you personally, is a man of no particular consequence for the world; the other man is a great scientist who, given a few more years of -life, is likely to do more than anyone else in the world in the fight to cure cancer. There is no doubt that the stranger would do far more good for the world than would your father. Which would it be your duty to rescue? There is hardly any doubt that utilitarianism is committed to saying that you should rescue the stranger and let your father burn. But most people would not agree: they would say (and don't we feel this ourselves?) that you should rescue your father, even though rescuing the other man would do more good for the world; *your* duty is toward your father, even though if someone else instead of you were on the scene — someone who was a stranger to both trapped men — that person would rightly rescue the scientist. It is not a question of which one you *would* rescue; 999 out of 1,000 people would rescue their fathers. The question is, which *should* you rescue? And here the conviction of many people would go against that of the utilitarian.

The utilitarian, of course, may say that to give this answer is merely to rationalize one's desires, since most people would prefer to rescue their father anyway (they don't know the stranger and so they have no feeling for him). By rationalizing, they bring their action into line with what they desire anyway — a favorite trick in moral behavior. He will tell you, "Rescuing your father, however noble the impulse, is — in the light of this particular situation — mere sentimentalism: your father is there before you, screaming for help, and he sees you; the sheer immediacy of this agonizing situation and the lifelong memories of your father that well up in your heart in one ghastly moment make the impulse well-nigh overwhelming." But think also of the people who would be saved by the scientist's cure: while you watch your father screaming for help in the burning building, think also, not only of the scientist who is also screaming for help, but of the thousands of people in hospitals all over the world who will scream in agony and in vain if the scientist's life is not saved. As Mill pointed out, that which is in close proximity to us in space and time is likely to exert a far stronger psychological effect on us than that which is remote; but, as Mill also pointed out, we should not let this fact deter us in our estimation of where our duty lies — we should not rationalize an understandable human frailty into a duty. One more example:

> Suppose that two explorers in the Arctic have only enough food to keep one alive till he can reach the base, and one offers to die if the other will promise to educate his children. No other person can know that such a promise was made, and the breaking or keeping of it cannot influence the future keeping of promises. On the utilitarian theory, then, it is the duty of the returned traveler to act precisely as he ought to have acted if no bargain had been made: to consider how he can spend his money most expediently for the happiness of mankind, and, if he thinks his own child is a genius, to spend it on him.[1]

[1] E. F. Carritt, *Ethical and Political Thinking*, p. 64.

Assuming that the returned explorer is financially unable to educate both his own children and those of the dead explorer and assuming that more good can be achieved by educating his own children, since they are worthy of it and the other man's children are dunces, we shall *still* probably feel that the explorer should keep his promise. He has made a solemn promise; a man has agreed to die on the strength of that promise being kept; and we feel that whatever happens that promise *should* be kept. Whatever happens? Well, almost; he should not keep it if keeping it would result in the downfall of civilization, certainly; but he should keep it even in the face of *some* greater good being achieved by his breaking it. He would not be justified in breaking the promise just because he was convinced, even with excellent evidence, that more good could be done by educating his own children than by educating those of the dead explorer.

Again, of course, a utilitarian could reply: "You are made to see half of the picture with great vividness — the dying man on the ice floe, the solemn promise that involves one man's death — but not the other half — the good that could be achieved by the promiser's children if they were given a thorough (and necessarily expensive) education. Since this aspect of the situation, especially since it is some years in the future, is not as vividly before our minds, we tend to the usual, 'sentimental' solution in favor of the immediate and the psychologically compelling appeal. But consider with equal vividness, if you can, the good the survivor can do by educating his own children — they are human beings too and they deserve a break — and the uselessness to everyone concerned that will result from educating dunces. Consider too that no one will ever know that he broke his promise so his breaking it won't have any adverse effect on future promise-keeping — the promiser will never reveal the secret, and no one else will ever know. Consider also the fact that the promisee is dead and will never know the difference; so in this situation, if one wants to be realistic and honestly do what is best rather than indulge in 'noble' sentiments, shouldn't one go against his initial (more human?) impulses and break this promise?"

It is against this background that we can best appreciate the contribution of a contemporary writer, Sir William David Ross. His theory follows closely that of Richard Price in the eighteenth century; but since Ross's is an explicit attempt to mediate between Kant and Mill, it will be most convenient to consider his. Here are several of Ross's main contentions:

1. Duty has a far more *personal* character than would appear from the utilitarian account. Though we have a duty to maximize good, we also have duties on specific occasions to specific people. For example, we have duties toward our parents, our children, those who have done things for us, duties which we do not have — at least not in the same degree — to people to whom we do not stand in such relations. Here Ross holds that common-sense ethics is correct and utilitarianism is mistaken.

2. Duty is *past-looking* as well as *future-looking*. That is to say, some of the acts which are our duty to perform are duties because of events that have occurred in the past, not because they may achieve future good. Not all duties arise *in order that* some future state may be brought about, as the utilitarians allege; some actions become duties *because of* some past action that has already occurred. I should keep a promise, not merely in order to produce the most good in the future (though doubtless more good is preserved by keeping promises than by breaking them), but *because* a promise was made. I should help out a benefactor, not only to produce good in the future, but *because* he has helped me. Ross illustrates the matter thus: Suppose that I have a choice between two acts, A and B. In doing A, I am keeping a promise and doing a total of 1,000 units of good; and in doing B, I am breaking a promise and doing a total of 1,001 units of good. According to the utilitarian, I should do whatever brings about the most good, and therefore I should choose B and break my promise. But to do so, according to Ross, is wrong: my duty is to keep my promise, even if it means that somewhat less total good will be achieved.

One can't escape this conclusion by saying, "Act A will produce the most good after all, because you have forgotten that keeping the promise will also have a favorable effect on future keeping of promises; so keeping the promise, in addition to producing the 1,000 units of good stated in the example, will produce more — say 100 units more — because of its effect on future promise-keeping." This reasoning is setting up new conditions which are not the ones given in the example. In the example, 1,000 units is the *total* amount of good that will be achieved after the bad has been subtracted and after whatever good effect this act has on future promises has been included. This last effect is already figured into the total; without it, the promise-keeping would have produced only 900 units of good. So we can't try to beat the game with this clever device. If we change the condition, then there is no moral problem — both Ross and the utilitarians would agree that we should keep the promise; and the problem generated by the specific example that Ross gives would still remain. Of course, if the amount of good to be achieved by breaking the promise is overwhelming — if by breaking a not-terribly-important promise I could cause a large sum of money to be donated to the muscular dystrophy fund — then I should break the promise. But no *small* edge of good in B over A would justify me in doing B, if it involved the breaking of a promise.

3. Kant got into difficulties because he considered certain kinds of acts, such as killing, lying, and breaking promises, to be wrong under all circumstances. The difficulties were these: (1) he erected certain prohibitions into unconditional rules, although they quite certainly have legitimate exceptions, and (2) he arrived at an impasse in situations of conflict of duty. Kant failed to distinguish absolute, or *unconditional,* duties — those things we must *always do,* no matter what — from *prima facie* duties — those things

which *tend* to be absolute duties. A prima facie duty *is* an absolute duty if no other prima facie duty conflicts with it. Thus, according to Ross, we have a number of prima facie duties. For example, we have a prima facie duty to keep promises and we also have a prima facie duty to produce good (our utilitarian duty). When the prima facie duty to produce good does not interfere with any other prima facie duty, it is our duty to produce the most good possible; but when — as in our example — they interfere with one another, one has to choose between the fulfillment of two prima facie duties; and these are situations of moral conflicts. In Ross's example, we chose the prima facie duty to keep promises over the duty to produce good because the difference in amount of good between A and B was very slight. In other examples — say, there are 10,000 units of good produced by doing B — the duty of producing good would outweigh that of keeping promises, and we should break the promise to promote the great good. Both are prima facie duties, and most situations of moral conflict occur when we have to choose between prima facie duties, neither of which can be simultaneously fulfilled in the action under consideration. We have, then, two prima facie duties, the greater of which should be fulfilled; but neither of them can be an absolute or unconditional duty, for we cannot simultaneously have two absolute but contradictory duties. It can't be our absolute duty both to keep the promise and to break the promise — this would involve a logical contradiction; but it can be, and sometimes is, our lot to have to choose between two prima facie duties.

Here is Ross's list of prima facie duties:

1. There are prima facie duties which arise because of *previous acts of my own*. These are of two kinds: (1) There are duties of *fidelity* to promises (or contracts, or other commitments) which I have voluntarily made and undertaken; these I have a prima facie duty to keep. I have this duty over and above the utilitarian duty to perform what will produce the most good. It is true that keeping promises usually tends to produce good, but keeping promises is not to be treated as simply a species of producing goods; it is a separate prima facie duty on its own. (2) There are duties of *reparation* for previous wrongful acts I have done to others. If I have injured someone or damaged his property, I have a special duty to make a fair reparation for the damage I have caused. For example, my baseball may have broken Mr. A's window. I owe him reparation for this and not Mr. B, even though Mr. A may be rich and in no financial need of such reparation; whereas Mr. B's windows, which I did not damage, are broken and Mr. B has no money to fix them. To make reparation is a duty incumbent on me *because of* a *past* act, not *in-order-that* a certain *future* condition should result. To make reparation is not merely a duty to produce the best possible results, although fulfilling a duty of reparation often succeeds in doing that as well.

2. There are duties which rest not on previous acts of my own but on

previous acts of others. If others have done good to me, I owe them a debt in return — a duty of *gratitude.* My parents have done more for me than my neighbors have, so I owe my parents more in return. If I could achieve 1,000 units of good by conferring some benefit on my parents or 1,001 units of good by conferring a similar benefit on my neighbors, my duty would be to my parents, in spite of the fact that the total *amount* of good produced would be slightly greater the other way.

The prima facie duties listed thus far have been past-looking. Although obeying them may have future effects, their being obligatory arises from past situations rather than from their presumed future effects. But Ross also includes on his list prima facie duties which are future-looking. Thus,

3. There is the duty of *beneficence,* that is, of promoting the maximum possible intrinsic good. This is the sole type of duty emphasized by the utilitarians. In Ross's ethics it is simply one type of duty among others.

4. There is the duty of *nonmaleficence,* or the duty of refraining from doing people harm. This duty is sharply distinguished from the duty of beneficence, and Ross considers it a stronger prima facie duty. I have a duty to help people, but I have an even stronger duty to refrain from harming them. Even if I had no duty to help a stranger, I certainly have a duty not to harm him. It would be wrong to do a certain amount of harm to A in order thereby to do the same amount (or even a greater amount) of good to B. It is wrong to rob Peter to pay Paul, even when doing so helps Paul more than it harms Peter. Ross says, "We should not in general consider it justifiable to kill one person in order to keep another alive, or to steal from one in order to give alms to another."

5. There is also the duty of *justice,* which Ross also believes to be separate from that of beneficence. The duty of justice has to do not with increasing the total *amount* of good to be produced by one's actions but with its *distribution.* Ross says that when there is "the fact or the possibility of a distribution of pleasure or happiness (or of the means thereto) which is not in accordance with the merit of the persons concerned, in such cases there arises a duty to upset or prevent such a distribution." Thus, if I can distribute some good equitably between A and B, I should do so, even if this means a slight decrease in the total amount of good that can be distributed. The concept of justice is a complex one, and we shall discuss it in Chapter 9.

6. There is the duty of *self-improvement.* If I can improve myself in respect of virtue or intelligence, I have a prima facie duty to do so. Presumably this means "even if thereby I did not increase the good of others," for otherwise Ross would not have listed it as a separate type of prima facie duty.

What would a utilitarian be likely to say about these last four — the future-looking members of the list? The duty of beneficence, of course, every utilitarian insists upon. The utilitarian would say that the duty of nonmaleficence was, in effect, already contained in the utilitarian concept of duty, because the duty of bringing about as much intrinsic good as possible already includes that of preventing as much intrinsic evil as possible; and the practice of not harming others is, in any case, amply justified by its consequences. The duty of justice can, perhaps, be fitted into the utilitarian scheme by a bit of amplification which is already implicit in the doctrines of Bentham and Mill; we shall say more about this in Chapter 9. The duty of self-improvement would be admitted, in fact insisted upon, by utilitarians, provided that improving oneself will affect happiness — either one's own or that of others — and this it almost certainly would do; even in those rare cases where improving yourself will not help others, it will probably tend to increase your own long-term happiness, which is also a consequence already included in the utilitarian criterion.

What would the utilitarian say about the past-looking duties? He would agree that paying one's debts and keeping one's promises and returning favors are good practices (with exceptions) for utilitarian reasons. But he cannot agree, while still remaining a utilitarian, that any duty is past-looking. Promises should usually be kept because, on the whole, keeping promises is more productive of good than is breaking them, but of course there are occasions on which promises should be broken, namely when keeping them will not do the most good, even when one has considered their effect on future trust in promises. (On this point there is a fundamental disagreement with Ross, which we have already discussed.)

Does this modification mean that the utilitarian is committed to the view that "we should always let bygones be bygones," that we should never bring up the past because our eyes should always be directed upon the future? Not at all. "You're always bringing up the *past*," says the delinquent child to his parents; "It's dead and gone, why keep dredging it up?" "But," the utilitarian parent might say, "I don't bring up the past simply because it's past but because by doing so, you may learn some lessons from it which you can put to good use in the future. By scrutinizing the source of past mistakes you may be helped to avoid future ones. To bring up the past simply because it's past would be pointless. In the same way, to hold a person to a promise *simply* because he made it, even though no good will come of it and perhaps evil will, would be not only pointless but immoral."

You may remain, after all these considerations, an unregenerate utilitarian; or you may be inclined to say that Ross's more complex set of ethical principles, though they make our duties more complicated than they are in the neat utilitarian system, do bring us nearer the truth than we were before we studied Kant and Ross. We are far from having finished discussing this question. Meanwhile, we may feel a certain dissatisfaction with Ross's ethics, not because his categories are less neat and tidy than the utilitarians' (the truth may be complicated and in fact quite messy, and there is no particular reason why one principle alone is better than many), but for quite different reasons:

1. Where, exactly, is one to draw the line? Between 1,000 and 1,001 units

of good, if choosing the first means keeping a promise and choosing the second means breaking it, we are to choose the first; but between 1,000 and 10,000, we are to choose the second, even if it means breaking the promise. What about 5,000 units, or 2,000, or 3,279? How much good must be produced before we are justified in breaking the promise for its sake? Since we are unable to quantify goods with any precision, the problem does not arise in practice in this numerical form. Still, if the surviving Arctic explorer was justified in breaking his promise if it meant saving civilization but not if it meant educating dunces, we would like to know under exactly *what* conditions he *would* be justified in breaking it, according to Ross. Would the bankruptcy of ten people, for example, be a consequence sufficiently great to entitle the promiser to break his promise? And if so, what criterion is to be employed to arrive at this conclusion?

One may suggest that the utilitarian is scarcely in a position to press this charge, since the consequences of human actions are so far-flung and so difficult to assess that it is impossible, in countless situations, to say definitely what is our duty according to the utilitarian criterion alone. In spite of this impossibility, at least the utilitarian answer to questions of right and wrong is to be determined only in terms of the *consequences* of actions, and, moreover, only those consequences that have to do with human happiness (or anything else that the ideal, or pluralistic, utilitarian may consider intrinsically good); the whole calculation proceeds at least on only one axis. But how are we to weigh the sanctity of promises against the production of good, as Ross's scheme requires? Are we not trying here to weigh and measure incommensurables? If so, how are we ever, especially in difficult situations, to arrive at a satisfactory solution?

2. Moreover, why does Ross list just the prima facie duties that he does? Ross does not claim that his list is complete. But if more could be added to the list, by what principle are we to guide our additions? Here is an example to illustrate the difficulty: Under duties of the first type, duties based on our own previous acts, we have two subdivisions, those based on past promises and those based on past wrongful acts. In the second type of prima facie duties, those based on previous acts of others, we might naturally expect to have two subdivisions also, gratitude for favors done us and revenge for wrongs done us. But the second of these subdivisions never appears on Ross's list: Ross apparently does not believe in vengeance and accordingly he lists no such prima facie duty. Perhaps he is right; few moralists in our century will insist upon a duty of vengeance. But *why* not? Ross gives no *reasons* why a certain type of suggested prima facie duty should or should not be included on his list. So the question remains: "Why, if good done you requires good from you, should not evils done you require evils from you in return?" To return evil for evil would at least make the whole scheme more symmetrical, and no reason has been given why it should not make the scheme better.

In short, no *criteria* are given for the inclusion or exclusion of candidates for the position of prima facie duty. Is there some overall standard by which to judge? Or are we simply to be left with a heterogeneous list of prima facie duties without any unifying principle or any *raison d'être?* It may be that such a list is all we can have and we must rest content with it; perhaps there are simply different kinds of prima facie duties whose nature we "intuit" (of this more in Chapter 11); but if so, what is to prevent others from coming up with a different and conflicting list of prima facie duties? Perhaps Ross is right; perhaps the utilitarian account of duty is too simple, and the Kantian account of duty too rigid; perhaps we do have special duties to special people for special things, and perhaps some of the duties are past-looking; perhaps we feel that we are now, at least, on the right track. But is there any way of pursuing that track, possibly by distilling what is best out of Ross's view and trying to set forth some criterion which he fails to supply?

EXERCISES

1. After reading the following list of moral situations, try to determine what solution a utilitarian would recommend. Then try to determine what solution a disciple of Ross would recommend and why. (Be sure to include a reference to prima facie duties. Do any of these examples impel you to add to Ross's list of prima facie duties?)

a. "I did you lots of favors, didn't I? Besides, I am your brother, and so you owe me something. And you also promised me that if I ever wanted you to do something for me, you would. Well, I'm asking you now. I want you to help me get even with this guy. You engage him in conversation during his walk through the park, and I'll come up from behind, knock him out, and then rob him."

b. "I certainly didn't want my wife to be unfaithful to me during my long absence in the army overseas. But she got lonely, and finally she was unfaithful. The fellow was her own cousin, so I guess it's all right, or at least a lot better than if it had been a total stranger. Blood is thicker than water."

c. Ordinarily you would not hesitate to tell the authorities where the escaped murderer is hiding. But he once saved your life, when he could just as easily have ignored you; in fact by saving yours, he risked losing his own. You feel that you should not do anything to cause him now to lose his. Should you reveal his location to the authorities?

d. A capable young actor who for years has been trying to get a break, is offered a part in a play which may bring him fame and fortune. But he strongly disapproves of the ideas he is called upon to express in his lines, and he believes the entire play is evil and immoral. He knows that if he turns down the part, other actors are ready to step into his place and perhaps handle the part less capably than he. The play is going to be performed anyway, regardless of what he does. Should he nevertheless turn down the part?

e. A man who made his fortune from running gambling establishments and houses of prostitution makes a gift of $500,000 to a church, offering to keep his náme (together with the source of funds) a secret. The church committee tries to decide whether to accept the gift. By accepting it they can do a great deal of good; at the same time they feel that "it's dirty money" and that it will never be blessed coming from such a source.

f. Should American soldiers (in World War II) dress the wounds and administer medication to Japanese prisoners, even though the Americans are almost out of supplies themselves and dressing the enemy's wounds may mean that their own soldiers will have to go without if supplies do not reach them in time?

g. Paying money to a rich creditor may not result in as much total happiness as a poor debtor's keeping it; is it therefore right to repudiate the debt? (How about a situation in which you have a choice between repaying a rich creditor and fulfilling a pledge you have made to a useful charity?)

h. "I can't understand why you are leaving so much money in your will to foreign organizations. Your first prima facie duty is toward your own country."

i. Assume that you know that one hour from now the world will be blown to bits. Are you morally justified in committing any crime you wish, such as rape or torture, since there will be virtually no consequences anyway?

j. A social worker in the slums tries to interest a rich man in giving a large gift for slum clearance and recreation halls to keep delinquents off the streets. But no matter how much the social worker tries, the rich man is not interested. Then the social worker accidentally stumbles onto information about the rich man — information which the rich man would pay heavily not to have published. Is the social worker justified in blackmailing him for the cause of social justice?

k. Should the Countess Walewski, who later became Napoleon's mistress, violate her moral and religious convictions and give herself to him in order that thereby — according to Napoleon's promise — Poland will be saved from destruction?

l. The Countess Walewski loves Napoleon and owes him all her wealth and finery, but she strongly disapproves of his plan to return with an army from Elba to retake France. Should she deliver a message for him which is essential to the success of his plan?

m. You know who murdered your uncle; you saw it happen. But if you testify in court, the gang who killed him will hunt you down and kill you too. The police have offered you protection, but they can't do it for a lifetime, and anyway they can't be foolproof in their protection so you are still in danger. Should you testify, or should you save your skin by refusing, thereby allowing murderers to run loose?

n. An old lady lives with her grandchildren and depends on them for support. She is a Christian, but they are not. As a Christian she feels it her duty to try to convert as many people as possible to Christianity, and she devotes all her spare time to this end. She attends meetings and rallies, is active in church groups and Salvation Army; but she asks herself what kind of a Christian she can call herself if she doesn't even pay attention to those in her own family. At the same time, she hesitates to try to influence her granddaughter and the granddaughter's husband, because she is beholden to them financially and depends on them for a roof over her head. Should she be less concerned for their souls because she depends on them for money?

o. A Catholic priest in Italy worked with the Allied underground, and one day bombed a supply train. As a result, the Nazis shot twenty hostages per day and promised to continue to do so until the culprit was found. But he did not give himself up to the authorities. When asked whether he failed to do so because of future deeds of valor which he would yet perform, he replied. "No. I am the only priest in this remote region, and the people depend on me for the sacraments. What dies is only the physical bodies of twenty hostages a day; we hope their immortal souls will be saved. But until there is another priest in this region to replace me, I must remain alive, for without me many souls cannot be saved; they depend upon me for absolution."

p. "But it was only because I owed you the money and had to get it back to you somehow — that is why I resorted to bribery and illegal manipulations."

"And am I expected to praise you for doing that? It's only because you took the money from me in the first place without my consent that you had to go to such lengths to return it; — if you hadn't performed that initial act, all that followed would have been unnecessary. If you do something wrong, should I praise you for doing other things, no matter what, to redress the wrong, to restore the balance you destroyed? It's not as if you had done anything to *increase* the balance in my favor by performing these acts."

q. In a story taken from life (made famous in the motion picture *Call Northside 777*), an aged mother scrubs floors for almost twenty years to earn the money required to get lawyers to reopen the case for her son, who has been sentenced to life imprisonment for a murder he did not commit. Would she have been entitled (or had a duty?) to gain the money by illegal means if she had been unable to do so in any other way?

r. The owner of a grocery store refuses to extend credit to any customer. His helper, nevertheless, extends credit to a poor family who, because of the husband's invalidism and the wife's illness, would otherwise go hungry. Would you say that the helper has both a prima facie duty to obey his employer's orders? and also a duty to produce good? Which should be paramount in this instance? (If there were no danger of the helper's being caught and losing his job, do you think this condition would make any difference?)

s. A soldier comes home from war and after considerable detective work discovers that it was his own brother who revealed to the Nazis that his (the soldier's) wife was a member of the underground, with the result that they tortured her to death. He swears to track down his brother and kill him. But his uncle says, "No, blame me. I won't live long anyway, and that way you'll keep the family together. Live for the future, not in the past, and let bygones be bygones." Should he accept the uncle's advice?

t. One of Caesar's trusted servants came to him when Pompey, who was threatening Caesar's rule, and his fellow conspirators were guests on board Caesar's ship, and said, "I can put something into their drinks, and get rid of them all at once" (or words to this effect). Caesar looked at him and said, "Alas, if you had done this without my knowledge, and come to me afterwards, I would have praised you. But now that you have mentioned it to me beforehand, it is my duty to condemn you for it and take whatever measures I can to prevent you from realizing your plan."

2. Do you think that the duty of nonmaleficence would prohibit you from ever inflicting harm on people in order that good may come out of it?

3. Assume that we have a prima facie duty of gratitude toward our parents because of the things they have done for us. Now suppose our parents are shiftless good-for-nothings who have caused us much harm and no good (other than bringing us into the world in the first place). Is it still our duty to benefit them — more than other people — just because they are our parents? (If your father were a drunken scoundrel, would you arrive at a different conclusion in the burning building example?)

4. If we have prima facie duties toward our parents for things they have done for us, do we have duties to our young children, who have as yet done nothing for us? (On what principle might you base the belief in a prima facie duty toward one's children?)

5. Does the duty of fidelity — for instance, to the wishes of the dead — require that we always abide by the terms of our parents' will? What if your father willed his entire estate to his cat?

6. Read Patrick Nowell-Smith's discussion, in his book *Ethics* (pp. 239-44), of situations involving desert islands and arctic explorers. Does it affect your estimate of Ross's theory?

7. A. C. Ewing, in his book *Ethics,* attempts to reconcile utilitarianism with Ross's modified formalism by simply saying that (1) it is always our duty to produce the most intrinsic good and that (2) keeping promises, doing return favors, behaving out of gratitude to parents, etc., are all intrinsically good. Do you find his solution satisfactory? Explain.

8. Comment on the following conversations in the light of Ross's theory.

a. "It's always wrong to refuse to help someone who needs help and to whom you can give it. As Brandt says (From Richard Brandt, *Ethical Theory.* Englewood Cliffs, N. J.: Prentice-Hall, 1959, p. 437. Reprinted by permission of the publisher.): 'If I meet an utter stranger . . . and he is in dire need or suffering, he has a moral right to my assistance.' "

"Maybe so, but why the emphasis? It puts such a premium on helping those people that I *happen to run across.* I may help a stranger suffering from a car accident, but what of my neighbor who needs help of various kinds but never seeks me out or appears bloodily on my doorstep? A professor friend of mine said, 'I don't go out of my way to help people, but I try to help them if they come to me.' But this is to reward the brash and penalize the timid. Why pick on just these to help?"

"Well, you have to draw the line somewhere. After all you can't spread yourself so thin that you don't succeed in really doing much for anybody."

"That's true, but why *this* principle of selection? Why those you happen to know well rather than those you don't, or those who come to you rather than those who need you just as badly but don't dare to?"

b. "I believe we have special duties of gratitude to those who have benefited us."

"What a merry-go-round that would cause: A helps B, B helps A back, A helps B again, and so on. Life is a series of curtsies and retreats. And meanwhile other people stand in the background needing help much more. One wealthy snob introduces another one to a person he wants to know; the second later returns the favor, and so on back and forth *ad nauseam* (this is like the Kentucky feuds that never end, only with favors instead of harm). Each person thinks he has a special duty to the other because of past favors, so he does it even though the other hasn't the slightest utilitarian *need* for it. Meanwhile others, who haven't been caught up in this stupid merry-go-round of favors, need the favors badly and never get them."

c. "Except in direst extremity, promises should be kept. Making a promise commits you to keeping it."

"Well, I should think it is more important to be sure you make the right promises in the first place. If you make a rash promise or a hasty one or an unreasonable one, you are less guilty for breaking it than you are for making such a promise in the first place. Suppose you promise someone you won't tell anyone what he is about to tell you, and he then confides in you that he is about to blow up the bank or kill his wife. Promises to keep a secret no matter what it is, are always unwise. What if you have promised to do something that injures another or violates his rights? Then, it would seem, you've put yourself in the position of violating some rule no matter what you do — breaking your promise or standing by and seeing a great injustice done. It is less important to keep promises once made than to be very careful about what promises we make to begin with."

d. "I believe in the motto 'Forgive and forget.'"

"I don't. I can forgive no end, but I never forget a thing."

(Do you consider this reply to be against past-looking duties, in favor of them, or neither? If the person explained, "I say this because if I forget one, I might make the same mistake again," how would you construe it?)

9. Do you feel that you have a stronger prima facie duty toward your mother than toward your father? toward your children than toward either parent? toward your stepchildren? toward a neighbor than toward an uncle you barely know? toward your aunt than toward your cousin? Do you have a duty toward the brother of a friend? toward a stranger recommended by a friend? to a third cousin you have never seen? toward someone you knew in childhood but haven't seen for years? In short, does blood relationship make any difference, over and above the fact that you know the person or care for him or that he has done things for you in the past?

10. To the question "Why did you do this?" each of the following answers refers to the past or present, not to the future. Evaluate each of them.

a. Because Grandfather would have wanted me to.

b. Because I said I would.

c. Because it's the law (not because obeying the law will have good results).

d. I used my influence to get theater tickets for him because he's a friend; I wouldn't do it for just anyone.

e. I didn't cheat him because — well, one just doesn't do such things.

f. Because that's the way I was brought up.

g. Because, though I admit I stole, I don't think it's as bad stealing from a stranger as from a friend.

h. I cheated him because people have been cheating me all my life.

READING LIST, SECTION 16

Blanshard, Brand. "The Impasse in Ethics and a Way Out." *Univ. of California Publications in Philosophy,* Vol. 28, No. 2 (1954), pp. 93-112.
Brandt, Richard. *Ethical Theory.* Englewood Cliffs, N. J.: Prentice-Hall, 1959, pp. 387-96.
Carritt, Edgar F. *Ethical and Political Thinking.* New York: Oxford Univ. Press, 1947, Ch. 9.
Ewing, Alfred C. *The Definition of Good.* New York: Macmillan, 1947, Ch. 6.
———. *Ethics.* New York: Macmillan, 1953, Ch. 5.
———. "Utilitarianism." *Ethics,* Vol. 58 (1948), pp. 100-11.
Pickard-Cambridge, W. A. "Two Problems about Duty." Pts. 1 and 2. *Mind,* Vol. 41 (1932), pp. 145-72, 311-40.
Price, Richard. *A Review of the Principle Questions in Morals* (1758). New York: Oxford Univ. Press, 1949.
Prichard, Harold Arthur. "Moral Obligation" and "The Obligation to Keep a Promise." In Prichard, H. A., *Moral Obligation.* New York: Oxford Univ. Press, 1949, pp. 87-163, 169-79.
Raphael, David Daiches. *Moral Judgment.* New York: Macmillan, 1955.
Ross, Sir William David. *Foundations of Ethics* (Gifford lectures, 1935-36). New York: Oxford Univ. Press, 1939.
———. *The Right and the Good.* New York: Oxford Univ. Press, 1930.

17. Rule-utilitarianism

We have now considered Ross's line of objection to the utilitarian ethics. Whether (at this stage) you agree with Ross or with the utilitarians or with neither, it will be interesting to consider a different line of criticism of utilitarianism, a criticism which attempts at the same time to make its peace with Kant and Ross. As usual, we can best bring out this line of criticism by considering several examples.

1. In order to receive a high enough grade average to be admitted to medical school, a certain student must receive either an A or a B in one of my courses. After his final examination is in, I find, on averaging his grades, that his grade for the course comes out a C. The student comes into my office and begs me to change the grade, on the ground that I have not read his paper carefully enough. So I reread his final exam paper, as well as some of the other papers in the class in order to get a better sense of comparison; the rechecking convinces me that his grade should be no higher than the one I have given him — if anything, it should be lower. I inform him of my opinion and he still pleads with me to change the grade,

but for a different reason. "I know I didn't deserve more than a C, but I appeal to you as a human being to change my grade, because without it I can't get into medical school, which naturally means a great deal to me." I inform him that grades are supposed to be based on achievement in the course, not on intentions or need or the worthiness of one's plans. But he pleads: "I know it's unethical to change a grade when the student doesn't deserve a higher one, but can't you please make an exception to the rule just this once?" And before I can reply, he sharpens his plea: "I appeal to you as a utilitarian. Your goal is the greatest happiness of everyone concerned, isn't it? If you give me only the grade I deserve, who will be happier? Not I, that's sure. Perhaps you will for a little while, but you have hundreds of students and you'll soon forget about it; and I will be ever so much happier for being admitted into a school that will train me for the profession I have always desired. It's true that I didn't work as hard in your course as I should have, but I realize my mistake and I wouldn't waste so much time if I had it to do over again. Anyway, you should be forward-looking rather than backward-looking in your moral judgments, and there is no doubt whatever that much more happiness will be caused (and unhappiness prevented) by your giving me the higher grade even though I fully admit that I don't deserve it."

After pondering the matter, I persist in believing that it would not be right to change the grade under these circumstances. Perhaps you agree with my decision and perhaps you don't, but *if* you agree that I should not have changed the grade, and *if* you are also a utilitarian, how are you going to reconcile such a decision with utilitarianism? *Ex hypothesi,* the greatest amount of happiness will be brought about by my changing the grade, so why shouldn't I change it?

Of course, if I changed the grade and went around telling people about it, my action would tend to have an adverse effect on the whole system of grading — and this system is useful to graduate schools and future employers to give some indication of the student's achievement in his various courses. But of course if I tell no one, nobody will know, and my action cannot set a bad example to others. This in turn raises an interesting question: If it is wrong for me to do the act publicly, is it any the less wrong for me to do it secretly?

2. A man is guilty of petty theft and is sentenced to a year in prison. Suppose he can prove to the judge's satisfaction that he would be happier out of jail, that his wife and family would too (they depend on his support), that the state wouldn't have the expense of his upkeep if he were freed, and that people won't hear about it because his case didn't hit the papers and nobody even knows that he was arrested — in short, everyone concerned would be happier and nobody would be harmed by his release. And yet, we feel, or at least many people would, that to release him would be a mistake. The sentence imposed on him is the minimum permitted by law for his offense, and he should serve out his term in accordance with the law.

3. A district attorney who has prosecuted a man for robbery chances upon information which shows conclusively that the man he has prosecuted is innocent of the crime for which he has just been sentenced. The man is a wastrel who, if permitted to go free, would almost certainly commit other crimes. Moreover, the district attorney has fairly conclusive evidence of the man's guilt in prior crimes, for which, however, the jury has failed to convict him. Should he, therefore, "sit on the evidence" and let the conviction go through in this case, in which he knows the man to be innocent? We may not be able to articulate exactly *why,* but we feel strongly that the district attorney should not sit on the evidence but that he should reveal every scrap of evidence he knows, even though the revelation means releasing the prisoner (now known to be innocent) to do more crimes and be convicted for them later.

x: It seems to me that some acts are right or wrong, not *regardless* of the consequences they produce, but *over and above* the consequences they produce. We would all agree, I suppose, that you should break a promise to save a life but not that you should break it whenever you considered it probable (even with good reason) that more good effects will come about through breaking it. Suppose you had promised someone you would do something and you didn't do it. When asked why, you replied, "Because I thought breaking it would have better results." Wouldn't the promise condemn you for your action, and rightly? This example is quite analogous, I think, to the example of the district attorney; the district attorney might argue that more total good would be produced by keeping the prisoner's innocence secret. Besides, if he is released, people may read about it in the newspaper and say, "You see, you can get by with anything these days" and may be encouraged to violate the law themselves as a result. Still, even though it would do more total good if the man were to remain convicted, wouldn't it be wrong to do so in view of the fact that he is definitely innocent of *this* crime? The law punishes a man, not necessarily because the most good will he achieved that way, but because he has committed a crime; if we don't approve of the law, we can do our best to have it changed, but meanwhile aren't we bound to follow it? Those who execute the law are sworn to obey it; they are *not* sworn to produce certain consequences.

y: Yes, but remember that the facts *might* always come out after their concealment and that we can never be sure they won't. If they do, keeping the man in prison will be far worse than letting the man go; it will result in a great public distrust for the law itself; nothing is more demoralizing than corruption of the law by its own supposed enforcers. Better let a hundred human derelicts go free than risk that! You see, *one* of the consequences you always have to consider is the effect of *this* action on the *general practice* of lawbreaking itself; and when you bring in *this* consequence, it will surely weigh the balance in favor of divulging the information that will release the innocent man. So utilitarianism will still account quite satisfactorily for this case. I agree that the man should be released, but I do so on utilitarian grounds; I needn't abandon my utilitarianism at all to take care of this case.

x: But your view is open to one fatal objection. You say that one never can be sure that the news *won't* leak out. Perhaps so. But suppose that in a given case one *could* be sure; would that really make any difference? Suppose you are the only person that knows and you destroy the only existing evidence. Since *you* are not going to talk, there is simply no chance that the news will leak out, with consequent damage to public morale. Then is it all right to withhold the information? You see, I hold that if it's wrong not to reveal the truth when others might find out, then it's equally wrong not to reveal it when *nobody* will find out. You utilitarians are involved in the fatal error of making the rightness or wrongness of an act depend on whether performing it will ever be publicized. And I hold that it is immoral even to consider this condition; the district attorney should reveal the truth regardless of whether his concealing it would ever be known.

y: But surely you aren't saying that one should *never* conceal the truth? not even if your country is at war against a totalitarian enemy and revealing truths to the people would also mean revealing them to the enemy?

x: Of course I'm not saying that — don't change the subject. I am saying that *if* in situation S it is wrong to convict an innocent man, then it is equally wrong whether or not the public knows that it is wrong; the public's knowledge will certainly have bad consequences, but the conviction would be wrong anyway even *without* these bad consequences; so you can't appeal to the consequences of the conviction's becoming public as grounds for saying that the conviction is wrong. I think that you utilitarians are really stuck here. For you, the consideration "but nobody is ever going to know about it anyway" *is* a relevant consideration. It has to be; for the rightness of an act (according to you) is estimated in terms of its total consequences, and its total consequences, of course, include its effects (or lack of effects) on other acts of the same kind, and there won't be any such effects if the act is kept absolutely secret. You have to consider all the consequences relevant; the matter of keeping the thing quiet is one consequence; so you have to consider this one relevant too. Yet I submit to you that it isn't relevant; the suggestion "but nobody is going to know about it anyway" is not one that will help make the act permissible if it wasn't before. If anything, it's the other way round: something bad that's done publicly and openly is not as bad as if it's done secretly so as to escape detection; secret sins are the worst. It is just as bad, if not worse, for the explorer to break his promise to the dying man in secret, as for him to break it publicly, even if publicly announcing it may tend to lead to more breaches of faith in the future.

y: I deny what you say. It seems to me worse to betray a trust in public, where it may set an example to others, than to do so in secret, where it can have no bad effects on others.

x: And I submit that you would never say that if you weren't already committed to the utilitarian position. Here is a situation where you and practically everyone else would not hesitate to say that an act done in secret is no less wrong than when done in public, were it not that it flies in the face of a doctrine to which you have already committed yourself on the basis of quite different examples.

4. Here is a still different kind of example. We consider it our duty in a democracy to vote and to do so as wisely and intelligently as possible, for only if we vote wisely can a democracy work successfully. But in a national election my vote is only one out of millions, and it is more and more improbable that *my* vote will have any effect upon the outcome. Nor is my failure to vote going to affect other people much, if at all. Couldn't a utilitarian argue this way: "My vote will have no effect at all — at least far, far less than other things I could be doing instead. Therefore, I shall not vote." Each and every would-be voter could argue in exactly the same way. The result would be that nobody would vote, and the entire democratic process would be destroyed.

What conclusion emerges from these examples? If the examples point at all in the right direction, they indicate that there are some acts which it is right to perform, even though by themselves they will not have good consequences (such as my voting), and that there are some acts which it is wrong to perform, even though by themselves they would have good consequences (such as sitting on the evidence). But this conclusion is opposed to utilitarianism as we have considered it thus far.

"But," you may object, "Ross takes care of all that, and we've discussed it already." True — Ross tries to account for all such situations in terms of prima facie duties. In the example of law-enforcement officials, there is the prima facie duty of fidelity to one's oath of office, in which one has sworn to observe and administer the law (not one's own theories of right and wrong); in the example of changing the student's grade, there is a duty of fidelity — to whom? well, to one's profession, and to one's employers, in grading entirely on the basis of achievement (even though the teacher may not have *explicitly* sworn to do this); and in the example of the Arctic explorers there is the duty of fidelity to one's promisee; in the example of the burning building there is the duty of gratitude. But we have already voiced some qualms about accepting prima facie duties as the answer and letting it go at that. We desired some principle in terms of which the prima facie duties are to be recognized as such — or perhaps a system which need not appeal to prima facie duties at all. We are now about to consider such a system.

A. Rule-utilitarianism and objections to it

The batter swings, the ball flies past, the umpire yells "Strike three!" The disappointed batter pleads with the umpire, "Can't I have four strikes just this once?" We all recognize the absurdity of this example. Even if the batter could prove to the umpire's satisfaction that he would be happier for having four strikes this time, that the spectators would be happier for it (since most of the spectators are on his side), that there would be little dissatisfaction on the side of the opposition (who might have the game clinched anyway), and that there would be no effect on future baseball games, we would still consider his plea absurd. We might think, "Perhaps baseball would be a better game — i.e., contribute to the greatest total enjoyment of all concerned — if four strikes were permitted. If so, we should change the rules of the game. But until that time, we must play baseball according to the rules which are now the accepted rules of the game."

This example, though only an analogy, gives us a clue to the kind of view we are about to consider — let us call it *rule-utilitarianism*. Briefly stated (we shall amplify it gradually), rule-utilitarianism comes to this: Each act, in the moral life, falls under a *rule;* and we are to judge the rightness or wrongness of the act, not by *its* consequences, but by the consequences of its universalization — that is, by the consequences of the adoption of the *rule* under which this act falls. This is the interpretation of Kant's categorical imperative which we promised (page 292) to discuss later — an interpretation which differs from Kant in being concerned with consequences, but retains the main feature which Kant introduced, that of universalizability.

Thus: The district attorney may do more good in a particular case by sitting on the evidence, but even if this case has no consequences for future cases because nobody ever finds out, still, the general policy or *practice* of doing this kind of thing is a very bad one; it uproots one of the basic premises of our legal system, namely that an innocent person should not be condemned. Our persistent conviction that it would be wrong for him to conceal the evidence in this case comes *not* from the conviction that concealing the evidence will produce less good — we may be satisfied that it will produce more good in this case — but from the conviction that the *practice* of doing this kind of thing will have very bad consequences. In other words, "Conceal the evidence when you think that it will produce more happiness" would be a bad rule to follow, and it is because this *rule* (if adopted) would have bad consequences, not because *this act* itself has bad consequences, that we condemn the act.

The same applies in other situations: Promises solemnly made, for which a man has paid his life, should be kept; if a policy of not doing so when nobody knew about it were to be introduced, the results would be bad, for nobody would any longer have reason to believe that a promise would be kept if the person who made the promise could break it in secret and thought he could do the most good by breaking it. And so too for the example of the student: perhaps I can achieve more good, in this instance, by changing the student's grade, but the consequences of the general practice of changing students' grades for such reasons as these would be very bad indeed; a graduate school or a future employer would no longer have reason to believe that the grade-transcript of the student had any reference to his real achievement in his courses; he would wonder how many of the high grades resulted from personal factors like pity, need, and irrelevant appeals by the student to the teacher. The same considerations apply also to the voting example: if Mr. Smith can reason that his vote won't make any difference to the outcome, so can Mr. Jones and Mr. Robinson and every other would-be voter; but if everyone reasoned in this way, no one would vote, and this *would* have bad effects. It is considered one's duty to vote, not because the consequences of one's not doing so are bad, but because the consequences of the general practice of not doing so are bad. To put it in Kantian language, the maxim of the action, if universalized, would have bad consequences. But the individual act of *your* not voting on a specific occasion — or of any *one* person's not voting, as long as *others* continued to vote — would probably have no bad consequences.

There are many other examples of the same kind of thing. If during a water shortage there is a regulation that water should not be used to take baths every day or to water gardens, there will be virtually no bad consequences if only *I* violate the rule. Since there will be no discernible difference to the city water supply and since my plants will remain green and fresh and pleasant to look at, why shouldn't I water my plants? But if everyone watered his plants, there would not be enough water left to drink. My act is judged wrong, not because of *its* consequences, but because the consequences of everyone doing so would be bad. If I walk on the grass where the sign says, "Do not walk on the grass," there will be no ill effects; but if everyone did so it would destroy the grass. There are some kinds of act which have little or no effect if any one person (or two, or three) does them but which have very considerable effects if everyone (or even just a large number) does them. Rule-utilitarianism is designed to take care of just such situations.

Rule-utilitarianism also takes care of situations which are puzzling in traditional utilitarianism, situations which we have already commented on, namely, the secrecy with which an act is performed. "But no one will ever know, so my act won't have any consequences for future acts of the same kind," the utilitarian argued; and we felt that he was being somehow irrelevant, even immoral: that if something is wrong when people know about it, it is just as wrong when done in secret. Yet this condition *is* relevant according to traditional utilitarianism, for if some act with bad consequences is never known to anyone, this ignorance does mitigate the bad consequences, for it undeniably keeps the act from setting an example (except, of course, that it may start a habit in the agent himself). Rule-utilitarianism solves this difficulty. If I change the student's grade in secret, my act is wrong, in spite of its having almost no consequences (and never being known to anyone else), because if I change the grade and don't tell anyone, how do I know how many other teachers are changing their students' grades without telling anybody? It is the result of the *practice* which is bad, not the result of my single action. The result of the practice is bad whether the act is done in secret or not: the result of the practice of changing grades in secret is just as bad as the results of the practice done in full knowledge of everyone; it would be equally deleterious to the grading system, equally a bad index of a student's actual achievement. In fact, if changing grades is done in secret, this in one way is worse; for prospective employers will not know, as they surely ought to know in evaluating their prospective employees, that their grades are not based on achievement but on other factors such as poverty, extra-curricular work load, and persuasive appeal.

Rule-utilitarianism is a distinctively twentieth-century amendment of the utilitarianism of Bentham and Mill, often called *act-utilitarianism*. (We have referred to the principles of Bentham and Mill simply as "utilitarianism" so far in this book.) Since this pair of labels is brief and indicates clearly the contents of the theories referred to, we prefer these terms to a second pair of labels, which are sometimes used for the same theories: *restricted utilitarianism* as opposed to *unrestricted* (or *extreme*, or *traditional*) *utilitarianism*. (Whether or not Mill's theory is strictly act-utilitarianism is a matter of dispute. Mill never made the distinction between act-utilitarianism and rule-utilitarianism, and his doctrine has always been interpreted as being act-utilitarianism. This is the interpretation taken by G. E. Moore in his very precise account of act-utilitarianism in Chapters 1 and 2 of his *Ethics*. Some of Mill's examples, however, have to do not with individual acts but with general principles and rules of conduct. Mill and Bentham were both legislators, interested in amending the laws of England into greater conformity to the utilitarian principle; and to the extent that Mill was interested in providing a criterion of judging rules of conduct rather than individual acts, he may be said to have been a rule-utilitarian.)

Much more must be said before the full nature of the rule-utilitarian theory becomes clear. To understand it better, we shall consider some possible questions, comments, and objections that can be put to the theory as thus far stated.

1. Doesn't the same problem arise here that we discussed in connection with Kant, the problem of *what* precisely we are to universalize? Every act can be put into a vast variety of classes of acts; or, in our present terminology, every act can be made to fall under many different general rules. Which rule among this vast variety are we to select? We can pose our problem by means of an imaginary dialogue referring back to Kant's ethics and connecting it with rule-utilitarianism:

A: Whatever may be said for Kant's ethics in general, there is one principle of fundamental importance which must be an indispensable part of every ethics — the principle of universalizability. If some act is right for me to do, it would be right for all rational beings to do it; and if it is wrong for them to do it, it would be wrong for me too.

B: If this principle simply means that nobody should make an exception in his own favor, the principle is undoubtedly true and is psychologically important in view of the fact that people constantly do make exceptions in their own favor. But as it stands I can't follow you in agreeing with Kant's principle. Do you mean that if it is wrong for Smith to get a divorce, it is also wrong for Jones to do so? But this isn't so. Smith may be hopelessly incompatible with his wife, and they may be far better off apart, whereas Jones may be reconcilable with his wife (with some mutual effort) and a divorce in his case would be a mistake. Each case must be judged on its own merits.

A: The principle doesn't mean that if it's right for one person, A, to do it, it is therefore right for B and C and D to do it. It means that if it's right for one person to do it, it is right for anyone *in those circumstances* to do it. And Jones isn't in the same circumstances as Smith. Smith and his wife would be better off apart, and Jones and his wife would be better off together.

B: I see. Do you mean *exactly* the same circumstances or *roughly* the same (similar) circumstances?

A: I think I would have to mean exactly the same circumstances; for if the circumstances were not quite alike, that little difference might make the difference between a right act (done by Smith) and a wrong act (done by Jones). For instance, if in Smith's case there are no children and in Jones's case there are, this fact may make a difference.

B: Right. But I must urge you to go even further. Two men might be in exactly the same *external* circumstances, but owing to their *internal constitution* what would be right for one of them wouldn't be for the other. Jones may have the ability to be patient, impartial, and approach problems rationally, and Smith may not have this ability; here again is a relevant difference between them, although not a difference in their external circumstances. Or: Smith, after he reaches a certain point of fatigue, would do well to go fishing for a few days — this would refresh and relax him as nothing else could. But Jones dislikes fishing; it tries and irritates and bores him; so even if he were equally tired and had an equally responsible position, he would not be well advised to go fishing. Or again: handling explosives might be all right for a trained intelligent person, but not for an ignorant blunderbuss. In the light of such examples as these, you see that under the "same circumstances" you'll have to include not only the external circumstances in which they find themselves but their own internal character.

A: I grant this. So what?

B: But now your universalizability principle becomes useless. For two people never *are* in exactly the same circumstances. Nor can they be: if Smith were in exactly the same circumstances as Jones, including all his traits of character, his idiosyncracies, and his brain cells, he would *be* Jones. You see, your universalizability principle is inapplicable. It would become applicable only under conditions (two people being the same person) which are self-contradictory, — and even if not self-contradictory, you'll have to admit that two exactly identical situations never occur; so once again the rule is inapplicable.

A: I see your point; but I don't think I need go along with your conclusion. Smith and Jones should do the same thing only if their situation or circumstances are the same in certain *relevant respects*. The fact that Jones is wearing a white shirt and Smith a blue one, is a difference of circumstances, but, surely, an *irrelevant* difference, a difference that for moral purposes can be ignored. But the fact that Smith and his wife are emotionally irreconcilable while Jones and his wife could work things out, would be a morally relevant circumstance.

B: Possibly. But how are you going to determine which differences are relevant and which are not?

Kant, as we saw on page 290, never solved this problem. He assumed that "telling a lie" was morally relevant but that "telling a lie to save a life" was not; but he gave no reason for making this distinction. The rule-utilitarian has an answer.

Suppose that a red-headed man with one eye and a wart on his right cheek tells a lie on a Tuesday. What rule are we to derive from this event? Red-headed men should not tell lies? People shouldn't lie on Tuesdays? Men with warts on their cheeks shouldn't tell lies on Tuesdays? These rules seem absurd, for it seems so obvious that whether it's Tuesday or not, whether the man has a wart on his cheek or not, has nothing whatever to do with the rightness of his action — these circumstances are just *irrelevant*. But this is the problem: how are we going to establish this irrelevance? What is to be our criterion?

The criterion we tried to apply in discussing Kant was to make the rule more *specific*: instead of saying, "This is a lie and is therefore wrong," as Kant did, we made it more specific and said, "This is a lie told to save a life and is therefore right." We could make the rule more specific still, involving the precise circumstances in which this lie is told, other than the fact that it is told to save a life. But, now it seems, the use of greater specificity will not always work: instead of "Don't tell lies," suppose we say, "Don't tell lies on Tuesdays." The second is certainly more specific than the first, but is it a better rule? It seems plain that it is not — that its being a Tuesday is, in fact, wholly irrelevant. Why?

"Because," says the rule-utilitarian, "there is no difference between the effects of lies told on Tuesdays and the effects of lies told on any other day. This is simply an empirical fact, and because of this empirical fact, bringing in Tuesday is irrelevant. If lies told on Tuesdays always had good consequences and lies told on other days were disastrous, then a lie's being told on a Tuesday would be relevant to the moral estimation of the act; but in fact this is not true. Thus there is no advantage in specifying the subclass of lies, 'lies told on Tuesdays.' The same is true of 'lies told by redheads' and 'lies told by persons with warts on their cheeks.' The class of lies can be made more specific—that is no problem—but not more *relevantly* specific, at least not in the direction of Tuesdays and redheads. (However, the class can be made more relevantly specific considering certain other aspects of the situation, such as whether the lie was told to produce a good result that could not have been brought about otherwise.)"

Consider by contrast a situation in which the class of acts can easily be made relevantly more specific. A pacifist might argue as follows: "I should never use physical violence in any form against another human being, since if everyone refrained from violence, we would have a warless world." There are aspects of this example that we cannot discuss now, but our present concern with it is as follows. We can break down violence into more specific types such as violence which is unprovoked, violence in defense of one's life against attack by another, violence by a policeman in catching a lawbreaker, violence by a drunkard in response to an imaginary affront. The effects of these subclasses of violence do differ greatly in their effects upon society. Violence used by a policeman in apprehending a lawbreaker (at least under some circumstances, which could be spelled out) and violence used in preventing a would-be murderer from killing you, do on the whole have good effects; but the unprovoked violence of an aggressor or a drunkard does not. Since these subclasses do have different effects, therefore, it *is* relevant to consider them. Indeed, it is imperative to do so: the pacifist who condemns *all* violence would probably, if he thought about it, not wish to condemn the policeman who uses violent means to prevent an armed madman from killing a dozen people. In any event, the effects of the two subclasses of acts are vastly different; and, the rule-utilitarian would say, it is accordingly very important for us to consider them—to break down the general class of violent acts into more specific classes and consider separately the effects of each one until we have arrived at subclasses which cannot *relevantly* be made more specific.

How specific shall we be? Won't we get down to "acts of violence to prevent aggression, performed on Tuesdays at 11:30 P.M. in hot weather" and subclasses of that sort? And aren't these again plainly irrelevant? Of course they are, and the reason has already been given: acts of violence performed on Tuesdays, or at 11:30 P.M., or by people with blue suits, are no different in their effects from acts-of-violence-to-prevent-aggression done in circumstances other than these; and therefore these circumstances, though more specific, are not relevantly more specific. When the consequences of these more specific classes of acts differ from the consequences of the more general class, it is this specific class which should be considered; but when the consequences of the specific classes are not different from those of the more general class, the greater specificity is irrelevant and can be ignored.

The rule, then, is this: we should consider the consequences of the general performance of certain classes of actions only if that class contains within itself no subclasses, the consequences of the general practice of which would be either better or worse than the consequences of the class itself.

Let us take an actual example of how this rule applies. Many people, including Kant, have taken the principle "Thou shalt not kill" as admitting of no exceptions. But as we have just seen, such principles can be relevantly made more specific. Killing for fun is one thing, killing in self-defense another. Suppose, then, that we try to arrive at a general rule on which to base our actions in this regard. We shall try to arrive at that rule the general following of which will have the best results. Not to kill an armed bandit who is about to shoot you if you don't shoot him first, would appear to be a bad rule by utilitarian standards; for it would tend to eliminate the good people and preserve the bad ones; moreover, if nobody resisted aggressors, the aggressors, knowing this, would go hog-wild and commit indiscriminate murder, rape, and plunder. Therefore, "Don't kill except in self-defense" (though we might improve this rule too) would be a better rule than "Never kill." But "Don't kill unless you feel angry at the victim" would be a bad rule, because the adoption of this rule would lead to no end of indiscriminate killing for no good reason. The trick is to arrive at the rule which, if adopted, would have the very best possible consequences (which includes, of course, the absolute minimum of bad consequences). Usually no simple or easily statable rule will do this, the world being as complex as it is. There will usually be subclasses of classes-of-acts which are relevantly more specific than the simple, general class with which we began. And even when we think we have arrived at a satisfactory rule, there always remains the possibility that it can relevantly be made more specific, and thus amended, with an increase in accuracy but a consequent decrease in simplicity.

To a considerable extent most people recognize this complexity. Very few people would accept the rule against killing without some qualifications. However much they may preach and invoke the rule "Thou shalt not kill" in situations where it happens to suit them, they would never recommend its adoption in all circumstances: when one is defending himself against an armed killer, almost everyone would agree that killing is permissible, although he may not have formulated any theory from which this exception follows as a logical consequence. Our practical rule against killing contains within itself (often not explicitly stated) certain *classes of exceptions:* "Don't kill *except* in self-defense, in war against an aggressor nation, in carrying out the verdict of a jury recommending capital punishment." This would be a far better rule — judged by its consequences — than any simple one-line rule on the subject. Each of the classes of exceptions could be argued pro and con, of course. But such arguments would be empirical ones, hinging on whether or not the adoption of such classes of exceptions into the rule would have the maximum results in intrinsic good. (Many would argue, for example, that capital punishment achieves no good effects; on the other hand, few would contend that the man who pulls the switch at Sing Sing is committing a crime in carrying out the orders of the legal representatives of the state.) And there may always be other kinds of situations that we have not previously thought of, situations which, if incorporated into the rule, would improve the rule — that is, make it have better consequences; and thus the rule remains always open, always subject to further qualification if the addition of such qualification would improve the rule.

These qualifications of the rule are not, strictly speaking, *exceptions to* the rule. According to rule-utilitarianism, the rule, once fully stated, admits of no exceptions; but there may be, and indeed there usually are, numerous classes of exceptions *built into the* rule; a simple rule becomes through qualification a more complex rule. Thus, if a man kills someone in self-defense and we do not consider his act wrong, we are not making him an exception to the rule. Rather, his act *falls under* the rule — the rule that includes killing in self-defense as one of the classes of acts which is permissible (or, if you prefer, the rule that includes self-defense as one of the circumstances in which the rule against killing does not apply). Similarly, if a man parks in a prohibited area and the judge does not fine him because he is a physician making a professional call, the judge is not extending any favoritism to the physician; he is not making the physician an exception to the rule; rather, the rule (though it may not always be written out in black and white) includes within itself this recognized class of exceptions — or, more accurately still, the rule includes within itself a reference to just this kind of situation, so that the action of the judge in exonerating the physician is just as much an application of the rule (not an exception to it) as another act of the same judge in imposing a fine on someone else for the same offense.

We can now see how our previous remarks about acts committed in secret fit into the rule-utilitarian scheme. On the one hand, the rule "Don't break a promise except (1) under extreme duress and (2) to promote some very great good" is admittedly somewhat vague, and perhaps it could be improved by still further qualification; but at least it is much better than the simple rule "Never break promises." On the other hand, the rule "Don't break a promise except when nobody will know about it" is a bad rule: there are many situations in which keeping promises is important (as in the example of the Arctic explorer), situations in which promises could not be relied on if this rule were adopted. That is why, among the circumstances which excuse you from keeping your word, the fact that it was broken in secret is not one of them — and for a very good reason: if this class of exceptions were incorporated into the rule, the rule's adoption would have far worse effects than if it did not contain such a clause.

2. Having explained how rule-utilitarianism applies to specific situations, we can hardly help being struck by its similarity, in the outcome of these situations, to the view of Ross which we considered in the preceding section.

As opposed to Kant, Ross and rule-utilitarians both agree that we should *sometimes* break our promises. As opposed to act-utilitarians, Ross and rule-utilitarians both agree that we should not break promises just because we think (even with good reason) that doing so will produce the most good in these particular situations.

Even though Ross and the rule-utilitarians agree on this point, they agree for different reasons. There is in rule-utilitarianism no reference to prima facie duties. Just as in act-utilitarianism, there is only one standard by which all particular moral questions are to be decided. In act-utilitarianism it is this: do that particular act which will produce the maximum good. In rule-utilitarianism it is this: act according to the rules whose adoption would produce the maximum good. Since there is no reference in rule-utilitarianism to prima facie duties, there is no problem about which prima facie duties are to take precedence or about how we are to be prevented from adding to the list of prima facie duties or subtracting from it.

Moreover, the rule-utilitarian does not agree with Ross that some duties are past-looking: all duties are in-order-that, not because-of. In this insistence, according to the rule-utilitarian, the act-utilitarian was right. But Ross was right too in holding that not all duties are encompassed by the concept of doing good by each individual act; that, for example, we have special duties to special people. For instance, we have special duties to persons to whom we have made promises, not simply because we have made them, but because the policy of keeping promises is a good policy. If people were permitted to break promises in those individual instances in which more good could be done by breaking them, *less* good would result from following such a rule than from following the rule that we should keep promises except under certain specifiable types of circumstances (which we have already discussed). The whole justification for *having* such a rule is that this rule produces the best consequences. The justification of a *rule* is always future-looking (good-production), though the justification of the individual act is neither future-looking nor backward-looking but simply the fact that it falls under the rule.

For example, in a given situation one might have a choice between doing some good for one's own children and doing a greater good for the neighbors' children. Viewed simply as an act, the second choice (*ex hypothesi*) produces the most good. Still, most people are convinced — and quite impartially, not simply because they love their own children more — that one should help his own children more than his neighbor's children. Ross would account for this conviction in terms of special prima facie duties, such as fidelity to an obligation one has undertaken by having children in the first place. The rule-utilitarian does not have this defense, for he never brings in prima facie duties. Instead he asks, "Which *rule* would have the best results — the rule of helping one's own children or of helping one's neighbors' children (even if the benefit to the latter were greater)?" The answer is not obvious, for the greater benefit to my neighbor's children may be considerable; they may need help far more than my own children. On the other hand, the policy of helping one's neighbors' children would have some effects that can mildly be described as dubious. The policy of helping one's neighbors' children with money, advice, punishment for infractions of rules, and so on, could become a policy of meddlesomeness and interference. Such acts, if they occurred on a widespread scale, would seriously undermine parental authority and frustrate the children's need for a certain *unity* of authority — some one person or pair of persons to whom they are responsible, even if that source of authority is far from good; to have no one person or pair of persons (typically the parents) to whom they are responsible but to have authority scattered about among neighbors and relatives, would be catastrophic for their developing personalities. Hence the general policy of noninterference, which prevails at present, would be justified by rule-utilitarianism (as against the policy of indiscriminate giving, advising, etc.), except in situations of extreme hardship, such as gross parental neglect or extreme poverty. This provision could be built into the rule so that the rule would read, "Do not interfere with your neighbors' children except . . ." rather than "Interfere with your neighbors' children whenever you can help them more than your own children." Thus Ross was right in thinking that we have a greater obligation toward our own children; but, according to rule-utilitarianism, we have the obligation because the policy of doing things for our own children is, on the whole, a better one (in its results) than the policy of doing things for everybody else's children.

The same considerations apply to helping one's own parents. The policy of helping one's parents, if one is able to support them and they need support, is better than that of each person trying to distribute his beneficence over the whole neighborhood; that is, the consequences of adopting "Support your parents" as a rule are better than those of "Try to support everybody in the vicinity." At least, *if* the effect of adopting the first rule of conduct is better, then rule-utilitarianism has justified our ordinary conviction that we should help our own parents at the expense of the neighbors. Which policy would in fact have the best consequences is, of course, an empirical matter; what we are concerned with here is the kind of principle involved in working out an answer.

3. In Ross's ethics there are certain prima facie duties, which apparently are the same for all men, at no matter what time or place. How does rule-utilitarianism stand on this matter? Is it more compatible with ethical relativism than Ross's ethics seems to be?

Rule-utilitarianism and act-utilitarianism are alike with regard to relativism. They are *not* relativistic in that they have one standard, one "rule of rules," one supreme norm, applicable to all times and situations: "Perform that act which will produce the most intrinsic good" (act-utilitarianism), "Act according to the rule whose adoption will produce the most intrinsic good" (rule-utilitarianism). But within the scope of that one standard, the recommended rules of conduct may well vary greatly from place to place. To use our example from Chapter 1: in a desert area the act of wasting water will cause much harm and is therefore wrong, but it is not wrong in a region where water is plentiful. In a society where men and women are approximately equal in number, it will be best for a husband to have only one wife; but in a society in which there is great numerical disparity between the two, this arrangement may no longer be wise. So much for act-utilitarianism; the same goes for rule-utilitarianism. The rule "Never waste water" is a good rule, indeed an indispensable rule, in a desert region but not in a well-watered region. Monogamy seems to be the best possible marital system in our society but not necessarily in all societies — it depends on the conditions. What are the best acts and the best rules at a given time and place, then, depends on the special circumstances of that time and place. Some conditions, of course, are so general that the rules will be much the same everywhere: a rule against killing (at least within the society) is an indispensable condition of security and survival and therefore must be preserved in all societies.

The situation, then, is this: Rule or Act A is right in circumstances C_1, and rule or Act B is right in circumstances C_2. In X-land circumstances C_1 prevail, so A is right; and in Y-land circumstances C_2 prevail, so B is right. Perhaps this is all the relativism that ethical relativists will demand.

4. Can't there be, in rule-utilitarianism, a conflict of rules? Suppose you have to choose between breaking a promise and allowing a human life to be lost. We have already seen what Ross says on this matter. What would the rule-utilitarian say? Which rule are we to go by?

No rule-utilitarian would hold such a rule as "Never break a promise" or "Never take a human life." Following such rigid, unqualified rules would certainly not lead to the best consequences — for example, taking Hitler's life would have had better consequences than sparing him. Since such simple rules would never be incorporated into rule-utilitarian ethics to begin with, there would be no conflict between these rules. The rule-utilitarian's rule on taking human life would be of the form, "Do not take human life except in circumstances of types A, B, C . . ." and these circumstances would be those in which taking human life *would* have the best consequences. And the same with breaking promises. Thus, when the rules in question are fully spelled out, there would be no conflict.

In any event, if there were a conflict between rules, there would have to be a second-order rule to tell us which first-order rule to adopt in cases of conflict. Only with such a rule would our rule-utilitarian ethics be *complete,* i.e., made to cover every situation that might arise. But again such a second-order rule would seldom be simple. It would not say, "In cases of conflict between preserving a life and keeping a promise, always preserve the life." For there might always be kinds of cases in which this policy would not produce the best consequences: a president who has promised something to a whole nation or who has signed a treaty with other nations which depend on that treaty being kept and base their own national policies upon it, would not be well advised to say simply, "In cases of conflict, always break your word rather than lose one human life." In cases of this kind, keeping the promise would probably produce the best results, though the particular instance would have to be decided empirically. We would have to go through a detailed empirical examination to discover which rule, among all the rules we might adopt on the matter, would have the best consequences if adopted.

5. Well then, why not just make the whole thing simple and say, "Always keep your promises except when breaking them will produce the most good," "Always conserve human life except when taking it will produce the most good"? In other words, "In every case do what will have the best consequences"—why not make this the Rule of Rules? To do so is to have act-utilitarianism with us once again; but why not? Is there anything more obvious in ethics than that we should always try to produce the most good possible?

"No," says the rule-utilitarian, "not if this rule means that we should always do the individual *act* that produces the most good possible. We must clearly distinguish rules from acts. 'Adopt the rule which will have the best consequences' is different from 'Do the act which will have the best consequences.' (When you say, 'Always do the most good,' this is ambiguous — it could mean either one.)" The rule-utilitarian, of course, recommends the former in preference to the latter; for if everyone were to do acts which (taken individually) had the best consequences, the result would *not* in every case be a policy having the best consequences. For example, my not voting but doing something else instead may produce better consequences than my voting (my voting may have no effect at all); your not voting will do the same; and so on for every individual, as long as most *other* people vote. But the results would be very bad, for if each individual adopted the policy of not voting, nobody would vote. In other words, the rule "Vote, except in situations where not voting will do more good" is a rule which, if followed, would *not* produce the best consequences.

Another example: The rule "Don't kill except where killing will do the most good"—which the act-utilitarian would accept—is not, the rule-utilitarian would say, as good a rule to follow as "Don't kill except in self-defense. . . ." (and other classes of acts which we discussed earlier). That is, the rule to prohibit killing except under special kinds of conditions specified in advance would do more good, if followed, than the rule simply to refrain except when not refraining will do more good. The former is better, not just because people will rationalize themselves into believing that what they want to do will produce the most good in a particular situation (though this is very important), but also because when there are certain standard classes of exceptions built into the rule, there will be a greater *predictability* of the results of such actions; the criminal will know what will happen if he is caught. If the law said, "Killing is prohibited except when it will do the most good," what could you expect? Every would-be killer would think it would do the most good in his specific situation. And would you, a potential victim, feel more secure or less secure if such a law were enacted? Every criminal would think that he would be exonerated even if he were caught, and every victim (or would-be victim) would fear that this would be so. The effects of having such a rule, then, would be far worse than the effects of having a general rule prohibiting killing, with certain classes of qualifications built into the rule.

There is, then, it would seem, a considerable difference between act-utilitarianism and rule-utilitarianism. Let us take a few more examples and see how the difference works.

a. A man is sick with some disease which makes him hideous to look at; his visage causes such extreme revulsion in others that the unpleasantness of the experience of looking at him far outweighs the pleasure he will have in his few remaining months of life. Therefore, some people decide to kill him. Assume that this act will have no effects on future acts because they will assassinate him secretly and never tell anyone else; and assume, if you like, that the murderers will then take a drug which blots the entire episode from their memory. Still, wouldn't the act be wrong? Why? Not, according to the rule-utilitarian, because the act wouldn't produce more intrinsic good in this case, but because such a *rule* (a rule permitting this type of act) could not be defended; in fact if such a rule were operative, it would have horrible effects on society.

b. If you don't pay the money you owe a rich man but give it instead to a poor man to whom you don't owe it, you may be doing more good: the rich man will never miss it and the poor man desperately needs it. And we can eliminate the effect on future actions (the causal factor) by specifying that no one will ever know. Yet would it be right to give the poor man the money if your act means not repaying the rich man? Some may say, "Yes"; but are they just as sure that this act would be right as they are that the act will produce the most good? Such a rule — that you should give money where it is needed rather than where you legally owe it — would have some very unfortunate effects if universalized; at least, it would upset the whole borrowing-and-lending policy upon which much of our economy depends.

c. Suppose that you decide to bypass the law, after you have driven your car through a red light, by paying the arresting officer a bribe instead of paying the fine in traffic court. In this particular case paying a bribe might do more good: the policeman needs the money more than the city does; and you won't have to take half a day off work to appear in court. The amount involved is so small that the city won't miss it. Yet the rule-utilitarian would argue that it would not be right to offer the bribe, because the general practice of bribery cannot be justified by the utilitarian criterion; it would in fact undermine our whole system of law.

d. The same applies in the case of cheating on your income tax. You may argue, "I need the money badly, and the amount is so small compared with the huge amounts in government finance that the government will never miss it." And all this may be true: you can do much more good with your money than by paying it to the government — at least as long as others continue to pay their tax to support a governmental structure. But such a *rule* could hardly be justified: for clearly we need money for public utilities, defense, and so on. Thus, the rule-utilitarian would say, it would be wrong to do it, in spite of the fact that you could put the money to good use otherwise.

e. There is a moral difference between actively *taking* a life and passively *permitting* someone to sacrifice his life willingly in the face of a great need. (Compare Ross's duty of beneficence to the duty of nonmaleficence.) In many instances, at least, the effects would be practically the same: the man is just as dead both ways, no one may know, and good effects may accrue from his death. Yet many feel that the first act is wrong, the second not necessarily. It would be wrong for a physician in an experiment with disease germs to *force* you to sacrifice your life for the advancement of medicine, whereas it would not be wrong for him to accept your sacrifice if freely made. The individual act of forcing you may have very good effects, when you consider the good done by it; why then is it wrong? Because the general *rule* permitting this compulsion to be exerted on people would have extremely bad effects. (Again, this is not to say that there are *no* conditions under which one should take a life. It is constantly done in war.)

6. "But," one may ask, "hasn't act-utilitarianism already taken care of all or most of these things, by including among the consequences of an act its effect upon *future actions of the same kind?* Thus, every instance in which a promise is broken tends to weaken confidence in promises (in the promisor as well as in others who know the promise was broken), and this bad result of the act of breaking promises may well outweigh all the other good results of breaking this particular promise. Assassinating an incompetent president, thus causing him to be replaced by an excellent vice-president, might have the best results in this instance and produce much good; but it is still wrong because this one act would set a very bad precedent — on the basis of it someone might later assassinate a president, thus automatically replacing him with an incompetent vice-president. Besides, consider the effects of this one act on public confidence in law, security of life and limb, and so on."

It is true, as we have seen, that act-utilitarianism includes a reference to *all* the consequences of this individual act, thus including the effects of this act on future acts. But still, the rule-utilitarian will say, this modification doesn't go far enough. For instance, it doesn't take care of those situations, already discussed, in which the violation of the rule is secret and will have no effects (except on the violator, and it may have little or no effect on him). The rule-utilitarian does not, in fact, use the criterion "What will be the effects of *this* act, including its effects on other acts of the same kind?" but rather "What would be the effects of the adoption of this rule (exemplified by this act) as a general rule?" The rule-utilitarian says that if the results of the adoption of this rule were bad, then the act falling under the rule is wrong *regardless* of whether or not it leads to other acts of the same kind.

Is the question whether or not this act leads to other acts (usually of the same kind) then irrelevant? Are we not even to consider whether or not this act will set a precedent for others? Yes, according to the rule-utilitarian, it *is* relevant, but only when it can be put into the rule itself — and it can. Thus, consider the rule "Never under any circumstances steal, except in order to preserve a life." In general, on the one hand, it would be better to steal than to allow a life to be lost, so the rule as it stands is certainly better than the rule *"Never* steal." On the other hand, it could be still further improved to read, "It is permissible to steal if thereby you can save a life (yours or another), *unless* doing so would lead (beyond a certain point) to other acts of theft which are *not* committed simply to preserve life." That would take care of the possibility that an act of theft, even under these unusual circumstances, would not be justified if it led to a great many *other* acts of theft which were *not* committed under these unusual circumstances.

In the terminology of one contemporary writer (A. K. Stout), the act-utilitarian principle is *causal:* it is concerned with other acts of the same kind only when this act will causally affect the commission of other acts of this kind. The rule-utilitarian principle is not causal but *hypothetical:* it appeals not to the consequences of this act but to the consequences of its universalization, that is, to the adoption of it as a general policy. It is hypothetical in that it says, *"If* this type of behavior were admitted as a general policy or rule, would it have better effects than the adoption of other rules we might think of?" If the consequences of this policy are on the whole better than that of any other policy, considering the total consequences of having such a policy, then this is the best policy and the acts falling under it are right.

But this position raises a new question: Is whether or not other people will follow the rule of no relevance at all to whether I should follow it? Must I act in splendid isolation of what other people are likely to do with regard to this rule?

7. Thus far we have been presenting rule-utilitarianism in its severely hypothetical form: not the effect of *this* act on other acts of the same kind, but the effect of the adoption of this *rule* as a general rule of conduct. Thus, we should not cheat on our income tax, we should not condemn an innocent man, we should not walk on the grass, we should not waste water dur-

ing a water shortage, we should not shirk our duties as voters, *not* because
any one such act would have bad consequences by itself (though it may),
but because the *rule* permitting such action would not be a good rule — the
consequences of its adoption would be bad, or less good than the consequences of the adoption of a different rule.

But, we may now be tempted to ask, doesn't what other people do matter at all? Suppose that everyone else, or almost everyone else, violates a
rule, should I keep it just the same, if the rule is good? Should I refrain
from walking on the grass even when almost everyone does walk on it and
the grass is destroyed anyway? Would this not be a useless gesture on my
part? Or suppose I am habitually prompt in keeping my engagements and
when I have an appointment for 2 P.M., I am there at 2 P.M. on the dot;
but most people are not very punctual. Should I continue to be punctual,
even though most people are not (and because they are not, most people
who issue invitations don't even expect promptness)? Or suppose I am extremely careful about writing the complete address on envelopes, including
the postal zone number, making my handwriting legible, and getting the
position of the lines right. I take such pains so that the postal authorities
won't have to spend valuable time trying to decipher my writing or figure
out where the letter is supposed to go. But I realize that most people are not
very careful about addresses: they cost postal clerks much added time and
energy, thus adding a bit to the tax bill for more hours of postal help. Now,
I know that practically everyone else is not going to address envelopes carefully, no matter what I do; those who know my habit may admire me for
my care, but they also think me a bit of a fool, and it's not going to change
their habits anyway. The question is, "Should I keep on being careful about
this matter all the same?" The time that *my* little bit of care will save the
postal authorities is negligible. Or suppose I live in a nation in which hardly
anyone pays his income tax, where it is a national habit or pastime to evade
it and (unofficially) no one is really expected to pay it in full. Should I be
a martyr and pay it in full anyway, thus, in effect, taking upon myself the
tax burdens of others, and in spite of the fact that my act would not set an
example to others but only make them call me a fool?

Of course, in those cases in which there is good reason to believe that
my doing the good deed will serve to set an example for others so that they
will follow suit, then clearly I should do the good deed. But what of those
cases in which it is clear that others won't follow my example? I may go
down fighting, I may give my life uselessly — but should I, when it is painfully apparent that nobody else is going to follow the rule, or even pay any
attention to what I am doing?

There is no general agreement, even among rule-utilitarians, as to what
one should do in such a situation. Here is one writer's view: Suppose that
a certain evil can be avoided only if a *large number of people* refrain from
acts of a certain kind. Then

If I have reason to suppose that the others will not refrain, I surely have reason not to refrain either, as my only reason for refraining is my desire to avoid causing the evil consequences. If these (evil consequences) cannot be avoided, I have no reason not to indulge myself. If the grass is not going to grow anyway, why should I make the detour?

It is no good arguing that I am not entitled to do wrong just because other people might or probably would. For I am not doing wrong. I have no moral reason for the sacrifice. I need no justification or excuse, for my behavior is wrong only if *I have no reason to think* that others will refuse to make the sacrifice. If I have reason to think they will refuse to make it, then I have reason to think that my own sacrifice will be in vain; hence I have reason against making it.

Of course, if the results are *very* undesirable and my sacrifice is *very* small, and I am not very certain what the others will do, I should take the risk of making the sacrifice even if it turns out to have been in vain. But, otherwise, reason will support the opposite course.[1]

But Baier's conclusion is not the end of the matter. Suppose that I break a rule just because I think that other people will do so too. (What I think may or may not be correct.) Other people, then, are entitled to do so just as I am: they may break a rule because they think that I will. And so we all break it. But surely this is not a desirable state of affairs if the rule is a good one. One suggestion, then, is this: I am justified in breaking a rule only if I *know* that all, or most, people will break it anyway, regardless of what I do; in that event my keeping it will serve no useful purpose and will indeed be a "useless gesture." But I am very seldom in a position to know this; usually I have to act on probabilities; the best I can usually say is that I *think,* with good reason (and I could state the reasons), that others will violate the rule. If I *did* know, then my violation of the rule would be all right; but if I only *think* it, even with good reason, my thinking would still not justify me in breaking it, for everyone else might think the same thing with equally good reasons.

The probability or otherwise of other people doing what I do *does* have a bearing on what my duty to do an action is, if it would have good consequences if everybody else did the same. It is true that, if I only have good reason for *thinking* that other people will not do what I do, then my duty to be just in a hard case still applies. For other people's reasons for thinking that theirs will not be the general practice are as good as mine, and if everybody failed to apply a rule in a hard case merely because they had good reasons for thinking that others would not do the same, bad consequences would result. But if I had *conclusive* reasons for thinking that other people would not do the same, then it would be my duty to relieve the hard case. For only *one* person can have conclusive reasons for thinking that other people will not relieve the hard cases he relieves, and, from one person's relieving a hard case, no disastrous consequences follow . . .

[1] From Kurt Baier, *The Moral Point of View.* Ithaca, N. Y.: Cornell Univ. Press, 1958, pp. 211-12. Reprinted by permission of the publisher.

My knowledge of the behavior of other people is a characteristic which relevantly specifies the class of actions, the consequences of which it is my duty to consider. I have a duty to perform a certain action, although believing that other people will *not* perform it, because *if everybody who believed that other people will not perform it were to do similar actions, good consequences would result.*[1]

In other words, the rule "If you think that other people won't do X, you need not do X either" is not a good rule to follow: everyone might then violate a good rule in the belief that others would do the same; whereas if everyone believed that others would violate the rule, but adhered to it anyway, good consequences would result from this adherence.

There is a kind of chain reaction here: Suppose I think that other people will violate a certain good rule, so I violate it; and you, thinking that I and others will violate it, therefore violate it yourself (whereas you wouldn't have if you hadn't thought this); and the same for everyone. The wide circulation of the belief that others will violate the rule, actually *causes* more people to violate it. This tendency shows that violating a rule because you think that others will do so is a very touchy sort of thing: it may generate an increase in the very violations which it is desirable to prevent. That is why we have to be so sure that others will violate it anyway before we indulge in a violation ourselves.

Consider this point also: If I may include among my deliberations on what it is right to do, the consideration of whether or not others will do the same, then *they,* for their part, may include a consideration of whether others will do the same, and for them *that "other" includes me.* In judging how they will act, I must judge how they believe I will act; and they in their turn must have a belief about what I believe they believe. But how can they have a true belief about what my belief is, when my belief in turn depends on what their belief is? Their belief includes a belief about me, but my belief does not include a belief about myself.

Following this line of reasoning, we conclude that we are *not* justified in breaking a rule just because we think (even with good reason, but short of certainty) that other people will break it. For suppose that these special circumstances — my belief about what others will do — were a good and sufficient reason for my breaking the rule.

> If these special circumstances are a good and sufficient reason for *my* breaking the rule, then they would be a good and sufficient reason for everyone else breaking it in similar circumstances. But I can see that if everyone else *did* break it, the consequences would be thoroughly bad, so they cannot be a good reason for everyone's breaking it. Therefore they cannot be a good reason for *my* breaking it. . . .
> If X (the special circumstances) is a good and sufficient reason for Y (my doing it) then it is also a good and sufficient reason for Z (everyone's doing it).

[1] J. Harrison, *Proceedings of the Aristotelian Society*, Vol. 53 (1952-53), pp. 128-29.

But Z has bad consequences and so there can be no good and sufficient utilitarian reason for Z. Therefore X is not a good reason for Z; therefore it is not a good reason for Y.[1]

Thus, in deciding whether or not to break the rule, you should not be deterred from following the rule by the belief that others will *probably* break it:

> When a utilitarian asks himself what others would probably do in his circumstances, consistency does not demand that he shall assume . . . that they will be asking the same question and will be guided by the degree of their assurance about the answer to it. The question for him is rather: "What ought *any* man to do in a world in which not all men do as they ought? [2]

On the one hand, then, we should not be deterred from following a good rule by the belief that others will probably not follow it; but, on the other hand, neither are we to base our actions on what things would be like in an ideal world: we have to consider what are the best rules to follow in *this* world, a world in which many others will not do what is right. We shall try to mediate between two extremes: not wasting ourselves uselessly, yet not being swayed from following a rule that has great utility because of the belief — even if that belief should turn out to be true — that others will fail to follow it; for if everyone acted on that principle, no one would follow the rule, and the welfare of the human race would be in a worse position than it would be in if a heroic few were to follow the rule in defiance of the many.

B. *Attitude-utilitarianism*

In conclusion, we may mention a recent view which on the whole supplements and reinforces rule-utilitarianism, a view which takes as its starting point not the acts which we perform but the attitudes which are determinants of actions.[3] According to *attitude-utilitarianism,* we should do our best to cultivate those attitudes which would be the most likely to produce the most good if generally adopted. One aspect of this view has already been alluded to in discussing the question "Why be moral" (pages 183-84).

If each person is interested in his own welfare and not at all in that of other human beings, it is virtually certain that less good will exist in the world than if each person is possessed of a genuine sympathy and concern for others, which (as we have already seen) will broaden the scope of his satisfactions. If people set a high value on cooperation — not merely to promote their own ends, but also because they have a sincere concern for human well-being — more good will exist in the world than if they are constantly engaged in cutthroat competition. It is true, of course, that there are some

[1] A. K. Stout, *Australasian Journal of Philosophy*, Vol. 32 (1954), p. 21.
[2] *Ibid.*, p. 22.
[3] The author of this view is Michael Scriven.

areas in which an egoistic attitude probably *is* conducive to the welfare of society. For example, in a society which encourages free competition, if a factory owner refrained from putting the latest improvements into his business lest he make more money than his competitor or if a contestant withdrew from a contest lest he win and thus prevent someone else from winning, progress would stop and life would become a series of curtsies and retreats. But even in these areas there would be more happiness all around if each person could take a certain pride in the accomplishments of others — if a person could say sincerely, "I have to hand it to him, he beat me to it but it's a wonderful idea he had, and I'm happy for him" — and if he could be genuinely concerned to help other human beings when they are in trouble or in need, without feeling that thereby *he* is being robbed or cheated.

The goal is not simply that people should help others — grudgingly, or even from a sense of duty — but that they should *enjoy* doing so. If people have developed within themselves an outgoing attitude which permits them to help others quite willingly and spontaneously, without begrudging it as a sacrifice, then there will be more happiness in the world than if they helped grudgingly or not at all. If I am the kind of a person who can help others in this spirit, *I* shall find life more rewarding than if I cannot (this point was already made in discussing "why be moral"); but also (and this is the point now) *others* will find life more rewarding. Since I should develop those attitudes which, if generally adopted, will result in the most happiness, clearly I should try to develop this one.

Consider the alternatives. (1) If I am genuinely concerned for the welfare of my fellow men, not only shall I not infringe upon their rights and do things that will injure them, but I shall not *want* to infringe upon their rights or to injure them. And this attitude, if I combine it with due exercise of intelligence, is the best guarantee that I *shall* not do so. Of course the same applies to their attitudes toward me. A universal attitude of mutual concern for one another — "no man is an island" — will yield a society in which the most possible good exists.

(2) If, however, I have not genuinely developed this attitude of mutual concern but only obey society's rules because I have to (in outward conformity only), then I shall be a far less happy person than if I can derive a genuine satisfaction from obeying them; and so will other people, insofar as they are aware of the attitude manifested in my actions. I shall still be an egoist at heart whose outer actions clash with his inner feeling; this conflict will decrease my happiness and also theirs; and I shall still behave on the basis of my egoistic attitude when I feel that I can get by with it, even to the detriment of others.

(3) Worse still, if I do not give even outward conformity but pursue my ends at the expense of others and have no thought for them when I injure them or when I advance myself to their detriment, then I shall be doing society even more harm. I shall probably be harming myself as well: for if

I break the law, I must live in a state of insecurity, not knowing when the law will catch up with me, even though I may pretend not to care; and if I cheat or swindle others, I shall thereby increase the chances that I shall be cheated and swindled by them. So much for their relation to me; but the same applies of course to my relation to them. There will then be a society of maximum friction, each person trying to outsmart and outmaneuver the other, with no one being able to count on any human sympathy. A society dominated by such an attitude would be the worst of all. The best society would be brought about through the cultivation of universal human sympathy. (Not pity, which is the feeling of the one on top for the miserable creatures down below; but sympathy, a concern by equals for equals.)

Indeed, the cultivation of such an attitude increases the chances not only of mutual well-being but, in extreme circumstances, of life itself, on which all well-being depends. When one person must give his life to enable others to live (as our Arctic explorer did), there is more chance for survival in a group possessing these attitudes. If you are one of three persons, one of whom must die to save the other two, your own chances of living are better if the others are not egoists; for if they are, they will be likely to try to destroy your life, in order that thereby they may live; whereas if they are genuinely concerned for your survival as well as for their own (not perhaps as much, yet genuinely concerned), then they will not kill you to achieve their own survival. Even if they die, their death will not be a total loss to them, for one of their values (your life) will still be preserved. The same is true for you, if you are the one who must die: you will not try to kill the others to attain your own survival, and if you must die, you can do so with greater equanimity, without complete despair or frustration, if the lives of others have value for you.

"But," you may ask, "isn't there a paradox here, analogous to the hedonistic paradox (page 134)? If the only reason you develop an attitude of concern for others is in order to gain more out of life yourself, aren't you an egoist still?" But remember that attitudes are relatively permanent things, not the kind of thing we can switch on and off at will or as the occasion demands. Once you *have* an attitude of genuine concern for others, you will no longer be an egoist — at least not in the sense of a person who is concerned only for his own welfare and has no concern for that of others. Your initial motive for having *become* a different kind of person may have been egoistic, but you can no longer be described as egoistic *after* you have fully developed the attitude of human sympathy and concern. For the sources of unhappiness to the egoist — such as seeing another person succeed if he has more ability than you — will no longer be sources of unhappiness to you. Having become the kind of person who genuinely cares about others, you will no longer experience the same unhappiness at his success as you would had you remained an egoist, nor will you be torn by envy and resentment. In other words, you will not *be* the kind of person you were before — you were an egoist before you cultivated the new attitude (from whatever motive), but you are one no longer.

"But how can we develop these attitudes?" you continue. "Since you say they *are* semipermanent things, how can we achieve them? Not by swallowing a pill." Certainly we cannot swallow a sympathy-pill, for no such pill exists. But we can, over a period of time, develop the habit of identifying ourselves with other people so that we can share their experiences and take joy in their successes. We do not have to remain the kind of person who can enjoy happiness only when others are unhappy, or who can take pride in his achievements only after he has strewn the field with the corpses of his competitors. We do not *have* to remain in the jungle. But the process is gradual and admittedly difficult to develop to a high degree. As Aristotle said, it is only by engaging in virtuous activity that one can become virtuous. At first we do it outwardly without inner willingness; but then, as we cultivate the habit, gradually "second nature becomes first nature" and we find ourselves enjoying what we once performed mechanically. (Learning to swim is not fun at first either, but as we develop the ability by being in the water, gradually we come to enjoy it.)

Unconvinced, you reply, "I can see how the best results would occur, both for you and for society, if you develop genuine sympathy and concern in a society in which *others have already done so*. But what if others are strictly out for themselves and get no satisfaction from your successes? Wouldn't you be a sheep in a den of wolves?" Admittedly things would be more difficult if nobody else has the human sympathy which you possess. You will have to "play it cautious" with them while yet retaining your concern for their welfare. But it is still to your own interest, and to that of society in general, for you to develop and retain your attitude even under these hard conditions. Even if you can instill sympathy in only a few others — say in your own children — you will increase the measure of the world's happiness by that tiny portion. If your child grows up possessing this sympathy, then there will be at least one person whom you can trust, one person whom you can rely on when in trouble or in need, one person with whom you can share your joys and troubles with no fear of envy or retaliation. There will be just that much more happiness in the world as a result of this one series of shared experiences. And for every other person whom you can lead into the cultivation of such an attitude, there will be that much more security, that much more shared experience, that much more reward to you and them mutually. Properly begun, such an attitude would tend to spread. And the more it spreads, the better it will be for society and for you. Ideally, you will have a state of society in which there is no conflict of interests, because what is to the interest of others will, because of the nature of your own attitudes, also be to your own.

EXERCISES

1. How would a rule-utilitarian handle the following situations? Pay special attention to the consideration "But suppose everyone did the same."

a. "If I do a bit of small pilfering from the office in which I work, the loss will be negligible. The few things I take mean more to me on my limited income than they would to the multimillionaire management."

b. "Why sell it legally? You can get much more for it on the black market."

c. The credit company spends thirty dollars tracking you down to pay a ten-dollar debt which you owe them. Is this foolish on their part?

d. "But it does make a difference whether everyone else does it too. I probably won't try to bribe a policeman on a traffic charge if no one else does, but if it's an accepted custom (however illegal) I shall be more inclined to do the same and to feel justified in doing it — especially if the money would only go for graft anyway if I paid it to the city and if my right action in refusing to bribe would not deter anyone else from doing it."

e. "But you can change my grade, can't you? just this once? Can't you *ever* make any exceptions to your confounded rules?"

f. "Sure I stole the money out of the pockets of the man who was lying drunk in the gutter. If I hadn't done it, the next person would have, and I might as well get it as he. Besides, I probably needed it more."

g. "Yes, I did want more Christmas cards of that particular design, but I thought that if I bought the whole supply (as I wanted to) nobody else would be able to buy any of that design. So I refrained." (Would you arrive at the same conclusion if it were a matter of buying the entire available supply of an essential foodstuff in a time of shortage?)

h. "What do I care what my apartment looks like after I've moved out of it? I don't know the next tenant from a hole in the ground. *Après moi le deluge.*"

i. "I'm going to stop eating beef and pork, on account of the inhumane way in which the animals are killed in slaughterhouses." "But how will *your* ceasing to eat meat cause more humane methods to be instituted?" "It won't; but if everybody stopped until such time as humane methods were introduced, they would be introduced soon enough."

j. A nation thinks it can gain an advantage by erecting tariff barriers against certain of the products of another nation. "The second country may, however, generally find it advisable to adopt retaliatory tariffs which tend to offset the effects of the initial tariff on the terms of trade, but which are likely to reduce the total quantity traded still further. The end result may be a tariff war which leaves the terms of trade substantially unaffected and yet adversely affects both parties by its effect on total quantities traded." (William J. Baumol, *Welfare Economics and the Theory of the State* [Cambridge: Harvard Univ. Press, 1952], p. 104.)

k. Labor union A demands a 25 per cent pay-increase for its members (for doing no more work than they did before). Union B then demands similar increases for its members; Union C and Union D do the same. The producer of product A proportionately increases the cost of the product to the consumer, and so do the producers of B, C, and D. (See Henry Hazlitt, *Economics in One*

Lesson [New York, Harper, 1946], Ch. 19. This book contains much excellent illustrative material for rule-utilitarianism.)

l. Laborers in a certain industry resist automation because some of them will thereby lose their jobs. The union threatens a boycott of the industry unless the employer resists automation or hires a number of useless workers. (You can easily figure out the effects of universalization for yourself.)

m. If it is right for you to have your dinner at 6:30, is it right for everyone to have it at that time? If so the nation's economy would stand still during that hour. (See K. Baier, *The Moral Point of View*, p. 209.)

n. "If everyone were celibate all his life, mankind would soon die out. . . . If everyone suddenly stopped smoking, drinking, gambling, and going to the pictures, some states might go bankrupt." Is abstinence from these things therefore wrong? (See *Ibid.*, p. 210.)

o. "Of course I'm not going to invest with them this year, because I don't think anyone else will either, and so they will go bankrupt. Why should I put my money into a sinking ship?"

2. Consider the following situations from the point of view of rule-utilitarianism. In which of them do you think the rule-utilitarian answer would be different from that of the act-utilitarian?

a. In Tennessee Williams's play *Suddenly, Last Summer,* a wealthy widow promises a large amount of money to support a much needed hospital, on condition that a certain female patient (who is quite sane) be committed as insane and have a lobotomy performed on her so that she will never make any trouble by revealing facts embarrassing to the wealthy widow. One life would be ruined, but many others, through the new hospital, would be saved.

b. You borrow a dozen eggs from a neighbor, promising to return her a dozen eggs next week. You do so, but in the meantime the price of eggs has dropped by half. The neighbor says, "Since the price has dropped, you owe me two dozen eggs, not one."

c. Your neighbor refuses to put a yard light on his back yard even though the yard is considerably used and the terrain is treacherous in the dark. Should you, his neighbor, do it for him even though you do not use his yard?

d. The miners, to be safe, take small quantities of condensed food with them into the mines each morning, to keep them going in case there should be a cave-in. A few of them, however, refuse, saying that this practice only serves to remind them that every day may be their last. One day there is a cave-in, and some of those entombed have no food with them. Should those who do share with those who don't, even though sharing might mean starvation for all of them before help comes, if it comes?

e. Should the airlines institute a policy that pilots over sixty years of age may not pilot commercial planes? True, most of them are experts by the time they have flown that long, and the regulation would do them an injustice. On the other hand, a small number of them beyond that age have had heart attacks during flight, thus endangering all the passengers in the plane.

f. "It is only on utilitarian principles that we can account for the anomalous difference which the morality of Common Sense has always made between the two sexes as regards the simple offense of unchastity. For the offense is commonly more deliberate in the man, who has the additional guilt of soliciting and persuading the woman; in the latter, again, it is far more often prompted by some motive that we rank higher than mere lust: so that, according to the ordinary canons of intuitional morality, it ought to be more severely condemned in the man. The actual inversion of this result can only be justified by taking into account the greater interest that society has in maintaining a high standard of female chastity. For the degradation of this standard must strike at the root of family life, by impairing men's security in the exercise of their parental affections: but there is no corresponding consequence of male unchastity, which may therefore prevail to a considerable extent without imperilling the very existence of the family, though it impairs its wellbeing." (Henry Sidgwick, *The Methods of Ethics* [New York: Macmillan, 1874], p. 451.)

g. "It is maintained by some . . . that the existence of a certain limited amount of . . . intercourse (with a special class of women, carefully separated, as at present, from the rest of society) is scarcely a real evil, and may even be a positive gain in respect of general happiness; for continence is perhaps somewhat dangerous to health, and in any case involves a loss of pleasure considerable in intensity; while at the same time the maintenance of as numerous a population as is desirable in an old society does not require that more than a certain proportion of the women in each generation should become mothers of families; and if some of the surplus make it their profession to enter into casual and temporary sexual relations with men, there is no necessity that their lives should compare disadvantageously in respect of happiness with those of other women in the less favoured classes of society.

"This view has perhaps a superficial plausibility; but it ignores the essential fact that it is only by the present severe enforcement against unchaste women of the penalties of social contempt and exclusion, resting on moral disapprobation, that the class of courtesans is kept sufficiently separate from the rest of female society to prevent the contagion of unchastity from spreading; and that the illicit intercourse of the sexes is restrained within such limits as not to interfere materially with the due development of the race. This consideration is sufficient to decide a utilitarian to support generally the established rule against this kind of conduct, and therefore to condemn violations of the rule as on the whole infelicific, even though they may perhaps appear to have this quality only in consequence of the moral censure attached to them. Further, the 'man of the world' ignores the vast importance to the human race of maintaining that higher type of sexual relations which is not, generally speaking, possible, except where a high value is set upon chastity in both sexes. From this point of view the virtue of purity may be regarded as providing a necessary shelter under which that intense and elevated affection between the sexes, which is most conducive both to the happiness of the individual and to the wellbeing of the family, may grow and flourish." (*Ibid.*, pp. 451-52.)

h. Is it wrong to deceive a man even though he is pursuing criminal ends? (Should he be able to rely on the assertions of others in pursuing those ends?) (*Ibid.*, p. 488.)

i. It is August 1945, and the Japanese have sued for surrender, though the war is not yet *officially* over; thus wartime regulations are still in effect throughout the American armed forces. On a lonely Pacific island, an American soldier is guarding a huge supply of materiel, and since danger from the enemy is over he relaxes his vigil somewhat and falls asleep at his post. The result is that he is court-martialed, and technically his offense (falling asleep on guard duty in time of war) is punishable by death. What should be done?

j. You ask someone to do an errand for you and give him ten dollars to buy the article you want; while he is on the way to the store, he is held up and robbed. Should he have to pay you the ten dollars? (Suppose you have already paid him for the job; would this make a difference?)

k. A driver asks you the way to X-ville, and you point to the road crossing the bridge, neglecting to tell him however that the bridge is now unsafe. As a result the driver is drowned. What should *the law* do: hold you liable if you said nothing to him, hold you liable only if you deliberately misled him when *asked* if the bridge was safe, or hold you liable (either for misdirecting him or for saying nothing about the bridge) only if you are a policeman whose official duty it is to give such information?

3. Evaluate the following interpretations of, or comments on, rule-utilitarianism.

a. According to rule-utilitarianism we really need only one rule: don't do the act in question unless performing it will (to the best of present available knowledge) result in the maximum intrinsic good. (Would the rule "Don't do X — steal, kill, etc. — except when X will do the most good" be the one whose adoption would produce the most good? Why?)

b. Rule-utilitarianism turns out to be the same as act-utilitarianism in the end; for each class of actions (e.g., breaking promises, breaking promises to save a life, breaking promises to save a life when another life will be lost by so doing, breaking promises in this special circumstance A, B, C. . . . — including just those particular circumstances I am in) can be so specified — relevantly specified — as to include *only that act* which I am performing or am about to perform. And thus rule-utilitarianism reduces to act-utilitarianism after all. All I have to do is circumscribe the rule sufficiently.

c. "According to rule-utilitarianism, I should not use water during the prohibited hours (in a time of water shortage), because if everyone did so, the water supply would be dangerously depleted."

"But what if everyone else uses the water during prohibited hours?"

"This makes no difference to me as a rule-utilitarian; I only reason, '*If* they did, the city would run out of water.' And that is why I refrain."

"On the contrary, according to rule-utilitarianism you *should* take into account what others will probably do; for if the water supply is already depleted, the little bit that you use won't make any difference anyway. Why make a useless sacrifice?"

d. Rule-utilitarianism suffers from an infinite regress (or from what A. K. Stout calls an "infinite shuttle"); for when I consider what to do (whether I should vote, whether I should use the water, whether I should walk on the grass, etc.), I must include among my deliberations the consideration of whether or not others will do the same; and they, for their part, must equally include a consideration of whether others will do the same, and for them "others" *includes me.* In deciding how they will act, I must judge how I believe they will act; and they in their turn, in deciding how they will act, must have a belief about how I will probably act; and so I must have a belief about how they believe I will act, and so on. But how can they have a true belief about what my belief is, when my belief in turn depends on what their belief is? Their belief includes a belief about how I will act, but how can my belief include a belief about their-belief-about-how-I-will-act?

e. "My duty to perform actions of a sort which would have good consequences if they were generally practised will thus depend, in some measure, upon my ignorance of the behavior of other people. I must not, for example, turn aside from applying a principle of justice in a difficult case when I do not know that other people will not do the same, because I have every reason to believe that they will have much the same reasons for failing to apply a rule of justice to similar difficult cases, as I have for failing to apply it to this one; and because, if everybody were to do what I propose doing, disastrous consequences would follow. But, *if I were omniscient* about the behavior of other people, then it would be my duty to do that action, *which itself* has good consequences. But this is not because the principle that we ought always to perform those actions which would have good consequences if generally performed, and to refrain from performing those actions which would have bad consequences if generally performed, is not applicable to people who have complete knowledge of the behavior of others. It is because, to people who have complete knowledge of the behavior of others, the two principles, (1) that we should perform those actions which themselves have good consequences, and (2) that we should perform those actions which are of a sort which would have good consequences if practiced generally, enjoin the same actions. If everybody having complete knowledge of the behavior of other people were to perform those actions which themselves had good consequences, good consequences would result; whereas, if all people not having complete knowledge of the behavior of other people were to perform those actions which themselves had good consequences, bad consequences would result." (J. Harrison, *Proceedings of the Aristotelian Society,* Vol. 53 [1952-53], pp. 129-30.)

4. Evaluate attitude-utilitarianism in relation to rule-utilitarianism. Do you think they would always lead to the same results? Where do you think they supplement each other? Can you think of any points on which they would clash?

READING LIST, SECTION 17

Aiken, Henry D. "The Levels of Moral Discourse." *Ethics,* Vol. 62 (1952), pp. 235-48.
Brandt, Richard. *Ethical Theory.* Englewood Cliffs, N. J.: Prentice-Hall, 1959, pp. 396-405.
———. "In Search of a Credible Form of Rule-utilitarianism." In Nakhnikian, G., and H. Castaneda, *Morality and the Language of Conduct.* Detroit: Wayne State Univ. Press, 1961.
Ewing, Alfred C. "What Would Happen if Everybody Acted Like Me?" *Philosophy,* Vol. 28 (1953), pp. 16-29.
Harrison, Jonathan. "Utilitarianism, Universalization, and Our Duty to Be Just." *Aristotelian Society Proceedings,* Vol. 53 (1952-53), pp. 105-34.

Harrod, R. F. "Utilitarianism Revised." *Mind*, Vol. 45 (1936), pp. 137-56.

Mabbott, J. D. "Interpretations of Mill's *Utilitarianism.*" *Philosophical Quarterly*, Vol. 6 (1956), pp. 115-20.

———. "Moral Rules" (Henrietta Hertz lecture). *Proceedings of the British Academy*, Vol. 39 (1953), pp. 97-118.

McCloskey, H. J. "An Examination of Restricted Utilitarianism." *Philosophical Review*, Vol. 66 (1957), pp. 466-85.

Nowell-Smith, Patrick. *Ethics*. Baltimore: Pelican Books, 1954, pp. 236-39, 271-73.

Rawls, John. "Two Concepts of Rules." *Philosophical Review*, Vol. 64 (1955), pp. 3-32.

Smart, J. J. C. "Extreme and Restricted Utilitarianism." *Philosophical Quarterly*, Vol. 6 (1956).

Stout, A. K. "But Suppose Everyone Did the Same." *Australasian Journal of Philosophy*, Vol. 32 (1954), pp. 1-29.

Toulmin, Stephen. *An Examination of the Place of Reason in Ethics*. New York: Cambridge Univ. Press, 1951, Ch. 11.

Urmson, J. O. "The Interpretation of the Moral Philosophy of J. S. Mill." *Philosophical Quarterly*, Vol. 3 (1953), pp. 33-39.

8. Political ethics

18. Democracy

Let us suppose that you are the only human being in the world; you live, like Robinson Crusoe, on a desert island. You would have many problems — how to survive alone, how to find food and shelter, how to amuse yourself, how to care for yourself when ill. Doubtless you would begin as a crude egoist, satisfying whatever desire was paramount at the moment; but as your life became more settled and predictable, you would start to deny yourself present pleasures in order to prevent future catastrophes. But you would have no one else to consider, and so you would have none of the moral problems which confront human beings in a society of other human beings. Your rules of life would be strictly prudential. (There would, of course, be questions about your relation to whatever animals existed on your island.)

A. The problem of power
But there are many people in the world, and very few of them live alone on islands. Therefore, some means must be found for them to get along with other people. If people's interests never conflicted, there would still be no problem. But notoriously interests do conflict. Many people want the same thing, and not all of them can have it; some things almost no one wants, such as collecting rubbish, but someone has to do it; and the means to some people's happiness often conflicts with that of others.

Each person might, of course, try to live in a state of splendid isolation, acting as if other people did not exist. But isolation would be extremely difficult, since the people on the earth are extremely numerous and there is not living space enough for each of them to wander around to his heart's content without bumping into somebody else. Besides, isolation would be unpleasant, for most people do not like to be alone; they desire the company of others, and moreover the perpetuation of the species requires at least occasional contact between the sexes. Thus, even if a no-contact rule were desirable, it would be impossible. When people were few and areas

344

were large, such a rule was possible to some extent; each hunter could have a domain of his own, not to be trespassed upon by other hunters, and the less contact between hunters the better. But even there problems would be bound to arise in the event that one hunter trespassed on another's domain.

Even though we are numerous and condemned to bump into one another constantly, it would still be possible to live in the complete absence of any enforceable agreements with one another — by "the law of the jungle," or in other words, the absence of any statutes whatever. In such a situation, people would live by strength and cunning; if one person found it to his interest to kill another or steal his grain or his cattle, there would be no law to protect the injured party. Each person would try to get the most for himself, and since there would be no law to stop him, he would do whatever he thought he could get by with without getting killed by the injured party or his family. He could plunder and murder at will, provided he was strong enough to kill his assailants and cunning enough to outwit them in their stratagems against him. Such a situation would be what the English philosopher Thomas Hobbes (1588-1679) described as a "state of nature."

At first blush the state of nature might seem quite appealing. There would be no law to check your actions, no danger of the police or the courts, no rein upon your depredations, nothing to prevent you from doing whatever (within the limits of physical possibility) your fancy might dream up. But your freedom to do as you like would be bought at a high price. You are free to kill others (or try to) without their recourse to law; but in the same way, others are free to kill you (or try to) and you have no recourse to law either. As long as you are stronger and cleverer than others, this arrangement might suit you; but the moment another arises who has more of these qualities than you have, you are doomed — as you would be also if several weaker persons decided to cooperate in eliminating you.

In a state of nature no one has any responsibilities to others; but no one has any rights either — he must be his own law and his own policeman and be constantly on guard against the destructive acts of others. There are no duties, but neither are there any rights. There is no redress against grievances, except private vendetta. Because of the lack of a central authority to guarantee security of life and limb, there is constant risk and insecurity; and without any protection, life in a state of nature is, as Hobbes put it, "nasty, brutish, and short."

To make matters worse, the fact that each person in a state of nature knows that others have unlimited freedom to exploit him causes him to do the same. Even if you don't happen to feel like killing your neighbor, you may decide to do so in order to beat him to the draw, thinking that if you don't kill him first, he will kill you. Of course he may have exactly the same idea about you, so he will try to kill you. Neither of you may desire the demise of the other, but each tries to kill the other only to prevent his own death at the hands of the other. Thus the state of nature is worse even than it would be otherwise because each party anticipates in the other a destructive behavior which might never have occurred in either one except for these predatory anticipations.

It seems clear by now that there is no long-run gain in living in a state of nature. Even if you are an ethical egoist (which we have assumed in this brief description), it seems better for you to live by rules which will restrict your freedom but also restrict that of others. If there is an organization — the state — which enacts laws and enforces them, prohibiting you from killing, stealing, and otherwise molesting others, this enforcement will mean occasional loss and frustration to you; but at the same time it will protect you against others as much as it protects them against you. Except for those few adventurous spirits who prefer to live dangerously (albeit briefly) and play the game for high stakes, the gain seems to be greater than the loss. Your being protected against the encroachments of others is worth more to you than your occasional desire to encroach upon others — particularly when you realize that the anticipatory or preventive action against them which you would take in a state of nature is now no longer necessary. The gains are well worth the sacrifice. Your freedom is limited, but within those limits you can express yourself with less fear and greater security.

The state of nature seems alluring at first because in it you have unbounded freedom and can do whatever appears to be to your own interest without interference. But since others have the same freedom, it soon turns out that their injuries to you (especially since there are many of them but only one of you) can far outweigh your injuries to them. And so, what seems to be to your own interest — the state of nature — turns out not to be to your interest at all. In a civilized society, with laws and law-enforcement, you refrain from doing some things that would be to your interest if there were no law and do instead what is to the mutual interest of the members of the group.

We have seen (pages 141-55) that most people are not complete egoists; people do, sometimes, desire the welfare of others even when their own welfare is not thereby enhanced. But even if everyone were a complete egoist — Hobbes assumed that everyone was — it would still be to your interest to belong to a social group in which certain rules of behavior, codified into laws and enforced by a central enforcing agency (the state), were adopted and acted upon. The state provides a check on aggressive desires in others as well as in yourself. It takes away much, but it gives back more. The happiness possible to a million beings in a state of nature, each in constant fear of the other, each constantly waging preventive war upon the other, is far less than the happiness possible to an organized society governed by laws which restrict in certain ways the behavior of each individual within it. Paradoxical as it may seem, a system which involves the surrender of some interests is what alone makes possible the gratification by everyone of the maximum possible range of interests. If you are in constant danger, most of your energies must be given over to self-defense, and the other interests which you are capable of developing cannot be developed at all. The limitations imposed by the state seem a small price to pay for so great an enlargement of the scope of one's interests.

We submit, then, to being governed, in some of our actions, by a central authority which, for the protection of all, decides upon certain rules of behavior and enacts them into laws. (Some of the rules, that is, become laws; others have only the force of custom or public opinion.) We submit so that thereby our total well-being may be increased. We must not, however, assume that *every* rule in *every* case works out so as to maximize our particular interests. Obeying the rule against theft (with qualifications built into the rule for situations like starvation) is generally advantageous, and having such a rule is better than not having one. But there are cases — for example, when the chance of detection is minimal — in which it *would* be to your interest to steal, and in which obeying the law is not at all to your own interest. Still, the rule requiring you to refrain from stealing even in this case is, under the circumstances, the best possible rule. Here, clearly, our account connects with rule-utilitarianism, which we discussed in the previous chapter.

But how is such a society to be formed, over what kinds of situations is it to legislate, and how is it to be governed?

1. *Formation of society.* According to the traditional Hobbesean account, a number of individuals, each a complete egoist, come together to form a "contract," realizing that though each will be giving up something, each will gain more than he loses. Since each person is an egoist, it would not be worth entering into the contract in the first place if the gain were not greater. Giving up some things means such an increase of benefits — chiefly security, the condition which makes civilized life possible — that it is to everyone's interest to enter into the contract.

This "social contract" theory of Hobbes has sometimes been presented as if the contract had been a historical event — as if at one time in the history of man some individuals banded together to form a centralized authority. Whether or not this is what Hobbes meant (and it is possible that he did not), the historical question is irrelevant to ethics. There is no time known to us in which men did not live in ordered groups with rules and regulations governing their behavior and penalties for the infringement of these rules (not necessarily written laws, but customs having the force of of law); but this historical fact does not matter. The point is that, whatever the historical sequence of events may have been, Hobbes's explanation is the rationale of the state: it is the consideration which justifies the existence of the state, however long or short may have been that existence.

2. *Areas of legislation.* Not all departments of human activity are best brought under the sway of law. Over what branches of human activity is

the government to have control? Opinions have always differed on this point, and the prevailing opinion differs from age to age. In Hobbes's view and in that of his contemporaries, the purpose of government was to provide the minimum benefit of *security* — and "security" meant not social security or unemployment compensation and the like but simply the physical security of life and limb, protection against murder, assault, theft, and the loss of the fruits of one's labor. In our own day, the function of government is usually conceived not only as that of preventing undesirable contingencies but also as that of positively bringing about desirable states of affairs — medical benefits, equitable distribution of economic goods, cultivation of the arts, providing for the needy and the aged. Whether more total good is brought about by having the government perform each one of these various functions or by leaving each to individuals, their families, and voluntary organizations, is an empirical matter too detailed and complex to go into here.

One point, however, is worth emphasizing. There are many things which would not be to a person's *individual* interest to perform, which are yet to people's *collective* interest to possess: that is, the total amount of good in a society is maximized by having these things. When a task is a huge one and beyond one person's power or when it is within one person's power but would affect a large number of people (so that it would be unfair if one had to do it for all), then the state should take over the task for the benefit of the individuals involved. Court procedure provides an obvious instance of this area of legislation. When grievances are to be settled, they should be arbitrated by some impartial body other than the individuals involved or their families, who are bound to be partial to their own cause; moreover, the court settles the case once and for all so that no private vendetta is either desirable or necessary. Protection of the individual against assault, murder, and theft by a police force is another obvious example: no one individual can protect himself against a multitude of others. If protection were left to organizations other than the state, such as clubs and churches, they would have no jurisdiction outside their own organization. There must then be some over-all organization, the state, which transcends the limits of all the various organizations, designed for specific purposes, which operate within it.

There are many tasks, from highway construction to waging war, which the state is in a position to perform because it has the means, the impersonality, and the means of enforcement. Hume gives an excellent example:

> Two neighbors may agree to drain a meadow, which they possess in common; because it is easy for them to know each other's mind; and each must perceive that the immediate consequence of his failing in his part, is the abandoning of the whole project. But it is very difficult, and indeed impossible, that a thousand persons should agree in any such action; it being difficult for them to concert so complicated a design, and still more difficult for them to execute

it; while each seeks a pretext to free himself of the trouble and expense, and would lay the whole burden on others. Political society easily remedies both these inconveniences. . . . Thus, bridges are built, harbours opened, ramparts raised, canals formed, fleets equipped, and armies disciplined, everywhere, by the care of government, which, though composed of men subject to all human infirmities, becomes, by one of the finest and most subtile inventions imaginable, a composition which is in some measure exempted from all these infirmities.[1]

Bridges have to be built to span rivers and lakes, but since they are used by everyone, it would be unfair for one individual or one organization to have to build them. Again, it is best for everyone if the smoke from factory chimneys is eliminated; but if one factory owner were to go to the enormous expense of doing this while the rest did not, very little good would be done by way of smoke alleviation; so there must be a central agency, the state, which requires that all equally eliminate smoke, thus legislating and enforcing what is to people's mutual interest to have performed (including that of the factory owners, taken collectively), even though it would not be to the interest of one heroic person acting alone.

3. *Form of government.* But what kind of government is the state to have? Rule by all the people together is far too unwieldy to be feasible; therefore there must be one person or a comparatively small number of persons who must make and administer the laws which are to be binding on the many. (In ancient Athens, all the citizens participated in the government, but they were the minority of the adult, male population; the slaves and foreign-born residents, who outnumbered them, had no part in the government at all.) But how is this person or persons to be chosen? Clearly those in power bear an enormous load of responsibility. We need people in positions of authority; but to whom are we to entrust this great power? Everything will depend on what kind of people they are. Leadership is vital in any organization, whether it be a school, a church, or a prison; but it is particularly so in government, since a government will have a certain measure of control (sometimes absolute control) over all these other organizations, including their leaders.

But at this point the common human impulse to *power* comes into play. Some people are not willing to assume power over other people and will not be willing to take high positions in government; but most people occupying such positions are very anxious indeed to assume power and even more anxious to retain it once they have it. In the assumption of power there lies an enormous danger.

Let us stop for a moment to consider what human impulses are of importance in political life. There is danger to others in the exercise of many human impulses, such as the sexual impulse: its expression may involve jealousy, bitterness, rape, murder, and various kinds of human misery. Still,

---

[1] David Hume, *Treatise of Human Nature* (Many editions), Bk. 2, Pt. 2, Sectn. 8.

the sexual impulse is not a *politically* important one; it may ruin many individual lives but not usually that of a state.

The impulse to acquire *money* can also be dangerous: the more so since the desire is not easily satisfied. (1) As a rule, the more one has of it the more he wants. One aims at acquiring a certain amount of money to achieve material comfort and security; but once he has them, other desires develop that can be satisfied only by more money, often because one has moved up into social strata where more money is required to keep up with one's neighbors. Thus the original goal is moved upwards, and when it is achieved, it is moved upwards once again; this process can go on indefinitely. The desire for money is, to use a medical term, a progressive disease rather than a self-limiting one. Still, the desire for financial aggrandizement is not normally the moving force which drives people into positions of government. Clever people can usually earn far more money in private industry or business and have far greater hopes of tenure. (Where corruption prevails or when the head of state is not subject to electoral procedure and can abscond with millions of dollars with impunity, government position can be extremely lucrative; but even then it is insecure.)

However, (2) the desire for money is not only progressive but usually *competitive* — it is satisfied at other people's expense. If some have more, others must have less. People who crave money do not merely crave to have a great deal but to have *more than* other people have. This competitive craving makes the desire for money (beyond a certain point) unfortunate, since even in a prosperous nation where it is possible for many to have much, it is impossible for many to have *more than* most other people have; and it is possible for only one person to have more money than anybody else has. Like all competitive desires, the desire to have more money than most other people is one which by its own nature is doomed, for most people, to frustration. Still, unfortunate though this fact is for the happiness of the people concerned — insofar as their happiness depends on the satisfaction of this desire — it is not usually of major political importance.

There is, again, the impulse of *vanity* which leads people to want positions of fame, glory, or glamour. The impulse to be famous or glamorous is also progressive — one cannot be *too* famous to suit himself: the more famous he is the more famous he wants to be; and, of course, the impulse to be famous is competitive as well, since one wants to be more famous or glamorous than others, and only a few people can be more famous than most. But political life is not normally the best one for satisfying this impulse. The life of a stage or movie star satisfies it much better, or the life of a boxing champion or a baseball player. In the United States these careers carry a maximum of fame and glamour — usually far more than that of a president or a prime minister — and a minimum of responsibility. Although this impulse is manifested in political life, it is not of prime political importance, since it can usually be more easily satisfied elsewhere.

Finally, there is the impulse to *power*. Many people who do not especially crave more money often crave more power; and those who do crave money are likely to want to use it to exert more power. Almost everyone likes to exert some power, but those who have been frustrated in other ways — little men who cannot compete intellectually with others, those who have acquired money but not been satisfied by it, those who have been rejected or cheated in love and feel that they have nothing else to live for, those who have been repudiated or humiliated by others during their lives — these people usually want more than anything else to have power so that they can use it to manage the lives of others, particularly those who have put them at a disadvantage. "You were successful in love, and you wouldn't pay any attention to me then, but now you'll have to pay some attention to me, because I can throw my weight around — I can annihilate you if I want to" is what many a power-seeker wants to be able to say.

The desire for power possesses, to an even greater degree, the unfortunate characteristics of the impulses mentioned before. It is progressive: the more power one has the more he is likely to want; very few persons in positions of power are content with the amount of power they have. Nothing would satisfy them short of omnipotence. Moreover, power is highly competitive: the more one has of it, the less others can have; only a few people can have a great deal of it; and only one person can be what many wish to be, the most powerful person in the world.

Power tends to attract the very people who are the least qualified to exert it. The risks involved are so great, especially if one wishes to be a tyrant or a dictator, that most people, even those who crave power, will hesitate to assume them. They prefer to live safer lives even without so much power. Often it is only the pathologically power-hungry man who will take the required risks: he will be so anxious to make up for real or imagined early frustrations, to get even with those who (he feels) have shoved him around, that he will risk death and destruction to get a position of power where he can shove them around. The moment one man becomes an absolute ruler, many others, yearning for his position, will already be plotting to unseat him. To protect himself, he will have to surround himself with armed guards and a large secret police force, with which to spy out and eliminate all those who threaten his power. But in thus securing himself, he may lead to his own undoing: for the men he kills have friends who will wish to assassinate him, and for every one he kills or has killed, ten more will arise to take their places; moreover, as this trend increases, an inflamed public will stand behind the rebels and demand the tyrant's head. Thus he pays a high price for his power: his life may be taken at any moment, and even while he lives he is in constant insecurity. The more insecure and threatened he feels, the more he will suppress the opposition and kill his opponents, which actions in turn will increase the bitterness and hatred directed against him, until finally he is killed and another power-hungry tyrant arises to take his place, and the whole cycle repeats itself. No wonder that few people, seeing the dangers of power, are willing to risk having this much of it; and no wonder that those who want the power in spite of these tremendous risks are seldom people who are qualified by character or training to exercise it wisely.

Here, then, we discover the tragedy of power. Even when those leaders who aspire to it have noble motives, their motives are interpreted simply as selfish ones, and in order to retain their power (which is precarious at first), they are forced to resort to the same protective devices as does the tyrant. If they do not protect themselves, they are killed or at least relieved of their command by others who do not hesitate to use force to gain their ends. The benevolent new ruler, let us say, does not wish to use force, but he must do so to fight the forces of evil that are ranged against him; and in fighting fire with fire, before long he himself has become as corrupt as those he replaced. Power is insidious: "bad" people do not hesitate to use it for their own selfish ends, and "good" people must use it to fight the bad people, and in so doing they become as bad as the people they opposed. "Power corrupts, and absolute power corrupts absolutely." At first a new regime, full of idealism and genuine concern for a downtrodden people, stirs the hope of a nation just released from the coils of a dictator; but some of the people, unwise and uninformed perhaps, misconstrue the aims of the new regime, oppose it, and rebel against it. The regime must then use force to crush opposition; but force once used creates enemies, and as the new regime uses greater force to protect itself against these enemies, the enemies increase. As a result the army and the secret police increase ("temporary measures" always), until the new regime becomes as tyrannical as the old. This development has occurred repeatedly in human history, most recently in the Soviet Union and in Cuba.

Nevertheless, power must be wielded by somebody. Someone must make laws, someone must execute them, someone must originate policies, and someone must enforce them, if we are not to return to a state of nature. It is easy to become moralistic and condemn power in all its manifestations, castigating all those who wield it and calling them wicked, as preachers and moralists perennially do. But to do so is to eschew power and leave it in the hands of others, permitting the very people whom one condemns to originate national policy. There is indeed a considerable human satisfaction in retreating from the arena and then condemning those who are in it, in excoriating the wielders of power and calling them vicious and then consoling ourselves with a morality of impotence and calling it virtue. To condemn power per se is no solution whatever; power is not evil in itself, it is only the use that is made of it that can be either good or evil. And if good people do not occupy positions of power, then bad people are certain to do so.

What, then, is the solution? The only solution, it would appear, is to make sure that those who assume power over other human beings (as some must) be of such a rare and noble stamp that they cannot be swayed from their high purpose or be corrupted by any means whatever; or, if this ideal is not possible, to devise a system in which, even if second-rate men come into positions of power, they can be replaced, and no catastrophe will result. In short, the solution would seem to be democracy.

We in a democracy are inclined to reason as follows: "Keep the power in the hands of the people. People don't want despots to rule over them; therefore, make it impossible to have dictators and tyrants by keeping the keys to power in the hands of the people. Permit them to elect to power the men whom they feel will be the most fitted to wield it; and give them at stated intervals the privilege of voting to continue these men in office if they do well and to replace them if they do not. The power must remain ultimately in the hands of the people and only be *delegated* to the men in government who wield the power. These men must execute the people's will; they are not the masters of the people but their servants. People will not willingly place themselves in a position of servitude to ruling masters. So, if the reins of power are in the people's hands, all is safe, for no one wants to inflict misery upon himself. The answer to the problem of power is not to have one group on the giving end and another on the receiving end of power; those who are on the receiving end of power, namely the people, must be the very ones who (through their elected representatives) are the wielders of the power. An absolute monarchy, in which a king rules from above, differs from a democracy, in which a president or prime minister carries out the will of the people below, because the source of power is in different hands."

This solution to the problem may seem to be so obvious, and its truth is so much taken for granted by citizens of democracies, that it may seem surprising that a plausible argument can be directed against it. The most famous, and the most thorough-going, argument was made by Plato, whose opposition to democracy was equaled only by his desire for an ideal state. What could Plato or anyone else possibly say in favor of any other arrangement?

B. Plato's attack on democracy

First, according to Plato, we must never forget that the profession of politics, or statecraft (the term "poltitics" has an unfavorable ring for us, as it did not in Plato's day), is the most important of all professions, for the well-being of all the others depends on the condition of this one. If the governing body of the state is stupid or selfish or corrupt, the disease affects all the enterprises taking place within the state. Tight government control, for example, can virtually destroy the happiness of the people and the healthy functioning of all the professions and organizations within the state.

It is, therefore, of the very first importance that those who occupy high positions of government be the very best men that the country can produce.

(1) They must be experts in their field, for a great deal of specialized knowledge is required for them to handle efficiently the complex problems daily confronting them in their high office. To be such experts, they must first undergo a long period of intensive training and preparation. It would be foolish and absurd to require physicians and lawyers to undergo long and intensive training for their professions but to permit people to go into politics, which requires even more skill and wisdom than these professions, without any training whatever. (Yet men allow this foolish practice in our own day as in Plato's.)

But even more important, (2) political leaders must be wise and incorruptible men, men of the best possible moral character, otherwise they might use their specialized knowledge to advance their own personal interests instead of the interests of the people they are governing. To insure the inviolability of their moral character after they are in office is a much more difficult task than to insure their having specialized knowledge and skill. Once they are in positions of power, they will be subject to the strongest temptation to abuse that power for their own ends. Power corrupts all but the very noblest natures. Their training, therefore, even from their earliest childhood years, must be such that they will never even desire to abuse the power that will one day be theirs. They must be protected when young against all evil moral influences, and their characters must be molded in such a way that they will be utterly incorruptible and immune even to the blandishments of the fawning admirers who would tempt them with lucrative offers.

These leaders then, must be trained in such a way that no stone is left unturned to insure their intellectual and moral excellence. This combination of characteristics is rare enough in human beings that we cannot afford to waste the small percentage of human material that possesses the potential for statecraft. We must nurture it and cultivate it with the utmost care, as the most precious of all our national possessions. To do so carefully and impartially requires the exertion of all our powers of discrimination and impartiality, but if the process seems difficult we must keep constantly in mind the supremely valuable end toward which such cultivation is the only possible means — an end which, if it is not achieved, means the corruption and decay of the entire state.

What, then, should this training be like? Plato describes every phase of it in detail in his *Republic*. In briefest outline it is this: Every child who shows the slightest promise must be thoroughly educated, in mind and spirit as also in body (for without a sound body his mind cannot function well throughout life). He must have a long and intensive training in mathematics, for by this means he learns objectivity in thinking and comes to know that truth is both difficult to attain and yet objectively there regardless of people's opinions. For the good of his soul, he must also be trained in the liberal arts — history, literature, music — so that he will become sensitive to human feeling and not like most athletes, who resemble wild beasts. During this early period there are influences which must be kept from him: sensuous music, for example, and tales about the gods (even if they occur in Homer) which are false or which portray the gods as being immoral or corrupt — for the child is impressionable ˙and evil must be kept from him from the beginning. Then, when he is eighteen or nineteen, he will undergo a course of military training to harden his body. From twenty to thirty he will go through an intensive course of studies, particularly in mathematics, to purify his mind and discipline his character. Then and only then will he be permitted to study philosophy (philo-sophia, literally, love of wisdom), particularly the study of true moral principles; for unless he has had considerable self-discipline from a long preliminary study of other objective truths, he will simply make sport of the difficult philosophical distinctions, using them as tools for rationalizing selfish ends, and doubt all that he has learned as a child. Then, from thirty-five to fifty he will cease his studies and return to the life of the people, taking jobs in public service in subordinate posts, applying what he has learned to the life around him. Only at the end of that time will he be in a position to sit in the Council of Rulers which governs the state.

Needless to- say, only a few will survive that grueling ordeal. Difficult competitive examinations (analogous to our civil service examinations) will have eliminated most of the contestants long before they reach the end of this long road. Only those most able and most conscientious will emerge triumphant at the end, fully equipped at last to assume the burdens of state.

It is clear that this long educational process can hardly be accused of lack of thoroughness; it produces leaders who, to say the least, are trained for their jobs. But can we be sure that even after this long process they will have all the qualifications necessary for assuming leadership in the most important of all human offices, that of leader of state?

Yes, according to Plato; if any process of education can eliminate those who are not desirable in every way, this one will. (1) The rulers have the most thorough possible knowledge required for the discharge of their all-important duties. (We might disagree on some points, for instance that mathematics is as important as Plato believed it to be; but these are matters of detail which could be argued separately.) (2) Not only are they thoroughly trained; they are no ivory-tower academicians. Before they can become rulers they must have spent fifteen years among the people, mixing with them, sharing their emotions, acquiring a first-hand knowledge of their problems and needs, and in every way applying their knowledge in a practical context. (3) In addition to their knowledge and practical experience, there is also a guarantee that they will be *morally* fit to rule. They have been carefully trained so that no evil influences could arise to develop undesirable tendencies in them. Their training throughout has aimed at the ennoblement of their character. Even the knowledge acquired through all those years of training has been principally a means toward this end.

As an example of this last point, consider Plato's discussion of why the student should not be exposed to philosophical discussion at an early age but must wait until he has had a thorough training first in other disciplines.

> You must have seen how much harm is done now by philosophical discussion — how it infects people with a spirit of lawlessness.
>
> Yes, I have.
>
> Does that surprise you? Can you not make allowances for them? Imagine a child brought up in a rich family with powerful connections and surrounded by a host of flatterers; and suppose that, when he comes to manhood, he learns that he is not the son of those who call themselves his parents and his true father and mother are not to be found. Can you guess how he would feel towards his supposed parents and towards his flatterers before he knew about his parentage and after learning the truth? Or shall I tell you what I should expect?
>
> Please do.
>
> I should say that, so long as he did not know the truth, he would have more respect for his reputed parents and family than for the flatterers, and be less inclined to neglect them in distress or to be insubordinate in word or deed; and in important matters the flatterers would have less influence with him. But when he learnt the facts, his respect would be transferred to them; their influence would increase, and he would openly associate with them and adopt their standards of behavior, paying no heed to his reputed father and mother, unless his disposition were remarkably good.
>
> Yes; all that would be likely to happen. But how does your illustration apply to people who are beginning to take part in philosophical discussions?
>
> In this way. There are certain beliefs about right and honorable conduct, which we have been brought up from childhood to regard with the same sort of reverent obedience that is shown to parents. In opposition to these, other courses attract us with flattering promises of pleasure; though a moderately good character will resist such blandishments and remain loyal to the beliefs of his fathers. But now suppose him confronted by the question, What does "honorable" mean? He gives the answer he has been taught by the lawgiver, but he is argued out of his position. He is refuted again and again from many different points of view and at last reduced to thinking that what he called honorable might just as well be called disgraceful. He comes to the same conclusion about justice, goodness, and all the things he most revered. What will become now of his old respect and obedience?
>
> Obviously they cannot continue as before.
>
> And when he has disowned these discredited principles and failed to find the true ones, naturally he can only turn to the life which flatters his desires; and we shall see him renounce all morality and become a lawless rebel. If this is the natural consequence of plunging the young into philosophical discussion, ought we not to make allowances, as I said before?
>
> Yes, and be sorry for them too.
>
> Then, if you do not want to be sorry for those pupils of yours who have

reached the age of thirty, you must be very careful how you introduce them to such discussions. One great precaution is to forbid their taking part while they are still young. You must have seen how youngsters, when they get their first taste of it, treat arguments as a form of sport solely for purposes of contradiction. When someone has proved them wrong, they copy his methods to confute others, delighting like puppies in tugging and tearing at anyone who comes near them. And so, after a long course of proving others wrong and being proved wrong themselves, they rush to the conclusion that all they once believed is false; and the result is that in the eyes of the world they discredit, not themselves only, but the whole business of philosophy. An older man would not share this craze for making a sport of contradiction. He will prefer to take for his model the conversation of one who is bent on seeking truth, and his own reasonableness will bring credit on the pursuit. We meant to insure this result by all that we said earlier against the present practice of admitting anybody, however unfit, to philosophic discussions, and about the need for disciplined and steadfast character.[1]

In spite of all this careful preparation, how can we be sure that the ruler-to-be will not go through all these years of training in order to gain monetary rewards at the end? Plato tries to take care of this possibility by making sure that the profession of statecraft will bring no such rewards. The rulers will receive no pay at all; they will receive enough clothing and food for their personal needs, not even for their comfort; and no luxuries will be permitted. Moreover — and this requirement is so demanding that many critics have felt that it is quite contrary to human nature — the rulers are not even permitted to have wives and families, lest the having of them distract their attention from the all-important matters of state to the comparatively unimportant concern with the well-being of their families and increase their craving for material possessions. Not that the rulers must live as celibates like monks: they may have intercourse with women when they choose, but a system must be devised to make sure that no ruler will ever know which children are his and which are those of other fathers. The Spartan rigor of this regime would hardly be likely to attract most people — certainly not for material rewards, comforts, and luxuries, for, as far as the rulers are concerned, there are none.

The ruler, then, will not be attracted to his office by hope of material gain. But how about another motive, desire for power? There are, as we have already seen, people who do not crave material rewards half as much as they crave power; they do not want wealth, they only want to throw their weight around and dominate the lives of other people. How are rulers to be kept from reaching high office through a desire for power? This possibility, too, Plato tries to take care of — partly by making the education of rulers a thorough training in morality, as we have already seen, so that they will not even desire the exertion of power; but partly also by making no

[1] From *The Republic of Plato,* translated by Francis MacDonald Cornford. Oxford University Press, 1941. Reprinted by permission, pp. 259-61.

one an absolute ruler. There is not one ruler but a whole council of rulers; no one of them alone would be able to exert enough power to make it worthwhile going through all those years of training just to satisfy the desire for power. People craving power could achieve it much more quickly and easily in private enterprise.

Thus Plato tried to make certain not only that his leaders were extremely well trained, mentally, physically, and morally, but also that no base impulses would move them to seek high positions because the rewards of money and power would be largely absent. Only one type of driving impulse would be sufficient to carry the ruler-to-be through all those years: a complete dedication, a wish to rule not for personal vainglory but simply and purely for the sake of doing well the most important job that could be done. A state cannot function without good rulers, and therefore those who are trained and worthy must rule, even if it means a life of personal hardship — this is the consideration which alone was to animate the men who achieved the high position of rulership.

So great is the dedication required of the rulers that we might think it surprising if any survived who would be willing to rule under the prescribed conditions. Yet Plato thought that nothing less was required: short of this herculean effort, no system could be guaranteed to produce rulers who were perfectly able and incorruptible. If the demands upon the rulers seemed so great as to be almost impossible of attainment, they were so because the end in view was greater still. The end of all this training was the very best government that it was possible for mortal beings to have. And the government in turn, including all the activities of rulership, was only a means to a further end — the well-being of the people who were governed. The best state was the state that brought about the best life for the people within it, just as the best shepherd was the one who served best the welfare of the sheep. The difference was that the art of ruling was far more difficult and exacting, and required much more training, experience, and nobility of purpose than the art of shepherding.

So much for Plato's system of government. Now let us return to democracy. Why does Plato set forth a political ideal in which there is no election by the people and in which the people do not determine the course of public affairs? The answer is simple: Democracy, according to Plato, fails as a system of government because of the nature of the people. The people are like sheep, ignorant, untrained, and easily led. Government is a task for those who are trained in this complicated art: to have rulers of state who are not properly trained for their jobs is even more tragic in its consequences than to entrust one's health not to well-trained physicians but to charlatans and quacks.

Imagine this state of affairs on board a ship or a number of ships. The master is bigger and burlier than any of the crew, but a little deaf and shortsighted and no less deficient in seamanship. The sailors are quarrelling over the control of the helm; each thinks he ought to be steering the vessel, though he has never learnt navigation and cannot point to any teacher under whom he has served his apprenticeship; what is more, they assert that navigation is a thing that cannot be taught at all, and are ready to tear in pieces anyone who says it can. Meanwhile they besiege the master himself, begging him urgently to trust them with the helm; and sometimes, when others have been more successful in gaining his ear, they kill them or throw them overboard, and, after somehow stupefying the worthy master with strong drink or an opiate, take control of the ship, make free with its stores, and turn the voyage, as might be expected of such a crew, into a drunken carousal. Besides all this, they cry up as a skilled navigator and master of seamanship anyone clever enough to lend a hand in persuading or forcing the master to set them in command. Every other kind of man they condemn as useless. They do not understand that the genuine navigator can only make himself fit to command a ship by studying the seasons of the year, sky, stars, and winds, and all that belongs to his craft; and they have no idea that along with the science of navigation, it is possible for him to gain, by instruction or practice, the skill to keep control of the helm whether some of them like it or not. If a ship were managed in that way, would not those on board be likely to call the expert in navigation a mere star-gazer, who spent his time in idle talk and was useless to them? . . . But our present rulers may fairly be compared to the sailors in our parable, and the useless visionaries, as the politicians call them, to the real masters of navigation.[1]

But even if the people themselves are untrained, will they not at least elect to positions of high office those who are? Not at all, according to Plato. How can the people put worthy men into office when they do not even know what qualifications the worthy men must possess? The people have no philosophy (love of wisdom), so how can they be expected either to recognize or to respect the kind of person who does?

. . . The multitude can never be philosophical. Accordingly it is bound to disapprove of all who pursue wisdom; and so also, of course, are those individuals who associate with the mob and set their hearts on pleasing it.

That is clear.

What hope can you see, then, that a philosophic nature should be saved to persevere in the pursuit until the goal is reached? Remember how we agreed that the born philosopher will be distinguished by quickness of understanding, good memory, courage, and generosity. With such gifts, already as a boy he will stand out above all his companions, especially if his person be a match for his mind; and when he grows older, his friends and his fellow citizens will no doubt want to make use of him for their own purposes. They will fawn upon him with their entreaties and promises of advancement, flattering him beforehand for the power that will some day be his.

Yes, that happens often enough.

What will become of a youth so circumstanced, above all if he belongs to

[1] *Ibid.,* pp. 195-96.

a great country and is conspicuous there for his birth and wealth, as well as for a tall and handsome person? Will he not be filled with unbounded ambition, believing himself well able to manage the affairs of the world, at home and abroad, and thereupon give himself airs and be puffed up with senseless self-conceit?

No doubt.

Now suppose that while this frame of mind is gaining upon him, someone should come and quietly tell him the truth, that there is no sense in him and that the only way to get the understanding he needs is to work for it like a slave: will he find it easy to listen, surrounded ·by all these evil influences?

Certainly not.

Perhaps, however, because there is something in a fine nature that responds to the voice of reason, he might be sensitive to the force which would draw him towards philosophy and begin to yield. But then those friends of his will see that they are in danger of losing one who might do so much for their party. Sooner than let him be won over, there is no engine of force or persuasion, from private intrigue to prosecution in the courts, that they will not bring to bear either upon him or upon his counsellor. How can he ever become a lover of wisdom?

He never will.

You see, then, I was not wrong in saying that, in a way, the very qualities which make up the philosopher's nature may, with a bad unbringing, be the cause of his falling away, no less than wealth and all other so-called advantages.[1]

Thus we see how even the noblest natures, those with the highest potential, are easily corrupted, and will be unless the utmost care is taken to prevent it. If it is so with the best, how can it be better with the people as a whole? With them the situation is entirely hopeless. They will never be able to recognize those men who are worthy to hold political office.

But even if the people were able to recognize those worthy of leadership, the people could not be trusted to elect them to the offices they were capable of holding. Those who are worthy to occupy positions in government are not usually the kind that attract the attention of the populace as a whole. The people, even those who are not indifferent to (as most are) and ignorant of (as most also are) the true qualifications for political office, are all too easily taken in by irrelevant considerations. They are not attracted by the capable man, who is usually too dedicated to be a "charming personality." Instead they gravitate toward the man who, regardless of his qualifications, exudes the most charm, or makes the most promises, or is a "simple soul" like themselves with whom they can identify and whom they like because they do not feel inferior to him. In democracy, says Plato, there is

. . . a contempt for all those fine principles we laid down in founding our commonwealth, as when we said that only a very exceptional nature could turn out a good man, if he had not played as a child among things of beauty

[1] *Ibid.*, pp. 201-02.

and given himself only to creditable pursuits. A democracy tramples all such notions under foot; with a magnificent indifference to the sort of life a man has led before he enters politics, it will promote to honor anyone who merely calls himself the people's friend.[1]

The people very seldom elect to high office a man worthy to hold it; on the contrary, they are much more likely to elect a mediocre man, for they do not recognize ability when it is there; and even if they do recognize it, they are too easily swayed by irrelevant considerations to put the man into the office where he belongs.

Suppose you are a storekeeper or restaurateur who, unlike most, does not desire merely to pile up the largest possible profit for himself but genuinely wishes to serve his clients a healthful and nutritious diet. Instead of cheap and nutritionally deficient substitutes, you use expensive but healthful oils in preparing the salads for your customers. Instead of offering them as topping for dessert inexpensive and indigestible sweetened grease and calling it "whipped cream," you offer them real whipped cream. But most people do not know the difference, and, what is more, they do not care. They never bother to inquire about the ingredients of your foods as long as the foods taste good to them. But because you use far better ingredients for the sake of their health, even if you accept a cut in profits, you must still charge somewhat higher prices than your less conscientious competitors. Soon your customers begin to complain about your prices and take their business to your competitors, who serve them nutritionally deficient foods at somewhat lower prices. In vain do you try to tell them about the importance of a sound diet; they neither listen nor care.

The same, according to Plato, happens in a democracy. Let us suppose that one candidate for office is capable, tells people the truth, and does not flatter their egos; he respects the truth too much to make extravagant promises which can never be fulfilled, and he tells them that if certain desirable ends are to be achieved they must face certain hardships and make certain sacrifices. But the people, too busy buying television sets and new automobiles on the installment plan, do not wish to hear these things; they turn from him to the other candidate, who smiles and repeats platitudes that they like to hear and assures them that everything will be all right and all fears are groundless. A few people see the truth through the tissue of deceptions, but they are not numerous enough to swing the election. The vast majority of the people vote for the second candidate because he has a charming smile, or because he brought the army safely home from the recent war, or because he is a white Protestant; and they vote against the first candidate because he has a solemn message which does not please their ears, or because he is divorced, or because he is well educated and is therefore presumed to lack the pioneer virtues and to be vaguely untrustworthy.

[1] *Ibid.*, p. 283.

That is Plato's point: the people — fallible, untrained, unwise, indifferent — are not the proper judges of their own best interests. They will elect to office a man who shirks his real duties while breathing smiling platitudes, a man who (as they do not discover until years later when it is too late) through negligence or ignorance has pushed their country to the brink of disaster. If the people *were* the best judges of what was best for them, then democracy would be an acceptable form of government, but they are not. They are like children; they have no conception which policies — complex and far beyond their comprehension — will be ultimately to their own collective best interests. Democracy puts government into the hands of the people, but unfortunately the people are not competent judges of what policies are best, even for themselves, in the complicated art of government. Democracy is government of the cattle, for the cattle, by the cattle.

Plato's analogy is that of the physician vs. the confectioner. The physician knows what is good for your body — what exercise you should have, what foods you should eat to remain strong and fit. The confectioner, however, offers you not the foods that are good for you but the foods that you like; he pleases your palate with ever new concoctions which make you fat and give you ulcers and heart trouble in the end, but you want them because you enjoy them and you lack the judgment and the discipline to forsake what you enjoy for the sake of what is good for your body. Democracy is government in the hands of the confectioners. Unfortunately it is not the confectioners of the state but the physicians of the state who alone are equipped to supervise the body politic. Most people, however, neither know nor care about this fact; as long as they get what they want at the moment and are told that it's all right, they are satisfied. A few people in the state know the truth, but they are shouted down when they try to tell the truth to others, so they remain forever a hopeless and helpless minority. Should the state, as Plato asks, be entrusted to the hands of such confectioners? As well to leave your physical care in the hands of the quack, or your prescriptions to the pharmacist who will give you the pills that have the sweetest taste.

C. A reply to Plato

CHAMPION OF DEMOCRACY: I feel quite repelled by this account of Plato's. It is government without the consent of the governed. It involves saying that a human being is to have no share in deciding how he shall be governed and who is going to do it. Even when the government is benevolent and the aims of the rulers are good, it is still government by others, imposed from the outside. True, we may sometimes govern ourselves badly, but then we have only ourselves to blame; but government imposed on us by those whom we have had no share in electing to office, is degrading, even when that government is good. We can feel respect for a government only when we have had some share in shaping its policies. We can obey laws with willingness and respect only if we ourselves, through our elected representatives, have had some share in passing them; we are - more *likely* to obey them too. After all, government plays a considerable part in our lives: it levies taxes, it provides benefits; in time of war it may even call upon us to die for our countries. If government has such an influence on us, shouldn't we, who do the paying and the dying, have a share in determining its policies and a chance to change the policies if enough of us disagree with them?

CHAMPION OF PLATO: The trouble is that when the people govern, it is mob rule, and there is no guarantee that the policies decided upon will be for the interests of the people themselves. It's true, I suppose, that the people will not *knowingly* legislate themselves into slavery or disaster; but, as Plato said, the people are often blind as to their own interests; they will follow the confectioners instead of the physicians; and thus, without meaning to, they will put into action stupid and shortsighted policies which may bring disaster upon them all.

D: Although I think your estimate of the people is unduly pessimistic, it's true that they will make mistakes. I contend, however, that if mistakes are made, it should be the people's mistakes, not the mistakes of those who rule over them without their consent. The people's welfare and their very lives are often in the hands of the government, and therefore they should have some share in shaping its policies. A government should reflect the views of its people; and when there are differing opinions within the nation, these differences should be reflected in governmental deliberations. In a democracy all points of view are represented. Not all of them may be equally represented, and of course they can't all win out on a specific issue, but at least the whole spectrum of popular opinion is present in the elected representatives.

P: It's true that democratic government is government by the majority. The majority win — not even the majority of the people, but the majority of their elected representatives — on each issue discussed. But what happens to the minorities? Democracies can be just as cruel to their own minority groups (who may, after all, be right) as a dictatorship can be to its people.

D: It is true that a democracy, involving the rule of the majority, is often unfair to its own minority groups. But at least a minority is more likely to have a voice there than in any other type of government. Where there is no democracy, a minority may be ruthlessly suppressed. In a democracy, issues are openly discussed by the elected representatives of a people, and the losing side is at least heard; the losers can agitate for a change and may later become the majority. So at least you have in democracy a better chance for representation of all shades of opinion.

P: You will indeed find all shades of opinion, and the party that can (by hook or by crook) muster the most votes on an issue will win. But numerical superiority does not mean that the decision arrived at is the right one. Legislators are answerable to their people and know that they won't be re-elected if they don't vote most of the time as the majority of their constituents desire them to, regardless of whether the majority of their constituents are right. And of course the majority — of the people, and through them their representatives in government — may well be wrong. One person may make a wrong decision, but if he can persuade a thousand others to share his convictions, there will be a thousand people in error. There is nothing in sheer numbers that makes it more likely that the most numerous will also be right. An error compounded a thousandfold is an error still. And quantity does not necessarily imply quality.

D: But even when the people are wrong, by having a share in government they have a chance to profit by their own mistakes. Their education will take time, and by the time they have learned, another generation will have arisen that has to learn all over again; true. But at least, since they do have a share in shaping policies, they have a *chance* to learn by their own mistakes. Memory is short, and complex causal relations, such as are involved in political policies, are difficult for most people to grasp; so often they won't learn. But at least there is some *educative* value in people's being able to make their own mistakes instead of having people above them dictating policies without their consent. The best reply to Plato's *Republic* is Mill's *Representative Government*. Mill argues that even if we had a perfect autocracy (meaning any government not elected by the people, whether it is the worst tyranny or Plato's ideal state), it would still be worse than a bad democracy because the people would be prevented from shaping their own destinies — even from legislating fickle and shortsighted policies, yes, even from unwittingly legislating themselves into destruction. Listen to Mill:

It has long . . . been a common saying, that if a good despot could be ensured, despotic monarchy would be the best form of government. . . . The supposition is, that absolute power, in the hands of an eminent individual, would ensure a virtuous and intelligent performance of all the duties of government. Good laws would be established and enforced, bad laws would be reformed; the best men would be placed in all situations of trust; justice would be as well administered, the public burdens would be as light and as judiciously imposed, every branch of administration would be as purely and as intelligently conducted, as the circumstances of the country and its degree of intellectual and moral cultivation would admit. I am willing, for the sake of the argument, to concede all this; but I must point out how great the concession is; how much more is needed to produce even an approximation to these results than is conveyed in the simple expression, a good despot. Their realization would in fact imply, not merely a good monarch, but an all-seeing one. He must be at all times informed correctly, in considerable detail, of the conduct and working of every branch of administration, in every district of the country, and must be able, in the twenty-four hours per day which are all that is granted to a king as to the humblest laborer, to give an effective share of attention and superintendence to all parts of this vast field; or he must at least be capable of discerning and choosing out, from among the mass of his subjects, not only a large abundance of honest and able men, fit to conduct every branch of public administration under supervision and control, but also the small number of men of eminent virtues and talents who can be trusted not only to do without that supervision, but to exercise it themselves over others. So extraordinary are the faculties and energies required for performing this task in any supportable manner, that the good despot whom we are supposing can hardly be imagined as consenting to undertake it, unless as a refuge from intolerable evils, and a transitional preparation for something beyond.

But . . . suppose the difficulty vanquished. What should we then have? One man of superhuman mental activity managing the entire affairs of a mentally passive people. Their passivity is implied in the very idea of absolute power. The nation as a whole, and every individual composing it, are without any potential voice in their own destiny. They exercise no will in respect to their collective interests. All is decided for them by a will not their own, which it is legally a crime for them to disobey. What sort of human beings can be formed under such a regime? What development can either their thinking or their active faculties attain under it? On matters of pure theory they might perhaps be allowed to speculate, so long as their speculations either did not approach politics, or had not the remotest connection with its practice. On practical affairs they could at most be only suffered to suggest; and even under the most moderate of despots, none but persons of already admitted or reputed superiority could hope that their suggestions would be known to, much less regarded by, those who had the management of affairs. A person must have a very unusual taste for intellectual exercise in and for itself, who will put himself to the trouble of thought when it is to have no outward effect, or qualify himself for functions which he has no chance of being allowed to exercise. The only sufficient incitement to mental exertion, in any but a few minds in a generation, is the prospect of some practical use to be made of its results. . . . Wherever the sphere of action of human beings is artificially circumscribed, their sentiments are narrowed and dwarfed in the same proportion. The food of feeling is action: even domestic affection lives upon voluntary good offices. Let a person have nothing to do for his country, and he will not care for it.[1]

p: Calling a bad democracy better than the best autocracy seems to me like cutting off your nose to spite your face. The object of government in the first place is to handle political affairs as wisely as possible for the good of the people; whichever form of government can do this best is the best government. And if autocracy of one kind or another can do it better than democracy, then that is what we should have. Certainly if a democracy legislates itself into catastrophe, it has lost its excuse for existing: it has given the ultimate proof that it is unworthy and that we had better have another form of government which would prevent such a disaster. Freedom of action isn't worth paying for at the price of catastrophe for the entire country.

d: But an autocracy will arrive at that result sooner than a democracy.

[1] From John Stuart Mill, *Representative Government*. Ed. by R. B. McCallum. Oxford: Blackwell, 1957, pp. 136-38. Reprinted by permission of the publisher.

When a despot misrules, he changes the people; when a president misrules, the people change him. Even if a despotic ruler, or council of such rulers, were to observe many of the rules and restraints of constitutional government,

> . . . he might allow such freedom of the press and of discussion as would enable a public opinion to form and express itself on national affairs. He might suffer local interests to be managed, without the interference of authority, by the people themselves. He might even surround himself with a council or councils of government, freely chosen by the whole or some portion of the nation; retaining in his own hands the power of taxation, and the supreme legislative as well as executive authority. Were he to act thus, and so far abdicate as a despot, he would do away with a considerable part of the evils characteristic of despotism. Political activity and capacity for public affairs would no longer be prevented from growing up in the body of the nation; and a public opinion would form itself not the mere echo of the government. But such improvement would be the beginning of new difficulties. This public opinion, independent of the monarch's dictation, must be either with him or against him; if not the one, it will be the other. All governments must displease many persons, and these having now regular organs, and being able to express their sentiments, opinions adverse to the measures of government would often be expressed. What is the monarch to do when these unfavorable opinions happen to be in the majority? Is he to alter his course? Is he to defer to the nation? If so, he is no longer a despot, but a constitutional king; an organ or first minister of the people, distinguished only by being irremovable. If not, he must either put down opposition by his despotic power, or there will arise a permanent antagonism between the people and one man, which can have but one possible ending. . . . However great an amount of liberty the citizens might practically enjoy, they could never forget that they held it on sufferance, and by a concession which under the existing constitution of the State might at any moment be resumed; that they were legally slaves, though of a prudent, or indulgent, master.[1]

It's true of course that democracy is often cumbersome, unwieldy, and irritatingly slow and inefficient, but it has to be so simply *because* it is the rule of the many and must represent the vast variety of opinions existing within it. When we are chafing at these weaknesses, it is all too easy to fall into a dangerous trap: we admire so much the ease and efficiency with which a complex policy can be put into operation by an autocracy that doesn't have to bother about elected representatives or congressional committees, that we sometimes wish we ourselves could do likewise, and have a benevolent despotism that would be equally efficient.

> It is not much to be wondered at if impatient or disappointed reformers, groaning under the impediments opposed to the more salutary public improvements by the ignorance, the indifference, the intractableness, the perverse obstinacy of a people, and the corrupt combinations of selfish private interests armed with the powerful weapons afforded by free institutions, should at times

[1] *Ibid.*, pp. 139-40.

sigh for a strong hand to bear down all these obstacles, and compel a recalcitrant people to be better governed. But (setting aside the fact, that for one despot who now and then reforms an abuse, there are ninety-nine who do nothing but create them) those who look in any such direction for the realization of their hopes leave out of the idea of good government its principal element, the improvement of the people themselves. One of the benefits of freedom is that under it the ruler cannot pass by the people's minds, and amend their affairs for them without amending them. If it were possible for the people to be well governed in spite of themselves, their good government would last no longer than the freedom of a people usually lasts who have been liberated by foreign arms without their own cooperation. It is true, a despot may educate the people; and to do so really, would be the best apology for his despotism. But any education which aims at making human beings other than machines, in the long run makes them claim to have the control of their own actions.[1]

P: Would you insist, then, that all governments should be democratic, even when democracy means ignorance and corruption and misgovernment of the most blatant sort? Remember recent events in Pakistan: the democracy was utterly corrupt; most of the people were illiterate and had no idea whom they were voting for and what their policies were, and the corruption was becoming intolerable to the people themselves. So a benevolent autocrat from the army came along, took the situation into his own hands, instituted countless badly needed reforms, brought efficiency to the government, got rid of the corrupt officials — and now for the first time the nation is thriving and prosperous; the people themselves are far better off, and they know it. Would you say that the autocrat should not have taken hold of the government and done these things, not even to save the country, for that is surely what he did?

D: Usually when an autocrat takes over he is far from benevolent, and he uses the people to serve his selfish ends. Even when he is benevolent, he seldom remains so for long — the power goes to his head. But even in that rare instance (Pakistan may be one) in which he not only begins as a wise and benevolent autocrat but remains one, there is only one excuse for his taking over: to train and educate the people so that as soon as possible *they* can take over. His rulership is only a kind of stewardship — a means to an end, the end being that the people themselves should take over from him at the earliest possible moment. In such a situation he is like a father to a nation of children, who must be trained to grow up into responsible adults. And of course, they must really *be* like children, unable yet to take care of themselves politically. Usually, however, they are just as fit to rule as he is, but he rationalizes himself into thinking they are children so that he can make use of them. Even in granting this much, I would probably be granting more than Mill would. Mill, if you remember, says that a good autocracy

[1] *Ibid.*, p. 140.

is really worse than a bad one, for a good one deludes the people into thinking that everything is all right; and they don't bother to prepare themselves
to take over —"leave it to Father" they will say — and they don't develop
the initiative and discipline they will need later in governing themselves —
an initiative and discipline which of course are vital in other aspects of their
lives as well.

p: I still think you are cutting off your nose to spite your face. You want
a democracy even when democracy is *not* the best for all concerned. But the
main reason why it is not the best for all concerned is one I haven't yet
mentioned — it is essentially Plato's reason: government is a highly specialized and difficult undertaking, and most people have no conception of
what it means to govern well. To be well run, this complex function must
be taken over by specialists. We don't elect doctors by popular vote on the
basis of a popularity campaign. We would not dare trust our health and
our very lives to people who didn't have the training for judging such matters. Even less should we put our lives into the hands of people who had
not (as in Plato's *Republic*) passed a severe series of tests to be sure that
they were adequately trained for the job. It comes to this: government, especially in the twentieth century (more than could even have been imagined
in Plato's day), requires the utmost in skill, patience, talent, courage, information, dedication — a combination of qualities which is rare indeed; and
to be sure that the few people who have the most of these qualities come
to the top, we cannot, we dare not, entrust the matter to a democratic popularity contest; we must only be sure that the men are completely qualified
for the positions they hold. Not just anybody can be entrusted to operate on
patients, and not just anybody can be trusted to rule states, no matter how
much they may be favored by the people.

d: I grant of course that rulers should be well trained for their jobs. But
I am suspicious of having just *one* ruler. No matter how good he is, power
is likely to compromise his ideals in the end. It takes a man of immense
strength not to be swayed by immense power once he has it in his grip.
Besides, even if he resists the temptation, what of those who come after him?
If the rulership is hereditary, there is no way of guaranteeing that the king's
son will be also a good king; and if it is left to chance (whoever is strong
enough to take over the government after the ruler is dead), the situation
is even worse; for then the succession comes about through revolution with
its accompanying chaos and anarchy, and the man who succeeds to power
under such conditions is already likely to be a ruthless man who rules to
serve himself and not the people.

p: Plato took care of the problems of despotism and succession by not
having one ruler with absolute power but by having a council of rulers
instead, each of whom arrived at his high office on the basis of a series of
super-civil-service examinations.

d: I know, but I am suspicious of that arrangement too. For one thing, who devises these examinations? This seems to me a crucial point, which Plato never discusses. Countless opportunities for corruption can enter here: "I'll pass you if you do so-and-so for me," "For a price I'll tell you what's in the next exam." What is going to guarantee the incorruptibility as well as the high level of intelligence required of the examiners? Another point: how is the system going to get started? How is the current ruler going to be pushed off the throne to make way for Plato's Council of Rulers? (In view of the long period of education required, it would take a long while for the system to get started even if it were known how the assumption of power was going to take place.) And what is going to control the Council of Rulers after they are in office? How are we going to make sure that they continue their severe Spartan regimen which Plato prescribed for them? What is to keep them from legislating that requirement out of existence? Who would stop them? The army? but the army is also corruptible; more so, probably, than the leaders themselves. The Council of Rulers is beholden to nobody. And the people, remember, are given no check on the rulers' activities.

Since the rulers are not answerable to the people for anything, what is to stop them from rescinding all the controls and requirements which Plato demanded of their high office — the lack of material rewards, the regulation about wives and children? It would take only one bad move of that sort to start a whole chain reaction of corruption and deterioration among the rulers; and sooner or later this bad move would be bound to occur. Once decay did set in, the people would have no recourse but bloodshed and revolution — revolution which would be difficult indeed because the rulers have at their disposal the guardians (the army) who are trained in physical combat as a full-time profession and who would surely support the rulers, no matter how corrupt, knowing full well on what side their bread was buttered. No, it would be a sticky business.

P: I grant you that there are difficulties in the system as Plato described it. But these are matters of detail; once you agree with me that his type of government is best, I think we could work out these details. Let's stick to principles.

D: Very well. I would urge, then, as an objection to *any* nondemocratic type of government, that as long as the rulers are not answerable to the people, sooner or later, in spite of Plato's precautions, corruption is bound to set in; and when it begins, it will run through the system like a cancer, and the people will be helpless to stop it, save by revolution. If corruption and revolution is the price we have to pay to have experts running the government, then the price is too high. Besides, it doesn't take experts to elect experts to the government. I don't have to be an expert in cookery to judge that a cook is bad; it is enough to taste the dinners she prepares. I can tell whether she prepared a good or a bad dinner without knowing how she prepared it.

p: That is where you're wrong. You can tell whether the dinner *tastes* good; but you can't tell without knowledge, *not* derived from your sense of taste, whether or not it is a *healthful* dinner. That is Plato's whole point in his analogy of the physicians and the confectioners. Of course if you don't care whether it's a healthful dinner but care only about the taste, you will be indifferent to what physicians and nutritionists may have to say about it. But government is a long-term affair, and surely one isn't interested in the welfare of the state only for the moment.

d: I see your point. Nevertheless, I have considerable qualms about your staff of experts as rulers. There are experts in the law, in medicine, in warfare, in horse-breeding, in automobile repair, and so on. The role of experts is always to serve as a means, and the most efficient possible means, toward a given end. Once we grant the end — say, the restoration of health to the sick — then of course we want experts (physicians) rather than nonexperts as the best possible means of achieving this end. But the expert himself cannot tell us what ends are worth pursuing. The expert's task is to provide the means toward a specified end, but not to specify the end. (In the example of the physician the problem doesn't arise since we all agree on the end.)

p: I should think that the end is as clear in statecraft as elsewhere. The end of government is to see to the welfare of the governed, to serve the collective interests of the people, exactly as in Plato's analogy the end of shepherding is to take the best possible care of the sheep. Surely you agree to that.

d: Of course: government is for the welfare of the governed, not for the aggrandizement of the governors. But all the same I doubt whether the similarity between government and the other skills is very great. The general proposition that the end of government is the best interest of the governed, of course I admit; but within the scope of that general proposition, it seems to me that those who govern not only serve admitted ends (as doctors, electricians, and plumbers do), they also shape and determine the ends themselves which the government shall pursue. And their decisions about which ends shall be pursued is not one for which their training as experts especially prepares them in the way it does their decisions about means. It is reasonable to consult an expert on what means we should adopt once the end is specified, but the situation is not the same with regard to the ends at which the governmental policies should aim. For example, whether or not giving financial aid to a certain backward nation is likely to win their friendship or help them fight evil ideologies is a question on which it takes an expert to inform us; only he knows the exact situation of that nation in all its causal complexity. But whether the end aimed at is itself a good thing — whether the ideology in question is really an evil one — is a moral question which is not the special prerogative of the expert. On that matter, an intelligent layman is just as likely to be a good judge as is the expert. I am all in favor of leaving decisions about means to experts, and we need (today more than ever before) experts in every branch of the increasingly complicated business of government. But the framing of the policies themselves requires people not only with expert knowledge but with wisdom, patience, moral dedication; and these qualities we are no more likely to find among experts than among ordinary laymen. Therefore I do not want to delegate to experts the task of framing these ends; experts are specialists in one field who may not even see in due proportion the other fields (and they can't be specialists in all); experts are notorious for not seeing the woods for the trees. It requires men of great vision and understanding, with the *assistance* of experts who can inform them of countless details that they themselves cannot possibly know, to rule the state. I gladly leave the choice of means to experts — that is what they are trained for; but I do not willingly leave the choice of ends to them. The freedom to choose ends must be left, ultimately, to the people themselves.

p: But I would remind you once again of Plato. The people, with all their ignorance and indifference and suggestibility, simply do not know what is good for them. They are like sheep. When left to themselves they are as likely to choose ends which do not serve their long-run mutual interest as those which do.

d: They are not as likely to choose proper *means* as experts are; the experts, as I have already suggested, should be the determiners of the means. But I am not at all confident that experts are any more likely than intelligent and conscientious nonexperts to choose the right ends. This, I repeat, should be left in the hands of the people through their elected representatives. Experts may inform me of facts which I did not know, which may well affect my decisions; but it would take more faith than I have in any expert to convince me that an expert's decision on an important matter of governmental policy, a decision which affects my prosperity and perhaps my very life, is a good one when it seems to me evil and misguided, unless, of course, he could show me that my rejection of his policy arose from my ignorance of some of the facts about which the expert could inform me.

p: But you surely admit that the people and their elected representatives are highly fallible and make countless mistakes.

d: Of course; the history of any democracy is too full of examples of this weakness for me to deny it. But I insist that any other form of government will make even more mistakes — through misuse of power, through highhanded decisions made without consulting the people affected by them, through failure to cultivate the people's own potentialities for self-government. The situation is, of course, an uncomfortable one no matter what type of government one has. When the people themselves cannot make all the decisions (and this is impossible in anything larger than a New England town meeting) but must have other people presiding over them and making decisions for them, then our problems multiply, and mistakes and abuses and corruptions are bound to enter in whether those presiding are kings or dictators or ruling councils or elected representatives. When some have to govern others, the situation is bad — and yet that situation cannot be prevented. Any form of government is an attempt to make the best of that bad situation. No government is perfect, or even very good; I only insist that, all things considered, democracy is less bad than the others.

P: Here lies the root of our disagreement. Democracy is *not* the best form of government because the people do not know their own true interests. We have already seen this to be so on the individual level, and it is the same way — multiplied many times over — on the social and political level. I admit that the government should serve the people's interests, but I don't believe that the people are wise enough or foresighted enough to know what these interests are or how they should pursue them. In matters of government at least, they must be led by the comparative few who do have the wisdom and foresight.

D: You are right that the judgment of democracy is the root of our disagreement. It is true that people are fallible, subject to persuasion and prejudice, and that they make countless tragic mistakes. But if they don't know their own interests, does the man who presumes to lead them know them better? If someone does know, who is to say that he does, and how does he know that he knows? And even if he does know and we know that he knows, it is still wrong for one man or ruling clique to impose his will on us. It is wrong for him to *make* us do even what *we* think is to our own best interests. Even if the planner plans much more wisely than we ourselves would and even if he plans for our welfare rather than for his own, the fact remains that *he* is planning *our* lives, and *we* are not free to make our own mistakes and exercise our prerogative of free and independent action. Even if a perfectly wise and benevolent individual — even a benevolent God — were at the head of a government and planning the citizens' lives far more wisely than they themselves could do, I would still consider such a government far worse than if the citizens themselves, limited and fallible as they are, were free to elect their own destiny.

But needless to say, those at the head of even the most benevolent dictatorship are far from being God. And the more power they retain in their own hands, without opportunity of being checked in free elections, the more they will plan and dominate the lives of those whom they govern. That is the ultimate ignominy and degradation: that my life and your life should be in the hands of another human being, who can rule your work, your activities, your very life, without consent from you. Again it is Mill who has said the last word on this subject:

> A fixed rule, like that of equality, might be acquiesced in, and so might chance, or an external necessity; but that a handful of human beings should weigh everybody in the balance, and give more to one and less to another at their sole pleasure and judgment, would not be borne unless from persons believed to be more than men, and backed by supernatural terrors.[1]

---

[1] J. S. Mill, *Principles of Political Economy,* Bk. 1, Ch. 2, par. 4.

D. *Relations between nations*

Within each nation, there is a certain amount of security simply because there is not a state of nature: there are laws, and a certain amount of law enforcement; the government undertakes many tasks which would be impossible for private individuals or other organizations to assume. Thus, highways are built, research is subsidized, retirement benefits are secured, and post offices and libraries are kept going. Many governments are mismanaged and headed by unworthy men; some of them assume too many functions and restrict the freedom of the people unnecessarily, whereas others provide less than the most elementary security; but at least there is, within the province of each government, not a state of nature. Even a bad government is better than no government at all.

Nevertheless there is, in the existence of separate nations side by side, each with complete power within its own borders, an ever-increasing danger. Consider:

1. As world population increases and nations become larger, government becomes a huge and sprawling affair, whose left hand often knoweth not what its right hand doeth. Its power increases in order to unify more completely an ever larger population. As life becomes ever more complex, more and more powers hitherto unthought of (such as the assigning of television channels) become vested in the government — but in appointed, not elected, government. In the United States, for example, more and more power centers in the executive branch of the government. The legislative branch, directly elected by the people, becomes too slow and cumbersome to make necessary quick decisions, while simultaneously it becomes less representative, since one member of Congress represents an ever larger number of constituents. The number of government bureaus and agencies — in the executive branch and not directly responsible to the people — grows and proliferates at a dizzying pace. The people, meanwhile, ever more numerous, become more distant from the workings of government and less able to comprehend them — they tend toward an attitude of resigned quietism ("let the experts take care of it"). They become increasingly indifferent as they become less and less able to control government directly. Letters and protests have little effect when the government is so vast and unwieldy that it takes a concerted and superhuman effort by thousands of people to make their influence felt even ever so slightly.[1]

2. The situation is even worse in nondemocratic governments. If there should be a rebellion, there are many devices available for suppressing it. The rebels can be subjected to refinements of torture such as no previous age has known — and all but a few will become quivering conformists rather than submit to more of it. But torture is already becoming out of date:

[1] For a detailed and dramatic illustration of this tendency in government, see Amaury de Riencourt, *The Coming Caesars* (New York: Coward-McCann, 1957).

there are subtle means of psychological conditioning (not to mention pills and opiates) which will sooner or later succeed in undermining the *mind* of the rebel until he becomes not a quivering conformist of no use to the state but an eager and willing disciple of the regime.

3. Any future Hitler could use these latest developments given him by the psychologists not only to suppress rebels but to insure the absolute and undeviating obedience of all his subjects so that a rebellion could not even get started. In the past, after years of chains and bondage, people could break out in rebellion and, either the first time or the tenth, finally succeed after much revolution and bloodshed. But today a clever dictator could convert people into sheep and take away from them the independence of mind that would be required to start a rebellion. A Gandhi, for example, would not be possible in the Soviet Union. Because he would not be given an opportunity to publicize his views, his cause could never become known. The government-controlled radios and newspapers would suppress all report of his actions, and no one would ever hear about him. The moment he tried to get even a few others to share his views, he would be taken off to prison and never heard of again. In a populous nation the people are dependent on modern means of communication for information about the world at large; but if these means of communication are controlled by the government, the information dispensed to the people will be only such information as the government wants the people to have.

4. With such powers, leaders can foment wars, even though their people do not want them. Consider the following situation: Two peoples do not want war with each other; they crave only peace. But the leaders, wishing to extend the range of their power, want war. Since they are not responsible to the people (except in a democratic government, but even there, as we have seen, they are becoming less so), they can, if they control a strong secret police, a strong army, and an efficiently run group of governmental agencies, get their vast armies to go to war and kill off the armies of the opposing nation. Each group will slaughter thousands of men in the other group, although the individuals in neither group have any desire to do so (except such desire as is whipped up in the government-controlled newspapers and radios). As individuals they have nothing against one another; yet they will slaughter one another by the million because of the predatory desires of a few leaders and their economic policies against one another.

Why should the leaders be so different in their desires and aims from the people as a whole or even from the army as a whole? Partly because the leaders are not likely to die — rather they will cause their subjects to die for them; but also because the entire system of power is such that it tends to perpetuate a ruling group — people who have ruthless ambition, craving for power, and animosity against other human beings. Only such people have the incentive to climb to the top of the organization that commands all the rest. With these ruthless men secure at the helm, one move from them can set the whole machinery of a vast and efficient organization in motion, causing millions of men who don't want to kill, to kill, nevertheless, millions of other men who don't want to kill either.

This tragic situation has always existed among nations, but modern conditions of governmental control exacerbate the disease.

In other words, although Hobbes's state of nature does not exist within nations, it does exist in the relation of every nation to every other. There is, of course, the United Nations, but it has no military power — only the power (greater than might at first appear) of airing disputes and mobilizing world opinion. But there is no central authority which has the power to arbitrate disputes and enforce its decisions. The result is that the nations of the world are in the same relation to one another that individuals were in at the (hypothetical) time before there were any tribes or nations, that is, in the state of nature:

a. Each nation fears and mistrusts the others; Nation #1, which has not the slightest desire to encroach upon any other nation, builds up huge armies and missile bases and spends half its national income on armaments in order to be protected against possible attack by Nation #2.

b. Nation #2, seeing Nation #1 arm against it, arms itself in turn, believing that Nation #1 means to attack it. In fact Nation #2 outdoes Nation #1 in order to guarantee victory against #1's attack. But Nation #1, seeing the activity of Nation #2 and believing its suspicions about #2's aggressive intentions to be confirmed, arms itself even more fully, further impoverishing its people in order to do so. Nation #2 in turn, observing this development, believes *its* suspicions about #1 to be confirmed and arms itself even further; the cycle is endless.

c. Although Nations #1 and #2 may not have aggressive intent toward each other, each one believes that the other does have aggressive intent. The newspapers and radios of each nation are full of propaganda material about the evil intentions and evil character of the other; and gradually popular opinion in each nation becomes inflamed against the other, requiring only a spark to set it off.

d. Voices begin to cry out in Nation #1, saying, "Nation #2 is going to attack us. Hadn't we better jump the gun on them by attacking them first? In modern war the one who strikes first has an enormous advantage. Therefore, if we strike first, we'll be much more likely to win." This military fact, of course, is no secret in Nation #2, and voices in #2 start to sing the same refrain. Sooner or later one of the nations will be bound to attack the other, waging a "preventive war" that has no rational cause and which would never have occurred if there had been an organization for arbitrating the disputes in the way that the courts of a nation arbitrate disputes between individuals and organizations within it. Since it takes only one nation to start a war, when many other nations are added to #1 and #2, the outbreak of war becomes even more likely.

Not only is this "state of nature" among nations extremely likely to lead to war — a war which, in the second half of the twentieth century, is likely to mean the end of civilization — the "state of nature" also demands and debases the character of the people in all the nations which are engaged in an arms race and in spreading hate-propaganda. Suppose that Nation #3, having achieved after a century of pioneer effort a measure of material comfort and security, can now devote more of its attention to culture and the humanities; it entertains no aggressive intent toward any other nation. Hating war and killing, it reduces its armed forces and spends the money thus saved on more education and social improvements for its people. Nation #4, observing this development, sees its opportunity: neglecting culture and the amenities of life, it trains its young people only in science and technology; it makes its people work many hours a day to increase its military production, and it sends into labor camps those who refuse to comply. Those who insist on voicing dissenting ideas are shot, and a large police force terrorizes most potential dissenters into submission. Meanwhile, the government wages an intensive fear-and-hate campaign against Nation #3 in the government-controlled press, a campaign which spurs on the people in Nation #4 to work even harder, to meet the attack by Nation #3 which their government has convinced them is coming. Nor does this government set much value on individual life: it is willing to sacrifice thirty million people if necessary in order to win victory against Nation #3.

What is Nation #3 to do? If it is to survive, it must go at least a considerable distance on the road that Nation #4 is taking. Nation #3 must shelve its emphasis upon culture (and the other ends toward which its benevolent government is a means) and concentrate on armaments; it must awaken its people to a tremendous effort, which is not likely to be accomplished unless it too starts an intensive hate-and-fear campaign. If war comes, it must be able to fight just as savagely as Nation #4, and with all the technical efficiency which Nation #4 has devoted its entire national effort to achieving. Nation #3 must take all these steps to have even a fair chance of winning. Assuming that it finally wins — as much as any nation can win in modern warfare — the danger is that after the war is over, the nation will have become so accustomed to the means it had to use to overcome its enemy that it will be almost impossible to go back to a life in which cultural values were looked upon with favor. That is the tragedy of modern war. It takes only one rotten apple to infect all the others in the basket, and it takes only one strong nation which refuses to cooperate peaceably and develops military values exclusively (such as Hitler's Germany) to plunge the rest of the world into a holocaust.

As long as the state of nature persists among nations, war will be a constant danger to all of them. Since there is no superpower to stop them, it takes only one or two powerful nations, animated each by the fear of attack by the other, to plunge all of them into war. The others then have the choice of meeting the challenge with blind force or capitulating and seeing their civilized values, developed long and arduously through the centuries, disappear in smoke. They must either do what they believe to be evil or see the evil triumph over them, perhaps forever.

Consider two children: Johnny would like to persuade Billy by argument, for Johnny is truly convinced that right is on his side. But Billy will not listen to him. Billy has no respect for arguments or for verbal persuasion; the only thing that Billy respects is force. If Johnny is able to beat Billy in a fight, then perhaps Billy will have enough respect for Johnny to listen to him or at any rate to do his bidding. So if Johnny is to have any chance for his reasoning to have any effect on Billy, he will have to learn to fight, even if he would prefer to do other things, even if he despises physical force as a way of settling disputes. If he does not learn to fight, Billy will have only contempt for him and whatever he stands for; besides, Billy, knowing of Johnny's unwillingness or inability to fight, will get together with other boys, gang up on Johnny, and mash him to a pulp.

To be sure, that Billy may win out over Johnny proves nothing about which of them is right. Perhaps Billy's side of the argument is better, and perhaps Johnny's is; but the fact that Billy wins in a fight with Johnny only shows that Billy is stronger or cleverer in fighting, not that reason is on his side. To *that* issue, the outcome of the fight is simply irrelevant.

Yet, in a hostile world, right is not *effective* unless it is backed up by might. Without might and all the deterioration of character and the misery and horror that go with war, right itself may be destroyed in the onslaught. If the Allies had not mustered the might to win over Nazi Germany, all the right in the world would not have enabled civilized values to survive against it. (We have the same situation on a smaller scale in countless television westerns: the reformed gunman tries to "go straight," but others will have no respect for him unless he wins over them in a gunfight; against his will, in order to make his love of peace effective, he must violate it by doing battle, thus compromising or destroying the very thing he is trying to preserve.)

Here then is another tragedy of war — that there is no guarantee that the side that has the most might is also the side that has the most right. Many worthwhile causes have been buried for centuries because, noble though they may have been, the nations espousing them did not also excel in the military might required to preserve themselves against the purely military might of less high-minded nations. The champions of such causes have been noble idealists who thought that the nobility of their cause alone would be sufficient to win in a struggle of might. They saw what ghastly evil and destruction war had wrought on the face of the earth in countless past cultures and civilizations, and they resolved to have no part of it. They hated war so much, as barbaric and stupid and wasteful beyond all other human acts, that they refused to employ it as a means to an end. Then other, cruder nations attacked them, and they collapsed completely. (The pacifist film,

Grand Illusion, is said to have been one of the causes of the French collapse in the face of Hitler in 1940.) Or, if their cause did win, it was through no efforts of their own: like the pacifists in America in World War II, they stood by and deprecated war — the very war, however, which made it possible for them to go on living and preaching pacifism after the war was over.

Yet surely these idealists were right in condemning war. What could possibly be worse than war? Were not people of intelligence and sensitivity to human values correct in judging it to be the worst of all possible evils? Yet, no matter how right they were, when another nation attacks yours, you must fight fire with fire or you don't survive. Indeed, in a tragic irony, by the very condemnation of war — war, which you justly hate above all other things — by that very act you make it less likely that the ideals you uphold will win out against naked power. Because you see the evils so clearly — war's effect on human character, the difficulty of regaining civilized values after you have resorted to it — with all the strength and passion within you, you condemn it. Yet your very condemnation of war may be instrumental in eliminating you and all those who share your views, when a ruthless power sees in your hatred of war an opportunity to destroy you. Then you must either participate in the great evil or be engulfed by it.

What is the solution to such a ghastly dilemma? The only solution, surely, is the abolition of Hobbes's state of nature among nations. The same united force which governs a nation, a force without which the life of the individuals within it would be "nasty, brutish, and short," is required in international relations; the nations would take the part of individuals and a supranational authority (probably restricted in scope to military matters) would take the place of national government. All nations agree on this plan in principle, and men in all countries see it clearly enough, but the difficulties of bringing it about seem well-nigh insuperable. The inertia of each nation, the prejudices instilled in the people by propaganda through the centuries, the many vested interests and envisoned advantages in selfish bargaining and jockeying for position, the understandable hatreds and mistrust caused by past wars and aggressions — all these combine to make each nation hold on to its own preserves rather than venture into an enterprise which, if everyone cooperated in it, would save everyone. The nations are like our hypothetical individuals before uniting into a state; they know that unity would give them mutual security, yet they fear unity because some of their own sovereign freedom of action would thereby be taken away, and they are afraid because everything untried is yet unknown and what is unknown is always feared. Just as individuals, if they had never united into tribes or nations, would long since (through personal aggression and attrition) have vanished from the face of the earth; so, if the nations do not give up some things — however much their people may cherish them and however much they may have been taught to revere national values and patriotism through many centuries — in order to gain mutual security against aggression, they will soon have to give up not a few rights but all rights, including their own existence, when they are destroyed in a nuclear war.

EXERCISES

1. Analyze and evaluate George Bernard Shaw's view of the ethics of power as contained in his play, *Major Barbara* (many editions).

2. Analyze and evaluate the following comments on the ethics of power in *Major Barbara* by Charles Frankel. (From Robert Morrison MacIver, ed., *Great Moral Dilemmas*. New York: Harper, 1956, pp. 18-20. Reprinted by permission of the publisher.)

"What bothers us, of course, is not that Shaw says that money and power are what actually count in the world. We all know that, or say that we do. Nor does it bother us too much that Shaw exhibits the disparity between the code of Power we live by and the code of Virtue which we profess. We all enjoy being called down for our vices, and we would in fact be much more comfortable if we could take ·*Major Barbara* simply as an attack upon our hypocrisy. What bothers us is that Shaw joyfully turns Power into a moral system and holds everything up to criticism in its light. He does not ask us to be more virtuous, to be more sincere about living up to our professions. He asks us to be more sincere about our actual practice, to take its principles seriously and to see them through to their logical conclusions, to regard poverty and weakness consistently as crimes, and to turn the love of money and power into a moral code. The universal regard for money, he tells us, is the one hopeful fact in our civilization, the one sound spot in our social conscience. . . .

"This, of course, is what hurts. While we may admit that we all love money, we hate to see ourselves glorified for it. It takes the fun — or should I say Sin? — out of it. . . .

"It would be comforting to believe that Shaw is saying all this with his tongue in his cheek. But he is, of course, in deadly earnest. He does not want us to stop loving money and power. He wants us to love money and power seriously and unashamedly, to commit ourselves to them, and to what the love of them entails. What are the reasons for this remarkably straightforward espousal of the morality of Power? The reasons are the classic ones — the reasons of Machiavelli and Hobbes and Marx and Nietzsche. And they show, I think, that Shaw is right.

"In the first place, most moral exhortation is majestically, indeed callously, irrelevant. It is irrelevant in the way in which it is irrelevant to tell a man playing football that hard tackling hurts. It is irrelevant because the standards which most moralists employ have almost nothing to do with the choices that men actually have to make. While moralists talk, history goes on behind their backs. For moral talk is relevant only when the individual can be held responsible for his choices, when it is possible for him to do otherwise than he is doing and to meet the standards that the moralist is imposing on him. But very little moral talk is really of this kind. And if it were, it would be rooted in facts and not in a priori ideals. It would be a morality of power and not of abstract goodness.

"Secondly, most moral exhortation is in the profoundest sense hypocritical. For only the love of power, as Shaw points out, stands the test of the Categorical Imperative. If everyone acted as Undershaft does, if everybody made it a point of honor to have money and power, if everybody would rather die than be poor and weak, the result would not be horrible at all. The result would be a revolution of incalculable beneficence. For it is an obvious and elementary fact that it is not power but weakness that makes men's lives nasty, brutish, mean, and short. 'I was a dangerous man,' says Undershaft, 'until I had my will. Now I am a useful, beneficent, kindly person. When that is the history of every Englishman, we shall have an England worth living in.' And as for our alleged love of Virtue, we do not, of course, really want everybody to be virtuous, come hell or high-water. Despite all our talk about the absolute character of morality, our moral judgments are in fact relative and circumstantial. We are all for truth and honor and brotherly love, for example, and we hope that our diplomats will go forth armed with these ideals. But we would complain, and we would have a right to complain, if they negotiated on this basis. . . .

"Moral preaching satisfies something it ostensibly opposes, namely, our love of power. This is the great secret weapon of the preacher. Hypocrisy, someone has said, is the tribute vice pays to virtue; well, moral talk is the poor man's substitute for power. Next to really having power, talk about Virtue is unbeatable as a way of building up a man's ego. This is true even when we flay that ego. For it makes the individual feel that he can change the world just by changing himself, that his struggle with his own soul is the struggle that will settle the destiny of mankind. Nothing could be more consoling. 'My dear, you are the incarnation of morality,' Undershaft says to his wife. 'Your conscience is clear and your duty done when you have called everybody names.'

"But moral exhortation serves these convenient purposes at a fearful price. Psychologically, it puts an extra, and unnecessarily cruel, burden of anxiety on people. Sociologically, it systematically misleads them, for the great trouble with most preaching is that it diagnoses the source of the trouble wrongly. It talks about walking upright, when the rooms in which men walk have low ceilings. It talks about individual regeneration, when the trouble is the social paths that are open. It substitutes, in a word, anxiety for action, and empty and indignant words for a political program. It seems to me, therefore, that Machiavelli and Hobbes and Nietzsche and Shaw are right. Conventional morality is generally the snare of the weak and the consolation of the powerless. And I say this seriously, and I hope soberly."

3. Evaluate the following assertions:

a. Leon Trotsky: "In a country where the sole employer is the State, opposition means death by slow starvation. The old principle, who does not work shall not eat, has been replaced by a new one: who does not obey shall not eat."

b. From *Commandant of Auschwitz: the Autobiography of Rudolf Hoess* (London: Weidenfeld and Nicholson, 1959), pp. 144-45: "It was certainly an extraordinary order; nevertheless the reasons behind the extermination program seemed to me right; whether this mass extermination of the Jews was necessary or not was something on which I could not allow myself to form an opinion. The Fuehrer himself had given the order for the 'final solution to the Jewish question.' For an SS officer there could be no question of considering its merits;

'The Fuehrer commands, we follow' was never a mere phrase or a slogan, it was meant in bitter earnest."

c. (From *Common Sense and Nuclear Warfare* by Bertrand Russell. Copyright © 1959 by Bertrand Russell. Reprinted by permission of Simon and Schuster, Inc., pp. 78-79.): "What should we think of an individual who proclaimed: 'I am morally and intellectually superior to all other individuals, and, because of this superiority, I have a right to ignore all interests except my own'? There are, no doubt, plenty of people who *feel* this way, but if they proclaim their feeling too openly, and act upon it too blatantly, they are thought ill of. When, however, a number of such individuals, constituting the population of some area, collectively make such a declaration about themselves, they are thought noble and splendid and spirited. They put up statues to each other and teach schoolchildren to admire the most blatant advocates of the national conceit."

d. When the citizens of a democracy do not legislate in their own best interest, they should be "forced to be free." (Rousseau.)

4. Which of the following political manifestations (or what they represent) do you consider the worst? Why?

a. Government officials suppress a report which is for the good of the people to know, because the officials think that making it public would result in their defeat in the next election.

b. A citizen votes for Candidate A because "he has an honest face" and is faithful to his wife but rejects Candidate B because he is "too intellectual" and "has no right to criticize the government."

c. The school board of a certain large city bans from the public schools all books containing the concept of "one world," replacing all these books with others recommending "America First."

d. The chairman of a senate investigating committee brands as "subversive" anyone who criticizes his methods. The frightened employers of the institutions being investigated then cause all such critical persons to lose their jobs.

e. The presidential candidates, instead of bringing crucial issues before the people, confine themselves to frequent five-minute television appearances, looking glamorous and repeating slogans, in order thereby to win the election.

5. Do you take the following to constitute arguments against democracy? Why?

a. You take a car to a garage for repair. The mechanic knows that you have no specialized knowledge of the car's working parts and that he can get by with making false statements about what is wrong with the car; he therefore charges you for repairs which he has never made and others which he has performed in a slovenly manner. The trouble persists, and you return the car to the garage, and the mechanic gives you an inane series of excuses. By now you are suspicious and no longer believe him. Later, when you make another complaint about the car's condition (to him or another mechanic), and he tells you what happens to be the truth, you no longer believe him.

Similarly, in a democracy, the workings of government are even more complex than those of a car, the effects more lasting, and misrepresentation more difficult to detect. It is easy for government officials to give false explanations, to conceal, to suppress information, knowing that the public won't know the difference anyway, at least until after the next election, at which time the new incumbent will be blamed. If the new incumbent then (correctly) blames it on the previous administration, the public will not believe him.

b. One political candidate makes promises which he knows he cannot keep, but which succeed in getting him into office. By the time his false promises are known, the harm is already done and he is in office.

Another, a very honest and conscientious candidate, makes one small mistake. On the one hand, he knows that if he admits it, he will be criticized by his enemies, the truth will be distorted and falsified out of all recognition, and he will not be elected. On the other hand, if he says nothing, no one will know. But he decides to be honest at all costs, and he admits his mistake. His admission of error is magnified and distorted by the press, and he loses the election.

c. A democracy cannot act with the speed and secrecy of a dictatorship and hence is far more likely to be the victim than the aggressor in a surprise attack.

6. Consider the following ethical problems which arise in political contexts:

a. Should a judge, when a point of morals is involved, consider his own moral convictions or those of his state or community? Should a legislator vote in accordance with his own convictions or with those of the majority of the constituents who elected him to office? (See Edmond Cahn, *The Moral Decision* [Bloomington, Ind.: Indiana Univ. Press, 1955], pp. 302 ff.)

b. If a nation makes a treaty with another nation, has it a moral obligation to keep this treaty? even when it seems certain that the other nation will violate it? even after the other nation has violated it? even if in the meantime another government has been elected to office whose officials did not make the treaty and were in fact opposed to it at the time? (See J. D. Mabbott, *The State and the Citizen*, pp. 141-42.)

c. Do you consider it morally objectionable to have laws on the books which are not enforced, or are enforced only spasmodically? Why? (One point is this: An official can enforce the law when he wishes to in order to settle a private grudge. Now list some other points.)

7. Which of the following do you take to be proper functions of government? Why?

a. providing medical care for the aged
b. building roads and bridges
c. maintaining public schools
d. providing free hospitals for those unable to pay
e. providing social security and unemployment insurance
f. maintaining an office of patents and copyrights
g. providing economic aid for depressed areas and victims of disasters
h. subsidizing agriculture and industry
i. maintaining national parks and Indian reservations
j. inspecting meats, foods, and drugs
k. setting standards (and providing examinations) for admission to the practice of law and medicine
l. providing financial assistance to foreign nations

8. What would you consider it right to do in the following situations?

a. You are in favor of Candidate X — so much so that you feel his election is needed to save your country from disaster. On a television program you are asked about a certain episode in the life of Mr. X. You know that this episode did occur, but if you say so the candidate has very little chance of getting elected. Should you lie about it, knowing that if you lie publicly now and the lie later is revealed, no one will ever trust your assertions again? Should you claim ignorance?

b. You are a hereditary monarch in a backward country. Unlike your father and grandfather, you wish to make life easier for your subjects instead of holding them down by illiteracy and repressive measures. But you have only recently ascended the throne, and unrest has been growing in the kingdom owing to the repressive measures taken by your father. You would like to appeal to the people by radio, but they have no radios; you would like to reason with them, but they cannot follow rational arguments. It will take considerable time to make the improvements you plan. Meanwhile, unable to convince your subjects of your good intentions, you must try to quell a growing rebellion among the people — the very people you plan to benefit, but people who still wish to unseat you because of carefully planted rumors that you will be a worse king than your father. You are tempted to continue the policy of harsh measures *temporarily,* to quiet things down until you can institute the much needed reforms. Unless you take some action, chaos will result; but if you act vigorously, you will be only perpetuating your father's tradition of tyranny and bloodshed. You want to introduce reason, benevolence, a better life for your people — but ends will take time and cannot even be begun without a considerable degree of order and security existing first. What should you do? What measures should you take now?

c. As a benevolent dictator you want to see your people govern themselves. But if they try, there will be inefficiency, corruption, bloodshed, chaos. Yet if they are not given the chance, they will never become acquainted with the democratic process by firsthand experience: they have to begin sometime. Should you take the risk, give them the vote, and abdicate?

9. There is a distinction between political democracy and social democracy: social democracy is government for the people and political democracy is government by the people. Government might be for the people but by others, as in Plato's ideal state, and it might be by the people but not for the people, as when the elected representatives are corrupted and sell out to pressure groups and lobbies. Do you think that, granted social democracy as an end, political democracy is the best means of achieving it? the only means? (See R. B. Perry, *Puritanism and Democracy,* especially Chapter 16.)

10. Consider a view such as Nietzsche's, which not only disapproves political democracy as a means but condemns social democracy as an end. Can you attack the view that government should not be for the people but only for the benefit of a certain group (a "natural aristocracy of ability" for example) along the same lines as we have attacked ethical egoism in Chapter 4?

11. Which of the following (or perhaps none but another alternative instead) would you consider the proper course for your country to take if it were invaded by an enemy more powerful than you are? (*1*) Repel the invaders even if half or two-thirds of the people in your country are killed. (Is the defense worth this price?) (2) Try to win over the enemy by love rather than hate; dissolve his aggressiveness and hatred by turning the other cheek. ("Overcome hatred by love" was Spinoza's motto and seems, at least sometimes, to be the Christian position. But this recourse may be successful only if you occupy a position of power. If you tell your conqueror that you love him he will only laugh at you and plunder your people all the more and will attribute your professed love to a desire to curry his favor.) (3) Passive resistance as Gandhi preached it: resist but not by military means; do not obey his commands even if disobedience means death; and finally, *absorb* the enemy. (Will this process work, in your opinion? It is slow, but there may be less loss of life this way.)

12. Which of the following "utopias" do you consider the more undesirable? Why?

a. George Orwell, *Nineteen Eighty-four* (many editions).

b. Aldous Huxley, *Brave New World* (many editions) and *Brave New World Revisited* (New York: Harper, 1958).

13. Give a critical evaluation of Plato's "utopia" as described in the *Republic*.

14. Compare the suggestions on world government to be found in B. Russell, *Common Sense and Nuclear Warfare*, with those in J. D. Mabbott, *The State and the Citizen*, especially pages 142-47. What should be the function and limitations of authority of a world government?

15. "From Mill's ardent championship of political freedom, it would appear that he considers freedom an intrinsic good and not merely an instrument to human welfare." Do you agree or disagree? Why?

16. In which of the following situations do you believe our country would be morally justified in retaliating against Nation X?

a. Our cities are bombed by another nation without warning. Should we retaliate against Nation X in the belief that it is the aggressor? (It seems probable but not certain.)

b. A nerve gas has killed the entire population of one of our cities, but we do not yet know whether this disaster occurred by accident; circumstances indicate that it *may* have. We know that *if* it was not an accident, Nation X was the aggressor, for it was the only nation possessing this gas. If we do not retaliate by bombing its source of supply, we may pay in millions of casualties for our delay if another of our cities is gassed. But if we do retaliate, we will be killing enemy millions and perhaps starting a world war unnecessarily. What should we do?

c. Nation X bombs Great Britain. Shall we sacrifice our cities to help Britain? (Assume that they would certainly be bombed if we did.)

d. Nation X controls the moisture in the atmosphere, turning the Middle West into a desert. (Or: Nation X melts the Arctic ice cap, flooding our coastal cities.) Should we retaliate?

e. Radar and other sources reveal that missiles from Nation X have just been launched, but we do not yet know whether they are destined for our shores. Should we assume that they are and therefore counterattack? (If we wait we may lose everything; the decisive advantage lies in speed.)

f. Nation X circles the globe with satellites containing television sets revealing every square mile of our territory to its gaze, making us a perfect target for any future aggression it may plan. Should we bomb it at once or wait till it has taken advantage of its near omniscience to inflict precision bombing on us?

READING LIST, SECTION 18

Lord Acton. *Essays on Freedom and Power.* Chicago: Free Press, 1948. (Meridian Books.)

Aristotle. *Politics.* Many editions.

Burkhardt, Jacob. *Force and Freedom.* New York: Pantheon Books, 1943. (Meridian Books.)

Carritt, Edgar F. *Ethical and Political Thinking.* New York: Oxford Univ. Press, 1947, Pt. 2.

———. *Morals and Politics.* New York: Oxford Univ. Press, 1935.

Dewey, John. *The Public and Its Problems* (1927). Denver: Swallow, 1957.

Ewing, Alfred C. *The Individual, the State, and World Government.* New York: Macmillan, 1947.

Field, Guy C. *Political Theory.* London: Methuen, 1955.

Green, Thomas Hill. *Lectures on the Principles of Political Obligation.* (1882) New York: Longmans, Green, 1942.

Hobbes, Thomas. *Leviathan.* Many editions, especially Chs. 13-19.

Laslett, Peter, ed. *Philosophy, Politics, and Society.* New York: Macmillan, 1956.

Locke, John. *First and Second Treatises Concerning Civil Government.* Many editions.

Mabbott, J. D. *The State and the Citizen.* London: Hutchinson, 1948.

Mill, John Stuart. *Principles of Political Economy.* Many editions.

———. *Representative Government.* Ed. by R. B. McCallum. Oxford: Blackwell, 1957. Many other editions.

Perry, Ralph Barton. *Puritanism and Democracy.* New York: Vanguard Press, 1944, especially Pt. 3.

Plato. *Republic.* Trans. by Francis Macdonald Cornford, New York: Oxford Univ. Press, 1945. Many other editions, especially Bks. 1 and 8.

———. *The Laws.* Many editions.

Russell, Bertrand. *Authority and the Individual.* New York: Simon and Schuster, 1949.

———. *Human Society in Ethics and Politics.* New York: Simon and Schuster, 1954.

———. *New Hopes for a Changing World.* New York: Simon and Schuster, 1952.

———. *Power.* New York: Simon and Schuster, 1938.

Sabine, George H. *History of Political Theory* (1937). Rev. ed. New York: Holt, 1950.

Sidgwick, Henry. *Elements of Politics.* New York: Macmillan, 1891.

19. Rights

We began the previous section by introducing the state as an instrument for serving the mutual interests of those who belong to it. But another account of the function of the state can be given as well: namely, as a protector of the rights of the individuals within it.

It is often said that all human beings have certain rights: the rights to life, liberty, the pursuit of happiness, property. Thus far we have not considered any of these rights, though if it is true that all people possess these rights, it is certainly within the province of ethics to discuss them.

What is meant by saying that we all have certain rights? If someone says, "You have no right to receive income from that source in California, but you do have a right in Nevada," he is obviously talking about a *legal* right: he means that you can legally claim such money according to the laws of the one state but not according to the laws of the other. But when people talk about rights that everyone equally possesses, they do not mean legal rights—that which existing law entitles you to claim. The laws of various states and nations notoriously differ from one another; and people alone on desert islands are not bound or protected by laws at all, yet it would be said that they too have rights. It might be said that some nations do not recognize certain human rights, which nevertheless exist, but such a statement can hardly mean that those nations do not recognize certain laws which they have. It is, of course, not legal rights that are being referred to (if you want to know what your legal rights are, consult a lawyer) but *moral* rights, sometimes called *natural* rights, rights to things to which all human beings are entitled simply because they are human beings.

A right is the reverse side, as it were, of an obligation. If one person has a certain right, then another person has an obligation not to interfere with its exercise. If all men equally have certain rights, then all men are obligated not to interfere with the behavior of others in their exercise of those rights. If I have a right to life, then others have an obligation not to deprive me of it; and if I have a right to free expression of my ideas, then others have an obligation not to interfere with this expression. The same is true, of course, for *their* rights: these imply obligations on the part of others, including myself.

Just as obligations have been divided into absolute obligations and prima facie obligations (pages 301-02), so the same distinction can be made about rights. As we consider some of the rights that have been alleged to be natural rights, we shall ask whether the right is unconditional (absolute)—that is, whether all people are entitled to its exercise under all conditions, or whether it is prima facie—that is, whether it has exceptions or qualifications and becomes an absolute right only if there is no competition from competing claims. We shall also consider whether, if these rights are accepted, they can be incorporated into the general framework of utilitarianism or whether utilitarianism must be revised to make provision for them. (Thus far, in our survey of political ethics, we have found no reason to revise rule-utilitarianism.)

A. *The right to freedom of speech*

Let us first consider in some detail the right of free speech, the right which has been championed by more people and with fewer qualifications and amendments than any other alleged right. "Every human being," the proponents of free speech claim, "has the right to express his opinions freely and without threat of coercion by other individuals or by the state. He does not have the right to force his opinions upon them, for then he is interfering with *their* rights; but he has the right to say what he pleases as long as others are not compelled to listen to him or to accept what he says."

The staunchest champion of this right of free speech was John Stuart Mill in his essay *On Liberty*. Mill contended that this right is virtually unlimited and that attempts to suppress the free expression of opinion are, under almost all circumstances, to be condemned. It makes no difference whether the opinion expressed is that of an overwhelming majority or that of a tiny minority or even that of one person against all the rest. "If all mankind minus one were of one opinion," says Mill, "and only one person were of the contrary opinion, mankind would be no more justified in silencing that one person, than he, if he had the power, would be justified in silencing mankind." [1]

Mill argues that first of all it is quite possible that the opinion which the authorities are trying to suppress is true. The people who are suppressing it of course do not believe that it is true; but they are not infallible. Yet by suppressing the opinion they are *assuming* their own infallibility. History abounds with examples of men in power who assumed their own views to be infallible and therefore suppressed a minority opinion which turned out in the course of time to be true (remember Galileo). Why, indeed, did these men in power think that their opinions were true? Their evidence was usually quite incomplete and sometimes lacking altogether. (Indeed, the less evidence there is for a view, the more vigorously the authorities who want it to be accepted will impose it on others and persecute dissenters; for the authorities cannot appeal to reason or evidence on behalf of their position and therefore must squelch the opposition by sheer force.) On political and religious opinions particularly, which are usually the ones suppressed, there are always intelligent and able men who will be able to adduce reasons for a contrary view. How, therefore, can anyone be so certain of his own infallibility?

[1] J. S. Mill, *On Liberty*, Ch. 2.

Besides, if the authorities have no fear that the opposing view is true, why are they so anxious to suppress it? Why not let it be discussed in the full light of day so that, if it is false, everyone can see its falsehood plainly exhibited? Rather, is it not likely that those in power are, perhaps unconsciously, afraid that the opinion they are trying to stamp out may be true and that their own view may be mistaken; is it not likely that fear of this possibility makes them suppress a contrary view rather than admit that they were mistaken?

"But," a critic of Mill may object, "it's true we can't be *certain* that an opinion is true; perhaps nothing in life is absolutely certain. But we have to act on the basis of probabilities. No one suggests that we should ignore a cry for help because we're not absolutely certain it wasn't an auditory hallucination. In the same way, if it seems overwhelmingly probable that a view is false, then we are justified in suppressing it. We act to the best of our ability, and we act on evidence we believe to be sufficient. There comes a point when for practical purposes we must act as if we *knew* our view was true; and in that situation we are justified in forcing everyone to accept it."

Not so, according to Mill. There is a big difference between assuming an opinion to be true because it has not been refuted even after every opportunity has been given for attacking it and assuming it to be true in order not to *permit* it to be attacked. The first grounds of assumption may be reasonable enough; the second grounds are always evil. Even with every opportunity for attacking your opinion, you still cannot be sure that your opinion is true, although you may assume it to be so until some evidence against it appears. But how can you possibly know that nothing can be said against it when you don't even permit criticism of it to be voiced?

Even if you do permit criticism, it is hard enough to find out the truth about matters of any importance. Even if you are as impartial as anyone can be, as intelligent as the best, and thoroughly conscientious and unswerving in your search for truth, the truth is still difficult to come by. How must it be then when the authorities in question are *not* impartial and conscientious and even persecute anyone who suggests criticism?

> In the case of any person whose judgment is really deserving of confidence, how has it become so? Because he has kept his mind open to criticism of his opinions and conduct. Because it has been his practice to listen to all that could be said against him; to profit by as much of it as was just, and expound to himself, and upon occasion to others, the fallacy of what was fallacious. Because he has felt, that the only way in which a human being can make some approach to knowing the whole of a subject, is by hearing what can be said about it by persons of every variety of opinion, and studying all modes in which it can be looked at by every character of mind. No wise man ever acquired his wisdom in any mode but this; nor is it in the nature of human intellect to become wise in any other manner. The steady habit of correcting and completing his own opinion by collating it with those of others, so far

from causing doubt and hesitation in carrying it into practice, is the only stable foundation for a just reliance on it. . . .[1]

"But surely," continues the critic, "there are some beliefs which, even though we cannot be absolutely certain that they are false, are so harmful to society that they must be suppressed in order to preserve morality or even civilization itself. For example, perhaps I cannot prove that my religious belief is true and that of others false or that religious belief of some kind is true and antireligious belief false; yet I may be convinced that the welfare of society depends on the continued teaching of such views. Therefore, for reasons of utility if not for reasons of truth, I shall be justified in suppressing the opponents of my view."

We have discussed elsewhere the question whether religious belief is necessary to morality (pages 249-56). But suppose the ruler is conscientious and utterly convinced that religious belief *is* essential to morality. We may even suppose there is some reason to believe his position is true. Is he not then justified in suppressing opposing beliefs for the sake of preserving moral values within his domain?

He is not, says Mill. "Those who thus satisfy themselves, do not perceive that the assumption of infallibility is merely shifted from one point to another. *The usefulness of an opinion is itself a matter of opinion* — as disputable, as open to discussion, and requiring discussion as much as the opinion itself." [2] In other words, the judgment that your religious belief is necessary to the preservation of morality is itself a fallible judgment and just as much entitled to the free light of open discussion as the belief itself.

Consider what has often happened in human history when those in power have been so certain of their beliefs that they suppressed all opposition to them. They have become, to subsequent history, standing examples of bigoted, if sincere, men who halted the progress of mankind by defending questionable views — questionable in regard to their truth and even more questionable in regard to the morality of suppressing opposition to them. During several centuries of European history, when the Church and state cooperated to enforce religious dogma, heresy was persecuted and religious tolerance virtually unknown. Those who doubted even the smallest article of the faith were scourged with whips, burned at the stake, broken on the rack, and subjected to every kind of fiendish torture that the ingenuity of the torturers could devise. Officially at least it was all done in the interest of truth and morality. Yet the effect has been one of the grossest immorality. Whether or not the doctrines upheld were true, a stigma was cast upon them throughout subsequent history by the means that were taken to uphold them; and the path of free inquiry into truth was halted or delayed for perhaps hundreds of years.

[1] *Ibid.*
[2] *Ibid.*

Who knows the harm that suppression of opinions — even false opinions — has done, even to those who were not victims of the suppression? When any intellectual view is persecuted, a tendency is set in motion toward intellectual timidity, toward not thinking things through and not trying to defend one's convictions at all lest the conclusions emerging from the process of thinking be at variance with the official opinion and one be persecuted in consequence. Who is intellectually so fearless as to be willing to endure torture and death for his views? A comparative few; but the vast majority, even of intelligent and honest people, will not play with the dangerous instrument (the intellect) whose use might bring on their own destruction. Who can tell how many people have held dissenting views secretly, unknown to their fellow men, but have kept them buried within themselves for fear of persecution if they revealed them? Yet many of such contrary views might well have been both true and morally helpful to mankind had they been permitted a voice; and the world is worse off for not having had the opportunity to receive them and examine them. Good ideas are rare enough so that humanity cannot afford to waste the intelligence of its best men until such time as the ruling authorities see fit to permit their open discussion. The suppression of views — *any* views — is a far more immoral thing than the willingness to see them examined and impartially considered, even if the views themselves seem morally subversive at the time.

Besides, how can we separate the truth of a view from its moral effects?

. . . It will not do to say that the heretic may be allowed to maintain the utility or harmlessness of his opinion, though forbidden to maintain its truth. The truth of an opinion is part of its utility. If we would know whether or not it is desirable that a proposition should be believed, is it possible to exclude the consideration of whether or not it is true? In the opinion, not of bad men, but of the best men, no belief which is contrary to truth can be really useful: and can you prevent such men from urging that plea, when they are charged with culpability for denying some doctrine which they are told is useful, but which they believe to be false? Those who are on the side of received opinions never fail to take all possible advantage of this plea; you do not find *them* handling the question of utility as if it could be completely abstracted from that of truth; on the contrary, it is, above all, because their doctrine is "the truth," that the knowledge or the belief of it is held to be so indispensable. There can be no fair discussion of the question of usefulness when an argument so vital may be employed on one side, but not on the other. And in point of fact, when law or public feeling do not permit the truth of an opinion to be disputed, they are just as little tolerant of a denial of its usefulness.[1]

Mill's critic counters, "But those who dissent from opinions which help to hold together the moral fabric of society are evil men — evil at least in that they set their own intellectual freedom above the well-being of the people."

[1] *Ibid.*

This charge too Mill declares to be without foundation. As we have already observed, the dissenting view *may* be true; if so, society will, in the long run, benefit more if the view is made known; then the truth can be squarely faced and there is not the danger that it might come out anyway and force the suppressors into a confession that they had been deceiving the people all along. But even if the view is false, more evil is caused by suppressing it (thus setting a precedent for the suppression of other and better views) than by permitting it to see the light of day.

Even if a view is *not* true, who is so wise or impartial that he can honestly be *sure* that it is not true? The suppressor may *feel* that he is infallibly right; but by suppresing the view he is not only assuming his own infallibility but trying to answer that question for others, who may be just as honestly convinced of their rightness as he is of his. It takes such rare impartiality and intelligence to arrive at even a reasonable probability that a view is true — and even then, with the best of intentions and judgment, it may be false. Consider, says Mill, the case of the Roman emperor Marcus Aurelius.

If ever any one, possessed of power, had grounds for thinking himself the best and most enlightened among his contemporaries, it was the Emperor Marcus Aurelius. Absolute monarch of the whole civilized world, he preserved through life not only the most unblemished justice, but what was less to be expected from his Stoical breeding, the tenderest heart. The few failings which are attributed to him were all on the side of indulgence: while his writings, the highest ethical product of the ancient mind, differ scarcely perceptibly, if they differ at all, from the most characteristic teachings of Christ. This man, a better Christian in all but the dogmatic sense of the word than almost any of the ostensibly Christian sovereigns who have since reigned, persecuted Christianity. Placed at the summit of all the previous attainments of humanity, with an open, unfettered intellect, and a character which led him of himself to embody in his moral writings the Christian ideal, he yet failed to see that Christianity was to be a good and not an evil to the world, with his duties to which he was so deeply penetrated. Existing society he knew to be in a deplorable state. But such as it was, he saw, or thought he saw, that it was held together, and prevented from being worse, by belief and reverence of the received divinities. As a ruler of mankind, he deemed it his duty not to suffer society to fall in pieces; and saw not how, if its existing ties were removed, any others could be formed which could again knit it together. The new religion openly aimed at dissolving these ties: unless, therefore, it was his duty to adopt that religion, it seemed to be his duty to put it down. Inasmuch then as the theology of Christianity did not appear to him true or of divine origin; inasmuch as this strange history of a crucified God was not credible to him, and a system which purported to rest entirely upon a foundation to him so wholly unbelievable, could not be foreseen by him to be that renovating agency which, after all abatements, it has in fact proved to be; the gentlest and most amiable of philosophers and rulers, under a solemn sense of duty, authorized the persecution of Christianity. To my mind this is one of the most tragical facts in all history. It is a bitter thought, how different a thing the Christianity of the world might have been, if the Christian faith had been adopted as the religion of the empire under the auspices of Marcus Aurelius instead of those of Constantine. But it would be equally unjust to him and false to truth to deny, that no one plea which can be urged for punishing anti-Christian teaching was wanting to Marcus Aurelius for punishing, as he did, the propagation of Christianity. No Christian more firmly believes that Atheism is false, and tends to the dissolution of society, than Marcus Aurelius believed the same things of Christianity; he who, of all men then living, might have been thought the most capable of appreciating it. Unless any one who approves of punishment for the promulgation of opinions, flatters himself that he is a wiser and better man than Marcus Aurelius — more deeply versed in the wisdom of his time, more elevated in his intellect above it — more earnest in his search for truth, or more single-minded in his devotion to it when found; let him abstain from that assumption of the joint infallibility of himself and the multitude, which the great Antoninus made with so unfortunate a result.[1]

But the critic of Mill may take another line of attack. "The truth gains by persecution;" "it has passed through the fiery ordeal, and every truth ought to pass through fire before it is accepted."

This position too, Mill would say, is a mistake. Truth should pass through the fiery ordeal of *open and unconcealed examination and criticism* but not through suppression, which may result in the truth being buried for centuries or lost forever to mankind. The idea that truth, simply because it is truth, has an inherent power of survival, is romantic nonsense. Views which were later proved true have been put down successfully many times in human history, and mankind has suffered as a result.

The dictum that truth always triumphs over persecution is one of those pleasant falsehoods which men repeat after one another till they pass into commonplaces, but which all experience refutes. History teems with instances of truth put down by persecution. If not suppressed for ever, it may be thrown back for centuries. To speak only of religious opinions: the Reformation broke out at least twenty times before Luther, and was put down. Arnold of Brescia was put down. Fra Dolcino was put down. Savonarola was put down. The Albigeois were put down. The Vaudois were put down. The Lollards were put down. The Hussites were put down. Even after the era of Luther, wherever persecution was persisted in, it was successful. In Spain, Italy, Flanders, the Austrian Empire, Protestantism was rooted out; and, most likely, would have been so in England, had Queen Mary lived, or Queen Elizabeth died. Persecution has always succeeded, save where the heretics were too strong a party to be effectually persecuted. No reasonable person can doubt that Christianity might have been extirpated in the Roman Empire. It spread, and became predominant, because the persecutions were only occasional, lasting but a short time, and separated by long intervals of almost undisturbed propagandism. It is a piece of idle sentimentality that truth, merely as truth, has any inherent power denied to error of prevailing against the dungeon and the stake. Men

[1] *Ibid.*

are not more zealous for truth than they often are for error, and a sufficient application of legal or even of social penalties will generally succeed in stopping the propagation of either. The real advantage which truth has consists in this, that when an opinion is true, it may be extinguished once, twice, or many times, but in the course of ages there will generally be found persons to rediscover it, until some one of its reappearances falls on a time when from favorable circumstances it escapes persecution until it has made such head as to withstand all subsequent attempts to suppress it.[1]

The discoverers of important truths have usually been suppressed, put down, tortured, or killed; is it desirable that these men should have had only the reward of being dealt with as the vilest of criminals? Rather, it is a shameful tragedy for which, says Mill, "humanity should mourn in sackcloth and ashes." Should the propounder of a new truth, one of mankind's greatest benefactors, be made to stand "with a halter round his neck, to be instantly tightened if the public assembly did not, on hearing his reasons, then and there adopt his proposition? People who defend this mode of treating benefactors cannot be supposed to set much value on the benefit." [2]

The critic of Mill offers one more argument: "Suppose that the belief that is suppressed turns out to be false. Were those who suppressed it not then acting rightly in suppressing it?"

Not in the least, according to Mill. The suppressors were wrong partly because at the time they suppressed the belief they could not have *known* that it was false — at least not without subjecting it to constant and impartial scrutiny; by suppressing that scrutiny they prevented the knowledge. They were wrong also, because true opinions are kept alive and vital in the public mind *not* through being taken for granted but through constantly being challenged by dissenting opinions. Truth must be constantly challenged in order to remain vital and alive. It is all too easy for an opinion to be held, even a true opinion, not as a deep conviction but merely as an inherited prejudice. But "this is not the way in which truth ought to be held by a rational being. This is not knowing the truth. Truth, thus held, is but one superstition the more, accidentally clinging to the words which enunciate a truth." [3] It requires falsehood to secure the truth and make its impact felt upon the mind; in doing this, falsehood is rendering the truth a great service. Even if the truth is not challenged from the outside, by the opinions of dissenters against it, it should be challenged from the inside by the believer himself, who should do everything within his power to place himself in the mental attitude of an intelligent dissenter against his view.

He who knows only his own side of the case, knows little of that. His reasons may be good, and no one may have been able to refute them. But if he is equally unable to refute the reasons on the opposite side; if he does not so much

[1] *Ibid.*
[2] *Ibid.*
[3] *Ibid.*

as know what they are, he has no ground for preferring either opinion. The rational position for him would be suspension of judgment, and unless he contents himself with that, he is either led by authority, or adopts, like the generality of the world, the side to which he feels most inclination. Nor is it enough that he should hear the arguments of adversaries from his own teachers, presented as they state them, and accompanied by what they offer as refutations. That is not the way to do justice to the arguments, or bring them into real contact with his own mind. He must be able to hear them from persons who actually believe them; who defend them in earnest, and do their very utmost for them. He must know them in their most plausible and persuasive form; he must feel the whole force of the difficulty which the true view of the subject has to encounter and dispose of; else he will never really possess himself of the portion of truth which meets and removes that difficulty. Ninety-nine in a hundred of what are called educated men are in this condition; even of those who can argue fluently for their opinions. Their conclusion may be true, but it might be false for anything they know; they have never thrown themselves into the mental position of those who think differently from them, and considered what such persons may have to say; and consequently they do not, in any proper sense of the word, know the doctrine which they themselves profess. They do not know those parts of it which explain and justify the remainder; the considerations which show that a fact which seemingly conflicts with another is reconcilable with it, or that, of two apparently strong reasons, one and not the other ought to be preferred. All that part of the truth which turns the scale, and decides the judgment of a completely informed mind, they are strangers to; nor is it ever really known, but to those who have attended equally and impartially to both sides, and endeavored to see the reasons of both in the strongest light. So essential is this discipline to a real understanding of moral and human subjects, that if opponents of all important truths do not exist, it is indispensable to imagine them, and supply them with the strongest arguments which the most skilful devil's advocate can conjure up.[1]

It can hardly be doubted that Mill presents a powerful argument for free expression of opinion. Probably that argument needs to be presented far more today than it did when Mill wrote the essay a hundred years ago, for the dangers to free speech today are far greater than they were then.

a. The dangers arise first of all from governments. Those who are in power usually wish to remain in power and increase it, as we have seen. In so doing it is easiest for them to suppress whatever opinions are unfavorable to their regime and to punish those who are bold enough to utter them. With modern methods of psychological conditioning, these devices can be used with far deadlier effectiveness than ever before in history.

b. But the dangers are not only from the state, enormous though these dangers are. Even when a state is fairly permissive with regard to public discussion, public opinion itself can wield as cruel a despotism upon free inquiry as any state can impose. It takes a daring and courageous intellect to

[1] *Ibid.*

dissent from majority opinion, if in doing so one is denied entrance to clubs and other social amenities, if one is looked upon with suspicion and distrust by one's neighbors and fellow workers, if one is withheld from promotions or even dismissed from his job on some pretext, if one is ostracized by everyone in his community and finds stones thrown through his windows. (Consider the plight of prointegrationists in the South.) Against this danger, governmental edict is an ineffective defense; the only long-term solution is education in freedom and fearless exposure to all points of view. And this goal, needless to say, cannot be achieved quickly.

c. Even when government does not intervene, the mass media of communication that exist today (as they did not in Mill's) can monopolize public opinion and public taste, thereby preventing all opposing views from reaching the attention of all but a few creative and independent minds. Consider the intellectual atrophy that inevitably descends on those who listen excessively to television programs: the viewer is fed a fictionalized and grossly oversimplified account of human nature and the problems of the world, an account which conveniently divides human beings into the good and the bad with no gradations in between. Of course, one is not compelled to watch television, but if one does so, there is no *alternative* to the intellectually stagnating fare that 90 per cent of it consists of. The sapping effects on the intellect and discrimination of the viewer occur so gradually that they are not apparent until it is too late. Or consider the fact that the news that comes to us is controlled by a few press syndicates, which can give us the news or refrain from doing so, as they choose. The head of one of the news syndicates can, it is said, break or make a man's reputation by releasing a news story about him (with damning implications suggested but not stated) or by not doing so. In the same way, these syndicates may delete, distort, or suppress news coming to us from all quarters of the globe. The government does not exercise the censorship, but the syndicates do. Most newspapers and broadcasting networks, though not owned by the state, are as biased as if they were. Being owned by multimillion-dollar corporations, they are naturally partial to the corporations' viewpoints and do not hesitate to delete news items favorable to the other side. More than 90 per cent of the nation's newspapers are of one political party; and radio and television networks do not hesitate to take off the air the news commentators who are unsympathetic to the point of view of the network.

What makes this situation so insidious to liberty?

(1) First, the fact that for international news, unlike the news about what our nextdoor neighbors are doing, we have no *other* sources of information. We cannot ourselves be stationed at all the capitals of the world to observe how events really occurred; for this knowledge we are utterly dependent on our press and radio, and these sources of information are controlled by organizations having a strong bias. The wells are poisoned at their source, and we have no other wells from which to draw water.

(2) Second, the fact that although we can always spread dissension by our own efforts — we have a tongue to speak, and usually there are other people who will listen — and even if we are placed under none of the restraints described in Mill's *On Liberty,* how are we to reach an audience large enough to make any difference in a nation of such tremendous size? We are stymied in spite of our best efforts because we have not the enormous amount of capital required to buy a radio or television network and state our position openly to an audience large enough to make a difference. To command this kind of audience, we would need many millions of dollars; but those who have that kind of capital usually no longer wish to represent the interests of those who do not. In view of all these difficulties, it is a little ironic to speak of "the right of free speech." It is not that the government interferes, as it does in some other countries; it is rather that the channels of communication, on which we depend to hear both sides of a dispute, are controlled by those who, in the absence of official coercion, censor the news as effectively as a government itself would be likely to do.

Is the right to freedom of speech, valuable and indispensable as it is, unlimited? Should one be permitted to express any opinion whatever at any time? Should one be permitted to agitate for the overthrow of the government or to undermine the morale of the people during wartime? Should one be permitted to reveal (or invent) details of his neighbor's private life to all those interested? Should one be permitted to shout oaths and filthy language from the balcony of a public theater without interference? Should one be permitted to say to motorists, "Go right ahead, the road's all right," thus causing them to speed down the hill, when you know that the bridge is washed out at the bottom of the hill and they will have no time to stop? Should you be free to advise people to take heroin or commit murder? Should you be free to yell "Fire" when there is no fire?

It would surely seem from examples such as these, that even the right to freedom of speech is limited. What limits your right of speech, like all rights, is that not only you but other people have rights. No individual who enjoys rights should deprive other individuals from enjoying them, for of course these rights belong equally to all. To tell someone else's secrets publicly would interfere with that person's right to have his personal life safeguarded from others except those whom he himself wishes to tell. To guide motorists to almost certain death certainly seems to compromise their right to life. (One might say, "But they don't have to take your advice," and of course they don't, but in the particular context described, do they not have a right to assume that the "information" you give them is true?) Yelling "Fire" in a theater when there is no fire compromises that same right, for many people may be trampled to death in the ensuing panic; in fact one might question whether a person has a right to yell "Fire" even when there *is* a fire, instead of reporting it to the authorities and letting them take such steps as they have devised for these occasions. It would seem, indeed, as if the utilitarian criterion is quite sufficient to deal with the question of when one has and when one has not the right to speak freely. To say that a person has a right (noun) under most circumstances to speak his mind, then, would be equivalent to saying that under most circumstances it is right (adjective) for a person to do so and that there are very few circumstances in which it would be wrong for others to prevent him from doing so. This position is, of course, that taken by Mill; and his essay *On Liberty* provides a detailed analysis of *why* it is wrong, under most circumstances, for people to prevent others from speaking.

The extent of the right to free speech, however, is still not clear. Ordinarily it means the right of each individual to say what he wants to say to anyone who will listen. It does not, of course, include the right to force people to listen against their will. Does the right to free speech also include the right to advertise an opinion in the newspapers and magazines — free of charge, or at the person's own expense if he can afford it? There are times when the right to state something to his fellow men by word of mouth is virtually useless — for example, when others will not listen or when nobody is nearby or when the few people who will hear what he says are vastly outnumbered by the millions who will read just the opposite in the newspapers. Suppose that the opposition has a channel, such as radio and the press, for publicizing its views which you, who cannot get your views into the newspapers because they won't print your side of the story, do not have. What then does your "right to free speech" amount to? Or do you have a right to equal time on a network? Do *all* opposing factions, even if there are dozens of them, have a right to equal time?

Today the very principle of freedom of speech is being questioned, especially freedom of speech for those who advocate views or political systems which, if adopted, would result in the removal of these rights (at least as legal rights). Should people be free to agitate for a police state which would put an end to everyone's right to agitate for anything whatever? Many people will say, "No," for if you grant this right, you will be preparing the funeral for most of the other rights (including right of these very same people to speak freely at a later date). But others will say, "Yes," at least when it is very unlikely that these agitators will succeed in their aims; people may argue that it is better to let agitators get their opinions out of their systems, at the same time providing a living demonstration of just how free we are. Thus, for example, while London was being bombed in the early 1940's, the police did not stop those agitators who stood in Hyde Park and cried, "Down with Britain! Down with the Empire!" The police only interfered with those who tried to interfere with the freedom of people to say these things. Not many modern nations would carry freedom of speech so far. Nevertheless, if these agitators had become anything like a majority, there is little doubt that they would have been forcibly stopped. If they had not been stopped, the rights to life and free speech of the entire nation would have been imperiled, and therefore the presence of these agitators constituted a "clear and present danger." But what constitutes a "clear and present danger" is admittedly vague; and once this reason is given, it is employed repeatedly by every dictator who wants to squelch the opposition.

One point emerges clearly from these considerations: the right to free speech, while not absolute, is far more nearly so than other rights which involve more than verbal activity. If you tell everyone that the government should be changed, people are still free to disagree with you, and you have not really interfered with their lives — they don't even have to listen to you. But if you implement your views by planting bombs to help bring about the demise of certain members of the government, then you are interfering with the rights of others by endangering their security and their very lives. If you think we should launch a preventive war against a foreign nation, people can argue with you; but if you start killing foreigners in this country, you are interfering with your victims' right to live — and incidentally making yourself like the very foreign leaders whom you hate. (Borderline situation: should you be free to distribute pamphlets denouncing foreigners if you know that the contents are false or if you have not bothered to investigate the truth?)

B. Other rights

We have just examined in some detail the right of freedom of speech. More briefly, we shall now consider some of the other alleged rights of all men. We shall see that they too are prima facie and not absolute but that some are more limited than others.

1. *The right to life.* This right is often said to be the most basic of all because all other rights depend upon it — one cannot enjoy them if he is dead.

But at once a problem arises: if we all have this right, what of the murderer who is condemned to die in the electric chair? If one says he still has his right to life, the right to life doesn't seem to come to much, seeing that his life is about to be taken away. ("You have a right to life" would be an ironic thing to remind him of as he was being led away to be executed.) Many would say, of course, that by taking a life he has forfeited his own right to life. Opponents of capital punishment will say that he has not forfeited his right to life but only his right to walk freely among his fellow men. But if a murderer forfeits his right to life, the right to life is not absolute — there are circumstances under which it no longer applies. In any event, one's right to life does not include the right to kill other people and thus deprive them of *their* right to life; for these rights are alleged to be universal in their extent, even if not absolute (exceptionless) in their conditions.

If one believes that the right to life is absolute, here is an even more puzzling (though very common) situation: What of the right of the state to place soldiers — and civilians as well, in modern war — in a position where there is a considerable probability that they will lose their lives?

What would one say if a few members of a drafted army who were holding a mountain pass against the enemy to cover their comrades' retreat were to exclaim, "But we have a right to life"?

One may say, of course, that the state has no right to take the lives of these soldiers, for they have committed no crime. Let us grant that the state has no right in an aggressive war; but what of a defensive war, when the enemy is invading your country? Then it might be said, that *others* have encroached upon *your* right to life so you have a right to take away their right. But, granting that they have forfeited their right to life (not the soldiers but their leaders), what about *yours* if you are one of the defending soldiers? Surely the person who claims an unlimited right to life is in a tough spot here. If you do not fight, your nation will be taken over by conquerors; and what happens to your right to life in the process? What point is there in saying that you still have the right to life if you are about to be killed? Is not the declaration of such a right, in these circumstances, mere empty words?

Confronted by such questions, one is tempted to exclaim, "Enough of this talk about rights! Let's talk only of utility — that's enough. When there is utility in waging war, as there seldom is, then it should be done — for example, in the Battle of Britain against Nazi Germany. When such a war occurs, lives have to be sacrificed; but let's not bring in any mythology by talking about rights!"

Such a conclusion, however, would be premature; for there are many who will still want to hold that people have rights to life and free speech, and other things, even *over and above* considerations of utility. For example: Suppose that a man, old and without much promise of longer life, could be painlessly put out of the way so that thereby a hundred men might have an easier livelihood for the next ten years. Although there would be great utility in this transaction, the supporters of absolute rights would say that it would be wrong; for it would interfere with the sacred, even if not absolute, right to life. The man has this right, according to the supporters, because he has not interfered with the right to life of others (thus taking care of the murderer example) nor have others (like the invaders) tried to take his right, thereby forcing him to risk his by combating them. So even if there is no maximum utility in the preservation of this one man's life, it should be preserved. To take it from him would be to violate his right to life.

Opponents of absolute rights, however, would still say that talk about "the right to life" is redundant, and that the instance of this one man being sacrificed is probably taken care of anyway, if not by act-utilitarianism then by rule-utilitarianism. (See pages 311-37.)

Utilitarian calculations have already acquainted us with the difficulties involved in weighing one value against another. It is particularly difficult to weigh the value of some gain against the loss of human life in rendering this gain possible. Some philosophers, such as Kant, have said that an individual human life is a thing not only of great value but of *infinite* value — that to preserve one human life it would be worthwhile not indeed to risk the collapse of civilization (for that would involve the loss of many lives), but to sacrifice for all mankind some convenience or source of happiness that would *not* involve loss of life.

What would the rule-utilitarian say about this position? He would, to be sure, insist upon the very great value of human life; if a person dies, he can enjoy no intrinsic goods whatever, and his death will probably cause grief to others and insecurity to society. But still, it is quite bold to say that each human life has not only value but infinite value. Consider the test pilots who risk their lives every day, some losing them, in order to test and perfect equipment for air travel. The result of their efforts enables us to reach our destination faster than ever before, even if we do not use our time any more wisely after we arrive. Is their risk worth it? There is, on the one hand, the suspense and grief of the wife and family — emotions more painful probably than the worries of the pilot himself, who voluntarily chose that profession and often enjoys taking risks and living dangerously or perhaps enjoys just the high income which he could earn in no other way. There is, on the other hand, the added convenience. Convenience is not even a moral good; yet most people would probably say that test flying, including even the loss of life, *was* worth it. Perhaps they would try to justify themselves by saying that, owing to speedy air travel, physicians or batches of vaccine can be shipped by air in time to reach patients hundreds of miles away and thus save their lives, and that thus the enterprise takes lives in order to save more. But suppose that planes were never used for this purpose — what then? Does *no* amount of convenience or pleasure balance the scales to make up for even a *little* loss of life — especially when such losses are among the calculated risks of a profession and joining the profession is strictly voluntary?

Does life, even one life, weigh so heavily on the scale of values that no amount of other value can tip the scales against it? Thousands of people die in automobile accidents every year, which would not happen if automobiles had never been invented or were never used. But would it be better on this account if there were no automobiles? Most people would probably say that the tremendous convenience and ease of transportation *is* worth even this heavy price. Are they mistaken? Would it be right for every American to leave his car at home, even on *one* specified day, no matter how much he needed it to get to his work, if an incorrect prescription which would cause one child in America to be poisoned would thereby be avoided? Would we be willing to do without telephones all over the world, thus inconveniencing millions of people and crippling business and industry, if this privation were required to save the life of one unknown person (of no value to society, let us say) in our country? To save this life, should we do without telephones even for a single day? Would we be justified in saving one human being who would otherwise perish, if to do so all Americans would have to forfeit a holiday on Thanksgiving Day? To many this day comes as a chance for rest and relaxation after a grueling business season, a chance to go out of town or see one's parents. Should this day be forfeited on a national scale in order to avoid one painless death? Or suppose that we could save the lives of thousands of soldiers in the army by means of a protective coating over the body made of a new impenetrable metal that would render soldiers immune to bullets, flame throwers, and radioactivity, but that such a protective coating would cost ten million dollars per soldier. (The army would never adopt it, that much is sure; lives are cheaper than materials.) Would we be justified in taking on the crushing tax burden required for years to come in order to save these soldiers? If Kant is right, we should take on ruinous taxation on a national scale even to save the life of *one* soldier.

Those of utilitarian persuasion would, with however much reluctance, say that for some worthwhile causes, even some ordinary conveniences if they are widespread enough, it *is* worthwhile to sacrifice lives. Even considering the loss of future intrinsic good brought about by the abrupt termination of one's existence, and the loss and grief caused to others, besides the loss of the fruits of one's subsequent labors to mankind, there are occasions when the gain is still worth the high price. Thus, again, the right to life is not unlimited. But it should be borne in mind, as we emphasized in discussing rule-utilitarianism, that there is a vast difference between voluntarily giving one's life (or entering a profession where one knows there is great risk) and forcibly taking away someone's life. The latter is justified only under the most extreme circumstances (page 329).

2. *The right to a minimum standard of living.* It is widely felt, more in this century than before, that all human beings, regardless of their station or their ability to find work, should receive, presumably from the state, an income that enables them to get along without going on a semi-starvation diet. How much this minimum should be is not clear: should it include a car for everybody, a bicycle, crutches for the infirm, or gin for those who prefer that to water? Presumably the minimum would vary: in a poor country not as much could be given as in a rich one. One might say that people are still *entitled* to as much in a poor country; but it would be pointless to insist on a right to something which the nation has no means to supply. Still, public opinion generally holds that everyone has a natural right not merely to live but to live in a state of not too great physical discomfort; nothing less than this state befits his dignity as a human being. This right is to apply equally to all human beings: even if they are unable to work because of severe physical or mental handicaps, even if they can find no work after repeated attempts to do so, and even (though some people would object to this last condition) if they are *unwilling* to work at all. If they are pathologically unwilling to work, perhaps they should not be helped

unless they consent to have psychiatric therapy that may cure them of this attitude; but even if therapy didn't work, the person should not be simply left to starve. Even the man who says, "I can work, but why should I? Let the state take care of me" deserves to live, and to live in a better way than in a cave with a crust of bread a day or than by begging and sleeping under bridges. It may be that there is not much utility in helping this kind of person — at least not much *economic* utility; the existence of such a person adds nothing to the world's work and only exacts additional work from others who have to support him. But it has been argued, nevertheless, that he has a right, which all human beings, industrious and indigent alike, possess. Almost no one would hold that such a man is entitled to an *equal* living with those who willingly work; neither, for that matter, will the livings of most other people be equal, for their abilities and energies differ. We shall discuss the reasons for justified inequality in the next chapter. Here we are only stating the position that all human beings have a right not only to life but to a minimal standard of living, however much inequality there may be or should be *above* that minimal level. There would not be much point in saying he has a right to life and then letting him starve to death.

3. *Economic rights.* Don't people have a right to do what they want with their money and their property? Shouldn't employers have the right to hire whom they like and fire whom they like? It's their money, isn't it, so why shouldn't they use it as they like?

Fashions in rights have changed. Not too many years ago the right to a minimum standard of living was hardly considered to be a right; public opinion thought it permissible to allow people who could not work to starve in the streets; the reasoning was that because such people were not adding to the world's produce they should take nothing from the world's produce. (This view pictures a kind of "moral symmetry" similar to the judgment "He took a life, so his life should be taken"). Today most people would feel differently about this issue. But not too many years ago, also, many believed that those who controlled money had an unlimited right to use it precisely as they pleased, even including the power of life or death over their slaves or employees. Today, however, this view is no longer so widely held in the Western world. Why this difference? Why is it that so many people believe that the state should *not* interfere with freedom of speech by putting political propagandists in jail and yet that it *should* interfere with predatory business practices that cause widespread misery in the form of periodic unemployment, dismissal of wage earners without security, and a substandard level of wages for work performed? The difference, surely, is that when a person utters political or other propaganda, he is not actually *interfering* with the rights of others — unless he shouts in loud tones in congested areas so that people can't sleep, in which event he is jailed for being a public nuisance but not for the things he says. You don't have to listen to propaganda, and if you do listen, you don't have to believe; that is up to you. But if an employer starves his employees, he *is* positively interfering with their lives; he is forcing upon them conditions of life which make it impossible for them to live like human bengs and to exercise their other rights. An economic system without any safeguards imposes terrible penalties on those who do not work, even though their not working is not the result of laziness. Some may object, "But if the state controls industry, isn't it then interfering too — with the rights of employers?" Yes, that is just the trouble. Not only do employers lose much by state control (including the incentive to increase production, which in turn would help create more wealth and help to alleviate the very conditions in question), but state control has countless disadvantages: red tape, inefficiency, graft, special favors for friends or relatives or in return for bribes, endless injustice owing to centralized control and ignorance of the full facts about each local situation, and perhaps most of all the fact that government bureaucrats who produce nothing can control the activities of those who do produce.[1]

Indeed it can be argued that if producers are left free to produce, unhindered by governmental restrictions, they will increase productivity and thus increase national wealth and employment and, through competition for able employees, wages as well. Conditions will improve, not because employers will voluntarily pay more to their workers, but because if one employer gives them bare subsistence wages, another employer will find it worth his while to offer them more, and they will go elsewhere unless the first employer meets the second one's price. This issue, however, must be left to the economists. The only point of relevance to human rights is that *to the extent* to which the activities of employers (or any other group of human beings) infringe upon the rights of other human beings, to that extent their exercise of such rights must be curtailed, inasmuch as the rights in question are the possession of all human beings equally.

The right to property is a special kind, or case, of an economic right — specifically, the right to own things (not necessarily real estate) of which you can dispose as you wish. It is sometimes thought that everyone equally has a right to property. But has he that right regardless of whether he works to earn it? How much property has he the right to? a stick? a pencil and paper with which to write letters of gratitude to the leaders of state? forty acres and a colonial mansion? Until it is made more specific, the alleged right has little content. Doubtless it is a good idea, from the standpoint of utility, for everyone to have something which he can call his own: people usually take better care of what belongs to them than of what does not (the latter including what belongs to the state). But if all men have the right to property, who is to confer it? and what are its limits? If everyone has a right to forty arable acres, there is not enough land in the world to

---

[1] See Ludwig von Mises, *Bureaucracy* and *Omnipotent Government* (both New Haven: Yale Univ. Press, 1944).

go round. Other questions arise also: Should those fortunate enough to inherit property be permitted to keep it, even though they have not earned it themselves? Should the discoverer of a Pacific island be entitled to keep the entire island for himself or for his country — even if the island should turn out to be very large — simply because he happened to discover it whereas other explorers were not so fortunate? Or perhaps no one has a right to any of these things; perhaps the only right that can be claimed is that of freedom to *work* (at what he likes? at just anything?) so that he may purchase property if he is so inclined.

Most talk about the right to property is extremely vague, yet extremely widespread; for those who do not have property usually want it, and those who have it want to hold on to it. However, the right to property is probably not one of the rights that should be insisted on over and above its utilitarian value: it would seem that the chief justification for having private property (including possessions of all kinds) is the utilitarian one that people have more of an interest in working for something which is their own than in working for someone else's property or for the state's — in other words, property creates an incentive to work, which is highly desirable from the utilitarian point of view and which would appear to be its main justification.

4. *Legal rights.* There are also certain rights before the *law* which, Western society holds, everyone possesses as natural rights: the right to a fair trial in the courts (*habeas corpus*), the right to vote for whoever you please by secret ballot, the right to be protected against certain grievances (not insults, but molestation, theft, burglary, perhaps slander). These rights include all rights to being protected by law from the encroachment upon one's other rights by other people.

It is generally felt that everyone has these rights — as natural rights, not as legal rights, for, of course, not every state provides them — whether one be rich or poor, black or white, humbled or exalted, thrifty or ne'er-do-well. The protection of these rights is the principal task of the state. Suspension of these rights, even temporarily, is fraught with danger to the freedom and security of the people, for civilized life is impossible without them; accordingly suspension of these rights is permissible only in conditions of *extreme* peril, such as imminent invasion or earthquake, when martial law is declared. When the danger is less extreme than in these instances, it is probably less than the danger to the public of having these rights suspended. Like the others, these rights are prima facie, since extreme conditions may call for their temporary suspension; but they are still extremely close to being absolute or unconditional rights. Since these legal rights have such enormous utilitarian value and suspension of them causes such great loss to human life and security, it would be difficult to imagine instances in which their preservation would *not* have utilitarian value.

It is sometimes thought that all this talk about human rights is adequately covered by one principle enunciated by Kant, that we should all "treat every human being as an end, not merely as a means." But Kant's principle does not specify to what rights people are entitled by this principle. To be useful, the principle requires interpretation. It *seems,* offhand, as if most of our interactions with other human beings in a civilized society consist in using them as a means to fulfill the purposes we have at the time. When a store-keeper sells to a customer, he is using the customer as a means — of gaining a profit for himself; and the customer is using the storekeeper as a means — of gaining the article he wants; neither is particularly interested in the other as a person. Does this situation violate Kant's principle? If so, almost every act performed in our business society would seem to violate it.

Probably the principle should be interpreted to mean that we should not use other people *merely* as a means. This provision would prohibit slavery, for example, where one group of people is used strictly as a means to the personal gain of others. But how, exactly, does this provision differ from a situation in which an employer pays his hired help as little as possible, not caring at all for their welfare but concerned only to give them just enough to keep them working for him? Is he not using them only as a means of personal gain? (Many slaves were better off than some paid employees.) But if this situation too violates Kant's principle, how about the employer who, because of union threats, hires only union help and so pays them more, but still only as little as possible in the circumstances? Isn't he using his employees only for personal gain just like the slaveowner — since his paying them more than slaves is through no merit of his own? Don't almost all employers follow this procedure, especially in a large factory where the employer doesn't know the employees personally? It is almost a basic principle of business practice that one pays one's employees as little as possible — and that one delivers to one's employers as little work as possible for the given wage. It is hard to see where to draw the line with this principle. All the parties in question would appear to use the others simply as means. Would Kant condemn them all?

Perhaps the correct interpretation of Kant's principle is that no one should use *compulsion* to force other human beings to do anything against their will. On this interpretation, there is much more to be said for the principle. It would of course prohibit slavery, for a slave is forced to work and not free to go elsewhere. The paid employee is always free to quit and work for someone else. In practice, however, this distinction sometimes does not come to much: in what sense were eighteenth-century employees free to go elsewhere if they were half starved, unable to afford travel even to the next city, and without any assurance that conditions were any better there than at home? In such a situation their "freedom to work elsewhere" is of about as much help to them as the fact that (in Anatole France's famous remark) the rich have as much freedom as the poor to sleep under bridges.

The intent of Kant's principle, however, seems clear enough: to protect the dignity of human beings so that they will not be used, as chattels or inanimate objects are used, only so long as they render service and then be thrown away. But if that is the intent, what is so vaguely asserted by this principle would seem to be better and more specifically stated (while yet including all that champions of the principle wish to preserve) by talking about human rights, as we have been doing in these last pages. Talk about human rights is, admittedly, vague enough.

We shall not attempt to discuss the "engineering" question of how and by whom these various rights should be enforced. Most of them are important enough, and easily enough violated, to require a guarantee by the state; and the state's chief function has often been held to be that of protecting people's rights. Some rights, such as the right of privacy in certain aspects of one's life, would be better upheld by custom or public opinion than by the state; yet when people go contrary to custom by violating these rights, the state must intervene to protect them if they are to be protected at all. It is worth noting, however, that some rights cannot at present be enforced even by the state. The right to life is not one that nations can guarantee as long as nationalism remains rampant in the world. In this respect the state has outlived its usefulness. Continuing nationalism may well put a quick end to all our lives and render useless all talk of our right to life, burying this right along with the others in radioactive oblivion.

C. Paternal legislation

There is, however, another side to the question of rights. The state attempts to guarantee the rights of individuals and organizations within it against encroachment by other individuals and organizations (including the state itself, as when individuals file lawsuits against the government). But is it also a function of the state to protect individuals against *themselves?* Should laws be enacted for the benefit of individuals even when the individuals do not desire the benefit and when they do not infringe upon the rights of others? Should there be laws controlling people's consumption of alcohol, for example, assuming that the people do not wish to be so controlled and that they are interfering with no one else's rights by their consumption of it? (Obviously there should be laws against the infringement upon the rights of others which occur when a person drives a car while intoxicated; but that is a law protecting the rights of *others,* not a law against drunkenness per se.) Should a person be forcibly prevented from doing something he very much wants to do, even if doing it is not to his long-run benefit and even if by doing it he does not interfere with others? Should he be permitted to consume alcohol, or commit suicide, or have others at his own request cause him a painless death if he is suffering from an incurable disease? Should the state take over and make him do what is good for him if he is so stupid that he won't do it for himself? This is the problem of *paternal legislation.*

Parents always assume this right in regard to infants and children, and society often assumes it in regard to hospital treatment of the physically and mentally ill. (The city ambulance may drive them against their will to a hospital, though unless they are declared mentally incompetent, they still have to give signed permission to have surgery performed.) But does the state have this right in the case of adult individuals of sound mind — even though some of them are such morons, scatterbrains, psychic masochists, or fools as to be called adults only in a chronological sense? If you believe that many adults are very much like children, you may also wish to have the state act toward them as parents do toward their children.

But there is enormous danger in this position. Many parents prohibit their children from doing certain things, not because it isn't best for them, but because it is inconvenient or bothersome for the parents; yet the parents rationalize their prohibitions by saying, "It's all for your own good." Similarly, leaders of states that have much paternal legislation often say in effect, "It's all for your own good" even when the law in question does not benefit others and the leaders are simply using the people to promote their own ends. As we have seen in the previous section, leaders who may begin their careers by legislating for the people's good may, after they are secure in their power, find themselves legislating strictly for themselves. Soon they may try to wipe out all opposition to their views, reasoning that the state must have a unified policy and not be threatened from within. To insure this unity, measures are taken which are ever more severe, culminating in a secret police — all to "protect" the people from "the cancers within the state." What begins as benevolent paternal legislation ends as vicious interference and domination; but the transition from the one to the other may go unnoticed because it is slow and gradual.

Even if those in power were not subject to such a danger, would they be wise enough not merely to *want* to legislate for the people's benefit but actually to *do* so? Many measures which one person or organization may *think* are for a person's benefit really are not; on this point other individuals, especially when they do not know the person's wants and needs intimately, are highly fallible. Most parents do not *purposely* command or encourage their children to do what is harmful to themselves, but they succeed in doing so all the same, not through lack of good will or good intentions, but through lack of detailed knowledge — knowledge about human nature, knowledge about the child's real problems and conflicts, knowledge of tactics (how best to go about doing it). If parents, who know their own children *comparatively* well, cannot be entrusted with the wisdom to guide them, how can we entrust the leaders of state, who do not know most of the individuals personally at all? Even if they are incorruptible and their intentions pure and unsullied, they cannot have the wherewithal to legislate wisely for each individual.

Suppose that the rulers have *both* good will *and* the detailed knowledge required for making wise decisions for each individual. The question remains, "Would they *then* have the right to enact such legislation?" No, because, according to many people, the rulers would be *interfering with the rights of individuals* — with the sacred right of each individual to indulge in trial and error, to make mistakes along the way, to harm himself, yes, even to destroy himself. The state is there to protect the rights of individuals against encroachment from the outside, but not to protect the individual against himself. If the state does undertake such protection, it is infringing upon the individual's private domain, just as one individual does when he reads another's personal mail without his consent. Some things should be left to the individual, and accordingly there should be no legislation on these matters, not even for the individual's own benefit.

A: There should be more laws — even against smoking. Cigarettes are harmful and habit-forming, and people who start smoking usually aren't able to break the habit after even a short time. If there were no cigarettes, people would not die so often from lung cancer. People start by taking a few, not even liking them, just taking them to keep up with the Joneses or (as children) to do the prohibited thing. Then a habit is formed which most people cannot break. The whole thing could be prevented if cigarettes weren't sold in the first place. And you must admit that most people who are victims of the habit wish that they had never begun.

B: But what would you do — limit a person's freedom entirely, even his freedom to do what he wants to, knowing full well that it is probably harmful to him in the long run? If people want to smoke, even to destroy their bodies, that is their own business, isn't it? The state is tampering with their rights if it refuses to permit them this indulgence. And not permitting so many things causes people to desire them even more than they would otherwise. Worse still, restricting the freedom of human beings makes it that much harder for human beings to discipline *themselves,* to develop *their own* habits (instead of having outside forces compel them), to let *their own* characters grow, each in its own unique way. True, a high price is paid for this freedom; some people fall by the wayside. But would you emasculate all men because some of them commit rape?

A: I see your point, but you know as well as I do that some things *have* to be prohibited by law for the person's own good. Narcotics, for example.

B: Doubtless they do. But even here I might suggest that if narcotics were not prohibited, fewer adolescents would use them than do now. Those who want narcotics badly manage to get hold of them anyway, and one reason they want them badly is that they desire what is forbidden — the lure of the forbidden fruit, which caused Eve's downfall. If this lure were taken away, the object would lose much of its attractiveness. Besides, when something is forbidden by law, an illegal traffic in it flourishes; the widespread use of narcotics in this country is caused more than anything else by the fact that illegal operators can make huge profits from its sale — and this possibility of profit motivates them to recruit new addicts. In Great Britain the use of narcotics is not illegal; anyone may take narcotics provided that he obtains them from the state and consents to state treatment; and as a result, there is only an infinitesimally small percentage there of the addicts we have in the United States.

A: What you say may be true; yet to permit the sale of such demoralizing merchandise is so immoral as to be monstrous. People just have to be forced to do things which they cannot see at the time to be wise. But later on these very same people will say, "At the time I thought you were persecuting me, but I can't tell you how grateful I am to you for preventing me from doing what I wanted to do. It would have ruined me, but I didn't see it then."

B: Well, at least let us try to agree that if the long-term consequences of passing a given piece of paternal legislation are worse (as regards the sapping of character, for instance) than the consequences of permitting the practice, the law is not justified. From that point on, we can leave it to rule-utilitarians who are also social engineers to find out whether or not a law should be passed in each individual situation.

EXERCISES

1. Would you say that a person has violated anyone's rights (and if so, which ones) if he

a. exceeds the speed limit

b. drives while intoxicated

c. poisons stray dogs? his own dog

d. raises sheep in his back yard

e. erects a high fence around his property, obscuring the neighbors' view

f. plays his hi-fi set loudly at midnight

g. distributes communist leaflets

h. sends anonymous letters to others containing vilifications of their friends

i. allows his wife to breast-feed their baby at a dinner party

j. sells aspirin under a different label at twice the price

k. eats dead cats

l. picks a fight with a stranger in a bar over a fancied insult

m. manufactures a new medication and sells it without listing the ingredients on the bottle

n. looks lasciviously at every attractive girl on the street

o. peeps at the windows of houses to watch good-looking girls

p. shouts obscenities at nobody in particular from his doorway

q. mixes sawdust with the meat loaf he serves his dinner guests, but tells them first

r. serves beer to a poor guest and champagne to a rich one?

2. Evaluate the following examples in terms of the right to life.

a. General Zhukov said to General Eisenhower that he had found a foolproof way of clearing areas of German mine fields: send a company of infantry through the mined area.

b. A famous surgeon gains a reputation for operating on his patients whether surgery is needed or not. He admits the charge, saying, "Sure, and some patients die who otherwise wouldn't have. But these few who die help me to save thousands. I learn by all these operations and experiments, and owing to these patients I have already developed a technique for saving thousands on whom surgery would otherwise have been fatal."

c. "If this man is released from the psychiatric hospital, there is a 1 per cent chance that he may go berserk and stab several people to death as he did once before. Therefore we should prevent the very possibility of this relapse by not releasing him. Even if the chance were 1/1000 of 1 per cent, we should still adopt this policy."

d. Chinese leaders: "Let there be a nuclear war. The Soviet Union and the United States will be destroyed, and even if two-thirds of the Chinese are killed besides, there will still be two hundred million of us left to dominate the earth."

e. "Since there flows in our veins largely the blood of generations of people who have managed to survive by the low cunning and treachery necessitated by the unnatural aspect of all past society, some kids will be unamenable even to the physical system of compulsory education. Taking away their desserts or knocking them on the head will not enliven them to any effectual effort at serious learning, even of their own language. These people should not be permitted to continue their schooling along general lines. An effort might be made to reclaim some of them after they reach maturity. But most should be prepared at once for the sedentary handicrafts — work in the trades, in the factories, in the iron seats of farm machines, and at the pump handles of filling stations. They have no aptitude for learning, make no use of what they do manage to be taught, and are a waste of tax money. A group of that group, the least stable and reasonable, should be politically disenfranchised. No one in the entire multitude should ever be permitted to hold public office. And a certain small percentage of this dreadful offal, much of which regularly accumulates in the bleachers of our ball parks, should be quietly put to sleep." From Philip Wylie, *Generation of Vipers,* copyright 1942, 1955 by Philip Wylie (New York: Holt, Rinehart and Winston, Inc., 1955), pp. 92-93. Reprinted by permission of the publisher.

f. "The only proper purpose of a government is to protect man's rights, which means: to protect him from physical violence. A proper government is only a policeman, acting as an agent of man's self-defense, and, as such, may resort to force *only* against those who *start* the use of force. The only proper functions of a government are: the police, to protect you from criminals; the army, to protect you from foreign invaders; and the courts, to protect your property and contracts from breach or fraud by others, to settle disputes by rational rules, according to objective law. But a government that *initiates* the employment of force against men who had forced no one, the employment of armed compulsion against disarmed victims, is a nightmare infernal machine designed to annihilate morality: such a government reverses its only moral purpose and switches from the role of protector to the role of man's deadliest enemy, from the role of policeman to the role of a criminal vested with the right to. the wielding of violence against victims deprived of the right of self-defense. Such a government substitutes for morality the following rule of social conduct: you may do whatever you please to your neighbor, provided your gang is bigger than his." (From *Atlas Shrugged* by Ayn Rand. © Copyright 1957 by Ayn Rand. Reprinted by permission of Random House, Inc., pp. 1062-63.)

g. An American explorer in the Amazon jungle is objecting to the practice of human slavery among the Indians. But a missionary disagrees: "'You see, my friend, slavery cannot be abolished. Our economy is built on it. As long as each tree will produce 30 kilos (75 lbs.) of rubber, there is no hope of relief. Slavery must always be deplored, but must never be abolished. At best we compromise, and make the life of the slaves a little less brutal.'

"'If this were known in the United States — surely something could be done.'

"'My poor friend! — the United States buys all our rubber!'" (From *The Rivers Ran East* by Leonard Clark. New York: Funk & Wagnalls, 1954, p. 142. Reprinted by permission of the publisher.)

h. A certain stretch of highway through the mountains has many dangerous turns, and there are more fatal accidents on it each year than in all the rest of the state put together. But to carve a new and safer road through these mountains, or even to change the course of the present one so as to remove the dangers, would cost several hundred million dollars of the taxpayer's money; many other much needed roads could be built for less than this amount. Should the road be built, or should we say, "It's the driver's own fault for going so fast"?

i. Suppose that by painlessly killing an innocent old man we could improve the economic status of ten thousand people, making life bearable for them, aiding them in their uphill struggle to earn enough to live on, and even preventing thereby numerous suicides among them. Would we be justified in killing him? (What would Kant say? Ross? act-utilitarianism? rule-utilitarianism?)

j. Even with lifeguards present, there are over a hundred drownings every season along this stretch of ocean, the only ocean beach within a hundred miles. The swimmers know that what they do is a calculated risk, but every season they prefer to take this risk and enjoy the swimming. Should swimming here be prohibited by law in order to save the lives?

k. A god comes down to earth and has a conference with the president of the United States. "I shall produce great good for your nation — ten thousand new housing projects instantaneously, opera houses for all your cities, longer paid vacations for all your people, almost anything you want — provided that you sacrifice to me the lives of 45,000 people per year." The president is aghast: "I will not accept your deal!" he cries in horror, "not even if you demanded only *one* life!" "I see," smiles the god; "the figure I quoted is what you are already sacrificing to me every year — they are the average number of annual deaths in automobile accidents on the highways of your nation."

3. Evaluate in terms of the concept of human rights the practices described in W. E. H. Lecky's *History of the Rise of Rationalism in Europe* (New York: Braziller, 1955), Chapters 4 and 5.

4. Do you consider the following to be encroachments on human rights? if so, to what extent?

a. preventing people who believe in the suppression of free speech from publicizing their views

b. banning criticism of the government in time of war

c. banning a movie because it is felt that children would be demoralized by seeing portions of it

d. banning the song "Gloomy Sunday" from the radio because many people are committing suicide as a result of hearing it

e. prohibiting the use of plastic coverings on clothes that come from the cleaners. (Many infants have accidentally been smothered to death by playing with these coverings.)

5. Do you consider a person's liberty to be increased or decreased by
a. laws limiting the speed at which one may drive on the highways
b. a law prohibiting people from taking narcotics
c. a law prohibiting people from smoking, for the sake of their health
d. a fence preventing people from walking over a cliff in the dark
e. a law prohibiting certain medications from being bought without a doctor's prescription
f. laws prohibiting sexual intercourse between consenting parties
g. laws against attempting suicide? (The penalty for committing suicide is death.)

6. Under what circumstances do you consider it morally permissible to require another person to do (or refrain from doing) something for his own good?
a. A parent prohibits the child from eating all the candy he wants, saying, "It isn't good for you."
b. "Some people may be led into a life of licentiousness by reading the passionate scenes in this novel, so there should be a law banning its sale."
c. "Murder and detective novels should be banned, lest some people be led into a life of crime by reading them."
d. "The Puerto Ricans are much better off in Puerto Rico, so we should pass a law preventing them from coming to our shores."
e. Should you forcibly prevent a foolish adult from going in deep water even though he cannot swim? (Suppose it were not an adult but a child — your child? another person's child?)
f. The custom of policemen is forcibly to prevent people from jumping off high ledges, bridges, etc. to kill themselves. Do you consider this custom justified or not?
g. "People shouldn't smoke marijuana. But some would if it were not prohibited by law. Therefore a law against it is a good thing."
h. "All theaters should be closed on Sundays so that people will observe the Sabbath."

7. Do you think you have the right
a. to open mail addressed to your son, aged five?
b. to open mail addressed to your son, aged fifteen?
c. to open mail addressed to your son, aged fifteen, marked "personal"?
d. to show to anyone you wish a letter addressed to you, containing insulting comments about the persons to whom you show it? (The writer has assumed, but not requested explicitly, that the letter be shown to no one else.)
e. same as (d), except that the writer has requested that the letter be shown to no one else.
f. to show to anyone you please a letter which you are writing, containing insulting remarks about the person to whom the letter is addressed?

8. Evaluate the following, with reasons:

a. "Since I have the right of free speech, I have the right to spread stories about Mr. X which I know to be false."

b. "I have the right to tell the truth but not lies. Therefore I have the right to tell to anyone I choose certain truths about the private lives of my friends and relatives."

c. "But of course we should censor non-Catholic publications. The truth should not compromise with error."

d. In the United States a man may sue another person for libel if the other person publicizes false or unproved stories about him. In Great Britain, he may sue even if the stories are known to be true. Which law do you consider preferable?

e. Does a presidential candidate have the right to make fake (composite) photographs of his opponent talking pleasantly with known communists, and have them published in the daily newspapers, in order to spread the opinion that his opponent is a communist?

f. "You have no right to come into my apartment without my consent." "But I do — I own the building." Yes, but you rented the apartment to me; if I were your house guest you would have the right, but seeing that I am a paying renter you don't." "But your rent is overdue and you haven't paid me yet." "Then you can sue me for nonpayment of rent, but you still have no right to enter without my consent."

g. "It's true that you worked for me faithfully for forty years and that you are too old now to find another job. But I am your employer and I have a perfect right to fire you without a reason."

h. "You didn't poison your wife?" "No, I didn't put the poison in her cup, but I admit that I knew there was poison in it when she lifted the cup to drink." "But why then didn't you stop her, or at least tell her?" "Because I have the right, not only to speak freely, but to keep silent when I choose. I admit I have no right to put poison into her cup, but the right of free speech includes the right to remain silent."

9. Do you believe that legislation against euthanasia (mercy killing) is paternal legislation? Do you believe that it would be morally right for an incurably ill person to be painlessly put to death, provided that he himself request it orally and in writing in the presence of impartial witnesses? Do you believe that physicians should be prosecuted in the courts for giving an incurably ill patient a lethal dose of a painless drug at his own request?

10. State your opinion on the following. (All the quotations are from Glanville Williams, *The Sanctity of Life and the Criminal Law* [New York: Knopf, 1957].)

a. "If it is true that euthanasia can be condemned only according to a religious opinion, this should be sufficient at the present day to remove the prohibition from the criminal law. The prohibition imposed by a religious belief should not be applied by law to those who do not share the belief, where this is not required for the worldly welfare of society generally" (p. 312).

b. "The fact is that there is no logical or moral chasm between what may be called shortening life and accelerating death. Once admit the principle that a physician may knowingly, for sufficient reason, shorten a patient's expectation of life — which cannot be denied — and one is compelled to admit that he may knowingly, for sufficient reason put an end to his patient's life immediately. If you may curtail a probable span of five years by one year, you may curtail a probable span of five days by one day, and of five minutes by one minute" (p. 324).

c. Some Roman Catholics accept the principle that "the will of the doctor is directed to the relief of suffering, an effect which he achieves; it is merely a secondary effect that the patient is killed. In just the same way St. Alphonsus Liguori, a Catholic theologian of the nineteenth century, thought a man justified in committing suicide by leaping from a window to get out of a blazing building, because the mode of death chosen is adapted to escape even though it will not succeed" (p. 321).

d. "A man drowned his incurably ill child, suffering from tuberculosis and gangrene of the face. He had nursed her with devoted care, but one morning, after sitting up with her all night, could no longer bear to see her suffering. The jury returned a verdict of 'not guilty' of murder. In the course of his summing-up, Mr. Justice Branson said: 'It is a matter which gives food for thought when one comes to consider that, had this poor child been an animal instead of a human being, so far from there being anything blameworthy in the man's action in putting an end to its suffering, he would actually have been liable to punishment if he had not done so'" (p. 328).

11. Under what conditions, if any, would you approve of censorship of (*1*) movies, (*2*) the press, (*3*) "subversive" literature, (*4*) pornography? (*Who* would do the censoring?)

12. Do animals have rights? all animals? under all conditions? Do animals have obligations as well as rights? If they have rights but no obligations, is this an exception to the rule that rights imply obligations? (Read the passages on the prima facie rights of animals in David Daiches Raphael, *Moral Judgment* [New York: Macmillan, 1955], pp. 52-53, 108-09.)

13. If you believe that animals have rights, evaluate the following practices:

a. hunting animals for sport

b. fishing

c. killing cattle in slaughterhouses

d. drowning unwanted baby kittens

e. killing poisonous snakes

f. painlessly killing aged or sick pets

g. vivisection of animals in medical laboratories

14. Do you agree or disagree with the following? Why?

a. All rights "are ultimately resolvable into the one supreme and unconditional right — the right to consideration." Hastings Rashdall, *Theory of Good and Evil,* 2nd ed. [New York: Oxford Univ. Press, 1924], 2 vols. Vol. 1, Bk. 1, p. 227.)

b. There is one absolute or unconditional right: to institutions which "provide general protection to all high-order goods and permit each individual member of the community to place the burden of proof upon those who would deny him his good or interfere with his pursuit of it." (Stuart M. Brown Jr., *Philosophical Review,* Vol. 64 [1955], p. 210.)

c. "If there are any moral rights at all, it follows that there is at least one natural right, the equal right of all men to be free. By saying that there is this right, I mean that in the absence of certain special conditions which are consistent with the right being an equal right, any adult human being capable of choice (*1*) has the right to forbearance on the part of all others from the use of coercion or restraint against him save to hinder coercion and restraint, and (*2*) is at liberty to do (i.e., is under no obligation to abstain from) any action which is not one coercing or restraining or designed to injure other persons." (H. L. A. Hart, *Ibid.*, p. 175.)

15. Having made up your mind (tentatively at least) on how close to absolute the various rights are, state, with reasons, whether you can defend your view best in terms of (1) Kant, (2) Ross, (3) act-utilitarianism, (4) rule-utilitarianism, or (5) some other view.

READING LIST, SECTION 19

Blake, Ralph M. "On Natural Rights." *Ethics,* Vol. 36 (1925), pp. 86-96.

Brandt, Richard. *Ethical Theory.* Englewood Cliffs, N. J. Prentice-Hall, 1959, Ch. 17.

Carritt, Edgar F. *Ethical and Political Thinking.* New York: Oxford Univ. Press, 1947, Chs. 6 and 15.

———. *Morals and Politics.* New York: Oxford Univ. Press, 1935.

Ewing, Alfred C. *The Individual, the State, and World Government.* New York: Macmillan, 1947, Ch. 2.

———. "The Rights of the Individual against the State." *Revue Internationale de Philosophie* (August, 1948), Special Issue, pp. 45-48.

Green, Thomas Hill. *Lectures on the Principles of Political Obligation.* (1882) New York: Longmans, Green, 1942.

Hart, H. L. A. "Are There Any Natural Rights?"; Stuart M. Brown Jr. "Inalienable Rights"; and William K. Frankena. "Natural and Inalienable Rights"; *Philosophical Review,* Vol. 64 (1955), pp. 212-32.

Hobbes, Thomas. *Leviathan.* Many editions, Chs. 13-19.

Locke, John. *First and Second Treatises on Civil Government.* Many editions, Bk. 2.

Macdonald, Margaret. "Natural Rights." *Aristotelian Society Proceedings,* Vol. 47 (1947-48), pp. 225-50.

Melden, Abraham I. *Rights and Right Conduct.* Oxford: Blackwell, 1959.

———, and William K. Frankena. "Human Rights." (symposium) *American Philosophical Association, Eastern Division, Proceedings,* Vol. 1 (1952), pp. 167-707.

Mill, John Stuart. *On Liberty.* Many editions.

Ross, Sir William David. *The Right and the Good* (1930). In Sellars, Wilfrid, and John Hospers, eds. *Readings in Ethical Theory.* New York: Appleton-Century-Crofts, 1952, pp. 197-203.

United Nations. *Universal Declaration of Human Rights.* Adopted by the General Assembly of the United Nations, December 10, 1948.

9. Justice

It will probably seem to many readers that rule-utilitarianism is the most satisfactory ethical view that has been presented. Some, as we saw in Chapter 8, will be convinced that certain human rights are so basic as to transcend any utilitarian ethics, even rule-utilitarianism; but others will see the basic character of these rights as occasions for having very strong rules about them and will justify these rules by their consequences — thus the issue of human rights will be assimilated into the structure of rule-utilitarianism after all. However one may feel about human rights, there is another concept we have not yet discussed, that of *justice*, which may present a challenge to rule-utilitarianism.

The words "just" and "unjust," though not used quite as often as "right" and "wrong," are used constantly enough to warrant a separate study of them. When a person receives a traffic ticket and another person does not after committing the same offense, the first person calls the inequality unjust; people condemn certain tax apportionments as unjust; some call it unjust when one man receives a grant for research while an equally capable man does not. "Justice" is one of our most frequently used moral terms, and we must now come to grips with it. Where does the concept of justice fit into the ethical picture?

Historically, the idea of justice is closely related to that of law and legality. The word "jus" in Latin means the same as "law," and the derived word "justitia" is the word for "justice." Though the term "justice" is still used somewhat more heavily in legal circles than in others, it does not function today as a primarily legal term but as a moral term. We often speak of certain laws, court decisions, and other legislative and judicial decisions as unjust, though there is no doubt that they are legal. When we say that the divorce laws in New York are unjust, we do not mean that they are illegal. Whether legal or not, we call certain acts, decisions, and situations unjust, and we intend this appellation as a moral condemnation.

But what kind of moral condemnation? When we speak of something as unjust, is this the same as calling it wrong? Surely not. "Wrong" and "unjust" are not synonymous, though they are related. We may think that something is right (driving carefully), though we would not think of applying the word "just" to it; and we can believe that something is wrong (suicide), although not unjust. We may even think of something as unjust (slavery in ancient times when the economy would have collapsed without it) without necessarily thinking of it as wrong; but of this matter, more shortly.

20. Justice and equality

There is no single unambiguous meaning for the word "justice." The word may seem at times to be a hopeless tangle; but we shall try to work our way into the complexities gradually, step by step. (Mill, for example, in Chapter 5 of his *Utilitarianism,* lists five separate senses of "justice," and other writers have isolated even more.) We shall attempt to handle every problem concerning justice under one or the other of two main headings: equality and desert.

There is no doubt that in daily life we associate the idea of justice with that of equality. If a parent is kind to one child and cruel to another, we call this treatment unjust. If a judge is severe to one prisoner and lenient to another for the same offense, this treatment too is called unjust. In both cases we attribute the injustice to "unequal treatment."

A. Equal treatment

If the judge fines you one hundred dollars and lets your neighbor go, and if the offense was the same, without mitigating circumstances in either case, we accuse him of injustice. "If the offense was the same, the treatment should be the same," we say. Or if the judge lets the second person go because that person happens to be his personal friend or relative, or because the judge happened to feel good on the one occasion but not on the other, again we cry "Injustice!" If the judge had a quarrel with his wife at breakfast that morning, felt a need to vent his aggression on somebody, and consequently imposed extra heavy fines that day, we consider this situation an example of injustice. We cannot, of course, escape entirely this human frailty: when we feel satisfied, we are inclined to be more benevolent toward the world; and if we are angry or resentful or envious, we take it out on innocent people, if circumstances or guilt feelings prevent us from taking it out on the guilty ones. No one is perfectly just, and people in positions of power are often less just than others; therefore we hear the popular complaint, "There ain't no justice."

But suppose that the judge sentences Smith heavily because he killed someone deliberately (homicide) but sentences Jones less heavily because he killed someone accidentally (manslaughter). Here we do not consider the sentence to be unjust. Why? We may be tempted to say that it is not unjust because Smith deserved a heavier punishment than Jones. This answer introduces the tangled concept of deserts, which we shall discuss later in the chapter. At the moment we are concerned with justice as equal treatment; and we do not consider the differential sentence in this instance to be an example of unequal treatment. Unequal treatment for the same offense we consider unjust; but unequal treatment for unequal offenses we do not. We could put the matter still otherwise in terms of impartiality: if the roles had been reversed and it had been Jones who was guilty of homicide and Smith of manslaughter, then the sentences too would presumably have been reversed; and so, thus far, there would have been no injustice.

But now a problem arises: If the judge lets Jones off more easily than Smith because Jones is a personal friend of his or Smith an enemy, or because Jones was a member of his national fraternity, or because he feels benign toward the world that day, we consider the sentences unjust; but if he lets off Jones more easily because his act was accidental or because someone forced him at the point of a gun, we do not consider the difference in sentences to be unjust. In other words, we consider the first group of reasons to be *irrelevant* ones (for a differential decision) and the second group to be *relevant*. But why? What is there about the first group of reasons that there is not about the second? Why does "He sentenced Jones more lightly because Jones is his personal friend" invoke a charge of unequal treatment, whereas "He sentenced Jones more lightly because Jones's act was accidental" does not? What is the criterion for making such a distinction? Consider the following imaginary dialogue.

A: Justice means equal treatment. For example: If both you and I are guilty of driving 45 miles an hour in a 30-mile-an-hour zone, it is unjust if one of us is fined for it and the other is not.

B: You mean, then, that if the two persons are equally guilty, they should be equally treated before the law.

A: Yes.

B: But I don't think that's true. Our situations may be somewhat different. Suppose you were driving someone to a hospital to save his life, while I was speeding just for the fun of it; doesn't that make a difference? Or suppose one of your friends agreed to give $100,000 to a worthy charity if you agreed to go 45 miles an hour for two miles in a 30-mile-an-hour zone.

A: Yes, of course, these circumstances make a difference. But the requirement of justice doesn't say that if you and I are in different situations we should be judged or treated in the same way. It says only that if you and I are *in exactly the same situation,* we should be treated the same way. For instance, if you and I are both speeding to get to a hospital to save someone's life, then the law should not exercise favoritism toward one of us; it should treat us both alike.

B: I see. We are to be treated the same only if our situations are the same. But now let's see: you and I might be in the same *external* situation but might still not be in the same *total* situation because of *internal* differences between our situations; we might have different temperaments, and sometimes this might make a difference as to what we should do or how we should be treated. Suppose that you and I have both been guilty of the same offense, namely driving through a stop light at Fifth Avenue and 42nd Street during the rush hour; and that this has caused inconvenience but no actual damage. Externally the situations are the same. And suppose neither of us has ever been in an accident before, or guilty of any traffic violation — so one of us can't be penalized for a "second offense." But suppose that you are a well-adjusted and reliable person, foresighted and sensible; and that I am nervous, jumpy, and accident-prone, and would have landed in traffic court much earlier if I had done much driving. Now, wouldn't the law be entitled to let you keep your driver's license but revoke mine, even though we had committed the same crime in a near-identical external situation?

A: Yes, I suppose so, since the difference here is in your and my internal set-up, which might well make a difference to a *future* external situation. By saying, then, that people in the same situation should be treated the same, we should include both the internal and the external situation.

B: Precisely. But now see how academic, how empty, how incapable of application our principle of justice has become. How could you and I ever be in the same situation, both externally and internally? I couldn't be in exactly your internal situation *unless I were you,* which, of course, is a logical impossibility. So, have your principle of justice if you want — much good may it do you! It will never be possible to apply it to any action.

A: I see your point. We shall then have to revise the principle so that it *will* be capable of some practical application to actual situations.

B: Right. And I don't see how you're going to do it.

A: Well, we'll just have to drop the proviso about you and me being in *exactly* the same situation, both internal and external. Shall we say, then, that you and I should be treated the same if we are both in a situation *of a certain type?* It needn't be identical situations, since in the strict sense this can never happen, only situations *similar* enough to each other to be classifiable under the same general heading — e.g., exceeding the speed limit to save a life, exceeding the speed limit for pleasure.

B: Yes, but then we find the difficulty we had before: even within the same general type, there are differences that would render a just verdict *different* in the two cases. You and I are, let's say, both in a situation of the same type, namely speeding in traffic; yet it would be just for you to be excused if you were rushing someone to a hospital, and unjust for me to be excused because I was speeding for fun.

A: True, but I've taken care of that — speeding to save a life is one class of actions (and not punishable), whereas speeding for pleasure is another (and punishable). Our two actions don't fall into the same class, you see.

B: But how wide or narrow do we want to make the classification? Suppose you are speeding one person to a hospital under conditions of very heavy traffic in which it is virtually certain that *more* than one person is going to die if you try to get through *that* traffic — at least more nearly sure than that your patient in the car is going to die if you don't try to buck the traffic to get him to a hospital. Then it would *not* be best to speed him toward the hospital, even to save his life, and the judge would be right to penalize you for doing so. So *not all* acts of the type you specify (speeding to save a life) are nonpunishable after all. You can always specify the class further and cook up examples in which exceptions occur even to the narrow class of actions you specify; even within that class there may be exceptions that should be treated differently.

A: Well, how about this proviso: all cases of speeding should be fined unless there is *some special reason* (e.g., saving a life) for not doing so; and even in the narrower class, all those accused of speeding to save a life should be exonerated unless, again, there is some special reason why they should not be.

B: Very neat, very plausible, very nice. But what is to count as a special reason? Speeding should be subject to a fine, you say, *unless* there is some special reason for not doing so, like rushing a patient to a hospital. But someone will say that everyone who qualifies for a certain job should be considered for that job entirely on the basis of his abilities, *unless* there is some special reason for not doing so, for instance if his skin happens to be black. Many Southerners would say that this is an excellent special reason. And yet you wouldn't consider this reason just, would you?

A: Of course not.

B: The problem, then, in formulating the principle of justice as impartiality, is to separate the *good* special reasons from the *bad* special reasons; or, in other words, the *relevant* special reasons (rushing someone to a hospital) from the *irrelevant* special reasons (having black skin). What I want you to produce is some *criterion* for distinguishing these from one another. That is what we need to put some teeth into our principle of justice. As long as we say, "Do X, unless there is some special reason not to do X" everyone can agree on it but everyone will act differently because they will not be agreed on what constitutes a satisfactory special reason.

There, that is our problem: to devise a test for relevance. But are we not already in a position to solve it, in the light of our discussion of rule-utilitarianism? Doesn't everything depend on the consequences of having such a policy? The policy of having the judge let off his friends would be a bad one because it would lead to many bad consequences (guilty people being acquitted and being free to commit crimes again, public distrust for law), whereas the policy of giving a stiffer sentence to the murderer than to the thief, and to the intentional act than the accidental one, is justified in that the consequences of such a policy are good — the value of having such a policy lies in its results. In the same way a consideration of the consequences should influence decisions about speeding: to fine speeders may deter them from breaking the speed laws in the future and thus from endangering the lives of others; but to fine those who are rushing patients to a hospital might well cause loss of life.

The concept of justice as equal treatment, however, is not limited in its application to courts of law or treatment of children by parents. It applies to human relations in general. Among the most flagrant injustices in human relations is the institution of slavery, for it involves a glaringly unequal treatment of human beings: some people are treated entirely as a means toward others' ends. (Remember our discussion of slavery in connection with Kant in the preceding chapter.) The injustice of slavery, then, will hardly be questioned. Nevertheless, many will claim, slavery is not *always* wrong. May not the institution of slavery sometimes have very great utility, even, in some circumstances, maximum utility? Perhaps it is the best possible arrangement in a preindustrial, agrarian society, with a labor shortage, not enough capital to hire people for money, and the danger of widespread starvation if there were no supply of slaves. Can we be absolutely sure that, on the whole, the institution of slavery in the American South lacked utility under pre-Civil War conditions — not, of course, after industrialization had dispensed with the need for unpaid labor? Even if we are sure that slavery was wrong in the antebellum South, what about slavery in the following circumstances? In ancient Babylon a large number of the people were slaves, and the minority had a life of leisure. This arrangement was unjust; but before we condemn it as wrong, let us reflect that it was *only* under the conditions in which a large number of people did not have to work for a living that certain difficult and complicated achievements, such as the invention of a written alphabet, were rendered possible. Suppose — and some historians have said that this is true — that a written language would not have been possible without the institution of slavery, would you still say that under those circumstances slavery was wrong? Wasn't it better to have a written language, which made civilization and culture possible, at the temporary expense of slavery (one might even say that it made slavery unnecessary later on), than to have no written language at all? How would the Industrial Revolution, which finally put an end to slavery, have been possible without writing and technical skills which required leisure? Or consider the Greeks: the institution of slavery made it possible for the citizens of Athens (again a minority of the adult, male population) to devote their time to art, drama, and mathematics; wouldn't you say that the immense cultural legacy that Athens has left us was worth paying the price of slavery to obtain?

But if slavery is always unjust and yet not always wrong, its wrongness cannot be entirely a function of its injustice. Does the distinction between wrongness and injustice contradict rule-utilitarianism? So far, not at all:

if the rules of behavior governing a certain society, under certain conditions, do not prohibit slavery, and if these rules are the best rules under the circumstances, then slavery is *not* wrong under these circumstances. Of course it is still unjust; but injustice is after all only a part or aspect of utility. The rules of equal treatment have very great utility indeed; but rule-utilitarianism would say that they *can* sometimes be suspended, or rather can give way to rules of still greater utility that do not include them, if some very great good is thereby achieved or some very great evil prevented. The good or evil in question must, of course, be very great — great enough to outweigh the tremendous disutility of suspending or transcending, even temporarily, the rules of equal treatment of individuals.

A different kind of example will illustrate the same problem of when to suspend the rules of equal treatment. A little over a hundred years ago a ship struck an iceberg and more than thirty survivors were crowded into a lifeboat intended to hold seven people.[1] In spite of the fact that some of the survivors took turns hanging over the side in the cold water, it soon became obvious — especially since a severe storm was approaching — that everyone in the lifeboat would be drowned unless the lifeboat were lightened by more than half its load. The agonizing question was, "How was it to be lightened?" All cargo had already been thrown overboard, down to the minimum of food and water for the number of people the lifeboat was designed to hold. It seemed probable indeed that no one would survive anyway; but unless the boat were lightened at once in the face of the approaching storm, it was not only probable but certain that nobody would survive — as certain as any empirical statement ever can be. But what specifically was to be done? It would have been possible to reason, "The just solution would be for us all to remain — justice means equal treatment for everybody — and so, when the storm breaks, we shall all drown. If we do, it will be an 'act of God,' and none of us (save God) will be responsible for any of our deaths. But if the captain were arbitrarily to select some of us for death in order to save the rest, their deaths would be on his head." The captain of the lifeboat did not share this view. Knowing full well that if anyone survived he would face criminal charges for his action (as he subsequently did), he reasoned thus: "If I don't do something, everyone is sure to drown. It is surely better to save some than none, though of course to do so would be to sacrifice the principle of equal treatment. The few who have volunteered to go over the side have already done so. So I shall have to *force* some individuals to go over the side and drown. Better that some be saved than none. Nor is it unjust to those selected for drowning; they would drown anyway."

Accordingly, amidst the universal hostility of the passengers, the captain selected some of them for death and forced them over the side; with the

---

[1] The case is described by Edmond Cahn, *The Moral Decision* (Bloomington, Ind.: Indiana Univ. Press, 1955), pp. 61-65.

ship thus lightened, the remainder survived the storm in the lifeboat and were picked up by a ship the next morning. (In the motion picture version of this story, *Abandon Ship,* the captain made his selection not on the chivalric principle "women and children stay" but on the basis of their ability to survive: those who were not already ill, those who were strong enough to row the two thousand miles to the African coast.) Here, then, is an example in which justice — in the sense of equality — was abandoned in favor of the maximum possible numbers of survivors. Do *you* think the captain acted rightly in sacrificing justice (equal treatment) to utility in order to save some rather than none? The judge — or those who made the laws on which the judge acted — apparently did not think so; he thought that justice, which the captain had sacrificed, was more valuable than lives and therefore found him guilty of manslaughter.

By the criterion of justice as equal treatment, there is no doubt that the captain was guilty of injustice. But did he, on that account, do wrongly by saving some instead of none, as equal treatment would have required? Some, putting justice ahead of utility, would doubtless say so. But others, perhaps most people, would agree that, difficult as his decision was, under the circumstances he did the best thing. Only by sacrificing justice could he produce the most good. This example shows once again, that, important as justice is, it is only a part of utility.

Thus far, then, we have found no compelling reasons for departing from rule-utilitarianism. But we have hardly yet begun our survey of the subject of justice. The idea of justice as equality is concerned not only with equal treatment but with equal distribution of the world's goods. And here some very thorny problems arise. It may be that on this point, if not before, justice will crack the rock of rule-utilitarianism.

B. *Equal distribution*

"There are some things that all men are equally entitled to, regardless of their rank or station in life, which it would be unjust for everyone not to have." "It is unjust for some to have caviar before everybody has bread." These and many similar sentiments are voiced every day, and they indicate that, however confusedly, the notion of equality is somehow tied up with that of justice.

But equality of what? Would it be desirable if everyone in the world had an equal supply of insulin, an equal number of electric fans, an equal number of potatoes, an equal number of books? Such equality would be about as absurd as anything could be: diabetics need insulin, while to nondiabetics it is not of the slightest use; some people desire many books, whereas others are unable or disinclined to read; some live in arctic climates and need no electric fans, and some live where no electricity is available and the fans would be useless. Nothing could be more ridiculous than to provide everyone with an equal number of each kind of material thing.

What these sentiments may mean is that everyone should have an equal amount not of instrumental goods but of intrinsic good. And if, again, we take happiness as intrinsic good, justice would then require that everyone be equally happy. But unfortunately, even if we could measure exact quantities of happiness, it would not be within our power, or within that of any human being or collection of human beings, to bring about such a state of affairs. In any practical scheme for equal distribution, happiness cannot figure directly, since it is something that no man can distribute. All that can be distributed is certain material things that may be a necessary *means* to happiness.

But if we distributed material things like potatoes equally among mankind, the happiness resulting would be far from equal. Some like potatoes; some hate them. The same would be true if we tried to distribute equally such intangible items as love: if we could somehow give every human being an equal amount of love, the happiness of the recipients would still be unequal, for some people are made happier by receiving love than others, and some prefer to give rather than receive.

It would seem, then, that the only thing that it would be practicable even to consider distributing equally is *money*. With money, people can buy what they want — they don't have to buy potatoes or electric fans; and people usually are more capable of buying the things they really want than other people would be capable of buying things for them. But not even the equal distribution of money will lead to equal happiness. Some of the main sources of happiness cannot be bought with money. Even ignoring these, a state of equality of distribution of money would last only a very short time: some would use money wisely and some would squander it at once so that very soon the amount would be unequal again, certainly long before the next generation; and so the next generation would once more begin with inequality. Besides, some people can be made quite happy with only a little money, and others are no happier, or even less happy, with a large amount. Some people require more money than others do to satisfy even their basic needs.

Still, in any possible scheme for equal distribution, money is about the only thing we can distribute, because people can satisfy so many, though not all, of their desires with it. Economists often assume that an equal distribution of money will come nearer to bringing about an equal distribution of happiness (or welfare) than would anything else. Therefore we shall be using the distribution of money in many of our examples, assuming for the moment the principle "If equal money, then equal happiness," even though this principle is not true.

At once, however, a possible conflict arises between the utilitarian ideal — even that of the rule-utilitarian — and the requirements of justice. For the acts in act-utilitarianism and the rules in rule-utilitarianism have one end in mind: the production of the *largest possible amount* (*quantity*) *of in-*

trinsic good. But does not justice require something additional that is not taken into account thus far at all, namely an equal *distribution* of that intrinsic good? This requirement can be illustrated as follows: Suppose you have a choice between two acts, A and B. If you do A, eleven units of intrinsic good will result, all going to Mr. Smith. If you do B, only ten units of intrinsic good will result, but instead of all going to Mr. Smith, they will be divided equally among ten people. Which is preferable? The follower of act- or rule-utilitarianism, it seems, will have to say that A is preferable, since the act of doing A or the rule which covers it will result in more intrinsic good than doing B. Yet many people would say that you should do B — not because B produces more good, for it doesn't, but because in B there is an equal *distribution* of good, and we tend to believe that there is some value in equality of distribution too, even *over and above* the total *amount* of good to be distributed.

Of course, we may try to beat the game by such maneuvers as this: if Smith gets all the intrinsic good, the other nine will be envious of him, and this unhappiness is sufficient to tip the scales in favor of doing B after all. But this solution won't work; for we have changed the original situation. If that were the situation, there would be no problem. The problem arises when the amount of good resulting from A *really is* greater. Suppose that the other nine will never know that Smith gets everything; or suppose that even if they do know, the total intrinsic good (happiness) to Smith is still greater, even when the envy is included in the total calculations as an already deducted minus quantity. Then our problem remains.

Perhaps it seems strange that this problem should arise: doesn't the utilitarian already provide for distribution of good — the greatest happiness (quantity) for the greatest number (distribution)? Aren't they both already included in the original Bentham-Mill principle of utility?

Let us try to unravel this matter. Bentham struck the egalitarian keynote in utilitarianism when he said that each person was to count for one, and only for one. Each person was to count equally; that is to say, in calculating the total good to be produced by an act, the good was to be counted no matter *to whom* it went — whether to your father or to the stranger in the burning building. (Indeed, it was for precisely this reason that Ross and the formalists objected to utilitarianism.)

However, in another way utilitarianism is not specifically egalitarian. We are never told that we should try to bring about an equal amount of happiness (or anything else) in all people; we are told only that we should aim at the *greatest possible* amount of happiness, *counting everybody's happiness into the total.* Perhaps Bentham and Mill meant to include equal distribution as well as maximum quantity into their principle; but if they did, they never said so. In fact, the motto "greatest happiness for the greatest number" is not very clear. It does not tell us what we are supposed to do in situations where the greatest total *amount* of happiness is achieved when not everyone has it or when it is unequally distributed; the motto does not tell us whether we should then decide for the largest amount or the most nearly equal distribution of what happiness there is.

The twentieth-century utilitarians, at any rate, have always interpreted the classical utilitarians as meaning that one should aim at the largest total quantity of intrinsic good, with no qualifications or additions saying that quantity of good is to be sacrificed when a more nearly equal distribution can thereby be achieved. (Why then did Bentham and Mill include the phrase "for the greatest number"? Probably to insure that every person was included in the calculations of the greatest total quantity.) Our problem, then, is this: does this classical utilitarian account of the matter (largest total quantity of good, with everybody being figured into the total) need revision in the light of the principle of equal distribution which we have said is included in our idea of justice?

Most thoughtful people, it seems, desire both ideals to be achieved: they would like to have a society in which the largest total *amount* of good is present, and if they had to choose between a society containing more good and a society containing less, they would unhesitatingly choose the first. Similarly, however, they would like to have a society in which good is, as nearly as possible, *equally distributed* (with exceptions we shall take up in the next section); and if they had to choose between a society in which good was equally distributed and one in which there were glaring inequalities, they would choose the first. The question is, what is to be done when the two ideals conflict? Are we — as the classical utilitarians would say, or at any rate as we are taking them to mean — always to select the alternative that contains the maximum total quantity of good, irrespective of its distribution? Or are we, as the supporters of justice would say, to select the alternative that contains the most nearly equal distribution of good, regardless of the amount? Or are we somehow to mediate between the two views by considering *both* principles and by believing that the right act should embody them both — the greatest total possible good that is compatible with the most nearly equal distribution thereof? It is probably fair to say that most people, once they have thought of it, would consider the third alternative — the one bringing in both principles — to be the best.

The possible clash between these two principles when each is taken alone is obscured because of the empirical fact that equal distribution is usually a *means* of achieving the greatest possible quantity. That is why classical utilitarians have usually been egalitarians. Mill worked all his life to break down the glaring inequalities between rich and poor; but, if one is to interpret his formula in the way that we have, he did so *in order* thereby to secure the largest total *quantity* of good in the nation as a whole. Whether equal distribution would or would not secure the largest total quantity of good is an empirical problem which is not ours at the moment. Our problem is, should we aim at two ideals or one? should we aim at maximum quantity of good (equal distribution being merely a means to it — perhaps a good means, perhaps not), or should we aim at maximum quantity of good *plus* equal distribution of good? Let us not make up our minds too quickly; in this section and the next one we shall pursue the matter with various examples and arguments.

Taking money again as an example, there is a long-standing economic controversy between those who want a maximum *amount* of money in a nation and those who want an equal, or nearly equal, *distribution* of it. Thus, a laissez-faire capitalist will argue: "I grant that a capitalist economy results in great inequalities: money comes to be concentrated in the hands of a few; big business tends to make out better than small business; and, as the big star becomes still bigger by its greater force of gravitational attraction, big money tends to get still bigger — 'to him that hath shall be given.' But wealth, or promise of wealth, provides the only *incentive* for taking risks, undertaking a new business, expanding an industry, and running it efficiently. If the government runs an enterprise, those in charge don't care if it loses money, they are not blamed anyway, they don't go bankrupt. To have a really expanding economy, with the *maximum quantity of wealth* in the nation, you need a free, capitalistic economy with a minimum of government interference and taxation so as not to dampen incentive toward expansion and more productivity. Such a system, in spite of great inequalities (which I admit are unavoidable), gives you the largest possible amount of wealth. Many of the inequalities are, to be sure, undeserved — the small business man suffers and is often forced out by Big Business — but in spite of this defect, this type of economy is the best because it permits a larger productivity and larger wealth than any other system. Even those who undeservedly suffer by comparison with Big Business still, as a rule, have more money than they would have in a more controlled economy."

The socialist, however, replies: "But in a laissez-faire capitalist state, the inequalities are so glaring, so *unjust,* that this type of economy will not do. In Great Britain, for example, there is a closer approach to equality in the distribution of life's goods. Since the state controls some industries, you don't have the cutthroat competition, with big industries gobbling up little ones, that you have in less controlled economies. It may be that the total *quantity* of financial good is not as great as it would be under laissez-faire capitalism. But whatever decrease in total quantity has come about through state control (as a result of smaller personal incentive) is more than made up for by the fact that the common run of people are at last getting decent treatment and certain guarantees of security, no matter what their station in life."

It is not our task, in a book on ethics, to debate the respective merits of various types of economy. We have used this discussion as an example only to illustrate the difference between two different ethical ideals: the one favoring the largest total quantity of (in this example, instrumental) good even at the expense of more nearly equal distribution, and the other favoring near-equality of distribution even at the expense of total quantity of good to be distributed. Neither view entirely ignores the opposing principle (socialists do allow inequalities if it means a much greater quantity of good will be distributed), but there is certainly a great difference in emphasis.

The difference between these ethical ideals can be illustrated in other ways than by a comparison of economic systems. If ten explorers are lost on an ice floe, the best distribution of the food supply would seem to be an equal one; each person shares equally in the food as long as it lasts, unless there is some special reason for inequality (for instance, one man is ill and can't eat his ration, or one man who will die in twenty-four hours unless he receives more than his ration of a certain food). But now suppose that there is only enough food for half of them to remain alive until the supply ship is due to arrive. Then it would be foolish to continue to distribute the food supply equally, for all of them would starve. A difficult decision would have to be made: whether to select some, by lot, to survive while the rest starve, or whether to ration the remaining food equally, with the result that all would starve.

The example is extreme, but the point is this: there is a bottom level of instrumental good (money, or in this instance, food) below which equality is useless because it is equality in nothingness, or something so near to nothingness that it would be of no use to any of the recipients. No good would be achieved by requiring equality under such conditions. On the one hand, a person who said, "I know we'll all starve, but we must share equally anyway" would really be running the equality principle into the ground! Precisely the same thing has been alleged of a socialistic economy: though it provides near-equality, the incentive is so low and, human nature being what it is, the system is inevitably so inefficient that after a while there will not be much left to divide equally: we shall have what has been called a state of "splendidly equalized destitution."[1] *If* it could be shown that an economy characterized by equal distribution produced this result, such an economy would be almost as useless to its members as the situation of ten men on the ice floe sharing substarvation rations.

On the other hand, a capitalist who said, "I don't care how many people suffer, I don't even care how many people starve, and I don't care how few people in the nation have practically all the wealth, as long as the total *quantity* of wealth is higher than in any other system," would surely be running the highest-total-quantity principle into the ground. Most people, as we have said, try to mediate, when there is a conflict, between achieving the highest total quantity of good (of whatever kind) and the most nearly equal possible distribution thereof.

How does one mediate between these principles? In the opinion of many

[1] L. Garvin, *A Modern Introduction to Ethics*, p. 460.

people, the principle of utility — interpreted as maximum total *quantity* of intrinsic good — will have to be revised. "For," they will allege, "it is not only the quantity of intrinsic good (happiness, knowledge, or whatever) that counts but also its *distribution:* it is just as important that there be a just distribution of intrinsic good as that there be a large quantity of it." If we accept this addition, we need not abandon rule-utilitarianism, but we will have to abandon it in the form in which we have thus far considered it. We can still retain it *if* we say that not only happiness (and according to the pluralist, certain other things as well) is intrinsically good but the *distribution* of happiness (or whatever else is intrinsically good) as well. In other words, justice is added to the list of things intrinsically worth attaining or producing. This revision of rule-utilitarianism is sometimes called *extended rule-utilitarianism.* And it is, indeed, an extension of rule-utilitarianism as we have considered it thus far. For the first time, we have a concept of intrinsic good that is not a state of consciousness of individuals (or a disposition to produce states of consciousness). X, Y, and Z may be states of consciousness of individuals, but the distribution of X, Y, and Z is not. Nevertheless, this fact need not deter us: it would be difficult to produce any reason why only states of consciousness can be intrinsically good or why the distribution of states of consciousness should not be.

Before we make up our minds whether to adopt extended rule-utilitarianism, another point needs to be developed. We have seen that there are occasions on which equality (equality of destitution, equality of death by drowning) should not be upheld, occasions on which justice should give way to utility. But are there not occasions on which equality is not just at all? If one man works hard and long while another is lazy, is it just that they should receive the same wage? Does not justice sometimes require *inequality*? Or, to return to our earlier example of the judge sentencing two men, suppose that the judge (assuming that he had the power) treated equally all persons who were convicted of the same traffic offense — he sentenced them all to death in the electric chair. We would consider such a sentence most unjust, *not* because the victims received unequal treatment (for he sentences them all equally to the same fate), but because the sentence is not in accordance with what the defendants *deserve*. In other words, in order to consider what is just, we have to consider the question of deserts. It is to this question, the most important strand in the concept of justice, that we must now turn.

EXERCISES

1. Indicate whether you think the following situations contain injustice in the sense of *unequal treatment*. Give your reasons.

a. A Negro is not hired for a certain job because (*1*) his skin is black. (*2*) he does not have the training required for the job. (3) there would be a strike among the white employees if he were hired.

b. A man who knows somebody on the hospital staff uses his influence to obtain preferential treatment for his brother, a patient in the hospital. Another patient, who lacks such influence, cannot obtain this treatment. (Does it matter that the second patient *would* use such influence if he had it?)

c. Some people volunteer for a dangerous medical experiment and some do not.

d. Two men, out of a whole platoon, are selected to go out on a dangerous mission with a 50 per cent chance of returning alive. They are selected (*1*) by the lieutenant because he holds a personal grudge against them. (2) by lot. (3) because they possess qualifications for the job which the other men in the platoon do not possess.

e. Ten men must die in order to hold off the enemy in a position that cannot be defended for long, in order that thereby one hundred men may escape to safety.

f. Certain draft laws may require only certain categories of adults to serve: (*1*) males but not females, (2) the healthy but not the unhealthy, (3) only men more than six feet tall, regardless of influence, position, wealth, or fame.

g. A rich widow leaves in her will one thousand dollars to every citizen of her community who is more than six feet tall.

h. A certain magazine, when the Republican presidential candidate makes a pre-election speech, devotes five or six glowing columns to a description of it; but when the Democratic candidate makes a speech, the magazine either ignores it or devotes one column or less to it, with disparaging remarks and excerpts selected in such a way as to distort the candidate's meaning. The magazine is (*1*) a weekly news magazine. (2) a Republican party periodical. (3) one which treats Hitler and Stalin in as insulting a fashion as it treats the Democratic candidate.

i. A national television and radio network gives equal free time to the Republican and Democratic parties, but refuses it to seven or eight minor political parties.

j. A Board of Education rejects a rich donor's offer to build a new public high school in his neighborhood, on the ground that all the neighborhoods in the city are entitled to equal treatment, and thus the acceptance of any offer which gave one neighborhood advantages not possessed by another would be an injustice.

k. "If a poor man were to leave one tradesman and deal with another because the first had turned Quaker, we should hardly call it an act of injustice, however unreasonable we might think it; but if a rich country gentleman were to act similarly towards a poor neighbor, many persons would say that it was unjust persecution." (H. Sidgwick, *The Methods of Ethics*, p. 270.)

l. You are driving on a turnpike which has a speed limit of 65 m.p.h. You are driving at 70 m.p.h., and another driver passes you at 80 m.p.h. The turnpike policeman arrests you. You say, "That's unjust! He was driving 80!" The policeman replies, "I know it, but you were both violating the speed limit. So you can't claim injustice. Besides, you were easier to catch."

2. We consider the fact that Smith is the judge's personal friend an irrelevant special reason for giving Smith a lighter sentence than Jones. But we consider

the fact that Smith was speeding to save a life a relevant special reason. What about the following reasons? (Assume that Smith and Jones are guilty of the same offense under the same conditions.)

a. Smith committed his crime many years ago, whereas Jones committed his recently.

b. Smith has mended his ways in the meantime, though Jones hasn't.

c. Jones gets punished more heavily (today) than Smith did for the same crime (last year), because crimes of this type are more prevalent today and there is a greater need for deterrence.

3. Which of the following do you consider justified special reasons for voting either for or against a presidential candidate?

a. He is a Catholic.

b. He is kind and generous to his wife.

c. He is divorced.

d. He is stingy with his money.

4. Are the following, in your opinion, justified special reasons? why?

a. "There should be laws requiring humane methods of killing cattle in slaughter-houses." "Yes, except for orthodox Jews, whose religion requires them to bleed the animal to death. That, surely, is a justified special reason."

b. "Surely Jewish circles were justified in requesting a ban on the movie *Oliver Twist,* since the villain, Fagan, is a Jew, and it might give some people the idea that all Jews are villains. Justice demands equal treatment for all races." "Yes, but what about all the other movies in which non-Jews are the villains? Should they all be banned too?"

c. "I suppose we do have to risk war to hold our position on Berlin and protect its citizens, but I have no enthusiasm for it. You see, I am a Jew, and not very many years ago the Germans were slaughtering my people. Therefore I have a special reason for not wanting us to go to war to protect them now."

d. "They wouldn't give you a job? You tried at twenty places and not one of them would hire you as a radio announcer? Why do you suppose they all turned you down?" "Th-th-they d-d-d-don't l-like the J-J-J-Jews."

5. The instructor gives the class a test containing ten questions. Some students can finish all ten in the allotted time; but as the period progresses, the instructor sees that most of them probably cannot, so he says, "Please omit question 10." Some students answer it anyway, though the instructor has told them that it won't count; for if he counts the answer for some, he must do so for all. Some students object that

a. it's all right to count the tenth question for those who have answered it and not to count it for those who haven't.

b. it is unjust to include the question, because to do so puts a premium on speed and this isn't just a speed test.

c. it is unjust to exclude the question, because some students are able to answer it and so should get credit for doing so; if some students are slow, the fast students shouldn't be penalized for it.

Evaluate these objections in the light of justice as equal treatment.

6. What decision would you make in the following situation? Why? You are in charge of an institution which gives free psychiatric help to those who can't afford to pay for it. Faced by a large group of candidates who all have an equal right to treatment and who all need it badly, you have to choose which of two policies to pursue; (a) providing infrequent sessions (say one every two weeks) for each of the one thousand people who desire and need help, although such a procedure will not provide enough treatment to cause any substantial improvement in the conditions of any except possibly a very few of them; (b) providing really effective psychiatric help for one hundred patients (at least several months of treatment, at least three sessions a week) and letting the remainder go untreated.

7. (a) If you had a choice between giving thirty people ten units of happiness apiece, and giving three people one hundred units of happiness apiece, which would you choose? Why? (b) If you had a choice between making thirty people happy for one year and making three people happy for ten years, which would you choose? Why?

8. It has been suggested (L. Garvin, *A Modern Introduction to Ethics*, pp. 461-64) that we need not only a principle of maximum quantity of good (utilitarianism) and a principle of equal or equitable distribution (justice) but still another principle. For example, suppose parents of limited economic means have a choice between having a small family of two children and having a large family of eight children. Suppose that the total *quantity* of good they can provide (economic good, but make it intrinsic good if you prefer) is the same in both situations, and that in both situations the good will be shared equally by all concerned. The first two criteria, then, are both fulfilled. But it is argued that we need still another principle, for clearly the smaller family, in which the limited means can be divided more comfortably, would be preferable to the large family, in which the same amount of good must be spread much more thinly, and the children may have to grow up in rags because there is less for each one. This third principle is called the Principle of Average Quantity, and it specifies that when the other criteria are met, the alternative to choose is the one in which each party receives the greatest quantity of good (though the *total* quantity of good is the same for both alternatives). In this situation the first alternative would clearly be the one to choose, since each member of the family would thereby enjoy more good.

In what specific types of situation will the Principle of Average Quantity have to be considered? (Why not in all cases of distribution?)

9. Now apply the Principle of Average Quantity to the following situation: If it were in your power to make the choice, which would you choose, (a) a world containing twenty billion people, each sharing the world's goods equally, but often hungry because there is not enough to go round in spite of equal sharing, or (b) a world containing two billion people, each sharing equally, but having enough for their needs because the resources would not have to be so thinly spread? (Can you think of any other situations in which the Principle of Average Quantity should be used?)

The reading list is at the end of the next section.

21. *Justice and desert: reward*

Why should people have unequal rewards and punishments? Why should A receive more money than B, and why should C move about freely among his fellow men while D is placed behind bars? Because of deserts, we say: A deserves more pay than B because A works harder or produces more, and D has committed a crime as a result of which he deserves punishment whereas C does not. We often speak of justice in terms of desert. We say that a certain individual has received his just reward — that is, the reward that he deserves; or that someone has been unjustly punished — that is, the punishment meted out is more than he deserves. We say that a father is unjust if he gives more to his spendthrift son than to his thrifty son — not only because he doesn't give them both an equal share, but because the inequality shown is not in line with their deserts. Christian theologians often say that the Dispensation of Justice (Old Testament) was supplanted by the Dispensation of Grace (New Testament) — that if we were all damned to hell forever, the sentence would be just, but that through grace some of us can attain the reward of heaven. In other words, according to these theologians, eternal punishment is what we all deserve, though, owing to divine grace, some of us are privileged to enjoy a better fate than we deserve.

Justice is getting what one deserves; what could be simpler? But here the simplicity ends. Often people do not agree on what rewards or punishments are deserved; nor is this disagreement always the result of partiality in their own favor. Even when they themselves are in no way involved, they often disagree on who deserves what and why. But at least they agree that justice has something to do with desert. They only disagree on what, in specific situations, is deserved.

To explore this issue, even in briefest outline, will be a sticky business. But there is no help for it; we cannot ignore it. Many would say that desert is the most important concept contained in the idea of "justice." Indeed, it is often held that the best possible state of society would be one in which each man gets what he deserves: he who deserves most is rewarded most (presumably with happiness, or whatever else is thought to be intrinsically good); he who deserves much is given much; and he who deserves little receives little. In other words, the ideal state of affairs would be one of *perfect apportionment* between one's desert and one's reward. It is quite clear (pages 175-83) that our present world does not fulfill such an exacting requirement; it often seems to come near the opposite, rewarding the wicked and punishing the guiltless. But it is often held by theologians that in the next world all the accounts will be set straight, that everyone will receive just what he deserves, and that therefore there will be "perfect justice." Kant, in fact, used this position as an argument for immortality: the moral law requires justice (apportionment of reward to desert), and in this world justice often does not triumph; therefore there must be a life after this one in which it does. As an argument, most philosophers agree that this one is not successful. But at least it is a testimonial to the widespread and deep-seated desire for justice.

But when we try to come down to cases, we are baffled at the outset. What *does* a person deserve, and why? What does a plumber deserve? two dollars an hour? five dollars? How is one to say? Shall we say of a man who has committed armed robbery that he *deserves* the ten-year prison sentence that the law prescribes for him — or five, or one, or twenty? and who is to say how much more time the armed robber deserves than the petty thief? It is not merely that cases differ, though they do; but that even in *one* case we seem to be utterly at a loss to say exactly *what* a person deserves. By what criterion are deserts to be estimated?

To guide our steps in this maze, let us restrict our discussion, for the moment, to reward for work performed; and let us consider only monetary rewards, assuming — though it is far from being true — that a greater monetary reward will result in greater intrinsic good to the person who receives it. What criteria, then, can be employed to determine who should receive the most money for his labor? [1]

The most straightforward and seemingly obvious criterion for determining the amount of one's reward is *work*. Surely, we say, what a person should be paid bears a relation to the work that he performs. But unfortunately the word "work" is ambiguous. It may refer either to the *achievement* — what one actually produces, whether it be crops, manufactured articles, or trained minds — or to the *effort* leading to that achievement. Let us consider these in order.

1. *Achievement* — what one has actually produced, accomplished or brought about through the expenditure of one's effort, regardless of how easy or difficult it was to produce or how long or short was the time required to produce it. Many people believe that actual achievement should be the only criterion for estimating reward. It *is* the only criterion employed (at least officially) in many areas, for example the assignment of grades to students in courses. The student who has accomplished the most in the course gets the A, regardless of whether he had to work hard or spend much time to get it. If he worked hard but, through lack of aptitude or stupidity, still did not accomplish much in the course, we may praise him for his effort but we still withhold the high grade. The winner of a hun-

---

[1] The criteria of justice which follow are in no way suggestions that any agency, such as a State Planning Commission, should attempt to regulate people's material rewards so as to bring about a state of justice. The results of such a procedure would doubtless be just as horrible as Mill thought (in the quotation on page 372). We are concerned here with what an ideal system of material rewards *would be,* not with how they should be brought about. If they were brought about by force, whim, or the arbitrary fiat of the bureaucrats on a regulatory commission, the results would probably be worse than that of the most flagrant injustices created without such fiat.

dred-yard dash may not have tried a tenth as hard as the competitor with a stiff knee, but he wins the trophy anyway. We admire the man with a stiff knee for his effort, but we reward the winner for his achievement. Normally, but not always, wages in industry tend to be in proportion to the achievement of the worker. And, some would say, this is the way it ought to be. Not only is reward according to achievement the only practicable system (it is easier to determine actual production than effort), but it has the highest utility; for in this way the people with the greatest capacity for achievement will be more likely to have the incentive to attain it.

The word "achievement" itself is somewhat ambiguous. It may refer to (1) the quantity of one's production — for example, the number of pieces of cloth one can stitch together during an eight-hour day; or it may refer to (2) the quality of one's production — for example, how good a teacher one is, or the wisdom and fruitfulness of the leadership the manager or administrator gives to his subordinates. Ordinarily, when one speaks of achievement, he includes both.

Practical difficulties, however, arise in attempting to estimate achievement. Can one measure one type of achievement against another? Should a good teacher receive less pay than a good lawyer, a good lawyer less than a good surgeon? In our society they are rewarded most unequally. But if we concede that this inequality is unjust, how *would* we propose to reward them? Perhaps we would do well to examine other possible criteria.

2. *Effort* — the other sense of the word "work." Some would say that the more effort you put forth, the higher the wage you deserve, regardless of the actual quality or quantity of what you produce. Effort, of course, is not a function only of the amount of time expended; it is also a function of the energy expended during that time. Two men can each spend eight hours at a certain job, but if one of them concentrates fully on it and gives it all he can during that time while the other works in a slovenly or half-hearted manner, clearly the amount of effort expended is not the same, even though the time spent is. If the two men work the same amount of time and at 100 per cent of their capacity, they may be said to have put forth equal effort.

How satisfactory is effort as a criterion for determining one's desert? Someone, let us call him A, may be inclined to reply as follows:

A: Not very. Suppose that you and your neighbor each put forth the same effort — same amount of time, same percentage of your full capacity during that time — and that by doing so you, who are more capable and intelligent than he is, accomplish three times as much work (production, achievement) as he does. Should you receive the same wage just because the effort expended is the same? What would such a procedure do to your morale, you, the capable worker? Wouldn't you be inclined to give the job less than your best, since by giving less you would still produce just as much as your neighbor would? Wouldn't a system based on effort rather than achievement reward the stupid and penalize the capable? Is it just that a person who can do three times as much as another should receive the same wage for his work? Should the dull student who works very hard but still gets everything wrong receive a better grade than the bright student who can grasp the content of the course and do all the required reading in half the time? Should effort per se be rewarded, even when it produces little of value?

B: It may be that in our present society and human nature being what it is, we have to reward to some extent on the basis of actual achievement. But I still think that it isn't the ideal system. Until recently there was a communistic settlement in the Midwest embracing several counties, a settlement in which people held all property in common. Everyone received the same wage from a common fund, provided that he exerted the same effort (insofar as effort could be determined, of course — everyone was expected to work as hard as he could, roughly the same number of hours per day). Some, of course, produced far more than others, for some followed professions to which they were not adapted. One day a physician in the settlement complained to the managing committee of the group (who also received the same wage as he and the others). "I'm a brilliant doctor, and everyone knows it. I work just as hard as Dr. X, who, on the whole, is rather stupid. I can diagnose diseases more quickly and accurately than he can; I can do surgery more skillfully. As a result I have far more patients — they are always waiting to avail themselves of my services. Yet I receive not a penny more than he does, although my service to the community is inestimably greater. I therefore request that you pay me more than you pay him." But his request was denied. "God has given you five talents, and has given your colleague, Dr. X, only one talent," he was told; "therefore He exacts from you five talents and from Dr. X only one talent. You are more intelligent, more capable; we know that. But this is no merit of yours, nor is it his fault that he has smaller capacities. To whom God has given more, from him He expects more in return."

A: I think that's a ghastly system. It penalizes ability and puts a premium on mediocrity. It provides no incentive for a person to do superior work. Remember that superior achievement is not only a result of superior ability but also of hard work, i.e., effort; and what incentive is there to prepare oneself for a skilled job or profession if the reward is no greater? The whole thing is against human nature, and it's no wonder that most of these settlements have broken up. The doctor in such a system would sooner or later go elsewhere, outside the settlement, where his superior talents would be recognized and rewarded.

B: But if the entire nation or world had the same type of socio-economic system as the settlement, he wouldn't be able to go elsewhere.

A: True. And do you call this system good? I think it would be most horrible.

B: No, it would be the ideally just system. People should be willing to work for the good of the community, the brilliant doctor no less than the mediocre one. Each should be willing to put forth his maximum effort in the service of mankind and not expect a greater reward if he happens to have more talent.

A: Talent — but it's not entirely a matter of talent. Even the most brilliant doctor can't reach the peak of achievement except by lots of hard work. And what incentive has he to put forth that hard work if he will receive nothing for it? Who will spend years of his life training for a profession? Who will perform jobs that are unpleasant or dangerous? We cannot afford to waste talent; able people must be encouraged; and the obvious way is by greater recognition and monetary reward. If you paid the drudge just as much as the genius, the effect would be to waste the genius; he would feel, "What's the use? I can get by just as well by not training my mind." The disutility of such a system would be deplorable. A society set up in such a way would be functioning with minimum utility when it could function with far more. By rewarding the genius as we should, we encourage him to develop his talents in such a way that society as a whole benefits — and even the drudge has a better life (economically, at least) than he would have had if talent had not been rewarded.

B: But the fact that my system, which does make severe demands on human nature without promise of greater reward, would not work — *if* indeed this is a fact — is no argument against it. It is still the only *just* system.

A: Perhaps it would be, in a society of angels, in a society in which people would need no personal incentive to lead them to great accomplishments. I see no point in discussing what would be just in a society of angels; surely what we are talking about is a society of human beings, with the psychological characteristics they now possess, including all their frailty and partiality in their own behalf. And for people, with the motives they have, the system you desire would decrease utility to such an extent that it would be self-defeating. By giving everyone the same reward for the same effort, regardless of the superiority of his product, you would put such a damper on talent that social and scientific improvements would cease, and even the majority who were comparatively untalented would be worse off. They owe what degree of comfort and welfare they have to the minds and work of men of ability; and if those minds ceased to be encouraged and spurred on to new efforts, the result would indeed be "splendidly equalized destitution."

B: I think you have too low a conception of human motives. I agree that people of ability should be encouraged, but I see no reason why this encouragement should be financial. You assume that people cannot be made to work for the good of the group by other than egoistic motives. I think you are unduly pessimistic. In the nineteenth century an American writer, Edward Bellamy (1850-98), wrote a book, *Looking Backward*, in which he envisoned a society animated by just such altruistic motives as I have been suggesting.[1]

---

[1] Discussed in M. S. Everett, *Ideals of Life*, Ch. 12, pp. 508-16.

"Some men do twice the work of others!" I exclaimed. "Are the clever workmen content with a plan that ranks them with the indifferent?"

"We leave no possible ground for any complaint of injustice," replied Dr. Leete, "by requiring precisely the same measure of service from all."

"How can you do that, I should like to know, when no two men's powers are the same?"

"Nothing could be simpler," was Dr. Leete's reply. "We require of each that he shall make the same effort, that is, we demand of him the best service it is in his power to give."

"And supposing all do the best they can," I answered, "the amount of the product resulting is twice greater from one man than from another."

"Very true," replied Dr. Leete; "but the amount of the resulting product has nothing whatever to do with the question, which is one of desert. Desert is a moral question, and the amount of the product a material quantity. It would be an extraordinary sort of logic which should try to determine a moral question by a material standard. The amount of the effort alone is pertinent to the question of desert. All men who do their best, do the same. A man's endowments, however godlike, merely fix the measure of his duty. The man of great endowments who does not do all he might, though he may do more than a man of small endowments who does his best, is deemed a less deserving worker than the latter, and dies a debtor to his fellows. The Creator sets men's tasks for them by the faculties he gives them; we simply exact their fulfillment."

"No doubt that is very fine philosophy," I said; "nevertheless it seems hard that the man who produces twice as much as another, even if both do their best, should have only the same share."

"Does it, indeed, seem to you?" responded Dr. Leete. "Now, do you know, that seems very curious to me? The way it strikes people nowadays is, that a man who can produce twice as much as another with the same effort, instead of being rewarded for doing so, ought to be punished if he does not do so. In the nineteenth century, when a horse pulled a heavier load than a goat, I suppose you rewarded him. Now, we should have whipped him soundly if he had not, on the ground that, being much stronger, he ought to. It is singular how ethical standards change." The doctor said this with such a twinkle in his eye that I was obliged to laugh.

"I suppose," I said, "that the real reason that we rewarded men for their endowments, while we considered those of horses and goats merely as fixing the service to be severally required of them, was that the animals, not being reasoning beings, naturally did the best they could, whereas men could only be induced to do so by rewarding them according to the amount of their product. That brings me to ask why, unless human nature has mightily changed in a hundred years, you are not under the same necessity."

"We are," replied Dr. Leete. "I don't think there has been any change in human nature in that respect since your day. It is still so constituted that special incentives in the form of prizes, and advantages to be gained, are requisite to call out the best endeavors of the average man in any direction."

"But what inducement," I asked, "can a man have to put forth his best endeavors when, however much or little he accomplishes, his income remains the same? High characters may be moved by devotion to the common welfare under such a system, but does not the average man tend to rest back on his oar, reasoning that it is of no use to make a special effort, since the effort will not increase his income, nor its withholding diminish it?"

"Does it then really seem to you," answered my companion, "that human nature is insensible to any motives save fear of want and love of luxury, that you should expect security and equality of livelihood to leave them without possible incentives to effort? Your contemporaries did not really think so, though they might fancy they did. When it was a question of the grandest class of efforts, the most absolute self-devotion, they depended on quite other incentives. Not higher wages, but honor and the hope of men's gratitude, patriotism and the inspiration of duty, were the motives which they set before the soldiers when it was a question of dying for the nation, and never was there an age of the world when those motives did not call out what is best and noblest in men. And not only this, but when you come to analyze the love of money, which was the general impulse to effort in your day, you find that the dread of want and desire of luxury was but one of several motives which the pursuit of money represented; the others, and with many the more influential, being desire of power, of social position, and reputation for ability and success. So you see that though we have abolished poverty and the fear of it, and inordinate luxury with the hope of it, we have not touched the greater part of the motives, which underlay the love of money in former times, or any of those which prompted the supremer sorts of effort. The coarser motives, which no longer move us, have been replaced by higher motives wholly unknown to the mere wage earners of your age. Now that industry of whatever sort is no longer self-service, but service of the nation, patriotism, passion for humanity, impel the worker as in your day they did the soldier. The army of industry is an army, not alone by virtue of its perfect organization but by reason also of the ardor of self-devotion which animates its members. . . ." [1]

Achievement and effort are the two principal competitors for criteria of distributive justice. Others, however, should be mentioned:

3. *Ability.* Perhaps rewards should be dispensed in proportion to one's ability. This view too sounds plausible. But the word "ability" is ambiguous.

(1) If "ability" means *native* ability, the abilities or capacities you were born with, it would hardly be recommended as a criterion. The abilities you were born with are something entirely outside your control. If you have considerable native ability, say in music, you are fortunate; but should rewards be dispensed on the basis of abilities which you had no part in creating? True, the criterion of achievement uses native ability, for (other things being equal) a person who has a great deal of native ability is more likely than others to reach higher levels of achievement. But at least achievement depends in part — and perhaps in greatest part — upon hard work. Thomas Edison said, "Achievement is 2 per cent inspiration and 98 per cent perspiration."

(2) There is also *acquired* ability. The ability to use the typewriter, to

[1] *Ibid.,* pp. 513-14.

master languages, to solve equations, to run a lathe, are acquired only after considerable effort, even in the most skillful. Acquired ability is a product of native ability and effort. But insofar as it depends on native ability, it is a matter of luck; and insofar as it depends on effort, it falls under the heading of "Effort" which we have already considered. In any event, what matters is surely not *having* the ability but *what you do* with the ability you have. Should ability per se, ability which produces nothing, be rewarded just as if it did?

4. *Need.* It may be suggested that one's reward should depend on how much one needs; the one who needs the most should receive the most. Some would doubt that need should be used as a criterion at all, and some would say that it should be used only sparingly or in extreme situations; but few would suggest that it should be the only criterion. If it were, work would soon come to a standstill, and there would be nothing left with which to reward anyone. Doubtless the needy should not be allowed to starve — especially if they desire work but, through no fault of their own, can find none. Doubtless even those who are able to work but refuse to do so ("Society owes me a living") should not be allowed to starve and if possible should be sent to a psychiatrist. (Some would say that they *should* be permitted to starve. But should their families too?) But at least, reward cannot be based entirely upon need. If nonworkers were rewarded as much as workers, who would desire to work? Some doubtless would, but would then have to work much harder, to make up for the large mass of the indigent. Moreover, if the neediest persons received the most money, they would probably spend it all at once in order to be needy again by the time the next paycheck came round. Rewarding in proportion to need would be rewarding the spendthrift and ne'er-do-well and penalizing the person who works hardest and tries most valiantly to prevent himself from becoming needy in the future.[1]

Thus far, all our criteria have had to do with the worker or what he can produce. Further suggestions, however, may come from another quarter: criteria may be found having nothing to do with the worker but with the society in which he lives.

5. *The open market.* Some have suggested that what a worker deserves depends entirely on the wage his work can command in an open market. When there is a great demand for engineers — a greater demand than the market can supply — then the wages of engineers go up, and (it is contended) so they should. The result is that more students become engineers, until the gap between supply and demand is closed. If too many become engineers — more than the market requires — the wages go down, incentive decreases, and fewer people become engineers, until the next engineer short-

---

[1] A dramatic illustration of the result of reward being based on need is contained in the Starnesville incident in Ayn Rand's *Atlas Shrugged* (New York: Random House, 1957), pp. 253-92, 654-97.

age causes the wages to go up again. (Other circumstances may cause changes in the market, such as whether there is much mining or bridge-building going on at the time, a circumstance which in turn depends on economic factors such as whether there is a depression or what the current Congressional fiscal policy is.) In this way, through the ebb and flow of supply and demand, each profession tends to attract roughly the number of members that are needed at that time — and, it is added, this is the only just solution. (This situation changes, of course, in a controlled economy; but that is precisely the reason that many people object to a controlled economy.)

As a criterion of justice, however, this scheme of supply and demand does not run without a hitch. People, once established in a profession for which long training was required, cannot suddenly change their profession no matter how overcrowded it has become. Many people are incapable, because of financial difficulties or lack of aptitude, of pursuing certain professions, no matter how great the shortage. Should persons who have dependents and therefore cannot afford the training required for a certain trade or profession be penalized throughout their lives because of this fact? Moreover, the open market, even in a completely free economy, can hardly be said in every situation to reward a person in proportion to his desert. Able teachers usually receive far less income than do incompetent surgeons; does this inequality mean that teachers *should* receive less — that their profession, or their individual achievement, is less worthy or deserving? Is it just that nurses specializing in tubercular patients should receive less or be unemployed because, owing to medical advances, tuberculosis has become easier to cure? Poets, even great poets, receive very little money from their life's work (in the United States, at any rate) — far less than farm hands and prostitutes. Does this inequality show that the oldest profession is more deserving than the less pecunious ones? Is an engineer less deserving of high wages because a sudden glut on the engineer market or a national depression forces his income down? Do teachers deserve less because they are usually hired by school boards, who are loath to spend money and increase their own tax burden and who tend to feel that a second television set is more important than that their children should have competent teachers?

6. Another criterion that we can note is *public need* for the product of one's labor. Perhaps not the need of the worker but the need of the public for the fruits of his labor should be a criterion of reward. Of course, people's needs differ; some need love more than money, some need money more than love. But everyone needs food; accordingly, farmers should receive the highest wages, for their work is the most indispensable: without them we would all starve. By the same criterion, the makers of expensive rings should receive little or nothing, for we could get along without them. But who is to decide whose services are the most needed? And most needed for what? For sheer survival? for the enrichment of life? for the spending

of leisure hours? for keeping up with the Joneses? Are Cadillacs less needed by everyone than Chevrolets or jeeps? Are handbags and hi-fi sets needed? Do not the manufacturers of exploding cigars render certain services to the community?

One must distinguish, of course, between the need for a certain *profession* and the need for given *individuals* within that profession. Farmers are certainly needed, but there is at present an oversupply of them, since agriculture has become mechanized and fewer men can produce more. Should farmers then receive much, because their work is vital, or little, because they are in oversupply? Moreover, some things are urgently needed, but by only a few people, whereas the products of agriculture are needed by everyone. The makers of antivenin for cobra poisoning have a product that is urgently needed by those who have just been bitten by cobras; but because this need is not particularly widespread, should they receive less than farmers do? Should the truck gardener receive as much pay as the man who daily walks the catwalk hundreds of feet above the water during fog and sleet to see if the bridge is still in first-class condition — assuming that these two workers are equally needed?

7. Yet a further criterion to be considered is *public desire* for the product of one's labor. Perhaps, then, it is not what people need but what they desire that should count. Desire is, of course, different from need: we may need food but not desire it, and we may desire alcohol but not need it. When we need something, it must be in some respect difficult or impossible to get along without it. (But often people say they need something when they merely desire it: "I need a drink!" a person may say every time he desires it.)

By the criterion of desire, one's reward should be in proportion to how much the consumer wants or desires the product — no matter how trivial or useless the product may be. "What would I pay rather than go without it?" is the question, regardless of whether one *should* go without it or not. But is desire a fair criterion? Many people would rather buy alcohol than food, even with their last dollar; if everyone had such a preference, would the distiller *deserve* more than the cook or the gardener? Is an individual's preference as to what he would rather have — or the preference of the majority of the population — to be taken as a criterion of either the worth of the product or the desert of its producer? If the majority of customers are unselective and easily taken in by false or misleading advertising, with the result that a first-rate product loses the market to a second-rate product because the first-rate product costs a few cents more and its makers have not stooped to false advertising, does this result show that the second-rate product really is a better buy for the money or that the producers of it deserve more income? Because most Americans prefer television to legitimate theater, does their preference show that stage actors deserve less pay than television actors? Because there is more demand for commercial art than for fine art, should the commercial artist receive more pay? We are tempted to say that the fact that people will pay more for Y than for X shows nothing whatever about whether Y is worth more than X or whether the maker or purveyor of Y deserves more than for X.

8. As if this difficulty were not enough, there are still other criteria that are sometimes used in estimating desert; no one suggests that they are sufficient by themselves, but it is often suggested that at least they are relevant to the question of deserts in income. Let us consider them briefly.

a. Anyone who is in a profession that requires *long training* at a considerable expenditure of money and years of his life is said to deserve a larger income, once he is in a position to earn, than one whose job is unskilled. This difference is not so much because we want to be snobbish or preserve class distinctions, or even because we want to provide incentive for going into the professions (some of them are overcrowded), but because we believe that a person deserves a reward for years of hard work spent in preparation for his profession, during which years other men his age were already earning money. Psychiatrists have a larger income than most people, but considering that very few of them can finish their long period of training before the age of thirty, even if they go to school all the time, it seems only reasonable that they should earn more once their training is completed.

b. Similarly, a position requiring *expensive equipment* for which the person must pay out of his own pocket (say, that of a physician or dentist in private practice) deserves more compensation; these added expenses are not luxuries but necessities for the professions in question, and they are there primarily for the benefit of the patient rather than the practitioner.

c. If a certain field of work involves great *risk of financial loss,* perhaps success in that field should be more heavily compensated. The people who earn the most in our society are not the salaried people but those who start new enterprises (or continue old ones) — manufacturing concerns, department stores, and restaurants. But when these ventures fail — as they often do through sudden overcompetition, increased taxes, or reasons other than carelessness or slovenliness on the part of the owner — probably those who take these risks deserve to earn more than they would if they worked equally hard in an enterprise where such risks were not involved. When the enterprise fails, years of money and labor go down the drain with nothing but debts to show for them — a fate which is hardly commensurate with their efforts and enterprise.

d. It would usually be agreed that a person whose job requires him to face considerable *physical danger* deserves a greater compensation than people in safer occupations. The worker who handles T.N.T., or works on steel girders sixty stories in the air, or helps to neutralize unexploded bombs, deserves more (other things being equal) than the worker whose job requires him to face no dangers. In a freely competitive society, such a worker *is* given more, to provide an incentive for going into such a hazardous occupation.

Outside the realm of free competition, however, this principle no longer applies: in the armed forces the infantry is exposed to the greatest danger, but its pay is among the lowest given to any branch of the service.

e. If a job is *unpleasant* — dirty, nerve-wracking, or in some way particularly taxing, such as collecting garbage or cleaning boilers or working eight hours a day next to a loudly blowing siren — it is felt that the person who endures the conditions of such a job deserves more than if his job is not unpleasant. Again, in a free economy this condition is likely to be fulfilled in order to provide incentive; but not otherwise — the army does not appear to feel this way about latrine duty.

All these factors, and doubtless others besides, have been considered relevant to the estimation of deserts. Many people would exclude some of these factors as irrelevant; many would include the majority of them but would differ with one another in the weight or importance to be attached to each of them. The estimation of the various factors depends, of course, on the ethical position that one accepts: specifically, whether one believes that the criteria of distributive justice are to be judged solely by their relevance to overall utility or whether one must consider more than utility in judging these criteria. Let us consider briefly both these possibilities:

1. According to the first position, people can say, "Utilitarianism, at least extended rule-utilitarianism, is adequate to cover all the situations considered; and the criteria of distributive justice are justified by their utility insofar as they can be justified at all. Thus, giving higher wages to people in dangerous or unpleasant jobs can be justified because such jobs are usually very necessary and only by providing higher wages can people be encouraged to take them. Again, production rather than effort is likely to be considered a principal criterion for distributive justice, since the use of this criterion tends to provide incentive and increase productivity, and thus (it is hoped) happiness. Even the desirability of equal, or at any rate equitable, distribution is considered as a handmaid of utility; for, according to the utilitarian, it is far more probable that the total amount of happiness (or other intrinsic good) will be increased by having the world's goods shared among men than by having them monopolized by a few. In every situation, utility decides. Since justice is a part of utility, an act may be right though still unjust, or even wrong and yet just; but in every situation rightness or wrongness is determined by utility — the utility of the act if one is an act-utilitarian, the utility of the rule under which the act falls if one is a rule-utilitarian."

This position is certainly the clearest, simplest, and neatest alternative, and aesthetically the most satisfying. But this fact, of course, provides no guarantee of its acceptability; the truth is often complex and extremely messy. Utilitarianism subsumes all moral rules, including those of justice, under one sweeping formula. But is the formula acceptable?

2. Those who uphold the second ethical position will not be content with

an analysis which disposes of all problems of justice as simply aspects of utility. "Justice," they will say, "is more than a handmaid to utility." Their reasoning will proceed somewhat as follows: "I fully admit that rewarding people for their actual production rather than for their effort has greater utility; such a principle provides incentive and encourages production; but *still it is unjust.* It's not merely that we require a principle of equitable distribution of good in addition to one of total quantity — this addition has already been suggested (pages 424-29). Our discussion of justice in terms of desert has bared a deeper conflict between justice and utility. It is this: When we consider what course of action has the greatest utility, we are concerned only with the *future* — and of course I admit we do have to consider the future. But when we consider what course of action is just — in the sense of 'in accordance with desert'— we are concerned not with the future but with the *past.* What a person deserves depends not on what will occur in the future as a result of his actions but on what he has done in the past. It is, like some of Ross's prima facie duties, past-looking. Thus, if you ask me what system of distribution of rewards has the greatest utility, I reply that rewarding actual production (as opposed to effort) has — and so does giving additional rewards to those in particular kinds of jobs such as dangerous and unpleasant jobs. But if you ask me what system of distribution of rewards is the most just, I reply that such a system would be one in which two people, of however unequal ability, receive the same wage for the same effort; and here of course I am not considering future effects, for the abler man will doubtless do the most good for society — I am considering the fact that in the past the two have expended an equal effort and worked for equal times to the limit of their respective capacities, and on this basis I say that they are *justly* entitled to the same wage. One man does not *deserve* to reap, more than his fellow man, the results of superior intelligence or other native capacity. If they both do the best they can with what they have, they both deserve the same reward. The type of society envisaged by Bellamy is far more just than ours; but perhaps, human nature being what it is, not the one with the highest utility — I admit that with regard to future consequences the man with ability should be rewarded in order to provide an incentive for him to do more in the future. The conclusion, then, is this: justice is at odds with utility. If we want a system of rewards with maximum utility, we must to some extent sacrifice justice; and if we want a just system of distribution, we must to some extent sacrifice utility."

If this point of view is accepted and we wish to incorporate desert as well as utility into our conception of rightness, we shall have to say that in considering what act or policy is right we must consider both desert (past) and utility (future), for rightness will be a function of them both. We shall then have a still further extension of rule-utilitarianism. For the time being, however, the reader must be left to make up his own mind on this point. The contrast will emerge much more sharply in the following section, where we shall once more consider the concept of desert, this time in connection not with reward but with punishment.

EXERCISES

1. "Justice requires equality when deserts are equal. But when they are unequal, reward must be proportioned to desert, and inequality is justified." In which of the situations below do you think the persons in question are giving good arguments for justified inequality and in which situations are they not? Why?

"I should get more than he does (or I should get it and he shouldn't) because

a. I'm rich and he's poor. (in appealing a case to a higher court)

b. I'm white and he's black. (in marrying a white girl)

c. I'm poor and he's rich. (in regard to getting the same merchandise for less money)

d. I'm an officer and he's an enlisted man. (in regard to getting better food)

e. I'm a professor and he's an instructor. (in regard to teaching fewer hours)

f. I'm intelligent and he's stupid. (in regard to having the right to vote)

g. I'm a property owner and he isn't. (in regard to eligibility for public office)

h. I'm a native American and he isn't. (in regard to becoming president of the United States)

i. I'm a writer and he's a hack. (in regard to receiving the Nobel Prize for literature)

j. I'm a man and she's a woman. (in regard to getting higher pay for equal work)

h. I'm a man and she's a woman. (in regard to obtaining a job as a truck driver)

i. I'm an adult and he's an adolescent. (in regard to obtaining a job as camp counselor)

j. I work harder than he does. (in regard to getting more pay for the same job)

k. I need more, since I was born a nobleman and he a peasant. (in regard to drawing more subsistence pay from the state)

l. I need more, since I have five dependents and he has none." (in regard to getting more pay for the same job)

2. Which of the following arguments for inequality of reward do you think are justified and why? Assume that each statement is made by the owner or manager of a factory to his employees, in response to a request for less inequality between his income and theirs.

a. We top executives bear a greater load of responsibility.

b. We have to take more risks.

c. We are more indispensable than you are; you need us more than we need you.

d. We deserve more than you do because there are fewer people with a talent for doing our job than there are for doing yours.

e. We have more training for our jobs than you do, so we deserve more money.

f. We have more ability than you; if we didn't we wouldn't be where we are now.

3. Conclude the following dialogue:

x: I think that need *is* a criterion for justice. The handicapped child gets more than his brothers and sisters in his father's will, and even the brothers and sisters don't consider this provision unjust, for they are earning their own money but he is unable to do so and needs expensive medication.

y: Very well, but try to use that criterion in business and employers would soon go bankrupt. "I have a wife and children and I need more than this other employee who has no dependents" is not usually a successful plea to an employer, nor should it be. If companies paid employees in proportion to their needs, they would soon have to quit hiring poverty-stricken applicants.

x: But even in business the criterion is applied somewhat. If an employer happens to know an employee personally and cares about him, he may give him a pay raise, not because he's a better worker, but because he needs it more.

y: To the extent that the employer follows such a principle, industrial efficiency is lost. To pay someone more though he does no more to earn it would be a disastrous policy. Consider the waste, the decreased production, the effect on the morale of the other workers.

x: Well, the Bureau of Internal Revenue follows this principle to some extent. It taxes one less the more dependents he has and the more medical expenses.

y: Yes, but what the government decrees is compulsory; that's just the trouble — in a free economy one would never get by with such a practice. Anyway, to give more to someone because he's needy is charity, not justice. You are giving him not what he deserves — he deserves no more than the others — but *more* than he deserves, and that is charity. Charity in industry causes waste, inefficiency, higher prices. Charity in private life may be necessary and desirable, but it is not justice.

4. Evaluate: "What a person deserves for his work should depend not on what he has accomplished nor on how much effort he has put into it but on what he *would* have accomplished if he had been given a chance." (See Mark Twain's Captain Stormfield's Visit to Heaven," in M. S. Everett, *Ideals of Life,* pp. 54-60. See also the discussion, p. 505.)

5. Evaluate the following assertions about justice:

a. "It's unjust for anyone to have caviar as long as anyone lacks bread."

b. "It's unjust for a person to be permitted to inherit wealth instead of earning it for himself."

c. "From each according to his abilities, to each according to his needs."

d. Rich man: "The income tax is unjust. I am taxed 80 per cent of my annual income just because I earn a great deal, whereas a poorer person is taxed 15 per cent or less. What could be more unjust?"

e. "You Americans have a much higher income than we do, in terms of what your wages will buy. Since you work no more hours than we do, and no harder, we deserve just as much as you do. You are lucky; your nation has space and natural resources; it rewards private enterprise; and it has escaped wartime privations. But is it just for rewards to be dependent on luck? Of course not. Therefore, it is just that you should give us a portion of your income — as much as is required to make other nations your equal in buying power."

f. "A morality that holds *need* as a claim, holds emptiness — nonexistence — as its standard of value; it rewards an *absence,* a defect; weakness, inability, incompetence, suffering, disease, disaster, the lack, the fault, the flaw — the *zero.* Who provides the account to pay these claims? Those who are cursed for being non-zeros, each to the extent of his distance from that ideal. Since all values are the product of virtues, the degree of your virtue is used as the measure of your penalty; the degree of your faults is used as the measure of your gain. Your code declares that the rational man must sacrifice himself to the irrational, the independent man to parasites, the honest man to the dishonest, the man of justice to the unjust, the productive man to thieving loafers, the man of integrity to compromising knaves, the man of self-esteem to sniveling neurotics. Do you wonder at the meanness of soul in those you see around you? The man who achieves these virtues will not accept your moral code; the man who accepts your moral code will not achieve these virtues." (From *Atlas Shrugged* by Ayn Rand. © Copyright 1957 by Ayn Rand. Reprinted by permission of Random House, Inc., p. 1032.)

6. Consider the following problems concerning the concept of distributive justice.

a. A merchant charges a single price for an item, whether the customer is rich or poor. This practice is not thought to be unjust. Is it? Would a system of taxation be just if it imposed the same burdens on all — say a thousand dollars a year, rich and poor alike?

b. A rich woman volunteers a portion of her time for Salvation Army work. A poor woman, who does the same work for the Salvation Army, is paid for it. (She would be unable to do it otherwise.) Is this arrangement just?

c. The interne works harder than the practicing physician, yet the interne receives far less money. Moreover, at his time of life, when he is planning to marry and set up an office requiring expensive equipment, he needs the money more. Is it unjust that his pay is less?

d. The internal medicine specialist does most of the basic work which makes surgery possible. In general, persons other than the surgeon do most of the work: the nurses, the anesthetist, the general practitioner who has followed the patient's progress from day to day and provides the entire case history, the chemist and research men who make most of the medical discoveries relevant to the patient's case. But after all this has been done, the surgeon spends an hour operating on the patient and collects perhaps 50 per cent of the entire fee. Is this practice just?

e. What would you think of the system of grading students not by their actual mastery of the subject matter of the course but by (a) the amount of effort expended? (b) the amount of improvement shown between the beginning of the course and the end?

f. One worker operates the machinery easily; a second worker is handicapped and is able to operate it only by having gone through a grueling set of exercises for many months and learning to operate the machines without using his right hand. Should the second worker receive a higher wage than the first?

g. The rich in a certain country had gold and jewels while the poor were starving. Finally there was a revolution and the rich became paupers. One planner of the new regime said that all should now share equally, former noblemen and peasants alike. Another said that the poor should have more than the former rich because the rich had had everything for so long that only by depriving them now could things be set right. A third said that even under the new regime the former rich should have somewhat more because they were used to having more and could not get along on as little as those who had never had much; after all, he said, the aim was equal happiness rather than equal goods, and the former rich needed more in order to make life bearable. Which point of view do you consider most just?

h. We would consider it unjust if we had to pay policemen for protection: we would protest if, in the event that our lives or property were threatened or attacked, we had to give up a large portion of our life's savings to buy police protection. Yet this is the system we have in regard to medical care: if you are poor and become ill for a considerable period, you may have to give up your entire life's savings in a few months to pay the doctor bills. Do you consider the medical situation to be like or unlike the police situation, in what respects, and why?

i. Is it just that the shiftless man's wife and children should suffer because the husband is lazy? Is it just that the families of hard workers should prosper because the husband is industrious?

j. A Japanese soldier can live on a smaller ration than an American soldier partly because the Japanese is smaller in stature and partly because he is accustomed to having less. Is it just to allot to him a smaller ration?

k. Assume that it is just for people performing extremely unpleasant jobs to receive higher wages. Would you also be willing to say that it is just for people who enjoy their jobs to receive lower wages? (Suppose the president of a college said to a professor, "I see that you enjoy your work. Since you find the work pleasant, I shall give you a cut in salary until such time as you hate your job.")

l. "My dear, I don't think you ought to take a job. Your husband earns enough for both of you, and though I know you enjoy the work, you are depriving others of a livelihood. Some men are unemployed because you, and others like you who don't need to, choose to work." "That may be true, but I have the right, and I would permit the same to anyone else. Even if I were an unemployed breadwinner I would still approve the practice of a person working if he or she can get a job and wants to do it, regardless of whether he or she has the money."

m. "It's unjust for only a small proportion of the youth to get an education, as occurs in some countries." "You mean when they can get it if their parents are wealthy and not if they're poor? I agree." "No, I mean even if they get it on the basis of merit. *All* should be educated, even through college, at public expense, regardless of merit, provided they wish to continue. Education should not be slanted so as to favor the better students; that's unjust to the poorer ones." "I think, on the contrary, that this method — which on the whole is the one practiced in the schools of the United States — is unjust to the better students, who are held back in their progress by the time and attention that must be paid to the slower ones. A superior student can grasp a point or a principle in a small fraction of the time, so time spent on him pays off much more handsomely. And yet, far more time is spent on the mediocre students, under the pretext that since we live in a democracy, everybody is equal."

n. "It is just for people who take financial risks in starting new business enterprises to have a higher income than others if they succeed, since if they lose, all the time and labor is for nothing." "Perhaps, but their success is not entirely the result of their careful planning; it may be the result of a fortuitous accident — for instance, that one's new store is located on a corner that's convenient and accessible." "Well, but to have put it there rather than elsewhere shows intelligent planning, which should be rewarded." "But — to the tune of $100,000 a year? when a brilliant teacher earns not a tenth that much? when a medical researcher who finds a cure for the common cold receives no more than increase in rank at his institution, plus some publicity? Besides, our new store owner may not have been clever at all; perhaps a competitor dies and a new superhighway is constructed in front of his store, without his foreseeing it. Does he deserve to reap the benefit of this unexpected windfall? I don't mean that someone should take it away from him, but still, do you think it's just?"

o. Assume that the inventor of an anesthetic has done more good for the world than a ditch digger could do in a thousand lifetimes. Should the inventor, if justice were to be served, receive the same income for his invention as the ditch digger would receive in a thousand lifetimes?

p. Some people have thought (Clive Bell, Henry James) that society would be better off if there were a hereditary leisure class whose members did not have to work, so that a high level of culture could be maintained. As for the more numerous class of people required to spend their lives in labor, they would be (except for the skilled technicians) better off without an education; for if they had an education, they would only be discontented and get ideas for improving themselves. Uneducated they would be more likely to be content with their lot, and since someone has to till the soil and prepare the food and wash the dishes, isn't it better (so it is reasoned) to have people who are content with doing these tasks? Analyze this suggestion in terms of distributive justice.

7. Consider all the examples in the preceding exercise and ask yourself not whether the acts described are just or unjust but whether they are right or wrong from the point of view of rule-utilitarianism.

8. Armed with the results of the preceding exercise, do you find that your judgments on these examples lead you to believe that rule-utilitarianism is sufficient to take care of all the situations or that you must extend it in one of the directions we have thus far considered? (Extended rule-utilitarianism, p. 429; desert, p. 445.)

READING LIST, SECTIONS 20 AND 21

Aristotle. *Nicomachean Ethics.* Many editions, Bk. 5.

Brandt, Richard. *Ethical Theory.* Englewood Cliffs, N. J.: Prentice-Hall, 1959. Ch. 16.

Drake, Durant. *Problems of Conduct.* Boston: Houghton Mifflin, 1935. Ch. 25.

Everett, Millard Spencer. *Ideals of Life.* New York: Wiley, 1954, Ch. 12.

Garvin, Lucius. *A Modern Introduction to Ethics.* Boston: Houghton Mifflin, 1953, Ch. 16.

Hume, David. *Treatise of Human Nature.* Many editions, Bk. 3, Pt. 2.

Kelsen, Hans. *What is Justice?* Berkeley: Univ. of California Press, 1957.

Mill, John Stuart. *Utilitarianism.* Many editions, Ch. 5.

Raphael, David Daiches. "Equality and Equity." *Philosophy,* Vol. 21 (1946), pp. 118-32.

Rashdall, Hastings. *Theory of Good and Evil.* 2nd ed. New York: Oxford Univ. Press, 1924. 2 vols., Vol. 1, Bk. 1, Ch. 8.

Rawls, John. "Justice as Fairness." *Philosophical Review,* Vol. 67 (1958), pp. 164-94.

Sidgwick, Henry. *Elements of Politics.* New York: Macmillan, 1891.

——. *The Methods of Ethics.* 7th ed. New York: Macmillan, 1874, Bk. 3, Chs. 5 and 13.

Singer, Marcus. "Generalization in Ethics." *Mind,* Vol. 64 (1955), pp. 361-75.

Wollheim, Richard, and Isaiah Berlin. "Equality." *Aristotelian Society Proceedings,* Vol. 56 (1955-56), pp. 281-326.

22. *Justice and desert: punishment*

We have now considered, albeit briefly, the criteria involved in saying "He deserved it" when what he deserved is a reward for something done. But what if he deserves not reward but punishment? Even more than of rewards, people say of punishments, "He deserved it" or "It's not what he deserves." What criteria are to be employed when the thing deserved is punishment? This aspect of the problem of deserts remains to be considered.

There is no universal agreement on which acts or kinds of acts should be punished, nor by whom. Children are usually punished by their parents — sometimes corporally, more frequently by loss of privileges or affection. But the other chief executor of punishment is the state. The state, of course, punishes people only for infractions of the law, even though there may be a thousand offenses which are morally worse. We shall not examine here which laws are good ones and which are bad, nor under what circumstances a bad law should be obeyed or disobeyed. Presumably our earlier discussion of rule-utilitarianism provides us with the principle by which these questions can be answered. Here we shall be concerned only with the following question: "Assuming that someone has violated a law and therefore deserves punishment, what considerations are relevant to determining the nature and the degree of the punishment which he deserves?" (*Usually* when a person breaks a law, he has violated one or more of the rights of others; but his violation is not always completely clear. What right of others has he violated when he attempts to commit suicide? or when he is arrested for vagrancy without having harmed anyone? or when he engages in nude swimming or in adultery by mutual consent?)

The oldest view on the subject, and the one that tends to be accepted uncritically by those who have given no special attention to the question, is that "he deserves to be punished *because* he has committed a certain offense." But why should he be punished? "Because," it is answered, "if he is not, there would be a *moral imbalance:* there would be something on the negative side of the moral ledger without anything done on the opposite side to balance the account again. There is an *injustice* in allowing a person to inflict harm on others without the others (usually through the law) being able to inflict harm on him in return."

The aim of punishment, then, is to right a wrong, to set the record straight again. How is this aim to be achieved? By *retribution;* by exacting a punishment from the offender, not *in order that* a certain result may occur, but *because* (in the past) the offender did something to upset the moral balance. This principle is called the *retributive* theory of punishment. The expression most commonly quoted to illustrate this view is the Old Testament command "An eye for an eye, and a tooth for a tooth." If you have taken a life, your life must be taken in return in order to satisfy the demands of justice; and if you have destroyed or damaged the property of others, you should be required to make due restitution for the damage done. You must be made to set the balance right again. But to restore the balance does not necessarily mean that you should have inflicted on you exactly the same offense that you inflicted on others. If you have killed someone, many would insist that it should be so: you have taken a life, so yours should be taken. But even those who insist upon this exact balance would be unlikely to insist that the man who steals fifty dollars from someone should be punished by having fifty dollars taken from him. If this were the only punishment, it would deter no one: for if the thief were caught, he would lose nothing but the fifty dollars he had just taken; and if he were not caught, he would be the gainer by fifty dollars. And if being killed is a just (retributive) punishment for killing, what is the just punishment for rape? "The punishment should fit the crime" — but what punishment fits? Is there a formula for every situation? Surely the punishment does not always have to be an exact mirror image of the crime itself. But when it is not, what is to determine what punishment fits? There appears to be no clear answer to this question.

Indeed, the formula "An eye for an eye and a tooth for a tooth" was not applied in a narrow way by the Hebrews themselves. In the Mosaic code it was simply a demand for adequate and equitable compensation to the injured. It did not imply that a person who knocked another's teeth out should have his own teeth knocked out in return. Judaic law took it to imply little more than that worse crimes demand worse punishments. Perhaps lifelong incarceration might even sometimes "fit" the crime of murder. In the Code of Hammurabi, however, several centuries earlier, a similar formula was carried out much more strictly:

> If the jerry-builder by his faulty construction of a house causes the death of the son or daughter of the owner, then not the jerry-builder but his own son or daughter is killed.[1]

To such an interpretation of the formula, however, one might well object: "How can it be justice, in any sense at all, if it is not the offender but *someone else* who is killed or penalized? Even if the death of the son or daughter is more dreaded by the offender than his own death would be, is this justice? is it even retribution? Doesn't retributive justice at least require that the retribution be on the person who committed the offense? Some desert tribes require that if a member of Tribe A (is killed by) a mem- ~~has killed~~ ber of Tribe B and the man from Tribe A is now dead or has fled, then *another* man from Tribe A must sacrifice his life in order to atone for the death of the man from Tribe B. Even though this man is innocent, the tribes feel that justice has not been done unless someone from Tribe A sacrifices his life in order to restore the state of moral imbalance.[2] But what kind of retribution is this, which penalizes not the offender but someone else in his place?"

Even if we insist, however, that genuine retribution requires the offender and no one else to be punished, the theory of punishment presupposed here is still retributive. Punishment is administered because of a past deed, and the justification given for the punishment is simply the fact that the past deed was committed. It is past-looking, not future-looking; because of, not in order that. If no good consequences were to result from the punishment, it should still be administered. This view of punishment is apparently very deeply rooted in human nature. It speaks to our blood; no matter how "enlightened" people may be in some things, when a particularly shocking crime has been committed, such as the kidnap-murder of an innocent victim for sport (the Loeb-Leopold case) or having millions of people killed in concentration camps (Hitler and his cohorts), we recoil in horror at such crimes; and we are inclined to say that those who perpetrated them should not only be killed but tortured to death. In order to produce good results? No: circumstances might be such that we would be quite sure that no good consequences would result; the retribution might even arouse such hatred among the tyrant's followers as would plunge the world into another blood bath later. We recommend drastic punishment simply out of vengeance — or, as people put it more euphemistically, "out of justice." "He had others tortured, so he should see what it's like to be on the receiving end of it," many of us would say — and many of us feel this sentiment even if we

[1] J. H. Hertz, *The Pentateuch and Haftorahs,* Hebrew text, English translation and commentary (London: Soncino Press, 1956), p. 405.
[2] See the T. E. Lawrence example on pages 3-4.

are far from convinced that carrying it out will help society in the slightest degree or deter anyone from crime. Mussolini, after he was shot, was hanged by his toes in the public square, not because he was any more dead that way, but because it was felt that this was a peculiarly deserving, fitting, appropriate, *just* fate for a man who had meted out a similar fate to so many others.

This view of punishment, however, has not gone unchallenged. Particularly in the nineteenth and twentieth centuries (although men continue to practice it, in war if not always in civil society), it has been called evil, barbaric, a return to the stone age. "If one man kills another," critics of the old principle will argue, "we have one evil; if the criminal is killed for his crime, we have not a canceling out of his crime, but *two* crimes, two evils on our hands instead of one. We are reminded of the traditional blood feuds among the Kentucky mountaineers, in which a man from one family kills a member of another for some real or fancied grievance, then a man from the second family must exact 'justice' by killing a member of the first, upon which a man from the first must again wreak vengeance by killing a member of the second — the process goes on indefinitely. Now what is the point of all this vengeance? Is it not a sure way of perpetuating evil and adding to the miseries of the human lot, which are already great beyond endurance? What better way to make sure that human conflicts and hatreds will continue and increase?"

"True," one may reply, "it is for this reason that we have an impartial authority, the state, to take vengeance out of the hands of individuals and administer it itself, settling the score once and for all. But even this improvement is pointless and immoral if no good is accomplished and no evil prevented by the second killing, the one by the state. What, indeed, could possibly justify punishing someone — whether taking his life or isolating him from society and submitting him to unpleasant conditions during his incarceration — if this punishment does not do some good — something, at any rate, far better than just enabling vengeful people to vent their aggressiveness, under the name of law and justice, upon other people through killing or torture?"

We come, then, to the *utilitarian* theory of punishment, which holds that an act or rule of punishing, like every other act or rule, is justified only if the act or the adoption of the rule produces good. Punishment involves an intrinsic evil, for it is the deliberate infliction of pain, discomfort, frustration, and other forms of unhappiness upon the person punished. Punishment is justified, however, by the effects it has; where its effects are not good, there is no excuse for indulging in it. Punishment should always be future-looking, not past-looking; always in order that, never simply because of. If someone has committed a crime, that is unfortunate, but punishment should be strictly *in order to* produce good consequences (which, again, includes the prevention of bad ones) in the future.

What factors will the utilitarian consider in assessing the rightness of punishing someone?

1. First of all, he will consider the future welfare of the wrongdoer himself. The offender may be *deterred* by being punished for his deed; certainly if he is *not* penalized for what he did, he is far more likely to do it again. Besides, punishment may improve his character. At present, prisons are hardly nurseries for moral improvement — thrown in with hardened criminals, by the time the first offender gets out of jail, the only trade he knows is crime, and he is sufficiently embittered and hates society enough by this time to want to injure those "on the outside." The utilitarian would argue that this situation, of course, is undesirable: it is better if the criminal is improved during his incarceration by such activities as recreation, learning a trade, and most of all psychiatric treatment so that his tendencies toward criminal activity will be turned into other and more fruitful channels.

2. Second, the utilitarian will consider not only the deterrent effect on the lawbreaker himself but also the deterrent effect on society. Even if he knew that punishment would not improve the lawbreaker and that it would not deter him in the slightest from committing future crimes when he had the chance, we must see to it that he does not *get* the chance. Imprisonment may substantially *reduce* the chances that *others* will commit such crimes; in other words, even if imprisonment acts as no deterrence on him, *it may deter others,* who, after reading about the case, may refrain from doing similar deeds in the future. Surely there are many people who would rob and plunder at will if they did not know that those who had already robbed and plundered were being punished for their deeds.

3. Third, the utilitarian will consider the protection of society. Suppose that punishment does not deter the lawbreaker from repeating his offense later, and suppose that it does not prevent others from committing offenses either. This is sometimes the effect in certain types of crimes: the psychopathic ax murderer or sex fiend is not deterred, for his criminality may result from overwhelming unconscious disturbances of which he is not aware — he may have a recurring compulsion to commit crimes of this kind, and no punishment deters him. Even if such a person knew that he would be caught and tortured for his crime, this prospect would not stop him any more than a stone can stop a cataract. The same is true of the *other* potential ax murderers and sex fiends: since their criminal tendency may arise from the same unconscious sources within them, they too may act from a sudden and overwhelming compulsion and not from choice (more accurately, the choice results from the compulsion). Punishment does not act as a deterrent for this type of criminal; passing a law that would increase punishment for such crimes would no more stop them than passing a law would stop a river from flowing downhill. Yet, in spite of punishment's lack of deterrent effect we clearly cannot let ax murderers and sex maniacs roam freely about through society. Perhaps they're "more to be pitied than censured"; they

can't help what they're doing, but still we have to isolate them from the rest of society — not in order to do *them* any good but in order to protect society from the future acts which they would commit if they were permitted to go free. Thus, even when punishment serves no deterrent function at all, it must often be inflicted just the same, for the protection of society. No good consequences may be brought about by the offenders' incarceration, but bad consequences would surely be brought about by their freedom.

The utilitarian theory of punishment seems so sane, so reasonable, so humane — how could it be challenged? Yet it can be, and has been:

RETRIBUTIVIST: If the sole aim of punishment is to produce good results (and avoid bad ones), what about those times when the best results can be obtained by railroading an innocent man to the chair or by making a public example out of some innocent scapegoat in order to prevent a crime wave?

UTILITARIAN: I wouldn't even call it punishment if the person isn't guilty; it's a miscarriage of justice.

R: Instead of punishment, let's call it telishment.[1] Imagine an institution such that "the officials set up by it have authority to arrange a trial for the condemnation of an innocent man whenever they are of the opinion that doing so would be in the best interests of society. The discretion of officials is limited, however, by the rule that they may not condemn an innocent man to undergo such an ordeal unless there is, at the time, a wave of offenses similar to that with which they charge him and telish him for." This is the institution we are calling telishment, and I think that you utilitarians will have to say, consistently with your doctrine, that occasionally telishment should be indulged in. Yet it seems to me shocking, immoral, and always wrong.

U: Speaking now as a rule-utilitarian, I would say that the rule permitting such a practice would be unjustifiable: consider what it would do to public morale if it were known that such a practice was being employed; any innocent person might be arrested at any time and might even be telished. Nor could the practice be kept secret; for one day a person might be telished and the next day the true offender might turn up and make a confession. No, I can't see any long-run utility in telishment; you might find isolated cases in which it might do more good than harm (say, if a crime wave of major proportions could be prevented by using it), but I don't think you could justify the rule permitting the practice. Thus a rule-utilitarian would certainly condemn it.

R: But he wouldn't under all circumstances. There might be circumstances in which the adoption of such a rule would have the best possible effects. The rule might say, "Telish in circumstances A, B, or C." And circumstance A, for example, might be one in which the lives of many people could be saved if that of one innocent person were taken.

[1] This term is taken from "Two Concepts of Rules," by John Rawls, *Philosophical Review*, Vol. 64, No. 1 (January, 1955), p. 11.

u: Of course — if you make the stakes high enough, you can find a rule providing circumstances in which it would be right to telish. But then it *would* be right. To take an extreme situation, suppose the fate of civilization depended on the telishment of one innocent man. Then it *would* be right to telish him, unfortunate and distasteful as that would be. (In wartime thousands of innocent people die.) Wouldn't you say it was right under those circumstances?

r: If I knew that the fate of civilization depended on it, I would reluctantly say, "Yes." But not just to produce *some* more good than would be produced by not doing it. It seems to me that you utilitarians would be committed to telishment far too often. And I would say the same about punishments — not telishments, but punishments — in which the penalty is far too severe. These punishments too are unjustified in my opinion, even though oversevere punishments may sometimes produce more good. Consider the Soviet practice in the 1930's of exacting extreme penalties, including death, for apparently minor infractions like coming late to work. Utilitarians, I would say, would have to justify it, though I, who say that punishment should be in proportion to one's desert, would not. Consider the circumstances: suppose you are sure, on the best of evidence, that an aggressor nation will invade yours in a few years; suppose they are militarily far stronger than you are; suppose that yours has, for centuries, been a backward, agricultural nation and that if you are to meet the challenge, you must equip yourself with superhuman speed to face the invader in time: in less than ten years you must go through the industrial revolution that took your enemy almost two hundred years. Assume, of course, that you *should* have the wherewithal to defend your land against such aggression which will take thousands of lives; suppose that you can do so (if at all) only with an absolute maximum of effort and the total cooperation of your people, most of whom are unaware of the urgency; but suppose too that most of them, with a rural background, have never developed the habits of punctuality and efficiency which are so necessary in a highly industrial nation, and will never do so in a short time unless the most extreme measures are taken. Under such circumstances, and assuming that the death penalty would successfully deter future latecomers to work, would not such treatment be justified according to utilitarianism? The Soviet leaders thought that such measures had to be taken against the inevitable Nazi invader, and history proved that their worst suspicions were justified.

u: But under such conditions — each life taken then causing the saving of hundreds or thousands later — it *would* be right, even from your point of view, wouldn't it? Provided, of course, that the measures were announced in advance, that everyone had fair warning, that the rule was applied impartially and not out of revenge or sadism or to work off private grudges, and (most important of all) *if* no less extreme measures could have been taken to bring about the same effect. (And it seems to me that they could.)

Do you doubt that *if* such measures were absolutely necessary to prepare the nation against Nazi enslavement, they were justified?

R: I do doubt it. Such measures, when taken at one time, set a terrible precedent for later occasions.

U: Oh, granted — but now you are speaking as a utilitarian. It is just the effect of such a practice on possible later practices of the same kind (under less justified conditions) that would be one major consideration against indulging in it. That is why I would, as a utilitarian, be opposed to such practices under all but the most extreme conditions, when survival was at stake. Remember that the utilitarian considers *all* the effects, of an action or policy, including its effect on subsequent practice.

R: Yes, I know. But you see my point, don't you? Punishment is not, in my opinion, an institution whose primary aim is to produce good consequences or avoid bad ones, though it may do that too. Its primary function is to do *justice* — to give a person what he *deserves*. And, make no mistake about it, the concept of desert is past-looking; it is not future-looking. A person deserves this or that *because of what he has done in the past,* not for the sake of something in the future. That is why telishment is always shocking and immoral, and overpunishment only slightly less so, because in both situations the person is not getting what he deserves. If you say that punishment is purely in-order-that, I say that this interpretation misses the whole essence of punishment. It is a consequence of past acts, not merely a preventative of future ones. The philosopher F. H. Bradley has put the matter better, perhaps, than anyone else:

> Punishment is punishment, only when it is deserved. We pay the penalty because we owe it, and for no other reason; and if punishment is inflicted for any other reason whatever than because it is merited by wrong, it is a gross immorality, a crying injustice, an abominable crime, and not what it pretends to be. We may have regard for whatever considerations we please — our own convenience, the good of society, the benefit of the offender; we are fools, and worse, if we fail to do so. Having once the right to punish, we may modify the punishment according to the useful and the pleasant; but these are external to the matter, they cannot give us a right to punish, and nothing can do that but criminal desert.[1]

What are we to say in the face of these conflicting views? Each of them may seem to have such a strong argument that it is tempting to wonder whether a compromise view is possible. The situation is this: According to the retributivist, on the one hand, punishment should depend on desert. *What* a person deserves in a specific situation has not yet been made clear: it is obvious enough that a person deserves more than a gentle scolding for the crime of murder and that he deserves something less than electrocution for driving through a red light. (Thus the judge on page 429 who sentenced

[1] From Francis Herbert Bradley, *Ethical Studies.* (1876), New York: Oxford Univ. Press, 1927, pp. 26-27 of 1876 ed. Reprinted by permission of the publisher.

everyone equally to the electric chair for a traffic offense would not be dispensing justice — not because the sentences were unequal, but because they were not deserved.) But what the specific desert is for a specific offense by a specific individual in a specific situation is, at the moment, far from clear. Perhaps it will remain so, though we shall discuss this point further when we discuss motives in the next chapter. At any rate, the important point at the moment is that the retributivist insists that punishment should depend solely on desert, and what one deserves depends solely on what has occurred in the past, without relation to what will occur in the future.

The utilitarian, on the other hand, is inclined not to talk about desert at all; for, according to him, the nature and degree of punishment administered should depend on probable future consequences: the punishment administered should be such as will promote the most good (which includes, of course, avoiding the most evil). He agrees with the retributivist that more serious offenses demand more serious punishments, but he disagrees about the reason: the reason is not (according to the utilitarian) that a serious offense was committed in the past but that when the offense is a serious one, there is a greater need for preventing similar offenses in the future — greater need for deterrence, greater security against repetition, hence longer isolation of the criminal from society and a greater attempt at rehabilitation so that he will not repeat his offense when he does return to society. Punishment should be future-looking, not past-looking, since the utilitarian is committed to maximizing future good; therefore the past should be considered only insofar as a consideration of it will be helpful in improving the future.

A compromise view can, in fact, be formulated in the following way. We can say that in order to justify punishment it must meet two conditions.

1. The punishment must be *deserved*. Whatever else this condition may imply, at least it implies that a person who is innocent of a certain offense should not be punished for it, since obviously a person who has not committed an offense does not deserve to be punished for it. Nor should the punishment be more severe than is deserved for the particular offense (though as we have just observed, it is as yet far from clear how what is deserved is to be estimated); for example, a person does not deserve to be hanged for poaching, as was often done in the nineteenth century, even if this punishment is effective (which it was not) in deterring future poachers. What is deserved depends entirely on the past — the nature of the offense and, as we shall see, the inner state of the offender.

2. But a punishment's being deserved is still not enough to justify its infliction. The infliction of punishment *must do some good* (or prevent some evil) — to the offender, to other potential offenders, to society, preferably to all. There are some instances in which a punishment is deserved but in which nevertheless it should be lightened or even suspended entirely, namely when the most good will be produced by this course of action. When punishment will not produce any good or avoid any evil — for example,

when a man has committed a crime, is too ill to repeat it, and his doctor has given him three months to live — then although the man deserves punishment because of his offense, there is no good reason for inflicting it.

Both of these conditions, then, must be fulfilled. Punishment does not conform to justice if it is undeserved, and it does not conform to utility if it produces no good result. Before we inflict punishment, then, which after all is the deliberate infliction of something *intrinsically* bad (displeasure), we should be sure that both of these conditions are met.

There are two related points which we should examine before leaving the subject of punishment. The first is an empirical one, but so important to the topic that it requires mention here.

1. Does punishment really deter? Even people who are not vindictive often cherish the belief that ten years behind bars will act as a deterrent to the offender and prevent him from committing similar offenses in the future. It is true, of course, that punishment and the threat of it *can* be a deterrent. When people park their cars in a prohibited area day after day because the parking laws have not been enforced and then suddenly the policemen start tagging their cars, after a few days not many cars will be found parked in that area. Here our common-sense egoism comes into play; it is less painful to park further away from work than it is to appear in court and pay frequent fines. But when legislators rely on this same common-sense egoism to succeed in deterring people from murder, there is every reason to believe, in the light of modern psychiatric and sociological studies, that they are mistaken about the facts. For most serious crimes, making the threatened punishments extremely severe does not usually have the effect of deterrence, and does not decrease the incidence of crime. It is noteworthy that the supposedly ideal deterrent to murder, capital punishment, has no useful effects at all, and the crime rate is in fact slightly lower in those states of the United States in which capital punishment has been abolished.

Why should the threat of punishment act as a deterrent in traffic violation but not in murder and other more serious crimes? Why isn't the threat of so great a punishment sufficient to scare people into being good? Psychiatrists know the answer well enough, though the public does not. A criminal personality (including the personality of those who are criminally inclined, even when circumstances do not permit them to go through with their acts) operates with a different set of values from that of common sense. The delinquent adolescent, more often than not the victim of a broken home, family dissension, and lack of warmth and trust by the parents, may have been conditioned

   . . . to believe that the chances of winning by undetected cheating are vastly greater than the probabilities of fair treatment and opportunity. He knows about the official threats and the social disapproval of such acts. He knows about the hazards and the risks. But despite all this "knowledge," he becomes involved in waves of discouragement or cupidity or excitement or resentment leading to episodes of social offensiveness. . . . In some instances the crime is the merest accident or impulse, expressed under unbearable stress. More often the offender is a persistently perverse, lonely, and resentful individual who joins the only group to which he is eligible — the outcasts and the anti-social.[1]

We, not recognizing the nature of his inner drives and the sources of his attractions and repulsions, continue to judge, advise, and blame him by standards that are foreign to him, and it is not surprising that these devices are ineffectual.

It is not only that the rewards that society offers to those who conform are not great enough to drive him into conformity. There is also, in many criminal cases, a positive attraction to crime — an allure stronger than that anything else possesses — not *in spite* of the fact that the crime will be punished and cause him suffering, but precisely *because* it will be, even *in order to* get such punishment. To "common sense" this attraction sounds fantastic, but it is a familiar fact to psychiatrists. The motivation is for the most part unconscious, but every psychiatrist will testify to the compelling power of this masochistic drive. There are thousands of case histories of people who are restless, insecure, and unhappy "on the outside," who are caught by the police for some stupid error (which the offender's "common sense" could easily have foreseen); once behind bars these people are much more content: it is as if they were atoning for their crime by being punished, that "guilt demands punishment" and they make themselves guilty in order to reap the punishment.[2]

The number of these offenders who are caught by the law — not a high percentage of individual offenses, though most habitual lawbreakers are caught sooner or later — is owing more to these stupid errors (unconsciously committed in order to be caught and punished, though consciously avoided) than to any special efficiency on the part of the police. These offenders are like those children who are not deterred by being spanked by their parents but who repeat the offense all the more when they have been punished for it, knowing full well that the punishment will only be repeated and intensified. This behavior is common-sense egoism working in reverse: instead of being repelled and deterred by the prospect of punishment, they are strangely attracted by it, and unconsciously do what they can to get it repeated. It is as if they said to themselves, "If I can't belong, I'll show them! I want to excel in something, so if I can't excel anything else I'll excel in frustration and torment!" They are like birds who are expected by the bird family to keep their nests dutifully clean; when, as little birds, things became unbearable because they couldn't keep up with the good and proper birds, no matter how they tried, they gave up the attempt and started to dirty their own nests instead with great fervor and intensity, even though they themselves would

---

[1] Karl Menninger, "Verdict Guilty — Now What?" *Harper's Magazine*, Vol. 219, No. 1311 (August, 1959), p. 61.
[2] See Edmund Bergler, *Principles of Self-Damage* (New York: Philosophical Library, 1959).

have to endure the stench. They would rather endure that displeasure than conform to the mores of the envied and hated Good Clean Birds Club.

The daily devices of blaming and punishing, back-slapping and pull-your-self-together talk, are no more effectual here than a drop of water in a desert. Yet, in spite of the complete failure of our legal practices in dealing with crime, we continue to beat the same old useless drums of blame and punishment, threat and deterrence. We put a man in prison for two years for a theft, five years for armed robbery, and twenty years to life (or the electric chair) for homicide, assuming smugly that these penalties will lessen his tendency to repeat his crime. We assume that being behind bars with nothing to do but build up resentments or go mad will make him emerge from prison a better man, renewed and chastened, and that when he does emerge from prison after the five years or the twenty, he will be able to resume his role in a society that refuses to employ him, spiritually prepared at last to conform to the moral ideals of middle age and the middle class.

Such a belief on our part, although it has been refuted by psychologists and criminologists for half a century, still persists in the majority of those who pride themselves on being useful and constructive citizens of the world's greatest democracy. The alternative, as psychiatrists have known for decades, is not punishment but treatment. To imprison a man for twenty years in the company of hardened criminals and to expect him to walk out at the end of that time without any deterioration of his character, is to retain an attitude harmful both to the offender and to society. But to try to mold him gradually into the kind of person that is not attracted by crime is to help both him and society. It is laborious and expensive, but far less so in the long run than to let him rot behind bars or to pay taxes for his re-incarceration after he has repeated his offense.

2. The preceding discussion leads us into the second consideration: who should administer the punishment, of whatever kind? Not, surely, a private individual. If one man has made love to another man's wife, the aggrieved husband's feelings will probably be so intense that he will retaliate out of all proportion to the offense; he may knock the offender's eye out or beat him to a pulp or shoot him. Worse still, private vengeance leads to its own indefinite continuation: one man kills another, the friends or family of the second man kill the first, and so on. There must be some *impersonal* authority administering the punishment, and the best candidate for this position would seem to be the state.

Determining the punishment and carrying it out, then, are duties of the state. Does this conclusion imply that the state should try to settle all matters of desert? Not at all. It is true that the most desirable state of affairs, as far as the distribution of intrinsic good is concerned, would be for those persons who deserve the most to have the most and those who deserve the least to have the least. But it does not follow that the state, because it exercises the legal power of punishment, should attempt to bring about such a state of affairs. It should punish criminals, for they have violated the rights of others, and the first function of the state is that of protecting the rights of individuals against those who have violated them. (Some would go so far as to say that this is the *only* function of the state.) But it is extremely questionable whether the state should seek to make any wholesale attempt to adjust the well-being of each individual in it to the degree of his deserts.

a. In the first place, it would be impracticable to make such an attempt. Who, except God, knows what each person deserves? We would have to know infinitely more than we now do about the private life of each individual to know (1) how much happiness he was having and had had throughout his life in relation to other individuals and (2) how much he deserved the amount of happiness he did enjoy; for this second judgment we would have to know how many wrong deeds he had committed, both publicly and in secret, throughout his life, not only those against the state, but wrong acts not punishable by law. The amount of knowledge we would have to have of each individual in the state would be simply staggering.

b. Even if we did have this knowledge, it is questionable whether the state should act upon it. Why the state to the exclusion of other organizations in the community — churches, unions, clubs, societies of all kinds — all of which help in limited ways to give some of life's rewards to those who are helpful and cooperative and deny them to those who are not? It is, in fact, questionable whether *any* agency should take it upon itself to apportion happiness to deserts, should try to play God in its own way. It is most of all doubtful whether the state, with all its power over the individual and its tendency to make mistakes, should do so. Why? Because even if it had the requisite knowledge, such action on the state's part would constitute *meddlesomeness* to the highest degree. Many people feel that the state meddles too much with our private lives as it is; it has to meddle with the private lives of offenders in order to preserve order, but imagine what life would be like if the state (Big Brother in George Orwell's *Nineteen Eighty-four*) kept an eye on all our daily activities—even on those having nothing to do with violations of the law — with a view to giving us all what we deserve. Would not life be unbearable? Even if Big Brother were watching us with the most benevolent eye, and the eye of omniscience besides, he would still be *watching* us; and this disadvantage would more than cancel out whatever benefits he might confer in the field of apportioning deserts. Besides, when a huge sprawling agency such as the state has to handle matters, there is likely to be endless red tape, waste, corruption, granting of favors for personal reasons, deprivation of jobs because of private feuds. It is enough that the state can exact from us a heavy burden of taxation, plus time and effort in the filling of forms and a thousand thankless laws regulating traffic, street cleaning, and property limits (all of which may be necessary) and that it can exact our full time and our very lives in time of war; is the state to take on, in addition to all these responsibilities, the onerous and meddlesome task of judging our respective moral merits and rewarding or punishing us accordingly?

One may agree, then, that justice as desert requires, ideally, an exact apportionment of our happiness (and whatever else may be intrinsically good) to what we deserve, without agreeing that the state or any organization should embark on such an enterprise. The state should limit its activities to certain areas. Rule-utilitarians can have a good time working out *which* rules for society are best made into law and enforced by the state, but the rules should involve at least the protection of the rights of individuals against their violation by other individuals or groups of individuals. To do *much* more than this is to invite an Orwellian nightmare.

We have now reviewed the main theories of punishment and assessed the function of the state in the administration of such punishment. We have also arrived at a view of punishment which considers both deserts (past-looking) and utility (future-looking) as separate principles. But we have not yet settled the question of *what* we deserve. To estimate what we deserve, it would seem, we have to consider not only the act itself, but its entire background in our personalities, whether it was done deliberately or through compulsion, whether it was done in ignorance, whether our motives were good or evil. This kind of consideration, however, carries us into the theme of the next chapter.

EXERCISES

1. Interpret as best you can the maxim "Let the punishment fit the crime." Do you think it has been done satisfactorily in the following excerpt from Gilbert and Sullivan's *The Mikado?*

> My object all sublime
> I shall achieve in time —
> To let the punishment fit the crime —
> The punishment fit the crime. . . .
>
> All prosy dull society sinners
> Who chatter and bleat and bore,
>   Are sent to hear sermons
>   From mystical Germans
> Who preach from ten to four.
> The amateur tenor, whose vocal villainies
> All desire to shirk,
>   Shall, during off-hours,
>   Exhibit his powers
> To Madame Tussaud's waxwork.
> The lady who dyes a chemical yellow,
> Or stains her gray hair puce,
>   Or pinches her figger,
>   Is blacked like a nigger
> With permanent walnut juice.
> The idiot who, in railway carriages,
> Scribbles on windowpanes,

We only suffer
To ride on a buffer
In Parliamentary trains.

The advertising quack who wearies
With tales of countless cures,
   His teeth, I've enacted,
   Shall all be extracted
By terrified amateurs.
The music-hall singer attends a series
Of masses and fugues and "ops"
   By Bach, interwoven
   With Spohr and Beethoven,
At classical Monday Pops.
The billiard sharp whom anyone catches,
His doom's extremely hard —
   He's made to dwell
   In a dungeon cell
On a spot that's always barred.
And there he plays extravagant matches
In fitless finger-stalls,
   On a cloth untrue
   With a twisted cue,
And elliptical billiard balls!

2. Consider the justice of the following allegations or situations having to do with punishment.

a. A person who commits robbery is sentenced to one to five years in jail; a person who commits armed robbery is sentenced to a minimum of five years. Do you consider this disparity just?

b. Read the literature on the Loeb-Leopold case (Meyer Levin's *Compulsion* [New York: Simon and Schuster, 1956]; Irving Stone's *Clarence Darrow for the Defense* [New York: Doubleday, 1941]; Clarence Darrow's *Attorney for the Damned* [New York: Simon and Schuster, 1957]; and others) and decide whether the punishment of life imprisonment given them was just in view of the total situation. State your reasons.

c. Suppose that more good was done through deterrence by having minor traffic violators suffer penalties as severe as those of armed robbers and rapists. Would you then recommend that such penalties be imposed?

d. "I know it won't do any good to punish him for his disobedience, but since I told him I would, I must do so." Do you consider this just?

e. "When punishment is deserved, it should be administered." "But how can punishment, which is of course painful (and hence the infliction of an intrinsic evil), possibly atone for crime? Don't we now have two evils instead of one — the one committed by the offender, and the other by those who punish him?" How would you answer?

f. Suppose we prefer not to punish a man because he is insane, but for some reason it is important for the public not to know about this fact — perhaps because failure to punish him will, we believe, result in outbreaks of the same kind of crime, with everyone committing it thinking he will be exonerated because this man was. Would we be justified in giving him a jail sentence in spite of his insanity?

g. Mr. A shoots Mr. B with intent to kill. But, unknown to Mr. A, Mr. B has just at that very moment died of a heart attack. What, if anything, should be done to Mr. B?

h. Would you be in favor of introducing, as legal evidence in court, the evidence obtained from a new mechanical device (similar to a lie detector) if you knew that the result of its use would be twofold: (1) to render twice as certain as now that no person innocent of a crime would be convicted for it, and (2) to increase (to double its present degree) the chances that a guilty man might go free?

i. If you knew that your nation had just been destroyed in a nuclear war and you were able to deliver a mortal blow to the aggressor nation which would destroy it completely, would you feel justified in doing so — not in order to produce good (which you would not) but simply because that nation had destroyed yours? (Bertrand Russell, *Common Sense and Nuclear Warfare* [Simon and Schuster, 1959], p. 33.)

j. Apartment owner: "But this woman is a psychotic. Repeatedly she has come down the fire escape into our apartment carrying a knife and threatening to kill us." Policeman: "I know, but that makes no difference. We can't punish her for something she hasn't yet done. You must first wait till she's done something. Besides, we don't know for sure whether she will, and you can hardly punish a person for a crime that has not been committed." If we had a much greater psychiatric knowledge than we now do — enough to be able to predict with 99 per cent certainty whether the woman would actually fulfill her threat — would we then be right in incarcerating her *before* she committed any overt offense? (Analogous case: We already have very reliable tests telling us which children are predelinquent, which ones are fairly certain to commit crimes, especially if they continue in their present slum environment under parental influence. Should the legal authorities have the right to institutionalize them against their parents' wishes in order to try to prevent crimes which have not yet occurred?)

3. Consider the following situations or precepts in the light of justice.

a. "He that killeth a beast shall make it good; and he that killeth a man shall be put to death." (Leviticus XXIV:21.)

b. "Ye shall take no ransom for the life of a manslayer which is guilty of death, but he shall surely be put to death." (Numbers XXXV:31.)

c. Uzzah touches the Ark of the Covenant, and he and all his fellow townsmen are put to death.

d. Eve ate the forbidden fruit, and as a result all mankind forever after are condemned to live in sin.

e. Eve sinned, and in consequence another life must be taken, through death by crucifixion, in order to atone for this. One being must die for the sins of another, to set right the moral balance.

f. "Justice requires that each person get what he deserves. But there is another and greater dispensation than that of Justice, and that is Grace. If God were *only* just, He would send us all to eternal damnation. But by Grace, a certain selected number of those who are justly damned, are saved by Grace — a salvation which none of them deserves."

4. State whether you accept or reject the rule-utilitarian account of punishment, with your reasons. Can you think of any other account of punishment than the one given in the text, which tries to mediate between the two extremes?

5. Retributive vs. utilitarian theories of punishment. What is your attitude toward the following case?

Adolf Eichmann, charged with the extermination of five million Jews in Hitler's concentration camps, claimed, "I will leap into my grave laughing because the feeling that I have five million human beings on my conscience is for me a source of extraordinary satisfaction." He was found in Argentina in June 1960 by Israeli government officials and taken to Israel for trial. An American newsmagazine (*Time,* Vol. 75, No. 23 [June 6, 1960], p. 29) remarked: "Remembering the stinking holes of Poland's Auschwitz, the smoking crematoriums of Germany, the boneyards and mass graves of the Ukraine, vengeful Israelis are not disposed to argue the fine points of the law. Instead, they debate what punishment could possibly fit the crime. Hanging, most agree, is too easy. Said one survivor of Eichmann's camps: 'He should be made to live under the very same conditions that we lived in the camps, eat the same crumbs of dried bread, work the same, smell the same putrid odors from the furnaces. Let's see how long he would last.' "

6. There are certain legal offenses classified as "strict liability," in which a person is considered guilty even if he had no intention of committing the offense, in fact even if he was ignorant of its commission. Examples: a bar owner who sells drinks to minors can have his bar closed by the authorities even if the minor showed a birth certificate which seemed genuine and which the bar owner did not know was forged. A landlord who does not keep his property in the condition required by law (e.g., if the hooks outside the windows of high buildings, on which the window-washer inserts the strap on which he leans, are not in safe condition) is fined even if he is ignorant of the condition of his property. A butcher who sells spoiled meat ignorantly (or even if it is sold by an employee and the butcher himself is out sick that day) is still prosecuted.

a. Do you agree that the above offenses should be "strict liability" offenses? Explain. Can you think of others that should be?

b. If you consider the whole concept of strict liability to be a mistake, give reasons. Or if you consider it justifiable, state your reasons.

7. What is your opinion of the following practices?

a. If a prisoner who is going to be electrocuted tomorrow gets appendicitis today, he is rushed to the hospital and taken care of until he is well again, then is electrocuted.

b. If a prisoner sentenced to electrocution becomes "mentally ill," his electrocution is postponed until such time as he is well again, in order that he can be electrocuted while he is of sane mind.

c. A pregnant woman cannot be electrocuted until after she has given birth to her child.

8. "The utilitarian theory of punishment is mistaken, for according to it crime is no different from disease, and imprisonment no different from quarantine." What do you think of this objection? In what way or ways do you consider imprisonment to be like quarantine, and in what ways unlike it? (Does it serve the same functions as quarantine? How, and how not?)

READING LIST, SECTION 22

Anshen, Ruth. *Moral Principles in Action*. New York: Harper, 1952.

Baier, Kurt. "Is Punishment Retributive?" *Analysis*, Vol. 16 (1955), pp. 25-32.

Benn, S. I. "An Approach to the Problems of Punishment." *Philosophy*, Vol. 33 (1958), pp. 325-41.

Bentham, Jeremy. *Principles of Morals and Legislation*. Many editions, Chs. 12-15.

Black, Charles L. *The People and the Court*. New York: Macmillan, 1960.

Brandt, Richard. *Ethical Theory*. Englewood Cliffs, N. J.: Prentice-Hall, 1959.

Carritt, Edgar F. *Ethical and Political Thinking*. New York: Oxford Univ. Press, 1947, Ch. 5.

————. *The Theory of Morals: an Introduction to Ethical Philosophy*. New York: Oxford Univ. Press, 1928, Ch. 12.

Ewing, Alfred C. *The Morality of Punishment*. London: Routledge & Kegan Paul, 1929.

Flew, Antony. "The Justification of Punishment." *Philosophy*, Vol. 29 (1954), pp. 291-307.

Friedmann, Wolfgang Gaston. *Legal Theory*. London: Stevens, 1953.

Hall, Jerome. *General Principles of Criminal Law*. Indianapolis: Bobbs-Merrill, 1947.

————. *Studies in Jurisprudence and Criminal Theory*. New York: Oceana Publications, 1958.

Hall, Livingston, and Sheldon Glueck. *Cases on Criminal Law and Its Enforcement*. St. Paul, Minn.: West, 1958.

Mabbott, J. D. "Free-will and Punishment." In Lewis, H. D., ed. *Contemporary British Philosophy*. Third series. London: Allen & Unwin, 1956, pp. 287-309.

Maclagan, W. G. "Punishment and Retribution." *Philosophy*, Vol. 14 (1939), pp. 281-98.

Mayers, Lewis. *The American Legal System*. New York: Harper, 1955.

Michael, Jerome, and Herbert Wechsler. *Criminal Law and Its Administration*. Brooklyn: Foundation Press, 1940.

Mundle, C. W. K. "Punishment and Desert." *Philosophical Quarterly*, Vol. 4 (1954), pp. 216-28.

Paton, George W. *A Textbook of Jurisprudence*. New York: Oxford Univ. Press, 1946.

Quinton, A. M. "Punishment." *Analysis*, Vol. 14 (1954), pp. 133-42.

Ross, Sir William David. "The Ethics of Punishment." *Philosophy*, Vol. 4 (1929), pp. 205-11.

————. *The Right and the Good* (1930), Ch. 2, Appendix. In Sellars, Wilfrid, and John Hospers, eds. *Readings in Ethical Theory*. New York: Appleton-Century-Crofts, 1952, pp. 203-09.

Stone, Julius. *The Province and Function of Law*. Cambridge: Harvard Univ. Press, 1950.

Turner, James William Cecil, ed. *Kenny's Outline of Criminal Law* (1902), 17th ed. New York: Cambridge Univ. Press, 1958.

Williams, Glanville. *Criminal Law*. London: Stevens, 1953.

————. *The Sanctity of Life and the Criminal Law*. New York: Knopf, 1957.

10. Moral responsibility and free will

Our discussion of justice has led us into a tangled nest of problems concerning deserts. We have examined the relation of desert to utility; but, except for the rather obvious remarks that more serious crimes deserve more serious punishment and that a person does not deserve punishment for something he hasn't done, we have not yet reached any conclusions about when a given punishment is deserved. And indeed, the prospect of doing more than this seems most discouraging. How on earth is one to estimate whether a certain punishment applied to a certain offender is deserved?

> We have heard talk of justice. Is there anybody who knows what justice is? No one on earth can measure out justice. Can you look at any man and say what he deserves — whether he deserves hanging by the neck until dead or life in prison or thirty days in prison or a medal? The human mind is blind to all who seek to look in at it and to most of us that look out from it. Justice is something that man knows little about. He may know something about charity and understanding and mercy, and he should cling to these as far as he can.[1]

23. Blame and excuse

We must try to pursue the matter somewhat further, for it takes us to the heart of an issue that we have not yet considered, that of moral responsibility: under what conditions shall we hold a person responsible for his actions? We shall consider two specific questions which are aspects of this problem: When does a person deserve to be blamed (or praised) for his actions? in other words, under what conditions is he blameworthy (or

[1] Clarence Darrow, *Attorney for the Damned* (New York: Simon and Schuster, 1957), p. 95.

469

praiseworthy) ? When does a person deserve to be excused for actions which he has performed?

A. Blame

The simplest theory of blame, and the one with which it is most convenient to begin, is the utilitarian theory.

1. *The utilitarian theory of blame.* According to the utilitarian, what must be said about blame is very similar to what he has already said about punishment. Indeed, the utilitarian would say that instead of talking about praise, blame, and punishment, as if they were substantives, we should talk about praising, blaming, and punishing, thus reminding ourselves that these words refer to actions. Blaming is something we *do*. Blaming is, in fact, according to the utilitarian, a special kind of punishing, namely punishing by means of words; and similarly praising is a special kind of rewarding. (From here on we shall be talking primarily about blaming, but parallel conclusions can be drawn about praising.) Blaming is often less effective than punishing by deeds — "sticks and stones may break my bones but words can never hurt me," but for many people harsh and condemning words are far more effective than sticks and stones. Usually we try blaming first, since it is easier to indulge in, involving as it does only the expenditure of a few words; most people rather enjoy doing it anyway, and it helps them "get it out of their system" ("it" being, presumably, aggressive impulses). If blaming fails, punishment comes next: corporal punishment or temporary loss of affection or attention or privileges for children, and a fine or prison sentence for adults. Which devices are most effective in which situations is, of course, an empirical matter of great complexity because people and conditions differ so greatly. The details of this matter must be left to child psychologists, psychiatrists, penologists, and social workers with wide experience in these matters. But in every situation, according to the utilitarian, the only justification for employing these devices is the production of good results (including, of course, the avoidance of bad ones).

Blaming and praising are not the only devices we use in trying to alter human behavior with words. We also advise, entreat, exhort, persuade, preach, teach, moralize, threaten, bully, and (in complex situations) psychoanalyze. The training of a child consists of one long series of these devices, constantly and persistently employed. Without them, the child would grow up as much of a demanding egomaniac as he began; indeed, sometimes he does anyway, in spite of these devices; but at any rate they are absolutely necessary if the child is to grow into a civilized human being. Nevertheless, these devices are sometimes greatly overused and used at the wrong times. The tendency of most human beings is to blame and advise and moralize even when these devices will have no effect or even a harmful effect. "Well, at least I've done my duty," parents say piously after delivering a moral sermon to their offspring, little realizing that the effect of this excoriation has been only to increase resentment and rebellion in the child.

"Do you see," the utilitarian may exclaim at this point, "how well we are getting along by talking only about blam*ing* and prais*ing?* These are actions we perform, actions which we justify by their consequences. We don't have to talk about desert at all. A child walks into the pond. 'Don't go in there!' shouts the angry parent. The child wades in anyway. 'Come back here or I'll mop the floor with you!' the parent shouts. But the child only continues to walk into the water. By this time the parent is convinced that the child deserves a thrashing. If we ask, 'Does the child deserve it or not?' we could argue far into the night without coming to any conclusion. But if we ask, 'Should the child be blamed or punished, and if so how?' we are on more solid ground; at least we know how to go about answering this question. We can consult our past experience of the child's responses to various stimuli, and if we are still puzzled we can consult child psychologists and other authorities on the effects of blaming and punishing."

Thus far, then, it would appear that blaming is a practice which is justified only by its results in changing behavior. We blame people in order that they will refrain from doing similar acts in the future, and we praise them in order to reinforce similar behavior in the future. When these devices will not have these effects, as often happens, we should refrain from using them.

But by this time we shall doubtless have thought of an objection: "That's all very well for blaming and praising. I agree that we should blame someone only when it produces good results. But there is still a distinction: to say that we should blame a person for his act is one thing; to say that he *deserves* blame is another. What I really want to know about is the latter. I want to know, not when to blame him, but when he is *worthy* of being blamed, or, in the usual phrase, when he is *blameworthy.* You have failed to make this distinction."

The utilitarian, however, may easily reply: "Very well, we can play that gambit if you like. To say that someone is blameworthy is merely to say that *it would be right to blame him.*" This formula is disarmingly simple, but it calls for a word of explanation. The act- or rule-utilitarian would say, "Whether an act is right or wrong depends upon the consequences of the act or of the adoption of the rule under which the act falls. This principle applies to the act of blaming as well as to the original act which is blamed. Let us assume that Smith has performed act A, which is a wrong act; it is wrong because of the consequences to which it leads (objective duty) or to which the agent could reasonably foresee that it would lead (subjective duty). Exactly the same consideration applies to the *second* act, namely the act of blaming Smith for having performed A: the rightness of the act of blaming too is judged by *its* consequences. There are many occasions on which an act is wrong, but yet it would not be right to consider it blameworthy. Conversely many right acts may not be praiseworthy. An act may be wrong; but if blaming the agent for it will produce no good consequences, the act of blaming the agent will not be right. A psychotic individual may have stabbed an innocent person to death, but yet his act would not be blameworthy because blaming him would do absolutely no good nor would it help to prevent him from performing similar acts in the future. Similarly, the assassination of a dictator may have been right — it may have prevented the infliction of suffering and death upon his helpless subjects, but the assassination would not be praiseworthy *if* the effect of praising the assassin for his act would be to encourage others to assassinate people when the act was *not* justified. Whether an act is blameworthy, then, does not depend at all on whether the original act was wrong; it depends entirely on whether the act of blaming it is wrong."

Does this utilitarian account apply to character-traits, habits, and dispositions as well as to overt acts? "Indeed it does," the utilitarian replies, "though it should be remembered that we ordinarily blame the person not for the possession of certain traits per se but for their manifestation in actions. Either way, however, the same analysis applies: a habit or character trait is blameworthy when it is right to blame it, that is, when the act of blaming it has maximally desirable consequences. It is true that habits and character traits are more difficult to alter through blame or any other devices than actions are; nevertheless they *can* sometimes be altered by this means, and in those situations it is right to praise or blame the person for them. Thus, we may blame a person for being lazy but not for being stupid; we may blame some for being overambitious but not for being six feet tall. Why? Because blaming (and the other devices for altering behavior) *can* achieve a useful result in the first kind of situation but not in the second.

"On the one hand, blaming a person for being stupid will not make him intelligent; if it would, we would be justified in blaming him. (Of course, our tempers may get the better of us and we may blame him for being 'a stupid lout'; but in our reflective moments we realize that blaming him for stupidity is not justified because no such action on our part can raise his I.Q., and such action may actually cause him to be hateful or resentful.) On the other hand, blaming him for being lazy *may* cause him to be less lazy in the future, for laziness is a trait that is, to a considerable extent at least, within his control. (When laziness is the result of a constitutional condition, such as anemia, then of course blaming him for it is as useless as blaming him for being stupid.) There are, unfortunately, many borderline situations in which it is far from clear whether blaming is justified because it is not clear whether the trait in question is alterable. Should we blame someone for being forgetful? for being worried or anxious? for being quick-tempered? for not 'taking things easy' or 'forgetting his troubles'? Consider the following dialogue:

SHE: Did you bring those light bulbs along with you today, as I asked you to?

HE: No, I forgot.

SHE: You forgot? Again? But I've asked you three days in a row!

HE: I know, but please don't blame me for that.

SHE: Blame you? Of course I blame you! Three times and still you forget!

HE: I'm sorry, but I can't help it if I'm forgetful. Some people are forgetful, some aren't. I happen to be one of those unfortunate people who is forgetful. Some people have blue eyes, some have brown. Don't blame me for that.

"We probably tend to sympathize with the husband, yet we see a point in his wife's claim as well, because we have doubts whether the husband's forgetfulness is a trait that is unalterable by praise and blame. The difficulty is that sometimes it is, to some extent, and sometimes it isn't at all, and we are not sure which it is in this instance. If the husband were an old man whose brain cells were deteriorating, we would not be justified in blaming him for being forgetful; blaming him would only make him tense and nervous and would aggravate the complaint. But if the husband is not old, then we are not sure — it is so easy to pretend or even to believe that one can't do things that one actually *can* do with some effort, when one doesn't want to exert the effort. So we hesitate: under the circumstances is it right to blame him or not? But our hesitation will occur, not because we doubt the moral principle involved (that a man should not be blamed for behavior that he cannot alter), but because we are not sure whether in his particular situation the behavior is alterable. Needless to say, this hesitation is very frequent."

The utilitarian conclusion, then, is that acts are blameworthy (it is right to blame them) only if they are alterable by blame — with the empirical precaution that traits and habits are not as directly alterable as actions are. If you have stolen something, you can usually refrain, with some effort, from doing so again — unless you are a kleptomaniac, in which event your habit is unalterable except possibly through psychotherapy. But if you are quick-tempered, it is extremely difficult to change this trait; and even at best it will take a great deal of self-discipline exercised over a considerable period of time to produce any appreciable result: for a long time you will find the angry words coming out of your mouth before you are able to stop them; and if someone keeps blaming you every time you lose your temper, it will be difficult for you to avoid feeling resentment toward the person who is so generous with his blame. Some traits, such as lack of human sympathy, are often imposible to alter, even over a considerable period, and therefore are not blameworthy: blaming people for them is quite useless, no matter how unfortunate the possession of such traits may be.

We should make one empirical point about the rightness of blaming and praising before we turn to criticism of the utilitarian position. This point can be phrased in the following way. One of the most universal traits of human beings, and one which unwittingly causes no end of misunderstanding and friction among us, is the tendency to assume that all other people are operating on the same psychological wave length as ourselves — that others are spurred to action by the same devices that we are and are deterred by the same considerations that deter us, that they are "wired up" the same way we are. Consequently, people tend to confer praise and blame on others in accordance with what would have been effective in changing *their own* behavior at an earlier period in their own lives. The father who was raised in poverty and pulled himself up through many difficult years into a state of affluence by ceaseless energy and labor blames his son for lack of the pioneer virtues. But the son, beset and overwhelmed by conflicts and problems of adjustment to the mores of his own society a generation later, problems which the father cannot understand — and which the father unwittingly helped to bring about by forcing the child to work even when other children were playing — has only contempt for the father and his advice; and the father blames the son bitterly for this attitude. The father thinks that by scolding and railing at his son he can modify the son's behavior; but the son is in such different circumstances, both internal and external, from the father that they never understand each other; no appeals or tongue-lashings by the father can affect the son except to make him more morose and embittered. This is the tragedy of misplaced blaming — people assume that what works as a modifier of behavior for them will also work as a modifier for others. But human nature is not so simple, and most people lack insight into the inner workings of others, with the result that a large percentage of the educative energies of parents is wasted. Often if the child turns out reasonably well, it is in spite of the parents' educative efforts rather than because of them. ("What an ungrateful child I have! Why, when I was his age I worked for ten cents an hour, and I was glad to get it too. I've given him every advantage and what do I get? He doesn't even appreciate it. How I would have appreciated a tenth as much at his age!" But what the father received in his childhood, understanding and love and confidence from his parents, he was too busy making money to give in turn to his son.)

So much, then, for the utilitarian theory of blaming and blameworthiness. What could be simpler or more reasonable? Has any other theory any plausibility at all beside it? Let us consider now the tenets of the opposition.

2. *Another view of blameworthiness.* We can best introduce the opposition by giving some possible counter-examples to the utilitarian's claims.[1]

One example: Let us begin by suggesting that there is a difference between saying that a person is *blameworthy* with respect to a certain act and saying that it is *right to blame him* for it. There are two things involved here and not one as the utilitarian says. A person may have committed an

[1] The position outlined here has been set forth with the greatest completeness by Richard B. Brandt. Thus far, the theory has not been graced with a name.

act for which he thoroughly deserves blame (that is, he may be blameworthy for it), and yet it might not be right to blame him for it. He may have committed a serious offense and be admitted by everyone to be blameworthy, and yet it does not follow that we ought to blame him. Suppose that he is incurably ill and about to die; or that he has had a nervous breakdown and blaming him (even more, punishing him) would make his state of mind even worse, perhaps irreparably so; or that for any other reason blaming will have no deterring effect upon him and will have positively bad effects. He is still blame*worthy,* but because to blame him would be useless, it would not be right to do so. "Shouldn't we blame him, anyway, to deter not him but others from performing similar acts?" you might ask. But suppose that nobody else ever knows about his blameworthy act or ever will? This supposition certainly decreases the utility of blaming him, but does it change his blameworthiness one iota? Is he less blame*worthy* because other people may not happen to know about what he did?

The utilitarian might make a slight amendment to his theory to try to take care of such cases. "A person is blameworthy," the utilitarian may say, "not when it is right to blame *this* person for *this* particular act, but when it is normally or *usually right* (has the best effects) to blame people for acts *of this kind.* Thus, even if this particular man cannot be deterred by blame or punishment and even if no one else knows about this particular offense, it is still true that *in general* it is right to blame people for offenses of this kind because to do so may deter others (though not in this particular case) and not to do so would be to invite others to commit crimes of this kind or even crimes in general. Won't such a provision take care of those cases in which neither the individual offender nor others will be deterred because this act does not become known?"

The provision does indeed take care of this limited class of situations, but not all situations. Consider offenses for which, even in general, there is little if any deterrent effect in blaming or punishing and for which we still believe that the person is as blameworthy as if blaming and punishing *did* have deterrent value.

For instance, a crime like parricide, which people think is highly reprehensible (remember the savage punishment the Romans reserved for parricide!), on the view in question should seem to be less reprehensible than ordinary murder, since ordinarily the offender will be too hardened or too abnormal psychologically to be improved by condemnation or punishment, and the general public is little tempted toward this crime and does not require to be deterred by a show of indignation. The utilitarian seems able to avoid awkwardness here only by urging that it is a good thing that people get indignant with crimes, and that their indignation should be indulged even when it serves no purpose, if no great harm is done![1]

[1] R. Brandt, in A. I. Melden, ed., *Essays in Moral Philosophy,* p. 7.

Another example: Offenses of type A (say, a hitchhiker robbing a driver on a deserted road) may be no more serious than offenses of type B (say, armed robbery of a house), and yet it may be that offenses of type A should be more severely punished than those of type B because in type-A offenses it is more difficult to find evidence that will convict. For utilitarian reasons, if an offender for one type of crime is more difficult to catch, the penalty for that type of crime should be correspondingly more severe; otherwise offenses of this type would be more frequent because the offenders would believe they would not be caught. Yet how does this practical utilitarian consideration affect blameworthiness? Is a person more blameworthy for committing offenses of type A just because they are more difficult to detect?

Besides, even when it seems clear that a person is blameworthy for some act, it is not equally clear that we should blame him or go around criticizing him to others. Suppose the person reacts adversely to blame; suppose that every time you blame him for something he is *more* likely to repeat the offense? (There are many such people.) This bad effect on him might still be counterbalanced by the salutary effects on society of blaming or punishing him; but suppose it has none of these effects either. Should we still indulge in blame, when all the effects are bad? Surely not; still, once again, isn't he nevertheless blameworthy? It would seem, then, that the utilitarian account, according to which a person is blameworthy for an act only when it is right to blame him, is mistaken.

But what then *does* constitute blameworthiness?

First, let us note that to blame is not necessarily to indulge in verbal punishment against people. It is, more often, to *take an attitude* of a certain sort.

> For notice how it is natural to say, "He has not said anything to me, and probably nothing to anyone else, but I think he blames me for. . . ." A cool handshake, a reproachful glance, would ordinarily be described rather as symptoms of blaming than as cases of it. And we say, "He blames himself for. . . ." without necessarily implying any internal preaching. It looks rather as if "blaming" refers, at least often, to a complex *state* of mind or attitude rather than to an *act*. And, in so far, it need not have a purpose — and all the speculations about the purposes of blaming are irrelevant to it. And further, then, the statement "I blame you" is not necessarily a performatory utterance like "I promise you" but can be what it seems to be, a *report* of an already present fact.[1]

We must try to take cognizance of this fact in giving an account of what it is to be blameworthy and at the same time try to refrain from mentioning in it the *effects* of blaming. So let us try this way of putting it: An act is blameworthy when those who are fully acquainted with the act (and, let us say, all the relevant conditions of its performance) are justified in having an unfavorable (condemning, censuring) attitude toward the agent on ac-

[1] *Ibid.*, pp. 6-7.

count of the act. Thus, you are blameworthy for killing your father, even though *you* will never kill your father again, and even though the effects of blaming or punishing, either in this instance or in instances of this kind, are zero. It is justified to call you blameworthy because of the seriousness of the offense, quite regardless of the effectiveness of blaming or punishing you for it.

Still, this account will not give us quite what we need, for it would include all manner of nonmoral offenses as blameworthy: I would be justified in blaming you for making an arithmetical error and so you would be blameworthy for it. So far, this account sounds all right; but we want some criterion of *moral* blameworthiness. We constantly blame people for things like not closing the windows when they leave the house or not wearing rubbers on a rainy day and for many other things which are irrelevant or marginal to morality. We want some criterion for holding that someone is *morally* blameworthy. What concept can we employ to distinguish moral blameworthiness? Perhaps we can find the answer if we think of blameworthiness in terms of a defect in the person's *character*.

What is a person's character? It is, we can safely say, the sum of all his character traits. But what are character traits, and how do they differ from other traits? We do constantly make this distinction: we consider kindness, scrupulousness, and fairness to be character traits, whereas mental celerity, good memory, and literary ability are traits of personality but not of character. Character traits, it would seem, differ from other personality traits in at least two respects: (1) They are social assets or social liabilities: for example, honesty is a social asset, dishonesty a social liability. Some character traits, like patience and persistence, *can* be cultivated in isolation, but when practised in a social context, they are, normally, social assets. But clearly this requirement is not enough: for the other traits we have listed — mental celerity, memory, literary ability — can have effects on the well-being of others also. So a further requirement is needed: (2) The trait, or rather the manifestation of it in our behavior, must be to a considerable extent within our voluntary control.

Can we act honestly if we wish? Of course: all we need do is pay our debts, refrain from deceit, and so on. Can we act generously if we wish? We can pay regard to the welfare of others; we can make gifts. Most non-character traits are different. We cannot act intelligently on order. We cannot become gay or effervescent just because we want to; we can try, and to some extent we can succeed, but if we are not naturally gay, we shall need histrionic skill in order to act as if we were.[1]

It is true, as we have already observed, that we sometimes become angered or incensed with people for displaying personality traits which are not character traits: for not having enough energy, for being forgetful or

---

[1] From Richard Brandt, *Ethical Theory.* Englewood Cliffs, N. J.: Prentice-Hall, 1959, p. 467. Reprinted by permission of the publisher.

depressed or stupid. It is also true that sometimes a person can fake these personality characteristics in order to escape responsibilities like working hard or making a necessary decision. But if a person genuinely has these traits, then to the extent that he cannot help having them (and a person can change these only to a very limited extent, if at all) we cannot accuse him of a defect of character. Once we realize his helplessness to change his personality traits, we tend to cease considering the person blameworthy for them, even though the possession of them may be a great social liability; or at least, we believe that we *should* not consider him blameworthy, inasmuch as he could not help having these traits.

To summarize, then: when we consider someone blameworthy, we are not necessarily committed to blaming him, but we do believe that he *deserves* blame, since he performed the act for which we blame him, and the act arises from a defect of character. When these conditions are actually fulfilled is, of course, another matter and often difficult to discover: sometimes people can help being forgetful and sometimes not (when they can, we consider it a defect of character); sometimes they can help being quick-tempered, sometimes not. We have to be astute students of human psychology and observers of the person in question in order to know. But at any rate, we now have a formula for blameworthiness, even though it is often difficult to determine whether an individual situation conforms to it.

We began presenting this account of blameworthiness as an alternative to the utilitarian account. But does it actually contradict what the utilitarian says? If we accept it, we need disagree with the utilitarian only at one point. (1) We can agree with the utilitarian that the right act or the rule under which it comes is the one which maximizes intrinsic good. (2) We can also agree with the utilitarian that we should indulge in blaming others only when there is more utility in doing so than in alternative modes of behavior. (3) We must disagree only if the utilitarian asserts that calling someone blameworthy is the same as saying that it would be right to blame him, for we have made a distinction between "X deserves blame" and "It is right to blame X."

So much, then, for blaming and blameworthiness. There are other questions in this area which are worth asking, but we can ask them more conveniently in the context of another concept, that of *excuses*. We have asked, and tentatively answered, the question "When is a person worthy of blame?" Another question, very closely related to it, is, "When should a person be excused for his acts?" To this question we now turn.

B. Excuses

When we offer an excuse for something we have done, we do not deny having done it — if we did, we would not need to be excused for having done it; but we do want to prevent ourselves from being blamed, punished, or in any other way condemned for having done it. Nor, unless our excuse is simply rationalization, are we merely trying to escape blame or punishment; on the contrary, we are convinced that there are circumstances in which we are morally *justified* in being exonerated from condemnation; in other words, we wish to exonerate ourselves from blame or guilt by showing that we do not *deserve* to be condemned for the act in question.

Under what circumstances do we deserve to be excused for our acts? According to Aristotle, the first philosopher to discuss the matter systematically, there are two types of circumstances in which people are justified in excusing us for our actions: they are ignorance and compulsion. We shall now examine each of these in turn.

1. *Ignorance.* We often ask to be excused for certain acts because they were performed in ignorance of the facts. "I didn't know he was allergic to feathers when I gave him the pillow, I thought I was doing him a favor!" "I'm sorry I invited them for the weekend, but please excuse me, I had no idea they were going to bring all their cats with them!" "But your honor, I didn't mean to bump into him on the street. I accidentally tripped over a tree root in the darkness and fell on him. I didn't know it was there." If the person really were ignorant of the facts in question, the excuses would probably be considered acceptable — that is, as genuinely excusing the person for having performed the act. But there are other situations in which ignorance does not excuse. "But I didn't know what the latest treatment of that disease was — I haven't looked at a medical journal for ten years, so how can you condemn me for not performing an operation I didn't know existed?" "But you honor, I didn't know he was an important official when I socked him in the jaw!" "But your honor, I didn't know when I aimed the gun at him that it was loaded." Even if the person *were* ignorant of these facts, his ignorance would not excuse him.

Why the difference? What is it about the first series of situations which renders the excuse acceptable when the excuse is not acceptable in the other series of situations? To try to answer this question, let us consider the difference between *avoidable* and *unavoidable* ignorance. On the one hand, when the ignorance was clearly unavoidable, like the ignorance of the fact that a bolt of lightning would strike him dead as he stepped from the car to the doorway, we exonerate (excuse) the person completely. On the other hand, when the ignorance was avoidable by the agent (with qualifications to be mentioned shortly), we tend not to do so. The judge does not excuse the defendant because he didn't know that the gun was loaded, for the defendant could have taken the trouble to inform himself on this point, and, in view of the fact (which the defendant knew) that loaded guns can kill people, he *should* have informed himself of it before playing around with the weapon. Again, the surgeon who pleaded that he was ignorant of any medical advances during the last ten years would on no account be excused: indeed, his ignorance of a subject on which he was supposed to be informed and which could mean life or death to many patients might well be considered morally worse than if he had known the facts but made a mistake during the operation. There is avoidable ignorance and unavoidable ignorance; and the physician's ignorance was not only avoidable but was made worse by the fact that he was ignorant in a field in which his paid clientele had every right to expect him to be competent.

These examples, however, bring out a further point: that not *all* avoidable ignorance is deemed inexcusable. If the surgeon had been ignorant of some fact of engineering, a field in which he was not expected to be competent and in which he was not required to pass any judgments, he would doubtless have been excused for his ignorance, in spite of the fact that he was probably *able* to inform himself on the subject. A person of any intelligence is able to inform himself of facts on countless subjects for which we nevertheless excuse him if he is ignorant, even though strictly speaking his ignorance is avoidable. A professor of chemistry is not excused for being ignorant of some fact of elementary chemistry, but a professor of Romance languages is excused (unless he poses as an authority on chemistry); we make this distinction in spite of the fact that both men *could* have informed themselves on the matter — they had the intelligence, and they could have taken the time.

Whether ignorance counts as an excuse, then, depends on the conditions. Consider the housemaid who pleads, "But, sir, you never told me before I emptied the wastebasket that you wanted to save that scrap of paper that was in it." Strictly speaking, her ignorance *was* avoidable, for she *could* have asked him and thus acquired the relevant information; indeed she *could* have asked him about every separate scrap of paper in the wastebasket. Nevertheless we find her excuse acceptable, for there was no reason why she should have known this: if something is in the wastebasket the presumption is that it can be thrown away, and it is the employer who needs an excuse for not telling her that this piece of paper was to be saved, or for not removing the paper himself. If, however, he was accustomed to preserving the contents of the wastebasket, and the maid knew it, then she would not be excused. Similarly, "I didn't know he was allergic to feathers" is considered an acceptable excuse, for there was no special reason why he should have known; on the other hand, if a large percentage of the human race were allergic to feathers so that there was a considerable probability that a given person would be, then a person would be considered less excusable for not informing himself on the matter. Excusability, like probability, is a matter of degree.

A student pleads, "But I didn't know, when I scheduled a student committee meeting in that room for that hour, that the Room Scheduling Office had already assigned that room to another group for the same hour." Here the student is not excused, for, we believe, he should have checked with the Room Scheduling Office before asking the committee to meet in that room; indeed, their permission is normally required before a meeting can be scheduled. We do not deny that the student was indeed ignorant of the fact that another group was meeting in that room, but we would assert that his was perfectly avoidable ignorance. Not only was it avoidable (he *could,* with some effort, have avoided ignorance of all the group meetings in all the hundreds of rooms on the campus by memorizing the schedule in the Room Scheduling Office); it was a matter on which he was reasonably expected to be informed — his ignorance on the matter was one which he had a positive duty to correct before inviting others to use the room. Suppose, however, that he had sincerely claimed, "But I didn't know that all such meetings have to be cleared through the Room Scheduling Office." In that event, whether we would excuse him would depend on whether under the circumstances he could reasonably have been expected to know of this rule — for example, whether he had been at the college a long time, whether he had once known but forgotten and whether the forgetting in turn was excusable, whether he had just come from another school which had no such rule, and so on.

Suppose I am chastised for not arriving on time at an important meeting, and I plead that I had to come in from out of town, and on the way, through no fault of mine, another car collided with mine and caused me to be late. This excuse, if true, would exonerate me completely, since of course I could not have known that this accident was going to happen: ignorance of the fact that another car was going to run into mine is certainly unavoidable ignorance. But suppose that instead I was delayed because of car trouble; should I be excused then? Now the question begins to get messy: "it depends." If the car trouble was the result of my negligence in not having the car properly serviced, then I cannot be completely excused (my ignorance of the state of my car was avoidable); still less can I be excused if I purposely neglected having the car serviced, hoping that a breakdown on the way would prevent my punctual arrival at the meeting. "But if you had been a mechanic, or even reasonably knowledgeable about cars, and bothered to look under the hood once in a while, you would have seen that the fan belt was about shot," someone might protest. But I'm not a mechanic, and should everyone who ventures on the road with his car be expected to be one? Though I *could* have lifted the hood of the car and given it a mechanical inspection before the trip, or for that matter every five minutes during the trip by stopping to recheck, isn't it true that in my position as nonmechanic car driver I cannot reasonably be expected to do this checking? Whether my exoneration is complete, however, will depend on whether the person judging me believes that every car driver should be enough of a mechanic to be able to forestall simple mechanical contingencies.

Ignorance of the law presents a somewhat unique problem. It is impossible within a lifetime for every person to become acquainted with every one of the laws of his nation, state, and community. Yet the law never permits ignorance of the law as an excuse. "But I didn't know that the speed limit in this state was fifty miles per hour," pleads the defendant caught for going fifty-five. There may be occasions when he is *morally* excusable for such ignorance — particularly when the law is an obscure one and seldom enforced, when signs are not posted, when he has never been in the region before; but legally, ignorance of the law is never considered an excuse. For this principle, of course, there is a simple utilitarian reason: if ignorance of the law *were* permitted as an excuse, who would ever be convicted for an offense? It would be impossible to prove that the agent was not ignorant of the law, and laws would become ineffective through inability to enforce them.

All the examples of ignorance mentioned so far have been ignorance of the relevant *facts* of the case. But suppose one knows all the relevant facts of the case but pleads excuse on the ground that he was ignorant of the *moral principles* involved. What if one were to argue, "Yes, I knew that the gun was loaded, and I shot him deliberately, but I had no idea that killing was wrong," or, "He stole my horse and so he deserved to hang; I didn't trust the law to do it and so I decided to take justice into my own hands; no, I didn't have any idea that it was wrong to do this." Such pleas leave the authorities, to put it mildly, somewhat cold. Such pleas may, in fact, boomerang against the user: we may think it worse for a man to kill in the belief that unprovoked killing is all right, than for him to believe that it is wrong and do it anyway in the heat of passion. "A person who commits a deed in the heat of passion," one might argue, "is not as bad a man as one who does it cold-bloodedly, 'with malice aforethought,' with no conviction that what he is doing is wrong. At least the man who kills in the heat of passion will not kill when he is *not* in such a state. A man who believes that unprovoked killing is right and acts on this belief, does not lack conscientiousness, but he is morally an even worse person than one who has better moral principles and lapses from them occasionally in his practice." Perhaps it is for this reason that ignorance of a moral principle is very seldom invoked as an attempted excuse. (More frequently, a person pleads *moral disagreement* with the law. In that event we would have to consider at length whether his moral principle or the law's was the more acceptable, and, if his was, whether he was not still causing more evil than good by encouraging others toward disrespect for law in general. This problem would be handled by considerations already discussed in connection with utilitarianism.)

2. *Compulsion.* The other factor which Aristotle mentions as excusing deeds is compulsion. "I couldn't help it, I was compelled to do it." Like unavoidable ignorance, compulsion too falls into the category of unavoidable actions, for if I was truly compelled to do it, I could not have avoided doing what I did. Nothing I could have done would have changed it; accordingly, I am excused for the act in question. But excuse by reason of compulsion is nevertheless a slippery business, far more complicated than

excuse by reason of ignorance; for compulsion is a matter of degree and is seldom complete, and even when it is complete, it is difficult if not impossible to establish. Let us consider in turn external compulsion, compulsion by other agents, and inner compulsion of the agent himself.

a. *External compulsion.* Talk about compulsion is most frequently in the context of other human agents. But, since this context is the simplest, an initial word is in order about compulsion by external forces other than human beings. Suppose that you fall from a height and while falling you inadvertently hit someone and injure him. Everyone would excuse you for your action, for quite literally you "couldn't help it." You were compelled to do as you did by conditions beyond your control. Indeed, it could hardly even be described as *your* act, since you were not the agent but the patient. In any event, since the conditions were beyond your control, no one would hold you responsible for what happened.

But "compulsion" by external circumstances is seldom as complete as the one just described. Consider Aristotle's example, "We were compelled to jettison the cargo of the ship." Here, unlike the case of falling, there *was* a choice: we could have dropped ourselves overboard instead of the cargo; so it is not true that nothing we could have done would have changed the outcome. Nevertheless, we often speak of cases like this one as if they were simon-pure cases of compulsion: we say that "circumstances compelled us" to do as we did. Between one unpleasant alternative and a still more unpleasant one, we often think of the latter as an impossible one and, discounting it, consider the other one to have been "forced upon us." Indeed, there is little practical difference between this case and one of complete compulsion. Even the insurance company paying the damages on the lost cargo would not hold out with the rejoinder, "You could have thrown yourselves overboard instead."

But the main area in which the concept of compulsion operates is that of human beings — either other human beings compelling one to act in certain ways, or one's own inner urges doing so.

b. *Compulsion by other agents.* If someone stronger than you places his hand over yours and forces your fingers to pull the trigger, you are excused from the charge of murder. It is a case of compulsion by a human being whose strength you cannot match; nor is his superior strength any reflection on your character. You resist as best you can, but you are not strong enough. What happened was, in fact, not so much your act as his. Or you could say it was your act, but compelled: quite literally you could say "I was compelled to pull the trigger."

The difficulty with compulsion by other agents is that there are not many cases of it that are as clear-cut as this one. A stranger enters your room with a loaded gun pointed at you and says, "Your money or your life!" Later on, in recounting the incident, you say, "I was compelled to give him my money." Your hearer says, "No, you weren't compelled; you could have sacrificed your life. There *was* a choice, though an unpleasant choice — between sacrificing your money and sacrificing your life (and probably your money as well)." Yes, you may think, so unpleasant that for all practical purposes you might as well say you were compelled to give up the money; in fact this *is* the way we speak about it ordinarily, and it would be most unusual to say, "No, I wasn't compelled to give up the money, I had a free choice." This case is similar to the one just considered about jettisoning the cargo of the ship.

But it is not always so with unpleasant alternatives. If you are an intelligence agent or an underground worker, you may be tortured for hours; but you are still not excused (if and when you return to your own men) by the plea, "But I was forced (compelled) to reveal the names of my companions, for I was tortured"; you are not excused in spite of the fact that being tortured is much more of a case of compulsion than being confronted by a gun. Why the difference? You had a choice in both cases, so why are you excused in the case of theft but not in this one? Because, surely, it is felt that you *should* have submitted to torture rather than reveal the names of your companions (who would be caught and tortured and perhaps killed as a result of your revelation), whereas there would have been no point in sacrificing your life along with your money. If you were not prepared to endure torture rather than reveal secrets more important than your life, you should not have undertaken to be an underground worker in the first place. Even this case, however, is not a clear one: it is usually agreed that there is a point beyond which torture cannot go on and still be voluntarily submitted to. Beyond a certain point — which is admittedly difficult to place, varying from person to person — you can no more stand to be tortured than you can help withdrawing your hand when someone places it over a flame. There are forms of torture, not always physical ones, which lessen one's power to resist, until finally one becomes like a blubbering idiot, revealing anything in order to be released. If such a point is reached, then it is actually true to say that one *could* not have done otherwise, and one is morally (even if not always legally) excused.

Most attempts to influence human behavior which are severe enough to be called "compulsion" are considerably more attenuated than physical torture. A person without a gun may threaten you with all kinds of dire consequences if you do not do as he says (telling your wife about your past, for instance), until finally you do his bidding, saying, "I was compelled to." A dynamic leader and propagandist may work on the minds of gullible or excitable people until they do things they would never have done if they had relied only on their own judgment or on reasoned advice; if such methods are used continuously enough, they too can be called "compulsion." A malicious husband systematically tries to break down the psychological defenses of his weak-willed wife, until, by subtly planted suggestions and rumors he spreads about her, she no longer cares to live and takes her own life. This form of influence too could be called compulsion — another will was exerted upon hers to make her do the deed. In every case of compulsion by other agents, the will of one person (or persons) is used to make others do things which they would not otherwise have done. But the kind and degree of this influence varies enormously, from torture or gunpoint at one end of the spectrum to influence by simple suggestion or calm reasoning on the other. The latter cases would not be said to be examples of compulsion because the person, though influenced, always made his own decision on the basis of what seemed to him relevant considerations. (Even so, he is often led to do things he would not otherwise have done, even if for no other reason than that he did not think of them.) The former cases would be considered examples of compulsion, because force or threat or other violent means were used to make the person act against his will. But where, in between these two extremes, is one to draw the line between compulsion and noncompulsion? When does strong suggestion become compulsion? It is no wonder that such cases are the despair of judges and juries. Not only is it frustratingly difficult to draw a line, but it is almost equally difficult to establish that a given act belongs at any one place on the continuum. About all we can say is, "The further away from rational persuasion you get, and the nearer to force (physical or psychological) imposed on the will from the outside, the more accurately the influence can be called compulsion." But even this account invites a question mark: a madman influences a suggestible and ignorant mob; isn't it their own choice to do what he says? "But that's not their real nature, it's his will imposed on them from the outside," someone may object. But a very important part of their "real nature" is this suggestibility itself; one cannot give a complete account of "their nature" without bringing in the fact that they are easily swayed by the wills of others.

Is hypnosis a case of compulsion by other agents? Suppose that you consent to be hypnotized, the hypnotist tells you that after you come out of the hypnotic state you will throw a kettle of boiling water on someone present, and this is just what happens. Can you excuse yourself from the charge on the ground that it was done under compulsion — "I wasn't myself, I wasn't in control of my faculties, I was acting under posthypnotic suggestion"? "But you could have refrained from being hypnotized; you did that voluntarily, didn't you?" "Yes, but how did I know he was going to suggest that I do a thing like that? [Plea of ignorance.] To the charge of throwing the water I plead excuse by reason of compulsion; to the charge of consenting to be hypnotized I plead excuse by reason of ignorance." One might then hold the hypnotist responsible; but what if he had no reason to believe that you would actually do what he said, that it was as much of a surprise to him as to anyone else? It is clear, at any rate, that you were led by the hypnotist's suggestion to do something (throwing the boiling water) which you would never have done of your own volition; it was the influence of another will, not your own, that made you do it. You would be excused for what you did once it was clear that you did it under hypnosis, though you might not be excused for consenting to be hypnotized in the first place (even if you had no reason to expect any danger) — just as a person, once intoxicated, may not be responsible for his action in driving a car and injuring a pedestrian, though he is certainly responsible for becoming intoxicated in the first place.

If cases of compulsion by other agents are puzzling, those of inner compulsion are even more so.

c. *Inner compulsion.* Usually one's impulses to do certain things are not so strong that one-cannot overcome them with effort. But sometimes they are. One could have refrained from starting to become addicted to drugs in the first place; once started, one could, with considerable effort, refrain from continuing; but beyond a certain point one finds it quite impossible to refrain; the person in need of drugs is under the sway of such an overpowering inner compulsion that he would do anything, kill his best friend or press the button that would blow up the world, in order to alleviate the agony, which he can do only by getting another fix. Once the addiction is formed, we do not hold the addict responsible for his actions, though we do hold him responsible for having started the habit or for not having stopped before he reached the point of no return. Here is a relatively clear case of an overpowering inner compulsion.

Or suppose that a man has a compulsion to wash; five hundred times a day he must wash his hands. He doesn't know why; psychiatrists say it is because of an infantile preoccupation with dirt, a charge which his "inner conscience" (superego) constantly makes and which he must constantly rebut by saying in effect, "But I'm not dirty! See how clean I am, see how I wash my hands?" But this charge and reply is unconscious. He does not know what drives him to wash his hands; all he knows is that he is driven, and he cannot help it. No one *else* forces him to do what he does; forces within his own personality exert the compulsion, but they do it just as effectively as if he had been forced at the point of a gun or on pain of torture in a concentration camp. Behaviorially, such external compulsion and his inner compulsion are indistinguishable.

Suppose that you are a timid and retiring personality, easily dominated by others, and that your wife or husband is a domineering personality who can get you to do almost anything. This state has come about gradually and imperceptibly, but by now your spouse has only to issue a peremptory command and you obey it unthinkingly, automatically. It is a difficult question to what extent you could have avoided this state of affairs. "By not marrying such a so-and-so in the first place," you might say. But so-and-so's don't come with labels on them, and many people are difficult to recognize for what they are until you have known them for a long time, by which time it may be too late. Besides, if you are of a personality type that has a great unconscious need to be dominated, then if you are not dominated by one person, you will undoubtedly find someone else to dominate you: you *un*consciously recognize, and therefore are consciously attracted to, the type of person who is domineering. Suppose now that under the influence of this domination you commit a deed for which you are summoned to appear in court. "But your honor," you protest, "I couldn't help it, I was under the influence of my domineering wife." If it is accepted as a fact (that you were under her domination), does it constitute an acceptable excuse for what you did? The judge may say that you could have prevented the domination from reaching that point, but is he correct in making such an assumption? Compulsion excuses, but to what extent is yours a case of compulsion? To what extent are you justified in saying that you *couldn't help* doing as you did? It's not as if you were in chains; yet isn't this domination a kind of chain? It operates with the same effectiveness as chains in dictating your behavior. When someone forced you to pull the trigger, you were compelled against your will; but now the compulsion has been exerted *upon your will itself*. Is it compulsion any the less?

If psychiatrists are correct, a tremendous number of acts are of this kind; indeed they often refer to such acts as *compulsive* behavior. The person has little or no more control over his behavior in such cases than he does during an epileptic fit. He may even *think* he has control (as in the case of the man with a compulsion to wash his hands), but he hasn't. The woman with a glass-phobia may not know that she is the victim of an unconscious compulsion; she thinks she can avoid her fear of glass, but she cannot. If she even gets close to glass she breaks out in a cold sweat, and if you force her to touch it she has a nervous collapse. She cannot avoid these reactions, which stem from unconscious identifications and traumatic experiences during infancy and early childhood. Or to take a more nearly "normal" case: a man who always "rubs people the wrong way" and, without consciously intending to, utters to each person he knows the very remarks that will most arouse their resentment, may think he can behave this way or not as he pleases, though if he gains a bit of insight into himself he will say, "I can't seem to help it — the remark is out of my mouth before I know it, and I can't seem to see when I say it that the person is going to take it badly." Even if he tries to correct his habit, he cannot — he only falls into the same trap again, when he least expects it. It seems to be in no way under his voluntary control — it is just as if some malicious demon forced him to utter the cutting remarks. On a conscious level the man may be neither intelligent nor discerning: he could not possibly figure out *consciously* which persons he could hurt the most by his remarks, he is not so clever. But without the slightest knowledge or cooperation of his conscious will, *unconsciously* he recognizes the psychologically vulnerable spots in the personalities of others and makes just the remarks which he *uncon-*

sciously sees will threaten and expose them and bring about a reaction of revenge and retaliation.

Psychiatric textbooks are full of case histories of acts like these, performed from inner compulsion. Psychiatrists and others aware of the nature and genesis of such cases are fairly well agreed that they are just as unavoidable as if a demon *had* put the cutting words into the man's mouth, and that, accordingly, the person cannot be held responsible for them. Most people, of course, totally unacquainted as they are with psychiatric facts, would not excuse him for such acts. But their error is not one of moral principle: they would not deny that *if* he could not avoid doing what he did, then he should be excused for it. Rather, their error is one of empirical fact: they do not know that under the circumstances (known to the psychiatrist) he cannot avoid it.

The number of acts which result from inner compulsion, then, far exceeds the uninformed layman's usual guess; he recognizes only the superficial or obvious cases and assumes that in all the other cases no inner compulsion exists. Still, his failure to recognize inner compulsion does not change the formula: *if* the act arises through compulsion, the agent is morally excusable for it. Or, as we can now state it in other terms, if the act arises through compulsion, the agent is not *responsible* for it. We say that a person is *responsible* for performing a wrong act unless he has an acceptable *excuse* for performing it. (We would hardly *excuse* someone for doing his duty, hence the restriction to wrong or undesirable acts.) The underlying idea in the concept of moral responsibility is simply this: a person is morally excusable for an action if he *couldn't help it.* We have considered the two main types of circumstance in which a person can be said not to help it: when he is unavoidably ignorant and when he is compelled. It is true, of course, that when a person couldn't help performing act B, he often *could* have helped performing a previous act, A, which led to B: he could have avoided taking drugs at the start, he could have refused to be hypnotized; in that event we hold him responsible for A but not for B.

Nevertheless, we cannot leave the matter here. Only a few moments' reflection will be sufficient to evoke some more probing questions: If we are not responsible for performing acts we can't help, how can we be responsible for our character traits, which, after all, we did very little to bring about and which (on our previous analysis) are involved in being blameworthy? Are we not all ultimately the products of forces that molded us, particularly our hereditary make-up and the influences of our early environment, which we did not create? Surely we couldn't help these forces; and if we couldn't, how can we help performing the acts which spring from them? On a deeper level, how can we be said to be responsible for any acts at all? When we consider all the factors that combined to make us what we are, doesn't the whole concept of responsibility collapse?

To answer this question, we must embark on a discussion of the timeworn controversy of determinism and free will.

EXERCISES

1. Why is it so difficult to ascribe responsibility in situations like the following? (Attempt it, nevertheless.)

a. After World War I the Allies imposed extremely harsh peace terms upon Germany in the Treaty of Versailles, including the "war guilt" clause. By keeping Germany in a state of poverty for a long time, conditions were brought about which rendered virtually inevitable the rise of Nazism. In desperation the people rallied round a leader, Hitler, who promised to improve their condition. Their support of Hitler led to the supremacy of the Nazi party, the concentration camps, and the outbreak of war in 1939 in which the Allies went to the defense of Poland.

b. During the American depression of the 1930's the tenant farmers, bankrupted by crop failures (due to dust storms and other problems) and unable to produce food or earn money, were forced bodily off their land by bulldozers which razed their houses and barns to the ground. The people tried to attack the drivers of the bulldozers. The drivers declared that they were only hired for the job, obeying the orders of others. "Get the men who hired us." But these men in turn were hired by the landlords. "So get the landlords." But the landlords were not private individuals but corporations — legal entities, not men. "Get the heads of the corporations." But these men were appointed by the stockholders, hundreds of them throughout the country, to keep the corporation afloat. The heads of the corporations had to show a profit or lose their jobs and bankrupt the company. (See John Steinbeck, *The Grapes of Wrath* [New York: Viking, 1939], pp. 42-47.)

2. One man submits to bribery and is considered blameworthy. Another man does not submit only because no one tried to bribe him. If anyone had, he would have submitted just as quickly as the first man. Do you consider him just as blameworthy (for something he didn't actually do) as the first man?

3. Evaluate the following assertion: "When they put up the price of gas ten cents a thousand, I do not know who will go to jail, but I do know that a certain number of people will go. When the meat combine raises the price of beef, I do not know who is going to jail, but I know that a large number of people are bound to go. Whenever the Standard Oil Company raises the price of oil, I know that a certain number of girls who are seamstresses, and who work night after night long hours for somebody else, will be compelled to go out on the streets and ply another trade, and I know that Mr. Rockefeller and his associates are responsible and not the poor girls in the jails." (C. Darrow, *Attorney for the Damned,* p. 8.)

4. Two bitter enemies meet in the desert and agree to bury their differences till they find the nearest water hole together. The water is poisoned, and the first man drinks it and dies. Later, the second man pleads excuse for the death of the first man. What would you think of the following pleas as excuses?

a. "I didn't know that the water was poisoned."

b. "I knew the water was poisoned and I told him so, but he didn't believe me, and drank it anyway. Did you expect me to *force* him not to drink it?"

c. "I knew the water was poisoned, but I said nothing. After all, I didn't actually *do* anything to kill him."

d. "I knew the water was poisoned, but I told him it was O.K. He didn't have to believe me, did he?"

5. "I know I didn't stop my car at the stop sign, but the sign was down — it had been washed out in the recent cloudburst." What do you think of the following countercharges?

a. "You should have known there was usually a stop sign there. You're a citizen of the community."

b. "You should have known that wherever a small road leads into a highway, there is a stop sign."

c. "You should have known that the law requires you to stop there, even though there was no sign. The sign is there only for your convenience in remembering, and if it happened to be down that's your tough luck. A city map containing the location of all the stop signs in town is posted in the City Hall."

6. To what extent are you excusable in the following situations?

a. Through carelessness you have neglected to have the brakes on your car fixed. While driving through an intersection you see, at the last moment, someone scurrying across the street against the red light. You slam down on the brakes, but they do not work properly, and as a result the pedestrian is killed.

b. You are driving your car on ice for the first time, quite carefully, and step on the brake to avoid running into someone. You are ignorant of the fact that brakes are worse than useless on ice; you skid into a pedestrian, who is killed.

c. You know that brakes are useless while driving on ice, but your reflexes are conditioned to ordinary conditions, and before you think of it you have stepped on the brake, killing a pedestrian.

d. You run over a dog on the highway. You could have avoided doing so, but you plead, "I don't see anything wrong with running over dogs."

7. Is intoxication a form of compulsion? After you have taken hold of the wheel while intoxicated and killed a pedestrian, should the judge look more leniently on your case than he would if you had run down the pedestrian while sober? Or should he hold you responsible for two offenses instead of one — first that of becoming intoxicated and then that of running down a pedestrian while in an intoxicated state?

8. A: But you were responsible for getting drunk in the first place.

B: But I wasn't drunk at first, I just had one drink — I didn't know that the person who bought me the drink had made it a double, and he didn't know (what I could have told him beforehand if he'd asked me) that I am no longer master of myself if I have more than one normal-sized drink.

A: But you were responsible for taking more than one.

B: No, after that first one I didn't even know what was going on; I just drank the others automatically as he gave them to me, without knowing what I was doing.

A: But you are responsible for having driven a vehicle while intoxicated.

B: But I'm not — by the time I got to the car I was going by instinct and was in no fit state to judge anything. I don't even remember doing it.

What *is* the person responsible for, then? Nothing?

9. A man accidentally shoots someone. To what extent do you consider the following considerations as (wholly or partly) excusing? Explain.

a. "I was drunk and thought it was a squirrel."

b. "I wasn't myself when I did it — I was irritable and depressed."

c. "I did it in the heat of passion — I would never have done it ordinarily, and never before in my life was I in such a state."

d. "I did it in the heat of passion." (But he is a person who regularly does things in the heat of passion. He is easily carried away.)

e. "What I did was contrary to my usual nature."

f. "I don't remember doing it, though I don't deny that I did it."

g. "I remember doing it, but it was as if some demon got hold of me and made me do it. I tried to resist but couldn't."

h. "I guess I just lost my head."

i. "I'm just a person with unusually strong aggressive impulses."

10. To what extent, if any, do you think the following plea constitutes a legitimate excuse for an offense? "I admit that I did it and that I acted wrongly, but almost *anyone in my position would have done the same.*" (For example, the man came home, found another man committing adultery with his wife, and shot him.)

11. Would you consider the following acceptable excuses? Why?

a. Pharmacist: "I know I filled the prescription incorrectly and that the person was poisoned, but after all I didn't do it deliberately; it was an accident."

b. Underground worker: "But I didn't know that the people I was telling the secrets to were the enemy. They said they were the underground, and they had the password, the insignia, everything. How was I to know that they had captured and killed some of our men and tortured others into giving away the password?"

12. Usually the law insists on the following rules. Do you agree with them or think they should be rescinded or amended? Can you give reasons why they should be held?

a. Ignorance of the law is never an excuse.

b. Conscientious objection to the law is never an excuse.

c. An act which would usually be punishable is not considered a crime if the agent performs it because someone threatened him with death or injury for failing to do it.

d. Lack of intent or ignorance of the relevant facts is not excusable (in crimes of strict liability).

13. Evaluate the following as excuses:

a. "But your honor, I was only a passenger, and I didn't know that the car I was riding in was stolen."

b. "I know that killing one's enemies is illegal, but your honor, I hold that it is my duty just the same. My conscience comes before the law."

c. A citizen before a Nazi court tries to hold out against the law that protecting Jews is punishable by death.

d. The person performing the act has no sense of right and wrong (e.g. a constitutional psychopath).

14. Evaluate the following as tests of moral responsibility:

a. The agent must know the "nature and character" of the act, and that it was wrong. (McNaughten Rules.)

b. The threat of future punishment (or promise of reward) must make some difference (causally) in the performance of the act.

c. A person is responsible for his deed if on that occasion he had the capacity to refrain from doing what he did. (Is he responsible for not having increased his capacity in the past?)

15. Evaluate the following pleas:

a. "I told the lie, but I did it only halfheartedly."

b. "I had my fingers crossed when I did it."

c. "I am naturally very shy, and I just couldn't make myself speak up."

d. "I would ordinarily have spoken to protect her, but her husband was in the room and he's stronger than I am."

16. Why are young children not held responsible for deeds for which their parents would be held fully responsible? (What things *do* parents nevertheless hold children responsible for? Rightly, in your opinion?)

17. An enemy invades a country. Most residents resist, and are shot by the invaders. A few, wishing to save their own lives, cooperate with the enemy. It doesn't pay them in the end, for they too are shot after they have served the enemy's purpose. But they didn't know their fate at the time, and collaboration seemed to be their only chance. Do you consider them blameworthy for collaborating? On what conditions do you think it would depend?

18. "But even the compulsive neurotic *can* avoid his compulsive behavior. With a great — a very great — effort, even the agoraphobe can force himself to go into the street." "Yes, but he will be in a state of nervous collapse for quite a while afterward. It's not that it *can't* be done but that the price exacted from him for doing it is too great. You *can* jump into a den of snakes, but nobody could blame you for not doing so." "Not even to save the world?"

19. Which of the following, in your opinion, are mitigating circumstances? Why?

a. He was born in the slums.

b. His parents never gave him any conception of right and wrong.

c. Well, that's just the way he is, and you can't expect him ever to be any different.

d. He was all right before he went to prison the first time (for a crime he didn't commit), but there he learned the techniques of crime from hardened criminals and learned to hate society for what it had done to him. Besides, no one would give him a job after he got out, so he had to turn to crime to stay alive.

20. To what extent, if any, do you think that people can be held responsible for (*1*) the thoughts or ideas that enter their minds? (*2*) their desires? (momentary ones? recurring ones?) (*3*) temperamental traits like having a quick temper? Justify your answers.

READING LIST, SECTION 23

Aristotle. *Nicomachean Ethics*. Many editions, Bk. 3.

Austin, John. "A Plea for Excuses." *Aristotelian Society Proceedings*, Vol. 57 (1956-57), pp. 1-30.

Barnes, Wriston H. F., W. D. Falk, and A. Duncan-Jones. "Intention, Motive, and Responsibility." (symposium) *Aristotelian Society Proceedings*, Supplementary Vol. 19 (1945), pp. 230-48.

Beardsley, Elizabeth L. "Excusing Conditions and Moral Responsibility." In Hood, Sidney, ed. *Determinism and Freedom*. New York: New York Univ. Press, 1958, pp. 133-37.

Brandt, Richard. "Blameworthiness and Obligation." In Melden, Abraham Irving, ed. *Essays in Moral Philosophy*. Seattle: Univ. of Washington Press, 1958, pp. 3-39.

————. *Ethical Theory*. Englewood Cliffs, N. J.: Prentice-Hall, 1959, Ch. 18.

Broad, C. D. "Conscience and Conscientious Action." In Broad, C. D., *Ethics and the History of Philosophy*. New York: Humanities Press, 1952, pp. 244-62.

Ewing, Alfred C. *Ethics*. New York: Macmillan, 1953, Ch. 8.

Farmer, Herbert H. "The Notion of Desert Good and Bad." *Hibbert Journal*, Vol. 41 (1942-43), pp. 347-54.

Frankena, William K. "Obligation and Ability." In Black, Max, ed. *Philosophical Analysis*. Ithaca, N. Y.: Cornell Univ. Press, 1950, pp. 157-75.

Ginsberg, Morris. "The Nature of Responsibility." In Ginsberg, M., *On the Diversity of Morals*. New York: Macmillan, 1957, pp. 97-129.

Hart, H. L. A. "The Ascription of Responsibility and Rights." In Flew, Antony, ed. *Essays in Logic and Language*. New York: Philosophical Library, 1951, Vol. 1, pp. 145-66.

————. "Legal and Moral Obligation." In Melden, Abraham I., ed. *Essays in Moral Philosophy*. Seattle: Univ. of Washington Press, 1958, pp. 82-107.

————. "Legal Responsibility and Excuses." In Hook, Sidney, ed. *Determinism and Freedom*. New York: New York Univ. Press, 1958, pp. 81-104.

Hughes, G. E. "Moral Condemnation." In Melden, Abraham I., ed. *Essays in Moral Philosophy*. Seattle: Univ. of Washington Press, 1958, pp. 108-34.

Lewis, H. D., J. W. Harvey, and G. A. Paul. "The Problem of Guilt." (symposium) *Aristotelian Society Proceedings*, Supplementary Vol. 21 (1947), pp. 175-218.

Nowell-Smith, Patrick. *Ethics*. Baltimore: Pelican Books, 1954, Chs. 19-20.

Raab, Francis. "The Moral Basis of Our Ascriptions of Responsibility." In Nakhnikian, G., and H. Castaneda. *Morality and the Language of Conduct*. Detroit: Wayne State Univ. Press, 1961.

24. Determinism and free will

Let us take stock of the situation thus far. We have been trying to state under what circumstances a person is responsible for his acts. We have concluded that if an act is performed as the result of compulsion, the person is not responsible for it. True, it is difficult to know when a genuine situation of compulsion is involved and even more difficult to know to what degree it operates in a specific instance. Still, at least a distinction has been preserved between acts for which we are responsible and those for which we are not. The kleptomaniac is not responsible for his acts of thievery, for he is the victim of a compulsion beyond his control; but the man who cleverly plots a theft and carries it through *is* responsible, for he knows what he is doing and could avoid it if he tried. If a student misses an examination because he is ill, circumstances compelled him to be absent and he is not held responsible for his absence; but if the student willfully missed the examination in order to have more time to study, he is held fully responsible for his absence.

At the end of our previous discussion we came across a suggestion far more radical than any we had confronted thus far — namely, that no one is ever responsible for his actions because, if we look sufficiently into the events preceding any act, we shall find that no matter what the person did, there was no alternative — he was always "compelled by circumstances" to do what he did. In this sense, it may be alleged, not only is the kleptomaniac not responsible; neither is the clever thief. It is true that he planned the theft whereas the kleptomaniac did not, but this difference is only superficial: the clever planner is just as much a victim as the compulsive; perhaps he had an overpowering impulse to "get even," to "show up" the cruel, fantasied mother of the nursery by performing antisocial acts. Whatever the cause, he did what he did just as inevitably as the kleptomaniac and is no more responsible for his act. "Well, perhaps he isn't responsible after all," one may say. "Perhaps the very planning itself is compulsive, so that the same analysis that applies to the kleptomaniac applies to him. But still it doesn't apply to *everybody*. Perhaps the thief and the kleptomaniac are both sick, but that doesn't mean that we all are. So there is still a distinction." "But," someone might urge in reply, "each of us, in all of his actions, could we but know all their secret springs, is compelled to do what he does; the circumstances being just what they were, he could do nothing else. In that event, none of us is ever responsible for any of his actions. In every situation there is something that *made* us do what we did. In the situation of the kleptomaniac, we know it and acknowledge it; but in the other situations we don't see it, so we keep talking about 'moral responsibility.'"

Clearly this is a challenge we must meet. Nor must we confuse the issue by warning that "to say nobody is ever responsible is to destroy the foundations of society." We are seeking the truth at whatever cost, whether or not we like what we may find. Nor need we fear that our conclusions will make human beings cease their activities of blaming, praising, punishing, rewarding, and excusing, for these practices have too much utility (in some instances at least) to be discarded. Even if the criminal is never responsible, we shall not on that account refrain from isolating him from society. These practices are justified by their utilitarian function — that at least is not now in question. What is in question is whether, in view of the total causal history of each human act, the agent is ever really responsible for the acts which he performs.

Consider the following imaginary conversation:

WHITE: When an act is performed from inner compulsion, isn't it the result of an impulse which, whether conscious or unconscious, was (under the circumstances) irresistible? Even the courts excuse an agent on grounds of "irresistible impulse" when it is quite clear to them that an impulse really was irresistible. Such things are sometimes faked, of course, and since lots of people can claim "irresistible impulse" after performing acts the impulse to which was far from irresistible, the law naturally prefers to err on the side of caution in such cases. But very few acts are induced by irresistible impulse. The impulse to do most acts, even those in which inner compulsion plays a part, *can* be resisted even if only by herculean efforts of will. Even the compulsive gambler *could* stop at a given moment if he were told that a bottle of acid would be thrown into his eyes if he kept on gambling.

BLACK: Yes, sometimes. But sometimes not. Some people have very poorly developed powers of resistance to impulses, but others have not. Some people really do have a very low resistance threshold so that impulses to acts which others are capable of resisting they cannot resist. Isn't an irresistible impulse, then, compulsion, and excusable? Most people find it impossible to imagine the strength and intensity of certain impulses, especially in neurotics and even more in psychotics. The average man, however much he may be attracted by a pretty girl, can control himself; but imagine his impulse suddenly to have twenty times its initial strength; could he resist it then? He may righteously say he could, but could he? He simply has no conception of the strength of the impulse, and the weakness of the built-in inhibitions, in the psychopathic rapist. Or if he could still resist at twenty times the strength, then increase the impulse to fifty times, a hundred — could he then? There is a point at which each person will break down and can master his impulses no longer — when they really do become irresistible.

As always, the average person makes the mistake of assuming that other people are wired up (psychologically) the same way he is. "I can resist, and therefore so can you." But he isn't the other fellow, and he can't know what the other fellow is or is not capable of at any moment. It is so very difficult to judge. Yet, of course, when such cases appear in court they have to be settled. The judge isn't God, and yet he must play God and try to decide whether or not it really was a case of irresistible impulse. Imagine a desire for alcohol so great that the person would trade his entire earthly fortune and his wife and family into the bargain, would even consent to see the world go up in smoke tomorrow, just so that he could have one more drink tonight. We have contempt for him and spit on him, we righteous, solid citizens. But can we really begin to comprehend the intensity of such an impulse? Who are we to sit in judgment and say that it is possible for him to resist it?

A young man calls at an apartment to make a delivery, rings the bell, talks to the girl who answers the bell, enters the apartment, and stabs her to death with a dozen jabs of an ice pick. "An unspeakable, foul murder," you say. And so it is. But is it excusable? "Of course it isn't excusable," you say, "what monstrous thing are you suggesting?" But you see, she wore a ring, which resembled his mother's wedding ring. And when he saw the ring he absolutely could not control himself. Why not? Because he had revered his mother, and dreamt of her even when she sent him to an orphanage to get rid of him, even when he was pushed around from one orphanage to another and wanted by no one. Then one day when he came to visit his mother unexpectedly, he discovered that she was a common whore. He could not take, psychologically, this awful ambivalence between hating her for what she was, shattering all his cherished illusions about her, and yet loving her and wanting her desperately as the only anchor in his life, weak as it was. Her wedding ring was the symbol of her sanctity, and nobody else could wear one in his eyes because it threatened that image of her which he wanted to preserve; yet at the same time he hated her, and this symbol of her sanctity was a mockery of what she really was — when he saw the ring he had to kill. Now do you still think he could have avoided it? Do you think he was personally to blame for what he did? Didn't that chain of tragic events in his history lead inevitably to what happened? And if the whole course of events was inevitable, surely you can't blame him personally for it — his act was a blind link in a long blind chain.[1]

w: Inevitable? Inevitable? What are you using that word to mean? Just that each event in the unfortunate series had a cause? Then I object.

b: No. "Inevitable" means the same as "unavoidable." I am saying that what he did was unavoidable, *given* the total background; and judges, juries, and common people all make the mistake of saying that it was avoidable because they look at the act *in isolation* or only in the light of its immediate antecedents but not in the light of *all* the factors that made it happen. He could not avoid his babyhood and childhood situations — he was the passive victim, not the agent, in these frightful circumstances. He was subject to influences — stresses, strains, conflicts, parental quarrels, neglect, hatred, then divorce and his mother's subsequent life. This series of influences, occurring in just the combination it did, and happening to a young child with just his biological and temperamental makeup (able to stand certain stresses but not others), *inevitably* led to his being rebellious, hating and loving the same object, envious of respectability yet contemptuous of it, each influence expressing itself in a different way. He was only the instrument of the influences; but all of them together were the cause.

[1] This is the first of five case histories related in Robert Lindner, *The Fifty-minute Hour* (New York: Rinehart, 1954).

w: But did that childhood situation, including its effects on him, inevitably bring about the act of murder at the age of twenty-one?

b: Not by itself, for many circumstances have yet to be mentioned. The situation might still have been salvaged to some extent had he not been bandied about unwanted from one orphanage to another, or had he not had such a deep-rooted longing for home, or had he not made the horrifying discovery about his mother and unconsciously (without his knowledge or control) focused his accumulated hatreds on that one object, the ring. Even that discovery wouldn't have led to the murder if he had not happened to see that girl with that ring. Each circumstance we know about makes us see more the inevitability of what followed; and if we knew all the relevant circumstances (we do, I think, know the most important ones), we would see that the act we condemn was really, and without qualification, inevitable, and hence, *morally* excusable.

w: So if we condemn him to death or life imprisonment, not as a protection for society but as a moral judgment against *him,* you would say, would you, that he didn't *deserve* it?

b: Of course. Constantly I see sick people railroaded to death or imprisoned who didn't deserve it. They were beaten from the beginning — they came into the world "scarce half made up," and the stresses and strains to which they were subjected from infancy were too much for them to take (not that it's easy even for the best of us), just as the weight of a ten-ton truck is too much for all but the strongest to bear. The delivery boy was a victim of an unfortunate situation and no more the master of it than a person who contracts scarlet fever or cholera.

w: Ah, but the situations are rather different. One contracts a disease through no fault of his own, except sometimes carelessness. But when one coldly and calculatingly plans a murder, he *does* have something to do with it, doesn't he? Since the murder was *his* act, and a most reprehensible one, he does deserve some punishment, whether it be death or imprisonment.

b: No. We have a duty to try to cure him as we would a sick person, and we should, for his own good and society's, isolate him from the outside world while this attempt is being made. If this treatment is punishment, then very well, we should punish him. But let's not add error to misfortune, and reinforce our feelings of self-righteousness into the bargain, by saying that he *deserves* it.

w: You don't believe that, quite apart from the requirement of isolation and society's duty to try to transform him into a better person, he *deserves* punishment simply and purely because of the deed he has done?

b: No. Superficially it may seem so. But when we look into the conditions that led up to the deed, we must conclude that *he* doesn't deserve it at all. When you investigate the slum background, the broken home, the lack of family feeling, the wanting to be loved and trusted when nobody would respond, the inevitable rebellion, the resolve to behave to the world as the world had behaved toward him, the need to restore his ego, his self-respect, his personal significance in a world that rejected him, you can see how all these circumstances led inevitably to the fatal result. Given those circumstances, the story couldn't have ended in any other way. So I can only repeat: we must isolate him to prevent a recurrence, and we must try therapy on him, but I cannot honestly find it within me to say that he *deserves* the sentence he receives. He was just unlucky. He got a raw deal all the way round, right from the start. Looking at the act alone, you say that he deserves what he gets; but can you say that, now that I have shown you that his act was the inevitable outcome of conflicts and rebellions thrust upon his sensitive nature by the intolerable conditions of those early years?

w: Well, I might excuse someone because he was born on the wrong side of the tracks, if there were not so many college presidents who were also born on the wrong side of the tracks. They overcame their disadvantages, and he didn't.

b: But not all the conditions were the same. The college president may have been raised in poverty, but perhaps he had at least parental trust and love to make him a sufficiently adjusted child to live on a fairly normal pattern. Perhaps he had someone outside who helped and trusted him at just the crucial time in his early life; perhaps he didn't have certain congenital defects that the murderer had. It would take a psychiatrist to tell you what the differential factors were, but they were there. I can only agree with Clarence Darrow:

> Back of every murder and back of every human act are sufficient causes that move the human machine beyond their control. . . .
>
> I know what causes the emotional life. I know it comes from the nerves, the muscles, the endocrine glands, the vegetative system. I know it is the most important part of life. I know it is practically left out of some. I know that without it men cannot live. I know that without it they cannot act with the rest. I know they cannot feel what you feel and what I feel; that they cannot feel the moral shocks which come to men who are educated and who have not been deprived of an emotional system or emotional feelings. I know it, and every person who has honestly studied this subject knows it as well. Is Dickie Loeb to blame because out of the infinite forces that conspired to form him, the infinite forces that were at work producing him ages before he was born, that because out of these infinite combinations he was born without it? If he is, then there should be a new definition for justice. Is he to blame for what he did not have and never had? Is he to blame that his machine is imperfect? Who is to blame? I do not know. I have never in my life been interested so much in fixing blame as I have in relieving people from blame. I am not wise enough to fix it.[1]

w: Very moving; but I must still insist on my point. There are people who have overcome early difficulties at least as severe as the murderer's. They

---

[1] C. Darrow, *Attorney for the Damned*, pp. 95, 55.

developed their characters, cultivated the right habits, disciplined themselves, and finally overcame these unfavorable early conditions enough to be accepted as members in a civilized society.

B: Yes, because they had it in them to overcome these difficulties. But not everyone can. A person who has *both* a bad early environment *and* a psychological incapacity to develop enough self-will and discipline to overcome them, is in a bad way. The college president had only the first difficulty, but not the second.

W: But all people have *some* capacity to overcome an unfavorable early environment. It's just that some people *use* these capacities and some don't. Whether they use their capacities is up to them. For not using them they can rightly be blamed.

B: But you still don't see: the psychological *wherewithal* to use the capacities they have is something they either have or they don't; if they don't have this capacity, there is nothing they can do about it. Having such a capacity is like a gift of God, and a far more important gift than a favorable early environment by itself. Because you and I have this capacity (to a considerable extent), we assume that our less fortunate brethren have it too, and we mistakenly blame them when they don't behave according to our standards. It all goes back to the capacities that God or Nature (in the form of heredity and early environment) gave us. If you don't have them, you can't develop them. Whether you have this capacity for self-development is something over which you have no control; psychiatrists tell us that our capacities are determined for us in infancy and early childhood, long before we arrive at what we euphemistically call "years of discretion." That is why, I say, the man does not *deserve* his penalty. Some people are lucky and some are unlucky. Some tin cans become jarred and dented and smashed on the grocer's shelf, and some escape. The dented ones, after they're dented beyond a certain point, can't be used again and have to be thrown away; that is no fault of the cans but of the many external forces that have acted upon them to make them as they are.

W: You mean it's not the fault of the person himself, but of his parents, of society, of those who might have tried to help him and didn't?

B: Precisely.

W: Aha! So somebody deserves something after all — not the child who later commits murder, but his parents, who provided the unfavorable conditions.

B: But the same is true of the parents in turn. It's like the family curse on the house of Atreus — it just goes back and back. The parents did what they did because of early forces that molded them, that worked on the inherited characteristics that they possessed. Because of these circumstances parents are neurotically overanxious, or authoritarian, or negligent, or secretly fascinated by their children's sins. You could blame the grandparents, in part, for what the parents were. But then you would have to go through the same story about the grandparents in turn.

w: So whether the murderer is hanged or sentenced, he still doesn't get what he, personally, deserves? Would you also say that if he becomes fabulously successful by dint of hard work, he doesn't deserve his success either?

b: Of course — that's just the other side of the same coin. It sounds strange, I know, to say he doesn't deserve it; but suppose for instance that he is a driving businessman because he has burning ambition inside of him and he is determined to outdo his successful father. Given these character traits and certain circumstances, he would naturally do what he does. We praise and reward him for it, for we look favorably upon success and want to encourage it; and of course his work may have high utility and we want to increase utility. But just as in the other case, if you delve into the details of how he became successful, you can see that the businessman no more *deserves* his rewards (in comparison to his less fortunate peers who didn't have this combination of characteristics plus these circumstances) than the man who turned out a killer deserves his punishment.

w: It's just a matter of luck, is it?

b: Yes, if you look back into the causes, that's what it is.

w: Do you consider it just luck that you've arrived at the position in life that you have?

b: Of course. One of my college classmates just this year entered a mental hospital, and in spite of repeated shock treatments he will probably be in and out of these hospitals all his life. He has had a severe melancholia for two years now, and nothing can snap him out of it. Psychiatrists know in a general way why it happened — early insecurity, being made to feel guilt in childhood for deeds that were quite innocent, being at one moment praised and the next punished for the same thing, the pressure of conformity to standards he didn't have it in him to conform to — and the inevitable outcome, a masochistic behavior pattern ("If I can't excel in pleasure, I'll excel in pain"). The world was just too much for him to handle with the limited psychological equipment he had at his disposal. I am grateful I don't have a psychological legacy from my early years like that, huge problems and a weak ego, just not enough psychological wherewithal to cope with the complex modern world. Poor fellow, it isn't his fault, he had just as much ability as I. Even during his college career a psychiatrist could have pegged him as a future psycho. Yes, I am just lucky.

w: But look, *you* made use of your capacities. And you did it through sheer hard work when you could have been lazy.

b: Yes, I had the capacity to do hard work, and I also was able (had the capacity) to *use* that capacity under certain circumstances — circumstances which, as it happened, actually did arise in my case (I can do hard work when there is keen competition and the reward is not too distant). But he didn't have those capacities: he didn't have the wherewithal to compete, and anyway his competitive drive was never as strong as mine. But that isn't his fault. He was like a soldier trying to face machine-gun fire with a wooden knife. The world was just too much for him.

w: Well, perhaps if someone had encouraged him at the right time . . .

b: Oh, for heaven's sake! You don't give a pep talk to a man who is trapped under ten tons of steel, saying "Try a little harder, buddy, and you can pull yourself out from under!" Pep talks may help a few people (those who could help themselves anyway), but to say that a case for the psychiatrists could be cured, or even helped, by a pep talk is just the perpetuation of a cruel fallacy. It makes people feel important to do it, and then they can turn around and blame the poor fellow if he doesn't wriggle out of the difficulty afterwards. It's time that we put such ignorant, medieval superstition behind us.

w: Perhaps. For the sake of the argument I will admit everything you say about the psychiatric cases you cite. Let us say they were all compelled to do as they did and are not morally responsible, at least not until after their condition has been corrected through therapy. But it's one thing to say that, and another thing to say that *none* of us is responsible for any of our actions. This seems to me to be plainly absurd. Of course we are responsible — most people are, for most of their actions, most of the time. You take a few cases from abnormal-psychology books and you apply the conclusions drawn from these cases to everybody at all times.

b: I only took the psychiatric cases because the conclusions there were so clear. But I hold that the same conclusions apply to all of us: that we are all what our heredity and environment make us, leading us through a long and complex chain of causation to do the things we do and think the things we think. Some of the influences on us, of course, include our conscious will; but our conscious will itself was made what it was by circumstances outside it. Given the circumstances in which he found himself, the psychotic murderer could do only what he in fact did; and given the circumstances in which you and I find ourselves, we can do only what we in fact do.

w: I don't follow you at all. You cite facts about inner compulsion, which apply to certain psychiatric cases. I ask you why the psychiatric cases should be extended to include all of us, and instead of answering my question you tell me things, not about compulsion, but about *causation:* you tell me that all our acts are caused. And this I don't deny. I just don't see what causation has to do with your talk about compulsion which was the original basis of your argument.

There is clearly a tangle here which we must try to unsnarl. Apparently we cannot put it off any longer: we must discuss the doctrine that has traditionally gone by the name of "determinism" and see what implications it has for moral responsibility.

A. Determinism

The philosophical doctrine called "determinism" is not always stated in the same way, and every way of stating it is fraught with pitfalls and mis-interpretations which will be extremely likely to entrap us when we apply this doctrine to ethics. It is most important, therefore, to proceed carefully in every step of our discussion.

1. In its simplest form, determinism merely says, "Everything that happens (every event) has a cause." We may not know what the cause is, and we may never find it, but it has one. Put in this way, one may well wonder how such a view ever got mixed up with discussions of ethics. What has ethics to do with such a purely scientific question as the causality of events?

Well, if everything that happens is caused, then every human act is caused, every desire, every thought, everything we ever do or think or feel. But somone may still remark, "So what? How does this principle affect ethics?" But if every human thought and act is caused, someone else may reply, "How can we be *free* to do anything? How can we help doing whatever it is we do? Doesn't ought imply can, and *can* we ever do otherwise than we actually do?" Here then is the connection, or alleged connection between causation and ethics; we shall explore it shortly.

2. Instead of the word "caused," some people use the word "determined" and state the view thus: "Everything that happens is determined." Put in this way it seems even more dangerous for ethics — for if everything that happens is determined to happen before it happens, what place is there left for human action, human choice, human volition? We shall have to analyze the unfortunate word "determined."

3. A more precise way of putting the doctrine is, "For every event in the universe, there is a set of conditions such that if the conditions were repeated, the event would be repeated." This formulation does not mention the word "cause," but attempts to define it. According to this formulation, if I now do some act, A, there were certain conditions preceding its occurrence which, if they were all to occur again exactly as before, would be followed by A exactly as before. Doubtless the conditions will never be exactly the same again; but this fact, of course, does not in any way count against the proposition that *if* they were to recur, the event in question would recur. Here the student of ethics may remark, "Now I see the connection! If the conditions were to be repeated exactly, then I'd do the same thing again — how could I *help* doing it?"

4. A still different way of putting it would be: "Everything that happens is an instance of some law (or laws) such that if *all* the laws of which this event is an instance were known and if all the states or conditions at any one moment (what physicists call the 'initial conditions') were known, then the event could be predicted." For example, we know the relative positions and velocities of all the planets in the solar system, and we know

the laws of their motion; from this knowledge we can predict exactly where they will be at any future time. Again, the apparent application to ethics is obvious: If everything I do can be predicted (at least in theory), in what sense can it be said that I am free to do it? If you, having this perfect knowledge of my nature and my environment, can predict everything I will do and say, how can you say that I do it freely? and if I don't do it freely, how can anyone be justified in praising or blaming me?

Some philosophers would prefer to state determinism exclusively in this last way, but one might question whether they are putting the cart before the horse. It would seem that predictability is the consequence of determinism rather than its meaning. If every event is predictable, it is so only because every event is caused by a uniform set of conditions; because, and only because, of this fact, someone who knew all the laws would be able to predict. Complete predictability would be impossible without determinism, but there might be determinism without complete predictability, for instance, if we were ignorant of some or all of the laws.

Such, then, are the alleged implications of determinism for ethics. Instead of going into a laborious investigation of whether determinism is true, an investigation which may turn out to be unnecessary if determinism does not have the alleged implications for ethics, let us ask first, "*Suppose* that it is true, what then? Does determinism have the consequences for ethics which many people fear?" Let us first, then, try to be quite clear about what determinism does and does not commit us to. There is a whole nest of popular fallacies and confusions connected with it, which turn up with monotonous regularity every time that determinism is discussed by people who have not studied very much philosophy. Here are the main ones:

1. "Isn't determinism the same as *fatalism?* Doesn't it say that every event is caused by conditions outside our control?"

Determinism is not fatalism. Determinism does not say that every event is caused by conditions outside our control but only that every event is caused; and causation is quite compatible with some causes being *ourselves* — our decisions, our acts of willing, our desires to do this or that. Eclipses occur outside our control, and there is nothing we can do about them; but whether you befriend someone in need depends on some conditions which are very much within your control, namely your voluntary decision as to whether to help him or not. (Of course if, as you start to help him, you suffer a paralytic stroke, then helping him is *not* in your control.) Your helping the person has causes, all right, but at least one of those causal factors is *you* — your decision to do it. If you hadn't decided to do it you wouldn't be doing it. Everything is caused, but some things are caused by you and through you. Determinism is committed only to the rather vanilla-flavored proposition that everything that occurs depends for that occurrence on a set of causal factors; it makes no assertion about what *specifically* those causes are. They may be physical, they may be mental or spiritual; they may be stones or suns, they may be people, or animals, or God.

2. "Doesn't determinism mean that everything is determined *in spite of* us, that somehow it *has* to happen, that the forces of nature *compel* it to happen?"

The word "determinism" is extremely misleading because it is associated with a whole set of verbs like "compel," "make," "force," "determine." If people take these verbs only as synonyms of the verb "cause," no harm is done. But people usually read into them far more than that. They seize upon the unfortunate word "determinism" — "universal causality" would have been a far less misleading term to use — and arrive at conclusions like that above. No such conclusion is warranted by the simple premise that everything has a cause.

As we saw in the preceding section, circumstances may "compel" you to do what you don't want to do (jettison the cargo), other agents may compel you to do what you don't want to do (by force or strong persuasion), and you yourself through "inner compulsion" may do things you would never dream of doing otherwise. But compulsion is not the same thing as *causation*. Suppose that I am given the choice between a vacation in June and a vacation in August, and I think it over for several weeks, listing the advantages and disadvantages of both alternatives, and finally I decide in favor of June. Doubtless my decision was caused (would anyone wish to deny it?), else my long process of reflection on the alternatives would be pointless. But was it compelled? Circumstances did not compel me, outside agents did not compel me, and as far as I know no inner compulsion was at work in me unknown to my conscious will causing me to do the one rather than the other. If I weren't sure about inner compulsion, I could get expert psychiatric opinion on this point. If all the evidence for inner compulsion was negative, how could the person back up his claim that in spite of all this reflection my act of choice was still compelled?

3. "But if every event, including my acts, is governed or controlled by laws of nature, how can I freely choose anything?"

But my behavior is not governed or controlled by laws of nature. To say so is to be guilty of a confusion between two senses of the ambiguous word "law." A statute law, such as is passed by Congress, prescribes that we shall do certain things under threat of certain penalties if we do not. But a law of nature is not like this. It prescribes nothing, it only *describes* the behavior of things and events in the universe. Matter does not *obey* laws of gravitation; the law of gravitation is a description of how particles of matter *do* move. They are not compelled to move, they *do* move in certain ways; and since this way is uniform, it can be stated in a law, which is simply a statement of uniformity. The laws of motion do not force the planets to move, under threat of prison sentences if they disobey. The notion of obeying laws, violating laws, defying laws, applies only to the other kind of law, statute

law. Exactly the same considerations apply to laws of human nature —
though at the present moment psychology can hardly be said to have these.
If a law of psychology said, "Whenever people in circumstances C do A,
then they always do B" and you were in circumstances C and did A but
then didn't do B, the law would be mistaken. The law would then be a
false description of the world, for it would not cover all situations.

4. "But even if laws of nature don't govern our behavior, isn't it still true
that, according to determinism, every event is caused? How is causality
compatible with freedom?"

This statement again is a confusion. As we daily use the term "free," we
do not distinguish free from unfree acts on the basis of whether they are
caused. To vary the example a bit, when I decide to go to the Grand Tetons
rather than to the Great Smokies for a vacation, I decide freely in the sense
that nobody forces me to do the one rather than the other. I weigh the
alternatives carefully and then I make my decision. If this is not free choice,
what is? Doubtless it was *caused* — it was caused by all sorts of considerations: a comparison of the scenic beauties of the two regions, a perusal of
the road maps, the wish for temporary isolation, the reflection that I have
already been to the Smokies but not to the Grand Tetons. But the fact that
my choice was caused in no way prevents it from being a *free* choice. When
a choice is *not* free, it is still caused, but it is caused in spite of me and not
as a result of my own decision. When the gunman forces me to pull the
trigger, I do not have a choice of alternatives. When the judge wants to determine whether the defendant did the deed of his own free will, he is not
trying to decide whether the act was caused; he probably assumes that it
was. He is trying to find out whether a certain *kind* of cause — coercion,
compulsion — was being exerted on the defendant in connection with the
act in question. Since that kind of cause is not operative in all situations,
some choices are free.

5. "If determinism is true, how could I help or avoid doing what I do?"

Often you can, even if determinism is true. You could have avoided having an explosion in your face if you had put a match to the oven the moment you turned on the gas. You could have avoided being fined if you
had not driven so fast. You could have avoided the doctor's verdict if you
had gone to see him sooner. Doubtless, according to determinism, there are
causes why you didn't do these things, and if you *had* done them there
would have been causes for that too. But this causation in no way commits
you to saying that you couldn't *help* doing them. Some things you can help
(like eating candy) and some things you can't (like fainting). Whether you
can or can't help the event in question has nothing to do with *whether* it
was caused but with *what kind* of cause it had. Some causes lie within your
control and some don't.

6. "But if determinism is true, can I ever truly say that I *could* have done
anything other than what I *did*? My act was preceded by a whole set of

causes. Those causes being what they were, they inevitably led up to my doing what I did. But in that event how could I have done differently, those causes being just what they were?"

Again there is a confusion. You *could* have, for "I could have done X" means roughly "I *would* have done X *if* I had decided to do it." For instance, I could have gone to the beach today, if I had decided to go there instead of coming to my classes. I didn't, but I could have. And I *can* stop talking to you now, though I am not doing so. If you think I can't, I'll prove to you that I can by walking out of the room without another word. To say that I *can* do something, or that I *could* have done something that I didn't actually do, does not in any way deny that whatever I *did* was preceded by a set of causes. It implies only that what I did was (at least in part) the result of my own decision — in other words, my decision was a causal factor in the event's occurring. I could have gone elsewhere today; that is, I would have if I had so decided. But I could not have turned myself into a cow: that is, this event would not occur no matter what I decided. In daily life we have no trouble with "can" and "could" words: we say, "I could have done it" if it was physically and psychologically possible for us to do it; and whether it was or wasn't is an empirical matter open to empirical investigation. If I actually do something, my action is conclusive proof that I *can* do it; but if my life depends on my doing something, if I try as hard as I can to do it and I still cannot succeed, my failure is good evidence that I *can't* do it. Such is the context in which the words "can" and "could" have application to the world. (Someone who says that I can't do other than I do faces a difficulty similar to the person who says I am always compelled. What does he mean by "can't"? Not what we ordinarily mean by it, surely, for I can show him that there are many things that I *can* do. But if he doesn't accept that meaning, what meaning *is* he attaching to the word? Is he just playing around with words to produce startling philosophical conclusions?)

But our questioner may still not be satisfied. "I still say you *couldn't* have done any other than what you did, in view of the *total* circumstances or conditions that led you to do it. I agree of course that you could have done something other than what you did, if some of the circumstances had been different. But could you have done anything other than you did if *all* the circumstances had been the same?"

This is the stock argument of the amateur determinist. But he does not realize that his question contradicts itself. We can answer him as follows: "To say that I *could* have done something different is to say that I *would* have done something different if I had decided to do so. And if I *had* decided to do so, then one of the conditions *would* have been different, and so the specification in the question (that *all* the conditions be the same) is not met. Your decision is certainly one of the conditions upon which the act depends; and if that had been different, your act would have been different."

"I see your point," the amateur determinist may say: "if your decision had been different, it would have changed one of the conditions on which the act depends. But now let me ask, not could, but *would* you have done differently if all the conditions had been the same?"

"*All* the conditions — including my decision?" we ask. "If everything, including my decision, were to be the same, then I suppose I *would* do the same. At least, that is what the true determinist would say. But what else would you want? For me to do one thing after I had decided to do something else?"

"So the determinist does say that much. And now: is what he says true?" the amateur determinist goes on.

"Ah — that's another question," we reply. "I've only tried to show that if what he says is true, it doesn't have the catastrophic consequences that you first thought. Whether it *is* true — nobody knows, I guess. Everything that happens, ever has happened, and ever will happen — that's a pretty big order. Who can say? I can only say that as far as ethics is concerned, I don't care."

"But if a person couldn't have — excuse me, wouldn't have — done differently if all the conditions had been the same . . ."

"That is what the true determinist says, but now I want to remind you how empty that statement is. For if the person *had* acted differently all the same, then at once we would say that one or more of the conditions leading up to it *was* different after all — and we would say this a priori, before trying to discover the difference in the causes; and we would continue to say it even though we never did find that difference."

"So it's an a priori truth, then?" the amateur determinist concludes.

"Perhaps. I am more inclined, however, to say that the deterministic principle is not a truth at all, nor a falsehood either, but a *rule* or guiding principle of scientific procedure. But that is no concern of ours now." [1]

B. Free will

With these confusions and ambiguities out of the way, let us approach once again the problem of free will.

If a person says, "Nobody is ever free," the first consideration that suggests itself is, "Free from what?" To be free from something implies some restraint from which one is free. Free from political oppression? free from economic exploitation? free from financial difficulties? free from the need of buying automobile insurance?

But the person who says that *nobody* ever is free can hardly be saying that we are never free from these things. He would have to admit the em-

[1] This position is developed in some detail in Chapter 4, especially pp. 249-62, in *Introduction to Philosophical Analysis*, by John Hospers (Englewood Cliffs, N, J,: Prentice-Hall, 1953).

pirical fact that sometimes, at least, people are free from these restraints, just as sometimes they are not.

Perhaps then he means to say, "One is never free to act in accordance with one's choices." Yet if this is what he means, what he says is plainly false. Although I am not free to do whatever I may please (such as jump over the moon), I am free to do some things, for when I choose to do them I do them. I can sit down or get up or walk about; I can have fish or chicken or beef for dinner, whichever I choose. True, my freedom is limited: I can't have steak if I lack the money, and I can't watch a certain movie if it isn't playing anywhere at the moment. I can't do what is logically impossible, like draw a square circle; I can't do what is empirically impossible, such as going faster than light; I can't do what is technically impossible, such as take a rocket ship to Mars this evening. All these restraints limit my actions. But within those limits, there are many things I am free to do — that is, I can do them if I choose to do them, and I am also free to refrain if I decide upon that. So this interpretation too can hardly be meant seriously by the person who denies that people are ever free.

Perhaps, however, the person is saying not that we aren't free to act as we choose but that we are not free to choose one thing rather than another. "We have freedom to *act* in accordance with our choices, but not freedom to *choose*." But to choose in accordance with — what? What does it mean, "not free to choose"? "I mean not free to choose in accordance with our desires," he replies. But this interpretation is simply false: I desire more light, I choose to turn on the light, I do turn on the light. People often do choose in accordance with their desires; they don't always, of course, but sometimes, as in the above example, they do. Often we choose between what we desire (sleep) and what we feel we ought to do (help a friend in need), and sometimes we choose one and sometimes the other. So don't we have freedom of choice?

But the person will object that this view is still not what he means. "We can act in accordance with our choices or decisions," he will say, "and we can choose in accordance with our desires. But we are not free to *desire*. We can choose as we please, but we can't please as we please. If my biological or psychological nature is such that at a certain moment I desire A, I shall choose A, and if it is such that I desire B, I shall choose B. I am free to *choose* either A or B, but I am not free to *desire* either A or B. Moreover, my desires are not themselves the outcomes of choices, for I cannot choose to have them or not to have them."

What can one say about this view? It is true, of course, that people are often victims of inner urges and desires they do not wish to have and from which they find it difficult to escape: a man may have a strong desire for alcohol and wish that he did not desire it so much. Nevertheless, to a very **limited** extent (varying considerably from person to person) and *over a* *considerable span of time,* we *are* free to desire or not to desire. We can choose to do our best to get rid of certain desires and to encourage other ones; and to a limited extent we may be successful in this endeavor. People who greatly desire alcohol, sometimes succeed, by joining Alcoholics Anonymous or by other means, in resisting the temptation to drink until finally they no longer desire it. So it is not true that we are *never* free to desire or that we are always the victims of whatever desires we happen to have.

What, more than this limitation, does out objector want? Perhaps he regrets that people's desires are not more directly under their control. We may agree that this lack of control is indeed regrettable: if more people were able to desire the welfare of others instead of their own welfare, the world would be a better place. But at least the contention that nobody ever has control over his desires has been refuted. We are able, within severe limits, to control many of our desires, and even in the course of time to change them. (Would our objector like it better if we acted *contrary* to our desires — if we desired A and found ourselves doing B instead, or desired B and found ourselves doing A? As things are, we can often desire A and as a consequence do A; what more freedom than this does he demand?)

But he may even yet not be content. "I grant," he may say, "that we can act in accordance with our desires and that to a limited extent we can sometimes change the course of our desires. But when we do change our desires, say for alcohol, we do it in accordance with *another* desire — our desire *not* to desire alcohol. We are free to desire some things and to change our desires to some extent, but we are not free in what we desire to desire." What does our objector want now? He admits that he is free to choose A rather than B in accordance with his desires and that he is sometimes even free to desire A rather than B (that is, he can sometimes do so by trying). Now he wants not only this freedom but also the freedom to desire to desire A rather than B. Let us say that he desires Cadillacs, but he desires (wants) to desire Chevrolets — it would be so much easier on his pocketbook if he did desire Chevrolets. But now suppose that, whatever this freedom would come to, we granted it to him; would he then be content? No, he would then want the freedom to desire to desire to desire, and so on. What kind of game is this? Once he is free to choose some things rather than others and even to desire some things rather than the things he now desires, isn't this all the freedom that he or anyone else could want? His worse self desires alcohol, his better self desires not to desire it; but how many selves-within-a-self does he want? How long does he want to peel the onion? Isn't he assuming that there is, beneath or behind one self, another "more real" or "more basic" self that has different desires? And isn't this "more basic" self just as much of a myth as the core of an onion — just as after you have peeled it for a while there is literally *nothing* left, since the onion just *is* its various peelings? The simple fact is that his actions are alterable by his choices, his choices are alterable by his desires, and even his desires are to some extent alterable by other desires. Isn't this freedom enough? What more than this can legitimately, or even meaningfully, be demanded?

Perhaps we can present what we mean by freedom in a somewhat different way.

(1) Sometimes we choose to do something, and something interferes to prevent us from doing it: we decide to vote for Mr. X and we suddenly become ill, preventing us from acting in accordance with our decision. This accident interferes with our freedom of *action,* that is, our freedom to act in accordance with our decisions.

(2) Sometimes we desire something and are prevented from choosing it, as when we want to vote for Mr. X but the ruling dictatorship prevents us from even having the choice because it prohibits free elections. This circumstance interferes with our freedom of *choice.*

(3) But still a third limitation of our freedom can be described: imagine the masses in a downtrodden country who are fed only the news the government wants them to have. Not that they are denied the vote — they are not prevented from fulfilling their desires the way they would be if the government forcibly prevented them from registering their opinions. They vote for whomever they want, but *what* they want has been determined for them through misinformation and censorship and such clever slanting of information that the people don't even know that what they're getting is falsehood and distortion. They are free to do what they want, but what they want has been decided for them without their knowing it. The chains are not on their actions, or on their decisions to act, but upon the desires which lead them to make the decisions. Would we describe such a people as free? Certainly not. The system under which they live interferes with their freedom to *desire.*

The kind of freedom one lacks, then, varies with the level at which the interference takes place. Nevertheless, on each of these levels, people are *sometimes* free: not always does something interfere between the decision and the act, or between the desire and the decision, or betwen the desires one would have if uninterfered with and the desires one actually has. Human freedom is limited — this is surely no news; but it is not *always* interfered with. Show me a situation in which it is, and I can show you a situation in which it isn't. Thus it is still false to say that nobody is *ever* free: people are, within limits, free to act, free to choose, and even free to desire.

C. Indeterminism

Our objector, however, may still not be satisfied. "I understand your analysis," he may say, "but what bothers me has not yet been discussed in your analysis. Consider this statement: if the causal principle (determinism) is true, then all my desires are caused. No matter what I do, no matter what I desire, it stems from causes — some immediate, some dating way back into my infancy and even before that. What I want, then, is freedom *from causality itself.*"

"Aha!" we reply. "I thought we would come to that sooner or later. You want indeterminism, or, as it is sometimes called, libertarianism. Let's first try to see whether what you want is desirable — whether you will still want it after you see through its implications. I doubt that you will. When parents train children, they are trying to *cause* certain changes in their children's behavior; if they thought for a moment that the children's actions were *un*caused, they might as well give up trying. The same is true when we try to reform the wayward: to reform is to cause a change in the other person; and to the extent that the other person's actions are uncaused, to that extent attempts at reformation are useless. (Often they are useless anyway, but that's only because our actions don't cause in people the responses we want.) Or take someone whom you've trusted all your life; you have never known him to violate any confidence; so naturally you trust him again. Suppose such a friend were to be seized by an attack of 'free will,' in the sense you now want; his actions, suddenly, are not caused by anything at all — not by his background, his habits, or his character as thus far developed. Then, I suppose, anything would be equally likely; at least you would no longer have the assurance that his habits of honesty hitherto developed would *cause* him to be honest at this time; for *ex hypothesi* his actions would now be uncaused. Good heavens! would you really want something like that? What we want is that people's actions should be caused not from the outside but from *within* them, by their whole character. Would you really want them not to be caused by anything at all?"

"I grant that causation operates in 99 per cent or more of human behavior," the objector goes on.

. . . We all realize that formed character has a great deal to do with the choices that we make; and formed character is, without a doubt, partly dependent on the external factors of heredity and environment. . . . No one denies that it determines, at least largely, what things we desire, and again how greatly we desire them. It may thus fairly be said to determine the felt balance of desires in the situation of moral temptation. But all that that amounts to is that formed character prescribes the nature of the situation *within* which the act of moral decision takes place. It does not in the least follow that it has any influence whatsoever in determining the act of decision itself — the decision as to whether we shall exert effort or take the easy course of following the bent of our desiring nature. . . . The agent . . . through his act of decision can oppose and transcend his own formed character in the interest of duty.[1]

"You see, I am only contending that in comparatively rare situations — rare enough not to disrupt at all the regular course of causality in the world —

[1] C. A. Campbell, "In Defense of Free Will," in Milton Munitz, ed., *Ethics* (Chicago: Free Press, 1959), p. 381.

there *is* such a thing as transcending one's character, of going above and beyond (so to speak) the course of causal influences as they have been operating on the person up to that time. This transcendence occurs, I think, in situations of moral crisis, when desire sways the person one way and duty another. In such situations I cannot find it within me to say that the person's act is simply the result of the causal influences operating on him up to that moment — the line of least resistance, as it were. Transcendence occurs, for example, when a bad man makes a sudden heroic move for which there is no basis in his background or character up to that point; perhaps it happened when St. Paul was converted."

"But I am afraid you are guilty of a confusion," we warn. "Don't confuse 'causality' with 'the line of least resistance.' I grant perfectly well that people *don't* always take the 'line of least resistance' (unless that phrase is *defined* in terms of what people actually do, and then it is a tautology to say it). But when they don't do the easiest thing (take the line of least resistance), as sometimes happens, then surely the fact that they don't is *caused* by something. There was *something* in them that caused them to take the sudden heroic move, even when that move was contrary to the *general trend* of that person's character as thus far expressed in his actions and could not have been predicted except perhaps by someone who knew him through and through (such as his psychiatrist). It may even have been God working in him, but then God was the cause. When St. Paul was suddenly converted to Christianity after a life of persecuting the Christians, I don't say that he was taking the line of least resistance, and certainly his act was not similar to his previous actions; but I am sure that it was caused by *something*. He was the kind of man who stuck to his convictions uncompromisingly, no matter how difficult; when he had a conviction, he shaped his actions accordingly, caring nothing for opposition or persecution. Probably he was also the kind of man who, though well disciplined, was temperamentally given to sudden changes or traumatic experiences; I don't know, but I think a trained psychiatrist could have told us. But whatever the causal factors, and they were many and deep-seated, surely what happened *was* caused. In fact, you want to praise him for his deed, don't you, and admire him for the courage and intensity with which he acted on his new belief? Or perhaps not — perhaps you want to condemn him. But *either* way, you presuppose the causality of his actions. If his action was uncaused, you could hardly admire *or* condemn him for it, for then it didn't spring from *his* character, and it had no more to do with *him* than if he had been struck by lightning. (Perhaps he was — divine lightning; but then it was God's act, not his.) No, if you have to start explaining moral triumphs by making them causeless, you cut yourself off from the only possible basis for praising the person for them. Freedom is not the opponent of determinism, but the other side of the same coin. Determinism says: 'My acts are caused — caused by *me*.'

Freedom says, '*I* cause my acts. If I did not cause my acts, then I am not their author, and I deserve neither praise nor blame for them.'"

D. *Final distinctions*

The mention of deserts brings us back once again to the subject we left on page 501 to enter upon a discussion of determinism and free will. After all these arguments and counterarguments, explanations, and distinctions, what can we now say about responsibility and desert? Is there any way to resolve the issue between our two disputants? Our objector, we may remember, did not talk about causality or free will at all; he was using moral terms, "responsibility" and "desert." He said that people are never, in the final analysis, responsible for their actions; and that, while we are justified in praising and blaming because of their (occasional) practical utility, we are never justified in saying that a person *deserves* what he gets (or what he doesn't get), because a complete knowledge of the causal antecedents of his act shows the act to have been *inevitable,* given the exact circumstances of the action. What can we now say about this position?

We can attempt to show that there is a recurring pattern of confusion running through the arguments we have considered. What has been happening is this: the disputant has used terms which, though often vague, have a definite meaning *within a certain context,* and he has then used them *outside that context,* assuming that they nevertheless had the same meaning as before. There are many examples of this confusion in daily life: People say, "This subject is interesting to you, but not to me," a statement which has a perfectly intelligible meaning ("It interests you, but it doesn't interest me"). But they assume without question that it is meaningful to say "This statement is true for you, but not for me." (See pages 161-62.) The moral judgments we make in daily life — "He *can* do it," "He did it *freely,*" "He is responsible" — are thoroughly embedded in the context of human *conduct,* and they all mark genuine distinctions within that context. Let us see what happens to the crucial terms in these judgments when they are pushed out of that context and used nevertheless.

1. We have already seen what happens with "can" and "could." "I *can* lift two hundred pounds" — that is, if I choose to, and try, I shall. The statement may not be *true* — I may try and yet fail — but at least we have no doubt what it *means* to say it. The same with "I *can* stop desiring alcohol" — that is, if I choose to, and try, I shall stop desiring it. But if someone (an amateur determinist who has not understood the distinctions presented on pages 503-10) comes along and says, "A person can't ever do anything other than what he does," in the usual meaning this statement is plainly false: I am standing still, but I *can* walk, and if you think I can't I'll show you. "But you *couldn't* have walked at that moment" the amateur determinist protests; "being just what you were at that moment, the product of all the forces playing on you up till just then, you *could* have done only what you

were doing, namely standing still." But what does "couldn't" mean here? It means "wouldn't, even if I chose to (and, sometimes, tried)." But if I had chosen to, I *would* have walked — does the objector wish to deny this? "You couldn't have done this" invites the reply "No? not even if I decided to?" and if I had decided to, I would have. It is true, of course, that my deciding to do it changes the causal conditions on which the action depends; without the decision, the act wouldn't have been performed, and with it, it is. "But that's what I mean!" the objector exclaims! "you *couldn't* have done it if even one of the causal conditions had been different!" But now the objector has put his foot in it, and his assertion has become nonsensical; for "couldn't" here implies a reference to a choice or decision; if there had been a different choice, the result *would* have been different, and the objector can no longer insist that *all* the conditions were the same. His assertion has become self-contradictory: it is self-contradictory to say "I couldn't have done it if all the causal conditions had been the same," for this means "I *wouldn't* have done it *if* all the causal conditions had been the same *if* one of the causal conditions had been different (namely my decision)." The two if's contradict each other.

We see, then, to what a pass the objector has come if he pushes his "couldn't" outside the context in which alone the expression has its meaning. (If, now, the objector says, "You could have done it if you'd chosen, but you couldn't have *chosen* to," we must go through the whole process again. See pages 506-07.)

2. The statement "What happened was *inevitable*" has a perfectly intelligible meaning in daily discourse: it was *unavoidable* — that is, we could not have avoided it however hard we tried. If someone says, *"Everything that happens is inevitable,"* taken in this meaning the assertion is plainly false: there are many things we can avoid by trying to — we can avoid being run over by a passing car by looking in both directions before we cross the street. "But this isn't what I mean," the objector persists; "I mean that every human act is inevitable, *given* exactly the circumstances that led up to it." But does he mean to include among these circumstances the fact that we try (or don't try) to avoid the thing in question? If so, his allegation is once again self-contradictory: if he says that some event which we did not try to avoid, was unavoidable, he is saying that it is unavoidable, given the exact circumstances (including our *not* trying), *even if we do try.* "Inevitable" ("unavoidable") implies a reference to trying, and this reference cannot be removed in the next breath without negating the meaning of the whole expression.

3. The statement "He did it *freely*" implies that his doing it (or deciding to do it, or desiring it) occurred partly as the result of his choice. If he chose to do it, his *act* was free. But was his *choice* free? Yes, if it sprang from his desires and was not coerced by threats and propaganda. But was his *desire* free? (Remember the conditioned subjects of the dictatorship who

genuinely desire what the rulers want them to desire.) Yes, if he desired what he *would* have desired if he had had full information about the subject in question. But was his desire to desire free? and his desire to desire to desire? But here once again the term "free" has lost its meaning, because it has been ripped from its context. We might say, "Show me what you mean by your request, and I'll show you an instance of free action. If you can't even describe what it would be like for an act (or desire) to be free, then I deny that your demand has any meaning, for you don't even know what you are demanding." A person might say, "We are not free, for we are human beings, chained to human wants and needs and desires; only gods are free." We would then have to explore what was involved in the use of the word "free" as applied to the gods. His assertion might well have a meaning, but at least it would have a *different* meaning from what it has with regard to human beings. Ordinarily when we talk about freedom we mean the kind of freedom of which *human* beings are capable, such as acting in accordance with their choices, choosing in accordance with their desires, and desiring in accordance with some standard like "more adequate information" or their "better" nature.

4. Consider the following: "I grant that an act is free if it is not *compelled,* but no act is ever uncompelled. All acts are compelled by the person's inherited characteristics, environment, temperament, . . etc." But in any ordinary sense of "compelled," these statements simply are not true. The ice pick murderer was compelled to do as he did because of certain circumstances over which he had no control, but these circumstances are precisely what made him psychotic. Not even a psychiatrist, who knows more about compelled behavior patterns than anyone else, would say that *all* human actions (including his own in making the judgment) are compelled. If in lecturing I walk toward the window, and no one made me do it, no one threatened me or even persuaded me against my will, and no inner compulsion was at work in me (and a psychiatrist might testify to this), then my act *was* uncompelled. Why assume that it must always be compelled? If the presence of certain circumstances A, B, C makes an act compelled, then the absence of these circumstances makes it uncompelled. The evidence suggests that there are thousands of compelled acts and thousands of uncompelled ones. They are caused, of course — caused, some of them, by my decision — but they were not compelled by any one or any thing. Let us not once more confuse causality with compulsion; compulsion is only one very special *kind* of causal influence. All compelled acts are caused, but not all caused acts are compelled.

Here the objector to free will picks up the argument. "But we *are* compelled, in the sense that, the circumstances being just what they were, we *couldn't help* doing what we did. We couldn't help doing what we did, deciding what we did decide, desiring what we did desire." "But 'couldn't help,'" we reply, "requires scrutiny. Ordinarily it means that we couldn't avoid it (whatever it was) even if we tried. But there are plenty of things we *could* have helped: we could have helped hitting the pedestrian if we'd been more careful in driving, we could have helped making the unfortunate decision if we'd thought about it a bit longer, we could even have helped desiring alcohol by trying over a period of time. We need not deny that our trying or not trying itself had causes; but once again 'caused' is not the same as 'compelled.' "

"Caused by you, yes; but *you* were caused," the objector goes on. "You are what you are because of factors beyond your control." "I beg your pardon," we reply. "I am what I am *partly* because of what I've made myself, through effort and self-discipline." "Yes," agrees the objector, "but your capacity to exert effort and self-discipline was not created by you but was a part of your natural endowment." "Yes, but I *used* that capacity, and some people don't." "But the fact that you used that capacity while others didn't," continues the objector, " — indeed, your capacity to use the capacities you were born with — is itself the result of causal circumstances having nothing to do with your conscious will. Anyway, you didn't create your will (and its capacities) — it is the product of forces outside you. You didn't originate your own character." "But in part I did — my character was *formed* by me. I certainly had something to do with the character traits I have now." "Yes I know, but you didn't cause your *original* traits, predispositions, and capacities, as a result of which your present character was formed." "All this is true enough," we conclude. "I did not cause my character — at least not my *original* character. But just try to imagine *what the opposite assertion would mean.* What would it be like to be the cause of my own character? To cause my original make-up, I must first have existed, and to exist I must already *have* some 'original make-up.' I can't cause myself unless I'm already there to do the causing. And if I already existed, then it wouldn't be my original make-up I was creating or choosing, and then where did I get the features or make-up which led me to choose the make-up which I chose? To choose a character, we must already *have* a character. Being the cause of our own original make-up is, we see, a self-contradictory notion. Once again we have pushed words outside their context and thus devoided them of meaning. In short: 'I am the cause of my *actions*' makes perfectly good sense, but 'I am the cause of my own original make-up' does not."

5. Let us look at the statement "Since you are not the cause of your original character or make-up, you are never *responsible* for any of your acts." But this is a *non sequitur.* If I had to be the cause of my original character in order to be responsible for my acts, what would it be like to be responsible? what actual or possible situation would it describe? And what then would the term "responsibility" refer to?

"I am responsible for this act, for I did it voluntarily and in full knowledge of the consequences . . ." makes perfectly good sense; so does "I am nót responsible for this act because I did it under compulsion (torture, threats, irresistible impulse)." But what about "I am not responsible for this act, your honor, because I am not the author of my original make-up"? (Again, what *would* it be like to be the author of one's own original make-up?) The word "responsible" has a perfectly intelligible meaning in the context of human conduct. But if being responsible is made to imply being the author of one's original make-up, then it involves (as we have seen) a contradiction. To such a pass, once again, we have come when we try to use a word whose meaning implies a certain context, and then proceed to remove the context.

Here is another instance of using words out of context. "In the *ordinary* sense, I admit, people are responsible. For instance, the teacher holds his students responsible for being at the exam at the specified time. But in the *ultimate* sense no one is responsible." There are, to be sure, ordinary and extraordinary senses of words, but what *is* the "ultimate" sense of "responsibility"? Being the author of one's own character? But this sense involves a contradiction as we just saw. We *do* hold people responsible for actions within their control (in the way we have described). They cannot achieve perfection, and some of them cannot even achieve a modicum of goodness, nor do we hold them responsible for failure if they are truly unable; but we do hold them responsible for *trying* the best they can. A man can do no more than try to the best of his ability; but he can be held responsible for doing less.

6. The most difficult of all these concepts remains that of *desert*. A resumption of the dialogue on page 501 will present both main points of view, after which the reader can make up his own mind.

BLACK: I still think that people don't deserve what they get.

WHITE: Sometimes they don't, I admit. Some victims of inner compulsion are executed for acts which they couldn't help performing. They were more sinned against than sinning.

B: I know, but I mean that *nobody* ever gets what he deserves.

W: This I deny. Doesn't a person who worked harder than anyone else for the first prize, and who has more ability besides, deserve the prize if he gets it?

B: No, he had more ability than the others, and they can't help it if they had less.

W: But he also worked harder. Doesn't he deserve it at least for that?

B: It seems so at first, yes; but he had, in addition to the talent, the *ability* to work hard; others didn't. Moreover, the circumstances were such that he could *use* this ability; for the others these circumstances were not so fortunate. So he doesn't actually deserve the prize — he's just lucky.

W: Luck has to do with things *outside* one's control, such as native ability and favorable environmental circumstances. (Who knows if our prize winner had favorable environmental circumstances? He might have had unfavorable ones and still surpassed those with more favorable ones. For this achievement, I'd say, he deserves even more credit.) But when it is not these outside things but one's own *work* that we are concerned with, we are concerned *not* with a matter of luck but of labor. Otherwise I don't know what in the world you mean by "luck."

B: All right. But I still say he doesn't deserve it — not that someone else *did* deserve it, but that nobody ever gets what he deserves.

W: This sounds puzzling to me. Are you making a statement about the injustice of the world — that one person deserves A but gets B, while another person deserves B but gets A? Do you mean that actual reward or punishment is always misplaced with respect to desert?

B: No, that's not what I mean; for if I did, I'd be saying that people *do* have deserts after all, only the deserts are misplaced. No, what I'm saying is more radical than that. I don't say that people have deserts but don't get them, I say rather that there are no deserts — period. The whole concept, or so-called concept, of desert is a snare and a delusion. I agree that there are processes of blaming and praising and punishing and rewarding, and that these are justified in general by their utility; but as to desert as a separate category from these processes — well, I believe there ain't no such animal.

W: I think that in saying that there is no such thing as desert, you are pushing the word out of its normal context, the evaluation of human motives and human conduct. Certainly we have had this word with us for a long time; we do mean something by it (or would you say that all sentences containing it are meaningless?), and the word *does* have a use. It makes a lot of difference whether we say "He deserved it" or "He didn't deserve it." We apply the latter sentence in cases where a person whose act was compelled, for example, was nevertheless sentenced, and the former in cases where a person was sentenced for a serious offense when the excusing conditions did not apply. If it is true, as you say, that there is no such animal as desert, you are in effect rubbing a word out of the language, and thereby erasing a distinction which we all make constantly.

B: Of course we make it, and we use it — vindictively or otherwise. But our use of it reflects the superficiality of our insight into the facts. If we knew all the causal factors leading to the act, none of us would say, "He deserves it" — except perhaps those who like to air their self-righteousness or thirst for blood. We make the distinction, true; but once the full facts are known the distinction disappears.

W: But there *is* a distinction which the word marks, and the word *does* have a use — so why not use it that way instead of putting it out of use forever by applying it to nothing?

B: For the same reason that knowing the facts is better than being ignorant. But most people are ignorant, so they continue to make distinctions which are rooted in that ignorance. The distinction is made only because we don't plumb deeply enough into the facts of the matter. Let me give you a similar situation. People when they hear or read about some unusual event, mouth the phrase, "It's a wonder!" It's a wonder he ever won the race, considering the obstacles in his way. It's a wonder he ever made out so well in the world, considering that he flunked out of high school. Such exclamations could go on and on. I remember that as a child I used to speculate about this phrase. I used to think, "What does that mean, 'It's a wonder'?" Just that it's unusual? But many unusual events can be explained perfectly well, and once they're explained we don't call them "a wonder" any more. That it's surprising? But that just means that the person is surprised — he wouldn't be surprised if he knew all the facts. "It's a wonder" — people say that just because they are ignorant. It's not a wonder that he won the race, considering his determination, his physical strength and stamina at the time, his girl watching him; given all these circumstances — and many more, about the other contestants as well — his victory was no "wonder" at all. "It's a wonder he turned out so well, considering he flunked out of high school." Even if it turns out that he was intelligent all the time but didn't have good teachers who stimulated him? Even if he was given a chance at a job which fitted his abilities perfectly and had a benevolent uncle who got him started? Even if his uncle died and he took over the business, and shortly afterward his sole competitor in town sold out, leaving him sole proprietor of this kind of business in the community? Considering all these circumstances, what happened was no "wonder," but precisely what was to be expected. Yes, the word has a "use," all right; it marks a distinction we make in daily life — a cat jumping over the fence is no wonder, a cow jumping over it is. But the distinction to begin with is made as a function of our ignorance, and it disappears once that ignorance is dispelled. Obviously now, I can say the same thing about your remarks on desert. If we were able to look into the secret springs of all human actions, the whole concept would disappear.

w: Aren't you confusing desert with predictability of events? If we knew *all* the causal circumstances, we wouldn't say anything was a wonder; and, you say, neither would we talk about desert, for we would be able to predict that one man would put forth the effort and win the prize and that another would lose it, and that one man (given his background and circumstances) would commit a certain crime and that another would refrain from it. To this conclusion I agree, of course — if we knew *all* the factors we could predict all the results. But you are stating an empty tautology (though most people who mouth it don't realize that it is), for the moment a prediction turned out to be mistaken, we'd automatically say that we *didn't* know all the circumstances. "All the circumstances" means "those that unerringly enable us to predict." So I can perfectly well grant your tautology that if we knew all the circumstances we could predict everything, including which people would do which things. But what does our ability to predict have to do with your other assertion that there is really no such thing as desert?

B: Just this. If I know that Smith is a person with this peculiar predisposition, this temperamental quirk, this tendency to respond to a certain stimulus, this strong habit, then I can predict that in this circumstance he will do act A. And if I know that Jones has that particular temperamental quirk, that strong habit . . . then I can predict that in another circumstance he will do act B. In view of the predictability of each act, given the conditions on which it depends, how can I talk about any difference in desert?

W: Quite easily. For among the conditions required to make the prediction must be included those having to do not with the man's role as *patient* but with his role as *agent:* for example, the amount of effort and labor which he puts forth to overcome difficulties, the kind of moral ideal he espouses, whether he has made himself into the kind of person who takes the easy way out or the hard heroic way. You will grant that to make the prediction I have to have this information too. And it is for his efforts and ideals that he is deserving.

B: But don't you see that he makes an effort only if he has it in him to do so; that if he has it in him and the conditions are right, he *will* do it?

W: Not necessarily. Many people have it in them to do good, and conditions are right, but because they are lazy or self-centered they still don't exert themselves.

B: Then that is because some other circumstances intervene — perhaps a weak ego or a natural timidity.

W: All these, I admit, must be considered in making the prediction. But not necessarily in the estimation of desert. What he *does* as agent, whether with unfavorable materials or with favorable ones, is all I need to estimate his desert.

B: But what he does as agent (in overcoming difficulties, for instance) depends in turn on other conditions, in whose creation he was *not* the agent. What he does as agent depends on conditions which were not of his doing — whether he has a certain brain structure, whether he had certain inherited capacities, whether he was confronted in babyhood by insuperable obstacles to the development of his ego, whether he has the ability to surmount odds. You see, in this *total* view of human beings, deserts disappear — or, if you prefer, all deserts are equal. This is the perspective of *ultimate moral equality*. If Jones rises above unfavorable conditions to do heroic deeds and Smith does not, Jones's victory is, *in the final analysis,* not to his credit.

> It is all very well, then, to judge that Jones performed a morally worthy act under great odds; but such a judgment is superficial and unstable. For, if determinism is true, these vaunted "odds" disappear upon examination; and Jones is seen to have done only what the causal factors in his situation, unknown as well as known, brought forth. So did Smith, and so do we all.[1]

[1] Elizabeth L. Beardsley, "Determinism and Moral Perspectives," *Philosophy and Phenomenological Research,* Vol. 21 (September, 1960), p. 11.

Knowing this fact will not keep us from praising and rewarding people, to spur them on to good deeds, or from blaming or punishing, to deter them and others and protect society. But nevertheless it will have an important moral effect upon us, I think. Since all *ultimate* moral distinctions are erased, we shall become more tolerant of the actions of other persons whose motivations we do not know or understand. "Feelings of admiration, contempt, guilt, and pride, will all be experienced more moderately by those who know that no man is ever the *first* cause of evil or good deeds, or *finally* responsible for winning or losing when confronted by odds."[1] If Jones rises to perform a heroic deed against great odds, we shall still admire him, but our admiration will be tempered by the fact that he had the capacity (which he did not give himself) to overcome these odds and that a situation arose favorable to the use or development of this capacity. Similarly if Smith fails where we expected him to succeed, our condemnation of him will be mitigated by considering that for this particular task at this particular moment and in this particular context, he did *not* have the capacity (and of this lack of capacity he is not the cause). Ultimately we are the kind of persons we are because of the countless circumstances that have molded us; and although we shall continue to praise actions of a˙ kind which we think need encouraging, we shall also keep in mind that when we consider questions of *ultimate* desert, "all men are equal."

Most of the time, of course, we do not view human conduct from the point of view of ultimate moral equality. We are too much involved in human affairs, not as spectators but as participants. And as participants we find it needful to encourage, blame, exhort, judge, advise, and condemn. But when we plumb deeply (as psychiatrists do) into the ultimate causes (what Hume called the "secret springs") of human conduct, we shall become aware that people are what they are and do what they do because of circumstances outside the control of their will — and that although the will itself is a causal circumstance, it in turn was fashioned by external circumstances which made it what it is. When we view other people's frailties and shortcomings in the light of this perspective, we shall no longer say, "He deserves what he's getting." Instead, we shall say, "There, but for the grace of God (and a favorable early environment) go I."

EXERCISES

1. Evaluate the following comments:

a. From Mark Twain, *What Is Man?* (New York: Harper, 1917), pp. 5-7: "Whatsoever a man is, is due to his *make,* and to the *influences* brought to bear upon it by his heredities, his habitat, his associations. He is moved, directed, *commanded,* by *exterior* influences — solely. He *originates* nothing, not even a *thought.* . . . A man's brain is so constructed that *it can originate nothing what-*

[1] *Ibid.*, p. 14.

ever. It can only use material obtained *outside*. It is merely a machine; and it works automatically, not by will-power. *It has no command over itself, its owner has no command over it."*

b. From Clarence Darrow, "Crime and Criminals": (To the prisoners in the Cook County Jail, 1902:) "You may not yourselves see exactly why it was you did this thing, but if you look at the question deeply enough and carefully enough you will see that there were circumstances that drove you to do exactly the thing which you did. You could not help it any more than we outside can help taking the positions that we take." (C. Darrow, *Attorney for the Damned*, p. 6.)

c. From Patrick Nowell-Smith, *Ethics*, p. 298: "Leopold Mozart was a competent musician; his son Wolfgang was given a good musical education and practised his art assiduously. Each of these facts helps to explain how he was able to compose and play so well. There is plenty of evidence that musical ability runs in families and still more of the effects of teaching and practice. But, having learnt these facts, we do not have the slightest tendency to say that, because Mozart's abilities were 'due' to heredity, teaching, and practice, his compositions were not 'really' his own, or to abate one jot of our admiration. In the same way, however a man came by his moral principles, they are still *his* moral principles and he is praised or blamed for them. The plea that, being what he is he cannot help doing what he does, will no more save the wicked man than it will save the bad pianist or actor who has the rashness to expose his incompetence in public. Nor is he saved by being able to explain how he has come to be what he is."

2. Resolve the following dispute:

"I still think that a man's behavior is completely determined — a certain act is caused by a series of circumstances A, and A by a preceding set of circumstances B, and B by C, indefinitely back, including his power of resistance and his other traits of character. Of course I know that we have (for practical reasons) to blame, to punish, to 'hold responsible.' But when we talk that language we are talking pragmatically only."

"No, it's not pragmatic; responsibility refers to a *fact* of the moral life. And I hold that a man's acts are, though caused, *his own* and that *he* is personally responsible for them."

3. Here are two people, each equally addicted to smoking. It is equally hard for them to stop the habit. But one of them succeeds in stopping, and the other does not. Would you say that (*1*) here are two different effects of the same cause or that (*2*) here are two different effects to which two different causes correspond? (If the latter, what difference in causation might you point out?)

4. At what point in the following examples would you say that a person's freedom is affected? (Freedom to act? to choose? to desire?)

a. You voluntarily take a pill which will keep you content and free of conflicts for the rest of your life.

b. You voluntarily submit to brain surgery which will make resistance to the regime under which you live impossible for you in the future.

c. Under threat of punishment or death, you submit to the surgery (b).

d. You voluntarily take a "truth serum" which renders you incapable of lying.

e. You perform an act as a result of posthypnotic suggestion.

f. An enemy tortures you into giving away state secrets.

g. You voluntarily lock yourself in an upper story and throw away the key.

h. Through habit and inertia, a slave refuses emancipation after it is granted.

i. Responding to a dare, you submit to hypnosis, not knowing that its effects will be lifelong. (Assume that this result is possible.)

j. A man accepts alcoholic drinks, not knowing their probable effects on him.

k. A man accepts alcoholic drinks, knowing their probable effects on him but, through long habit and the strong desire to overcome inferiority feelings, unable to resist.

l. "I'll give you a million dollars if you can refrain from thinking about a hamburger during the next minute." The person tries, but in trying thinks of the hamburger.

m. A man with a compulsion to wash *can* refrain from washing his hands, but breaks into a sweat and becomes tense and irritable, finally "going to pieces" emotionally, until he washes his hands again.

n. A hungry dog smells the meat on the table, almost takes it, but, on the command of his master, refrains.

o. A man cannot bring himself to go to the movies on Sunday, not because he any longer considers it wrong, but because of strong guilt feelings caused by his early training.

p. A man eats regularly a harmful food, thinking it to be nutritious. He could check these opinions against medical advice, but refuses to do so.

5. Which of the following statements do you consider true? Why? "If determinism is true, then . . .

a. I could not have done anything other than what I did."

b. I could have done other than what I did, if some of the causal circumstances had been different."

c. I could have done other that what I did, even if all the causal circumstances leading up to my act had been the same."

d. I would not have done other than what I did, even if all the causal factors leading up to my act had been the same."

e. everything I do is compelled by previous events in my history."

f. if I were omniscient I could predict every act I would perform for the rest of my life."

6. Read all the five case histories described in Robert Lindner's *The Fifty-Minute Hour* and attempt to assess the degree (and kind) of freedom, if any, that the agent had in each of the major actions he performed. (There are many other psychiatric case books which will do just as well.)

7. Evaluate the following passage: "It is assumed sometimes that if it can be shown that deliberation determines choice and deliberation is determined by character and conditions, there is no freedom. This like saying that because a flower comes from root and stem it cannot bear fruit. The question is not what are the antecedents of deliberation and choice, but what are their consequences. What do they do that is distinctive? The answer is that they give us all the control of future possibilities which is open to us. And this control is the crux of

our freedom. Without it, we are pushed from behind. With it we walk in the light." (John Dewey, *Human Nature and Conduct* [New York: Modern Library, 1930], p. 311.)

READING LIST, SECTION 24

Austin, John. "Ifs and Cans." (lecture) *Proceedings of the British Academy,* Vol. 42 (1956), pp. 109-32.

Ayer, Alfred Jules. "Freedom and Necessity." In Ayer, A. J. *Philosophical Essays.* New York: St. Martin's, 1954, pp. 271-84.

Beardsley, Elizabeth L. "Determinism and Moral Perspectives." *Philosophy and Phenomenological Research,* Vol. 21 (1960), pp. 1-20.

Broad, C. D. "Determinism, Indeterminism, and Libertarianism." In Broad, C. D., *Ethics and the History of Philosophy.* New York: Humanities Press, 1952, pp. 195-217.

Campbell, Charles Arthur. "Is Free-will a Pseudo-problem?" *Mind,* Vol. 60 (1951), pp. 441-65.

———. "In Defense of Free-will" (1938). In Munitz, Milton K., ed. *A Modern Introduction to Ethics.* Chicago: Free Press, 1959, pp. 375-86.

———. "Prolegomena to a Theory of the Moral Criterion." In Sellars, Wilfrid, and John Hospers, eds. *Readings in Ethical Theory.* New York: Appleton-Century-Crofts, 1952, pp. 631-44.

Ekstein, Rudolf. "Psychological Laws and Human Freedom." *Journal of Social Psychology,* Vol. 25 (1947), pp. 181-91.

Ewing, Alfred C. "Can We Act Against Our Strongest Desire?" *Monist,* Vol. 44 (1934), pp. 126-43.

Farrer, Austin. *The Freedom of the Will.* New York: Scribner, 1958.

Gallie, W. B. "Free-will and Determinism Yet Again." (lecture) Printer to the Queen's Univ. Belfast, Northern Ireland, 1957.

Hampshire, Stuart, W. G. Maclagan, and R. M. Hare. "The Freedom of the Will." (symposium) *Aristotelian Society Proceedings,* Supplementary Vol. 25 (1951), pp. 161-215.

Hobart, R. E. (Dickinson Miller). "Free-will as Involving Determinism and Inconceivable without It." *Mind,* Vol. 43 (1934), pp. 1-27.

Hook, Sidney, ed. *Determinism and Freedom.* New York: New York Univ. Press, 1958, Pts. 1 and 4.

Hospers, John. "Free-will and Psychoanalysis." In Sellars and Hospers. *Readings in Ethical Theory,* pp. 560-75.

Ladd, John. "Free Will and Voluntary Action." *Philosophy and Phenomenological Research,* Vol. 12 (1952), pp. 392-405.

Lewis, H. D. "Moral Freedom in Recent Ethics" and "Guilt and Freedom." In Sellars and Hospers. *Readings in Ethical Theory,* pp. 576-620.

Mandelbaum, Maurice. "Determinism and Moral Responsibility." *Ethics,* Vol. 70 (1960), pp. 204-19.

Matson, Wallace I. "The Irrelevance of Free-will to Moral Responsibility." *Mind,* Vol. 65 (1956), pp. 489-97.

Montefiore, Alan. " 'Ought' and 'Can.' " *Philosophical Quarterly,* Vol. 8 (1958), pp. 224-40.

Moore, George Edward. *Ethics.* New York: Holt, 1912, Ch. 6.

Nowell-Smith, Patrick. "Free-will and Moral Responsibility." *Mind,* Vol. 57 (1948), pp. 45-61.

———. "Determinists and Libertarians." *Mind,* Vol. 63 (1954), pp. 317-37.

Paul, G. A. "H. D. Lewis and the Problem of Guilt." In Sellars and Hospers. *Readings in Ethical Theory,* pp. 621-28.

Raab, Francis. "Free-will and the Ambiguity of 'Could.' " *Philosophical Review,* Vol. 64 (1955), pp. 60-77.

Ross, Sir William David. *Foundations of Ethics.* (Gifford lectures, 1935-36) New York: Oxford Univ. Press, 1939.

Schlick, Moritz. *The Problems of Ethics.* Englewood Cliffs, N. J.: Prentice-Hall, 1939, Ch. 7.

Sidgwick, Henry. *The Methods of Ethics.* 7th ed. New York: Macmillan, 1874, pp. 56-66.

Stevenson, Charles Leslie. *Ethics and Language.* New Haven: Yale Univ. Press, 1945, Ch. 14.

———. "Ethical Judgments and Avoidability." In Sellars and Hospers. *Readings in Ethical Theory,* pp. 549-69.

Stout, A. K. "Free-will and Moral Responsibility." In Sellars and Hospers. *Readings in Ethical Theory,* pp. 537-48.

11. The problem of verification

We must now attempt to consider a question which has probably occurred to every reader many times: "How can any of the theories we have been discussing possibly be proved?" We have examined the outlines and some of the details of the major historical views on moral questions, we have ventured some defenses and some attacks, and perhaps we have formed some opinions as a result. Doubtless it has been fruitful to examine the implications of each of these views, to see how they compare and contrast with one another, and to see to what criticisms they are subject. But once we have attempted to do all this examining, can we definitely establish as true one or another of the views on the various questions with which we have been concerned? Is there any way to go about such a project?

NORTH: It seems to me that it's all a matter of opinion from here on in. We can describe each view, trace its implications, and compare it with others, and that's that. From here on, "You pays your money and you takes your choice."

SOUTH: Well, you've brought up a long, long story — I scarcely know where to begin. Let me point out at the beginning that there are clearly *some* statements which can be definitely established, and empirically at that. I mean statements about *means* as opposed to statements about *ends*. I can say that giving you a thousand dollars is a means of satisfying at least one of your desires, whereas giving you an igloo is not. I can say that shooting a man at close range is a better means of killing him than sticking him with pins.

N: Granted. Statements about means are, of course, empirical statements about what leads to what. When A is said to be a means toward B, we can investigate empirically whether in fact A does lead to B, and whether it does so (1) with greater probability and (2) more efficiently than something else would. But surely such statements are not ethical statements at all.

526

Whether the end, B, is good or valuable or worth pursuing — *that* is an ethical statement and I don't see how it can be proved.

s: Wait a moment. B may in turn be a means to something else, C; and C a means to D. Anything can be a means to something else. Having an operation may be a means toward restoration of health, and that in turn may be a means toward increased strength, happiness, and peace of mind. These possessions in turn may (though they were probably not intended to) be a valuable means toward the endurance of more surgery in the future, if that becomes necessary.

n: All right. Whenever the statement is one about a means toward an end, then it is an empirical statement. But the moment that the B or C or D in question is considered as an end and not as a means toward something else, then I think it is unprovable. You can prove to me that what I am doing is not a good means to the attainment of something that I want, but you cannot prove to me that I should not *want* what I do want — unless, again, what I want in turn is a means toward something further which I also want.

s: Hold on — there are several confusions here. In the first place, an end, even an end which *you* pursue, isn't at all the same as what you want. You may not desire or want the end at which you are aiming, but you may pursue it just the same.

> It may be my end to track down the murderer although I know that it is my brother and although I dread the moment when I shall succeed. In one sense of "desire" and "want," I do of course desire and want to find him, for it could not be my end to find him if I did not (in any sense) desire or want to find him. But in another, more obvious, more literal sense, I do not want or desire to find him. I abhor, I dread, I hate to think of the moment of success. Nevertheless, I overcome all this in pursuing my end.[1]

In the second place, statements about ends can be defended, and reasons given for them, just as much as statements about means. If, on the one hand, I take exercise as a means toward improving my health, I can use the end in view as a reason for engaging in the exercise. If, on the other hand, I don't exercise as a means toward any end but just because I enjoy it, then again I have given a reason. I can give you a reason for pursuing certain ends just as I can give you a reason for pursuing certain means toward those ends.

n: I think you are changing the subject on me a bit. I said that statements about means could be proved to be *true* (empirically) whereas statements about ends could not. You didn't deny my statement, but you said that I could *defend* the having of certain ends as well as the taking of certain means. Perhaps; but then I would still want to say that *ultimate ends* cannot be defended. Intermediate ends, which are means toward further ends,

---

[1] From Kurt Baier, *The Moral Point of View*. Ithaca, N. Y.: Cornell Univ. Press, 1958, p. 263. Reprinted by permission of the publisher.

can. Even when I take exercise for enjoyment, the exercise is the means and the enjoyment the end — at least it is the end in the sense that it occurs as the direct result of my activity, the exercise. But if you ask me to defend enjoyment as an end, I couldn't do it, and neither could you. It was Mill who said that statements about ultimate ends could not be proved.[1]

s: I'm afraid I must stop you again. First, I am very dubious about all talk concerning ultimate ends. As far as I know, I don't have any such thing; do you? We each pursue many ends, and some of these ends are in turn means toward still further ends; each of our lives is a tangled network of means and ends. But is there just one ultimate end toward which all the subsidiary ends are means? I doubt it — except in a few monomaniacs. There may be a few lives so tightly organized that every act is a means toward an end which is in turn a means toward some further end, and so on till you reach one end toward which all the rest converge; but even that is doubtful. Even the man so bent on revenge that everything he does seems to have this one end in mind still aims at other ends, such as earning his living.

But let that be as it may. I don't really care which things are means and which are ends or which are both simultaneously. I suggest that what you mean could be much better stated in the following way: statements about what is intrinsically good cannot be proved, but statements about what actions of ours will in fact *lead* to the attainment of these things (whatever things are intrinsically good) are capable of empirical proof. (For example, that A will make you happier than B will, is an empirical fact.) Once that is said, isn't it what you want to say? Then it no longer matters which are means and which are ends — though normally, of course, intrinsic goods are pursued as ends and instrumental goods as means toward them.

n: Very well; I accept your amendment. But I do want to say that statements about what is intrinsically good are incapable of any kind of proof.

s: Though I admit that Mill first denied that such statements can be proved, he nevertheless tried one maneuver for proving them. He argued, you may remember, that just as the only proof that a thing is visible is that people see it, and the only proof that a thing is audible is that people hear it, so the only proof that something is desirable is that people desire it.

n: But this argument, of course, was a monstrous piece of bad reasoning. To say that something is visible is to say that it is *capable* of being seen, and to say that it is audible is to say that it is capable of being heard; but to say that it is desirable is *not* the same as to say that it is capable of being desired. If it were, everything in the world would be desirable, for what is there that is not capable of being desired by somebody or other? To say that something is desirable is, of course, to say that it *ought* to be desired (the same as with "contemptible," "admirable," "abominable"). From the

---

[1] John Stuart Mill, *Utilitarianism* (many editions), Ch. 4.

fact that something is capable of being desired it certainly does not follow that it ought to be desired or is worthy of being desired.

s: If you interpret Mill's argument in that way, of course it is ridiculous. But Mill himself, being the author of *A System of Logic,* the most famous treatise on logic of all time next to Aristotle's, surely knew that formally his argument was fallacious. I think he was trying to do something else. He was asking, "What better evidence is there that something is desirable than the fact that people do desire it?" Suppose it could be shown that the only thing that people ever desire for its own sake is happiness (their own or that of others). If happiness were really their sole desire, (and I don't maintain that it is), wouldn't it be the best possible evidence that happiness is intrinsically good or worthwhile? This, I think, was what Mill was trying to say.

n: Who knows, perhaps it was. But I still think he was mistaken. The fact that people, even all people, desire something is no *proof* that it is good or desirable. If some people can desire things which aren't good, why couldn't all people? His argument is a kind of *argumentum ad hominem* rather than a proof.

s: I admit that at any rate it does not offer deductive proof: from the fact that something is desired you cannot *deduce* that it is desirable. But before we proceed further let me correct you on one more point: I think you make your thesis unduly narrow by saying that it is statements about intrinsic good that cannot be proved. In a utilitarian ethics, intrinsic good is the foundation stone of the structure, instrumental good is built upon it, and the notion of right is interpreted as also being an instrumental good, for the right act is the one that leads to the most intrinsic good. However, in other theories the concept of duty or obligation is fundamental, and that of goodness is subsidiary or interpreted, say, as that which we *ought* to aim at. You don't want to limit your argument to one type of ethics. What you want to say is, I think, that certain basic ethical principles in each system (whether or not they be statements about intrinsic good) cannot be proved. The derived or subsidiary principles can of course be deduced from the basic principles with the aid of empirical premises; for example,

> Human happiness is good. (basic principle about good)
> What maximizes human happiness is right. (basic principle about right)
> Cooperation tends to maximize human happiness. (empirical premise)
>
> *Therefore,* Cooperation tends to be right. (subsidiary principle)

But the *underived,* or *ultimate* premises of an ethical theory — those which cannot be deduced from any other propositions in the theory — these, I think you would want to hold, are incapable of proof.

n: Exactly. Ultimate principles of ethics can't be proved. You can logically prove some statements by deriving them from other ones, and then of course you haven't proved them to be *true* unless the premises from which you deduce them are also true. But obviously this process of logical derivation can't go on forever. Where it stops, you have your unprovable ethical principles, your ultimate premises. No matter whether you're an egoist, a utilitarian, a Kantian, or something else, you will run into them. That happiness (or for the pluralistic utilitarian, other things as well) is intrinsically good, is an ultimate premise of utilitarianism; that acts whose maxims are universalizable are right is a first premise of the Kantian system; other systems have other first premises. None of these premises can be proved.

s: How else could this situation be? If you really have a first premise, then it *cannot* possibly be deduced from others; if it could, it would not be a first premise but a derived proposition. By saying that it is the first premise of a system, you are already implying that it is, that it must be, nondeducible from other ones; a derived first premise is a contradiction in terms. Thus it should be no surprise that the utilitarian cannot prove his ultimate premise or premises about intrinsic good.

> What kind of things ought to exist for their own sakes? . . . No relevant evidence whatever can be adduced; from no other truth, except themselves alone, can it be inferred that they are either true or false. We can guard against error only by taking care, that, when we try to answer a question of this kind, we have before our minds that question only, and not some other or others. . . .[1]

People often express surprise or regret that you can't prove ultimate premises by logically deriving them from other premises; what they don't realize is that if you could, they wouldn't be ultimate premises; what such people want is self-contradictory. But please don't cry out, "So ethics is unprovable!" as if the unprovability of ultimate premises were a cause for surprise or distress, or as if we might through some herculean effort achieve what is in the very nature of the case a logical impossibility.

n: I grant that it's a logical impossibility. Still, that admission doesn't change the point, does it — that the fundamental premises of an ethical system are unprovable?

s: Oh dear. It doesn't change *that* purely logical point, to be sure. But I am afraid you are making an illicit inference here: you are saying to yourself, at least in the back of your mind, "Statement S can't be proved (in the sense of being deduced from other statements), therefore it can't be known to be true." Of course no such conclusion follows. Indeed, there must be some statements whose truth is known *without* being deduced from other statements, else we would be left with an infinite chain of statements each dependent on still another one. People

> seem to have thought . . . that no proposition can ever be known to be true, unless it follows from some other proposition or set of propositions already

[1] G. E. Moore, *Principia Ethica*, pp. 63-64.

known to be true. But it is, I think, easy to see that, if this view were true, no man ever has known any proposition whatever to be in the slightest degree probable. For if I cannot know any proposition whatever to be either true or probably true, unless I have first known some other proposition, from which it follows, to be so; then, of course, I cannot have known this other proposition, unless I have first known some third proposition, before *it;* nor this third proposition, unless I have first known a fourth before it; and so on *ad infinitum.* In other words, it would follow that no man has ever known any proposition whatever to be even probably true, unless he has previously known an absolutely infinite series of other propositions. And it is quite certain that no man ever has thus known a really infinite series of propositions. . . . Therefore . . . it must be the case that we are capable of knowing at least *one* proposition to be true, *without* knowing any other proposition whatever from which it follows.[1]

N: But if it can't be proved, how can it be known?

s: Proved, proved. You are too attached to the deductive model of proof by derivation from other propositions. That's all very well in mathematics. But in most situations in daily life, when we say that something can be proved we don't mean that it can be deduced logically from true premises. When the attorney in court says, "Prove that you were at home the night of the murder," he doesn't mean "Deduce that proposition from other propositions." He means, "Give empirical evidence to show that you were home that evening." Giving evidence is proof too—empirical proof; don't assume that all proof conforms to the deductive model. Moreover, there are times when I cannot even offer you other propositions, and yet I may be said to know: if you ask me to *prove* that we are sitting here talking with one another, I cannot offer you other propositions, I can only ask you to look for yourself. No further evidence than looking, hearing, etc. is possible — or, if you prefer, the looking itself provides the evidence. What more evidence could be given? What more should you need or want? (If you take a picture of the room to make sure, you have to use your senses in looking at the picture.)

N: That's all very well for empirical propositions like "We are sitting talking with each other," but how about ethical propositions like "This act is right"? How can one possibly prove such a proposition in the sense of "empirical proof"? It doesn't seem to be an empirical proposition at all. Nor does it seem to be an analytic proposition or a tautology like "Black is black" or "You're not both here and not here." How then can one possibly verify such propositions?

Thereby hangs our tale — a very long and complicated tale, which we shall have time in the short space remaining to consider only in the sketchiest way. Yet we shall have to begin to tell the tale in order to glean even a hint of the answer to our question. The assumption with which we shall

[1] From G. E. Moore, *Some Main Problems of Philosophy.* New York: Macmillan, 1953, pp. 122-23. Reprinted by permission of The Macmillan Company and Allen & Unwin, Ltd.

begin is that in order to know how we can verify ethical statements, we first have to know how to *define* the ethical terms which they contain. This is a separate field of investigation, called *metaethics,* on which we have not yet touched in this book. It is in this area that most of the work on ethics in the twentieth century has been done; but all we shall be able to do here is to outline its major positions and trends.

25. *Nonnaturalistic theories*

In every system of morality which I have hitherto met with, I have always remarked that the author proceeds for some time in the ordinary way of speaking, and establishes the being of a God, or makes observations concerning human affairs; when of a sudden I am surprised to find, that instead of the usual copulations of propositions, *is,* and *is not,* I meet with no proposition that is not connected with an *ought,* or an *ought not.* This change is imperceptible; but is, however, of the last consequence. For as this *ought,* or *ought not,* expresses some new relation or affirmation, it is necessary that it should be observed and explained; and at the same time that a reason should be given for what seems altogether inconceivable, how this new relation can be a deduction from others, which are entirely different from it.[1]

So wrote David Hume more than two hundred years ago, and the question he posed in this passage is as alive today as it was then. How do we get ethical conclusions from nonethical premises? "He will cause her a great deal of suffering if he leaves her" is a statement of empirical fact (which may be true or false); but how do we get from this the ethical conclusion "Therefore he *ought not* to leave her"? The attempt to bridge the gulf between the "is" and "ought" Moore has called the *naturalistic fallacy.*

A. *The naturalistic fallacy*
If only we could deduce ethical statements (containing "good," "right," "ought," "duty") from statements of empirical fact, there would be no problem; but it seems that we cannot. After all, isn't it a principle of logic that you can't derive a conclusion containing a term (such as "right") which did not appear somewhere in the premises from which that conclusion is deduced?

But perhaps we don't need to deduce a conclusion, perhaps we can know by empirical observation that it is true. Can't we be said to know by experience that war is evil? But this suggestion, though it sounds promising as long as we don't stop to think about it, doesn't seem to stand up either. Not that we deny that war is an evil; but is this statement really an empirically observed fact? What we observe empirically is that many people die, that many others are injured, that much property is destroyed, that hate and bit-

[1] David Hume, *A Treatise of Human Nature* (many editions), Bk. 3, Pt. 1, Sect. 1.

terness are engendered, that ruinous taxation occurs; all these occurrences are empirical facts which can be verified by detailed observation. But in spite of our unquestioned conviction that war is evil, can we honestly say that we *observe* it to be true? What we observe are the empirical facts just described. How would you convince someone that war is evil if he admits all the empirical facts described, and yet denies the conclusion that war is evil? Suppose he said that these things are good, or indifferent? You couldn't change his mind by showing him more facts because he admits all these facts already.

If ethical statements are not empirical ones, perhaps we can try another maneuver, and say that they are definitions. When you say "A yard is three feet," you do not have to deduce the truth of this statement from other statements, nor do you observe empirically that it is true; indeed, "three feet" is the way the word "yard" is defined. You would not have to show a person empirically that everything a yard long has always turned out to be three feet long; you would simply have to tell him that the word "yard" is so defined in our language as to be interchangeable with the expression "three feet" — the one could be substituted for the other without change of meaning. Now, if we can make this substitution with "yard" (and countless other words), why not with moral words such as "right"? Surely "right" has a definition, and if so we have only to substitute the definition for the term to be defined.

But the matter is not so easy. In the first place, what *is* the definition of "right"? We can say that "right" means the same as "not wrong," but this definition is of no help because now we have to define "wrong," which is as much an ethical term as "right" is. Defining "right" is not as easy as defining "yard." Those who do attempt to give a definition would probably give different ones — again as they would not for "yard." The utilitarian, for example, would define "right" as "productive of the maximum possible intrinsic good." But not everyone would assent to such a definition, as we have abundantly seen in discussing opposing ethical theories in Chapters 6 and 7. Besides, even if this definition were accepted, it still contains an ethical term, namely "good" — and how is "good" to be defined?

"Well," someone might suggest, "why not do the same with 'good' as we did with 'right'? Happiness alone, according to hedonistic utilitarianism, is intrinsically good. So why not identify 'intrinsic good' with 'happiness' just as we earlier identified 'productive of maximum intrinsic good' with 'right'? If we make this identification, it would seem, we shall be in a most fortunate position: we shall have defined 'intrinsic good,' we shall have defined 'right' in terms of intrinsic good, and we shall have defined 'instrumental good' as that which leads to intrinsic good. A brilliant stroke!"

But it won't work. For even if everyone agreed that happiness alone is intrinsically good, which of course they do not, "happiness" would still not *mean* the same as "intrinsic good." Happiness would be an *instance* of intrinsic good — in this example, the one and only instance; but an instance of the application of the term is not the same thing as the meaning of the term. (To use the language of semantics, happiness would be a *denotation* of the term — that is, an instance of intrinsic good, but not the designation of the term.) If someone denied that a yard is three feet, we would refer him to a dictionary or to observation of common usage of the word to show that this is indeed what people mean by it; but if someone denied that happiness was the sole intrinsic good, it would not help at all to send him to a dictionary. For we have in mind some meaning attaching to the word "good" even before the investigation begins, and we are trying to discover whether "happiness" covers the same ground that "good" does; and of course it does not. If someone were to deny that a yard is three feet (that is, that "yard" is so used by those who speak the English language), we could show empirically that he was mistaken; we could do no such thing for a person who denied that happiness was intrinsically good. Even if the utilitarian definition of "right" were accepted — as "whatever maximizes intrinsic good" — the attempt at definition would break down with "intrinsic good" itself: for even if happiness alone is intrinsically good, it does not follow that "happiness" *means* the same as the phrase "intrinsic good." (Even if all equilateral triangles are equiangular and all equiangular triangles are equilateral, it does not follow that "equilateral" *means* the same as "equiangular," for the first word refers to a property of the sides and the second word to a property of the angles.)

Lest we be misled, what we have just said in no way shows that utilitarianism is mistaken as a theory of normative ethics. That is not the subject we are now discussing. Promotion of intrinsic good may be an acceptable theory about right actions, and happiness may be the one and only thing worth having for its own sake — that is another matter. All that we have shown here is that utilitarianism fails if it attempts to go further and say that the term "happiness" gives the *meaning* (not just the denotation) of the term "intrinsic good." Most of those who have espoused utilitarianism have not been so foolhardy as to equate these terms. Hedonistic utilitarians have not said that happiness is the *meaning* of the phrase "intrinsic good." In the same way, people would say that snow is white, without ever meaning to suggest that the word "snow" means the same as the word "white."

Well, perhaps the utilitarian criterion, turned into a definition, will not do; but how about others? Perhaps "right" means the same as "consistently universalizable" or "in accordance with nature" or "in the direction of evolution" or any of a number of other criteria we have already examined — the difference being now that they are being suggested as *definitions* of the term "right." But these other definitions must be rejected by the same test. "Right" does not *mean the same* as "in accord with nature" or "consistently universalizable," because it makes sense to ask, "This act is in accord with nature *but is it right?*" and "This act is consistently universalizable

but is it right?" Even if the answer is always, "No," it is still a sensible —
that is, a nonself-contradictory — question to ask. "Right" cannot *mean* the
same as any one of these other expressions, else there would be no controversy (as there notoriously is) as to whether everything that fulfills the criterion in question *is also* right. If any of these proffered definitions were acceptable, then arguing about them pro or con would be as pointless as arguing about whether a yard was three feet: those who asserted that it was
would be defending a tautology, and those who denied it would be saying
something self-contradictory.

This is G. E. Moore's famous "open question" argument.[1] No matter
what property, P, according to Moore's reasoning, you give as the meaning
of an ethical term such as "good," you will always be faced with the question, "What if someone agrees that the thing in question has the property P, but denies or doubts that it is good? Clearly he is not contradicting
himself (saying "It has property P but has it property P?"); and yet that is
just what he must be doing if what you have given is a definition." You may
be able to tell me what things are good; you may be able to point to many
instances of the word's application; perhaps you can even give me a complete list of things which are good (both intrinsically and instrumentally);
but one thing you cannot do is *define* the term — if giving a definition is
giving a phrase or other set of words which have the same meaning as the
original term so that they could be substituted for it in all its occurrences in
sentences without any change in meaning, the way "three feet" can always
be substituted for "yard."

There is an important caution, however: you *may* be able to define some
ethical terms by means of *other* ethical terms or phrases. For example, you
can define "right" as "not wrong." And *perhaps* you can define "right" as
"productive of the maximum intrinsic good" (not happiness, which is an
empirical term, but intrinsic good, which is an ethical term). But you cannot define ethical terms into *non*ethical ones. Thus, "intrinsic good" can be
defined as "that which is desirable for its own sake," but this definition still
contains an ethical term, "desirable." It's not that you can't define ethical
terms — at least some of them — but rather that you can't define them by
means of *non*ethical ones; you can't, then, turn ethical sentences into empirical ones by getting rid of all the ethical terms in them and substituting
for them empirical terms. (For example, you can't define "desirable," an
ethical term, as meaning the same as "desired," an empirical term.) Some
of the ethical terms, perhaps, can be got rid of by equating them with
phrases containing *other* ethical terms; but you can't get rid of all the ethical terms. That is to say, ethical sentences are *irreducible* to empirical sentences, and indeed to any other kind of nonethical sentences, such as theological or mathematical.

[1] G. E. Moore, *Principia Ethica*, Ch. i.

Why are ethical sentences thus irreducible? Simply because (according to the view we are considering) they do not have the same meaning that nonethical sentences do. The concepts involved are simply different. When you say that a certain state of affairs is good or that a certain act is a duty or an obligation, you are not saying anything that can be expressed by a purely empirical sentence. Between saying that war causes death and destruction and saying that war is evil, there is an unbridgeable gulf of meaning. As long as two people can agree on the same empirical facts and yet disagree on the ethical conclusion derived from it, how *could* the ethical conclusion have the same meaning as the sentences which merely state the empirical facts?

B. *Criticism of the naturalistic fallacy*

This fallacy, or alleged fallacy, has been interpreted in several ways:

1. According to one interpretation, the naturalistic fallacy is the fallacy of trying to deduce ethical statements from nonethical ones. It is, of course, a fallacy — a logical fallacy — to try to derive a proposition containing ethical words like "good" or "right" or "duty" in the conclusion of a deductive argument when no such words have appeared in the premises. Thus, we cannot deduce "He is a good man" from "He is always helping other people" unless we also supply a premise saying that a man who is always helping other people is good. But this fallacy is in no way peculiar to ethics. From the propositions "He is tall" and "He is sandy-haired" we cannot deduce the proposition "He is thirty years old" either, since no reference to his age appears in the premises of the argument. It is *always* a logical fallacy to deduce conclusions containing terms which are not contained in the premises.

Suppose someone ventured a *definition* of "good"? Suppose he said, for example, that "good" means the same as "pleasant." Then he could argue that

> What's pleasant is good. (definition)
> This is pleasant.
Therefore, This is good.

He may have given a ridiculous definition of "good," but at least we can deduce a conclusion about good from this definition. The naturalistic fallacy would appear to be a fallacy, then, *only* if "good" is indefinable in terms of nonethical concepts. This indefinability, of course, remains to be shown. We cannot assume the indefinability of ethical terms before we have demonstrated it.

2. The above discussion leads us to a second interpretation of the naturalistic fallacy, the so-called *definist* fallacy, which attempts to *define* "good" (or other ethical terms).[1] If "good" *can* be defined, then conclusions can be

---

[1] See W. K. Frankena, in Sellars and Hospers, *Readings in Ethical Theory*, pp. 103-14.

deduced from statements, one of which includes the definition, as above. The nonnaturalist, then, can be construed as declaring that "good" *cannot* be defined and that *because* it cannot, one cannot deduce propositions about good from nonethical propositions. (The first interpretation of the naturalistic fallacy, then, is a logical consequence of the second.)

But *can* "good" be defined? Nonnaturalists — those who believe that the "naturalistic fallacy" in one form or another *is* a fallacy — think that it cannot, but naturalists in ethics, as we shall see, think that it can. We are only begging the question if we *assume* at the outset of the discussion that the term cannot be defined. We shall first have to examine naturalistic theories to see whether any of them succeed. The definist fallacy is the fallacy of trying to define the indefinable, and of course this *is* a fallacy; but if "good" should turn out to be definable, then the attempt to define it is not guilty of this fallacy. Before one can paste the label "Fallacy" on something, one must know not only what the fallacy is but whether this particular example is an instance of it; and that is precisely what we have yet to find out.

3. More plausibly, then, the naturalistic fallacy can be interpreted in a third way as the fallacy of trying to reduce *two* characteristics or properties to *one*. If there are two characteristics, for example, goodness and pleasantness, and we define goodness in terms of pleasantness, we are making the mistake of assuming that there is only one property, pleasantness (or goodness, said to be identical with it), when actually there are two properties, goodness *and* pleasantness.

Of course it is always a fallacy, and not only in ethics, to confuse things with one another, or, as in this instance, to assume that there is one property when there are two. But *are* there two properties? That is the question. Nonnaturalists say there are two; naturalists say there is just one — that e.g., "goodness" and "pleasantness" are just two names for the same thing. Doubtless this contention is absurd in regard to pleasantness, since we obviously don't mean the same thing by the two words. But is it equally absurd for *all* attempts, however complex, to identify goodness with some other property or set of properties? This identification too we cannot judge in advance; we just have to wait for the naturalists to speak their piece. Nonnaturalists, on the one hand, are quite certain that goodness is different from any nonethical property or set of properties:

> All I can say is that when I try to see what I mean when I use ethical terms I find that I have present to my consciousness an idea generically different from any empirical psychological concepts, and that I am as clearly aware of this as I am of what I mean in almost any other case of meaning.[1]

Naturalists, on the other hand, are just as certain that nonnaturalists think there are two properties just because there are two different words or sets of

---

[1] A. C. Ewing, "Subjectivism and Naturalism in Ethics," in Sellars and Hospers, *Readings in Ethical Theory,* p. 123.

words. Is it a fallacy, according to nonnaturalists, to assume that Zeus and Jupiter must be two different gods just because there are two different names? It is just as much of a fallacy to assume that there are two when there is only one, as it is to assume that there is one when there are two. Which of these fallacies is being committed cannot, unfortunately, be settled by an a priori dictum; the pronouncement that the naturalist is guilty of trying to reduce two things or properties to one is something that might be said at the end of an exhaustive investigation of naturalistic theories, but not at the beginning of it. Once again, we shall just have to see what the naturalists have to say. Presumably they are neither stupid nor blind and are perfectly aware of the nonnaturalist's arguments, yet they are not convinced by these arguments that there are ethical properties and nonethical properties with an unbridgeable gulf between them.

Before we leave the nonnaturalists, however, we must consider one further problem. If there are ethical properties and nonethical properties, then of course it would be a mistake to define the former by means of the latter. But if so, how do nonnaturalists propose to find out what things ethical terms apply to? How will they discover what things are good or bad, what acts are right or wrong? They cannot say, "By empirical observation." Naturalists can make this statement, for they believe ethical properties to be identical with nonethical ones (as Zeus and Jupiter were identical gods), and usually (though not always) these nonethical properties have turned out to be *empirical* properties like being pleasant or being desired or being approved. But the nonnaturalist can give no such answer, for he insists that goodness and rightness are not to be identified with any empirical properties, nor indeed with any nonethical properties whatever. He cannot, then, say, that we can find out whether something is good or desirable the way we find out that something is approved or desired. Nor can he say that we can find out by deducing conclusions about goodness or desirability from given premises; for if the premises contain no ethical term, we cannot deduce a conclusion containing such a term, and if they do contain an ethical term we have the same question over again — how do we find out whether that premise is true?

Since neither reason nor observation will do the trick for the nonnaturalist, how about *intuition?* This solution has been suggested so often that "ethical intuitionism" has often come to be another name for ethical nonnaturalism. It has often been held that human beings have an inner faculty, a "moral sense," which tells them what is good, bad, right, and wrong. Just as we see physical objects with the physical eye and are enabled by this means to state true propositions about them, so, according to this position, we can "see" moral truths with an "inner eye" and thus state true propositions about good and right. When we truly discern some moral fact, such as that killing is wrong, with this faculty of intuition, the corresponding ethical proposition, "Killing is wrong," is true. Of course, many people commit errors in intuition because they do not truly allow their inner faculty to speak: they rationalize, they hear what they want to hear or see what they want to see — whatever it is easy or convenient or pleasant for them to see; or they are blinded by habit and tradition, accepting without question what they have been told by others rather than trying to have a genuine intuition of their own. Their moral vision is blurred or distorted by all sorts of personal factors which get in the way of a true vision. Nevertheless, moral truths are there to be discerned, and the trained and impartial inner eye can see them.

It is sometimes held that the moral truths thus seen are *self-evident*. A moral philosopher whose views we have already considered, Sir David Ross, maintains such a position. *Particular* moral judgments — that this particular act is right, that a certain thing is my duty — are, he believes, never certain; what *is* self-evident, at least to anyone who has focused his attention on the matter, is what our *prima facie* duties are. It is the application of these prima facie duties to the actual situations in daily life which must always be accompanied by some degree of doubt.

> That an act, *qua* fulfilling a promise, or *qua* effecting a just distribution of good, or *qua* returning services rendered, or *qua* promoting the good of others, or *qua* promoting the virtue or insight of the agent, is *prima facie* right, is self-evident; not in the sense that it is evident from the beginning of our lives, or as soon as we attend to the proposition for the first time, but in the sense that when we have reached sufficient mental maturity and have given sufficient attention to the proposition it is self-evident without any need of proof, or of evidence beyond itself. It is self-evident just as a mathematical axiom, or the validity of a form of inference, is evident. The moral order expressed in these propositions is just as much part of the fundamental nature of the universe (and, we may add, of any possible universe in which there were moral agents at all) as is the spatial or numerical structure expressed in the axioms of geometry or arithmetic. In our confidence that these propositions are true there is involved the same trust in our reason that is involved in our confidence in mathematics; and we should have no justification for trusting it in the latter sphere and distrusting it in the former. In both cases we are dealing with propositions that cannot be proved, but that just as certainly need no proof.[1]

Here, however, our difficulties begin. The analogy with arithmetic and geometry is less than fortunate: few mathematicians today hold that mathematical propositions are self-evident truths. In any event, they prove nothing about the status of ethical propositions. More important is the following consideration: what is to be done when disagreement occurs — when one person claims to intuit that we should return good for evil and another claims to intuit that we should return evil for evil? It is useless to say that one of

---

[1] W. D. Ross, *The Right and the Good*, Ch. 2, in Sellars and Hospers, *Readings in Ethical Theory*, p. 184.

them must be mistaken and therefore has the wrong intuitions; for how is one to know which person? What if both persons are trying hard to arrive at the truth about the matter, both are sincere, both are intelligent and informed concerning the empirical facts of the moral situation? What now? We appear to have reached an impasse. Each disputant can accuse the other of having a mistaken intuition, and there seems to be no way of discovering which one is right. (Through another intuition? but how does one discover whether *that* intuition is right?) If intuition justifies the view of the first person, it also justifies the view of the second which contradicts the first; and if the second intuition is condemned as fraudulent or an intuitional error, why cannot the first be condemned in exactly the same way?

Of course, not *all* ethical statements are held to be known by intuition. It may be that only one is: for example, perhaps "Happiness is good" is intuited to be true, and right can be defined as what is productive of maximum happiness. In that event, you never have to intuit what is right — you discover that empirically by finding out what leads to the most happiness; you intuit only that happiness is good. But even this single-intuition view is vulnerable: (1) Many persons would not agree that "right" means the same as "productive of maximum happiness"; hedonistic utilitarians might, but not pluralistic utilitarians, Kantians, or for that matter Ross himself. (2) Even if only one intuition is needed, the problem about intuition has not been solved. If we can know how to validate *one* intuition, presumably we would have no trouble with the others. It is the introduction of the first one that brings in problems about validation, and one intuition is just as much in need of justification as a thousand would be.

The problem, moreover, is more serious here than it is in the empirical sciences or in mathematics. In empirical science, epistemologists usually agree, we ultimately reach reports of sense experience (protocol statements, as Carnap calls them) on which our scientific assertions are based; and though reports of sense experiences sometimes differ (one person may call an object red and a color-blind person may call it gray), there are elaborate techniques that have been worked out for deciding which sense experience is to be taken as veridical and why.[1] In any event, relying on sense experience is hardly the same thing as relying on intuition.

In mathematics, which is a deductive system, we do begin with certain axioms and definitions which are unproved. It has sometimes been said that the axioms are known to be true by intuition. The dispute is too complex to enter into at this point; (1) it would be more usual to say that the axioms are simply *postulated* at the beginning of the system; (2) however that may be, people do not disagree about mathematical conclusions as they do about ethical ones. We do not find some mathematical schools holding that two plus two is four whereas others hold that two plus two is five. But in ethics,

---

[1] See John Hospers, *Introduction to Philosophical Analysis* (Englewood Cliffs, N. J.: Prentice-Hall, 1953), Ch. 6.

when someone says that people should return good for evil, there are others who sincerely deny it, and thus there is a serious problem about how to find out whose view is the right one.

EXERCISES

1. The Oxford English Dictionary defines the word "good" as "the most general word of commendation in the English language." Do you find this definition helpful in solving the metaethical problem of the meaning of "good"? Explain.

2. If "good" is indefinable (at least in nonethical terms), does this indefinability make any difference, pro or con, to any of the theories of normative ethics we have examined in the preceding chapters? Explain.

3. Trace as many similarities and differences as you can between basic or ultimate principles in ethics and those of (*1*) mathematics, (*2*) the empirical sciences.

4. Which basic principle do you consider the more fundamental, the concept of goodness or that of obligation (right, duty)? Why?

5. Does it seem to you that Moore's argument concerning the naturalistic fallacy refutes ethical naturalism? Explain.

6. What kind of fallacy, if any, is involved if the naturalistic fallacy is interpreted as that of

a. trying to deduce ethical from nonethical statements?

b. trying to define ethical terms by means of nonethical ones?

c. assuming that ethical concepts are reducible to nonethical ones?

(See the article by Frankena on the reading list below.)

7. Do you agree or disagree with Moore's "open question" argument? Give your reasons.

8. List as many things as you can that people mean by the word "prove" when they state their demand, "Prove it!"

READING LIST, SECTION 25

Brandt, Richard. *Ethical Theory*. Englewood Cliffs, N. J.: Prentice-Hall, 1959, Ch. 8.

Broad, C. D. "Is 'Goodness' the Name of a Simple Non-natural Quality?" *Aristotelian Society Proceedings*, Vol. 34 (1933-4), pp. 249-68.

Ewing, Alfred C. *The Definition of the Good*. New York: Macmillan, 1947, especially Ch. 5.

———. *Ethics*. New York: Macmillan, 1953, Chs. 6 and 7.

———. "Naturalism and Subjectivism in Ethics." In Sellars, Wilfrid, and John Hospers, eds. *Readings in Ethical Theory*. New York: Appleton-Century-Crofts, 1952, pp. 115-33.

Field, G. C. "The Place of Definition in Ethics." In Sellars and Hospers. *Readings in Ethical Theory*, pp. 92-102.

Frankena, William K. "The Naturalistic Fallacy" (1939). In Sellars and Hospers. *Readings in Ethical Theory*, pp. 103-14.

Hall, Everett W. *What Is Value?* New York: Humanities Press, 1952, especially Chs. 2-4.

Johnson, O. A. "Ethical Intuitionism — a Restatement." *Philosophical Quarterly*, Vol. 7 (1957), pp. 193-203.

Kretzmann, Norman. "Desire as Proof of Desirability." *Philosophical Quarterly*, Vol. 8 (1958), pp. 246-58.

Moore, George Edward. *Philosophical Studies*. New York: Harcourt, Brace, 1922, Ch. 8.

———. *Principia Ethica* (1903). New York: Cambridge Univ. Press, 1959 (also paperbound), especially Ch. 1.

Nowell-Smith, Patrick. *Ethics*. Baltimore: Pelican Books, 1954, especially Chs. 2-4.

Prichard, H. A. "Does Moral Philosophy Rest on a Mistake?" (1912). In Sellars and Hospers. *Readings in Ethical Theory*, pp. 149-62.

Prior, Arthur N. *Logic and the Basis of Ethics*. New York: Oxford Univ. Press, 1949, especially Ch. 1.

Ross, Sir William David. *Foundations of Ethics*. (Gifford lectures, 1935-36) New York: Oxford Univ. Press, 1939.

———. *The Right and the Good* (1930). Especially Chs. 1 and 2. In Sellars and Hospers. *Readings in Ethical Theory*, pp. 163-209.

Strawson, P. F. "Ethical Intuitionism" (1949). In Sellars and Hospers. *Readings in Ethical Theory*, pp. 250-59.

26. Naturalistic theories

Let us see, then, whether we can escape any of these difficulties by adopting a naturalistic theory of ethics. It will not be enough for us to succeed in defining an ethical term; what is required is that it be defined by means of *non*ethical terms. To say that "good" means the same as "desirable" would not be naturalistic, for "desirable," as we have already seen, means approximately the same as *"ought* to be desired," and "ought," of course, is an ethical term. But to say that "good" means the same as "desired" would be naturalistic, for to say that something is desired is not to say anything about what ought to be: drunkenness may be desired but need not therefore be desirable; helping people in distress may be desirable but may not be desired.

The difficulty is to find a naturalistic theory that is in the least degree plausible. For it certainly *seems* as if ethical terms do not have the same meaning as any nonethical terms do. Nobody uses "good" to mean the same as "desired" (though it is a rough synonym of "desirable"), and to say that something is good as long as somebody desires it is quite absurd. Yet, just because "good" doesn't mean the same as "desired," or "pleasant," or "enjoyed," it doesn't follow that *no* definition of "good" or other ethical terms can be given.

A. Unsatisfactory naturalistic theories

Let us try a few rather obvious candidates for theories that will define ethical terms. The first suggestions will all turn out to be defective, and in rather obvious ways; but it is important to go through them nevertheless and see why they are defective so that we shall know what to watch out for when we come to more sophisticated attempts at definition. Since the word "right" has had simpler suggested definitions than "good," we shall begin with "right." (Actually it makes very little difference which term we use as an example, for as long as we are able to give an adequate definition of *one* ethical term, we shall have achieved our naturalistic breakthrough. Non-naturalism contends, remember, that *no* ethical term can be defined by means of nonethical terms. So if we find even *one* exception to this rule, nonnaturalists will have been refuted.)

1. The first suggested theory is that when you say that an act is right, all you mean is that *you morally approve the act.* ("Morally approve," not just "approve," for there is an experience we all have of conferring upon an act our *moral* approval, and what is being suggested is that morally approving something is the same as calling it right.) But this view will not stand inspection: to say that something is right is a very different thing from saying that we approve it. (1) In the first place, if it were the same, all you would have to do to discover whether an act was right would be to ask yourself whether you morally approved it, and that would settle the matter. If you morally approved it on Tuesday and (on further reflection) disapproved it on Wednesday, then the act would be right on Tuesday and wrong on Wednesday. (2) Second, what would the reflection be *about?* About whether the act is right or not; not about whether you approve it. People often know that they approve or disapprove something but still wonder whether they *ought* to — whether their approval is *justified* — in other words, whether the act is really right after all. They will approve it only if they also think it to be right — their thinking it right is not the same thing as their approving it, and the approval can be distinguished from the conviction that it is right. (3) Third, if all that the ethical statement amounts to is that the person in question approves it, then people never really disagree about matters of right and wrong — which seems plainly contrary to fact. Why does this conclusion follow? Because if Smith says he approves something and Jones says he disapproves it, they are not disagreeing at all: Smith doesn't deny that Jones disapproves it and Jones doesn't deny that Smith approves it; there is no proposition which one of them believes to be true which the other believes to be false. But when Smith says it was wrong of Brutus to kill Caesar and Jones says it was right of Brutus to do so, they *are* surely disagreeing about something. They may argue far into the night about the rightness or wrongness of the act, though they would never think about arguing about their respective moral approvals; each disputant al-

ready knows whether the other approves or disapproves the act in question. (There are many other objections, but these are sufficient.[1])

What superficial plausibility this view possesses arises from a confusion. When we say (sincerely) that an act is right, it is probably *also* true that we morally approve it — it would be strange to call something right and yet morally disapprove it. But this equation in no way shows that when we call an act right, what we *mean* is that we approve it. Our approval is not the *meaning* of the sentence we utter; rather, it is a *causal condition* for our *uttering* the sentence at this particular time. The conditions under which we say something are not at all the same as what we mean by the sentence when we say it. I would not be writing a book about ethics unless I were breathing — breathing is a condition that is always present when I write. But this fact doesn't show that what I mean by the sentences I write is simply that I am breathing. Once we keep in mind the difference between what we mean by a sentence and the conditions under which we utter the sentence, there will probably be not much temptation left to believe that "Act X is right" means no more or less than "I morally approve X."

2. Another possible theory is that when we say that an act is right, all we mean to say is that *most people* (the majority?) *morally approve it.* If majority approval did make an act right, there would be a comparatively easy way to discover whether an act was right or wrong — just take a poll and ask people whether or not they approve the kind of act in question. But taking a poll, while it does settle the question of what the majority of people *do* approve, does not begin to settle the question of what they *should* approve. A person who believes strongly that mandatory school segregation is wrong will not be convinced that it is right if he is told that the majority of people (in his state, in the South, even in his nation) approve segregation. Quite the contrary: he will hold his belief all the more firmly and will publicize it in order to cause other people to disapprove it as he does. Yet, if the theory we are now considering is correct, a person who has learned that the majority approve segregation would *have* to believe that it was right, since, according to the theory, "right" means no more than that the majority approve it. More than this: if he asserted that segregation was wrong, while it was true that the majority approved it, he would, according to the theory, be contradicting himself; for he would be saying, "I believe segregation is wrong, but nevertheless it is right (i.e. the majority approve it)." But of course, when people who are in the minority disagree with the majority, they are not uttering any such rank nonsense as this. Therefore, the proposed analysis cannot be correct.

This second theory does escape one difficulty of the first theory, namely that disagreement on matters of right and wrong is impossible according to the theory. For, according to our second theory, people can and do disagree. The trouble is, however, that disagreeing about whether something is right or wrong is one thing, and disagreeing about whether the majority approve or disapprove it is quite another thing; the second dispute can be settled by a public opinion poll, whereas the first one cannot.

It is plain, then, that the truth about matters of right and wrong cannot be discovered by simply introspecting or by taking a public opinion poll. But perhaps there are other possibilities.

3. A third suggested theory of the definition of ethical terms is that when we say that an act is right, the meaning of this assertion is that *God commands (or approves)* the act. At first this possibility may come as a surprise: "I thought you were talking about naturalistic theories, and this view is *super*naturalistic." But this surprise results from a confusion of terminology: in one common meaning of the word "naturalistic," it is opposed to "supernaturalistic." But that is not the meaning given the term in ethics. The so-called naturalistic fallacy is that of equating the meaning of an ethical term with that of *any nonethical terms whatever;* and, of course, theological terms like "God" are just as much nonethical terms as empirical terms are. Thus, the view that "The act is right" means the same as "God commands or approves it" is just as much a naturalistic theory as the view that "The act is right" means "Society approves it" or "I approve it."

We have already discussed the problem of divine commands (pages 31-34, 184-89) — not, however, as the *meaning* of right (we discuss that now for the first time), but as the criterion for *testing* the rightness of an act. Clearly what I *mean* by a word or sentence need not be the same as the criterion I use for testing the truth of a sentence in which the word appears. For example, when I say that there is a full moon above the horizon, what I mean to say is that there is a real physical object, many thousands of miles away, visible to me now; but the criterion I use for testing the statement is sense experience: I observe whether a round yellowish shape appears in my visual field when I look in the appropriate direction. In a world in which all red objects were round and all round objects were red, a blind man's criterion for discovering whether something was red would be to feel it and discover whether it was round; but, though he could use this criterion without making mistakes as long as the correlation of redness with roundness held true, the criterion used would be different from the meaning: for what is meant by calling it red is that it has a certain color, not that it has a certain shape. When a physicist reports on what is going on in the cyclotron, he *means* by his assertion certain things going on in the cyclotron, but the criterion he uses for judging what goes on is observation of readings on his various instruments.

Nevertheless, though the meaning of a sentence and the criterion we use for verifying it are not the same, we run into many of the same objections that were already cited in discussing divine command as a criterion of right. Indeed, if it is implausible to hold that divine command constitutes a satisfactory *criterion* of rightness, it is even less plausible to hold that it constitutes the very *meaning* of the sentence "The act is right." Thus: people who don't believe in God can still believe that something is right, so at least *they* don't mean by saying "It's right" the same as "God commands it." Are religious people declaring that nonreligious people cannot attach any meaning to ethical sentences or that they mean something without knowing it? Moreover, which God do they mean? Would they believe that what God commanded was right *no matter what* it was that (they believed) God commanded? [1]

Once the existence of divine commands had been established and the goodness of the Deity had also been established (so as to be sure that He would not issue bad commands), the nature of the divine commands would provide a reliable *indicator* or *criterion* of what was right; but it would still not show that the commands constitute *the very meaning* of sentences about right acts.

B. The Ideal Observer theory

But perhaps we can remedy some of our previously rejected theories by being a bit subtler. Instead of saying, "I approve the act," let us say, "I have a *tendency* or *disposition* to approve the act." That is, we *would* approve it under certain specified circumstances, even though we may not now approve it; we would approve it if we thought about it more, for instance. And let us refine our definition still further to read, not "I have a tendency to approve this act," since you could hardly have had the tendency to approve it before you knew it existed, but "I have a tendency to approve *acts like this one.*" This definition is admittedly vague, for how much (and in what respects) like this act does an act have to be before it is said to be really like this one? Nevertheless, these changes may be counted as improvements, for with one more change we can come up with a much more plausible naturalistic theory, the Ideal Observer theory.

According to this theory, not I, but *anyone* who was impartial (and perhaps fulfilled some other conditions as well, which we shall discuss below), *would* approve acts like this one (or perhaps even this act). This statement is a hypothetical one: it does not assert that there actually *is* anyone who is impartial, etc. but that *if* anyone were, *then* what he morally approved would be (by definition) right. The theory does not guarantee, then, that we can consult with actual people to determine their views and find what is right, because no actual people may live up to the required specifications. Although the view is sometimes called the Ideal Observer theory, there may be no Ideal Observers. Whether there are or not, however, makes no difference to the theory. It may be, of course, that only God is an Ideal Observer. That too is admitted by the theory as a possibility, but it is not required by the

---

[1] For a detailed and careful discussion of this topic, see R. Brandt, *Ethical Theory*, Ch. 4.

theory. Correcting the previous theory (the third), which assumes the *existence* of God in order to make ethical statements meaningful, the present theory says, *"If* there is or were an Ideal Observer (perhaps God, perhaps not), what this Ideal Observer morally approves is (by definition) right."

The fact that the theory is couched in a hypothetical form may make some persons suspicious. This hypothetical form alone, however, is not a decisive objection; many empirical statements, in fact, are hypothetical in character and yet not even the most tough-minded scientist objects to them: for example, "If you drop this lump of sugar into water, it will dissolve," or even "If you walk to the corner, you will see a mailbox." These statements, of course, are predictions as to what will happen if we do something else first, but something nevertheless within our power to do — unlike being Ideal Observers. These statements do not state anything *contrary to fact.* Yet even contrary-to-fact hypothetical statements are constantly used in daily life: "If you had been here last night, you would have seen Mr. Robinson." "If we had been stationed on the moon, the earth would have been visible to us as a disk considerably larger than the moon appears from the earth." In the same way we might say, "If you were an Ideal Observer you would say . . ." or "If you met an Ideal Observer he would say . . ."

So far so good. But there is a difficulty: in practice, the theory is in great danger of running in a logical circle. If we were convinced that something was right and that we were quite impartial in so thinking, we would probably reject the opinion of anyone else, rejecting his verdict as "not being impartial." He, of course, would return the compliment. The theory can very easily be used as a way of making one's own moral convictions infallible by definition.

Suppose, however, that this difficulty is overcome — that we are on to this trick, and that we are prepared to defer in our judgments to others who have passed the tests for being Ideal Observers. Precisely what are these tests?

a. As already indicated, a person would not be said to be an Ideal Observer unless he were *impartial* — that is, unless he were entirely free of bias. Bias is most likely to occur when the person himself is involved in the situation, and judges it in his own favor in order to rationalize what he wants to do. As we have observed in previous chapters, a good test of impartiality to put to someone in this situation would be to ask: "Would you still say the same thing if the roles were reversed?" Another is: "Would you still say it was right if you were not personally involved in the situation and had nothing to gain or lose either way?"

b. A person would not be said to be an Ideal Observer if he were lacking in knowledge of the facts relevant to the situation. For example, a person might condemn Mr. A for attacking Mr. B but would not have condemned him had he known that Mr. B had assaulted Mr. A's wife. You might praise someone for passing an examination with honors, until you discovered that he had achieved this result by means of cheating. Clearly, an Ideal Observer must have before him *all* the relevant facts of the situation. There might, of course, be some difficulty in deciding which facts were relevant. But if we specified that our Ideal Observer must know *all* facts (in other words, be omniscient), this difficulty would be taken care of.

c. But information is not enough. A man might know that thousands of people are starving in another part of the world, yet the knowledge might not move him in the slightest — it would be "just a pile of meaningless statistics." To be an Ideal Observer, he must be able to project himself vividly, in his imagination, into the problems and feelings of other human beings. He must be able, in fact, to be fully aware of their situations, their feelings, their total experience. People differ greatly in their capacity for imaginative sympathy, but it is probably safe to say that no human being possesses it with regard to others as much as he does with regard to himself. Yet the requirement specifies that he do this equally with regard to all those involved in the situation in which he must make a choice.

d. The Ideal Observer must be in a certain frame of mind — calm, dispassionate, reflective, able to weigh all the evidence pro and con, able to see both sides of an issue, not blinded by passion and special interests. This is, to be sure, a rather vague requirement, but some such requirement must be met before we can call anyone an Ideal Observer. He would not be an Ideal Observer all the time but only when his state of mind was such as we have specified. Nor does this requirement seem to be an impossible one: most people, it would seem, *can* be in such a frame of mind at some times — at least when their own interests are not involved; some people have these qualities to a very high degree when evaluating the acts of others, but they cannot seem to "get out of themselves" long enough to possess them in evaluating their own past or future acts. Other people, however, seem to be unable ever to fulfill the requirement: they look at every issue with some vested interest and are unable ever to be calm and dispassionate; they see every issue that arises only insofar as it affects *them*. (Man to his wife: "I don't like women; they take everything you say personally." Wife: "*I* don't.") This inability to be dispassionate may be a matter of inadequate childhood training and bad habits, but sometimes it may be a matter of native temperament and is relatively unchangeable. Such persons are not equipped to be Ideal Observers.

e. Are these requirements enough? Some have suggested that still another requirement is necessary: that the person be psychologically *normal*. Suppose a person is a gambler or adventurer by temperament, or a ne'er-do-well, who nevertheless is intelligent and perceptive and has many moments of calm and dispassionateness. No matter how calmly he reflects on a matter, no matter how he puts himself in another's place and visualizes the other's difficulties, his answer still comes out differently from that of other people. He wants life to be exciting and dangerous. No matter how impartial he tries to be, even in judging policies in which he is in no way personally involved, he will tend to make decisions which expose people to a great amount of danger and risk because he thinks that life is more interesting and exciting that way and because he thinks that nothing is worse than dullness and humdrum. He knows, of course, that most people most of the time don't particularly like this much excitement and risk and playing for high stakes; but he believes that if they did develop an appetite for excitement through experience or conditioning, they *would* enjoy it. Every judgment he makes, including moral judgments, will be colored by this basic temperamental penchant of his.

Some critics say that such people should be excluded as Ideal Observers because they have this kind of temperament. But this exclusion generates problems. (1) Does the possession of *any temperament whatever* prevent them from being Ideal Observers, or Ideal Judges? If so, then, since everyone has some temperamental characteristics, there can be no such thing as an Ideal Observer among the ranks of human beings. Indeed, what would such a person be like? Can we even imagine one? Only God, we might say, fulfills this condition. But even to choose God is a difficulty: can we really imagine how a timeless being who had no infancy and no childhood, no conditioning, no habits, would judge? Can we imagine what such a being would be like? (2) But if only people with *some specified type* of temperamental trait are to be excluded from the ranks of Ideal Observers, then which ones? and by what criterion? If we say that we are "normal" and the adventurous man is not because we are in the majority and he in the minority, our statement is doubtless true in the statistical sense of "normal," but what does it prove? The frequency of something proves nothing about its desirability. (See pages 75-77.) But on what other basis can we show that we are in a better position to be Ideal Observers than our adventurer? What if he were to turn the tables on us by saying that it is he who has the desirable type of temperament, even though he *is* in the minority, and that we are biased by our temperamental penchant toward safety and middle-class respectability? How are we going to show him that we are more "normal" in a *non*statistical sense than he is? If we can show him, does it really show that we are better equipped to be Ideal Observers than he is?

Perhaps this cascade of objections is fatal to the Ideal Observer theory. But let us assume that the difficulties can be overcome; is the theory then satisfactory as a naturalistic account of the meaning of ethical terms?

Having described the Ideal Observer theory, if we were to ask people "Is this description what you meant all along by calling something good or right?" they would probably say, "Of course not." They would say that they first asked themselves whether an act was right, and then thought of how it would be judged by an Ideal Observer (as described), and *then* compared the two to see whether in their opinion the two judgments would always coincide. But if this procedure is truly what most people follow, it would seem that there are still *two* characteristics, (1) that of being right and (2) that of being approved by an Ideal Observer. The two may have the same denotation, just as "equilateral triangles" and "equiangular triangles" have the same denotation, but they still do not *mean* the same; two characteristics may always go together, but that doesn't make them one characteristic. If there really are two characteristics, then the Ideal Observer theory has not succeeded as a naturalistic theory, which claims to give us the meaning of the ethical term. If it does not define the term but only tells us what *other* property is regularly associated with that of rightness, then it no more tells us what rightness is than a definition of equiangularity tells us what it is to be equilateral. We are back once more with Moore's "open question" argument: can't one always significantly ask, "I know that this act has property X (being approved by an Ideal Observer), but still, *is* it right?" If the question is not self-contradictory, and it surely seems not to be, then once again we have two characteristics on our hands rather than one, and the naturalistic approach has not succeeded.

The "open question" technique, designed by Moore to refute all naturalistic theories, has not gone uncriticized. Consider just one example. If we are given the definition of the word "circle" as "a plane, closed figure, all of the points on whose circumference are equidistant from a point within called the center," we shall probably accept this definition without hesitation. Yet can we truthfully say that this definition was *what we had in mind all along* when we called a figure a circle? Surely we did not think of this rather technical definition when as children we correctly identified circles on the blackboard and easily distinguished them from squares, ellipses, and parabolas. We did not, then, have the definition *consciously* in mind during the years before we studied plane geometry. Yet in *some* way we must have had it in mind, for it was no accident that we always performed the identification with 100 per cent accuracy. (In Plato's dialogue *Meno* and elsewhere, Socrates argues that we must have had such definitions in mind in some sense, else we would not be able to recognize an acceptable definition when we came across it.) In what way? Perhaps somewhat as follows: we had never before actually thought of the suggested definition, but once we did come across it we found that (1) the definition covered everything to which we had applied the name, (2) the definition did not cover anything to which we had not applied the name, and (3) we had been *using* all along the specifications given in the definition without consciously thinking of them — we had been aware of them only in the sense that we *used* them, without, however, having *verbalized* them, and therefore without having the exact words of the definition before our minds. We might suggest that if these three conditions are met by a definition, then it is perfectly satisfactory and acceptable as a definition in spite of the fact that we had never previously thought of it and therefore could not have had it before our minds all the time. Was it "what we had meant all along"? It was, in the sense of satisfying the three conditions above; but it was not, in the sense of having it verbally articulated before our minds all along. "But I didn't (consciously) mean that!" is, therefore, no objection to its acceptability as a definition of the term in question. But whether the Ideal Observer theory gives us "what we had meant all along" even in this modified sense, can, of course, still be questioned.

C. Ralph Barton Perry's theory

Let us examine, in conclusion, a rather different kind of naturalistic theory, one whose emphasis is upon the nature of the act or situation itself, rather than on the nature of the observer or judge of the act. The late Ralph Barton Perry has undertaken to give us a naturalistic account not only of moral values ("good," "right," "duty") but of aesthetic value, economic value, and all other kinds of value, by defining the value term "value" itself. (Its relation to "good" will be seen shortly.) What is it for something to have value, or to be valuable? According to Perry, anything has value *when it is the object of an interest* — any interest. To the cat, the cream has value; to a drug addict, the drug has value. "Thus the valuableness of peace is the characteristic conferred on peace by the interest which is taken in it, for what it is, or for any of its attributes, effects, or implications." [1] Since "interest" is an empirical term, Perry *has* given us a naturalistic definition.

But what, next, is interest? It is not the same as what we have described in the previous pages as *self*-interest; self-interest is only one special kind of interest, interest directed toward some state of the self. Interest, says Perry, is "a train of events determined by expectation of its outcome. Or, a thing is an object of interest when its being expected induces actions looking to its realization or non-realization. Thus peace is an object of interest when acts believed to be conducive to peace, or preventive of peace, are performed on that account, or when events are selected or rejected because peace is expected of them." [2] Anything is good in the widest sense of that word, when it is an object of pro-interest, bad when it is an object of anti-interest.

But aren't there good pro-interests and bad ones? Of course there are. But how then can value attach to *any* object of an interest, and goodness to any object of a pro-interest? A certain drug has value to the addict because he has an interest in it; but is it good just because he has a pro-interest? Perry replies that the drug, considered *merely* an object of pro-interest, has positive value and is good. But it is also an object of strong anti-interest by other people, and to that extent it is bad; already, probably, the bad outweighs the good. Moreover, the addiction prevents the person himself from either taking or fulfilling countless other interests which he *might* have ful-

[1] From Ralph Barton Perry, *Realms of Value*. Cambridge: Harvard Univ. Press, 1954, p. 3. Reprinted by permission of the publisher.
[2] *Ibid.*

filled if he did not have the interest in this one fatal thing; that is, this interest is deleterious to the whole *system* of his own interests. Similarly, an unpleasant-tasting medicine is bad in that it is dreaded and has an unpleasant taste; yet if it cures the patient, enabling him to pursue his other interests, it must be counted as more good than bad, on the whole. Indeed a person may have a pro-interest in taking something that turns out to be poisonous: in respect of having the pro-interest directed toward it, the poison is good, but nevertheless, no matter how much its taste may be enjoyed, it is bad when the *total interest pattern* is considered, since the imbibing of it puts an end forever to all his other interests. *"Whatever is desired, liked, enjoyed, willed, hoped for, is thereby good,"* says Perry;[1] but the opposite of each of these states is bad, and the bad may outweigh the good even though the good is present.

Almost everything in the world, then, has both its good and its bad aspects, and there is virtually nothing known to man that is not good in some respect or other. But the question whether it is good *on the whole,* or *on balance,* is the question whether the pro-interests (being liked, enjoyed, willed, hoped for) predominate over the anti-interests. The object of one person's pro-interests may be the object of everyone else's anti-interests; and even within the person himself, a thing may be an object of his pro-interest but may be at odds with all his *other* pro-interests — it does not "harmonize" with them — and when this situation is true, the pursuit of the thing in question must be condemned as *on the whole* bad.

Considering only the individual himself, the most desirable state of affairs is for his entire life to consist of *one harmonious pattern of interests,* with each individual interest cooperating with every other interest, rather than for some of the interests to be obstructive of the others. Such a life will be the best possible for the individual concerned.

But just as one interest in a man's life may be obstructive of others, so it is possible for the sum total of a man's interests, even if they form one total harmonious pattern, to be obstructive of the interests of other human beings. The interests of an individual *may* be centered in, and harmonized around, safe-cracking; but this object of *his* harmoniously integrated pro-interests may be the object of everyone *else's* anti-interests, so his activity is still, on the whole, bad. It frustrates more total value (interests) than it achieves. The best society, then, is the one containing the maximum possible fulfillment of pro-interests. Finally (bringing in "right" for the first time), that act is right which makes possible the maximum fulfillment of pro-interests of everyone concerned.

By this time Perry's theory will have a familiar ring: it turns out to be a somewhat refined version of utilitarianism — indeed, an interesting general theory housing (social) utilitarianism and (individual) self-realization

[1] *Ibid.*

together under the same roof. Why then are we discussing it at this late stage of our inquiry? Because Perry presents his account not merely as a true theory of normative ethics but as a *definition* of "value," and thence, indirectly, of "good" and more indirectly of "right." As such, his account falls under our present subject, naturalistic theories of ethics.

As a theory of normative ethics, Perry's is a fascinating and exciting one. But objections have been made to it on the grounds of what it purports to be, a naturalistic definition of ethical terms. Does Perry's theory really give us "the *meaning* of these ethical terms"? Utilitarians — those who not only accept utilitarianism as a theory of normative ethics but accept it also as an account of the meaning of ethical terms — may say that it does. But others will not. Most people, it seems, believe that some things are not good even though they do fulfill Perry's criterion of maximum fulfillment of pro-interest, and they certainly do not believe that they are good *in proportion to* the degree to which they fulfill Perry's criterion. Most people consider incest wrong, but does it really violate Perry's criterion as much as other things such as tax evasion, which they condemn much less? Perhaps people are mistaken in so thinking; but as long as they do, it would seem that they cannot mean by "good" and "right" the same thing that Perry means by them. In fact, even many people who *would* agree with Perry about what things are good and what acts are right, would disagree with Perry's view that fulfillment of pro-interest is our very meaning in calling them good or right.

Such is, in brief, the main line of attack on Perry's view that his theory gives us a *definition* of value terms. But Perry, in offering us his definitions, does not claim that these definitions are what people *actually mean* by these value words. He does not consider the question "What does 'X' mean?" to be the same as the question "What do people (you, I, others) *mean* by 'X'?" This point is an extremely important one in a consideration of Perry's theory, and indeed of naturalistic theories in general.

> Some philosophers, unfortunately, put the question concerning value in the form "What *is* meant by 'value'?" or "What *does* one mean by 'value'?" as though that meaning were already determined, and it was only necessary to call attention to it. Those who approach the matter in this way are accustomed to challenge a proposed definition of value by saying, "But this is not what is meant by 'value'" or "This is not what one means by 'value.'" The fact is, however, that there is no such established and universal meaning. Different people mean different things in different contexts. The problem is not to discover a present meaning — there are only too many meanings.
>
> The problem is not solved, however, by simply enumerating these many meanings. This job is already done by the unabridged dictionaries which list, in fine print, all the varieties of meaning which appear in literature and ordinary speech. Theory of value is in search of a preferred meaning. The problem is to define, that is, *give* a meaning to the term, either by selecting from its existing meanings, or by creating a new meaning.

But one must not then leap to the conclusion that this giving of a meaning to the term "value" is an arbitrary matter, dictated by the caprice, or mere personal convenience, of the author. One can, it is true, make the term mean "anything one likes," but this would not advance knowledge, or be of the slightest importance, or be capable either of proof or of disproof. The man who said "When I say 'value' I mean a purple cow" would not even be listened to, unless by a psychiatrist or a kindergarten teacher. There must, in other words, be a control or set of criteria, by which the definition is justified or rejected.[1]

At this point Perry proposes the definitions of "value" and "interest" which we have already considered.

In view of these remarks, how are Perry's definitions to be construed? (1) Are they *stipulative* definitions — merely a statement of how *he* is going to use the terms? If so, why should we accept his stipulations? But in view of his remarks about "purple cow," it is quite certain that he is not merely giving us new stipulative definitions. (2) Are they *reforming* definitions? Is he just saying "it would be a good thing if everybody adopted my definitions"? But by what criterion would it be "good" if everyone adopted his definitions? By the criterion of "good" which he himself sets forth? But in this case he would be arguing in a circle. (3) No, it seems fairly certain that he is trying to give *reportive* definitions of these terms — he is trying to state what these terms mean as people actually *do* use them in daily life; but as we have seen, this is not the same as stating what people say they mean by them, or even what they consciously do mean by them, for of course most people have never heard of these definitions until they read Perry's work. What Perry offers us is rather an *explication* of the criteria people employ (though not with their own conscious knowledge) in using these terms — in distinguishing what they call "good" from what they call "bad," in distinguishing situations containing value from those which do not. In other words, Perry is offering us something analogous to the definition of "circle" which the geometer gives to people who have never studied geometry; the definition he gives does not correspond to what they have consciously meant by the term, but it does give the criteria they themselves have used all along in distinguishing circles from non-circles.

OBJECTOR: I agree with you about "circle," but not about "value" and "good."

ADVOCATE OF PERRY: Let me first remind you of this fact: everywhere in the special disciplines, terms are taken from daily life and used with more precise meanings than they have in ordinary contexts. Physics uses terms such as "matter," "energy," "mass," "resistance," all in a more precise way than the laity uses them. Science could not proceed very far without this precision. There is a continuity between the ordinary usage and the scientific usage of these terms, but it is not the same: don't expect to exclaim after you've heard the scientific definition, "Why, that's what I meant by the term all along!" Can't philosophy do what the sciences constantly do,

[1] *Ibid.*, p. 2.

take as much as possible from the ordinary meaning of a term and then, in the interest of clarity and precision, decide on a precise meaning which still operates to a large extent in the same area as its ordinary usage?

o: Of course; but to the extent that you are doing this, your definitions *are* stipulative — you are stipulating a new meaning for a term which still has much in common with its ordinary meaning. I don't deny you the right to do this, but I do deny your right to impose it on others; why should *we* accept these definitions of yours? Specifically, why should we accept them in the case of "good"? Why should *I* favor X because you say, "X is good according to *my* definition of 'good'?"

p: True; I merely made my remark about definitions in science as a precautionary measure. What I really contend is that my definitions aren't stipulations at all. I contend that they report the meanings of value terms as you and I and others use them and have used them all along; that is, they state the criteria that you use as well as I in deciding whether something is to be called good or valuable.

o: But this is clearly false! Suppose I am a Kantian and I claim that lying is always wrong, even when a certain act of lying fulfills *your* requirement for goodness (preponderance of pro-interests); then certainly I am not going by *your* definition of "good."

p: This doesn't follow. All the students in the class may agree that one plus one is two and that adding one to any integer gives the next highest integer, and yet some of them may make mistakes in doing complicated feats of addition; they agree to certain premises, and yet don't always stick to them in the application. So here: if I can get you to agree on my basic definitions, and I think I can once you understand them, then you are only being inconsistent when you deny their implications at a later stage of the inquiry.

o: Granted; but suppose I deny your basic definitions. In other respects, I admire your theory very much; with a few basic definitions you have organized the whole field of human values, including ethics, in such a way that every item now springs into place — a frustratingly complex area of inquiry has become simplified and clarified, like an image suddenly brought into focus. All the concepts in the value scheme derive from the concept of interest; and, into the bargain, all ethical issues have become empirical issues, decidable in principle by the methods of science instead of being left in the limbo of intuition. You have heroically endeavored to touch the nerve of all talk about value, and, in so doing, to bridge the gap between the empirical and the ethical. You have achieved unity and given us a naturalistic theory, all in one brilliant stroke. In view of this achievement, it may seem ungrateful of me to say that I doubt whether you've really brought it off. But I must, for I doubt whether the definitions you give *do* give an explication of the meanings of value terms.

p: Then we must start over again, going way back to the cat and the cream. Don't you agree that value arises only when a subject (a conscious being) takes an interest in an object (not necessarily a physical object)? that the mountain has no value to anyone until someone sees it and admires its beauty (intrinsic value) or finds mineral deposits in it from which he can profit (instrumental value)? Without consciousness there is no value. And don't you agree that an object has positive (or plus-) value when a pro-interest is taken in it, and a negative (or minus-) value when an anti-interest is taken in it (e.g., when the observer finds it ugly, or a barrier to travel)? Having granted so much, don't you agree that the *more* pro-interests an object satisfies or fulfills, the more value it has? and that it may have plus-value for some and minus-value for others? and that we must estimate its *overall* value by considering its relation to the *entire* system of interests involving everyone concerned? and thus that it is good (on the whole, on balance) if it fulfills a preponderance of all the pro-interests? and, when the thing in question is an act, that it's right when it helps, more than any other possible act, to achieve such a preponderance?

o: I admit that this all sounds very plausible. . . .

p: And I suggest that you hesitate to accept it *in toto* because of its strangeness and unfamiliarity. I submit that the basic building blocks of the system (the definitions of "value," "good," "right") *are* acceptable. But these are the premises from which my entire system follows; and you cannot accept the premises without also accepting their implications. If some of the moral beliefs you hold (e.g., that lying is *always* wrong) conflict with my system, I suggest that the reason for this conflict is that you haven't thought the whole system through. You haven't seen how the goodness or badness of anything in the world can be empirically tested in terms of my theory (though it is often difficult in practice owing to the complexity of the world); and particularly, you haven't seen how, owing to these complexities, it is easy to grant the initial premises and yet deny their implications in complicated cases. If you find the premises acceptable (and I think you do — at least I have heard no arguments against them), then in consistency you must accept the conclusions that follow from them — just as the student who accepts certain basic principles of addition must grant that 84,938 plus 59,027 equals 143,965, and only fails to get that result through a mistake in his addition. I submit to you that it is not my premises that are mistaken, but your addition.

Here we must rest Perry's case. If, on reflection, you find his view acceptable, then you have reached one goal — a satisfactory naturalistic theory of ethics. If, however, you do not accept it, you will have to continue the search. Either way, another type of theory remains to be discussed — one quite different from either of the two types that we have thus far considered.

EXERCISES

1. Which of the following would be naturalistic theories? "Good" means

a. what is desired.

b. what is desirable.

c. what would be desired by an ideal observer.

d. what is reasonably desired.

e. what all men desire to desire.

Evaluate each of the above theories as a claim to render the meaning of "good."

2. In your opinion, are psychological and anthropological investigations helpful in an understanding of the meaning of ethical terms? Explain.

3. Evaluate the view that "right" *means* (*1*) what is in the direction of evolution; (*2*) what is to the interest of the strongest (Thrasymachus in Plato's *Republic*); (*3*) what is ordained by God.

4. Large numbers of ethical disagreements occur because the disputants have inadequate and fragmentary knowledge of the full facts of the situation. Do you think that most, or all, ethical disputes would be resolved if all parties to the dispute were acquainted with *all* the facts that might conceivably have a bearing on the moral judgment in question?

5. Now add, one by one, the other specifications set forth by the Ideal Observer theory. Do you think that two people who fulfilled *all* the requirements for an Ideal Observer would (or could) ever disagree in their moral judgments? Explain.

6. Do you think the last two requirements for the Ideal Observer are needed on their own, or are needed (if at all) only as necessary conditions for the fulfillment of the first three requirements?

7. Explain exactly why Perry's view is incompatible with the belief that the goodness or badness of something depends on anyone's *opinion* about whether it is good or bad ("there's nothing good nor bad but thinking makes it so").

8. After hearing Perry's definition of "value," someone says, "But that's not what I mean by the word! I never even heard of a definition like this before!" Why is this objection not a good refutation of Perry's definition?

9. A theory of right is said to be *subjectivistic* when the rightness of the act depends on the *attitude* of some conscious being or beings toward the act (the agent, an observer, or many observers, or ideal observers, or God); it is said to be *objectivistic* when the rightness of the act depends, not on anyone's attitude toward it, but on the nature of the act itself (its characteristics, its consequences, its causes or motives, its universalizability, etc.). Classify all the theories discussed in this section as subjectivistic or objectivistic, and justify your answer in each case.

10. Do you agree or disagree with the following? Why? "What is it that is missing from any naturalist or subjectivist account? . . . Most important . . . is the concept of obligation. 'Good' in its non-natural sense or senses carries with it the notion that the good thing *ought* not to be wantonly sacrificed but, other things being equal, pursued. Now to say that I wish for something or that I have a certain kind of emotional feeling about it . . . does not entail that I am under any obligation whatever to produce the objects of this wish or emotion." (A. C. Ewing, "Subjectivism and Naturalism in Ethics," in Sellars and Hospers, *Readings in Ethical Theory*, p. 125.)

READING LIST, SECTION 26

Brandt, Richard. *Ethical Theory*. Englewood Cliffs, N. J.: Prentice-Hall, 1959, Ch. 7.

―――. "The Status of Empirical Assertion Theories in Ethics." *Mind,* Vol. 61 (1952), pp. 458-79.

Broad, C. D. "Some Reflections on Moral-sense Theories in Ethics." In Sellars and Hospers. *Readings in Ethical Theory*, pp. 368-88.

Campbell, C. A. "Moral and Non-moral Values." (1935) In Sellars and Hospers. *Readings in Ethical Theory*, pp. 340-62.

Dewey, John. "The Construction of Good." In Sellars and Hospers. *Readings in Ethical Theory*, pp. 272-91.

Field, Guy C. *Moral Theory*. London: Methuen, 1921, Ch. 11.

Firth, Roderick. "Ethical Absolutism and the Ideal Observer." *Philosophy and Phenomenological Research*, Vol. 12 (1952), pp. 317-45.

Harrison, Jonathan. "Empiricism in Ethics." *Philosophical Quarterly*, Vol. 2 (1952), pp. 289-306.

Lewis, Clarence Irving. *An Analysis of Knowledge and Valuation*. (Paul Carus lectures, 1945) LaSalle, Ill.: Open Court Publishing, 1946, Chs. 12-17.

Pepper, Stephen C. *The Sources of Value*. Berkeley: Univ. of California Press, 1959.

Perry, Ralph Barton. *General Theory of Value* (1926). Cambridge: Harvard Univ. Press, 1954.

―――. *Realms of Value,* especially Chs. 1-8. Cambridge: Harvard Univ. Press, 1954.

―――. "Value as Any Object of Any Interest." In Sellars and Hospers. *Readings in Ethical Theory*, pp. 292-309.

Ross, Sir William David. "The Nature of Goodness." In Sellars and Hospers. *Readings in Ethical Theory*, pp. 310-31.

Russell, Bertrand. *Human Society in Ethics and Politics*. New York: Simon and Schuster, 1954, Chs. 8 and 9.

Santayana, George. "Hypostatic Ethics." In Sellars and Hospers. *Readings in Ethical Theory*, pp. 263-71.

Sharp, Frank C. "Voluntarism and Objectivity in Ethics." *Philosophical Review*, Vol. 50 (1941), pp. 253-67.

Westermarck, Edvard A. *Ethical Relativity*. New York: Harcourt, Brace, 1932, Ch. 5.

White, M. G. "Value and Obligation in Dewey and Lewis." In Sellars and Hospers. *Readings in Ethical Theory*, pp. 332-39.

Ziff, Paul. *Semantic Analysis*. Ithaca, N. Y.: Cornell Univ. Press, 1960, especially Ch. 5.

27. *The emotive theory*

What, then, is the next step? When we utter ethical sentences, we *seem* to be saying things which are not at all the same as when we utter empirical sentences or mathematical sentences or any other kind of nonethical sentences; so nonnaturalistic theories have the greatest initial plausibility. But the concept of intuition and the difficulties about verification may lead us to abandon nonnaturalism in favor of naturalism. Yet naturalism, though it overcomes the verification problem by making ethical statements ultimately empirical, fails to convince many people that what it provides us with is a translation of ethical sentences in their original meaning; we ask for bread and we get cake, but it is not bread. So, at least, the critics of naturalism are inclined to believe. But what alternative is there?

Let us consider now an alternative, which, whatever we may think of it in the final analysis, contains many helpful suggestions and calls attention to important points at which we have not even hinted up to now; the *emotive* theory. (Sometimes it is called "noncognitive," in opposition to the two types of theory already considered, which are called "cognitive" because they both hold that ethical sentences are used to *state* something.) The fact to which the emotive theory appeals, and which it says has not even been considered by the other theories, is that language is employed for purposes other than to inform us of facts. When we say, "The movie lasted an hour and forty-five minutes," we are stating a fact about the movie; but when we say, "The movie was boring," we are, *primarily*, not stating a fact about it, but rather expressing our own reaction to it. If we were asked, "What property of the picture are you referring to in calling it boring?" you might answer, "I wasn't talking about a property of the picture itself at all. I was expressing my own attitude to it, the way I felt about it." The theories considered thus far make the mistake, according to the emotive theory, of assuming that adjectives are always the names of properties, or qualities. Some adjectives indeed *are* the names of properties — "large," "green," "heavy" — but some are not — "boring," "interesting," "gorgeous." Previous ethical theories have assumed without question that moral adjectives like "good" and "right" belong to the first group rather than to the second.

If, according to the ethical emotivist, we broaden our conception of the function of language and try to see what we are really *doing* when we use sentences containing ethical terms, it will be clear that we are not so much *stating facts* about the things we call good as *taking an attitude* toward them. When the child is told by its mother not to do something because "It's wrong," particularly when the utterance is made in a threatening tone, he probably has no idea of any property of the act that the mother is referring to in calling it wrong. But what comes through to the child without any difficulties whatever is that the mother, in using the word "wrong," is expressing a disapproving and condemning attitude toward the act in question. She is not describing the act; she is not even describing her own reactions to it in saying, "It's wrong"; she is not describing anything at all but expressing her attitude toward it and trying to instill a similar attitude toward it in the child. Let us consider these two factors separately:

1. Ethical words and sentences are used to *express* people's feelings and attitudes. Usually when we use words like "good" and "right" we are expressing our approval of the acts or people or situations to which we apply the words, and in using "bad" and "wrong" we express disapproval. In moral situations, we are expressing *moral* approval and disapproval; we may approve someone's swimming technique, but this is not moral approval as is the approval of beneficent action. The word "good" is customarily used for both kinds of approval.

We should be especially careful, at this point, not to confuse the emotive theory with our first naturalistic theory, according to which "X is wrong" means the same as "I morally disapprove X." According to that naturalistic theory, when you say something is wrong you are *stating* that you disapprove it — a statement which of course is false if you do not actually disapprove it. But according to the emotive theory, you are not stating anything at all; you are expressing an attitude toward it but not stating that you have the attitude. "I feel sad" states how you feel, but "Alas!" expresses your feeling without stating anything. According to the emotive theory, ethical utterances are like the second, not like the first.

2. Ethical words and sentences are used not only to express feelings and attitudes but to *evoke* or generate them in others. Evocative language is not speaker-directed but audience-directed. When you say, "Better see that movie, it's good," you are not so much expressing your own liking of the movie as encouraging your hearer to see it. When you say to a child, "It's wrong to steal that candy, it doesn't belong to you," you are not so much expressing your own disapproval of stealing (you don't need to remind yourself that *you* disapprove of it) as trying to get the child to disapprove of it enough to refrain in the future. In other words, you are using language *directively* — to direct the course of other people's attitudes and feelings. You are trying, by your use of language, to exert an influence upon others and thus to change their behavior. Children are encouraged to do certain things and refrain from doing others by this verbal means perhaps just as much as by punishment or threat of punishment.

According to the expressive version of the emotive theory, when we use ethical sentences like "Stealing is wrong," we are not stating any fact about stealing; we are merely expressing our own disapproving attitude toward acts of this kind. It is as if we were to say "Stealing!!!" in an indignant and disapproving tone of voice. It is quite clear that when we say "Stealing!!!" we are not saying anything that could possibly be true or false; and the same is true, according to the expressive version of the emotive theory, with "Stealing is wrong."

According to the evocative version of the emotive theory, when we say "Stealing is wrong" we are, in effect, giving a command, "Don't steal!" But commands and prescriptions are, of course, no more true or false than are utterances like "Stealing!!!" If I say to you, "Shut the door!" it would be most inappropriate for you to reply "That's false!" You may criticize my command as unjustified, by saying that the air is stifling and the door should be left open; or as superfluous, by saying that the door is already shut; or as impossible to carry out, because you are unable to get up from your chair; but you cannot say that it is *false*. This difference distinguishes emotive statements from all statements of fact, like "The table is black" and "This act caused widespread suffering," which *are* either true or false, though we are not always in a position to say which.

The expressive and evocative aspects usually go together, and from here on we may consider them together as "the emotive theory." The emotive theory has been developed and amplified in numerous and subtle ways. It would take an entire book to trace these separate developments and the controversies engendered by each one. Here we can consider only a few of the main features which all or most versions of the emotive theory possess in common.

The emotive theory probably strikes a responsive chord in most people in at least one respect: we *do* use language in the way the theory describes, and we do so constantly. Every child understands the emotive import of ethical terms (not, of course, the fact *that* the terms are being used emotively); he knows what types of behavior are being discouraged and which ones encouraged. But if you asked him the *meaning* of the ethical term in any of these sentences, he would be quite unable to answer. For that matter, the mother who utters the sentence in addressing her offspring would also be unable to answer: if you said to her, "I know that when you tell your child that stealing is wrong you are trying to get him to change his attitude (and thus his behavior) toward stealing, and doubtless you are expressing your own disapproval at the same time; but aside from that, what are you *saying* about stealing when you say that it is wrong? What property does the word 'wrong' stand for?" she would probably stare at you in blank astonishment. She knows the job that sentences like this perform — and the child knows as well as she does — but she could not tell you, even after having used ethical sentences all her life, what property of acts she is referring to when she calls them right or wrong. Isn't this example a confirmation of the emotive theory — doesn't it give an accurate account of how ethical terms and sentences are used in actual practice?

Moreover, the emotive theory offers another advantage, at least for philosophical analysis of ethical language. Perhaps in our various attempts to discover naturalistic definitions of ethical terms, we had the feeling through-

out that there was "something missing" from every suggested analysis —
hard to put one's finger on, perhaps, but still, some inadequacy in all the
accounts. Can it be that in the light of the emotive theory we have now
found it? The ethical terms always have emotive meaning, and the nonethical terms into which naturalists attempt to translate them do not, or
at least not nearly as much. When you say, "The movie has features A, B,
C . . . ," you are describing the movie; when you say "Better see it, it's
good," you are encouraging others to see it, and the function of your language is different; there is an expressive-persuasive character attaching to the
ethical sentence that does not attach to the other. It's no wonder, then, that
we may feel dissatisfied at all attempts to reduce the one to the other.

Nonnaturalists, of course, also believe there is something missing from
all naturalistic accounts: the *nonnatural property* which they say the ethical
word names. But we have already seen what difficulties are encountered
in trying to find what that nonnatural property is and how its existence is
to be verified. Doesn't the emotive theory provide a way out of the difficulty?
Doesn't it give us a much easier way of accounting for the feeling of "something missing"? The emotive meaning of the ethical terms supplies the
answer, so we need look no further for nonnatural properties. If a simple
and easy-to-find explanation will do, we need not look for a mysterious one.
If the sound at the window at night was caused by a stranger crying for
help, we need not look for a ghost.

What are we to conclude from all this discussion? Shall we accept the
emotive theory, lock, stock, and barrel? Let us make a distinction at once:
If the view being considered is that ethical terms *are* used emotively, then
it would be difficult indeed for anyone to deny it — every example of people
being encouraged, discouraged, blamed, praised, advised, cajoled, wheedled,
or threatened by the use of ethical sentences will provide another example
of the emotive theory. Nor can we easily deny that this emotive flavor is
largely missing from all attempted naturalistic accounts. One cannot deny
that there is *an* emotive function of ethical terms; but one can very well
deny that the emotive function is their *only* function. That is, if the view
being considered is that ethical terms are being used *only* in an emotive
manner, this claim has not been established; indeed, not a shred of evidence
has been presented in favor of it. Let us consider a few points about this
claim.

1. People constantly use emotive language, whether their discussions and
disputes have to do with ethics or not. Yet usually they are not *merely* using
emotive language; they are, in addition, using language to *state* something.
If I simply say, "Hurrah!" or "Damn!" of course I am not stating (asserting) anything but simply using emotive language — interjections are the
purest example in our speech of emotive language. But, rather than cheer-
ing or cursing, I may produce my intended effect much more surely and
precisely by stating some fact. If I say, "There is a time bomb in this room,

set to go off in two minutes," I am not intending merely to convey information; my intention is to make you leave the room at once, and I have failed to achieve my intention if you sit still and say, "So what?" But if I do achieve my intended effect, I shall have done so not by uttering emotive language, or by gesticulating wildly, but simply by stating a cold, hard fact. Language is most effective at evocation when it is not *merely* emotive but states something quite independent of the emotion.

Here emerges a most important distinction. The purpose or intention I have in uttering the sentence is one thing; the effect it actually has on my hearers is another; but what the sentence *means* (or I, through the utterance of it, mean), is a still different thing, not·to be confused with either of the others. My intention in saying what I do may be to make you change your attitudes, to alter your behavior, or perhaps just to express my own feelings; but all these purposes that I may have in saying what I do, do not even touch the question of *what* it is that I am saying, what the *meaning* of my sentence is. Anyone who understands the English language knows what I mean by my sentence about the time bomb. If there are any words in the sentence that he does not understand, he can ask me. But if he asks me *why* I said it, then I can tell him what my purpose or intention was in uttering the sentence. In telling him my purpose, however, I am answering a *different* question. What I mean by the words I utter is one thing; my purpose in uttering them is another. In my statement to you I am obviously trying to change your attitudes, but I don't try by saying just *anything* that could be true or false. On the contrary, it is precisely by saying *what* I do — by communicating to you in words the fact about the time bomb — that I am able to achieve the intended effect upon your behavior. I can achieve the effects I desire only if you understand the meaning of the words that I am uttering; my tone of voice, gestures, and the emotive character of my language (if any) *alone* will not do it.

"But it isn't that way in ethics," someone protests. There is, of course, a difficulty in regard to ethical language — a difficulty with which we have become familiar enough in this chapter! — of discovering exactly what ethical sentences mean. We do not have this kind of difficulty with empirical sentences. That is why the emotive theory is such a tempting way out of the difficulties. But let us not jump to conclusions. Just because it is hard to give an account of what a person is saying when he utters a sentence, it doesn't follow that what he says has no meaning and that he is only "emoting." Or, to put it another way: it doesn't follow that his words have *only* "emotive meaning" — though it would be far less confusing if instead of "emotive meaning" we said "emotive effect" and distinguished this effect clearly from meaning. Indeed, we may well ask whether the emotive language would be likely to have the desired effect if it were not accompanied by *some* descriptive meaning — especially when used by mature persons who don't want to have people work on their feelings but want simply to discover the truth. It may be that the ethical words that parents use when they are addressing young children are used in a purely or primarily emotive manner; certainly this manner is what is most obvious about them to the child. But when two mature individuals sit down and ask whether it would be wrong of one of them to break a solemn promise when the effects of doing so will cause more happiness to all concerned than if the promise were kept, they are not trying to express their attitudes of approval or disapproval to each other nor to influence one another to accept their own attitudes; they do not — yet — *have* any attitudes to express, and they don't yet know what attitudes they would like the other to adopt; they are not trying to express or evoke an attitude, nor even to acquire one, but to learn or discover something on the basis of which they could have an attitude they would feel to be justified. The emotive theory may be all very well in certain contexts, when you already know what your own attitude is and you are trying to persuade someone else to share it — as in the parent-child relationship; but how does it fare when you are not trying to inculcate an attitude at all but to have some factual basis for having an attitude toward the thing in the first place?

"A factual basis," we say. But this attempt seems to show once again that in making ethical utterances, we *are* making statements of fact; at least that we believe we are doing so. "It's not true that it's right to do that!" someone protests. But how can it be true when, according to the emotive theory, ethical utterances are neither true nor false?

2. It is true that we use ethical sentences to persuade, intimidate, encourage, and in general to work on people's feelings and attitudes. But do we *always* use them for this purpose? (1) "It's wrong for you to stay out late, at least without phoning me and telling me!" the wife exclaims to her husband. Here she is certainly trying to persuade him (perhaps even to command him) to behave differently in the future. But suppose instead she says (2) "It was wrong of you to have stayed out late last night." This remark cannot be construed as a command, "I order you to have come in earlier last night," since one cannot change the past by commanding. Nothing can now change what he did; however, her remark could still be construed as an attempt to persuade him not to perform similar acts in the future. But now suppose she says, (3) "It was wrong of Father to have farmed me out to an orphanage when I was a child." Is she still trying to change someone's behavior? Whose? The father is dead, and she will never be a child again, nor does she have any children of her own whose behavior the remark might affect. Whom is she trying to influence? Herself? Does she need to influence herself? Perhaps then she is just expressing a feeling; but perhaps not — must we assume that she is expressing a feeling every time we can find no other explanation within the bounds of the emotive theory? If a person says (4) "It was wrong of Brutus to kill Caesar" or something equally remote, the point is even plainer. It may be said that the speaker is trying

to influence potential wrongdoers in the future, to deter them; but is this explanation really plausible? Must this influence be the function of the utterance? Or perhaps she is only expressing her own disapproval. (Not *stating* her disapproval, as our first naturalistic theory would have it, but simply expressing it.) But must the speaker be expressing disapproval every time he says this phrase, any more than a person must sigh every time he is sad? The emotive theory, as a theory covering all situations, seems to be not very plausible.

3. Even more serious problems confront us when we consider ethical disagreement; for according to the emotive theory, there can be no such thing. True, if one person says "Shame!" or "Alas!" and another says "Hurrah!" about the same thing or event, the two persons are not taking the same attitude toward the thing in question; but there is no *disagreement* between them, since thus far no propositions have been uttered — nothing has yet been said which one of them believes to be true and the other not. Similar considerations, according to the emotive theory, apply to ethical utterances. When a person says that something is wrong but formerly said it was right, what he says at this moment does not contradict what he said before, according to the emotive theory. For there are no ethical *opinions,* just *attitudes;* and all we can or need say is that his present attitude is different from his previous one. One cannot say that his previous view was mistaken (or that his present one is), because there is no view in the first place, only a difference in attitudes — his present attitude vs. his former one, his attitudes vs. those of others. But is this account plausible? Surely, one may object, his present utterance contradicts his previous one; and there is not merely an *attitude* toward something, but an ethical *opinion* — something that *can* be true or false. Suppose, for example, that a person comes to doubt a previous moral view or opinion; then there must be a view or opinion to doubt — and there cannot be one if, as the emotive theory says, there are only differing attitudes, not contradictory views.

4. Since, according to the emotive theory, there are no ethical beliefs but only attitudes, how are we to describe the process which is usually called "trying to change somebody's opinion" about a moral question? Well, a supporter of the emotive theory would say that it is simply a matter of trying to change their attitudes toward the thing in question — by whatever means. Partly, we may persuade them to change their attitude by using emotively tinged ethical terms. But this method will seldom do by itself; people want facts. They can, of course, be given *empirical* facts, and these will do the trick, provided the facts cited will appeal to them sufficiently. "That's a good movie; you should see it." "Why?" "Well, Miss X is in it and you like her. Also it has lots of suspense, and you like suspense pictures. Besides, it's in Cinemascope. . . ." You would go on in this vein, appealing to whatever facts you think may induce the desired change in attitude. You may follow the same procedure in moral matters: "You ought

to be more careful about hurting people's feelings." "Why?" "Well, in the first place, it doesn't help them — they don't enjoy having their feelings hurt any more than you do. Besides, it doesn't do you any good; the last time you said something that hurt your boss's feelings you didn't get the raise he was planning to give you." The empirical facts cited may appeal to the other person's feeling for others (like the first one) or to his self-interest (like the second one), but either way they are cited in the hope that they will change the person's attitude.

Superficially this account may seem to be extremely plausible. But is it an accurate account of what it is to give reasons in ethics? Is *any* statement, true or false, which will help the person change his attitude toward X, a reason for doing X? Do reasons vary with people's whims in this way? If a person won't accept a certain medicine (which will cure him) unless he is told that it tastes good, will our telling him that it tastes good constitute a *reason* (much less a good reason) for him to take it? True, it may supply a *motive;* it may alter his desires and attitudes; but will that make it a reason?

The emotivist denies that there are any such things as reasons in ethics; or, if you prefer, he says that there *are* reasons, but anything that may motivate someone to do something counts as a reason for doing it. (These are two ways of saying the same thing.) But is the emotivist's position true? Is the fact that he will take the pill if he thinks it will taste good a *reason* for taking it? a *good* reason? Surely one must distinguish between (1) reasons for doing X and (2) whatever will induce the person to do X. Can't something be a good reason for doing X even if it doesn't in any way cause the person to perform it? Isn't the fact that an act, if performed, will cause widespread and needless suffering a good reason for not performing it — a good reason even though it induces *no* change in the agent's behavior because he is indifferent to human suffering? Can we really identify a reason for doing something with providing a motive for doing it? May not a person have a *motive* for doing something without having a reason — when he gambles away the family fortune but could not give one reason in defense of this course of action? — and may he not have a reason, and know the reason, and yet not be moved toward doing it in the slightest degree?

5. Emotivists do, however, have a theory about disagreement in ethics; or, since there is, according to emotivists, no specifically ethical disagreement, let us say a theory about sentences containing ethical terms which differ only in the presence or absence of the word "not." When one person says "X is right" and another says "X is not right," there is no property of X, its rightness or wrongness, for them to disagree about; nevertheless, what makes them "come to agreement," or, more accurately, what makes one of them stop uttering his sentence and come to utter the sentence of his opponent? According to emotivists, this can happen if they come to agreement on what the nonethical facts of the situation are; if they come to agreement on this point but still utter "conflicting" ethical sentences, there

is nothing more to be done. The first situation is called "disagreement in belief," and the second is called "disagreement in interest." [1] Let us see how this distinction operates.

Suppose you say that a certain student should not be allowed to graduate, and I say that he should. But now suppose that you present to me conclusive evidence that the student has cheated in examinations, bribed an employee in the registrar's office to change some of the grades on his record (otherwise his grade average would have been too low to enable him to graduate), and forged the signature of several physicians on letters requesting that he be excused from tests on account of illness. Once I am acquainted with these facts, I "change my mind" — that is, I now utter the sentence, "He should not be permitted to graduate," and thus the controversy ends. It ends, because once you and I agree on what the nonethical facts of the situation are, we reach the same verdict. (Or, if a verdict must be a proposition, let us say "we utter the same sentence" and leave it at that.)

But now suppose that even after you have informed me of all these facts about the student, and we agree on all the facts that could possibly have any relevance, I still do not give in: suppose I still say "He should be permitted to graduate." Perhaps I have a favorable attitude toward cheating and forgery, and thoroughly approve it as long as it enables a person to achieve his ends; and nothing you or anyone else can say to me can make me change my attitude. In such a case, according to emotivists, further argument is futile: there is no disagreement about matters of fact any more (for I assent to all the facts about the case that you point out to me), but only a "disagreement in attitude" which cannot be resolved by argument. Disputes rooted in disagreement (or ignorance) about the facts can be resolved, once we come to agree on what the facts are; but disputes which remain after all the facts have been adduced cannot — here nothing more can be done by way of argument, and each disputant must be content to go his separate way with the dispute unresolved, or try to change his opponent by other devices than by presenting facts, e.g., by force or by hypnosis or other psychological conditioning.

To call this second type of dispute "disagreement" is certainly misleading, since, in any usual sense of "disagreement," when two people disagree, there is a proposition which one of them thinks is true and which the other thinks is false; and, by the emotivist's own account, in the case of "disagreement in attitude" there is no such proposition — there is only a clash of attitudes, with one disputant pro-X and the other anti-X, and that is all. Since, according to the emotivist, there are no ethical facts, there can be no disagreement about ethical facts; there can only be disagreement about nonethical facts which may lead people to utter their ethical sentences.

What can be said of the emotivist's account of ethical "disagreement"?

[1] See Charles L. Stevenson, "The Emotive Meaning of Ethical Terms," in Sellars and Hospers, *Readings in Ethical Theory,* p. 426-28.

A critic could make the following points: (1) The emotivist may have shown that there comes a point where *argument* ends; but it does not follow that therefore *disagreement* ends. Indeed, it seems obvious that disagreement still persists. But surely our aim in arguing is not merely to reach the end of argument, but to resolve disagreement. The emotivist's examples do not show that disagreement, as opposed to argument, has ceased. (2) "But how can there still be disagreement when there is no proposition that is the subject of disagreement but only a clash of attitudes?" But that is just the point — is this really so? Would it not be better to say, "There *is* still a subject of disagreement, namely whether or not the student should be permitted to graduate"? The difference between the examples of "disagreement in belief" and "disagreement in interest" is that in the first case the nonethical facts presented led to an agreement on the ethical issue, and in the second case they did not. In the second case there was no *non*-ethical disagreement, but (it is contended) an *ethical disagreement* remained, concerning the morality of cheating, forgery, and other fraudulent action; the difference in attitude was the *result* of the ethical disagreement. Even in the first case, where agreement on nonethical facts led to ethical agreement one need not assume that the nonethical facts were what the disagreement was *about;* the disagreement was still an ethical one, but in this case it was resolved by a presentation of nonethical facts on which it was based. (3) But what then *are* these ethical facts about which disagreement in the second case still remains? It is easy to say, "There is still disagreement, namely about whether the student should be permitted to graduate." But what does it mean to say this? What exactly *are* they disagreeing about? Having reached this point, we are led back into either naturalism or nonnaturalism: either to a nonnaturalistic view (e.g., Ross), that we are disagreeing about the presence of an ethical property irreducible to any nonethical ones, or a naturalistic view (e.g., Perry), that we are still disagreeing about some *further* empirical facts, however complex.

Here an interesting possibility arises: can't we combine the emotive theory with either of the two other types of theory? If the emotive theory is interpreted in its purest or "strongest" sense — as saying that *the* distinctive use of ethical sentences is emotive, that *no* cognitive meaning is attached to them, and that there is therefore no ethical disagreement (since ethical terms have no cognitive meaning anyway) — then the emotive theory cannot be reconciled with either of the other ones. But if we take the emotive theory in its "weaker," or "modified," sense — as saying only that ethical words and sentences *do* have "emotive meaning" (or emotive effects), and that they are used to persuade, express, intimidate, and so on, but not necessarily *only* in this way — then it can readily be combined with either of the other types of view already considered. For example, suppose we are inclined toward a naturalism like that of Perry and hesitate to accept it only because of a lingering suspicion that no naturalistic definition really gives an adequate translation of ethical terms or sentences. Then we can hold a combined view as follows: we can say that ethical terms like "good" do have emotive meaning ("an aura of favorable feeling hovering about them") that no nonethical terms possess, just as the emotive theory says, and that is why no translation lacking emotive meaning is quite adequate; but that there is, in addition to the emotive meaning which is always (or almost always) present when ethical terms are used, a cognitive component as well — which is weak or even nonexistent in cases where people are merely trying to work on others' feelings and attitudes, but strong when they are trying "in a cool hour" to arrive at a tenable moral view — and that this cognitive component is the real subject of disagreement when disagreement occurs. That people have clashing or conflicting attitudes toward an act or situation when they utter opposed ethical sentences is, then, true, but it is not the whole truth; they have clashing attitudes *because* they disagree about a matter of genuine fact, e.g., whether the thing in question does or does not possess some property: for example, whether it does or does not contain (or in the case of an act, lead to) a preponderance of total pro-interests. If such a view is held, it does not differ greatly from Perry's naturalism, and there is nothing in it that is inconsistent with Perry's theory. Perhaps you will find such a combination of one aspect of the emotivist thesis with a non-emotivist thesis (if not Perry's, then some other) the solution to the meta-ethical problems we have been concerned with in this chapter.

If we accept this solution, however, let us do it with our eyes open and not assume that all our problems can be solved in a pleasantly eclectic manner. A great deal depends on how strong a place we give to the emotive component of the meaning of ethical terms. Shall we say that the emotive "meaning" of ethical terms is so strong as to be the determinant of whether these terms are used, or shall we say that they are merely an accompaniment? If we say that the emotive meaning is primary and the cognitive secondary (as emotivists do), then we shall be tempted to say that it is the emotive meaning that remains constant throughout all the contexts in which ethical terms are used, and that the cognitive varies from case to case. It does seem to be true that the word "good" always, or almost always, carries with it a favorable emotive meaning; but if we also say that the cognitive meaning is secondary and varies from case to case, then we must conclude that (to the extent that this occurs) people disputing about ethical matters are not really disagreeing any more than they were in the "pure" emotive theory. Suppose, for example, that Ross and Perry are disputing about whether a certain act is right. According to the view we are now considering, Ross, in saying "X is right," will be (1) using the word "right" to express his pro-attitude toward X and try to get others to share it (emotive component) and also (2) *asserting* that X has a certain non-natural property, rightness (cognitive component); and Perry, on his part, in saying "X is not right," will be (1) using the word "right" to express his pro-attitude toward X and try to get others to share it (emotive component) and also (2) *asserting* that X fails to lead to the maximization of pro-interests of everyone involved (cognitive component). But here, again, they are not really disagreeing — any more than you and I are disagreeing if you say "It's blue" and I say "No, it isn't round," for each one is attaching a different *cognitive* meaning to "right." Doubtless this kind of thing does occur; people sometimes think they are disagreeing when they aren't. But if this happens most or all of the time, then we must conclude that there is no genuine ethical disagreement. And is such a position really plausible? If two people hold opposing ethical views, are they really attaching different cognitive meanings to "right" and only attaching the same emotive meaning? When one person says X is right and another denies it, aren't they, normally at least, disagreeing about *the same thing?* But if they are, then the view cannot be correct which says that emotive meanings remain constant while cognitive meanings change. There must be some stable subject on which agreement and disagreement can occur. It is easy, whenever we are at loggerheads, to assume that we are being tricked by some ambiguity; and of course, often we are; but if we are in this case — if "right" is as multiply ambiguous (cognitively) as the present theory requires — then we must admit that we seldom if ever disagree on ethical matters. Indeed, if ethical words are as ambiguous as all that, it is quite amazing that we are ever able to use them intelligibly in our daily conversations.

This last modification of the emotive theory, then, faces great difficulties. Yet it is not easy, once we have assented to a modified emotive theory by granting that ethical terms have both emotive and cognitive meaning, to stop short of the next modification which says that it is the emotive meaning that remains constant while cognitive meaning varies; yet this modification generates difficult, perhaps insuperable, problems.

EXERCISES

1. List a dozen terms used in ethics which carry a strong "emotive meaning." Of what practical importance is it to be aware of the emotive nature of their use? (Example: the term "freedom." "See how free we are? We have no laws at all." "But true freedom is possible only under law. We are therefore freer than you are.")

2. Read Chapter 3, "Pragmatic Aspects of Meaning," of C. L. Stevenson's *Ethics and Language,* and apply any of its analyses that you can to problem dealt with in preceding chapters.

3. Analyze the concept of persuasive definition (C. L. Stevenson, "Persuasive Definitions," *Mind,* Vol. 48, No. 187 [1938], pp. 331-50). Think of some persuasive definitions you have met with in discussions on ethics.

4. Do you take the following as a confirmation of the emotive theory? Explain.
a. "While it makes sense to say of any two objects that they are the same in

every respect except one, namely that one is red and the other is not, it does not make sense to say of any two objects that they are exactly the same with the single exception that only one of them is good. This is because while the use of a term like 'red' is sufficient to mark a factual difference between any two objects (or events etc.), the use of a term like 'good' is not. If someone tells us that he has painted two pictures only one of which is good, we are naturally led to ask him what is the difference between them. Suppose he replied 'that just is the difference, one is good and the other is not'; most people would find this quite unintelligible." (A. Montefiore, *A Modern Introduction to Moral Philosophy,* pp. 58-59.)

b. If I, an American, go to England and start using the words "garter" and "suspender" as they are used in America, an Englishman reminds me, "What you call 'garters' we call 'suspenders,' and what you call 'suspenders' we call 'braces'." I then accept his statement about verbal usage, and agree while in England to use the words in their English meaning to avoid confusion. But what if I, an American, visit Nazi Germany in 1938 and object on utilitarian grounds to the persecution of minority groups, and my host replies, "In Greater Germany we call the persecution of minority groups 'right' "? In this case I decline to go along with his usage. (Paraphrased from Patrick Nowell-Smith, *Ethics.*) (Do you find the two cases analogous? Explain.)

5. Emotivists sometimes say that what *all* the uses of the word "good" have in common is emotive meaning and nothing else, and that the cognitive (descriptive) meaning — if any — attaching to the term varies from case to case. Examine, in the light of this,

a. Aristotle's view that the common meaning of "good" is fulfilling a function. (E.g., a good job of surgery is one which fulfills to a high degree the criteria for surgery; a good tennis player is one who fulfills to a high degree the criteria for tennis-playing, and so on.)

b. Paul Ziff's view that "good" always means "ministering to certain interests." (P. Ziff, *Semantic Analysis,* Ch. 5.)

6. Do you agree or disagree with the following statements? What do you think is their bearing on the tenability of the emotive theory?

a. According to the emotive theory, the distinctive function of ethical terms is emotive. But this is clearly untrue; for there are lots of terms — "appeaser," "nigger," "communist," for example — which have a much stronger emotive meaning than ethical terms do, yet have little or nothing to do with ethics.

b. If a person first believes that killing is *never* right (pacifism), then later comes to believe that it is sometimes right (however rarely), he has surely changed his mind *about the same thing,* namely the wrongness of killing. So there must be some *uniform* cognitive meaning attaching to the word "wrong," else his former view and his present view would not be incompatible with each other, as they obviously are.

c. All the emotivist can say is that he has a different attitude toward killing now from the one he had before. He could not say that he has a different *view* (for this implies a proposition), nor could he say his former view was *mistaken.* He could only say that his present attitude toward killing was different.

d. If the last view described is correct (that of the modified emotivist who says that the emotive meaning remains constant and the cognitive meaning shifts from case to case), then a person who ceased being a Kantian and became a disciple of Mill (for example), and said "I used to think that lying is always wrong, but I don't think so any longer," would have to be construed as saying "I used to believe that lying is not universalizable, but now I think that it doesn't always have bad consequences." But what a curious thing this would be to say! What would be the point of the "but"? The two clauses of his sentence don't contradict each other at all. In fact he could perfectly consistently believe *both* that lying is not universalizable *and* that it sometimes produces the maximum intrinsic good in the specified circumstances.

e. (Emotivist in reply): When a person says that killing is never right, and later says it sometimes is, one thing is clear: he had an attitude of unqualified disapproval toward it before, and he doesn't now. That much we can definitely infer — and that's just what we would expect of the emotive theory. To infer more than this we would have to know more facts about the person in question, but this much we would know for sure.

f. Moreover, the attitude he has toward something is the sole determinant of whether he calls the thing in question good or bad, right or wrong. He may change his beliefs about the consequences of killing, about the causes or motives of killing, about other people's approval or disapproval of killing, and as long as none of these things change *his own* attitude toward killing he will still say that killing is wrong. But once he *changes* his attitude toward killing — even if his changed attitude results from no changed nonethical beliefs — he will *no longer* say that killing is always wrong. Can anything be a clearer proof that the emotivist is completely right in saying that the attitude he has is the sole determinant for the use of ethical terms, and that *everything else* — such as what particular properties of the thing in question he has in mind in calling it wrong, e.g., its universalizabilty or its consequences for human happiness — is secondary and accidental?

7. Read R. M. Hare's *The Language of Morals* (together with Chapter 9 of Richard Brandt's *Ethical Theory*) and indicate, with reasons, whether you think that Hare's amendments to the emotive theory remove some or all of its difficulties. (According to Hare, "You ought to do X" is a prescription — "Do X!" — but a *generalized* prescription applying to all acts of the same kind, and one we are prepared to back up with reasons.)

READING LIST, SECTION 27

Aiken, Henry D. "Emotive 'Meanings' and Ethical Terms." *Journal of Philosophy*, Vol. 41 (1944), pp. 456-70.

Ayer, Alfred J. "Critique of Ethics" and "The Emotive Theory of Values." In Sellars and Hospers. *Readings in Ethical Theory*, pp. 393-402, 430-31.

———. "On the Analysis of Moral Judgments." In Ayer, A. J. *Philosophical Essays*. New York: St. Martin's, 1954, pp. 231-49.

Barnes, Winston H. F. "Ethics Without Propositions." *Aristotelian Society Proceedings*, Supplementary Vol. 22 (1948), pp. 1-30.

———. "A Suggestion about Value." In Sellars and Hospers. *Readings in Ethical Theory*, pp. 391-92.

Brandt, Richard. "The Emotive Theory of Ethics." *Philosophical Review*, Vol. 59 (1950), pp. 305-18, 535-40.

———. *Ethical Theory*. Englewood Cliffs, N. J.: Prentice-Hall, 1959, Ch. 9.

Carritt, Edgar F. "Moral Positivism and Moral Aestheticism." In Sellars and Hospers. *Readings in Ethical Theory*, pp. 405-14.

Edwards, Paul. *The Logic of Moral Discourse*. Chicago: Free Press, 1955.

Ewing, Alfred C. *Ethics*. New York: Macmillan, 1953, Ch. 7.

Falk, W. D. "Goading and Guiding." *Mind*, Vol. 62 (1953), pp. 145-71.

Hare, R. M. *The Language of Morals*. New York: Oxford Univ. Press, 1952.

Harrison, Jonathan. "Can Ethics Do Without Propositions?" *Mind*, Vol. 59 (1950), pp. 358-71.

Kaplan, Abraham. "Are Moral Judgments Assertions?" *Philosophical Review*, Vol. 51 (1942), pp. 280-303.

Moore, George Edward. "A Reply to My Critics." (excerpt) In Sellars and Hospers. *Readings in Ethical Theory*, pp. 432-40.

Robinson, Richard. "The Emotive Theory of Ethics." *Aristotelian Society Proceedings*, Supplementary Vol. 22 (1948), pp. 79-106.

Ross, Sir William David. "Critique of Ayer." In Sellars and Hospers. *Readings in Ethical Theory*, pp. 493-504.

Stevenson, Charles Leslie. "The Emotive Meaning of Ethical Terms" (1937). In Sellars and Hospers. *Readings in Ethical Theory*, pp. 415-29.

———. *Ethics and Language*. New Haven: Yale Univ. Press, 1944.

Tomas, Vincent. "Ethical Disagreements and the Emotive Theory of Values." *Mind*, Vol. 60 (1951), pp. 205-22.

Urmson, J. O. "On Grading." *Mind*, Vol. 59 (1950), pp. 145-69.

28. Final considerations

Perhaps by this time you will have found some form of naturalism, non-naturalism, or emotivism acceptable. Or perhaps you have not yet arrived at any conclusions on metaethics. At any rate, you have some idea by now what the alternatives are and how each one has been defended and attacked. Ethical theory is still in a state of flux, and no final answers can be given in an area in which each issue is still so hotly debated. Our task here is only to consider various views and the main arguments for and against each of them. The main portion of our task has now been completed, insofar as this can be done in one chapter.

A. Other approaches to the problems of metaethics

But there is still some tidying up to be done. Our account would not be complete if we did not mention still other approaches to the problems of metaethics.

1. "You have considered so far what ethical sentences mean. I think a good rule is that you know what a sentence means when you know what *other* sentences are used to support it. When you know all the sentences which are used to support a given sentence, then you know what that sentence

means." Thus, if you want to know the meaning of a pacifist's sentence when he says that killing is always wrong, the thing to do is to assemble all the sentences he gives or might give in support of what he says, and when you have done that you will know what his sentence (containing the ethical term) means. For example, if in defending his pacifistic view he appeals to the consequences of killing to human happiness, then you know what his sentence means: it is a disguised empirical statement about the consequences of certain actions.

This suggestion will have a familiar ring to all those who are acquainted with the problems of contemporary epistemology. Nevertheless, there is reason to doubt that it is an adequate account of the meaning of ethical sentences. Mr. B may agree to the reasons which Mr. A gives in support of an ethical statement and yet may disagree with him about the ethical statement itself. "I accept everything you say about the consequences of killing," Mr. B may say, "and all the other empirical facts you bring forth in favor of your ethical assertion, but I still do not admit that killing is always wrong." This statement shows, certainly, that in saying that killing is not always wrong, Mr. B is *not* merely asserting the empirical statements used in support of the judgment, since he already agrees with Mr. A about these. The relation of an ethical statement to the reasons presented in its support is more complex than this; the ethical statement is not merely a summary of the reasons in its favor. It is more like the relation of a verdict in court to the evidence on which the verdict is based. The verdict is something different from the evidence, even from the sum total of the evidence. Two judges or juries may listen to exactly the same evidence and yet arrive at opposing verdicts. Therefore, it cannot plausibly be said that the verdict is only a summary of the evidence. (Indeed, if the ethical statement amounts to nothing more than a summary of the statements given in support of it, what would the evidence be given in support *of?*)

This view derives its initial plausibility from apparently parallel situations in epistemology and the philosophy of science. But even there it could be questioned. When I say that there is a tree in the yard, my reason for saying so is that I have certain visual and tactual sense experiences; but the sentence "There is a tree in the yard" is not *about* any sense experiences, mine or anyone else's. Sense experience may be invoked in support of my statement, but it does not constitute its meaning. When I say there is a tree in the yard, I am talking not about sense experience but about a physical object which (I believe) exists whether any sense experiences do or not. Undoubtedly I could not *know* that there is a tree in the yard without having certain sense experiences; but these are not what I *mean* when I say there is a tree in the yard. One must not confuse what a sentence means with how one finds out whether it is true. The same considerations can be used to apply to ethics: when I say that an act is wrong, I may support this assertion with reasons, but my reasons for saying something are not the same as what I mean by the statement when I say it.

2. But there is a more promising possibility. One might reason as follows: Of course ethical sentences don't mean the same as the sentences used in support of them. In fact, it is impossible to *define* most ethical words at all (although sometimes we can give approximate synonyms). Consider: it would tax the ingenuity of any logician to define the term "relevance," and although every scientist uses the concept of evidence he is not usually expected to give a strict *definition* of the term "evidence." Definitions of our most crucial terms are often impossible to provide; and indeed, why should they be required? A definition is simply a group of words (the definiens) which can be used interchangeably with the word being defined (the definiendum), and it is not always true that there exists a group of words in the language which can be used interchangeably with another word. When exact definitions are possible, they can be extremely helpful; but where they are not possible, it does not follow that the words in question have no meaning or that we don't know what we mean by them. To demand this rigor in metaethics only results in an endless naturalism vs. nonnaturalism controversy, which, in the opinion of many students of the subject, leads to a dead end. Perhaps another approach should be tried. In scientific situations, philosophers of science go about trying to see how scientific propositions are confirmed and verified and by what means (often involving a complex interplay of sense experience and reasoning) conflicting scientific hypotheses are actually resolved. Similarly, in ethics, let us try to see how we use ethical words, how they function in our language, and how we actually go about attempting to settle conflicting ethical claims.[1]

There is in fact a method of arbitrating these claims, which is called the Qualified Attitude method. What is this method? Briefly it comes to this: We form the moral judgments (or verdicts) that we do in response to the promptings of attitudes which we find persisting in ourselves. But not just any attitude will serve; some attitudes must be discounted. Under what conditions, then, can we say that our "persisting attitudes" are *not* reliable guides in discovering what is right and wrong, and must therefore be discounted? We "discount" an attitude (1) if it is not impartial; (2) if it is uninformed as to the facts of the situation, (3) if it is a consequence of an abnormal state of mind such as "illness, insanity, fatigue, anger, grief, and depression." [2]

Have we not discussed this view before? Isn't this the Ideal Observer

---

[1] This approach in ethics, whose systematic exposition is relatively recent, has tended in recent years to supersede the naturalism-nonnaturalism-emotivism controversy. It is set forth in detail in books by Toulmin, Hare, Nowell-Smith, Baier, and others. See the reading list at the end of this section.

[2] From Richard Brandt, *Ethical Theory.* Englewood Cliffs, N. J.: Prentice-Hall, 1959, p. 250. Reprinted by permission of the publisher. A full account of the Qualified Attitude method is given in Brandt's Chapter 10.

theory again with a new name? Not quite. The Ideal Observer theory is a theory about the *meaning* of ethical terms. It says that the statement "X is right" means the same as the statement "An Ideal Observer (defined in terms of the possession of certain characteristics) would morally approve X." This position is, of course, a naturalistic theory of ethics; and as such, arguments have been made against it, some of which we have examined (pages 549-51). But the Qualified Attitude method is not a theory about the meaning of ethical terms. It is identical with the Ideal Observer theory only insofar as that theory specifies the requirements which an Ideal Observer must fulfill. It does not go on to say that the Ideal Observer's utterances give us what our ethical sentences *mean*. Thus the method retains the relatively unobjectionable feature of the Ideal Observer theory while dispensing with the claim to give an account of the meaning of ethical terms and sentences.

The Qualified Attitude method does, indeed, provide an account of the way thoughtful and conscientious persons do go about attempting to resolve ethical questions. They discount attitudes which are not impartial or fully informed, for instance; and when ethical disagreement occurs, they look again for the presence of attitudes that need discounting. One may question, however, whether the method is of much practical use when disagreements persist. Suppose that one person, as impartial as he knows how to be, aware of all the relevant facts of the situation, possessing great imaginative sympathy into the experiences of others, and in a calm and dispassionate state of mind, still attaches more value to individual lives (would not risk them in combat even to achieve great gains) than a second person, who possesses the same qualifications, does. Or suppose that the first person is more anxious to have a large amount of knowledge or happiness in the world, even at the price of great pain to others, than the second person is. What are we to do in this situation? Both men, apparently, have passed the Qualified Attitude test. Of course, one of them can always say to the other, "You haven't really passed the test; examine your attitudes again," and the second can give the same reply back to the first. In the absence of any independent evidence that either of them is deficient in his qualifications for using the Qualified Attitude method, it would appear that nothing more can be done to resolve the issue. Well, perhaps this kind of ultimate disagreement is what we shall have to settle for. (It can be fully admitted, however, that *most* ethical disputes would be resolved if people were truly impartial, knew all the relevant facts, had great imaginative sympathy with others. The problem is that it is by no means clear that *all* the disputes would be resolved.)

One more gambit remains to be explored. Thus far we have considered ethical statements occurring more or less in isolation; we have not discussed systems or hierarchies of such statements. But this topic, which will be our final one, cannot be embarked upon until we have first prepared the way for it by a further discussion of a topic that was introduced in Chapter 1, a topic on which further discussion was postponed until we were in a position to reintroduce it — the topic of ethical relativism.

B. Relativism again

In the light of the intervening chapters, let us look once again at relativism. We shall consider sociological relativism first; and there are several versions:

1. *Sociological relativism*

a. Do different individuals, groups, tribes, or cultures hold moral views which contradict one another? It certainly *seems* that they do (pages 34-36). Some groups believe, for example, that parricide is always wrong, and some groups do not believe it. But before we conclude that relativism in this sense is a certain fact, we might do well to stop and ask whether it is in every situation *the same kind of act* which is considered right in one society and wrong in another.

> Thomas Jefferson said, approximately, "A revolution every few years is a fine thing." But suppose Karl Marx also said, "A revolution every few years is a fine thing." Could we assume that these two men were necessarily saying the same thing? Of course not. Or again, suppose Mr. A, a resident of the South Pacific, says it is right to bury one's father alive on his sixtieth birthday, irrespective of his state of health; and suppose I say this is not right. Are we talking about the same thing? Not necessarily. The kind of situation Mr. A has in mind is likely to be very different from the kind of situation I have in mind. Perhaps he is assuming that the body one will have in the next world will be exactly like the kind one has just before departing this life (and hence, may think it advisable to depart before feebleness sets in); whereas I may think one has no further existence at all after one's earthly demise. He is talking about burying alive a father who will exist in the next world in a certain kind of body; and I am not. In this situation, it is only confusing to say that our ethical opinions "conflict." [1]

The acts in question are conceived so differently that it would seem to be a mistake to call them the *same kind* of act at all; though whether we decide to call them the same kind of act because of certain external similarities or different kinds of act because of their different context and the different beliefs leading to them, is ultimately a matter of how we choose to classify them. One thing at least is clear: before we say (as many people do with considerable glibness) that one group considers acts of kind A to be right and another group considers acts of the same kind, A, to be wrong, we should be quite clear in what respects the acts in question can be classified as belonging to "the same kind."

b. Do different individuals, groups, tribes, or cultures really hold *basic* moral views which contradict one another? If it can be doubted whether they disagree on any moral views, it can certainly be doubted whether they

[1] *Ibid.*, p. 273.

disagree on basic moral views (pages 35-36). For example, some groups seem to attach much more value to the preservation of the individual life (as opposed to the survival of the group) than other groups do — though some end may be promoted by this attachment which is not promoted where the attachment is not so strong, so that the moral view of the groups are not basic after all. Again, some tribes and cultures are more opposed to permitting human beings and animals to suffer pain than other tribes and cultures are; but this difference *may* be because there are different religious or metaphysical beliefs accompanying the two moral convictions, in which event this example is like the father-burial example cited above. It is very difficult to be sure. But it *seems* that different groups do disagree on at least some basic moral beliefs and convictions, and the burden of proof is on him who says that there is an underlying agreement behind the apparent disagreement.

c. Whether or not any two *actual* individuals or societies disagree in their moral views (and they certainly seem to), would any two *hypothetical* individuals — even from different cultures — who were both impartial, had knowledge of all the relevant facts, had perfect ability at imaginative identification, and were in a calm dispassionate frame of mind, ever disagree in their moral views? In other words, would any two Ideal Observers disagree?

This situation is tricky: a person may say, "No, they wouldn't, and in this sense at least there is no relativism." But he might make this statement simply on the basis of the reasoning that if two persons did disagree, at least one of them could not be an Ideal Observer. But this reasoning would be a tautology, for then one defining characteristic of Ideal Observers would be that they could not disagree with one another. Clearly we cannot settle the question this way without circularity.

One would first have to ascertain *independently* whether the two persons possessed the attributes of an Ideal Observer, and *then* put the matter to the test by seeing whether they ever disagreed. If two persons were both known to be Ideal Observers, and they still disagreed, then sociological relativism (in the sense we are now considering) would be true. The difficulty is, of course, that this test cannot be performed, since no two Ideal Observers exist in this world — or, if they do exist, people will probably disagree as to who they are. About all we can do in the circumstances is to ask ourselves, "Does it seem to be true that the nearer people attain to the ideals of impartiality, knowledge etc. required of the Ideal Observer, the nearer they come to complete agreement on moral matters?" (Analogy: "Is it true that the nearer we come to a perfect vacuum, the more nearly it is true that the stone and the feather fall at the same rate?" The answer would be, "Yes, but we cannot demonstrate it.") Seemingly they do, but it is far from established that they always do agree. Perhaps if they went *all* the way to being Ideal Observers, they would completely agree. But there is no way for us to know if they would, and we cannot therefore say with confidence that it would be true — except, once again, by the circular procedure of *defining* the Ideal Observer in terms of complete agreement.

All these three versions, however, have to do with whether people (even ideal people) *do* disagree, so the question of *ethical* relativism has not yet been touched. Ethical relativism too can take various forms — more than were indicated in our preliminary survey of ethical relativism on pages 36-38.

2. *Ethical relativism*

a. According to one version of ethical relativism, acts of a certain kind, such as stealing a loaf of bread or killing one's father, may *be* right in one society (or in one set of circumstances) and wrong in another. (Not only be *thought* right — this position would be sociological relativism — but *be* right.) But, on the one hand, if this is all this version means, virtually everyone would agree to it. Surely if the circumstances are different, act A may be right and act B wrong, even though A and B are both acts of the same kind. For instance, take our example of wasting water in a desert society (page 35) — who would not agree that such waste would be wrong where water is scarce but not wrong where water is plentiful? Or this example: killing one's father may be right if one is a member of a tribe that cannot survive the long migrations necessary for survival if its journeys are encumbered by the aged who cannot travel with the necessary speed; but the practice may be wrong under less necessitous conditions. We might not agree on all the possible examples, but we surely would about some: for example, cutting into the body of a living person is wrong if a thug does it but right if a surgeon does it. (Once again, these *could* be classified as different types or kinds of actions, depending on the basis of our classification.)

b. On the other hand, the proposition "If A is right when done by one person, it can be wrong when done by another person in *exactly the same* circumstances (both internal and external)" would be assented to by virtually no one. Even the anthropologists and sociologists who proudly proclaim their "relativism" would probably deny it, for the examples *they* continually exhibit are those in which members of one tribe think that acts of kind A are right *in one set of circumstances* (those in which the members of the tribe find themselves) whereas members of another tribe think that acts of kind A are wrong, in what are clearly very different circumstances. For example, in one tribe the food supply may be insufficient without permitting a diet of human flesh, but these are not the circumstances in another; or torture is permitted by one tribe in the belief that it will purify the soul, but not by another tribe which does not share this religious belief. Presumably the anthropologists would not deny — at least no "facts of the case" would require them to deny — that *if* the circumstances of the act were exactly the same in both situations, what would be right for the one would also be right for the other. The difference in rightness and wrongness (right in this tribe, wrong in that one) can always be attributed to some differences or other in the circumstances, for differences aplenty in the circumstances can always be found. (The same principle applies, of course, not only to tribes or cultures but to individuals.)

Whenever a person alleges that a certain act, A, is right and that another act of the same kind, B, performed in the same circumstances, is wrong, the question we always ask immediately is, "Why? What's the *difference* between the two situations?" thus showing that we believe that there cannot be two acts, one of which is right and the other wrong, if there is not some difference between them to account for the difference in moral judgment. Usually, of course, it is easy enough to find numerous differences.

Let us, then, turn our inquiry in a somewhat different direction. Let us interpret ethical relativism, not as another theory of ethics, but as a *meta-*ethical theory: a theory about the *meaning* of ethical terms or sentences. Perhaps then we shall arrive at some formulation on which intelligent disagreement is possible.

c. Let us take "relativism" to mean this: if you assert a moral rule or principle and another person denies it, *both views may be correct* (or valid, or justified, or true). But how is this difference possible? There are several versions of this position:

(1) It might be held that the sentence "X is right" (or "Acts of kind X are right") means the same as "I (or the members of my society or tribe or culture) *think* that X is right." In other words, there's nothing good nor bad but thinking makes it so. This theory, however, suffers from a patent logical defect: it uses the term to be defined (the definiendum) in the phrase that does the defining (the definiens). The error is the same as if one were to define "house" as "anything that one thinks is a house." "What's right is what I think is right"; but what does this sentence mean? What's right is what I think is — what? Right. And what's that? What I think is right. What I think is what? Right. And so on indefinitely, in an infinite regress. Substituting the definition for the term each time, we get "what I think is right," that is, "what I think is what I think is right," that is, "what I think is what I think is what I think is right," that is. . . . We are reduced to an infinite series of stutters.

(2) Why not, then, go back to the autobiographical approval theory (the first of the naturalistic theories we examined) and instead of saying "what I think is right," say "what I approve"? To be sure, this is a naturalistic theory, but isn't it relativistic too? For it *does* permit us to say that one person may call an act right and another person may call it wrong and yet they are both correct in so saying. When Smith says "X is right" he means that he, Smith, approves X, and when Jones says "X is wrong" he means that he, Jones, disapproves X; and of course both Smith's and Jones's state-

ments may both be true. Thus this naturalistic theory is as relativistic as anyone could wish.

The only trouble is, that Smith and Jones are not talking about the same thing. For Smith is talking about Smith's approval, and Jones is talking about Jones's disapproval. Between them there is no disagreement whatever. For how can they be disagreeing when both of their statements may well be true — each being about his own attitude of approval or disapproval toward X? When Smith utters the sentence, it is about Smith, and when Jones utters it, it is about Jones. So there is nothing to disagree about — there is no one proposition which the one thinks is true and the other thinks is false. (This is a situation we do not encounter in the other theories. Even in the second naturalistic theory [pages 544-45], the public-opinion poll theory, the two opposing moral judgments are at least about the same thing, namely whether the majority of the group do or do not approve X, and either they do or they don't. But on the autobiographical theory, there are not even any opposing moral judgments!)

(3) Let us consider, then, the following view: moral judgments really do disagree with one another — they *are* about the same thing — and yet they can both be true: "X is right" may be true for you; "X is wrong" may be true for me.

But this insipid cliché lands us once again in the miserable sinkhole of confusions which were already exposed in Chapter 4 (pages 160-61). We may remind ourselves here of just two pertinent points: first, statements aren't true for you but not true for me; they are true or they are not true, period. Confusion about this matter — which often leads people to use the language of "true for me" — arises usually from the following fact, that a statement *about* you may be true and a precisely similar statement (except for the proper name) *about* me may be false. It may be true that you like strawberries and false that I like them; but these statements are not true for one of us and false for the other — they are both true, and to deny either of them would be to utter a false statement. Or, second, "true to you" may mean simply "true *according to* you." But this phrase leaves open the question whether the statement really is true or not. It may be that according to you there will be a depression in the next two years and according to me there will not be, but then one of us is mistaken. Either there will be a depression or there won't be. To say that there will be "according to me" is simply a way of saying that *"I think* there will be" or *"it is my opinion* that there will be" — and of course my opinion may be false. It is not true for you and false for me.

Our inquirer, however, may persist: "I don't really mean to say that a statement can be true for you but false for me. What I mean when I assert relativism is that all that you and I or anyone else can do in the field of ethics is simply to compare our attitudes — our moral attitudes, if you like — to various acts and situations. You may approve of euthanasia, I may not.

I may try to persuade you or argue you out of your opinion by citing certain facts, and you may do the same with me. But there is no way in which I can prove to you that my view is the correct one, and neither is there any way in which you can prove to me that your view is. Nothing can be proved in ethics. I am a relativist because I believe that *there is no rational method of settling moral disputes.*"

d. But with this last assertion we have before us an ethical relativist of a different stripe. He does not allege that one and the same moral principle can be both true and false, both correct and incorrect, both justified and unjustified. For all he knows, one or another moral principle may be perfectly justified; but if it is, how is anyone going to demonstrate this fact? This variety of ethical relativist is a relativist about the *method of verification* of moral statements. He says that there *is* no method of verification, and thus his position is that of the ethical skeptic discussed in Chapter 1 (page 38). We can continue to call him a skeptic if we like, but the usual philosophical term for him is *methodological relativist.* What can we say about his view?

Methodological relativism, of course, is *not* acceptable if there *is* a rational method of settling moral disputes. The upholder of the Qualified Attitude method, for his part, says that there is such a method and that he has already described what it is. It is not a method which in practice enables us to settle all our moral disputes, but this inability may be because it is so very difficult to be sure whether a person is really fulfilling the requirements laid down by the method. Can we really deny that people who did live up to the requirements *would* find their moral disputes resolved? Until we can be sure that they wouldn't, we cannot be sure that there is no rational method for settling moral disputes and therefore that the relativist is right. But neither, of course, can we be sure, until the Qualified Attitude method has been successfully applied, that the relativist's opposite number, the absolutist, is right in saying that the use of this method will enable us to resolve all our moral disputes.

Much more, however, can be said on the matter than we have said. Everything depends on the *level* of controversy at which the dispute is being conducted. The question of level brings us to the further analysis promised on page 38, to which we now turn for a final attempt at clarification of the absolutism-relativism controversy. Consider the following conversation:

WEST: I believe that if a person is suffering from an incurable disease and he himself requests in writing in front of witnesses that he be painlessly put out of his misery, his wish should be granted. I also believe that the person doing it should not be haled into court and accused of murder for his merciful deed.

EAST: And I believe that such acts are always wrong. There is always the possibility of a frame-up (to get the sick person out of the way); and there is always the possibility, however remote, that a sudden medical advance may occur and a cure be found for the disease from which the patient is suffering.

w: I grant that these things are possible, although cures from someone suffering from the *last stages* of a disease are virtually unknown, and a frame-up is practically impossible when the safeguards I am recommending are observed. Still, I admit that something might go wrong once in a ten thousand times. But that disadvantage is small compared with the inconceivable amount of suffering that would be avoided if euthanasia under controlled conditions were permitted.

e: Your main reason, then, for being in favor of euthanasia is that suffering is thereby prevented? And you would change your opinion if someone convinced you that it did not decrease suffering after all?

w: Yes, I would.

e: But tell me, why are you against suffering?

w: I am not necessarily against *all* suffering. Perhaps the man born with a silver spoon in his mouth who has never known suffering himself, and who shoves people around and doesn't care about the feelings of others should suffer a bit to see what it's like. But I am against all useless and unnecessary suffering, suffering which achieves *no* such constructive purpose, and I believe that (with possible exceptions, as usual) the suffering undergone by the dying falls into this class.

e: Well, it seems that you and I disagree on our moral principles. I believe that it's wrong to take a life under all circumstances, and you believe that life can occasionally be taken when doing so prevents great suffering. So let me ask you again, just why are you against suffering, at least avoidable suffering and suffering that will serve no useful purpose? Or can you give no defense of this conviction of yours — do you consider it self-evident, or axiomatic, or what?

w: No, my disapproval of avoidable and useless suffering, along with many of my other moral convictions, are all parts or aspects of my utilitarian ethics. My views about euthanasia, about war, about sexual behavior, about government, about cruelty to animals, and about countless other matters affecting morality are all part of a system, the utilitarian system. I consider the principle "produce the maximum possible intrinsic good" to be basic, and I make all my moral evaluations in terms of it. That is to say: I *verify* particular moral judgments — about this or that act — in terms of moral rules having to do with *kinds* of actions; and then I *validate* these rules, in turn, by reference to the utilitarian principle, which is my supreme norm or standard.

e: I have no objection to the verification and validation of moral judgments, as you are using those terms. But once you have the supreme norm, for you the utilitarian principle, the process of validation comes to an end, doesn't it? I mean, there is nothing more you can do. What if I don't assent to the principle? How are you going to prove it to me?

w: You already know the answer to that, don't you (pages 529-31)? Don't ask the impossible — and the logically impossible at that. You can't prove the supreme norm of an ethical system by deducing it from any higher norm, for if you could, it wouldn't be the supreme norm.

e: Well, you admit then that you can't prove your supreme norm. So how are you going to make me accept it?

w: I'm not sure that I can; anyway, I'm not yet quite at the end of my rope. It's true that I can't validate a supreme norm in terms of any other ethical norms — to do so, as I said before, is logically impossible. But although I cannot validate it — validation applies only to the subsidiary or derived principles — I *can* do something else: I can *vindicate* it. That is, the utilitarian principle is the apex of my moral system, and there is nothing above it in terms of which to validate it; but I can try to justify *my adoption of it* — and this justification is called vindication. But remember, one doesn't vindicate propositions, one vindicates *actions* — in this instance, my adoption of the supreme norm that I do.

e: How are you going to vindicate the adoption of your supreme norm?

w: First of all, by simply asking you, "Look here, what kind of a world do you *want*? Do you want to live in a world in which there is much avoidable suffering, or in which there is less or none? a world with freedom (within certain limits) to speak and act as one wishes, or a world governed by a police state? a world in which man can develop his capacities — at any rate those whose development doesn't interfere with an equal development of others, or a world in which they are constantly impeded and frustrated? I would ask you to study the nature of man and of the world in which he lives and then to ask yourself as honestly as you can what way of life you find best for man. In short, I am trying to vindicate my adoption of an ethical system in terms of a *way of life*. And a way of life includes much more than a moral code — it encompasses all possible aspects of human life and behavior.[1]

e: Perhaps you can vindicate it to yourself, but not to me. Suppose I don't share these basic ideals? Suppose I say, "I don't want the kind of world that you want." Suppose I say, "You haven't shown me a shadow of *reason* why you should want this kind of a world." Suppose I say "Your choice of a way of life, by means of which you wish to vindicate the adoption of a moral system, is entirely irrational."

w: And suppose I say it isn't; for I think that there is one more step. I think that even a way of life can be justified — not proved, the way you can prove a particular moral statement in terms of rules covering it or the rules in terms of a supreme norm or norms, but yet seen to be *more rational* than another way of life. Whether I can actually perform the justification is another question: but at least I think I can show you that the

---

[1] From this point on I am greatly indebted to Paul Taylor, *Normative Discourse*.

choice of a way of life, by means of which I vindicate the adoption of a moral system, is not just an arbitrary or irrational decision. Thus I propose these four steps: verification of a particular moral statement by certain rules (often containing many qualifications, of course); validation of the rule by means of a supreme norm or norms; vindication of the adoption of a supreme norm (and thus of the entire system which it supports) in terms of a way of life; and a justification of the way of life by showing it to be more rational than others.

E: You have outlined a most ambitious program — particularly the last part. Suppose you tell me how you propose to go about it.

W: I shall try. But let me first indicate that I think *it is here that the basic issue of absolutism vs. relativism really lies.* On reflection, I think, no one will doubt that we do validate our moral rules in terms of supreme norms of conduct; or, probably, that we can vindicate the adoption of these norms in terms of a way of life. But the relativist, as I think he should be defined, is one who says that a way of life itself cannot be justified — that the choice among ways of life is wholly arbitrary or irrational. This statement, I think, is what the relativist really means when he says (page 582) that there is no rational basis for resolving disputes in ethics. We have to advance to this level before we encounter the honest-to-goodness relativist.

> Are values relative or absolute? If we can trace the logical foundations of our value judgements back to our commitment to a certain way of life but cannot justify this commitment itself, then all values are said to be relative. They are relative to our way of life. (More accurately, they are relative to our value systems, and our value systems are themselves relative to our way of life.) This relativistic position holds that, if we find (as we do) that different societies and cultures have conflicting ways of life, then the struggle between them is a matter of brute force, unless they voluntarily decide to tolerate each other's differences. No rational choice can be made between them. If one has a moral code (i.e., a moral value system) which contradicts the moral code of the other, so that acts of a certain sort are right in the one culture and wrong in the other, we cannot talk about acts of that sort being "really" right or "really" wrong. They *are* right (not merely believed to be right) in one culture and wrong in the other. Good reasons can be given *for* doing the acts if one accepts the supreme norms of the value system vindicated by the way of life of the first culture. Similarly, good reasons can be given *against* doing the same acts in the framework of the way of life of the second culture. Since good reasons cannot be given in support of one whole way of life rather than the other, these "good reasons" are themselves relative to value systems and (finally) to ways of life. They are valid only in so far as one adopts a certain value system and accepts a certain way of life.[1]

There — does that strike you as going to the heart of the issue between relativism and absolutism?

[1] *Ibid.,* Ch. 6.

E: It does indeed. You have stated the argument for relativism so well that I don't see how you are ever going to pull yourself out of it or convince me that it isn't the only acceptable view.

W: Perhaps I can't — but let's see.

E: Remember that you can't say that one way of life is better than another because it is governed by utilitarian principles or anything of the kind, for that would be begging the question. Your supreme norm, or the adoption of it, has been vindicated in terms of a way of life, so you can't turn around and try to justify that way of life by means of a supreme norm.

W: I'm aware of that, of course.

E: Nor can you any longer invoke any parallel between what you are trying to do now and the justification of the basic rules of argument (in logic) or of inductive procedures (in scientific method). We can't prove the principles of logic by means of themselves — that would be circular. But we can justify the rules or principles of logic by saying that discourse would be impossible without them and that any attempt to deny them presupposes them in the very denial.[1] Similarly, we can justify inductive procedure by saying that, although the existence of an order of nature continuing into the future cannot be demonstrated nor even shown to be inductively probable because the very laws of probability are based on the assumption of such an order, we can say that *if* there is an order of nature, then the inductive methods of science will disclose that order.[2] Thus induction has a pragmatic justification, that is, we have vindicated our use of it. But these vindications quite clearly are vindications for everyone — for everyone using language (which means all of us) in the matter of the principles of logic and for everyone interested in discovering laws wherewith to predict the future in the matter of induction; they are vindications as much for Chinese scientists as for American scientists. But ways of life, unlike inductive procedures, seem to differ from culture to culture and even from person to person so that when you vindicate a way of life, it seems that you are doing it only for yourself or for like-minded persons. My charge a while ago, you remember, was that you haven't justified your way of life *to me*. The justification of inductive procedures is the same for everyone; but the justification of a way of life, it seems to me, is not. What justifies it to one person or culture will not justify it to another. Thus you see I'm a relativist. I take it that you are not.

W: That's correct. Absolutism, as opposed to relativism, claims that a way of life can be justified in the sense of being *rationally preferred* to others, or rationally chosen over against others. My task now, as I see it, is not to defend one particular way of life to you (for instance, my own) as rationally preferable but rather to try to show you *what a rational choice*

---

[1] See J. Hospers, *Introduction to Philosophical Analysis*, pp. 123-31.
[2] H. Feigl, in Sellars and Hospers, *Readings in Ethical Theory*, p. 676.

is with regard to a way of life and thus to *give meaning* to the expression "justifying a way of life." If I succeed, then you can no longer say that I am simply recommending a way of life without reason or vindicating my supreme norm to myself but not to you.

E: Let's see whether you can bring it off. I don't think you can.

W: Well, let me see how far I can get. Let me first define "rationality" with regard to a way of life: let me say that a way of life is rational if the choice of it is (1) free, (2) enlightened, and (3) impartial. I'll say a few words about each of these qualifications. First, to be *free,* a choice of a way of life must not be determined by external constraint: no person or circumstances in the physical or social environment must be putting any pressure on me to accept one way rather than another. In practice this requirement, like all the rest of them, is very difficult to fulfill — especially that of social constraint. We are probably all so conditioned by our own training and early environment, even when we think we're not, that we tend to prefer whatever way of life we've been brought up in, or else to rebel irrationally against it. Both of these tendencies are forms of social constraint, dating far back into our childhood, but yet they are very much with us in our adult lives. So much for external constraint. But neither must the choice be determined by internal constraint, such as irresistible impulse or extreme desire; the person must be in a state of mind in which he can weigh all the alternatives carefully and with due consideration.

E: What about unconscious motivation? Nobody can escape from that.

W: True, it always plays a role, but the role must not be decisive if the choice is to be free. What must be decisive is the person's own preference. He must choose in accordance with what he really prefers, not with what he is conditioned to think but would reject under different circumstances.

E: A man's real preference is very difficult to know; who can say what he would prefer under different circumstances?

W: Admittedly it is difficult — rational choice is not easy. But let me go on to the second main requirement: his choice must be enlightened. And to be enlightened, the nature of each way of life must be fully known; its probable effects in actual living must also be fully known; and so must the means necessary to bring it about. Every aspect and manifestation of the alternative ways of life must be known — again, an impossible condition to realize perfectly. But to achieve such knowledge as much as possible, a wide acquaintance with people living different kinds of lives is extremely helpful; one can hardly make an enlightened choice if he knows only people who share his own way of life, for then he has a most inadequate conception of what alternatives he must choose among. It is also helpful to have a thorough acquaintance with biographies and works of art expressing or elucidating various aspects of different ways of life, for from information one often gains an insight into ways of life greater even than one derives from long personal acquaintance with people.

Now to the third and most important condition: impartiality. The choice must be impartial, that is, disinterested, not determined by favoritism or desire to protect one's own privileges.

E: Suppose I said to you that the way of life I want is one in which I am the supreme master of everyone else and can shove others around as I want to without interference. What would you say?

W: I would say that this choice won't do because it fails to fulfill the condition of impartiality. Ask yourself instead: Would you want a world in which one person lorded it over all the others? Put in that way, I don't think you'd want it at all. You would want it only if you knew that *you* would be the ruler. But that condition goes against the requirement of impartiality. Impartiality requires that you choose the kind of world you want *without yet knowing what your role in it will be* or what position in society you will occupy (pages 282-83); thus you won't want slavery in it because you might turn out to be the slave and not the master. The world you choose must be the world that you impartially want.

E: You don't demand much, do you? Who in the history of the world has ever been entirely free, enlightened, and impartial in his choice, as you define these terms?

W: No one, probably. And it would take such a person to make a completely rational choice. But I am in no way committed to saying that such a person has ever existed or will exist, any more than a geometer is committing to saying that a perfect circle will ever be drawn by human hands. But, just as the idea of a perfect circle has meaning, so, I claim, the idea of a rational choice has meaning; and that is all I am trying to show. Actual people are, to varying degrees, irrational; witness the wide variety of ways of life we find in the world. But, even though it may be that no actual person lives up to the requirements, the requirements do have meaning. I have sketched briefly what I take to be the requirements of a rational choice among ways of life, and thus I think I have substantiated my claim that the choice is not entirely arbitrary or irrational, as you relativists contend.

E: But suppose I ask you how you substantiate the claim that these requirements of yours are what rationality (in choosing a way of life) consists of? Have you just invented them? Are you simply giving the term "rational" a stipulative definition of your own?

W: I don't think so. Most people, to be sure, haven't thought much about the definition of "rational," but when they reflect about it, I suspect that they would agree that a choice that does not fulfill these requirements is not a rational choice. I haven't just stipulated a definition at random; I have only made explicit a concept that was already present in people's thinking, one which they used more or less unconsciously without verbalizing with any precision. I have explicated a concept, not invented one. Do you think I was mistaken in any of the requirements I laid down about a rational choice? Can you think of a better way of explicating the concept of rationality?

E: I'm not sure that I can. I think that the requirements you set forth are excellent ones. But I wonder whether they aren't *necessary* conditions without being *sufficient* conditions. I am inclined to return once again to the point that people not only have different early environments (different conditioning, different types of indoctrination which leave a lifelong stamp on them) but different *basic temperaments*. A happy-go-lucky person will not prefer the same way of life that a more cautious person will, even if we correct for the effects of parental and other conditioning. Or again, the way of life chosen by a person who is old and set in his ways will be different from that chosen by one who is young and full of spirit.

W: True, but isn't this difference because they are both lacking in certain aspects of impartiality and enlightenment? The young person does not have the experience of life and the wide acquaintance with various ways of life that are required to make a fully rational choice; and the old person is already so habit-ridden that he has probably forgotten (if indeed he ever possessed) much of his acquaintance with diverse ways of life which is required to make such a choice. It seems probable then that both are lacking in the requirements, though in somewhat different ways. But that's not all. I am not saying that an old person and a young person should live in the same way; in some respects of course they should live differently. Does this difference mean that they should have different ways of life? I would prefer to say that one way of life should be inclusive enough to be suited to a diversity of conditions: not only to environmental conditions (some ways of behaving that are appropriate on the desert are not on the sea), but also to one's sex and age (some acts appropriate for the young would be most inappropriate for the aged, and vice versa), and certainly to one's temperament (a person of a slow and cautious temper should not behave in all respects like a person of mercurial temper). I am certainly not saying that everyone should behave alike — what a dull world that would be! A full description of a way of life would spell out how different kinds of people should behave in different circumstances.

E: Suppose I grant all this. Now: in defining rationality as you have, haven't you imposed your own way of life on your hearers in defining that very ideal itself?

W: I don't think so. What I have specified are the conditions which anyone, in any way of life, would accept as *defining* a rational choice. The concept of a rational choice is independent of the various ways of life; it provides a method for *arriving* at a rational choice, but it does not in any way prejudge what the content of that choice will be. It doesn't even say that the way of life that is rationally chosen will itself be a life dedicated to rational pursuits or that it will exclude the satisfaction of irrational desires, whatever those may be. There is no necessity that a rationally preferred way of life will have the same characteristics as the rational choice itself. Thus, when you ask me, "Why ought I to accept your conditions of rationality?" my answer is, "They are not *my* conditions of rationality, but yours too. Isn't this what *you* would mean by an ideally rational choice?" If you say it isn't, then I urge you to give me a better explication of the concept of a rational choice.

E: I think I misphrased my question to you. The question I really meant to ask is this: "Assume that a certain way of life is rationally preferable to another. Now show me *why I should live in accordance with it*. I grant, at least until further notice, that it is rationally preferable. But why, therefore, should I do anything about it? You have shown me how, in principle, I can arrive at a rational choice of a way of life, but you haven't shown me why I should adopt it.

W: Yes, I thought that would come up sooner or later. (We discussed the question "Why be moral?" on pages 174-95.) In the first place, I'm not trying to make you or anyone live a certain kind of life; I am trying first and foremost to spell out what a rational choice among ways of life *is*. If you don't elect to follow it, I can't help it. But the question at the moment is not whether you're *going* to follow it but *why you should* follow it. In other words, how do you get from "A is rationally preferred to B" to "A *ought* to be preferred to B," and from this in turn to "I *should choose* A in preference to B"? There is quite a tangle here. As to the first of these two transitions:

When we say that A is rationally preferred to B we mean that whenever the conditions of a rational choice hold, A is preferred to B. Now let us assume that the conditions of a rational choice as I have specified them do correctly explicate the justification of a way of life (and this assumption is not now in question). Then it would follow that A is more justified than B. This means that there are better reasons for choosing A than for choosing B. If a person, knowing this, were still to prefer B to A, his preference would be a paradigm of an irrational choice. The person might want to persist in his choice nevertheless, claiming that he honestly does prefer B to A. There is no logical error in his doing this, so long as he does not claim that he has good reasons, or is being rational, in doing it. He is saying in effect that he does not care to be rational about this matter. But then he must not ask "Why be rational?" For as soon as he asks "Why?" *he is demanding reasons and thus presupposing rationality*. To ask such a question is to speak as if only a rational answer will be acceptable. But in the present situation he already knows what a rational preference is (namely, the preference of A over B) and that his own preference runs counter to the rational one. What more does he need to know? His question appears to be expressed in words outside any context for their possible use.[1]

[1] P. Taylor, *Normative Discourse*, Ch. 6. (Italics mine.)

So much for the first transition; now as to the second: if we already know that we ought to prefer A to B (since that is the rational choice), what point is there left in the question, *"Why* ought we to do it?" Surely that reason has already been given — namely that it is what we ought to do. True, that we *ought* to do it doesn't guarantee that we *will* do it; perhaps rational considerations will not be as effective as persuasion or psycho-analysis. Nevertheless, as far as reason is concerned, we have done all that we can do or need to do. (See pages 193-95.)

E: Yes, but I still want to ask, "Why live according to A? Why not just ignore rational choice and select a way of life that is *not* rationally prefer-able? What happens if I do that?"

W: You mean will something happen to you? Is this really your question? Consider what you are asking. You are asking *"Why* should I?" "Why" is a request for reasons. But I have already given you the reasons. Presumably if you were not interested in seeking reasons but just wanted to act irration-ally, you would not ask for reasons. What you do with them is something else again. The fact that I give you reasons and that you accept them will not automatically make you *act* on them; that's true. But I *can* point out to you that once you have agreed that a certain way of life is rationally preferable, it is redundant to ask for *reasons* for living it.

E: I think I see your point. But now comes the question that I want to ask you most: "Which way of life is the one that *is* the most rationally justified?"

W: Well — I was expecting that one too. I may be able to list the require-ments for a rational choice without being able to make one — I am human and biased and a slave of my background, probably, as much as the next person. Let me also point this out: if you ask a philosopher of science what procedures and methods he uses in establishing scientific theories, he can give you an explication of the methods used — perhaps not those used all the time by actual scientists (for they all make mistakes) but those that would be employed by an ideal scientist. But if you go on to ask him *what particular* laws or theories he arrives at by the use of these methods, he will say to you: "Go to the practicing scientist; it is not for me to say what things he discovers by means of the methods which I have explicated." I am inclined to do the same thing with your request. I have described to you what a rational choice is among ways of life; I have tried to show you that the concept of a rational choice is a meaningful one and therefore that those who say that there *is* no rational procedure for resolving such questions (the relativists) are mistaken. If you now ask me to turn from the method to the content, and give you the actual results of applying ra-tional procedure in this field, I can't say that I am particularly competent to do it; once again, the "personal equation" operates as much in me as it does in you. How can I say what a person who was completely free, en-lightened, and impartial in his choice would choose, since I am none of these things?

E: But as far as you can, taking into account the inevitable human equation, what way of life would you choose — I mean, freely, impartially, and in as enlightened a manner as possible, what way of life would you choose for mankind?

W: Very well, I'll attempt briefly to sketch an answer; but remember that if you disagree with me on the way of life I think it is rational to choose, it does not follow that you must disagree with me in my description of what a rational choice *is*. I may not be using the method properly, but at least I believe I have given a fair account of the method. Remember too that a way of life includes far more than a moral code — to know a person's whole way of life one must know about how he enjoys himself, how he works, what he does with his leisure time, what company he prefers and how he gets along with people, and a host of other things. Moral codes only impose certain strictures upon people's behavior so that they will be able to live together in harmony; moral codes are primarily a means toward making their individual developments possible.

Speaking, then, only of the moral aspect of a way of life, I would say that a rationally chosen way of life, particularly under the conditions of the world in the second half of the twentieth century, would be one, in Bertrand Russell's words, "inspired by love and guided by knowledge." Not wishy-washy sentimental love that consists in giving in to everyone's demands no matter how unreasonable, or in making a doormat out of oneself, or in turning the other cheek in a way that makes one an easy victim to the depredations of the next stupid aggressor and thus destroys whatever good is left in the world. I mean love in the sense of equal consideration for everyone and an acknowledgment to everyone equally of certain basic rights — giving others as much consideration as one would oneself, doing to them as one would be done by, and not interfering with their lives (in the name of morality) more than is required to retain peace among men. This kind of life is indispensable if man is to survive in the face of the means he now possesses for destroying all life in one stroke. But equally indispensable are intelligence and knowledge; for without it people, no matter how much love they bear their fellow men, will commit deeds which are stupidly short-sighted and just as disastrous to mankind as if they possessed knowledge but no love. To achieve a combination of these qualities is, of course, far from easy, and yet they must somehow be combined if the human race is to live together in harmony or even to survive at all on this planet. Within this frame which I have outlined there is, of course, tremendous scope for the development of individual differences, and these should be encouraged as much as possible within the frame. Nevertheless the way of life I am outlining as an irreducible minimum for a way of life for mankind requires a considerable change in the present habits of human beings, since

. . . for love of domination we must substitute equality; for love of victory we must substitute justice; for brutality we must substitute intelligence; for competition we must substitute cooperation. We must learn to think of the human race as one family and further our common interests by the intelligent use of natural resources, marching together towards prosperity, not separately towards death and destruction. The mental change required is difficult and will not be achieved in a moment, but if the need is recognized by educators, and if the young are brought up as citizens of this world and not of a bygone world of predatory warriors, the change can be achieved within a generation, so that we may hope to save at least a portion of mankind from the universal destruction with which we are threatened by the pursuit of obsolete ideas.[1]

EXERCISES

1. An anthropologist writes that relativism teaches us the lesson of tolerance toward the moral customs of all other peoples. Can a consistent relativist say that tolerance is preferable to intolerance? (Should he be tolerant of those who believe in intolerance?) Answer as well as you can on your own, then turn to R. Brandt, *Ethical Theory*, pp. 288-92.

2. Evaluate the following statements (of the kind that people who call themselves relativists often utter):

a. Each tribe's or nation's set of norms is right for those who hold them.

b. Any set of rules is right which meets the needs of the society that holds it.

c. Any set of rules is right which enables the society holding it to survive.

d. "What's good is what I feel good after, and what's bad is what I feel bad after." (Hemingway.)

3. "One can give *reasons* to support his ethical assertions." But what constitutes a reason in ethics? What makes one reason better than another? (In answering this question, study Kurt Baier, *The Moral Point of View*.)

4. Trace the relations among the following:

a. X is the rational choice.

b. X is better than any other act I could choose.

c. I should do X.

d. I shall do X.

5. Do you agree or disagree with the following?

a. "Reason does not furnish you with reasons why you should act reasonably. It does not pretend to. There is no argument in favor of rationality, for all argument is based upon it and presupposes it. Reason makes no offer to bribe you into obedience. It speaks, that is all. If you disobey, that is the kind of man you are." (From James B. Pratt, *Reason in the Art of Living: a Textbook of Ethics*. New York: Macmillan, 1949, p. 207. Reprinted by permission of the publisher.)

b. "If pressed to justify a decision completely, we have to give a complete specification of the way of life of which it is a part. This complete specification it is impossible in practice to give; the nearest attempts are those given by the great religions, especially those which can point to historical persons who carried out the way of life in practice. Suppose, however, that we can give it. If the inquirer still goes on asking 'But why *should* I live like that?' then there is no

---

[1] *New Hopes for a Changing World* by Bertrand Russell. Copyright 1950 by Bertrand Russell. Reprinted by permission of Simon and Schuster, Inc., p. 165.

further answer to give him, because we have already, *ex hypothesi,* said everything that could be included in this further answer. We can only ask him to make up his own mind which way he ought to live; for in the end everything rests upon such a decision of principle. He has to decide whether to accept that way of life or not; if he accepts it, then we can proceed to justify the decisions that are based upon it; if he does not accept it, then let him accept some other, and try to live by it. The sting is in the last clause. To describe such ultimate decisions as arbitrary, because *ex hypothesi* everything which could be used to justify them has already been included in the decision, would be like saying that a complete description of the universe was utterly unfounded, because no further fact could be called upon in corroboration of it. This is not how we use the words 'arbitrary' and 'unfounded.' Far from being arbitrary, such a decision would be the most well-founded of decisions, because it would be based upon a consideration of everything upon which it could possibly be founded." (R. M. Hare, *The Language of Morals,* p. 69.)

5. First describe and then evaluate the "way of life" expressed in two or more contemporary novels.

Example: The following, or something like it, could be said to be (at least in part) the "way of life" expressed in Jack Kerouac's novel *On the Road:* Do whatever will give you fun; fun is the only thing worth living for. It's fun to sleep with any woman you meet and to get her to do so by means of any false promise that will convince her. Don't engage in constructive activities like building things or being an honest politician or setting up a business, that's only for squares. Don't learn anything that's hard, leave that to the eggheads. Life is crazy, don't try to figure it out. Do whatever you feel like doing at the time, you only live once. Never think about tomorrow, tomorrow will take care of itself. People who think about tomorrow are bores or phonies and you shouldn't bother with them. If you've spent your last nickel the night before on liquor or women, or given your last dollar to the drummer in a jazz combo if you liked his number, and you need food for the next day or gasoline for your car, just distract the attention of the guy at the counter or go to the filling station while the attendant is asleep, and steal what you want.. It's o.k. as long as you don't get caught. The important thing is to get what you want and have fun doing it. If others suffer or are brokenhearted that just shows they're not with it, but don't let them spoil your fun.

READING LIST, SECTION 28

Baier, Kurt. "Good Reasons" and "Proving a Moral Judgment." *Philosophical Studies,* Vol. 4 (1953), pp. 1-15, 33-44.
———. *The Moral Point of View.* Ithaca, N. Y.: Cornell Univ. Press, 1958.
Brandt, Richard. *Ethical Theory.* Englewood Cliffs, N. J.: Prentice Hall, 1959, Chs. 10 and 11.
Duncker, K. "Ethical Relativity." *Mind,* Vol. 48 (1939), pp. 39-57.
Edel, Abraham, and Douglas B. Dryer. "Ethical Reasoning." (symposium) *American Philosophical Association, Eastern Division, Proceedings,* Vol. 2 (1953), pp. 127-57.

Feigl, Herbert. "Validation and Vindication." In Sellars and Hospers. *Readings in Ethical Theory,* pp. 667-80.

Findlay, J. N. "The Justification of Attitudes." *Mind,* Vol. 63 (1954), pp. 145-61.

Gardiner, Patrick L. "On Assenting to a Moral Principle." *Aristotelian Society Proceedings,* Vol. 55 (1954-5), pp. 23-44.

Griffiths, A. Phillips. "Acting with Reason." *Philosophical Quarterly,* Vol. 8 (1958), pp. 289-99.

———. "Justifying Moral Principles." *Aristotelian Society Proceedings,* Vol. 58 (1957-8), pp. 103-24.

Hall, Everett W. "Practical Reason(s) and the Deadlock in Ethics." *Mind,* Vol. 64 (1955), pp. 319-32.

Hampshire, Stuart. "Fallacies in Moral Philosophy." *Mind,* Vol. 58 (1949), pp. 466-82.

———. *Thought and Action.* London: Chatto & Windus, 1959.

Hare, R. M. *The Language of Morals.* New York: Oxford Univ. Press, 1952.

Kluckhohn, Clyde. "Ethical Relativity." *Journal of Philosophy,* Vol. 52 (1955), pp. 663-77.

Mandelbaum, Maurice. *The Phenomenology of Moral Experience.* Chicago: Free Press, 1955.

Mayo, Bernard. *Ethics and the Moral Life.* New York: St. Martin's, 1958.

Montefiore, Alan. *A Modern Introduction to Moral Philosophy.* New York: Praeger, 1958.

Nielsen, Kai. "The Functions of Moral Discourse." *Philosophical Quarterly,* Vol. 7 (1957), pp. 236-48.

———. "The 'Good Reasons' Approach and 'Ontological Justification' of Morality." *Philosophical Quarterly,* Vol. 9 (1959), pp. 116-30.

Nowell-Smith, Patrick. *Ethics.* Baltimore: Pelican Books, 1954, especially Pts. 1 and 2.

Sachs, David. "On Mr. Baier's 'Good Reasons.'" *Philosophical Studies,* Vol. 4 (1953), pp. 65-69.

Taylor, Paul. "Four Types of Ethical Relativism." *Philosophical Review,* Vol. 63 (1954), pp. 500-16.

———. *Normative Discourse.* Englewood Cliffs, N. J.: Prentice-Hall, 1961.

———. "Social Science and Ethical Relativism." *Journal of Philosophy,* Vol. 55 (1958), pp. 32-44.

Terrell, D. B. "A Remark on Good Reasons." *Philosophical Studies,* Vol. 4 (1953), pp. 58-63.

Toulmin, Stephen. *An Examination of the Place of Reason in Morals.* New York: Cambridge Univ. Press, 1951.

INDEX

596

F
G
H
I
J
K